Second Workshop on Domain Adaptation for NLP (Adapt-NLP 2021)

Online
20 April 2021

ISBN: 978-1-7138-2956-0

Printed from e-media with permission by:

Curran Associates, Inc.
57 Morehouse Lane
Red Hook, NY 12571

Some format issues inherent in the e-media version may also appear in this print version.

Association for Computational Linguistics
209 N. Eighth Street
Stroudsburg, Pennsylvania 18360

Phone: 1-570-476-8006
Fax: 1-570-476-0860

acl@aclweb.org

Additional copies of this publication are available from:

Curran Associates, Inc.
57 Morehouse Lane
Red Hook, NY 12571 USA
Phone: 845-758-0400
Fax: 845-758-2633
Email: curran@proceedings.com
Web: www.proceedings.com

Adapt-NLP 2021

The Second Workshop on Domain Adaptation for NLP

Proceedings of the Workshop

April 20, 2021

Our Sponsors:

Google

Introduction

The growth in computational power and the rise of Deep Neural Networks (DNNs) have revolutionized the field of Natural Language Processing (NLP). The ability to collect massive datasets with the capacity to train big models on powerful GPUs, has yielded NLP-based technology that was beyond imagination only a few years ago.

Unfortunately, this technology is still limited to a handful of resource rich languages and domains. This is because most NLP algorithms rely on the fundamental assumption that the training and the test sets are drawn from the same underlying distribution. When the train and test distributions do not match, a phenomenon known as domain shift, such models are likely to encounter performance drops.

Despite the growing availability of heterogeneous data, many NLP domains still lack the amounts of labeled data required to feed data-hungry neural models, and in some domains and languages even unlabeled data is scarce. As a result, the problem of domain adaptation, training an algorithm on annotated data from one or more source domains, and applying it to other target domains, is a fundamental challenge that has to be solved in order to make NLP technology available for most world languages and textual domains.

Domain Adaptation (DA) is hence the focus of this workshop. Particularly, the topics of the workshop include, but are not restricted to:

- Novel DA algorithms, for existing as well as new setups.
- Extending DA research to new domains and tasks through both novel datasets and algorithmic approaches.
- Proposing novel zero-shot and few-shot algorithms and discussing their relevance for DA.
- Exploring the similarities and differences between algorithmic approaches to DA, cross-lingual and cross-task learning.
- A conceptual discussion of the definitions of fundamental concepts such as *domain*, *transfer* as well as *zero-shot* and *few-shot* learning.
- Introducing and exploring novel or under-explored DA setups, aiming towards realistic and applicable ones (e.g., one-to-many DA, many-to-many DA, and DA when the target domain is unknown when training on the source domain).

Adapt-NLP would not have been possible without the dedication of its program committee. We would like to thank them for their invaluable effort in providing timely and high-quality reviews on a short notice. We are also grateful to our invited speakers and panelists for contributing to our program.

The Adapt-NLP workshop organizers,
Eyal Ben-David, Shay Cohen, Ryan McDonald, Barbara Plank, Roi Reichart, Guy Rotman, and Yftah Ziser

Organizing Committee:

- Eyal Ben-David, Technion - Israel Institute of Technology
- Shay Cohen, University of Edinburgh
- Ryan McDonald, ASAPP Research
- Barbara Plank, University of Copenhagen
- Roi Reichart, Technion - Israel Institute of Technology
- Guy Rotman, Technion - Israel Institute of Technology
- Yftah Ziser, Amazon Research

Program Committee:

- Reut Apel, Technion - Israel Institute of Technology
- Isabelle Augenstein, University of Copenhagen
- Steven Bethard, University of Arizona
- Danushka Bollegala, University of Liverpool
- Xia Cui, University of Manchester
- Kevin Duh, Johns Hopkins University
- Jacob Eisenstein, Google AI
- Amir Feder, Technion - Israel Institute of Technology
- Alexander Fraser, University of Munich
- Milica Gasic, Heinrich Heine University Düsseldorf
- Suchin Gururangan, Allen Institute for AI
- Roman Klinger, University of Stuttgart
- Mirella Lapata, University of Edinburgh
- Ana Marasović, University of Washington
- Timothy Miller, Harvard University
- Preslav Nakov, Qatar Computing Research Institute
- Mariana Neves, University of Potsdam
- Farhad Nooralahzadeh, University of Oslo
- Nadav Oved, Technion - Israel Institute of Technology
- Yuval Pinter, Georgia Institute of Technology
- Sebastian Ruder, DeepMind
- Benoit Sagot, ALMAnaCH Research
- Anders Søgaard, University of Copenhagen
- Idan Szpektor, Google Research

Invited Speakers:

- Isabelle Augenstein, University of Copenhagen
- Jacob Eisenstein, Google AI
- Hinrich Schutze, University of Munich (LMU)

Panel:

- Jacob Eisenstein, Google AI
- Mari Ostendorf, University of Washington
- Roi Reichart, Technion - Israel Institute of Technology
- Sebastian Ruder, DeepMind
- Anders Søgaard, University of Copenhagen

Table of Contents

Multidomain Pretrained Language Models for Green NLP

Antonis Maronikolakis
CIS, LMU Munich
antmarakis@cis.lmu.de

Hinrich Schütze
CIS, LMU Munich

Abstract

When tackling a task in a given domain, it has been shown that adapting a model to the domain using raw text data before training on the supervised task improves performance versus solely training on the task. The downside is that a lot of domain data is required and if we want to tackle tasks in n domains, we require n models each adapted on domain data before task learning. Storing and using these models separately can be prohibitive for low-end devices. In this paper we show that domain adaptation can be generalised to cover multiple domains. Specifically, a single model can be trained across various domains at the same time with minimal drop in performance, even when we use less data and resources. Thus, instead of training multiple models, we can train a single multidomain model saving on computational resources and training time.

1 Introduction

Domain adaptation in the form of training on unlabeled data has been prevalent in recent work (Rietzler et al., 2020; Han and Eisenstein, 2019). When given a task T in domain D, it is useful to adapt our model on raw text data pertinent to D before supervised training on the labeled data of T.

Unfortunately, domain adaptation is expensive and costly. So even though results do get better, there needs to be a balance between use of computational resources and model performance.

Accentuating the issue is the rising dominance of increasingly larger models (Devlin et al., 2019; Brown et al., 2020). These large models require a lot of data and computational resources to train. Not only have these resources been prohibitive for smaller labs, but the environmental impact of training such large models cannot be understated either (Strubell et al., 2019; Lacoste et al., 2019).

There is therefore a need to build models that can tackle tasks across multiple domains, much in the same way multilingual models are able to operate across multiple languages. These multidomain models, to be useful, need to exhibit performance comparable to models adapted to a single domain. Then, these models can be trained and deployed with reduced computational costs.

In this paper we explore such multidomain models. We compare multidomain DistilBERT (Sanh et al., 2019) models with single-domain DistilBERT models[1]. In our analysis, we test the multidomain model on tasks from multiple domains (including MultiNLI), we examine how important adaptation order is for performance and we show that training on the domains jointly or sequentially does not impact effectiveness. We also reproduce findings in Rietzler et al. (2020), where the authors showed that pretraining on an irrelevant domain is not beneficial. Finally, we show that much like multilingual BERT, multidomain models can be used for better performance in low-resource domains, with the low-resource domain leveraging the larger pretrained model.

2 Related Work

It has been shown empirically that domain adaptation improves model performance (Gururangan et al., 2020). Specifically, the authors experimented on RoBERTa (Liu et al., 2019) and eight tasks ranging across four domains (computer science and biomedical papers, reviews and news). Performance increased when adapting to a domain pertinent to the domain of the task, compared to when the two domains were not as related.

Work has also been done to alleviate the environmental impact of training larger models. In Poerner et al. (2020), an inexpensive method was proposed for domain adaptation, which can be performed on

[1] Code and instructions for data acquisition are available at https://github.com/antmarakis/multidomain_green_nlp.

Proceedings of the Second Workshop on Domain Adaptation for NLP, pages 1–8
April 20, 2021. ©2021 Association for Computational Linguistics

a CPU and significantly reduces training cost.

Finally, MobileBERT is a downsized BERT model with around 4 times fewer parameters (Sun et al., 2020) than the original BERT-base model. There is a need to fit larger models in low-capacity machines, with MobileBERT and our work being a step in that direction, alongside other work in the pruning area (Sanh et al., 2020; Zhao et al., 2020).

3 Data

3.1 Raw Text Domain Data

In Gururangan et al. (2020), the authors showed that adaptation using domain data improves performance on a downstream task. In our work, we trained two types of models, *single-domain* models (one for each domain) and a *multidomain* model. All models were pretrained from scratch.

For the single-domain models, we used around 4GBs of each dataset, adapting DistilBERT on each domain for 1 epoch. This resulted in four distinct models. For our multidomain model, we adapted our model successively on all domains, using around half of the available data (approximately 2GBs from each domain) for 1 epoch as well.

The datasets we used for adaptation are: *Amazon* (He and McAuley, 2016), *Arxiv* (Cohan et al., 2018), *Realnews* (Zellers et al., 2019), *CS* (Lo et al., 2020) and *Reddit Comments* (Völske et al., 2017).

The original datasets were truncated for our experiments, using approximately only the first 4GBs of text. For the *Amazon* dataset, which contains reviews across multiple products (eg. books, music, clothing), we took care to balance data across all categories, by sampling at random n=50,000 reviews from products with more reviews than n.

3.2 Supervised Task Data

Models were evaluated on eight supervised classification tasks in total, spanning four domains. An overview and description of the tasks can be found in Appendix A. Each model was trained on each task separately. For most of the datasets, train/dev/test splits are already provided. Where such splits are not available, we randomly sample 60/20/20 sets from the original data for train/dev/test splits respectively.

4 Training

The training of our models is broken up in two steps: domain adaptation and supervised task learning. Furthermore, we have two setups for our experiments: a) perform domain adaptation on four models in parallel and then train them on each individual task, and b) perform domain adaptation on a single model for all domains successively before task learning.

We also perform ablation studies on irrelevant and low-resource domain adaptation, domain adaptation order and finally investigate whether joint instead of sequential adaptation performs better.

4.1 Domain Adaptation

In our experiments we used DistilBERT (Sanh et al., 2019). DistilBERT is a lightweight BERT-based model that showcases performance remarkably close to BERT, with around 40% fewer parameters. Training was performed on a publicly available[2] pretrained model.

First, we perform domain adaptation on each of the four domains separately. This results in four distinct models, each adapted to a different domain. Hyperparameters can be found in Appendix B. We also train a single model successively on all four domains, resulting in a multidomain model. All possible domain adaptation orders were compared and for our comparisons we chose the order with the worst overall performance, which is *Amazon* $\rightarrow$ *Reddit Comments* $\rightarrow$ *Realnews* $\rightarrow$ *Arxiv* (*Am-RC-R-Ar*). Further details on order comparison can be found in 5.4.

4.2 Supervised Task Learning

After the domain adaptation phase, the single-domain and multidomain models were trained on the training data of each task. Training took place over 1 or 2 epochs, trying to keep training time approximately equal across all tasks. Namely, all tasks required 1 epoch to train, except the *ACL-ARC* and *HyperPartisan* tasks, for which the models were trained for 2 epochs. More details on the hyperparameters are available in Appendix C.

5 Results

5.1 Base vs. Single-domain vs. Multidomain

Evaluation took place across eight tasks, covering all four domains. As an added experiment, we also evaluated on the MultiNLI dataset (Williams et al., 2018). MultiNLI is a dataset for textual entailment consisting of sentence pairs spanning multiple genres. We made three runs over each task and averaged the results, shown in Table 1.

[2]Accessible online here.

Note that the multidomain model used here (*Am-RC-R-Ar*) comes from the lowest-performing domain adaptation order. We chose it to illustrate that even in the worst case scenario, there is still a substantial improvement over the base model. On average, the gains are even larger (Section 5.4).

	Base	**Single**	**Multi**
ACL-ARC	$68.0_{0.3}$	$\mathbf{74.1_{1.5}}$	$70.5_{2.1}$
SciCite	$84.9_{0.8}$	$86.0_{0.3}$	$\mathbf{86.1_{0.2}}$
SARC	$75.3_{0.1}$	$\mathbf{78.6_{0.6}}$	$76.1_{0.3}$
TalkDown	$86.1_{0.7}$	$\mathbf{86.5_{0.1}}$	$86.1_{0.7}$
HyperPartisan	$78.9_{0.8}$	$\mathbf{81.4_{2.0}}$	$80.5_{1.4}$
AG-News	$94.0_{0.1}$	$94.1_{0.1}$	$\mathbf{94.3_{0.1}}$
IMDB	$86.3_{0.1}$	$\mathbf{87.2_{0.2}}$	$86.7_{0.1}$
Clothing	$68.9_{0.2}$	$\mathbf{69.8_{0.3}}$	$69.3_{0.3}$
MultiNLI	$77.0_{0.4}$	$77.8^{*}_{0.2}$	$\mathbf{79.1_{0.3}}$
Average	79.7	**81.7**	81.1

Table 1: Accuracy in percentage for task/model combinations. Standard deviation is shown in subscript (based on three runs). With *Base* we denote the original model, with *Single* the model trained on the corresponding domain and with *Multi* the multidomain model. For the *Single* model, we show the best accuracy out of all the models in MNLI.

When adapting DistilBERT to a single domain, performance is greater compared to the base model. When adapting to all domains, performance still increases, although by less on average. The average increase from base DistilBERT to single-domain DistilBERT is 2.0, whereas the multidomain model shows an improvement of 1.4 over the respective base model.

Overall, performance increases across tasks when adapting to all domains and in some cases the multidomain model is better than the single-domain model. Also, performance never drops for the multidomain model which, in the worst cases, still achieves marginally higher accuracy than the base model. At the same time, on MultiNLI the multidomain model scores higher than both base and all single-domain models, showcasing its domain-agnostic capabilities.

It is thus shown that multidomain models provide a boost in most tasks while never hindering performance in any task. They do so while requiring less data; from the 16GBs needed to train the four single models (4GBs for each domain), we only require 8GBs (2GBs for each domain) to train the multidomain model with comparable results.

5.2 Low-resource Domains

One of the advantages of multilingual models is that low-resource languages can leverage the multilingual model. A model is trained on multiple languages before the low-resource language is added. The resulting model performs better than a model trained only on the low-resource language.

We examine whether this holds true for multidomain models as well. For this experiment, we include the biomedical domain by further adapting our multidomain model to the *Pubmed* (Lo et al., 2020) dataset. Namely, we experiment with 10MB, 100MB and 500MB *Pubmed* datasets added to *Am-RC-R-Ar*. After pretraining on each of the new, smaller *Pubmed* sets, we test our models on *ChemProt* (Kringelum J, 2016) and *Pubmed-RCT* (Dernoncourt and Lee, 2017). As a baseline, we pretrain DistilBERT on solely the *Pubmed* datasets. We also evaluate how the original multidomain model does without any biomedical data. Finally, we examine if training on the low-resource domain has a catastrophic effect on the previously learned domains. Results are shown in Table 2.

Due to differences in dataset sizes, care was taken to keep training times approximately equal for all setups. For *Pub-500*, we trained for 1 epoch. For *Pub-100* we trained for 5 epochs and for *Pub-10* we trained for 50 epochs.

When pretraining only on *Pubmed*, the amount of training data used does not have an impact on performance. All of *Pub-10/100/500* perform similarly. Performance on *ChemProt* is higher than the multidomain model by around 0.6, while on the rest of the tasks accuracy is not as high.

If we further adapt the multidomain model to the *Pubmed* sets, we get a larger improvement over the original multidomain model, not only on the tasks in the biomedical domain, but over all examined tasks. In *ChemProt*, the improvement is around 2.4 over the original multidomain model and around 1.0 over the single-domain *Pubmed* models. For the rest of the tasks we see marginal improvements across the board and on average the new multidomain model (*Am-RC-R-Ar-P*) performs the best out of all models.

Results here indicate that performance is improved when continuously adapting to a low-resource domain than simply pretraining a model on it, regardless of domain data size. In fact, performance improves overall, possibly because of the increased amount of training data.

	Multi	**Pub-10**	**Pub-100**	**Pub-500**	**+Pub-10**	**+Pub-100**	**+Pub-500**
ACL-ARC	$70.5_{2.1}$	$68.7_{1.7}$	$68.5_{1.4}$	$68.5_{2.0}$	$70.7_{1.2}$	$70.7_{1.8}$	$\mathbf{71.0_{1.7}}$
SciCite	$86.1_{0.2}$	$85.7_{0.2}$	$85.9_{0.3}$	$85.5_{0.2}$	$86.1_{0.2}$	$\mathbf{86.3_{0.3}}$	$86.2_{0.2}$
SARC	$\mathbf{76.1_{0.3}}$	$75.2_{0.2}$	$75.2_{0.2}$	$75.7_{0.1}$	$\mathbf{76.1_{0.3}}$	$\mathbf{76.1_{0.3}}$	$\mathbf{76.1_{0.2}}$
TalkDown	$86.1_{0.7}$	$86.0_{0.5}$	$85.9_{0.4}$	$86.0_{0.5}$	$86.1_{0.3}$	$\mathbf{86.2_{0.4}}$	$86.1_{0.4}$
HyperPartisan	$80.5_{1.4}$	$78.8_{1.2}$	$79.0_{2.3}$	$78.8_{1.3}$	$80.5_{1.8}$	$80.5_{2.0}$	$\mathbf{80.6_{1.6}}$
AG-News	$\mathbf{94.3_{0.1}}$	$94.0_{0.1}$	$94.1_{0.1}$	$94.0_{0.1}$	$\mathbf{94.3_{0.1}}$	$\mathbf{94.3_{0.1}}$	$\mathbf{94.3_{0.1}}$
IMDB	$86.7_{0.1}$	$86.4_{0.1}$	$86.3_{0.1}$	$86.3_{0.1}$	$86.7_{0.1}$	$\mathbf{86.8_{0.1}}$	$86.7_{0.1}$
Clothing	$69.3_{0.3}$	$66.7_{0.4}$	$67.2_{0.5}$	$66.9_{0.3}$	$\mathbf{69.5_{0.4}}$	$69.3_{0.4}$	$69.4_{0.3}$
ChemProt	$77.0_{0.6}$	$78.3_{0.1}$	$78.5_{1.1}$	$78.3_{0.2}$	$79.2_{0.1}$	$79.4_{0.5}$	$\mathbf{79.6_{0.4}}$
Pubmed-RCT	$86.4_{0.1}$	$86.4_{0.1}$	$86.4_{0.1}$	$86.4_{0.1}$	$86.4_{0.0}$	$\mathbf{86.5_{0.1}}$	$86.4_{0.1}$
MultiNLI	$79.1_{0.3}$	$76.9_{0.3}$	$77.1_{0.3}$	$77.1_{0.3}$	$79.2_{0.4}$	$\mathbf{79.7_{0.5}}$	$79.3_{0.3}$
Average	81.1	80.3	80.4	80.3	81.3	81.4	**81.5**

Table 2: Comparison of a) our main multidomain model (**Multi**), b) models pretrained solely on *Pubmed* (**Pub-10/100/500**), and c) models after continued adaptation to *Pubmed* (**+Pub-10/100/500**).

5.3 Adaptation to Irrelevant Domain

To establish whether the multidomain model is indeed benefiting from exposure to multiple domains, or whether this is a case where more data means better modeling, we train a model on solely *Amazon* using as much data as the total amount of data in the main multidomain model (roughly 8GBs). We show that this model performs worse than the multidomain model (Appendix D). Thus, it is the use of multiple domains that is beneficial in this setting and not strictly the amount of data.

5.4 Domain Adaptation Order

Experiments were conducted to determine how much domain adaptation order affects performance. In our main comparisons, the domain order was *Amazon* → *Reddit Comments* → *Realnews* → *Arxiv* (*Am-RC-R-Ar*). Here we examine the accuracy of the rest of the possible adaptation orders.

The average performance of all orders across the given tasks is 81.4, with a minimum of 81.1 and a maximum of 81.7, whereas base DistilBERT scores an average of 79.3. In the worst case, there is still an improvement of 1.8, while on average we see an improvement of 2.1 over the base model.

In general, performance didn't fluctuate substantially between different orders. A plausible assumption is that the last adapted domain would have a large effect on performance, especially on tasks in that domain. This is not the case though; there seems to be no correlation between last adapted domain and task accuracy. Extensive results are presented in Appendix F.

5.5 Joint Domain Adaptation

So far we have only the case where we continuously adapt to domains in succession. After Domain A, we adapt to Domain B, then C, etc. What happens when we adapt on all domains at the same time? When training sequentially, it is plausible that a later domain will overpower an earlier one. Maybe this will be mitigated by training on all domains jointly. For this experiment, domain datasets are merged into the same training set via the following scheme: the first batch is comprised of Domain A samples, the second batch of Domain B and so on. We observe that performance remained unchanged. We showcase this experiment in Appendix E.

6 Conclusion

In this work we show that domain adaptation can be extended to multiple domains. These multidomain models are able to tackle tasks across various domains with minimal performance drop compared to single-domain models, while using fewer resources and reducing our carbon footprint.

In addition, based on Zhao et al. (2020), we can use several finetuned instances of a multidomain model for a number of tasks, with negligible increase in memory usage. So our multidomain models are also beneficial on low-resource devices.

Finally, we show that adapting to multiple domains always provides a performance increase and that tasks in low-resource domains receive a boost from multidomain models.

Acknowledgments. This work was supported by ERCAdG #740516.

References

Nick Brooks. 2018. Women's e-commerce clothing reviews. Accessed: 23-06-2020.

Tom B. Brown, Benjamin Mann, Nick Ryder, Melanie Subbiah, Jared Kaplan, Prafulla Dhariwal, Arvind Neelakantan, Pranav Shyam, Girish Sastry, Amanda Askell, Sandhini Agarwal, Ariel Herbert-Voss, Gretchen Krueger, Tom Henighan, Rewon Child, Aditya Ramesh, Daniel M. Ziegler, Jeffrey Wu, Clemens Winter, Christopher Hesse, Mark Chen, Eric Sigler, Mateusz Litwin, Scott Gray, Benjamin Chess, Jack Clark, Christopher Berner, Sam McCandlish, Alec Radford, Ilya Sutskever, and Dario Amodei. 2020. Language models are few-shot learners.

Arman Cohan, Waleed Ammar, Madeleine Van Zuylen, and Field Cady. 2019. Structural scaffolds for citation intent classification in scientific publications. In *NAACL*.

Arman Cohan, Franck Dernoncourt, Doo Soon Kim, Trung Bui, Seokhwan Kim, Walter Chang, and Nazli Goharian. 2018. A discourse-aware attention model for abstractive summarization of long documents. In *Proceedings of the 2018 Conference of the North American Chapter of the Association for Computational Linguistics: Human Language Technologies, Volume 2 (Short Papers)*, pages 615–621, New Orleans, Louisiana. Association for Computational Linguistics.

Franck Dernoncourt and Ji Young Lee. 2017. PubMed 200k RCT: a dataset for sequential sentence classification in medical abstracts. In *Proceedings of the Eighth International Joint Conference on Natural Language Processing (Volume 2: Short Papers)*, pages 308–313, Taipei, Taiwan. Asian Federation of Natural Language Processing.

Jacob Devlin, Ming-Wei Chang, Kenton Lee, and Kristina Toutanova. 2019. BERT: Pre-training of deep bidirectional transformers for language understanding. In *Proceedings of the 2019 Conference of the North American Chapter of the Association for Computational Linguistics: Human Language Technologies, Volume 1 (Long and Short Papers)*, pages 4171–4186, Minneapolis, Minnesota. Association for Computational Linguistics.

Suchin Gururangan, Ana Marasović, Swabha Swayamdipta, Kyle Lo, Iz Beltagy, Doug Downey, and Noah A. Smith. 2020. Don't stop pretraining: Adapt language models to domains and tasks.

Xiaochuang Han and Jacob Eisenstein. 2019. Unsupervised domain adaptation of contextualized embeddings for sequence labeling. In *Proceedings of the 2019 Conference on Empirical Methods in Natural Language Processing and the 9th International Joint Conference on Natural Language Processing (EMNLP-IJCNLP)*, pages 4238–4248, Hong Kong, China. Association for Computational Linguistics.

Ruining He and Julian McAuley. 2016. Ups and downs. *Proceedings of the 25th International Conference on World Wide Web - WWW '16*.

David Jurgens, Srijan Kumar, Raine Hoover, Dan McFarland, and Dan Jurafsky. 2018. Measuring the evolution of a scientific field through citation frames. *Transactions of the Association for Computational Linguistics*, 6:391–406.

Mikhail Khodak, Nikunj Saunshi, and Kiran Vodrahalli. 2018. A large self-annotated corpus for sarcasm. In *Proceedings of the Eleventh International Conference on Language Resources and Evaluation (LREC 2018)*, Miyazaki, Japan. European Language Resources Association (ELRA).

Johannes Kiesel, Maria Mestre, Rishabh Shukla, Emmanuel Vincent, Payam Adineh, David Corney, Benno Stein, and Martin Potthast. 2019. SemEval-2019 task 4: Hyperpartisan news detection. In *Proceedings of the 13th International Workshop on Semantic Evaluation*, pages 829–839, Minneapolis, Minnesota, USA. Association for Computational Linguistics.

Brunak S Lund O Oprea TI Taboureau O Kringelum J, Kjaerulff SK. 2016. Chemprot-3.0: a global chemical biology diseases mapping.

Alexandre Lacoste, Alexandra Luccioni, Victor Schmidt, and Thomas Dandres. 2019. Quantifying the carbon emissions of machine learning.

Yinhan Liu, Myle Ott, Naman Goyal, Jingfei Du, Mandar Joshi, Danqi Chen, Omer Levy, Mike Lewis, Luke Zettlemoyer, and Veselin Stoyanov. 2019. Roberta: A robustly optimized bert pretraining approach.

Kyle Lo, Lucy Lu Wang, Mark Neumann, Rodney Kinney, and Daniel Weld. 2020. S2ORC: The semantic scholar open research corpus. In *Proceedings of the 58th Annual Meeting of the Association for Computational Linguistics*, pages 4969–4983, Online. Association for Computational Linguistics.

Andrew L. Maas, Raymond E. Daly, Peter T. Pham, Dan Huang, Andrew Y. Ng, and Christopher Potts. 2011. Learning word vectors for sentiment analysis. In *Proceedings of the 49th Annual Meeting of the Association for Computational Linguistics: Human Language Technologies*, pages 142–150, Portland, Oregon, USA. Association for Computational Linguistics.

Nina Poerner, Ulli Waltinger, and Hinrich Schütze. 2020. Inexpensive domain adaptation of pretrained language models: Case studies on biomedical ner and covid-19 qa.

Alexander Rietzler, Sebastian Stabinger, Paul Opitz, and Stefan Engl. 2020. Adapt or get left behind: Domain adaptation through BERT language model finetuning for aspect-target sentiment classification. In *Proceedings of The 12th Language Resources and Evaluation Conference*, pages 4933–4941, Marseille, France. European Language Resources Association.

Victor Sanh, Lysandre Debut, Julien Chaumond, and Thomas Wolf. 2019. Distilbert, a distilled version of bert: smaller, faster, cheaper and lighter.

Victor Sanh, Thomas Wolf, and Alexander M. Rush. 2020. Movement pruning: Adaptive sparsity by finetuning.

Emma Strubell, Ananya Ganesh, and Andrew McCallum. 2019. Energy and policy considerations for deep learning in NLP. In *Proceedings of the 57th Annual Meeting of the Association for Computational Linguistics*, pages 3645–3650, Florence, Italy. Association for Computational Linguistics.

Zhiqing Sun, Hongkun Yu, Xiaodan Song, Renjie Liu, Yiming Yang, and Denny Zhou. 2020. Mobilebert: a compact task-agnostic bert for resource-limited devices.

Michael Völske, Martin Potthast, Shahbaz Syed, and Benno Stein. 2017. Tl;dr: Mining Reddit to learn automatic summarization. In *Proceedings of the Workshop on New Frontiers in Summarization*, pages 59–63, Copenhagen, Denmark. Association for Computational Linguistics.

Zijian Wang and Christopher Potts. 2019. TalkDown: A corpus for condescension detection in context. In *Proceedings of the 2019 Conference on Empirical Methods in Natural Language Processing and the 9th International Joint Conference on Natural Language Processing (EMNLP-IJCNLP)*, pages 3711–3719, Hong Kong, China. Association for Computational Linguistics.

Adina Williams, Nikita Nangia, and Samuel Bowman. 2018. A broad-coverage challenge corpus for sentence understanding through inference. In *Proceedings of the 2018 Conference of the North American Chapter of the Association for Computational Linguistics: Human Language Technologies, Volume 1 (Long Papers)*, pages 1112–1122. Association for Computational Linguistics.

Rowan Zellers, Ari Holtzman, Hannah Rashkin, Yonatan Bisk, Ali Farhadi, Franziska Roesner, and Yejin Choi. 2019. Defending against neural fake news. In H. Wallach, H. Larochelle, A. Beygelzimer, F. d'Alché Buc, E. Fox, and R. Garnett, editors, *Advances in Neural Information Processing Systems 32*, pages 9054–9065. Curran Associates, Inc.

Xiang Zhang, Junbo Zhao, and Yann LeCun. 2015. Character-level convolutional networks for text classification.

Mengjie Zhao, Tao Lin, Martin Jaggi, and Hinrich Schütze. 2020. Masking as an efficient alternative to finetuning for pretrained language models.

A Task Data Overview

In *ACL-ARC* (Jurgens et al., 2018), the task is to classify citation intent in excerpts from ACL papers. *SciCite* (Cohan et al., 2019) is also a citation intent classification task, covering multiple scientific domains. *HyperPartisan* (Kiesel et al., 2019) is a news dataset, where given an article the task is to predict whether it is hyperpartisan (ie. one-sided) or not. In *AG-News* (Zhang et al., 2015), we need to predict one of four possible news topics given the article text. In *IMDB* (Maas et al., 2011) and *Clothing Reviews* (Brooks, 2018), given a review text the corresponding rating must be inferred. In *SARC* (Khodak et al., 2018), we are tasked with identifying whether a Reddit comment contains sarcasm or not. *TalkDown* (Wang and Potts, 2019) presents Reddit comment pairs and we are tasked with identifying if the reply is condescending to the original comment. *PubMed-RCT* (Dernoncourt and Lee, 2017) is a dataset containing sentences from biomedical paper abstracts alongside their role in the abstract (for example, 'background', 'result'), while for *ChemProt* (Kringelum J, 2016) we are tasked with identifying relations between proteins and chemicals.

B Domain Adaptation Hyperparameters

For domain adaptation, hyperparameters are the same for both setups (single-domain and multidomain), across all domains. Minimal hyperparameter tuning was performed, with the main goal being to keep training as computationally efficient as possible. Batch size and sequence length were set to 32 and the learning rate to $1e$-5. Models were trained for a single epoch. The multidomain model was therefore trained for 4 epochs in total, one for each domain.

C Supervised Task Learning Hyperparameters

Apart from the difference in epochs and the number of classifier neurons, all other hyperparameters are the same for all models during supervised task learning. Learning rate was kept at $4e$-5, as suggested in Devlin et al. (2019). Maximum sequence length was set to 128 while we used 32 batches for training and testing. All hyperparameters were selected upon evaluation on the development sets.

D Irrelevant Domain Adaptation Results

Results for adaptation to an irrelevant domain. In this case, DistilBert is pretrained entirely on *Amazon* (8GBs). As in Gururangan et al. (2020), we find that when adapting to an irrelevant domain, performance does not increase.

	Multi	**Amazon**
ACL-ARC	$\mathbf{70.5_{2.1}}$	$68.2_{1.3}$
SciCite	$\mathbf{86.1_{0.2}}$	$85.1_{0.3}$
SARC	$\mathbf{76.1_{0.3}}$	$75.3_{0.2}$
TalkDown	$\mathbf{86.1_{0.7}}$	$\mathbf{86.1_{0.5}}$
HyperPartisan	$\mathbf{80.5_{1.4}}$	$79.3_{1.1}$
AG-News	$\mathbf{94.3_{0.1}}$	$94.1_{0.1}$
IMDB	$\mathbf{86.7_{0.1}}$	$\mathbf{86.7_{0.1}}$
Clothing	$69.3_{0.3}$	$\mathbf{69.5_{0.1}}$
ChemProt	$77.0_{0.6}$	$\mathbf{77.4_{0.8}}$
Pubmed-RCT	$\mathbf{86.4_{0.1}}$	$86.1_{0.1}$
MultiNLI	$\mathbf{79.1_{0.3}}$	$77.2_{0.3}$
Average	**81.1**	80.4

Table 3: Comparison between our main model (**Multi**) and a model pretrained entirely on **Amazon** data.

E Joint Domain Adaptation Results

Here we compare results between sequential (*Am-RC-R-Ar*) and joint domain adaptation. Results remain similar, showing that there is no substantial difference between the two adaptation methods.

	Sequential	**Joint**
ACL-ARC	$70.5_{2.1}$	$\mathbf{72.6_{1.9}}$
SciCite	$86.1_{0.2}$	$\mathbf{86.5_{0.2}}$
SARC	$\mathbf{76.1_{0.3}}$	$76.0_{0.2}$
TalkDown	$\mathbf{86.1_{0.7}}$	$86.0_{0.6}$
HyperPartisan	$80.5_{1.4}$	$\mathbf{80.9_{1.2}}$
AG-News	$\mathbf{94.3_{0.1}}$	$94.2_{0.1}$
IMDB	$\mathbf{86.7_{0.1}}$	$\mathbf{86.7_{0.1}}$
Clothing	$69.3_{0.3}$	$\mathbf{69.4_{0.2}}$
ChemProt	$77.0_{0.6}$	$\mathbf{77.9_{0.7}}$
Pubmed-RCT	$\mathbf{86.4_{0.1}}$	$\mathbf{86.4_{0.1}}$
MultiNLI	$79.1_{0.3}$	$\mathbf{79.2_{0.3}}$
Average	81.1	**81.4**

Table 4: Comparison of sequential and joint models.

F Domain Adaptation Order Results

Results for adaptation order experiments are given in Tables 5, 6, 7 and 8 (alphabetical order).

	Am-Ar-R-RC	Am-Ar-RC-R	Am-R-Ar-RC	Am-R-RC-Ar	Am-RC-Ar-R	Am-RC-R-Ar
ACL-ARC	$74.1_{1.2}$	$71.0_{2.4}$	$72.7_{3.0}$	$75.1_{0.3}$	$72.7_{2.1}$	$70.5_{1.0}$
SciCite	$86.0_{0.3}$	$86.3_{0.1}$	$85.7_{0.5}$	$85.9_{0.3}$	$85.5_{0.2}$	$86.1_{0.2}$
SARC	$75.9_{0.1}$	$76.2_{0.1}$	$76.0_{0.3}$	$75.9_{0.2}$	$75.7_{0.3}$	$76.1_{0.1}$
TalkDown	$86.4_{0.5}$	$86.1_{1.2}$	$85.9_{0.6}$	$86.1_{1.0}$	$85.9_{0.7}$	$86.1_{0.6}$
HyperPartisan	$80.1_{2.5}$	$78.4_{0.7}$	$80.5_{3.8}$	$81.6_{1.3}$	$81.3_{1.4}$	$80.5_{1.7}$
AG-News	$94.2_{0.2}$	$94.4_{0.1}$	$94.3_{0.1}$	$94.2_{0.0}$	$94.5_{0.1}$	$94.3_{0.1}$
IMDB	$86.5_{0.1}$	$86.6_{0.1}$	$86.7_{0.1}$	$86.6_{0.1}$	$86.6_{0.2}$	$86.7_{0.1}$
Clothing	$69.2_{0.2}$	$69.4_{0.4}$	$69.4_{0.4}$	$69.2_{0.1}$	$69.5_{0.3}$	$69.3_{0.4}$
ChemProt	$78.2_{0.3}$	$77.7_{0.3}$	$77.5_{0.5}$	$77.7_{0.8}$	$77.7_{0.6}$	$77.0_{0.3}$
Pubmed-RCT	$86.4_{0.1}$	$86.4_{0.0}$	$86.5_{0.1}$	$86.5_{0.1}$	$86.4_{0.1}$	$86.4_{0.1}$
MultiNLI	$79.3_{0.2}$	$79.1_{0.3}$	$79.3_{0.3}$	$79.2_{0.1}$	$79.3_{0.3}$	$79.1_{0.2}$
Average	81.5	81.1	81.3	81.6	81.4	81.1

Table 5: Domain adaptation order comparison - Orders commencing with *Amazon*.

	Ar-Am-R-RC	Ar-Am-RC-R	Ar-R-Am-RC	Ar-R-RC-Am	Ar-RC-Am-R	Ar-RC-R-Am
ACL-ARC	$72.9_{0.7}$	$70.5_{1.2}$	$72.9_{1.5}$	$71.2_{1.6}$	$74.8_{1.8}$	$72.4_{1.4}$
SciCite	$86.1_{0.1}$	$86.5_{0.5}$	$85.8_{0.2}$	$85.9_{0.4}$	$86.1_{0.2}$	$86.2_{0.3}$
SARC	$75.9_{0.3}$	$76.2_{0.2}$	$76.1_{0.1}$	$75.8_{0.4}$	$76.1_{0.2}$	$76.0_{0.3}$
TalkDown	$86.3_{0.3}$	$86.3_{0.3}$	$85.9_{0.8}$	$86.7_{0.3}$	$85.9_{0.9}$	$86.2_{0.7}$
HyperPartisan	$81.5_{2.1}$	$82.1_{1.5}$	$82.7_{1.5}$	$80.3_{1.9}$	$78.5_{1.8}$	$79.3_{2.3}$
AG-News	$94.4_{0.2}$	$94.3_{0.1}$	$94.2_{0.2}$	$94.3_{0.2}$	$94.4_{0.1}$	$94.3_{0.1}$
IMDB	$86.6_{0.2}$	$86.4_{0.0}$	$86.6_{0.1}$	$86.6_{0.2}$	$86.6_{0.2}$	$86.7_{0.2}$
Clothing	$69.6_{0.3}$	$69.3_{0.2}$	$69.5_{0.5}$	$69.7_{0.4}$	$69.3_{0.2}$	$69.5_{0.2}$
ChemProt	$77.7_{0.3}$	$78.3_{0.4}$	$77.7_{0.8}$	$78.9_{0.4}$	$78.3_{0.7}$	$77.4_{1.2}$
Pubmed-RCT	$86.5_{0.1}$	$86.4_{0.1}$	$86.5_{0.1}$	$86.5_{0.1}$	$86.5_{0.1}$	$86.5_{0.0}$
MultiNLI	$78.9_{0.3}$	$79.4_{0.2}$	$79.2_{0.2}$	$79.3_{0.3}$	$79.4_{0.3}$	$79.0_{0.1}$
Average	81.5	81.4	81.6	81.4	81.5	81.2

Table 6: Domain adaptation order comparison - Orders commencing with *Arxiv*.

	R-Am-Ar-RC	R-Am-RC-Ar	R-Ar-Am-RC	R-Ar-RC-Am	R-RC-Am-Ar	R-RC-Ar-Am
ACL-ARC	$74.8_{1.7}$	$72.4_{1.3}$	$70.7_{2.4}$	$72.2_{2.9}$	$73.1_{3.2}$	$72.7_{1.2}$
SciCite	$85.8_{0.4}$	$85.6_{0.4}$	$86.2_{0.1}$	$86.0_{0.3}$	$85.9_{0.4}$	$86.3_{0.2}$
SARC	$76.4_{0.3}$	$76.3_{0.2}$	$75.9_{0.3}$	$75.9_{0.3}$	$76.1_{0.1}$	$75.8_{0.4}$
TalkDown	$86.3_{0.2}$	$86.4_{0.1}$	$86.4_{0.7}$	$85.9_{0.4}$	$86.7_{0.4}$	$85.8_{0.9}$
HyperPartisan	$81.5_{2.1}$	$83.5_{2.9}$	$80.4_{1.2}$	$80.6_{1.3}$	$81.0_{3.1}$	$81.3_{1.8}$
AG-News	$94.2_{0.1}$	$94.2_{0.1}$	$94.4_{0.1}$	$94.2_{0.1}$	$94.3_{0.1}$	$94.4_{0.1}$
IMDB	$86.7_{0.0}$	$86.7_{0.1}$	$86.4_{0.2}$	$86.6_{0.0}$	$86.6_{0.1}$	$86.7_{1.5}$
Clothing	$69.7_{0.2}$	$69.2_{0.2}$	$69.6_{0.1}$	$68.8_{0.6}$	$69.2_{0.3}$	$68.8_{0.3}$
ChemProt	$77.8_{0.8}$	$77.1_{1.0}$	$77.9_{0.9}$	$77.9_{0.8}$	$79.0_{1.0}$	$79.0_{0.3}$
Pubmed-RCT	$86.5_{0.1}$	$86.4_{0.1}$	$86.5_{0.1}$	$86.5_{0.1}$	$86.5_{0.1}$	$86.4_{0.0}$
MultiNLI	$79.1_{0.1}$	$79.2_{0.2}$	$79.1_{0.2}$	$79.4_{0.3}$	$79.0_{0.4}$	$78.8_{0.2}$
Average	81.7	81.6	81.2	81.3	81.6	81.5

Table 7: Domain adaptation order comparison - Orders commencing with *Realnews*.

	RC-Am-Ar-R	RC-Am-R-Ar	RC-Ar-Am-R	RC-Ar-R-Am	RC-R-Am-Ar	RC-R-Ar-Am
ACL-ARC	$70.7_{1.2}$	$72.9_{2.5}$	$72.0_{1.0}$	$71.0_{3.4}$	$76.0_{2.1}$	$74.3_{1.2}$
SciCite	$86.5_{0.1}$	$86.4_{0.2}$	$85.9_{0.3}$	$86.2_{0.2}$	$86.0_{0.2}$	$86.0_{0.3}$
SARC	$76.2_{0.2}$	$75.9_{0.3}$	$76.3_{0.1}$	$75.9_{0.3}$	$76.1_{0.3}$	$76.3_{0.3}$
TalkDown	$86.1_{0.5}$	$86.6_{0.3}$	$85.9_{1.0}$	$86.7_{0.8}$	$86.0_{0.5}$	$86.1_{0.4}$
HyperPartisan	$82.3_{2.0}$	$82.1_{1.6}$	$80.9_{2.3}$	$80.6_{0.9}$	$81.2_{1.3}$	$78.8_{1.4}$
AG-News	$94.1_{0.1}$	$94.2_{0.1}$	$94.1_{0.1}$	$94.4_{0.1}$	$94.4_{0.1}$	$94.3_{0.2}$
IMDB	$86.6_{0.2}$	$86.7_{0.2}$	$86.7_{1.5}$	$86.7_{1.5}$	$86.7_{1.5}$	$86.4_{0.2}$
Clothing	$69.5_{0.4}$	$69.9_{0.5}$	$69.3_{0.7}$	$69.5_{0.4}$	$69.1_{0.1}$	$69.1_{0.4}$
ChemProt	$79.2_{0.4}$	$78.3_{0.6}$	$78.6_{0.3}$	$78.7_{0.9}$	$77.9_{0.5}$	$78.0_{0.9}$
Pubmed-RCT	$86.5_{0.1}$	$86.4_{0.1}$	$86.5_{0.1}$	$86.5_{0.1}$	$86.4_{0.1}$	$86.4_{0.1}$
MultiNLI	$79.2_{0.4}$	$79.3_{0.1}$	$79.3_{0.2}$	$79.1_{0.2}$	$79.0_{0.4}$	$78.9_{0.3}$
Average	81.5	81.7	81.4	81.4	81.7	81.3

Table 8: Domain adaptation order comparison - Orders commencing with *Reddit Comments*.

Pseudo-Label Guided Unsupervised Domain Adaptation of Contextual Embeddings

Tianyu Chen[1], Shaohan Huang[2], Furu Wei[2], Jianxin Li[1]*
Beihang University[1], Microsoft Research Asia[2]
tianyuc@buaa.edu.cn shaohanh@microsoft.com
fuwei@microsoft.com lijx@buaa.edu.cn

Abstract

Contextual embedding models such as BERT can be easily fine-tuned on labeled samples to create a state-of-the-art model for many downstream tasks. However, the fine-tuned BERT model suffers considerably from unlabeled data when applied to a different domain. In unsupervised domain adaptation, we aim to train a model that works well on a target domain when provided with labeled source samples and unlabeled target samples. In this paper, we propose a pseudo-label guided method for unsupervised domain adaptation. Two models are fine-tuned on labeled source samples as pseudo labeling models. To learn representations for the target domain, one of those models is adapted by masked language modeling from the target domain. Then those models are used to assign pseudo-labels to target samples. We train the final model with those samples. We evaluate our method on named entity segmentation and sentiment analysis tasks. These experiments show that our approach outperforms baseline methods.

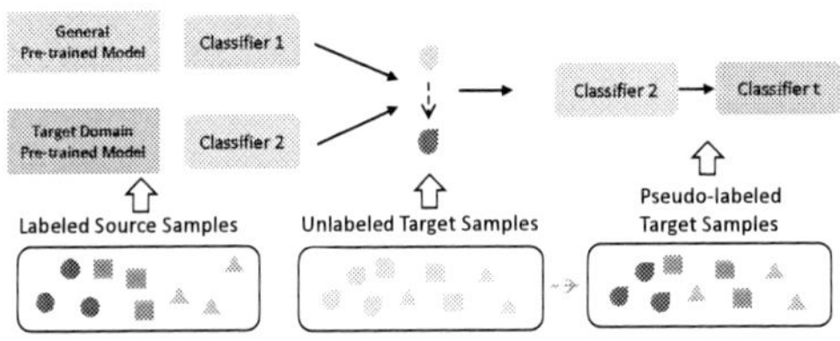

Figure 1: Overview of our training framework. We jointly fine-tune general pre-trained model and target domain pre-trained model with labeled source data. Then we generate pseudo-labels on target samples. Finally, we train the final model with the pseudo-labeled samples.

1 Introduction

Contextualized embeddings have become the foundations of many state-of-the-art natural language processing technologies (Devlin et al., 2018; Han and Eisenstein, 2019; Straková et al., 2019). Pre-trained contextualized embeddings can be used for many downstream tasks and be incorporated into an end-to-end system, allowing the embeddings to be fine-tuned from task-specific labeled data (Akbik et al., 2019a,b, 2018; Beltagy et al., 2019).

One of the problems with contextual embedding models is that although fine-tuned models perform well on the samples generated from the same distribution as the training samples, they suffer considerably from unlabeled data when applied to a different domain (Saito et al., 2017; Rietzler et al., 2019; Ruder and Plank, 2018). For example, a named entity segmentation model trained on a news dataset fails to predict correctly on social media data such as Twitter. Because collecting many labeled samples in various domains is expensive, it is important to adapt contextual embedding model to different domains in unsupervised setting.

Many domain adaptation methods of neural networks in NLP have been proposed in the past several years (Li, 2012; Ziser and Reichart, 2019, 2018; Cui et al., 2018; Louizos et al., 2015; Ganin et al., 2015; Mou et al., 2016). Our work focuses on unsupervised domain adaptation of contextual embeddings. We aim to fine-tune a pre-trained model that works well on a target domain when provided with labeled source samples and unlabeled target samples. With no access to the labels in target domain data, it is very difficult to adapt when the divergence of the label distribution between the source domain and the target domain is huge.

Some of current methods propose a simple unsupervised domain-adaptive method, using a masked language modeling objective over unlabeled text in the target domain (Rochette et al., 2019; Han and Eisenstein, 2019; Gururangan et al., 2020). They first learn discriminative representations for the tar-

*Corresponding author.

Proceedings of the Second Workshop on Domain Adaptation for NLP, pages 9–15
April 20, 2021. ©2021 Association for Computational Linguistics

get domain and then fine-tune a domain-adapted model with labeled source samples. Although self-supervised fine-tuning in the target domain improves the generalization of the pre-trained model for the target domain, an adapted model cannot capture the task-specific pattern of the target domain only using labeled source samples to fine-tune. We expect the adapted model to not only acquire some target-discriminative language representations but also to obtain some task-specific features of target domain.

In this paper, we propose a pseudo-label guided method for unsupervised domain adaptation. As shown in Figure 1, two models are jointly fine-tuned on labeled source samples as pseudo labeling models. We design a multiview constraint loss to encourage those two model to make predictions based on different view-point. To learn representations for the target domain, one of those models is adapted by masked language modeling from the target domain. Then those models are used to assign pseudo-labels to target samples. Pseudo-labeled target samples will provide target discriminative information to the model. We train the final model with the pseudo-labeled samples.

We evaluate our method both on named entity segmentation (NES) and sentiment analysis (SA) tasks. We find that our pseudo-label guided method outperforms baseline methods. Moreover, we demonstrate the multiview constraint significantly improves performance of our method.

2 Methodology

2.1 Overview

In unsupervised domain adaptation, we aim to train a model that works well on a target domain when provided with labeled source samples and unlabeled target samples.

As illustrated in Figure 1, **P**seudo-label **G**uided unsupervised **A**daptation (**PGA**) consists of three steps: jointly fine-tuning, pseudo label generation and final adaptation. First, we initialize two pre-trained models with the same architecture as the general pre-trained model and the target domain pre-trained model (TDPM) which leverages language modeling objective on unlabeled data from target domain. In the second step, we use those two fine-tuned model to make predictions for unlabeled target samples. If both models agree with the prediction and two prediction scores exceed a threshold, the prediction is regarded as a pseudo label. Finally, all pseudo labels are collected to fine-tune the target domain pre-trained model and complete the adaptation.

2.2 Jointly Fine-tuning

In the first stage, we jointly fine-tune the general pre-trained model and the target domain pre-trained model on the source domain data to obtain two classification models F_1 and F_2. Their predictions are utilized to give pseudo-labels. We assume each sample in the source domain can be denoted as (X_i, Y_i), where X is a text sequence and Y is a label sequence for NES task or a label for SA task.

For named entity segmentation task, the token representations are fed into an output layer at the output. For sentiment analysis, the [CLS] representation is fed into an output layer for classification (Devlin et al., 2018).

Inspired by the asymmetric tri-training adaptation method (Saito et al., 2017), we design a multiview constraint loss to encourage model F_1 and F_2 to make predictions based on different viewpoints. We add the term $|W_1^T W_2|$ to the cost function, where W_1, W_2 denote output layers weights of model F_1 and F_2. With this constraint, each model learns from different features. The objective of learning F_1, F_2 is defined as:

$$E(\theta_{F_1}, \theta_{F_2}) = CE_{loss}(F_1(x_i), y_i) + CE_{loss}(F_2(x_i), y_i) + \lambda |W_1^T W_2| \quad (1)$$

where CE_{loss} denotes the standard cross entropy loss and we decide the trade-off parameter λ based on validation split. With the multiview learning objective, the pseudo labels can be more informative and improve model accuracy.

2.3 Pseudo Label Generation

After jointly fine-tuning, classification model F_1 and F_2 are used to generate pseudo labels. Pseudo labels will provide target-discriminative information to the model. However, since they certainly contain false labels, we have to pick up reliable pseudo-labels.

For text sequence X in the unlabeled target domain data, we add pseudo annotations Y to the sequence in the NES task and add single pseudo label Y to the sequence in the SA task.

There are two requirements for pseudo label assignment. Take the NES task as an example. First, for each token X_i in the text sequence, when C_i^1 and C_i^2 denote the class which have the maximum predicted probability for X_i from model F_1 and model F_2 respectively, we require $C_i^1 = C_i^2$, which means the two models agree with the prediction. The second requirement is that the probability of C_i^1 or C_i^2 exceeds the threshold parameter, which we set as 0.5 in the experiment. We suppose that unless two models are confident of their predictions, the prediction is not reliable. If the two requirements are satisfied, the label is added to the pseudo target samples.

Intuitively, if the two domains are closely related, the pseudo labels are assigned to a large portion of target samples while distant domains will reduce the amount of agreement. We expect the threshold of agreement to keep the pseudo labels reliable and maintain a probable number of samples.

2.4 Final Adaptation

We use the pseudo-labeled target samples to construct a training set of the target domain and further fine-tune the target domain pre-trained model with this training set. Since the accuracy of pseudo labels can not be assured, we use a smaller learning rate and fewer training steps to fine-tune F_2 with pseudo labels.

The whole training algorithm is depicted in Algorithm 1, where we take labeled source samples and unlabeled target samples and output the adapted model.

Algorithm 1 We jointly fine-tune two models and generate pseudo labels for final adaptation.

```
Input:
S = {(x_i, t_i)}_{i=1}^m, T = (x_j)_{j=1}^n
Train TDPM on T with language modeling objective
Initialize F_1 with original BERT
Initialize F_2 with TDPM
Train F_1, F_2 with Equation 1
Initialize T_l = ∅
for x_j in T do
    y_j^1 = F_1(x_j)
    y_j^2 = F_2(x_j)
    C_j^1 = argmax(y_j^1)
    C_j^2 = argmax(y_j^2)
    if C_j^1 == C_j^2 and max(y_j^1, y_j^2) > threshold
    then
        Add (x_j, y_j^1) to T_l
    end if
end for
Train F_2 on T_l with supervised learning
Output: F_2
```

3 Experiments

3.1 Datasets

Named Entity Segmentation (NES) The named entity segmentation is a typical task of the sequence labeling task. Different from named entity recognition, we only predict the "BIO" format in a sequence, which divides the sequence into entity chunks without deciding which class the entity chunk belongs to. We choose the shared task of the 2016 workshop on Noisy User Text (WNUT; Strauss et al., 2016) as target domain and the canonical CoNLL 2003 shared task (Tjong Kim Sang and De Meulder, 2003) as the source domain. In the WNUT task, the corpus was from Twitter, which is an open-domain source and the data of the CoNLL 2003 task was annotated on a corpus of newstext.

Sentiment Analysis (SA) The sentiment analysis is a sequence classification task. Since we need to assign a sentiment class to each whole sentence, the task is more relied on contextualized level information. We choose 3 domains from open Amazon review data (He and McAuley, 2016) including books, electronics and kitchens, following the settings of Ruder and Plank's domain adaptation survey (Ruder and Plank, 2018). The data statistics and hyper-parameters see Appendix A and B. The source code* and sentiment analysis data set will be released at a future date.

3.2 Baselines

We evaluate the following systems:

Source only: This baseline directly fine-tunes the pre-trained BERT on the source domain.

Frozen BERT: This baseline first learns from unlabeled data from target domain by language modeling. Then it freezes the BERT encoder and only optimizes the classifier layer.

AdaptaBERT: This baseline first learns from unlabeled data from target domain by language modeling. Then it fine-tunes target domain pre-trained model with labeled source samples†.(Han and Eisenstein, 2019).

PGA: Our pseudo-label guided unsupervised adaptation method in Section 2.

*Implementation retrieved from `https://github.com/huggingface/transformers`

†Use the released code to conduct our experiment `https://github.com/xhan77/AdaptaBERT`

Model	WNUT (target)	CoNLL (source)
Source only	56.52	97.69
AdaptaBERT	63.81	97.67
PGA w/o MC	64.12	96.89
PGA	**64.32**	96.82
Upper Bound	65.81	82.64

Table 1: Named entity segmentation performance on the WNUT test set (target) and CoNLL test set A (source). The F1 score of our method is very close to the upper bound of the **target domain**.

Model	Books ↓ Electronics	Electronics ↓ Books	Books ↓ Kitchens	Kitchens ↓ Books
Source only	45.68	47.84	45.28	49.56
Frozen BERT	30.52	31.76	30.16	31.44
AdaptaBERT	46.56	49.32	47.76	51.32
PGA w/o MC	45.33	50.61	48.60	53.18
PGA	**50.81**	**50.62**	**49.28**	**53.74**
Upper Bound	60.04	57.44	59.68	57.44

Table 2: Multi-domain sentiment analysis adaptation. All results are evaluated with accuracy score.

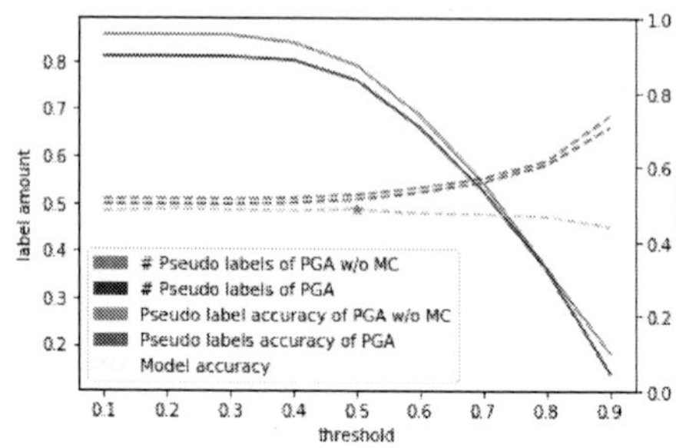

Figure 2: The threshold influences the amount of pseudo labels. We evaluate on books to electronics domain adaptation of sentiment analysis.

Domain Adaptation	PGA	PGA w/o MC
Books → Electronics	52.97	51.25
Books → Kitchens	51.94	51.03
Electronics → Books	56.72	55.34
Kitchens → Books	59.26	58.32

Table 3: The accuracy of pseudo labels.

PGA w/o MC: Our pseudo-label guided unsupervised adaptation method. Notice that the multiview constraint (MC) is not used.

Upper Bound: In *supervised learning*, we fine-tune the target domain pre-trained model directly on target training set and evaluate.

3.3 Results

As indicated in Table 1, AdaptaBERT shows strong performance of unsupervised adaptation, achieving a much better F1 score than zero-shot setting in source only. Moreover, even without multiview constraint, our PGA method performs better than AdaptaBERT. With multiview constraint, our method learns a higher quality of pseudo labels, which pushes the F1 score closer to the upper bound.

We present the domain adaptation results of sentiment analysis at Table 2, without a multiview constraint, the quality of pseudo labels can not be assured and sometimes leads to a drop in performance for target domain. However, our PGA method with multiview constraint can improve model accuracy in most scenarios. We can observe that supervised learning still greatly outperforms unsupervised methods. There is more room to improve for unsupervised domain adaptation in sentiment analysis task.

3.4 Pseudo Labels Quality

We scientifically evaluate the quality of pseudo labels generated by our method. First, we find the amount of pseudo labels is closely related to the value of our threshold in Figure 2. When the threshold is set above 0.5, the number of pseudo labels drops quickly while the accuracy of pseudo labels increases a lot. With multiview constraint, our PGA method tend to generate fewer labels with higher accuracy. It is observed that higher threshold may not benefit the final model accuracy, partly due to the significant drop of the number of pseudo labels.

We also evaluate the accuracy of pseudo labels in the SA task. The results are illustrated in Table 3. We find in different domain adaptation settings, the multiview constraint can improve the quality of pseudo labels.

4 Conclusion

We propose a new unsupervised domain adaptation method guided by pseudo labels. Generated by general pre-trained model and target domain pre-trained model with multiview constraint, the pseudo labels of unlabeled target data are more reliable and benefit model performance on the target domain. Experiments show that our approach achieves very promising results on different NLP downstream tasks.

References

Alan Akbik, Tanja Bergmann, Duncan Blythe, Kashif Rasul, Stefan Schweter, and Roland Vollgraf. 2019a. Flair: An easy-to-use framework for state-of-the-art nlp. In *Proceedings of the 2019 Conference of the North American Chapter of the Association for Computational Linguistics (Demonstrations)*, pages 54–59.

Alan Akbik, Tanja Bergmann, and Roland Vollgraf. 2019b. Pooled contextualized embeddings for named entity recognition. In *Proceedings of the 2019 Conference of the North American Chapter of the Association for Computational Linguistics: Human Language Technologies, Volume 1 (Long and Short Papers)*, pages 724–728, Minneapolis, Minnesota. Association for Computational Linguistics.

Alan Akbik, Duncan Blythe, and Roland Vollgraf. 2018. Contextual string embeddings for sequence labeling. In *Proceedings of the 27th International Conference on Computational Linguistics*, pages 1638–1649, Santa Fe, New Mexico, USA. Association for Computational Linguistics.

Iz Beltagy, Kyle Lo, and Arman Cohan. 2019. Scibert: A pretrained language model for scientific text. In *Proceedings of the 2019 Conference on Empirical Methods in Natural Language Processing and the 9th International Joint Conference on Natural Language Processing (EMNLP-IJCNLP)*, pages 3606–3611.

Xia Cui, Noor Al-Bazzas, DANUSHKA Bollegala, and FP Coenen. 2018. A comparative study of pivot selection strategies for unsupervised domain adaptation. *The Knowledge Engineering Review*.

Jacob Devlin, Ming-Wei Chang, Kenton Lee, and Kristina Toutanova. 2018. Bert: Pre-training of deep bidirectional transformers for language understanding.

Yaroslav Ganin, Evgeniya Ustinova, Hana Ajakan, Pascal Germain, Hugo Larochelle, François Laviolette, Mario Marchand, and Victor Lempitsky. 2015. Domain-adversarial training of neural networks.

Suchin Gururangan, Ana Marasović, Swabha Swayamdipta, Kyle Lo, Iz Beltagy, Doug Downey, and Noah A. Smith. 2020. Don't stop pretraining: Adapt language models to domains and tasks. In *Proceedings of ACL*.

Xiaochuang Han and Jacob Eisenstein. 2019. Unsupervised domain adaptation of contextualized embeddings for sequence labeling. In *Proceedings of the 2019 Conference on Empirical Methods in Natural Language Processing and the 9th International Joint Conference on Natural Language Processing (EMNLP-IJCNLP)*, pages 4229–4239.

Ruining He and Julian McAuley. 2016. Ups and downs: Modeling the visual evolution of fashion trends with one-class collaborative filtering. In *proceedings of the 25th international conference on world wide web*, pages 507–517.

Qi Li. 2012. Literature survey: domain adaptation algorithms for natural language processing. *Department of Computer Science The Graduate Center, The City University of New York*, pages 8–10.

Christos Louizos, Kevin Swersky, Yujia Li, Max Welling, and Richard Zemel. 2015. The variational fair autoencoder.

Julian McAuley, Christopher Targett, Qinfeng Shi, and Anton Van Den Hengel. 2015. Image-based recommendations on styles and substitutes. In *Proceedings of the 38th International ACM SIGIR Conference on Research and Development in Information Retrieval*, pages 43–52.

Lili Mou, Zhao Meng, Rui Yan, Ge Li, Yan Xu, Lu Zhang, and Zhi Jin. 2016. How transferable are neural networks in nlp applications?

Alexander Rietzler, Sebastian Stabinger, Paul Opitz, and Stefan Engl. 2019. Adapt or get left behind: Domain adaptation through bert language model finetuning for aspect-target sentiment classification. *arXiv preprint arXiv:1908.11860*.

Alexandre Rochette, Yadollah Yaghoobzadeh, and Timothy J Hazen. 2019. Unsupervised domain adaptation of contextual embeddings for low-resource duplicate question detection. *arXiv preprint arXiv:1911.02645*.

Sebastian Ruder and Barbara Plank. 2018. Strong baselines for neural semi-supervised learning under domain shift. *CoRR*, abs/1804.09530.

Kuniaki Saito, Yoshitaka Ushiku, and Tatsuya Harada. 2017. Asymmetric tri-training for unsupervised domain adaptation. In *Proceedings of the 34th International Conference on Machine Learning-Volume 70*, pages 2988–2997. JMLR. org.

Jana Straková, Milan Straka, and Jan Hajic. 2019. Neural architectures for nested NER through linearization. In *Proceedings of the 57th Annual Meeting of the Association for Computational Linguistics*, pages 5326–5331, Florence, Italy. Association for Computational Linguistics.

Benjamin Strauss, Bethany Toma, Alan Ritter, Marie-Catherine de Marneffe, and Wei Xu. 2016. Results of the WNUT16 named entity recognition shared task. In *Proceedings of the 2nd Workshop on Noisy User-generated Text (WNUT)*, pages 138–144, Osaka, Japan. The COLING 2016 Organizing Committee.

Erik F. Tjong Kim Sang and Fien De Meulder. 2003. Introduction to the CoNLL-2003 shared task: Language-independent named entity recognition. In *Proceedings of the Seventh Conference on Natural Language Learning at HLT-NAACL 2003*, pages 142–147.

Yftah Ziser and Roi Reichart. 2018. Pivot based language modeling for improved neural domain adaptation. In *Proceedings of the 2018 Conference of the North American Chapter of the Association for Computational Linguistics: Human Language Technologies, Volume 1 (Long Papers)*, pages 1241–1251, New Orleans, Louisiana. Association for Computational Linguistics.

Yftah Ziser and Roi Reichart. 2019. Task refinement learning for improved accuracy and stability of unsupervised domain adaptation. In *Proceedings of the 57th Annual Meeting of the Association for Computational Linguistics*, pages 5895–5906.

A Hyperparameters

We use a bert-base-cased model from huggingface ‡ as initial parameter checkpoint. In supervised learning stage, we fine-tune the model for 3 to 5 epochs with batch size between [16, 32] and learning rate between [2e-5, 5e-5]. The weight decay of model parameters has been set as 0.1. Adam optimizer has been adopted with a warm up ratio of 0.1. In the unsupervised language modeling stage, the rate of masking tokens has been set as 0.15.We train the model for 3 epochs and adopt the same optimizer settings in supervised learning. We set the threshold parameter as 0.5 for the best performance model in both NES and SA task.

B Data Statistics

In this section, we will introduce the data statistics of our named entity segmentation and sentiment analysis . In Table 4, the data are from origin AdaptaBERT (Han and Eisenstein, 2019), of which Twitter dataset has more unlabeled dev data than labeled train data. In Table 5, the data is collected from open Amazon review (He and McAuley, 2016; McAuley et al., 2015). We process the data into 3 domains of balanced datasets. In the pre-processing stage, we exclude the text whose length is too short (shorter than 1 valid token) or too long (more than 256 valid tokens). The sentiment analysis data has been shared via google drive §.

Dataset	Train	Dev
CoNLL	14986	10,000
Twitter	2394	3852

Table 4: Data statistics of named entity segmentation.

Dataset	Train	Dev
Books	100,000	10,000
Electronics	100,000	10,000
Kitchens	100,000	10,000

Table 5: Data statistics of sentiment analysis. The train data and dev data of each domain is balanced, which means the number of samples of each class is the same.

‡https://github.com/huggingface/transformers

§https://drive.google.com/drive/folders/1fdmD08pZUzN3WbgxEu_Hv9lq4ZKmq7J3?usp=sharing

C Experiment details

We use a single Tesla P40 card to conduct all our experiments. The average runtime of each approach is 3 minutes for named entity segmentation and 30 minutes for sentiment analysis. The number of parameters in our model is about 110M , same as the bert-base model.

Conditional Adversarial Networks for Multi-Domain Text Classification

Yuan Wu [1], **Diana Inkpen** [2] **and Ahmed El-Roby** [1]
[1]Carleton University, Ottawa, Ontario, Canada
[2]University of Ottawa, Ottawa, Ontario, Canada
{yuan.wu3, Ahmed.ElRoby}@carleton.ca Diana.Inkpen@uottawa.ca

Abstract

In this paper, we propose conditional adversarial networks (CANs), a framework that explores the relationship between the shared features and the label predictions to impose stronger discriminability to the learned features, for multi-domain text classification (MDTC). The proposed CAN introduces a conditional domain discriminator to model the domain variance in both the shared feature representations and the class-aware information simultaneously, and adopts entropy conditioning to guarantee the transferability of the shared features. We provide theoretical analysis for the CAN framework, showing that CAN's objective is equivalent to minimizing the total divergence among multiple joint distributions of shared features and label predictions. Therefore, CAN is a theoretically sound adversarial network that discriminates over multiple distributions. Evaluation results on two MDTC benchmarks show that CAN outperforms prior methods. Further experiments demonstrate that CAN has a good ability to generalize learned knowledge to unseen domains.

1 Introduction

Text classification is a fundamental task in Natural Language Processing (NLP) and has received constant attention due to its wide applications, ranging from spam detection to social media analytics (Pang et al., 2002; Hu and Liu, 2004; Choi and Cardie, 2008; Socher et al., 2012; Vo and Zhang, 2015). Over the past couple of decades, supervised machine learning methods have shown dominant performance for text classification, such as Naive Bayes Classifiers (Troussas et al., 2013), Support Vector Machines (Li et al., 2018) and Neural Networks (Wu et al., 2020). In particular, with the advent of deep learning, neural network-based text classification models have gained impressive achievements. However, text classification is well known to be highly domain-dependent, the same word could convey different sentiment polarities in different domains (Glorot et al., 2011). For example, the word *infantile* expresses neutral sentiment in baby product review (e.g., *The infantile cart is easy to use*), while in book review, it often indicates a negative polarity (e.g., *This book is infantile and boring*). Thus a text classifier trained on one domain is likely to make spurious predictions on another domain whose distribution is different from the training data distribution. In addition, it is always difficult to collect sufficient labeled data for all interested domains. Therefore, it is of great significance to explore how to leverage available resources from related domains to improve the classification accuracy on the target domain.

The major line of approaches to tackle the above problem is multi-domain text classification (MDTC) (Li and Zong, 2008), which can handle the scenario where labeled data exist for multiple domains, but in insufficient amounts to training an effective classifier. Deep learning models have yielded impressive performance in MDTC (Wu and Guo, 2020; Wu et al., 2021). Most recent MDTC methods adopt the shared-private paradigm, which divides the latent space into two types: one is the shared feature space for all domains with the aim of capturing domain-invariant knowledge, the other one is the private feature space for each domain which extracts domain-specific knowledge. To explicitly ensure the optimum separations among the shared latent space and multiple domain-specific feature spaces, the adversarial training (Goodfellow et al., 2014) is introduced in MDTC. By employing the adversarial training, the domain-specific features can be prevented from creeping into the shared latent space, which will lead to feature redundancy (Liu et al., 2017). In adversarial training, a multinomial domain discriminator is trained

Proceedings of the Second Workshop on Domain Adaptation for NLP, pages 16–27
April 20, 2021. ©2021 Association for Computational Linguistics

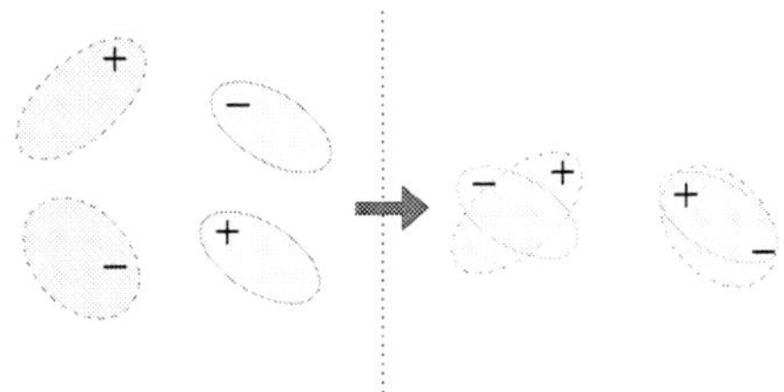

Figure 1: The mismatch risk when aligning the marginal distributions in MDTC, we present the case containing two domains D_1 and D_2. The blue regions denote distributions of D_1, and the yellow regions denote distributions of D_2. (a) The scenario before performing domain alignment. (2) When aligning the marginal distributions, a mismatch may occur with regard to the label.

against a shared feature extractor to minimize the divergences across different domains. When the domain discriminator and the shared feature extractor reach equilibrium, the learned shared features can be regarded as domain-invariant and used for the subsequent classification. The adversarial training-based MDTC approaches yield the state-of-the-art results (Liu et al., 2017; Chen and Cardie, 2018). However, these methods still have a significant limitation: when the data distributions present complex structures, adversarial training may fail to perform global alignment among domains. Such a risk comes from the challenge that in adversarial training, only aligning the marginal distributions can not sufficiently guarantee the discriminability of the learned features. The features with different labels may be aligned, as shown in Figure 1. The critical mismatch can lead to weak discriminability of the learned features.

In this paper, motivated by the conditional generative adversarial networks (CGANs), which aligns distributions of real and generated images via conditioning the generator and discriminator on extra information (Mirza and Osindero, 2014), we propose conditional adversarial networks (CANs) to address the aforementioned challenge. The CAN method introduces a conditional domain discriminator that models domain variance in both shared features and label predictions, exploring the relationship between shared feature representations and class-aware information conveyed by label predictions to encourage the shared feature extractor to capture more discriminative information. Moreover, we use entropy conditioning to avoid the risk of conditioning on the class-aware information with low certainty. The entropy conditioning strategy can give higher priority to easy-to-transfer instances. We also provide a theoretical analysis demonstrating the validity of CANs. Our approach adopts the shared-private paradigm. We validate the effectiveness of CAN on two MDTC benchmarks. It can be noted that CAN outperforms the state-of-the-art methods for both datasets. Finally, we empirically illustrate that CAN has the ability to generalize in cases where no labeled data exist for a subset of domains. The contributions of our work are listed as follows:

- We propose conditional adversarial networks (CANs) for multi-domain text classification which incorporate conditional domain discriminator and entropy conditioning to perform alignment on the joint distributions of shared features and label predictions to improve the system performance.
- We present the theoretical analysis of the CAN framework, demonstrating that CANs are minimizers of divergences among multiple joint distributions of shared features and label predictions, and providing the condition where the conditional domain discriminator reaches its optimum.
- We evaluate the effectiveness of CAN on two MDTC benchmarks. The experimental results show that CAN yields state-of-the-art results. Moreover, further experiments on unsupervised multi-source domain adaptation demonstrate that CAN has a good capacity to generalize to unseen domains.

2 Related Work

Multi-domain text classification (MDTC) was first proposed by (Li and Zong, 2008), aiming to simultaneously leverage all existing resources across different domains to improve system performance. Currently, there are two main streams for MDTC: one strand exploits covariance matrix to model the relationship across domains (Dredze and Crammer, 2008; Saha et al., 2011; Zhang and Yeung, 2012); the other strand is based on neural networks, sharing the first several layers for each domain to extract low-level features and generating outputs with domain-specific parameters. The multi-task convolutional neural network (MT-CNN) utilizes a convolutional layer in which only the lookup table is shared for better word embeddings (Collobert and Weston, 2008). The collaborative multi-domain sentiment classification (CMSC) combines a classifier that learns common knowledge among domains with a set of classifiers, one per domain, each of which captures domain-dependent features to make the final predictions (Wu and Huang, 2015). The multi-task deep neural network (MT-DNN) maps arbitrary text queries and documents into semantic vector representations in a low dimensional latent space and combines tasks as disparate as operations necessary for classification (Liu et al., 2015).

Pioneered by the generative adversarial network (GAN) (Goodfellow et al., 2014), adversarial learning has been firstly proposed for image generation. (Ganin et al., 2016) applies adversarial learning in domain adaptation to extract domain-invariant features across two different distributions (binary adversarial learning). (Zhao et al., 2017) extends it to multiple adversarial learning, enabling the model to learn domain-invariant representations across multiple domains. However, only considering domain-invariant features can not provide optimal solutions for MDTC, because domain-specific information also plays an important role in training an effective classifier. (Bousmalis et al., 2016) proposes the shared-private paradigm to combine domain-invariant features with domain-specific ones to perform classification, illustrating that this scheme can improve system performance. To date, many state-of-the-art MDTC models adopt the adversarial learning and the shared-private paradigm. The adversarial multi-task learning for text classification (ASP-MTL) utilizes long short-term memory (LSTM) without attention as feature extractors and introduces orthogonality constraints to encourage the shared and private feature extractors to encode different aspects of the inputs (Liu et al., 2017). The multinomial adversarial network (MAN) exploits two forms of loss functions to train the domain discriminator: the least square loss (MAN-L2) and negative log-likelihood loss (MAN-NLL) (Chen and Cardie, 2018). The multi-task learning with bidirectional language models for text classification (MT-BL) introduces language modeling as an auxiliary task to encourage the domain-specific feature extractors to capture more syntactic and semantic information, and a uniform label distribution-based loss constraint to the shared feature extractor to enhance the ability to learn domain-invariant features (Yang and Shang, 2019).

Adversarial learning has several advantages, such as Markov chains are not needed and no inference is required during learning (Mirza and Osindero, 2014). However, there still exists an issue in adversarial learning. When data distributions embody complex structures, adversarial learning can fail in performing the global alignment. The conditional generative adversarial network (CGAN) is proposed to address this problem (Mirza and Osindero, 2014). In CGAN, both the generator and discriminator are conditioned on some extra information, such as labels or data from other modalities, to yield better results. The conditional adversarial training mechanism has been explored in transfer learning. The conditional domain adversarial networks (CDANs) condition the domain discriminator on a multilinear map of feature representations and category predictions so as to enable discriminative alignment of multi-mode structures (Long et al., 2018). The conditional generative adversarial networks for structured domain adaptation learn a conditional generator to transform the feature maps of source domain images as if they were extracted from the target domain, and a discriminator to encourage realistic transformations for the semantic segmentation of urban scenes (Hong et al., 2018). Sharing some spirit of CGAN, this paper extends conditional adversarial learning in MDTC, enabling a domain discriminator on the shared features while conditioning it on the class-aware information conveyed by the label predictions. Moreover, in order to guarantee the generalizability of the learned features, we also utilize the entropy conditioning strategy.

3 Approach

In this paper, we consider MDTC tasks in the following setting. Assume there exist M domains $\{D_i\}_{i=1}^{M}$. For each domain, both labeled and unlabeled samples are taken into consideration. Specifically, D_i contains two parts: a limited amount of labeled samples $\mathbb{L}_i = \{(\mathbf{x}_j, y_j)\}_{j=1}^{l_i}$; and a large amount of unlabeled samples $\mathbb{U}_i = \{\mathbf{x}_j\}_{j=1}^{u_i}$. The challenge of MDTC lies in how to improve the system performance of mapping the input $\mathbf{x}$ to its corresponding label y by leveraging all available resources across different domains. The performance is measured as the average classification accuracy across the M domains.

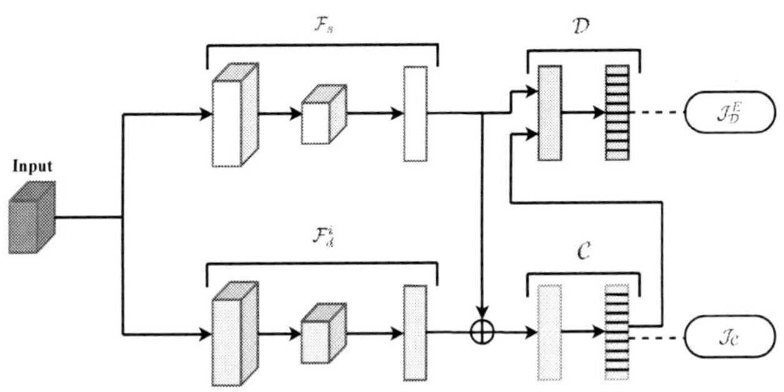

Figure 2: The architecture of the CAN model. A shared feature extractor $\mathcal{F}_s$ learns to capture domain-invariant features; each domain-specific feature extractor $\mathcal{F}_d^i$ learns to capture domain-dependent features; a conditional domain discriminator $\mathcal{D}$ models shared feature distributions by conditioning on discriminative information provided by label predictions; a classifier $\mathcal{C}$ is used to conduct text classification; $\mathcal{J}_\mathcal{C}$ is the classification loss function; $\mathcal{J}_\mathcal{D}^E$ is the entropy conditioning adversarial loss function which guides the domain-invariant feature extraction.

3.1 Model Architecture

We propose conditional adversarial networks (CANs), as shown in Figure 2, which adopt the shared-private scheme and consist of four components: a shared feature extractor $\mathcal{F}_s$, a set of domain-specific feature extractors $\{\mathcal{F}_d^i\}_{i=1}^M$, a conditional domain discriminator $\mathcal{D}$, and a text classifier $\mathcal{C}$. The shared feature extractor $\mathcal{F}_s$ learns to capture domain-invariant features that are beneficial to classification across all domains, while each domain-specific feature extractor $\mathcal{F}_d^i$ aims to learn knowledge that is unique to its own domain. The architecture of these feature extractors are flexible and can be decided based on the practical task. For instance, it can adopt the form of a convolutional neural network (CNN), a recurrent neural network (RNN), or a multi-layer perceptron (MLP). Here, a feature extractor generates vectors with a fixed length, which is considered as the hidden representation of certain input. The classifier $\mathcal{C}$ takes the concatenation of a shared feature and a domain-specific feature as its input and outputs label probabilities. The conditional domain discriminator $\mathcal{D}$ takes the concatenation of a shared feature and the prediction of the given instance provided by $\mathcal{C}$ as its input and predicts the likelihood of that instance coming from each domain.

3.2 Conditional Adversarial Training

Adversarial learning has been successfully investigated in minimizing divergences among domains (Chen and Cardie, 2018; Zhao et al., 2017). In standard adversarial learning for MDTC, a two-player mini-max game is conducted between a domain discriminator and a shared feature extractor: the domain discriminator is trained to distinguish features across different domains, and the shared feature extractor aims to deceive the discriminator. By performing this mini-max optimization, the domain-invariant features can be learned. The error function of the domain discriminator corresponds well to the divergences among domains. Most MDTC methods align the marginal distributions. However, the transferability with representations transition from general to specific along deep networks is decreasing significantly (Yosinski et al., 2014), only adapting the marginal distributions is not sufficient to guarantee the global alignment. In addition, when the data distributions embody complex structures, which is a real scenario for NLP applications, there is a high risk of failure by matching features with different labels.

Recent advances in the conditional generative adversarial network (CGAN) disclose that better alignment on two different distributions can be obtained by conditioning the generator and discriminator on class-aware information (Mirza and Osindero, 2014). The discriminative information provided by the label prediction potentially reveals the structure information underlying the data distribution. Thus, conditional adversarial learning can better model the divergences among domains on shared feature representations and label predictions. Unlike the prior works that adapting the marginal distributions (Liu et al., 2017; Chen and Cardie, 2018), our proposed CAN framework is formalized on aligning joint distributions of shared features and label predictions. There exist two training flows in our model. Due to the nature of adversarial learning, the conditional domain discriminator is updated with a separate optimizer, while the other components of CAN are trained with the main optimizer. These two flows are supposed to complement each other. Denote $\mathcal{L}_\mathcal{C}$ and $\mathcal{L}_\mathcal{D}$ as the loss functions of the classifier $\mathcal{C}$ and the conditional domain discriminator $\mathcal{D}$, respectively. We utilize the negative log-likelihood (NLL) loss to encode these two loss functions:

$$\mathcal{L}_\mathcal{C}(\widetilde{y}, y) = -\log P(\widetilde{y} = y) \tag{1}$$

$$\mathcal{L}_\mathcal{D}(\widetilde{d}, d) = -\log P(\widetilde{d} = d) \tag{2}$$

where y is the true label, $\widetilde{y}$ is the label prediction, d is the domain index and $\widetilde{d}$ is the domain label prediction. Therefore, we formulate CAN as a minimax optimization problem with two competitive terms defined as follows:

$$\mathcal{J}_\mathcal{C} = \sum_{i=1}^{M} \mathbb{E}_{(\mathbf{x},y)\sim\mathbb{L}_i}[\mathcal{L}_\mathcal{C}(\mathcal{C}_i, y)] \tag{3}$$

$$\mathcal{J}_\mathcal{D} = \sum_{i=1}^{M} \mathbb{E}_{\mathbf{x}\sim\mathbb{L}_i\cup\mathbb{U}_i}[\mathcal{L}_\mathcal{D}(\mathcal{D}([\mathcal{F}_s(\mathbf{x}), \mathcal{C}_i]), d)] \tag{4}$$

where $[\cdot,\cdot]$ is the concatenation of two vectors, $\mathcal{C}_i = \mathcal{C}([\mathcal{F}_s(\mathbf{x}), \mathcal{F}_d^i(\mathbf{x})])$ is the prediction probability of the given instance $\mathbf{x}$. $\mathcal{C}$ and $\mathcal{D}$ adopt MLPs with a softmax layer on top. For the domain-specific feature extractors $\{\mathcal{F}_d^i\}_{i=1}^M$, the training is straightforward, as their objective is simple: help $\mathcal{C}$ perform better classification. While the shared feature extractor $\mathcal{F}_s$ has two goals: (1) help $\mathcal{C}$ reduce prediction errors, and (2) confuse $\mathcal{D}$ to reach equilibrium.

3.3 Entropy Conditioning

We condition the domain discriminator $\mathcal{D}$ on the joint variable $(f, c) = (\mathcal{F}_s(\mathbf{x}), \mathcal{C}_i)$. For brevity, here we use f and c to denote $\mathcal{F}_s(\mathbf{x})$ and $\mathcal{C}_i$, respectively. If we enforce different instances to have equal importance, the hard-to-transfer instances with uncertain predictions may deteriorate the system performance (Saito et al., 2019). In order to alleviate the harmful effects introduced by the hard-to-transfer instances, we introduce the entropy criterion $E(c) = -\sum_{k=1}^{2}[c_k log c_k]$ to quantify the uncertainty of label predictions, where c_k is the probability of predicting an instance to category k (negative: k = 1, positive: k = 2). By using the entropy conditioning, the easy-to-transfer instances with certain predictions are given higher priority. We reweigh these instances by an entropy-aware term: $w(c) = 1 + e^{-E(c)}$. Therefore, the improved $\mathcal{J}_\mathcal{D}$ is defined as:

$$\mathcal{J}_\mathcal{D}^E = \sum_{i=1}^{M} \mathbb{E}_{\mathbf{x}\sim\mathbb{L}_i\cup\mathbb{U}_i}[w(c)\mathcal{L}_\mathcal{D}(\mathcal{D}([\mathcal{F}_s(\mathbf{x}), \mathcal{C}_i]), d)] \tag{5}$$

Therefore, the mini-max game of CAN is formulated as:

$$\min_{\mathcal{F}_s, \{\mathcal{F}_d^i\}_{i=1}^M, \mathcal{C}} \max_{\mathcal{D}} \quad \mathcal{J}_\mathcal{C} + \lambda \mathcal{J}_\mathcal{D}^E \tag{6}$$

where λ is a hyperparameter balancing the two objectives. The entropy conditioning empowers the entropy minimization principle (Grandvalet and Bengio, 2005) and controls the certainty of the predictions, enabling CAN have the ability to generalize on unseen domains with no labeled data. The CAN training is illustrated in Algorithm 1.

Algorithm 1 Stochastic gradient descent training algorithm

```
1: Input: labeled data L_i and unlabeled data U_i
   in M domains; a hyperparameter λ.
2: for number of training iterations do
3:    Sample labeled mini-batches from the multiple domains B^ℓ = {B^ℓ_1, ··· , B^ℓ_M}.
4:    Sample unlabeled mini-batches from the multiple domains B^u = {B^u_1, ··· , B^u_M}.
5:    Calculate loss = J_C + λJ^E_D on B^ℓ and B^u;
      Update F_s, {F^i_d}^M_{i=1}, C by descending along the gradients Δloss.
6:    Calculate l_D = J^E_D on B^ℓ and B^u;
      Update D by ascending along the gradients Δl_D.
7: end for
```

3.4 Theoretical Analysis

In this section, we present an analysis showing the validity of the CAN approach for MDTC. All proofs are given in the Appendix. The objective of CAN is equivalent to minimizing the total divergence among the M joint distributions. First, we define different joint distributions as $P_i(f, c) \triangleq$

$P(f = \mathcal{F}_s(\mathbf{x}), c = \mathcal{C}_i | \mathbf{x} \in D_i)$. Combining $\mathcal{L}_\mathcal{D}$ with $\mathcal{J}_\mathcal{D}$, the objective of $\mathcal{D}$ can be written as:

$$\mathcal{J}_\mathcal{D} = -\sum_{i=1}^{M} \mathbb{E}_{(f,c)\sim P_i}[\log \mathcal{D}_i([f, c])] \quad (7)$$

where $\mathcal{D}_i([f, c])$ yields the probability of the vector $([f, c])$ coming from the i-th domain. We first derive that CAN could achieve its optimum if and only if all M joint distributions are identical.

Lemma 1. *For any given $\mathcal{F}_s$, $\{\mathcal{F}_d^i\}_{i=1}^M$ and $\mathcal{C}$, the optimum conditional domain discriminator $\mathcal{D}^*$ is:*

$$\mathcal{D}_i^*([f, c]) = \frac{P_i(f, c)}{\sum_{j=1}^{M} P_j(f, c)} \quad (8)$$

Then we provide the main theorem for the CAN framework:

Theorem 1. *Let $\widetilde{P}(f, c) = \frac{\sum_{i=1}^{M} P_i(f,c)}{M}$, when $\mathcal{D}$ is trained to its optimum $\mathcal{D}^*$, we have:*

$$\mathcal{J}_{\mathcal{D}^*} = M \log M - \sum_{i=1}^{M} KL(P_i(f, c)||\widetilde{P}(f, c)) \quad (9)$$

where $KL(\cdot)$ is the Kullback-Leibler (KL) divergence (Aslam and Pavlu, 2007) of each joint distribution $P_i(f, c)$ to the centroid $\widetilde{P}(f, c)$.

Finally, considering the non-negativity and convexity of the KL-divergence (Brillouin, 2013), we have:

Corollary 1. *When $\mathcal{D}$ is trained to its optimum $\mathcal{D}^*$, $\mathcal{J}_{\mathcal{D}^*}$ is $M \log M$. The optimum can be obtained if and only if $P_1(f, c) = P_2(f, c) = ... = P_M(f, c) = \widetilde{P}(f, c)$.*

Therefore, by using conditional adversarial training, we can train the conditional domain discriminator on the joint variable (f, c) to minimize the total divergence across different domains, yielding promising performance on MDTC tasks.

4 Experiments

We evaluate the effectiveness of the CAN model on both MDTC and unsupervised multi-source domain adaptation tasks. The former refers to the setting where the test data falls into one of the M domains, and the latter refers to the setting where the test data comes from an unseen domain without labels. Moreover, an ablation study is provided for further analysis of the CAN model.

Domain	Train	Dev.	Test	Unlabeled	Avg. L	Vocab.
Books	1400	200	400	2000	159	62K
Electronics	1398	200	400	2000	101	30K
DVD	1400	200	400	2000	173	69K
Kitchen	1400	200	400	2000	89	28K
Apparel	1400	200	400	2000	57	21K
Camera	1397	200	400	2000	130	26K
Health	1400	200	400	2000	81	26K
Music	1400	200	400	2000	136	60K
Toys	1400	200	400	2000	90	28K
Video	1400	200	400	2000	156	57K
Baby	1300	200	400	2000	104	26K
Magazine	1370	200	400	2000	117	30K
Software	1315	200	400	475	129	26K
Sports	1400	200	400	2000	94	30K
IMDB	1400	200	400	2000	269	44K
MR	1400	200	400	2000	21	12K

Table 1: Statistics of the FDU-MTL dataset

4.1 Experimental Settings

Dataset We conduct experiments on two MDTC benchmarks: the Amazon review dataset (Blitzer et al., 2007) and the FDU-MTL dataset (Liu et al., 2017). The Amazon review dataset consists of four domains: books, DVDs, electronics, and kitchen. For each domain, there exist 2,000 instances: 1,000 positive ones and 1,000 negative ones. All data was pre-processed into a bag of features (unigrams and bigrams), losing all word order information. In our experiments, the 5,000 most frequent features are used, representing each review as a 5,000-dimensional vector. The FDU-MTL dataset is a more complicated dataset, which contains 16 domains: books, electronics, DVDs, kitchen, apparel, camera, health, music, toys, video, baby, magazine, software, sport, IMDB, and MR. All data in the FDU-MTL dataset are raw text data, tokenized by the Stanford tokenizer. The detailed statistics of the FDU-MTL dataset are listed in Table 1.

Implementation Details All experiments are implemented by using PyTorch. The CAN has one hyperparameter: λ, which is fixed as 1 in all experiments, the parameter sensitivity analysis is presented in the Appendix. We use Adam optimizer (Kingma and Ba, 2014), with the learning rate 0.0001, for training. The batch size is 8. We adopt the same model architecture as in (Chen and Cardie, 2018). For the Amazon Review dataset, MLPs are used as feature extractors, with an input size of 5,000. Each feature extractor is composed of two hidden layers, with size 1,000 and 500, respectively. The output size of the shared feature extractor is 128 while 64 for the domain-specific ones. The dropout rate is 0.4 for each component. Classifier

Domain	CMSC-LS	CMSC-SVM	CMSC-Log	MAN-L2	MAN-NLL	CAN(Proposed)
Books	82.10	82.26	81.81	82.46	82.98	$\mathbf{83.76 \pm 0.20}$
DVD	82.40	83.48	83.73	83.98	84.03	$\mathbf{84.68 \pm 0.16}$
Electr.	86.12	86.76	86.67	87.22	87.06	$\mathbf{88.34 \pm 0.14}$
Kit.	87.56	88.20	88.23	88.53	88.57	$\mathbf{90.03 \pm 0.19}$
AVG	84.55	85.18	85.11	85.55	85.66	$\mathbf{86.70 \pm 0.11}$

Table 2: MDTC classification accuracies on the Amazon review dataset.

Domain	MT-CNN	MT-DNN	ASP-MTL	MAN-L2	MAN-NLL	MT-BL	CAN(Proposed)
books	84.5	82.2	84.0	87.6	86.8	**89.0**	87.8 ± 0.2
electronics	83.2	81.7	86.8	87.4	88.8	90.2	$\mathbf{91.6 \pm 0.5}$
dvd	84.0	84.2	85.5	88.1	88.6	88.0	$\mathbf{89.5 \pm 0.4}$
kitchen	83.2	80.7	86.2	89.8	89.9	90.5	$\mathbf{90.8 \pm 0.3}$
apparel	83.7	85.0	87.0	**87.6**	**87.6**	87.2	87.0 ± 0.7
camera	86.0	86.2	89.2	91.4	90.7	89.5	$\mathbf{93.5 \pm 0.1}$
health	87.2	85.7	88.2	89.8	89.4	**92.5**	90.4 ± 0.6
music	83.7	84.7	82.5	85.9	85.5	86.0	$\mathbf{86.9 \pm 0.1}$
toys	89.2	87.7	88.0	90.0	90.4	**92.0**	90.0 ± 0.3
video	81.5	85.0	84.5	89.5	**89.6**	88.0	88.8 ± 0.4
baby	87.7	88.0	88.2	90.0	90.2	88.7	$\mathbf{92.0 \pm 0.2}$
magazine	87.7	89.5	92.2	92.5	92.9	92.5	$\mathbf{94.5 \pm 0.5}$
software	86.5	85.7	87.2	90.4	90.9	**91.7**	90.9 ± 0.2
sports	84.0	83.2	85.7	89.0	89.0	89.5	$\mathbf{91.2 \pm 0.7}$
IMDb	86.2	83.2	85.5	86.6	87.0	88.0	$\mathbf{88.5 \pm 0.6}$
MR	74.5	75.5	76.7	76.1	76.7	75.7	$\mathbf{77.1 \pm 0.9}$
AVG	84.5	84.3	86.1	88.2	88.4	88.6	$\mathbf{89.4 \pm 0.1}$

Table 3: MDTC classification accuracies on the FDU-MTL dataset.

and discriminator are MLPs with one hidden layer of the same size as their input ($128 + 64$ for classifier and $128 + 2$ for discriminator). ReLU is used as the activation function. For the FDU-MTL dataset, CNN with a single convolutional layer is used as the feature extractor. It uses different kernel sizes $(3, 4, 5)$, and the number of kernels is 200. The input of the convolutional layer is a 100-dimensional vector, obtained by using word2vec (Mikolov et al., 2013), for each word in the input sequence.

4.2 Multi-Domain Text Classification

Comparison Methods We first conduct experiments of multi-domain text classification. The CAN model is compared with a number of state-of-the-art methods, which are listed below:

- MT-CNN: A CNN-based model which shares the lookup table across domains for better word embeddings (Collobert and Weston, 2008).
- MT-DNN: The multi-task deep neural network model with bag-of-words input and MLPs, in which a hidden layer is shared (Liu et al., 2015).
- CMSC-LS, CMSC-SVM, CMSC-Log: The collaborative multi-domain sentiment classification method combines an overall classifier across domains and a set of domain-dependent classifiers to make the final prediction. The models are trained on least square loss, hinge loss, and log loss, respectively (Wu and Huang, 2015).
- ASP-MTL: The adversarial multi-task learning framework of text classification, which adopts the share-private scheme, adversarial learning, and orthogonality constraints (Liu et al., 2017).
- MAN-L2, MAN-NLL: The multinomial adversarial network for multi-domain text classification (Chen and Cardie, 2018). This model uses two forms of loss functions to train the domain discriminator: least square loss and negative log-likelihood loss.
- MT-BL: The multi-task learning with bidirectional language models for text classification, which adds language modeling and a uniform label distribution-based loss constraint to the domain-specific feature extractors and the shared feature extractor, respectively (Yang and Shang, 2019).

All the comparison methods use the standard partitions of the datasets. Thus, we directly cite

Method	Books	DVD	Electr.	Kit.	AVG
CAN (full)	83.76	84.68	88.34	90.03	86.70
CAN w/o C	82.45	84.45	87.30	89.65	85.96
CAN w/o E	83.60	84.80	87.70	89.40	86.38
CAN w/o CE	82.98	84.03	87.06	88.57	85.66

Table 4: Ablation study analysis on the Amazon review dataset.

the results from (Chen and Cardie, 2018; Yang and Shang, 2019) for fair comparisons.

Results We conduct MDTC experiments following the setting of (Chen and Cardie, 2018): A 5-fold cross-validation is implemented for the Amazon review dataset. All data is divided into 5 folds per domain: three of the five folds are used as the training set, one is the validation set, and the remaining one is treated as the test set. The 5-fold average test accuracy is reported. All reports are based on 5 runs.

Table 2 and Table 3 show the experimental results on the Amazon review dataset and the FDU-MTL dataset, respectively. From Table 2, it can be seen that our model yields state-of-the-art results not only for the average classification accuracy, but also on each individual domain.

From the experimental results on the FDU-MTL dataset, reported in Table 3, we can see that the CAN model obtains the best accuracies on 10 of 16 domains and achieves the best result in terms of the average classification accuracy. The experimental results on these two MDTC benchmarks illustrate the efficacy of our model.

Ablation Study The CAN model adopts the conditional domain discriminator and entropy conditioning. In this section, we investigate how these two strategies impact the performance of our model on the Amazon review dataset. In particular, three ablation variants are evaluated: (1) CAN w/o C, the variant of the proposed CAN model without conditioning the domain discriminator on label predictions, which utilizes the standard domain discriminator and entropy conditioning; (2) CAN w/o E, the variant of the proposed CAN model without the entropy conditioning, which hence imposes equal importance to different instances; (3) CAN w/o CE, the variant of the proposed CAN model which only uses standard adversarial training for domain alignment. The results of the ablation study are shown in Table 4, where we can see that all variants produce inferior results. Thus, it indicates that both strategies contribute to the CAN model.

4.3 Unsupervised Multi-Source Domain Adaptation

In the MDTC scenario, the model requires labeled training data from each domain. However, in real-world applications, many domains may have no labeled data at all. Therefore, it is important to evaluate the performance of MDTC models on unseen domains (Wright and Augenstein, 2020).

In the unsupervised multi-source domain adaptation setting, we have multiple source domains with both labeled and unlabeled data and one target domain with only unlabeled data. The CAN has the ability to learn domain-invariant representations on unlabeled data, and thus it can be generalized to unseen domains. Since the target domain has no labeled data at all, the domain discriminator is updated only on unlabeled data in this setting. When conducting text classification on the target domain, we only feed the shared feature to C and set the domain-specific feature vector to 0.

We conduct the experiments on the Amazon review dataset. In the experiments, three of the four domains are regarded as the source domains, and the remaining one is used as the target one. The evaluations are conducted on the target domain. In order to validate CAN's effectiveness, we compare CAN with several domain-agnostic methods: (1) the MLP model; (2) the marginalized denoising autoencoder (mSDA) (Chen et al., 2012); (3) the domain adversarial neural network (DANN) (Ganin et al., 2016). These methods ignore the differences among domains. And certain state-of-the-art unsupervised multi-source domain adaptation methods: (4) the multi-source domain adaptation neural network (MDAN(H) and MDAN(S)) (Zhao et al., 2017); (5) the multinomial adversarial network (MAN-L2 and MAN-NLL) (Chen and Cardie, 2018). When training the domain-agnostic methods, the data in the multiple source domains are combined together as a single source domain.

In Table 5, we observe that the CAN model outperforms all the comparison methods on three out of four domains. In terms of the average classification accuracy, the CAN method achieves superior performance. This suggests that our model has a good ability to generalize on unseen domains.

5 Conclusion

In this paper, we propose conditional adversarial networks (CANs) for MDTC. This approach can perform alignment on joint distributions of shared

Domain	MLP	mSDA	DANN	MDAN(H)	MDAN(S)	MAN-L2	MAN-NLL	CAN(Proposed)
Books	76.55	76.98	77.89	78.45	78.63	78.45	77.78	**78.91**
DVD	75.88	78.61	78.86	77.97	80.65	81.57	82.74	**83.37**
Elec.	84.60	81.98	84.91	84.83	**85.34**	83.37	83.75	84.76
Kit.	85.45	84.26	86.39	85.80	86.26	85.57	86.41	**86.75**
AVG	80.46	80.46	82.01	81.76	82.72	82.24	82.67	**83.45**

Table 5: Unsupervised multi-source domain adaptation results on the Amazon review dataset.

features and label predictions to improve the system performance. The CAN approach adopts the shared-private paradigm, trains domain discriminator by conditioning it on discriminative information conveyed by the label predictions to encourage the shared feature extractor to capture more discriminative information, and exploits entropy conditioning to guarantee the transferability of the learned features. Experimental results on two MDTC benchmarks demonstrate that the CAN model can not only boost the average classification accuracy for MDTC but also promote the generalization ability when tackling unseen domains.

References

Javed A Aslam and Virgil Pavlu. 2007. Query hardness estimation using jensen-shannon divergence among multiple scoring functions. In *European conference on information retrieval*, pages 198–209. Springer.

J. Blitzer, M. Dredze, and F. Pereira. 2007. Biographies, bollywood, boom-boxes and blenders: Domain adaptation for sentiment classification. In *Proc. of the annual meeting of the association of computational linguistics.*

K. Bousmalis, G. Trigeorgis, N. Silberman, D. Krishnan, and D. Erhan. 2016. Domain separation networks. In *Advances in Neural Information Processing Systems.*

Leon Brillouin. 2013. *Science and information theory.* Courier Corporation.

M. Chen, Z. Xu, K.Q. Weinberger, and F. Sha. 2012. Marginalized denoising autoencoders for domain adaptation. In *Proc. of International Conference on International Conference on Machine Learning.*

X. Chen and C. Cardie. 2018. Multinomial adversarial networks for multi-domain text classification. In *Proc. of the Conference of the North American Chapter of the Association for Computational Linguistics: Human Language Technologies.*

Yejin Choi and Claire Cardie. 2008. Learning with compositional semantics as structural inference for subsentential sentiment analysis. In *Proceedings of the 2008 Conference on Empirical Methods in Natural Language Processing*, pages 793–801.

R. Collobert and J. Weston. 2008. A unified architecture for natural language processing: Deep neural networks with multitask learning. In *Proc. of the inter. conference on Machine learning.*

Mark Dredze and Koby Crammer. 2008. Online methods for multi-domain learning and adaptation. In *Proceedings of the Conference on Empirical Methods in Natural Language Processing*, pages 689–697. Association for Computational Linguistics.

Y. Ganin, E. Ustinova, H. Ajakan, P. Germain, H. Larochelle, F. Laviolette, M. Marchand, and V. Lempitsky. 2016. Domain-adversarial training of neural networks. *The Journal of Machine Learning Research*, 17(1):2096–2030.

X. Glorot, A. Bordes, and Y. Bengio. 2011. Domain adaptation for large-scale sentiment classification: A deep learning approach. In *Proc. of the international conference on machine learning.*

I. Goodfellow, J. Pouget-Abadie, M. Mirza, B. Xu, D. Warde-Farley, S. Ozair, A. Courville, and Y. Bengio. 2014. Generative adversarial nets. In *Advances in neural information proc. systems.*

Yves Grandvalet and Yoshua Bengio. 2005. Semi-supervised learning by entropy minimization. In *Advances in neural information processing systems*, pages 529–536.

Weixiang Hong, Zhenzhen Wang, Ming Yang, and Junsong Yuan. 2018. Conditional generative adversarial network for structured domain adaptation. In *Proceedings of the IEEE Conference on Computer Vision and Pattern Recognition*, pages 1335–1344.

Minqing Hu and Bing Liu. 2004. Mining and summarizing customer reviews. In *Proceedings of the tenth ACM SIGKDD international conference on Knowledge discovery and data mining*, pages 168–177.

D.P. Kingma and J. Ba. 2014. Adam: A method for stochastic optimization. *arXiv preprint arXiv:1412.6980.*

Lingling Li, Yuan Wu, Yi Yang, Lian Li, and Bin Wu. 2018. A new strategy to detect lung cancer on ct images. In *2018 IEEE 3rd International Conference on Image, Vision and Computing (ICIVC)*, pages 716–722. IEEE.

S. Li and C. Zong. 2008. Multi-domain sentiment classification. In *Proc. of the Annual Meeting of the Association for Computational Linguistics on Human Language Technologies.*

P. Liu, X. Qiu, and X. Huang. 2017. Adversarial multi-task learning for text classification. In *Proc. of the Annual Meeting of the Association for Computational Linguistics*.

X. Liu, J. Gao, X. He, L. Deng, K. Duh, and Y.Y. Wang. 2015. Representation learning using multi-task deep neural networks for semantic classification and information retrieval. In *Proc. of the Conference of the North American Chapter of the Association for Computational Linguistics: Human Language Technologies*.

Mingsheng Long, Zhangjie Cao, Jianmin Wang, and Michael I Jordan. 2018. Conditional adversarial domain adaptation. In *Proceedings of the 32nd International Conference on Neural Information Processing Systems*, pages 1647–1657.

T. Mikolov, K. Chen, G. Corrado, and J. Dean. 2013. Efficient estimation of word representations in vector space. *arXiv preprint arXiv:1301.3781*.

Mehdi Mirza and Simon Osindero. 2014. Conditional generative adversarial nets. *arXiv preprint arXiv:1411.1784*.

Bo Pang, Lillian Lee, and Shivakumar Vaithyanathan. 2002. Thumbs up?: sentiment classification using machine learning techniques. In *Proceedings of the ACL-02 conference on Empirical methods in natural language processing-Volume 10*, pages 79–86. Association for Computational Linguistics.

Avishek Saha, Piyush Rai, Hal DaumÃ, Suresh Venkatasubramanian, et al. 2011. Online learning of multiple tasks and their relationships. In *Proceedings of the Fourteenth International Conference on Artificial Intelligence and Statistics*, pages 643–651.

Kuniaki Saito, Donghyun Kim, Stan Sclaroff, Trevor Darrell, and Kate Saenko. 2019. Semi-supervised domain adaptation via minimax entropy. In *Proceedings of the IEEE International Conference on Computer Vision*, pages 8050–8058.

Richard Socher, Brody Huval, Christopher D Manning, and Andrew Y Ng. 2012. Semantic compositionality through recursive matrix-vector spaces. In *Proceedings of the 2012 joint conference on empirical methods in natural language processing and computational natural language learning*, pages 1201–1211. Association for Computational Linguistics.

Christos Troussas, Maria Virvou, Kurt Junshean Espinosa, Kevin Llaguno, and Jaime Caro. 2013. Sentiment analysis of facebook statuses using naive bayes classifier for language learning. In *IISA 2013*, pages 1–6. IEEE.

Duy-Tin Vo and Yue Zhang. 2015. Target-dependent twitter sentiment classification with rich automatic features. In *Twenty-Fourth International Joint Conference on Artificial Intelligence*.

Dustin Wright and Isabelle Augenstein. 2020. Transformer based multi-source domain adaptation. In *Proceedings of the 2020 Conference on Empirical Methods in Natural Language Processing (EMNLP)*, pages 7963–7974.

F. Wu and Y. Huang. 2015. Collaborative multi-domain sentiment classification. In *IEEE International Conference on Data Mining*.

Yuan Wu and Yuhong Guo. 2020. Dual adversarial co-learning for multi-domain text classification. In *Proceedings of the AAAI Conference on Artificial Intelligence*, volume 34, pages 6438–6445.

Yuan Wu, Diana Inkpen, and Ahmed El-Roby. 2020. Dual mixup regularized learning for adversarial domain adaptation. In *European Conference on Computer Vision*, pages 540–555. Springer.

Yuan Wu, Diana Inkpen, and Ahmed El-Roby. 2021. Mixup regularized adversarial networks for multi-domain text classification. *arXiv preprint arXiv:2102.00467*.

Qi Yang and Lin Shang. 2019. Multi-task learning with bidirectional language models for text classification. In *2019 International Joint Conference on Neural Networks (IJCNN)*, pages 1–8. IEEE.

Jason Yosinski, Jeff Clune, Yoshua Bengio, and Hod Lipson. 2014. How transferable are features in deep neural networks? In *Advances in neural information processing systems*, pages 3320–3328.

Yu Zhang and Dit-Yan Yeung. 2012. A convex formulation for learning task relationships in multi-task learning. *arXiv preprint arXiv:1203.3536*.

H. Zhao, S. Zhang, G. Wu, J.P. Costeira, J. Moura, and G.J. Gordon. 2017. Multiple source domain adaptation with adversarial training of neural networks. *arXiv preprint arXiv:1705.09684*.

A Appendix

A.1 Proofs for CAN

Assume there exist M domains, for each domain $\mathcal{D}_i$, we have a joint distribution defined as:

$$P_i(f, c) \triangleq P(f = \mathcal{F}_s(\mathbf{x}), c = \mathcal{C}_i | \mathbf{x} \in \mathcal{D}_i) \tag{10}$$

where $\mathcal{C}_i = \mathcal{C}([\mathcal{F}_s(\mathbf{x}), \mathcal{F}_d^i(\mathbf{x})])$ is the prediction probability of the given instance $\mathbf{x}$, $[\cdot, \cdot]$ is the concatenation of two vectors. The objective of $\mathcal{D}$ is to minimize $\mathcal{J}_\mathcal{D}$:

$$\mathcal{J}_\mathcal{D} = -\sum_{i=1}^{M} \mathbb{E}_{(f,c)\sim P_i}[\log \mathcal{D}_i([f, c])] \tag{11}$$

where $\mathcal{D}_i([f,c])$ is the probability of the vector $([f,c])$ coming from the i-th domain. Therefore, we have:

$$\sum_{i=1}^{M} \mathcal{D}_i([f,c]) = 1 \tag{12}$$

Lemma 1. *For any given $\mathcal{F}_s$, $\{\mathcal{F}_d^i\}_{i=1}^M$ and $\mathcal{C}$, the optimum conditional domain discriminator $\mathcal{D}^*$ is:*

$$\mathcal{D}_i^*([f,c]) = \frac{P_i(f,c)}{\sum_{j=1}^M P_j(f,c)} \tag{13}$$

Proof. For any given $\mathcal{F}_s$, $\{\mathcal{F}_d^i\}_{i=1}^M$ and $\mathcal{C}$, the optimum

$$\begin{aligned}
\mathcal{D}^* &= \arg\min_{\mathcal{D}} \mathcal{J}_{\mathcal{D}} \\
&= \arg\min_{\mathcal{D}} -\sum_{i=1}^{M} \mathbb{E}_{(f,c)\sim P_i}[\log \mathcal{D}_i([f,c])] \\
&= \arg\max_{\mathcal{D}} \sum_{i=1}^{M} \int_{(f,c)} P_i(f,c) \log \mathcal{D}_i([f,c]) d(f,c) \\
&= \arg\max_{\mathcal{D}} \int_{(f,c)} \sum_{i=1}^{M} P_i(f,c) \log \mathcal{D}_i([f,c]) d(f,c)
\end{aligned}$$

Here, we utilize the Lagrangian Multiplier for $\mathcal{D}^*$ under the condition (12). We have:

$$L(\mathcal{D}_1, ..., \mathcal{D}_M, \lambda) = \sum_{i=1}^{M} P_i \log \mathcal{D}_i - \lambda(\sum_{i=1}^{M} \mathcal{D}_i - 1) \tag{14}$$

Let $\nabla L = 0$, we have:

$$\begin{cases} \nabla_{\mathcal{D}_i} \sum_{j=1}^M P_j \log \mathcal{D}_j - \lambda \nabla_{\mathcal{D}_i}(\sum_{j=1}^M \mathcal{D}_j - 1) = 0 \\ \sum_{i=1}^M \mathcal{D}_i = 1 \end{cases}$$

From the two above equations, we have:

$$\mathcal{D}_i^*(f,c) = \frac{P_i(f,c)}{\sum_{j=1}^M P_j(f,c)} \tag{15}$$

□

Theorem 1. *Let $\widetilde{P}(f,c) = \frac{\sum_{i=1}^M P_i(f,c)}{M}$, when $\mathcal{D}$ is trained to its optimum $\mathcal{D}^*$, we have:*

$$\mathcal{J}_{\mathcal{D}^*} = M \log M - \sum_{i=1}^{M} KL(P_i(f,c)||\widetilde{P}(f,c)) \tag{16}$$

where $KL(\cdot)$ is the Kullback-Leibler (KL) divergence of each joint distribution $P_i(f,c)$ to the centroid $\widetilde{P}(f,c)$

Proof. Let $\widetilde{P}(f,c) = \frac{\sum_{i=1}^M P_i(f,c)}{M}$. We have:

$$\sum_{i=1}^{M} KL(P_i(f,c)||\widetilde{P}(f,c)) = \sum_{i=1}^{M} \mathbb{E}_{(f,c)\sim P_i}[\log \frac{P_i(f,c)}{\widetilde{P}(f,c)}]$$

When $\mathcal{D}$ is updated to $\mathcal{D}^*$, we have:

$$\begin{aligned}
\mathcal{J}_{\mathcal{D}^*} &= -\sum_{i=1}^{M} \mathbb{E}_{(f,c)\sim P_i}[\log \mathcal{D}_i^*([f,c])] \\
&= -\sum_{i=1}^{M} \mathbb{E}_{(f,c)\sim P_i}[\log \frac{P_i(f,c)}{\sum_{j=1}^M P_j(f,c)}] \\
&= -\sum_{i=1}^{M} \mathbb{E}_{(f,c)\sim P_i}[\log \frac{P_i(f,c)}{\sum_{j=1}^M P_j(f,c)} + \log M] \\
&\quad + M \log M \\
&= M \log M - \sum_{i=1}^{M} \mathbb{E}_{(f,c)\sim P_i}[\log \frac{P_i(f,c)}{\frac{\sum_{j=1}^M P_j(f,c)}{M}}] \\
&= M \log M - \sum_{i=1}^{M} \mathbb{E}_{(f,c)\sim P_i}[\log \frac{P_i(f,c)}{\widetilde{P}(f,c)}] \\
&= M \log M - \sum_{i=1}^{M} KL(P_i(f,c)||\widetilde{P}(f,c))
\end{aligned}$$

□

In our model, a mini-max game is implemented to achieve the optimum:

$$\min_{\mathcal{F}_s, \{\mathcal{F}_d^i\}_{i=1}^M, \mathcal{C}} \max_{\mathcal{D}} \quad \mathcal{J}_{\mathcal{C}} + \lambda \mathcal{J}_{\mathcal{D}} \tag{17}$$

Therefore, by the non-negativity and convexity of the KL-divergence, we can have the corollary:

Corollary 1. *When $\mathcal{D}$ is trained to its optimum $\mathcal{D}^*$, $\mathcal{J}_{\mathcal{D}^*}$ is $M \log M$. The optimum can be obtained if and only if $P_1(f,c) = P_2(f,c) = ... = P_M(f,c) = \widetilde{P}(f,c)$.*

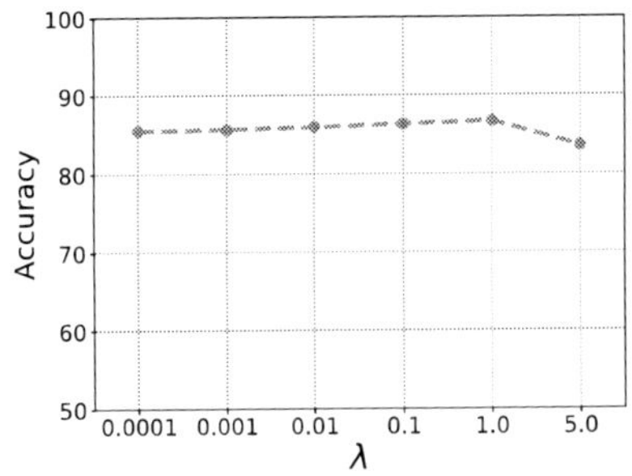

Figure 3: The parameter sensitivity analysis.

A.2 Parameter Sensitivity Analysis

The proposed CAN approach has one hyperparameter λ, which is used to balance $\mathcal{J}_C$ and $\mathcal{J}_D^E$. We conduct parameter sensitivity analysis on the Amazon review dataset. The λ is evaluated in the range $\{0.0001, 0.001, 0.01, 0.1, 1.0, 5.0\}$. The experimental results are shown in Figure 3. The average classification accuracies across the four domains are reported. It can be noted that from 0.0001 to 1.0, the performance increases with λ increasing, the performance change is very small. Then the accuracy reaches the optimum at the point $\lambda = 1.0$, while the further increase of λ will dramatically deteriorate the performance. This suggests that the selection of λ has an influence on the system performance.

The impact of domain-specific representations on BERT-based multi-domain spoken language understanding

Judith Gaspers, Quynh Do, Tobias Röding, Melanie Bradford
Amazon Alexa AI
{gaspers, doquynh, rodingtr, neunerm}@amazon.com

Abstract

This paper provides the first experimental study on the impact of using domain-specific representations on a BERT-based multi-task spoken language understanding (SLU) model for multi-domain applications. Our results on a real-world dataset covering three languages indicate that by using domain-specific representations learned adversarially, model performance can be improved across all of the three SLU subtasks domain classification, intent classification and slot filling. Gains are particularly large for domains with limited training data.

1 Introduction

Spoken Language Understanding (SLU) is a key task in voice-controlled devices, such as Amazon Alexa or Google Home. It is often divided into the two subtasks intent classification (IC) determining the user intent and slot filling (SF) extracting semantic constituents. For instance, given an utterance "play madonna", IC should determine *PlayMusic* as the intent, while SF should label "play" and "madonna" as *Other* and *Artist* slots, respectively. The third subtask, domain classification (DC) which classifies user utterances into different domains, is sometimes required, especially in large-scale industry applications. DC helps when the data comes from different domains and the SLU labeling results require some domain-specific post-processing steps.

Aiming at reducing model building efforts, in this paper, we focus on single multi-task models solving the three subtasks of DC, IC and SF jointly for multi-domain data. Traditionally, these models learn shared-representations for all domains (e.g. Kapoor and Tirkaz (2019); Hakkani-Tür et al. (2016); Kim et al. (2017)). However, using only domain-shared representations may limit model performance as it ignores potentially useful domain-specific knowledge. For instance, let us consider two user requests "play madonna" and "play star wars", belonging to the *Music* and *Video* domains, respectively. In this case, the carrier phrase "play" is shared while the slot values "madonna" and "star wars" are specific to *Music* and *Video*, respectively. Thus, both domain-shared and domain-specific representations could potentially be useful.

In order to shed a light on whether (missing) domain-specific knowledge may play an impact on the model performance, we carry out a wide range of experiments on real-world data comparing the performances of DC-IC-SF multi-task models with and without domain-specific representations. To assure that the models used in the experiments are close to the current state-of-the-art systems, we adapt one of the most recent BERT-based language-adversarial approaches for IC-SF (Do et al., 2020) to our problem. In particular, we use its adversarial architecture to learn domain-shared and domain-specific representations, and extend the model to solve DC in addition to IC and SF.

Our contribution in this paper is studying the impact of using domain-specific representations on a modern multi-task DC-IC-SF model for multi-domain data. Our experiments on a real-world dataset covering three languages (German, English, Japanese) indicate that the domain-specific representations can improve model performance across all of the three SLU subtasks, especially for domains with limited training data.

2 Related Work

A majority of existing work in SLU has focused on modeling IC and SF only, for which mostly DNN-based joint models are currently used (e.g. Liu and Lane (2016); Do and Gaspers (2019); Chen et al.

Proceedings of the Second Workshop on Domain Adaptation for NLP, pages 28–32
April 20, 2021. ©2021 Association for Computational Linguistics

(2019a)). There have been also several researches studying the use of different representation types in these DNN models. He et al. (2020); Chen et al. (2019b); Do et al. (2020) used adversarial training to learn language-shared and language-specific representations for SLU in multilingual settings. Our model architecture can be considered as an extension of the BERT-based language-adversarial model proposed by Do et al. (2020). However, instead of focusing on only IC and IF, our model can deal with an extra DC subtask, which can be used effectively in real-world applications. Moreover, the adversarial training is applied on multi-domain data instead of multilingual data.

Multi-domain joint SLU models have been explored aiming to solve all three tasks via multi-task learning (e.g. Kapoor and Tirkaz (2019), Hakkani-Tür et al. (2016), Kim et al. (2017)). However, none of these studied the impact of domain-shared and domain-specific representations on model performance.

While some previous work followed the idea of leveraging domain-specific representations, we are not aware of a previous study using a full BERT-based multi-domain SLU model with domain-adversarial learning. Liu and Lane (2017) explored adversarial training in multi-domain SLU, but focus on SF only. In another work, Lee et al. (2019) applied adversarial training to obtain locale-specific and locale-agnostic features for the DC task. More recently, Qin et al. (2020) explored domain-specific parametrization for multi-domain SLU in a cascade approach, i.e. a domain classifier is applied as a first step instead of a completely joint system like our focus.

3 Method

In the following, we first describe the multi-domain baseline SLU model, which uses BERT as a single shared feature extractor, and subsequently the adversarial approach, where additionally a domain-specific feature extractor is used for each domain.

3.1 Multi-domain SLU model

We started from a common BERT-based IC-SF architecture (Do et al., 2020), and extended it for DC. In particular, our model (see Fig. 1) consists of: i) a single BERT encoder to learn domain-shared representations for words and utterances. ii) a CRF-based slot decoder for SF, iii) a 2-layer perceptron for both IC and DC. Since DC and IC are both sentence level classification tasks and there is a strong interaction between the two, as usually the intent is conditioned on the domain, we simply use the DC-IC decoder to predict a joint label of domain and intent which is of format DOMAIN_INTENT.

3.2 Domain-adversarial SLU model

We adapted the language-adversarial BERT-based architecture for joint SF and IC from Do et al. (2020) to our problem. In particular, in our system, the IC decoder predicts the DC-IC joint labels instead of only IC labels, and the language identification information is changed to domain identification information.

Our model (see Fig. 2) comprises: i) a regular pre-trained BERT encoder (enc_{bert}), ii) a 1-layer CNN encoder (enc_{shared}) to learn domain-shared representations, iii) n 1-layer CNN encoders ($enc_X, ...$) to learn domain-specific representations for n domains, iv) a 1-layer CNN encoder (enc_{domain}) is used to learn features for predicting the domain, v) a domain predictor, vi) a domain discriminator, vii) a DC-IC decoder, and viii) an SF decoder. Here, the decoders have the same architectures as in 3.1, while the domain predictor and domain discriminator are simply soft-max output layers. The information flow of the token and sentence representations between the model components can be seen in Fig. 2. Given the sentence representations from enc_{domain}, the domain predictor predicts the domain distributions of the input data, which are in turn used as weights to compute the domain-specific features from the token-level outputs of $enc_X, ...$. Meanwhile, the domain discriminator receives the sentence representations from the shared encoder as inputs and also predicts domain distributions. However, the discriminator is trained to fool the system such that the domains become indistinguishable. The domain-shared and domain-specific representations are concatenated before being fed to the DC-IC and SF decoders.

The model is trained via an adversarial training strategy. For the SF task, we use CRF loss L_s, and for the DC-IC decoder, language predictor and language discriminator we use cross-entropy loss denoted by L_{di}, L_p and L_d, respectively. Given training data annotated with intent, slot and domain labels, and $\alpha_d, \alpha_{di}, \alpha_s, \alpha_p, \beta_d$ being model hyper-parameters, i) some data batches are generated randomly, ii) $L = \alpha_d L_d$ is computed, iii) weights are updated, iv) some data batches are generated ran-

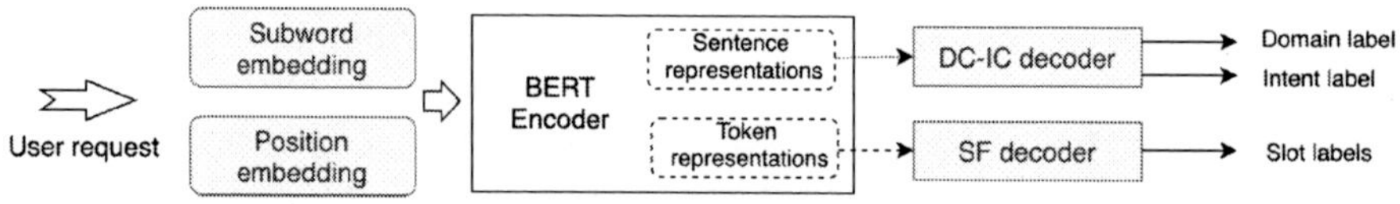

Figure 1: A BERT-based multi-task multi-domain SLU model.

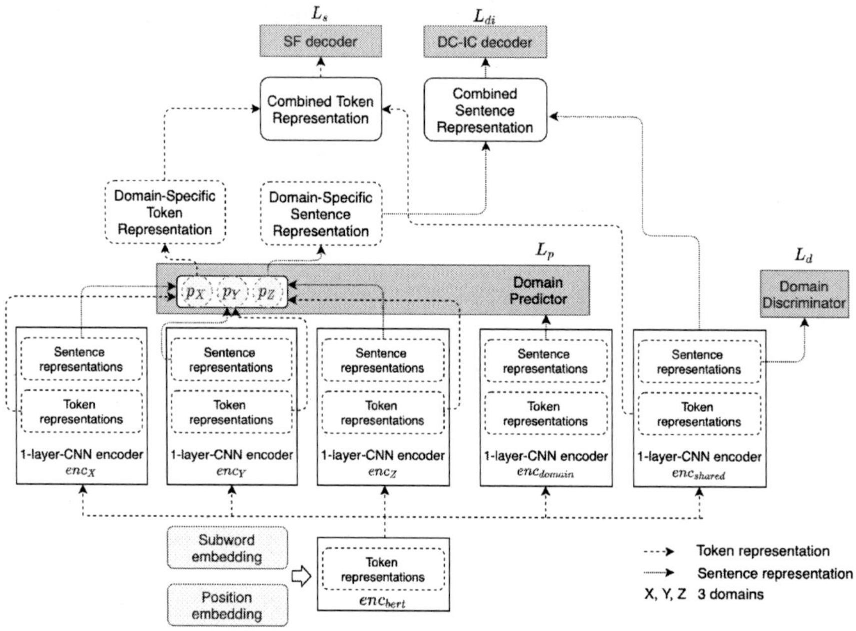

Figure 2: An adversarial model architecture for multi-domain SLU. The figure is adapted from Do et al. (2020).

domly, v) $L = \alpha_{di}L_{di} + \alpha_s L_s + \alpha_p L_p - \beta_d L_d$ is computed, and vi) model weights are updated.

4 Experiments

4.1 Datasets and settings

We extracted random data samples from large-scale commercial SLU systems for English, German and Japanese. The data is comprised of user requests to voice-controlled devices which were suitably anonymized, and each request was manually annotated with domain, intent and slot labels. For each language we used data from three domains, namely *Music*, *Books* and *Video*. In each experiment, the data is composed from all of these three domains with different data distributions. To reflect a real-world scenario, we randomly sampled different training and development data amounts per domain. For *Video*, we randomly sampled data samples of 100, 500, 1,000 and 5.000 utterances. to study domain bootstrapping with growing data amounts. For each sample, we used 90% and 10% of the data to create a training and a development set, respectively. The dataset statistics per domain are summarized in Table 2. Note that for *Video* we have different samples with growing data amounts.

For our experiments, we use pre-trained multilingual BERT (size 768) (Devlin et al., 2018). We use two dense layers of size 768 with gelu activation for the task decoders, and dropout values of 0.5 and 0.2 for the DC-IC and SF decoders, respectively. Each domain decoder has one dense layer of size 768 with gelu activation and a dropout value of 0.5. Each CNN encoder has one layer with a kernel size of three and a hidden dimension of 512. Max-pooling is used in all encoders for computing sentence representations. For adversarial models, the $\alpha_d, \alpha_{di}, \alpha_s, \alpha_p$, and β_d hyper-parameters are set to 1.0, 1.0, 1.0, 1.0, and 0.2, respectively. We train our models with a batch size of 64 for 80 epochs with early stopping using Adam optimizer with a learning rate of 0.1 and a Noam learning rate scheduler. We report F1 score for SF (computed with the CoNLL2002 script) and accuracy for IC

Lang.	#Video samples	Music DC acc.	Music IC acc.	Music SF F1	Books DC acc.	Books IC acc.	Books SF F1	Video DC acc.	Video IC acc.	Video SF F1
German	100	-0.58	+2.11	+6.14	+0.79	+7.44	+2.56	+338.65	+10.5	+13.13
German	500	+0.03	+2.14	+5.98	-0.35	+5.29	+4.11	+75.62	+26.26	+24.92
German	1,000	-0.37	+1.93	+6.3	+1.09	+6.2	+4.09	+32.5	+22.76	+17.34
German	5,000	+0.7	+2.1	+4.32	+1.05	+4.37	+5.21	+1.69	+6.37	+6.73
German	Avg.	-0.06	+2.07	+5.69	+0.64	+5.82	+3.99	+66.38	+16.47	+15.53
English	100	-0.3	+2.02	+3.55	+1.15	+5.23	+2.65	+504.9	+153.31	+27.15
English	500	-0.61	+1.59	+4.9	+1.39	+5.25	+2.36	+47.69	+41.83	+12.85
English	1,000	-1.49	+0.46	+5.74	+0.88	+3.67	+2.31	+27.98	+29.7	+13.32
English	5,000	-2.1	-0.43	+4.57	+0.83	+3.66	+3.12	+4.44	+7.51	+5.12
English	Avg.	-1.12	+0.91	+4.69	+1.06	+4.45	+2.61	+146.25	+58.9	+14.61
Japanese	100	+0.03	+3.99	+19.84	+1.96	+8.42	+15.57	+191.02	+3.1	+100.24
Japanese	500	+0.77	+2.4	+11.62	+0.88	+5.61	+7.62	+23.53	+17.61	+44.6
Japanese	1,000	+1.2	+3.25	+14.22	+2.15	+6.61	+8.88	+4.68	+11.12	+40.6
Japanese	5,000	+1.17	+1.58	+17.31	+2.75	+6.11	+10.33	+2.72	+15.07	+19.93
Japanese	Avg.	+0.79	+2.8	+15.75	+1.93	+6.69	+10.6	+55.49	+11.72	+51.34
Avg.	Avg.	-0.13	+1.93	+8.71	+1.21	+5.65	+5.73	+89.37	+29.03	+27.16

Table 1: Relative change in domain classification (DC) accuracy, intent classification (IC) accuracy and slot (SF) F1 for domain-adversarial training compared to multi-domain training using a single shared feature as the baseline. For the *Music* domain 10,000 samples are used for model training, and 5,000 are used for *Books*. For *Video*, a growing amount of samples is used, ranging from 100 to 5,000.

Domain	Train	Dev.	Test
Music	9,000	1,000	3,000
Books	4,500	500	3,000
Video - samples 100	90	10	3000
Video - samples 500	450	50	3000
Video - samples 1,000	900	100	3000
Video - samples 5,000	4,500	500	3000

Table 2: Number of utterances per domain and dataset (available in English, Japanese and German).

and DC tasks.

5 Results

In our experiments *Video* is considered as a new domain, where initially few domain data samples are available, and data amounts are growing over time. In particular, we consider samples with sizes of 100, 500, 1,000 and 5,000 utterances for the new domain. For each experiment, the total data amounts for the domains *Music* and *Books* are kept constant at 10,000 and 5,000 utterances, respectively. For each considered Video sample size, we combine the corresponding *Video* training and development data with the other domain's training and development data, respectively. We then train i) a multi-domain SLU model as described in Section 3.1, and ii) an adversarial SLU model as described in Section 3.2, which are subsequently applied on the test datasets for all domains. The results are presented in Table 1. Due to confidentiality reasons, relative numbers are reported.

Overall, the domain-adversarial approach consistently outperforms the baseline model across all tasks and languages, except for some small fluctuations for the DC task in the *Music* domain, which has the largest data amounts in our scenario. In turn, DC performance is improved slightly for *Books* and greatly for *Video*. In particular, averaged across languages and sample sizes, DC accuracy is improved by 1.21% and 89.37% relative for the *Books* and *Video* domains, respectively. Performance gains in the *Video* domain are particularly large for smaller samples sizes. For the IC and SF tasks, the largest gains are also achieved for the *Video* domain. Averaged across languages and sample sizes, we achieve relative improvements in IC and SF of 29.0% and 27.16%, for the *Video* domain. Again, the largest relative improvements are achieved when only a few *Video* samples are available.

The results suggest that the adversarial approach is particularly useful to boost performance of domains with a limited amount of data, which could be new or low-frequency domains. While the highest gains are achieved when only few domain data is available, consistent gains in IC and SF performance are achieved for all domains and data sizes, with gains being larger for the SF task. A potential reason could be that the amount of relevant domain-specific information is higher for SF than for IC, and thus larger gains are possible by adversarial training. Note that domain-shared information can also be leveraged by the baseline model (though it may not be domain-agnostic). The results also reveal that there are language-specific differences. Specifically, the domain-adversarial training approach seems to be particularly useful for Japanese. Averaged across sample sizes, relative improvements in slot filling performance of 15.75% and 10.6% for *Music* and *Books*, respectively, are achieved.

6 Conclusion

We studied the impact of using both domain-specific and domain-shared representations vs. using only domain-shared representations on the application of multi-domain SLU. In particular, we compared a baseline which uses BERT as a single shared feature extractor to learn domain-shared representations to an adversarial model which additionally uses a domain-specific feature extractor for each domain to learn domain-specific representations in addition to the standard domain-shared representations. Our results on a real-world dataset covering three languages indicate that by using a domain-adversarial approach, model performance can be improved across all of the three SLU subtasks. Performance gains were particularly large for the use case of bootstrapping a new domain, where little target domain data are available.

References

Q. Chen, Z. Zhuo, and W. Wang. 2019a. Bert for joint intent classification and slot filling. *arXiv:1902.10909*.

Xilun Chen, Ahmed Hassan Awadallah, Hany Hassan, Wei Wang, and Claire Cardie. 2019b. Multi-source cross-lingual model transfer: Learning what to share. In *Proceedings of the 57th Annual Meeting of the Association for Computational Linguistics*, pages 3098–3112, Florence, Italy. Association for Computational Linguistics.

Jacob Devlin, Ming-Wei Chang, Kenton Lee, and Kristina Toutanova. 2018. BERT: pre-training of deep bidirectional transformers for language understanding. *CoRR*, abs/1810.04805.

Quynh Do, Judith Gaspers, Tobias Roeding, and Melanie Bradford. 2020. To what degree can language borders be blurred in BERT-based multilingual spoken language understanding? In *Proceedings of the 28th International Conference on Computational Linguistics*, pages 2699–2709, Barcelona, Spain (Online). International Committee on Computational Linguistics.

Quynh Ngoc Thi Do and Judith Gaspers. 2019. Cross-lingual transfer learning for spoken language understanding. *Proceedings of the 2019 IEEE International Conference on Acoustics, Speech and Signal Processing, ICASSP*.

Anuj Kumar Goyal, Angeliki Metallinou, and Spyros Matsoukas. 2018. Fast and scalable expansion of natural language understanding functionality for intelligent agents. In *Proceedings of the 2018 Conference of the North American Chapter of the Association for Computational Linguistics: Human Language Technologies, Volume 3 (Industry Papers)*, pages 145–152, New Orleans - Louisiana. Association for Computational Linguistics.

Dilek Hakkani-Tür, Gökhan Tür, Asli Çelikyilmaz, Yun-Nung Chen, Jianfeng Gao, Li Deng, and Ye-Yi Wang. 2016. Multi-domain joint semantic frame parsing using bi-directional RNN-LSTM. In *Interspeech 2016, 17th Annual Conference of the International Speech Communication Association, San Francisco, CA, USA, September 8-12, 2016*, pages 715–719. ISCA.

K. He, W. Xu, and Y. Yan. 2020. Multi-level cross-lingual transfer learning with language shared and specific knowledge for spoken language understanding. *IEEE Access*, 8:29407–29416.

Shubham Kapoor and Caglar Tirkaz. 2019. Bootstrapping nlu models with multi-task learning.

Young-Bum Kim, Sungjin Lee, and Karl Stratos. 2017. ONENET: joint domain, intent, slot prediction for spoken language understanding. In *2017 IEEE Automatic Speech Recognition and Understanding Workshop, ASRU 2017, Okinawa, Japan, December 16-20, 2017*, pages 547–553. IEEE.

Jihwan Lee, Ruhi Sarikaya, and Young-Bum Kim. 2019. Locale-agnostic universal domain classification model in spoken language understanding. In *Proceedings of the 2019 Conference of the North American Chapter of the Association for Computational Linguistics: Human Language Technologies, NAACL-HLT 2019, Minneapolis, MN, USA, June 2-7, 2019, Volume 2 (Industry Papers)*, pages 9–15. Association for Computational Linguistics.

Bing Liu and Ian Lane. 2016. Attention-based recurrent neural network models for joint intent detection and slot filling. In *INTERSPEECH*.

Bing Liu and Ian Lane. 2017. Multi-domain adversarial learning for slot filling in spoken language understanding.

Libo Qin, Minheng Ni, Yue Zhang, Wanxiang Che, Yangming Li, and Ting Liu. 2020. Multi-domain spoken language understanding using domain- and task-aware parameterization.

Bridging the gap between supervised classification and unsupervised topic modelling for social-media assisted crisis management

Mikael Brunila* **Rosie Zhao*** **Andrei Mircea*** **Sam Lumley** **Renee Sieber**
McGill University / Montreal, QC, Canada
{rosie.zhao,andrei.romascanu,sam.lumley}@mail.mcgill.ca
mikael.brunila@gmail.com
renee.sieber@mcgill.ca

Abstract

Social media such as Twitter provide valuable information to crisis managers and affected people during natural disasters. Machine learning can help structure and extract information from the large volume of messages shared during a crisis; however, the constantly evolving nature of crises makes effective domain adaptation essential. Supervised classification is limited by unchangeable class labels that may not be relevant to new events, and unsupervised topic modelling by insufficient prior knowledge. In this paper, we bridge the gap between the two and show that BERT embeddings finetuned on crisis-related tweet classification can effectively be used to adapt to a new crisis, discovering novel topics while preserving relevant classes from supervised training, and leveraging bidirectional self-attention to extract topic keywords. We create a dataset of tweets from a snowstorm to evaluate our method's transferability to new crises, and find that it outperforms traditional topic models in both automatic, and human evaluations grounded in the needs of crisis managers. More broadly, our method can be used for textual domain adaptation where the latent classes are unknown but overlap with known classes from other domains.

1 Introduction

1.1 Social Media for Crisis Management

As climate change increases the frequency of extreme weather events and the vulnerability of affected people, effective crisis management is becoming increasingly important for mitigating the negative effects of these crises (Keim, 2008). In the general crisis management literature, social media has been identified as a useful source of information for crisis managers to gauge reactions from and communicate with the public, increase situational awareness, and enable data-driven decision-making (Tobias, 2011; Alexander, 2014; Jin et al., 2014).

1.2 The Need For NLP

The large volume and noise-to-signal ratio of social media platforms such as Twitter makes it difficult to extract actionable information, especially at a rate suited for the urgency of a crisis. This has motivated the application of natural language processing (NLP) techniques to help automatically filter information in real-time as a crisis unfolds (Imran et al., 2013; Emmanouil and Nikolaos, 2015).

Other work has investigated the use of NLP models to automatically classify tweets into finer-grained categories that can be more salient to crisis managers and affected people in rapidly evolving situations (Ragini and Anand, 2016; Schulz et al., 2014). Training such classification models typically requires large-scale annotated corpora of crisis-related tweets such as that made available by Imran et al. (2016), which covers a variety of countries and natural disasters including flooding, tropical storms, earthquakes, and forest fires.

1.3 Limitations of Current Methods

Whereas supervised approaches work well for classifying tweets from the same event as their training data, they often fail to generalize to novel events (Nguyen et al., 2017). A novel event may differ from past events in terms of location, type of event, or event characteristics; all of which can change the relevance of a tweet classification scheme.

Various methods of domain adaptation have been suggested for addressing this issue (Li et al., 2018; Sopova, 2017; Alrashdi and O'Keefe, 2020). However, this type of supervised classification assumes that relevant classes remain the same from event to event. Probabilistic topic modelling approaches such as Latent Dirichlet Allocation (LDA) can overcome this limitation and identify novel categorizations (Blei et al., 2003). Unfortunately, these unsupervised methods are typically difficult to apply to tweets due to issues of document length and non-standard language (Hong and Davison, 2010).

*Equal contribution.

Proceedings of the Second Workshop on Domain Adaptation for NLP, pages 33–49
April 20, 2021.

Furthermore, the categorizations produced by these models can be difficult to interpret by humans, limiting their usefulness (Blekanov et al., 2020).

1.4 Our Contributions

To address these issues, we propose a method for the unsupervised clustering of tweets from novel crises, using the representations learned from supervised classification. Specifically, we use the contextual embeddings of a pretrained language model finetuned on crisis tweet classification.

Our method bridges the gap between supervised approaches and unsupervised topic modelling, improving domain adaptation to new crises by allowing classification of tweets in novel topics while preserving relevant classes from supervised training. Our model is robust to idiosyncrasies of tweet texts such as short document length and nonstandard language, and leverages bi-directional self-attention to provide interpretable topic keywords.

We assess our approach's transferability to novel crises by creating a dataset of tweets from Winter Storm Jacob, a severe winter storm that hit Newfoundland, Canada in January 2020. This event differs significantly from past crisis tweet classification datasets on which we finetune our model, and allows us to evaluate domain adaptation for novel events. We find that our approach indeed identifies novel topics that are distinct from the labels seen during supervised training.

In line with human-centered machine learning principles (Ramos et al., 2019), we also create a novel human evaluation task aligned with the needs of crisis managers. We find that, with high interrater reliability, our model provides consistently more interpretable and useful topic keywords than traditional approaches, while improving cluster coherence as measured by intruder detection. Automated coherence measures further support these findings. Our code and dataset are available at `https://github.com/smacawi/bert-topics`.

2 Related Work

2.1 Topic Modelling

Topic modelling in a variety of domains is widely studied. Although there are many existing approaches in the literature, most innovations are compared to the seminal Latent Dirichlet Allocation (LDA) model (Blei et al., 2003). LDA is a generative probabilistic model that considers the joint distribution of observed variables (words) and hidden variables (topics). While LDA has well-known issues with short text, approaches such as Biterm Topic Modelling (BTM) have been developed to address these (Yan et al., 2013). BTM specifically addresses the sparsity of word co-occurrences: whereas LDA models word-document occurrences, BTM models word co-occurrences ('biterms') across the entire corpus.

2.2 Clustering

Topic modelling can be distinguished from clustering, where documents are usually represented in a multi-dimensional vector space and then grouped using vector similarity measures. These representations are typically formed through matrix factorization techniques (Levy and Goldberg, 2014) that compress words (Mikolov et al., 2013b; Pennington et al., 2014) or sentences (Mikolov et al., 2013a; Lau and Baldwin, 2016) into "embeddings". Recently, language representation models building on Transformer type neural networks (Vaswani et al., 2017) have upended much of NLP and provided new, "contextualized" embedding approaches (Devlin et al., 2019; Peters et al., 2018). Among these is the Bidirectional Encoder Representations from Transformers (BERT) model, which is available pretrained on large amounts of text and can be finetuned on many different types of NLP tasks (Devlin et al., 2019). Embeddings from BERT and other Transformer type language models can potentially serve as a basis for both topic modelling (Bianchi et al., 2020) and clustering (Reimers et al., 2019), but many questions about their usefulness for these tasks remain open.

The use of embeddings for clustering in the field of crisis management has been explored by Demszky et al. (2019) using trained GloVe embeddings. Zahera et al. (2019) used contextualized word embeddings from BERT to train a classifier for crisis-related tweets on a fixed set of labels. Using BERT to classify tweets in the field of disaster management was also studied by Ma (2019) by aggregating labelled tweets from the CrisisNLP and CrisisLexT26 datasets. While the aforementioned work requires data with a gold standard set of labels, our proposed clustering approach using finetuned BERT embeddings is applied in an unsupervised environment on unseen data — it invites domain expertise to determine an appropriate set of labels specific to the crisis at hand.

2.3 Topic Keyword Extraction

A significant issue when clustering text documents is how the keywords of each cluster or topic are determined. Unlike standard topic models such as LDA, clustering approaches do not jointly model the distributions of keywords over topics and of topics over documents. In other words, clusters do not contain any obvious information about which keywords should represent the clusters as topics. While the previous generation of embedding models has been leveraged for interpretable linguistic analysis in a wide variety of settings (Garg et al., 2018; Hamilton et al., 2016; Kozlowski et al., 2019), the interpretability of language models in general and BERT in particular remains a contested issue (Rogers et al., 2020).

One promising line of research has been on the attention mechanism of Transformer models (Bahdanau et al., 2015; Jain and Wallace, 2019). Clark et al. (2019) found that the attention heads of BERT contained a significant amount of syntactic and grammatical information, and Lin et al. (2019) concluded that this information is hierarchical, similar to syntactic tree structures. Kovaleva et al. (2019) noted that different attention heads often carry overlapping and redundant information. However, if attention is to be useful for selecting topic keywords, the crucial question is whether it captures semantic information. Jain and Wallace (2019) found that attention heads generally correlated poorly with traditional measures for feature importance in neural networks, such as gradients, while Serrano and Smith (2019) showed that attention can "noisily" predict the importance of features for overall model performance and Wiegreffe and Pinter (2019) argued that attention can serve plausible, although not faithful explanations of models. To the best of our knowledge, there is no previous work on leveraging attention to improve topic modelling interpretability.

2.4 Model Coherence

Whether based on clustering or probabilistic approaches, topic models are typically evaluated by their coherence. While human evaluation is preferable, several automated methods have been proposed to emulate that of human performance (Lau et al., 2014). In both cases, coherence can be thought of formally as a measure of the extent to which keywords in a topic relate to each other as a set of semantically coherent *facts* (Röder et al., 2015; Aletras and Stevenson, 2013; Mimno et al., 2011). If a word states a fact, then the coherence of a set of topic keywords can be measured by computing how strongly a word W' is confirmed by a conditioning set of words W^*. This can be done either directly where W' is a word in a set of topic words and W^* are the other words in the same set (e.g. Mimno et al., 2011), or indirectly by computing context vectors for both W' and W^* and then comparing these (e.g. Aletras and Stevenson, 2013). In a comprehensive comparison of different coherence measures, Röder et al. (2015) found that, when comparing the coherence scores assigned by humans to a set of topics against a large number of automated metrics, indirect confirmation measures tend to result in a higher correlation between human and automated coherence scores.

2.5 Human Evaluation of Topic Models

While automated coherence measures can be used to rapidly evaluate topic models such as LDA, studies have shown that these metrics can be uncorrelated — or negatively correlated — to human interpretability judgements. Chang et al. (2009) demonstrated that results given by perplexity measures differed from that of their proposed 'intrusion' tasks, where humans identify spurious words inserted in a topic, and mismatched topics assigned to a document. Tasks have been formulated in previous works to meaningfully enable human judgement when analyzing the topics (Chuang et al., 2013; Lee et al., 2017).

The latent topics given by these methods should provide a semantically meaningful decomposition of a given corpus. Formalizing the quality of the resulting latent topics via qualitative tasks or quantitative metrics is even less straightforward in an applied setting, where it is particularly important that the semantic meaning underlying the topic model is relevant to its users. Due to our focus on the comparison between the labels in the CrisisNLP dataset and novel topics discovered by our model, we restrict this part of the analysis to nine topics.

Our work is motivated by structuring crude textual data for practical use by crisis managers, guiding *corpus exploration* and efficient information retrieval. It remains difficult to verify whether the latent space discovered by topic models is both interpretable and useful without a gold standard set of labels.

3 Methodology

In this section we describe the dataset of snowstorm-related tweets we created to evaluate our model's ability to discover novel topics and transfer to unseen crisis events. We then outline the process by which our model learns to extract crisis-relevant embeddings from tweets, and clusters them into novel topics from which it then extracts interpretable keywords.

3.1 Snowstorm Dataset

On January 18 2020, Winter Storm Jacob hit Newfoundland, Canada. As a result of the high winds and severe snowfall, 21,000 homes were left without power. A state of emergency was declared in the province as snowdrifts as high as 15 feet (4.6 m) trapped people indoors (Erdman, 2020).

Following the Newfoundland Snowstorm, we collected 21,797 unique tweets from 8,471 users between January 17 and January 22 using the Twitter standard search API with the following search terms: `#nlwhiteout`, `#nlweather`, `#Newfoundland`, `#nlblizzard2020`, `#NLStorm2020`, `#snowmaggedon2020`, `#stormageddon2020`, `#Snowpocalypse2020`, `#Snowmageddon`, `#nlstorm`, `#nltraffic`, `#NLwx`, `#NLblizzard`. Based on past experience with the Twitter API, we opted to use hashtags to limit irrelevant tweets (e.g. searching for `blizzard` resulted in half the collected tweets being about the video game company with the same name). We filter retweets to only capture unique tweets and better work within API rate limits. We make the dataset publicly available with our code.

3.2 Finetuned Tweet Embeddings Model

Our proposed approach, Finetuned Tweet Embeddings (FTE) involves training a model with bidirectional self-attention such as BERT (Devlin et al., 2019) to generate embeddings for tweets so that these can be clustered using common off-the-shelf algorithms such as K-Means (Lloyd, 1982; Elkan, 2003). We then combine activations from the model's attention layers with Term frequency-Inverse document frequency (Tf-Idf) to identify keywords for each cluster and improve model interpretability.

3.2.1 Model Finetuning

To build a model that extracts tweet embeddings containing information relevant to crisis management, we finetune a pretrained BERT language representation model on classifying tweets from various crisis events. Similar to Romascanu et al. (2020), we finetune on CrisisNLP, a dataset of Crowdflower-labeled tweets from various types of crises, aimed at crisis managers (Imran et al., 2016). These show a significant class imbalance with large amounts of tweets shunted into uninformative categories such as `Other useful information`, further motivating the need for unsupervised topic discovery. CrisisNLP label descriptions and counts are included in Appendix A for context. To address the issue of class imbalance, we create a random stratified train-validation split of 0.8 across the datasets, preserving the same proportions of labels.

To finetune BERT, we add a dropout layer and a linear classification layer on top of the `bert-base-uncased` model, using the 768-dimensional `[CLS]` last hidden state as input to our classifier. We train the model using the Adam optimizer with the default fixed weight decay, and a batch size of four over a single epoch. Our model obtains an accuracy of 0.78 on the withheld validation dataset. One advantage of BERT is its subword tokenization which can dynamically build representations of out-of-vocabulary words from subwords, allowing a robust handling of the non-standard language found in tweets.

3.2.2 Tweet Embedding

Once the model is trained, we use a mean-pooling layer across the last hidden states to generate a tweet embedding, similar to Reimers and Gurevych (2019) who found mean-pooling to work best for semantic similarity tasks. Whereas the hidden state for the `[CLS]` token contains sufficient information to separate tweets between the different CrisisNLP labels, the hidden states for the other tokens in the tweet allow our model to capture token-level information that can help in identifying novel topics beyond the supervised labels. For example, tweets that use similar words — even those not occurring in the CrisisNLP dataset — will have more similar embeddings and thus be more likely to cluster in the same topic.

3.2.3 Clustering

Given the embeddings for each tweet, we apply an optimized version of the K-Means clustering algorithm to find our candidate topics (Elkan, 2003). We use the K-Means implementation in `Sklearn` with the default 'k-means++' initialization and n_int equal to 10.

3.2.4 Keyword Extraction

To extract keywords from topics generated by our model and ensure their interpretability, we experiment with two approaches and their combination.

We first identify relevant keywords for each cluster using Tf-Idf (Spärck Jones, 2004), combining each cluster into one document to address the issue of low term frequencies in short-text tweets. During automatic evaluation, we perform a comprehensive grid search over Tf-Idf and other hyperparameters:

1. maximum document frequency (mdf) between 0.6 and 1.0 with intervals of 0.1 (to ignore snowstorm related terms common to many clusters);
2. sublinear Tf-Idf (shown to be advantageous by Paltoglou and Thelwall (2010));
3. phrasing (grouping of frequently co-occurring words proposed by Mikolov et al. (2013b))

We find an mdf of 0.6 and sublinear Tf-Idf perform best for FTE with our number of topics, and we use these hyperparameters in our experiments. Phrasing makes no significant difference and we only include unigrams in our keywords.

However, Tf-Idf only uses frequency and does not leverage the crisis-related knowledge learned during finetuning. Based on the observation by Clark et al. (2019), we use BERT's last layer of attention for the `[CLS]` token to identify keywords that are important for classifying tweets along crisis management related labels. For each cluster, we score keywords by summing their attention values (averaged across subwords) across tweets where they occur, better capturing the relevance of a keyword to crisis management.

We also experiment with the combination of Tf-Idf and attention by multiplying the two scores for each token, allowing us to down-weight frequent but irrelevant words and up-weight rarer but relevant words. For all three approaches, we drop stopwords, hashtags, special characters, and URLs based on preliminary experiments that found these contributing substantially to noise in the topic keywords.

4 Evaluation

In this section we describe the baselines, as well as the automatic and human evaluations used.

4.1 Baselines

We report on two standard topic modelling techniques: BTM and LDA, for which we train models ranging from five to fifteen topics under 10 passes and 100 iterations, following the work of Blei et al. (2003). For LDA, we generate clusters of tweets by giving a weighted topic assignment to each word present in a given document according to the topic distribution over all words present in the corpus. Clusters can be generated similarly with BTM, but according to the topic distribution over biterms (with a window size of 15).

We also report on BERT, which is simply our method without the finetuning step, i.e. using vanilla pretrained BERT embeddings with K-Means clustering and keyword extraction based on Tf-Idf and attention. For further comparison with the FTE model, we focus our analysis on trained baselines with nine topics, the number of labels in the CrisisNLP dataset (Imran et al., 2016).

4.2 Automatic Evaluation

To evaluate topics we calculate C_{NPMI} and C_V, two topic coherence metrics based on direct and indirect confirmation respectively (Röder et al., 2015). These are described in Appendix B. For subsequent human evaluation, we select the configuration (§3.2.4) of each model with the highest C_V for nine topics. This allows us to directly compare with the nine labels from the CrisisNLP dataset and assess our model's ability to learn novel topics. We focus on C_V as Röder et al. (2015) found it to correlate best with human judgements (in contrast to $UMASS$, another commonly used coherence metric that was not included in our analysis due to poor correlation with human judgements).

4.3 Human Evaluation

We performed anonymous evaluation through four annotators[1]. Since these models are primarily for use by crisis managers, we aim to concentrate our evaluation from the perspective of annotators working in the field. Specifically, we propose two evaluation methods focused on (1) topic keywords and (2) document clustering within topics.

[1]Student researchers familiar with the crisis management literature and the needs of crisis managers as described in §1.1

4.3.1 Keyword Evaluation

To assess the quality of topic keywords, annotators were presented with the top 10 keywords for each topic (Table 1) and asked to assign an interpretability score and a usefulness score on a three-point scale. Following the criteria of Rosner et al. (2013), we define interpretability as **good** (eight to ten words are related to each other), **neutral** (four to seven words are related), or **bad** (at most three words are related). Usefulness in turn considers the ease of assigning a short label to describe a topic based on its keywords, similar to Newman et al. (2010) except we further require the label should be useful for crisis managers. We score usefulness on a three-point scale: **useful**, **average**, or **useless**.

4.3.2 Cluster Evaluation

The second task assesses — from the perspective of a crisis manager — the interpretability and usefulness of the actual documents clustered within a topic, instead of only analyzing topic keywords as done in previous work.

Given an anonymized model, for each topic we sample 10 sets of four documents within its cluster along with one document — the 'intruder' — outside of that topic. For each set of documents, all four annotators were tasked with identifying the intruder from the sample of five documents, as well as assigning an interpretability score and a usefulness score to each sample.

The task of intrusion detection is a variation of Chang et al. (2009). However, instead of intruder topics or topic words, we found that assessing intruder tweets would give us a better sense of the differences in the clusters produced by our models. Participants were also given the option of labeling the intruder as 'unsure' to discourage guessing.

The interpretability score was graded on a three-point scale: **good** (3-4 tweets seem to be part of a coherent topic beyond "snowstorm"), **neutral**, and **bad** (no tweets seem to be part of a coherent topic beyond "snowstorm"). The cluster usefulness score was similar to the keyword usefulness score, but formulated as a less ambiguous binary assignment of **useful** or **useless** for crisis managers wanting to filter information during a crisis.

4.4 Model agreement

While our human cluster evaluation provides a good estimate of how topic clusters appear to humans, it does not necessarily establish the difference between two models' document clusters due to the random sampling involved. In other words, two models may have different cluster evaluation results, but similar topic clusters. We define 'agreement' as a measure of the overlap between two unsupervised classification models.

Given a model A, its agreement Agr_A with a model B is

$$\mathrm{Agr}_A(B) = \frac{\sum_{i=0}^{N} \max_j \mathrm{p}(A_i, B_j)}{N} \tag{1}$$

where A_i is the set of documents in the ith cluster of A and $\mathrm{p}(A_i, B_j)$ is the proportion of documents in A_i that are also in B_j. We further define model agreement between A and B as the average of $\mathrm{Agr}_A(B)$ and $\mathrm{Agr}_B(A)$.

5 Results

5.1 Automatic Evaluation

Figure 1 shows that combining attention and Tf-Idf produces the highest automated C_V coherence scores for our method, across a range of topic numbers. However, the improvement of adding attention is marginal and attention alone performed much worse, suggesting it is suboptimal for identifying keywords. Recent work by Kobayashi et al. (2020) proposes a norm-based analysis which may improve upon this.

Figure 2 shows that FTE significantly outperforms the LDA and BTM baselines, with similar scores to the BERT baseline. We observed similar trends for C_{NPMI}. However, despite BERT's high C_V scores, we found that the topics it generated were of very low quality, as described below.

5.2 Qualitative Analysis of Keywords

Topic keywords are shown in Table 1. By restricting the number of topics to the number of labels in the CrisisNLP dataset, we were able to ask our annotators to identify overlap with these original labels. Conversely, this allows us to show that our approach indeed bridges the gap between supervised classification and unsupervised topic modelling by identifying novel topics in addition to salient topics from supervised training.

5.2.1 FTE Keywords

Annotators identified overlap between generated topics and relevant classes from the CrisisNLP dataset: Topic 4 capturing donation needs and volunteering services, Topic 5 expressing sympathy

Model					Topic				
	1	2	3	4	5	6	7	8	9
FTE	reporting	ivyparkxadidas	outage	assistance	prayer	blowingsnow	trapped	monster	bread
	monster	mood	campus	assist	praying	alert	stranded	meteorologist	song
	snowiest	song	widening	troop	pray	advisory	hydrant	drifting	coffee
	recorded	blackswan	advisory	volunteer	wish	caution	ambulance	perspective	milk
	peak	le	reported	providing	wishing	advised	dead	stormofthecentury	feelin
	temperature	snowdoor	impassable	relief	humanity	stormsurge	garbage	mood	pin
	cloudy	perspective	remaining	aid	brave	wreckhouse	rescue	snowdrift	enjoying
	reported	ode	thousand	request	surviving	surge	permitted	climate	laugh
	equivalent	music	reporting	offering	loved	drifting	body	windy	favorite
	meteorologist	adidasxivypark	suspended	rescue	kindness	avoid	helped	snowdoor	girl
BTM	emergency	eminem	safe	cbcnl	people	like	nltraffic	closed	cm
	state	photo	stay	today	today	storm	road	st	st
	st	click	blizzard	thank	storm	snow	power	tomorrow	winds
	city	learn	newfoundland	people	need	time	st	john	pm
	cityofstjohns	saveng	storm	day	like	day	street	remain	today
	says	michelleobama	canada	home	day	newfoundland	drive	january	km
	declared	sexeducation	weather	work	grocery	going	pearl	update	airport
	john	ken	nlstorm	help	food	blizzard	roads	emergency	yyt
	mayor	starr	warm	storm	open	house	line	state	snowfall
	roads	pin	snowstorm	nltraffic	know	today	mount	today	blizzard
BERT	shareyourweather	pin	thankful	lay	metro	mood	glad	thankful	monster
	ivyparkxadidas	feelin	bank	justintrudeau	campus	hutton	looked	glad	stormsurge
	saturdaythoughts	taxi	yo	save	provincial	cute	apartment	sharing	le
	saturdaymotivation	mayor	mayor	suck	mayor	compound	cloudy	favourite	wreckhouse
	snowdoor	metro	neighbor	radiogregsmith	remain	lovely	law	shareyourweather	newfoundlandlabrador
	bcstorm	en	walked	kettle	operation	spread	snowblowing	grateful	ode
	titanscollections	blowingsnow	wa	anthonygermain	pharmacy	stream	honestly	monster	snowiest
	badboysforlife	ivyparkxadidas	bus	kilbride	region	design	as	feelin	ottawa
	bingo	bus	glad	kaylahounsell	taxi	ivyparkxadidas	eat	neighbor	historic
	blackswan	dannybreennl	pharmacy	campus	advisory	crisis	weird	mom	explorenl

Table 1: Topic keywords for our FTE model and the BTM and BERT baselines used in human evaluation.

and emotional support, Topic 7 covering missing or trapped people, and Topic 2 seemingly covering unrelated information. Distinct novel topics were also identified in the meteorological information in Topic 1, and information about power outages and closures in Topic 3. Topics 8 and 9 were less clear to annotators, but the former seemed to carry information about how extreme the storm was thought to be and the latter about citizens bundling up indoors with different foods and activities.

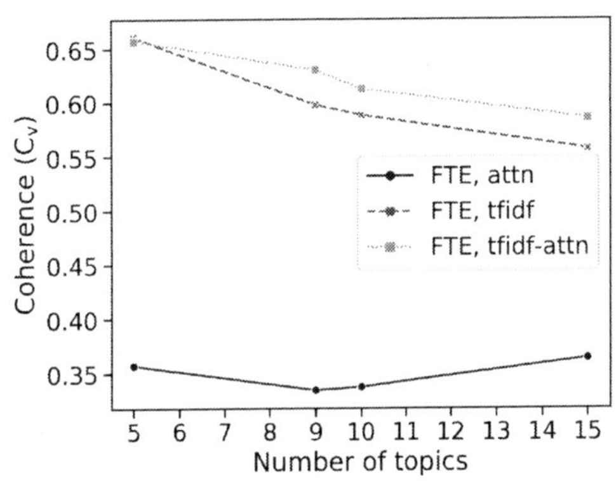

Figure 1: Effect of keyword extraction strategies.

5.2.2 BTM Keywords

The topics in BTM were less semantically meaningful to annotators, although they found interesting topics there as well, with Topic 5 showing information about the need to stockpile provisions, Topic 7 relating to traffic conditions, and Topic 8 potentially providing information about a state of emergency and closed businesses.

5.2.3 BERT Keywords

The topics in BERT were largely incoherent for annotators, with the exceptions being Topic 9 (positive sentiment) and Topic 5 (services and advisories). This is in stark contrast to the large automated coherence scores obtained by this method, indicating the importance of pairing automatic evaluation with human evaluation.

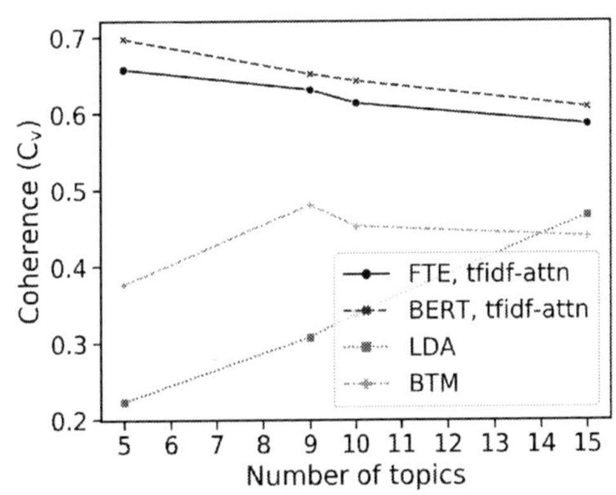

Figure 2: Comparison of FTE with baselines.

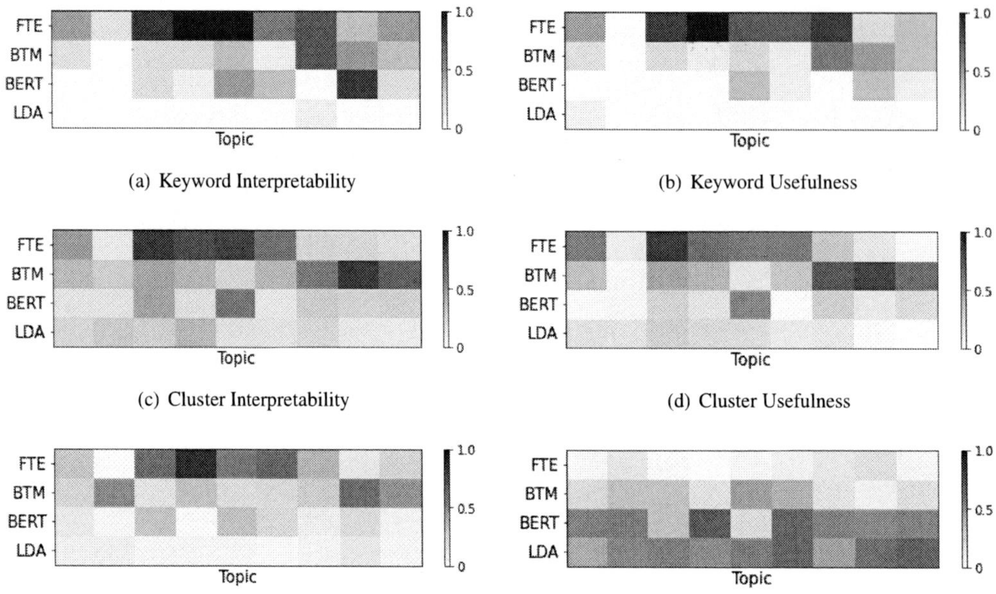

(a) Keyword Interpretability (b) Keyword Usefulness (c) Cluster Interpretability (d) Cluster Usefulness (e) Correct Intruders (f) Unsure Intruders

Figure 3: Topic-level results for keyword and cluster evaluations, aligned with topics from Table 1. All scores are rescaled to values between 0 and 1, then averaged across annotators and samples.

	Average Score		Topic Count		Fleiss' κ	
Score	BTM	FTE	BTM	FTE	BTM	FTE
Interpretability	31.94	**65.28**	1	**5**	15.01	**17.97**
Usefulness	27.78	**59.72**	1	**5**	12.36	**21.55**

Table 2: Keyword Evaluation scores averaged across topics, number of topics with average scores greater than 0.5, and inter-rater agreements (Fleiss' κ).

	Average Score		Topic Count		Fleiss' κ	
Score	BTM	FTE	BTM	FTE	BTM	FTE
Interpretability	50.28	**51.53**	3	**4**	11.05	**23.45**
Usefulness	45.46	**46.11**	3	**5**	**21.82**	21.60
Correct Intruders	35.28	**44.17**	2	**4**	25.78	**31.50**
Unknown Intruders	26.39	**8.89**	0	0	-	-

Table 3: Cluster Evaluation scores averaged across topics, number of topics with average scores greater than 0.5, and inter-rater agreements (Fleiss' κ).

5.3 Human evaluation

In Figure 3, we compare topic-level results for keyword evaluations (averaged across annotators), and for cluster evaluations (averaged across samples and annotators). We summarize these results for BTM and FTE in Table 2 and Table 3, leaving out LDA and BERT due to significantly lower scores.

We find that our method outperforms the various baselines on both the keyword and cluster evaluations. In particular, the improvement over BERT further confirms the importance of the finetuning step in our method. In contrast, the improvements in average scores over BTM reported in Table 3 are marginal. Nevertheless, we find that the number of interpretable and useful topic clusters was greater for our approach. Indeed, while the BTM baseline had more semi-interpretable (i.e. only a subset of the sampled tweets seemed related) but non-useful topics, our method had a much clearer distinction between interpretable/useful and non-interpretable/non-useful topics, suggesting that tweets marked as hard to interpret and not useful are consistently irrelevant. This may be preferable for downstream applications, as it allows users to better filter our irrelevant content.

The annotators also identified intruder tweets in topic samples from FTE more reliably and with less uncertainty, as measured by the number of correct intruders predicted and the number of times an intruder could not be predicted. Interestingly, BTM topics rated for high interpretability had lower rates of correct intruder detection, suggesting that these topics may seem misleadingly coherent to annotators. Inter-rater agreements as measured by Fleiss' κ further confirm that annotators more often disagreed on intruder prediction and interpretability scoring for BTM topics. This is undesirable for downstream applications, where poor interpretability of topics can lead to a misinterpretation of data with real negative consequences.

5.4 Model agreement

Agreement for the models was 32.7% between FTE and BERT, 26.5% between FTE and BTM, 19.9% between FTE and LDA and 20.7% between BTM and LDA. This confirms that the different models also generate different clusters.

6 Conclusion

This paper introduces a novel approach for extracting useful information from social media and assisting crisis managers. We propose a simple method that bridges the gap between supervised classification and unsupervised topic modelling to address the issue of domain adaptation to novel crises.

Our model (FTE, Finetuned Tweet Embeddings) incorporates crisis-related knowledge from supervised finetuning while also being able to generate salient topics for novel crises. To evaluate domain adaptation, we create a dataset of tweets from a crisis that significantly differs from existing crisis Twitter datasets: the 2020 Winter Storm Jacob.

Our paper also introduces human evaluation methods better aligned with downstream use cases of topic modelling in crisis management, emphasizing human-centered machine learning. In both these human evaluations and traditional automatic evaluations, our method outperforms existing topic modelling methods, consistently producing more coherent, interpretable and useful topics for crisis managers. Interestingly, our annotators reported that several coherent topics seemed to be composed of related subtopics. In future work, the number of topics as a hyper-parameter could be explored to see if our approach captures these salient subtopics.

Our method, while simple, is not specific to crisis management and can be more generally used for textual domain adaptation problems where the latent classes are unknown but likely to overlap with known classes from other domains.

Acknowledgements

We are grateful for the funding from Environment and Climate Change Canada (ECCC GCXE19M010). Mikael Brunila also thanks the Kone Foundation for their support.

References

Nikolaos Aletras and Mark Stevenson. 2013. Evaluating Topic Coherence Using Distributional Semantics. In *Proceedings of the 10th International Conference on Computational Semantics (IWCS 2013) – Long Papers*, pages 13–22, Potsdam, Germany. Association for Computational Linguistics.

David E. Alexander. 2014. Social Media in Disaster Risk Reduction and Crisis Management. *Science and Engineering Ethics*, 20(3):717–733.

Reem Alrashdi and Simon O'Keefe. 2020. Automatic Labeling of Tweets for Crisis Response Using Distant Supervision. In *Companion Proceedings of the Web Conference 2020*, WWW '20, pages 418–425, New York, NY, USA. Association for Computing Machinery.

Dzmitry Bahdanau, Kyunghyun Cho, and Yoshua Bengio. 2015. Neural machine translation by jointly learning to align and translate. In *3rd International Conference on Learning Representations, ICLR 2015, San Diego, CA, USA, May 7-9, 2015, Conference Track Proceedings*.

Federico Bianchi, Silvia Terragni, and Dirk Hovy. 2020. Pre-training is a Hot Topic: Contextualized Document Embeddings Improve Topic Coherence. *arXiv:2004.03974 [cs]*. ArXiv: 2004.03974.

David M. Blei, Andrew Y. Ng, and Michael I. Jordan. 2003. Latent Dirichlet Allocation. *Journal of Machine Learning Research*, 3(Jan):993–1022.

Ivan S. Blekanov, Svetlana S. Bodrunova, Nina Zhuravleva, Anna Smoliarova, and Nikita Tarasov. 2020. The Ideal Topic: Interdependence of Topic Interpretability and Other Quality Features in Topic Modelling for Short Texts. In *Social Computing and Social Media. Design, Ethics, User Behavior, and Social Network Analysis*, Lecture Notes in Computer Science, pages 19–26, Cham. Springer International Publishing.

Jonathan Chang, Sean Gerrish, Chong Wang, Jordan L. Boyd-graber, and David M. Blei. 2009. Reading Tea Leaves: How Humans Interpret Topic Models. In Y. Bengio, D. Schuurmans, J. D. Lafferty, C. K. I. Williams, and A. Culotta, editors, *Advances in Neural Information Processing Systems 22*, pages 288–296. Curran Associates, Inc.

Jason Chuang, Sonal Gupta, Christopher Manning, and Jeffrey Heer. 2013. Topic Model Diagnostics: Assessing Domain Relevance via Topical Alignment. In *International Conference on Machine Learning*, pages 612–620. PMLR. ISSN: 1938-7228.

Kevin Clark, Urvashi Khandelwal, Omer Levy, and Christopher D. Manning. 2019. What Does BERT Look at? An Analysis of BERT's Attention. In *Proceedings of the 2019 ACL Workshop BlackboxNLP: Analyzing and Interpreting Neural Networks for NLP*, pages 276–286, Florence, Italy. Association for Computational Linguistics.

Dorottya Demszky, Nikhil Garg, Rob Voigt, James Zou, Jesse Shapiro, Matthew Gentzkow, and Dan Jurafsky. 2019. Analyzing polarization in social media: Method and application to tweets on 21 mass shootings. In *Proceedings of the 2019 Conference of the North American Chapter of the Association for Computational Linguistics: Human Language Technologies, Volume 1 (Long and Short Papers)*, pages 2970–3005, Minneapolis, Minnesota. Association for Computational Linguistics.

Jacob Devlin, Ming-Wei Chang, Kenton Lee, and Kristina Toutanova. 2019. BERT: Pre-training of Deep Bidirectional Transformers for Language Understanding. In *Proceedings of the 2019 Conference of the North American Chapter of the Association for Computational Linguistics: Human Language Technologies, Volume 1 (Long and Short Papers)*, pages 4171–4186, Minneapolis, Minnesota. Association for Computational Linguistics.

Charles Elkan. 2003. Using the triangle inequality to accelerate k-means. In *Proceedings of the Twentieth International Conference on International Conference on Machine Learning*, ICML'03, pages 147–153, Washington, DC, USA. AAAI Press.

Dontas Emmanouil and Doukas Nikolaos. 2015. Big data analytics in prevention, preparedness, response and recovery in crisis and disaster management. In *The 18th International Conference on Circuits, Systems, Communications and Computers (CSCC 2015), Recent Advances in Computer Engineering Series*, volume 32, pages 476–482.

Jonathan Erdman. 2020. Crippling Newfoundland, Canada, Blizzard From Bomb Cyclone Smashes All-Time Daily Snow Record. *The Weather Channel*.

Nikhil Garg, Londa Schiebinger, Dan Jurafsky, and James Zou. 2018. Word embeddings quantify 100 years of gender and ethnic stereotypes. *Proceedings of the National Academy of Sciences*, 115(16):E3635–E3644. ISBN: 9781720347118 Publisher: National Academy of Sciences Section: PNAS Plus.

Sedigheh Khademi Habibabadi and Pari Delir Haghighi. 2019. Topic Modelling for Identification of Vaccine Reactions in Twitter. In *Proceedings of the Australasian Computer Science Week Multiconference*, ACSW 2019, pages 1–10, New York, NY, USA. Association for Computing Machinery.

William L. Hamilton, Jure Leskovec, and Dan Jurafsky. 2016. Cultural Shift or Linguistic Drift? Comparing Two Computational Measures of Semantic Change. In *Proceedings of the 2016 Conference on Empirical Methods in Natural Language Processing*, pages 2116–2121, Austin, Texas. Association for Computational Linguistics.

Liangjie Hong and Brian D. Davison. 2010. Empirical study of topic modeling in Twitter. In *Proceedings of the First Workshop on Social Media Analytics*, SOMA '10, pages 80–88, New York, NY, USA. Association for Computing Machinery.

Muhammad Imran, Shady Elbassuoni, Carlos Castillo, Fernando Díaz, and Patrick Meier. 2013. Extracting information nuggets from disaster- Related messages in social media. In *ISCRAM 2013 Conference Proceedings – 10th International Conference on Information Systems for Crisis Response and Management*, pages 791–801, KIT; Baden-Baden. Karlsruher Institut fur Technologie. ISSN: 2411-3387 Journal Abbreviation: ISCRAM 2013.

Muhammad Imran, Prasenjit Mitra, and Carlos Castillo. 2016. Twitter as a Lifeline: Human-annotated Twitter Corpora for NLP of Crisis-related Messages. In *Proceedings of the Tenth International Conference on Language Resources and Evaluation (LREC'16)*, pages 1638–1643, Portorož, Slovenia. European Language Resources Association (ELRA).

Sarthak Jain and Byron C. Wallace. 2019. Attention is not Explanation. In *Proceedings of the 2019 Conference of the North American Chapter of the Association for Computational Linguistics: Human Language Technologies, Volume 1 (Long and Short Papers)*, pages 3543–3556, Minneapolis, Minnesota. Association for Computational Linguistics.

Yan Jin, Brooke Fisher Liu, and Lucinda L. Austin. 2014. Examining the Role of Social Media in Effective Crisis Management: The Effects of Crisis Origin, Information Form, and Source on Publics' Crisis Responses. *Communication Research*, 41(1):74–94. ZSCC: 0000391 Publisher: SAGE Publications Inc.

Mark E. Keim. 2008. Building Human Resilience: The Role of Public Health Preparedness and Response As an Adaptation to Climate Change. *American Journal of Preventive Medicine*, 35(5):508–516.

Goro Kobayashi, Tatsuki Kuribayashi, Sho Yokoi, and Kentaro Inui. 2020. Attention is not only a weight: Analyzing transformers with vector norms. In *Proceedings of the 2020 Conference on Empirical Methods in Natural Language Processing (EMNLP)*, pages 7057–7075, Online. Association for Computational Linguistics.

Olga Kovaleva, Alexey Romanov, Anna Rogers, and Anna Rumshisky. 2019. Revealing the Dark Secrets of BERT. In *Proceedings of the 2019 Conference on Empirical Methods in Natural Language Processing and the 9th International Joint Conference on Natural Language Processing (EMNLP-IJCNLP)*, pages 4365–4374, Hong Kong, China. Association for Computational Linguistics.

Austin C. Kozlowski, Matt Taddy, and James A. Evans. 2019. The Geometry of Culture: Analyzing the Meanings of Class through Word Embeddings. *American Sociological Review*, 84(5):905–949.

Jey Han Lau and Timothy Baldwin. 2016. An Empirical Evaluation of doc2vec with Practical Insights into Document Embedding Generation. In *Proceedings of the 1st Workshop on Representation Learning for NLP*, pages 78–86, Berlin, Germany. Association for Computational Linguistics.

Jey Han Lau, David Newman, and Timothy Baldwin. 2014. Machine Reading Tea Leaves: Automatically Evaluating Topic Coherence and Topic Model Quality. In *Proceedings of the 14th Conference of the European Chapter of the Association for Computational Linguistics*, pages 530–539, Gothenburg, Sweden. Association for Computational Linguistics.

Tak Yeon Lee, Alison Smith, Kevin Seppi, Niklas Elmqvist, Jordan Boyd-Graber, and Leah Findlater. 2017. The human touch: How non-expert users perceive, interpret, and fix topic models. *International Journal of Human-Computer Studies*, 105:28–42.

Omer Levy and Yoav Goldberg. 2014. Neural word embedding as implicit matrix factorization. In *Proceedings of the 27th International Conference on Neural Information Processing Systems - Volume 2*, NIPS'14, pages 2177–2185, Cambridge, MA, USA. MIT Press.

Hongmin Li, Doina Caragea, Cornelia Caragea, and Nic Herndon. 2018. Disaster response aided by tweet classification with a domain adaptation approach. *Journal of Contingencies and Crisis Management*, 26(1):16–27. _eprint: https://onlinelibrary.wiley.com/doi/pdf/10.1111/1468-5973.12194.

Yongjie Lin, Yi Chern Tan, and Robert Frank. 2019. Open Sesame: Getting inside BERT's Linguistic Knowledge. In *Proceedings of the 2019 ACL Workshop BlackboxNLP: Analyzing and Interpreting Neural Networks for NLP*, pages 241–253, Florence, Italy. Association for Computational Linguistics.

S. Lloyd. 1982. Least squares quantization in PCM. *IEEE Transactions on Information Theory*, 28(2):129–137. Conference Name: IEEE Transactions on Information Theory.

Guoqin Ma. 2019. Tweets Classification with BERT in the Field of Disaster Management. page 15.

Tomás Mikolov, Kai Chen, Greg Corrado, and Jeffrey Dean. 2013a. Efficient estimation of word representations in vector space. In *1st International Conference on Learning Representations, ICLR 2013, Scottsdale, Arizona, USA, May 2-4, 2013, Workshop Track Proceedings*.

Tomas Mikolov, Ilya Sutskever, Kai Chen, Greg Corrado, and Jeffrey Dean. 2013b. Distributed representations of words and phrases and their compositionality. In *Proceedings of the 26th International Conference on Neural Information Processing Systems - Volume 2*, NIPS'13, pages 3111–3119, Red Hook, NY, USA. Curran Associates Inc.

David Mimno, Hanna Wallach, Edmund Talley, Miriam Leenders, and Andrew McCallum. 2011. Optimizing Semantic Coherence in Topic Models. In *Proceedings of the 2011 Conference on Empirical Methods in Natural Language Processing*, pages 262–272, Edinburgh, Scotland, UK. Association for Computational Linguistics.

David Newman, Jey Han Lau, Karl Grieser, and Timothy Baldwin. 2010. Automatic evaluation of topic coherence. In *Human Language Technologies: The 2010 Annual Conference of the North American Chapter of the Association for Computational Linguistics*, HLT '10, pages 100–108, USA. Association for Computational Linguistics.

Dat Tien Nguyen, Kamela Ali Al Mannai, Shafiq Joty, Hassan Sajjad, Muhammad Imran, and Prasenjit Mitra. 2017. Robust classification of crisis-related data on social networks using convolutional neural networks. In *Proceedings of the 11th International Conference on Web and Social Media, ICWSM 2017*, Proceedings of the 11th International Conference on Web and Social Media, ICWSM 2017, pages 632–635. AAAI press.

Georgios Paltoglou and Mike Thelwall. 2010. A Study of Information Retrieval Weighting Schemes for Sentiment Analysis. In *Proceedings of the 48th Annual Meeting of the Association for Computational Linguistics*, pages 1386–1395, Uppsala, Sweden. Association for Computational Linguistics.

Jeffrey Pennington, Richard Socher, and Christopher Manning. 2014. GloVe: Global Vectors for Word Representation. In *Proceedings of the 2014 Conference on Empirical Methods in Natural Language Processing (EMNLP)*, pages 1532–1543, Doha, Qatar. Association for Computational Linguistics.

Matthew Peters, Mark Neumann, Mohit Iyyer, Matt Gardner, Christopher Clark, Kenton Lee, and Luke Zettlemoyer. 2018. Deep Contextualized Word Representations. In *Proceedings of the 2018 Conference of the North American Chapter of the Association for Computational Linguistics: Human Language Technologies, Volume 1 (Long Papers)*, pages 2227–2237, New Orleans, Louisiana. Association for Computational Linguistics.

J. Rexiline Ragini and P. M. Rubesh Anand. 2016. An empirical analysis and classification of crisis related tweets. In *2016 IEEE International Conference on Computational Intelligence and Computing Research (ICCIC)*, pages 1–4. ISSN: 2473-943X.

Gonzalo Ramos, Jina Suh, Soroush Ghorashi, Christopher Meek, Richard Banks, Saleema Amershi, Rebecca Fiebrink, Alison Smith-Renner, and Gagan Bansal. 2019. Emerging Perspectives in Human-Centered Machine Learning. In *Extended Abstracts of the 2019 CHI Conference on Human Factors in Computing Systems*, CHI EA '19, pages 1–8, New York, NY, USA. Association for Computing Machinery.

Nils Reimers and Iryna Gurevych. 2019. Sentence-BERT: Sentence Embeddings using Siamese BERT-Networks. In *Proceedings of the 2019 Conference on Empirical Methods in Natural Language Processing and the 9th International Joint Conference on Natural Language Processing (EMNLP-IJCNLP)*, pages 3982–3992, Hong Kong, China. Association for Computational Linguistics.

Nils Reimers, Benjamin Schiller, Tilman Beck, Johannes Daxenberger, Christian Stab, and Iryna Gurevych. 2019. Classification and Clustering of Arguments with Contextualized Word Embeddings. In *Proceedings of the 57th Annual Meeting of the Association for Computational Linguistics*, pages 567–578, Florence, Italy. Association for Computational Linguistics.

Anna Rogers, Olga Kovaleva, and Anna Rumshisky. 2020. A primer in BERTology: What we know about how BERT works. *Transactions of the Association for Computational Linguistics*, 8:842–866.

A. Romascanu, H. Ker, R. Sieber, R. Zhao, M. Brunila, S. Greenidge, S. Lumley, D. Bush, and S. Morgan. 2020. Using deep learning and social network analysis to understand and manage extreme flooding. *Journal of Contingencies and Crisis Management.*

Frank Rosner, Alexander Hinneburg, Michael Röder, Martin Nettling, and Andreas Both. 2013. Evaluating topic coherence measures. In *Topic Models: Computation, Application, and Evaluation.*

Michael Röder, Andreas Both, and Alexander Hinneburg. 2015. Exploring the Space of Topic Coherence Measures. In *Proceedings of the Eighth ACM International Conference on Web Search and Data Mining*, WSDM '15, pages 399–408, Shanghai, China. Association for Computing Machinery.

Axel Schulz, Eneldo Loza Mencía, Thanh-Tung Dang, and Benedikt Schmidt. 2014. Evaluating multi-label classification of incident-related tweet. In *# MSM*, pages 26–33. Citeseer.

Sofia Serrano and Noah A. Smith. 2019. Is Attention Interpretable? In *Proceedings of the 57th Annual Meeting of the Association for Computational Linguistics*, pages 2931–2951, Florence, Italy. Association for Computational Linguistics.

Oleksandra Sopova. 2017. Domain adaptation for classifying disaster-related Twitter data. Report, Kansas State University.

Karen Spärck Jones. 2004. A statistical interpretation of term specificity and its application in retrieval. *Journal of Documentation*, 60(5):493–502. Publisher: Emerald Group Publishing Limited.

Ed Tobias. 2011. Using Twitter and other social media platforms to provide situational awareness during an incident. *Journal of Business Continuity & Emergency Planning*, 5(3):208–223. Publisher: Henry Stewart Publications LLP.

Ashish Vaswani, Noam Shazeer, Niki Parmar, Jakob Uszkoreit, Llion Jones, Aidan N. Gomez, Łukasz Kaiser, and Illia Polosukhin. 2017. Attention is all you need. In *Proceedings of the 31st International Conference on Neural Information Processing Systems*, NIPS'17, pages 6000–6010, Red Hook, NY, USA. Curran Associates Inc.

Günter Wallner, Simone Kriglstein, and Anders Drachen. 2019. Tweeting your Destiny: Profiling Users in the Twitter Landscape around an Online Game. In *2019 IEEE Conference on Games (CoG)*, pages 1–8. ISSN: 2325-4289.

Sarah Wiegreffe and Yuval Pinter. 2019. Attention is not not Explanation. In *Proceedings of the 2019 Conference on Empirical Methods in Natural Language Processing and the 9th International Joint Conference on Natural Language Processing (EMNLP-IJCNLP)*, pages 11–20, Hong Kong, China. Association for Computational Linguistics.

Xiaohui Yan, Jiafeng Guo, Yanyan Lan, and Xueqi Cheng. 2013. A biterm topic model for short texts. In *Proceedings of the 22nd international conference on World Wide Web*, WWW '13, pages 1445–1456, Rio de Janeiro, Brazil. Association for Computing Machinery.

Hamada M Zahera, Rricha Jalota, Ibrahim Elgendy, and Mohamed Ahmed Sherif. 2019. Fine-tuned BERT Model for Multi-Label Tweets Classification. page 7.

Jichuan Zeng, Jing Li, Yan Song, Cuiyun Gao, Michael R. Lyu, and Irwin King. 2018. Topic Memory Networks for Short Text Classification. In *Proceedings of the 2018 Conference on Empirical Methods in Natural Language Processing*, pages 3120–3131, Brussels, Belgium. Association for Computational Linguistics.

A CrisisNLP Dataset

Here we include class distributions (Table 4) and descriptions (Table 5) from the CrisisNLP Dataset.

	Label Id								
Crisis Dataset	1	2	3	4	5	6	7	8	9
2013_pak_eq	351	5	16	29	325	75	112	764	336
2014_cali_eq	217	6	4	351	83	84	83	1028	157
2014_chile_eq	119	6	63	26	10	250	541	634	364
2014_odile	50	39	153	848	248	77	166	380	52
2014_india_floods	959	14	27	67	48	44	30	312	502
2014_pak_floods	259	117	106	94	529	56	127	698	27
2014_hagupit	66	8	130	92	113	349	290	732	233
2015_pam	143	18	49	212	364	93	95	542	497
2015_nepal_eq	346	189	85	132	890	35	525	639	177
Total	2510	402	633	1851	2610	1063	1969	5729	2345

Table 4: Label counts for the different datasets labeled by Crowdflower workers in (Imran et al., 2016)

B Automated Coherence Metrics

The direct confirmation C_{NPMI}, uses a token-by-token ten word sliding window, where each step determines a new virtual document. Co-occurrence in these documents is used to compute the normalized pointwise mutual information (NPMI) between a given topic keyword W' and each member in the conditioning set of other topic keywords W^*, such that:

$$NPMI = \left(\frac{PMI(W', W^*)}{-log(P(W', W^*) + \epsilon)}\right)^{\gamma}$$

$$PMI = log\frac{P(W', W^*) + \epsilon}{P(W') * P(W^*)}$$

The coherence of a topic is then calculated by taking the arithmetic mean of these confirmation values, with ϵ as a small value for preventing the log of zero.

The indirect confirmation C_V is instead based on comparing the contexts in which W' and W^* appear. W' and W^* are represented as vectors of the size of the total word set W. Each value in these vectors consist of a direct confirmation between the word that the vector represents and the words in W. However, now the context is just the tweet that each word appears in. The indirect confirmation between each word in the topic is the cosine similarity of each pair of context vectors such that

$$\cos(\vec{u}, \vec{w}) = \frac{\sum_{i=1}^{|W|} u_i \cdot u_i}{||\vec{u}||_2 ||\vec{w}||_2}$$

where $\vec{u} = \vec{v}(W')$ and $\vec{w} = \vec{v}(W^*)$. Once again, the arithmetic mean of these similarity values gives the coherence of the topic.

C_V was found by Röder et al. (2015) to be the most interpretable topic coherence metric when compared to human judgement and has later been used extensively on assessing the coherence of short texts like tweets as well (Zeng et al., 2018; Habibabadi and Haghighi, 2019; Wallner et al., 2019). We also use C_{NPMI}, which has been one of the most successful topic coherence measures based on direct confirmation (Röder et al., 2015; Lau et al., 2014). See Röder et al. (2015) for further details on both C_V and C_{NPMI}.

Label	Id	Description
Injured or dead people	1	Reports of casualties and/or injured people due to the crisis
Missing, trapped, or found people	2	Reports and/or questions about missing or found people
Displaced people and evacuations	3	People who have relocated due to the crisis, even for a short time (includes evacuations
Infrastructure and utilities damage	4	Reports of damaged buildings, roads, bridges, or utilities/services interrupted or restored
Donation needs or offers or volunteering services	5	Reports of urgent needs or donations of shelter and/or supplies such as food, water, clothing, money, medical supplies or blood; and volunteering services
Caution and advice	6	Reports of warnings issued or lifted, guidance and tips
Sympathy and emotional support	7	Prayers, thoughts, and emotional support
Other useful information	8	Other useful information that helps one understand the situation
Not related or irrelevant	9	Unrelated to the situation or irrelevant

Table 5: Label descriptions and id's in (Imran et al., 2016)

C Human evaluation tweet samples

Here we present one of the set of tweets presented to human annotators for each model and topic. We also show the ground truth intruder tweet which the annotators were asked to predict. Non-ASCII characters were removed here, but included in tweets shown to human annotators.

C.1 FTE

C.1.1 Topic 0

- How bad was the blizzard in St. John's, Newfoundland? Here's what a seniors home looks like the day after. photo: https://t.co/6n8txqnuWl
- East End of St. Johns 4 days post blizzard. #NLwx #NLtraffic #snowmegeddon2020 https://t.co/5s2p9Ivejf
- Well here's the big mother storm en route. Currently the size of Nova Scotia, nbd. #nlwx https://t.co/CFi9szzunK
- INTRUDER: I hope I don't have to go to work on Monday because I don't remember my password anymore. #nlwx #stormageddon2020 https://t.co/BswQppEFVh
- #StJohns declares #StateOfEmergency and #Newfoundland and #Labrador get pounded with #SnowFall with more to come https://t.co/JNxnIF5mNx

C.1.2 Topic 1

- Gentle heart of Jesus #nlwx https://t.co/cEbvv3it5f
- This was the moment I fell in love with #Newfoundland, #Canada when I first entered the Gros Morne National Park. https://t.co/2mSD79u6qC
- #nlwx https://t.co/md4pRSafW5
- @UGEABC families-send a pic of what youre reading!!! @NLESD @PowersGr6 @AndreaCoffin76 @MrBlackmoreGr1 https://t.co/FwEbRe9YJs
- INTRUDER: So much for the snow I was really hoping to make a snowman Did anyone get their snowman built? #wheresthesnow https://t.co/FT3IJqIVsS

C.1.3 Topic 2

- Garbage collection in the City of St. John's is cancelled for the rest of the week. It will resume on Monday, Jan 2 https://t.co/nvWHGHcrwJ
- City of St. Johns Snow Clearing on Standby :Due to deteriorating conditions and reduced visibility snow clearing o https://t.co/UC7GV2wFrw
- Memorial Universitys St. Johns, Marine Institute and Signal Hill campuses will remain closed all day. #nlwx
- Current outages. St. Johns area. https://t.co/wEwJKWKxpF #nlwx https://t.co/FsIieBLzGw
- INTRUDER: $SIC Sokoman Minerals Provides Winter 2020 Exploration Update at Moosehead Gold Project, Central Newfoundland https://t.co/ma9Ai4PLeE

C.1.4 Topic 3

- Not everyone has the funds to go to the grocery store (not just during a SOE) Hats off to the food banks that are o https://t.co/sljOgZZUmf
- Up to 300 troops from across Canada will be asked to work on the response to the unprecedented #nlblizzard2020. Gag https://t.co/Yw7jUAWUJE
- INTRUDER: Beautiful @DowntownStJohns the morning after #Snowmageddon https://t.co/HS7jhLIt4l
- So pleased to see the joint efforts of @GovNL with the cities/towns during #snowmaggedon2020. From calling it a SOE https://t.co/0oKer9CLmo
- Updated story: Five days is a long time without food for people who can't afford to stock up. Staff at one St. John https://t.co/gNJSXMsv3B

C.1.5 Topic 4

- Were quite buried in Paradise right now! Luckily still have power for now. Stay safe everyone! #nlwx https://t.co/sOC7TL4Al7

- Hoping everyone's pets are safe inside your homes. #nlblizzard2020
- @IDontBlog Yikes! Hoping everyone there stays safe.... #nlblizzard2020 #NLStorm2020
- @DanKudla The weather channel is calling for snow in Toronto, but nothing like that. Hope youre all safe in Newfou https://t.co/0KN2AD3JrS
- INTRUDER: BREAKING — Province is calling in the military @NTVNewsNL #Nlwx https://t.co/ggfOlrbYCz

C.1.6 Topic 5

- We've made it through the worst of the storm, but #yyt's State of Emergency remains in effect. Pls stay inside & sa https://t.co/YGVxNOEzf1
- INTRUDER: How COLD is it? Coby took less than 30 seconds to use the facilities this morning! #snowmaggedon2020 #snowstorm https://t.co/f4zZ38MJol
- Stay safe St. Johns! #Newfoundland #snowmaggedon2020
- Take your time cleaning this up, Newfoundland friends! It is a brutal amount of snow! Be safe! #nlwx https://t.co/POwfBYWHFy
- Meanwhile in ON, 15-25cm w/ 50km wind forecast and asked to stay off streets. #nlblizzard2020 https://t.co/wwKVnqmM3F

C.1.7 Topic 6

- @VOCMNEWS This is amazing. In the next couple of days we could really get so many of our neighbourhood hydrants dug https://t.co/7Z2TOfwpwB
- @weathernetwork batteries charging and camera gear drying out after 16 hours shooting in blizzard. @MurphTWN #nlwx https://t.co/yGUMV93Yrw
- So we visited friends last night and left at the height of the storm ... somewhere under there are a couple of cars https://t.co/NYHHxXT4EI
- @KrissyHolmes #nltraffic just like any other weekday morning coming out of Cbs. Two solid lines of traffic
- INTRUDER: @BrianWalshWX so its 7:00 pm , how much more snow potentially will fall before noon tomorrow? #nlblizzard2020 #nlwx

C.1.8 Topic 7

- @StormchaserUKEU A glimpse into the future @yyt #nlwx
- Its official - weve named this storm #BettyWhiteOut2020 in honour of #BettyWhitesBirthday #nlwx
- Even for just a moment with the front door open, snow is hitting you in the face and the wind is taking your breath https://t.co/pJkpwwqDfF
- INTRUDER: #nlwx https://t.co/2mnaF7TkSl
- Open those curtains, let all the sunshine heat in that you can! Solar gain will help us through. #nlwx https://t.co/AFAubBvWwg

C.1.9 Topic 8

- INTRUDER: Plow came by and then the neighbours started a snow clearing party. So thankful #nlblizzard2020 #nlwx https://t.co/QpIapG1N4Y
- Y seguimos con la supernevada (fuera de lo comn, tambin hay que decirlo) de #Newfoundland , en #Canad ! Laia ll https://t.co/O1adKSXbFa
- If you have to wear a full snowsuit to go shopping, STAY HOME. You do NOT need to be out. You do NOT need a fondue https://t.co/qig24xkrK5
- @NewfieScumbag Pretty much... love of God! In case you didnt get the memo, keep your packin vehicle off the roads https://t.co/AJe6RpgWBS
- So our front door looks like a neat little burrow now, at least. #nlwx #Snowmageddon2020 https://t.co/qUCdntRJgE

C.2 BTM

C.2.1 Topic 0

- THIS!! #nlwx #nltraffic https://t.co/fGPl0DDJWF

- 2/2 During a State of Emergency the public is advised to contact their nearest emergency hospital department for em https://t.co/MTbO1MHF2K
- there's a house in there somewhere #snowmaggedon2020 https://t.co/r36lWxJPzd
- INTRUDER: @PaulDoroshenko Yup, sorry as a proud Newfoundlander living on Vancouver Island for the last ten years they totally https://t.co/eNdNvtnJUI
- Move over, CBC announcers! #NLStorm2020 https://t.co/TTvE0LZgIG

C.2.2 Topic 1

- INTRUDER: Snowmageddon 2. The return of the snowstorm! Now playing...#nlwx #nlsnowstorm2020 #snowdoor #blizzard https://t.co/EvBlOdrg23
- If you're NOT feelin this? Then you have NO "PULSE" @therealbigthump #SaturdayMorning #Eminem https://t.co/r1orKgKGar
- Click On Photo To Learn More #michelleobama Eminem #SAvENG Ken Starr #SexEducation #nlwx How Cheap https://t.co/jCYbHGDKM1
- If you're NOT feelin this? Then you have NO "PULSE" @therealbigthump #SaturdayMorning #Eminem #WomensMarch https://t.co/su8qA0qjP0
- If you're NOT feelin this? Then you have NO "PULSE" @therealbigthump #SaturdayMorning #Eminem #WomensMarch https://t.co/pORhRKunhs

C.2.3 Topic 2

- Stay safe, Newfoundland. Stay warm. Stay home. Stay off the roads. #Newfoundland
- Newfoundland peeps - the CBC in Toronto is warning that Toronto is about to be walloped with snow, and that Envir https://t.co/NmWRu8t6rL
- INTRUDER: #NLStorm2020 #nltraffic Thanks for coming and doing some cleanup on Gower St right now. Many fans in windows watch https://t.co/FZBsIaN7v1
- My thoughts go to those who need to serve the communities during #Snowmageddon in NFLD today. Stay safe while you do what you need to do.
- @DrAJHalifax They're getting absolutely walloped! #nlstorm

C.2.4 Topic 3

- Have woken up ... and grateful that the power is still on in the house. I'm also grateful that the noise of the w https://t.co/xQjXoz3qED
- A huge THANK YOU to all of the deputies, officers, troopers, medics, firefighters, dispatchers, plow operators and https://t.co/mCnFbDUHd8
- Watch what happened at 1:56:51 in @DaHonestyPolicy's broadcast: Come Talk With the Ladies #DaAngels #DaNation https://t.co/L4zsDuzTHe
- What do you expect when graduate with good cgpa don't have a job after graduating, Efcc free guys to hustle jor. Dr https://t.co/DYGlpBBmHe
- INTRUDER: Weve made the Washington Post #nlwx https://t.co/sjqdJkR7XL

C.2.5 Topic 4

- INTRUDER: Its a brand new day #nlwx https://t.co/l30WBqLHIE
- Whos up for a twitter game: give us your best movie title related to #snowmaggedon2020 pls use #snowmoviesnl so we can retweet you #nlwx
- somebody should make a video of #snowmaggedon2020 with Greata saying how dare you
- Doing my civic duty as a Minnesotan today....storming @Target and battling the masses for the last cart to stock up https://t.co/D72nJ0I3em
- My 13-yr old got tickets to tomorrow night's @Raptors game for Xmas but will miss b/c all flights are grounded at https://t.co/NsvWNwcIix

C.2.6 Topic 5

- Mom look! One of my videos made the @BBCWorld news! Bys, tis a rough way to get famous! #nlwx #blizzard2020 https://t.co/Y0jx2pycO7
- Very cool! #Newfoundland $gold $SIC.B #mooseheadmadness https://t.co/YKfIBIMCaA
- The morning after. Pictures from my Daughter and my Sister. Both live in St. John's NL #NLWX #Blizzard #NL https://t.co/UhtFlddTXn
- It's #SaturdayMorning and the storm has died down here in Newfoundland. Still blowing hard out there but not as bad https://t.co/Qkoj6XjBc3
- INTRUDER: We are still in a SOE - STAY OFF THE ROADS so all of the emergency & essential workers can do their jobs! Even thou https://t.co/2TSmfKYlnZ

C.2.7 Topic 6

- @590VOCM several reports of very slippery conditions at the intersection of Carrick Drive and Stavanger Drive. Ple https://t.co/pDlCBjvLfi
- Dave says there's a car off the road and now on top of a snowbank on the ORR WB just before Paradise turnoff #nltraffic
- Is @MaryBrowns open in Mount Pearl? #nlwx #companylunch
- Power outage here in Bonavista. #nlwx #nlblizzard2020 #snowmaggedon2020
- INTRUDER: The #nlwx hashtag is making me really appreciate our mildly inconvenient snowstorm here in Wisconsin. 27 inches of https://t.co/dzV0elcy6y

C.2.8 Topic 7

- INTRUDER: @CBCNews #nlwx #snowmaggedon2020 might be a while before things return to anything close to normal. Main road throu https://t.co/1vHX2B9oPo
- MUN's St. John's, Signal Hill campuses and Marine Institute will be closed until Jan. 27 #nlschools #YYTSOE #nlstorm2020 #nlwx
- #SOEYYT remains in place for tomorrow, Jan 23. #nlwx
- Bell island ferry update #nltraffic https://t.co/pTFo4FuxfM
- MUN closed METROBUS OFF THE ROADS SCHOOLS CLOSED https://t.co/G3rvNoXVt5

C.2.9 Topic 8

- With a 9:30pm snow total of 20cm, today is #Gander's snowiest day so far this winter. #NLWx https://t.co/ZYhyV2Xpsm
- #nlblizzard2020 #nlstorm look at the winds... the gusts are Cat 4 hurricane equivalent https://t.co/JjFbiMJAdg
- 10min avg wind speeds of 132.0km/h with max gust of 167.4km/h through 12:10pm at Green Island, Fortune Bay. #nlwx https://t.co/GtisE875av
- INTRUDER: This is Lovely. I have always had a soft spot in my heart for #Newfoundland and the wonderful people there. https://t.co/CqPyzW3vLH
- There has been the equivalent of 32.7 mm of precipitation since Fri 04:30 at "ST JOHNS WEST CLIMATE" #NLStorm

Challenges in Annotating and Parsing Spoken, Code-switched, Frisian-Dutch Data

Anouck Braggaar
University of Groningen
a.r.y.braggaar@student.rug.nl

Rob van der Goot
IT University of Copenhagen
robv@itu.dk

Abstract

While high performance has been obtained for dependency parsing of high-resource languages, performance for low-resource languages lags behind. In this paper we focus on the parsing of the low-resource language Frisian. We use a sample of code-switched, spontaneously spoken data, which proves to be a challenging setup. We propose to train a parser specifically tailored towards the target domain, by selecting instances from multiple treebanks. Specifically, we use Latent Dirichlet Allocation (LDA), with word and character N-gram features. The best single source treebank (NL_ALPINO) resulted in an LAS of 54.7 whereas our data selection outperformed the single best transfer treebank and led to 55.6 LAS on the test data. Additional experiments consisted of removing diacritics from our Frisian data, creating more similar training data by cropping sentences and running our best model using XLM-R. These experiments did not lead to a better performance.

1 Introduction

As parsers are improving (with currently scores higher than 96 (Mrini et al., 2020)), parsing scores for low-resource languages lag behind. In recent years there has been an increase in interest in ways to parse and annotate these languages. This paper will focus on parsing the low-resource language Frisian (Germanic language spoken in the north-western part of the Netherlands, approximately 612.000 speakers[1]). We will use spontaneous speech data containing code-switches from the FAME! corpus created by Yilmaz et al. (2016). We annotate a small portion of this data with UPOS tags and Universal Dependencies (Zeman et al., 2020) for evaluation purposes. An example of such an utterance can be seen in Figure 1.

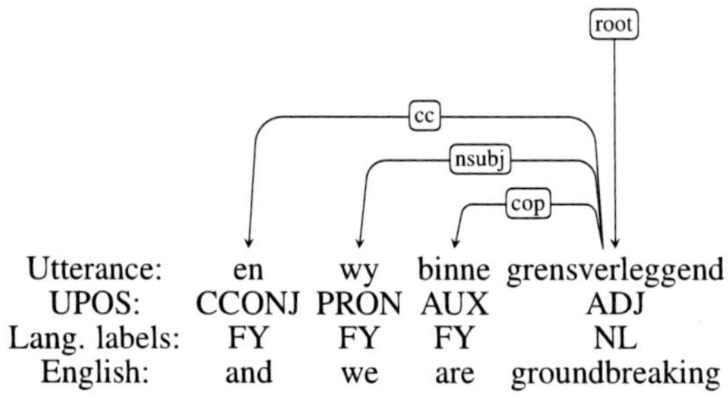

Figure 1: Example of annotated utterance.

Because it is unclear which (parts of) datasets are likely to be good candidates for training a parser for spoken Frisian, we propose to use instance-based selection from a variety of sources. This leads to our main research question: Can automatic data selection on the instance level outperform selection on the treebank level for training a parser for a new target domain/language? After finding our best model, we will try to improve our results by removing diacritics in our Frisian data and by making our train data more similar to spoken Frisian. All data and code are available on GitHub[2].

2 Related Work

Previous work on dependency parsing for spoken data created English annotations for conversational agents (Davidson et al., 2019) and Slovenian data (Dobrovoljc and Martinc, 2018). Partanen et al. (2018) create a treebank for spoken Komi-Zyrian with code-switching to Russian. Contemporary to our treebank, Çetinoğlu and Çöltekin (2019) created a treebank for spoken code-switched Turkish-German. They adapt the guidelines to deal with the spoken and code-switch nature of the data. Seddah et al. (2020) create a treebank for an Arabic dialect that contains a high amount of code-switching.

[1]https://fy.wikipedia.org/wiki/Fryske_talen

[2]https://github.com/Anouck96/ParsingFrisian

Proceedings of the Second Workshop on Domain Adaptation for NLP, pages 50–58
April 20, 2021.

Meechan-Maddon and Nivre (2019) and Blodgett et al. (2018) show that annotating a small amount of target language and target domain data outperforms a cross-lingual setup, but we focus on a pure zero-shot scenario instead. Previous work on zero-shot parsing has mainly focused on annotation projection using parallel data (Barry et al., 2019) and selecting transfer treebanks (Meechan-Maddon and Nivre, 2019). Previous work exploring more fine-grained selection methods are either focusing only on 3 domains (and multiple topics within the news) and 3 corpora (Plank and Van Noord, 2011), or focus on parser selection during test time (Litschko et al., 2020).

3 Data & Annotations

3.1 Data

The creators of the FAME! corpus (Yilmaz et al., 2016) had already transcribed and segmented the data and annotated the code-switches. We copied their word-level language labels to our miscellaneous column. The data consists of broadcasts from Omrop Fryslân (Frisian radio broadcaster) and mainly contains spontaneous interviews. The manually annotated radio broadcasts contain approximately 18.5 hours of speech and contains 3837 word- and sentence-level code-switches (Yilmaz et al., 2016). The majority of these switches are from Frisian speakers who switch to Dutch, because as Yilmaz et al. (2016) also mention it is not common for Dutch speakers to switch to Frisian. 67.8% of the words are Frisian and 26.1% are Dutch. The remainder of the words are annotated as being Frisian-Dutch, are hesitations (like "eh") or are of a different language. From this corpus we randomly selected and annotated 400 utterances. Each utterance contains at least one switch from Frisian to Dutch or the other way around. In our selection there are 144 different speakers, 135 of them Frisian speakers (the other 9 Dutch). Most of the speakers only occur one, two or three times. In the corpus 3,067 tokens are Frisian, 625 Dutch and 37 are other languages or annotated as Frisian-Dutch. The distributions over the languages for POS tags can be found in Appendix A.

3.2 Annotations

As a starting point, 150 utterances where annotated by two annotators (the authors of the paper, who have backgrounds in NLP, parsing and linguistics), in three batches of 50 utterances. After each batch, disagreements where discussed and resolved. Afterwards, 250 more utterances where annotated by one of the annotators and checked by the other. Table 1 shows the inter-annotator agreement between the three initial batches of annotation. We report accuracy over Universal Part-of-speech tags, Unlabelled Attachment Score (UAS) and Labelled Attachment Score (LAS) (Zeman et al., 2018). Most of our disagreements were due to difficulties with non-standard constructions, sentence segmentation, ambiguities of utterances and the fact that the guidelines had to be applied consistently, and in some cases had to be adapted. Adaptations to the guidelines can be found in Appendix B. For a more detailed discussion regarding the annotations we refer to Braggaar and van der Goot (2021).

	POS	UAS	LAS
Round 1	69.5	72.3	60.9
Round 2	87.1	76.1	64.6
Round 3	89.7	80.1	71.4

Table 1: POS, UAS and LAS scores between the two annotators.

3.3 Analysis of disagreements

To find trends in the disagreements, we calculated confusions over all labels (POS tags and Universal Dependency relations). The most occurring confusion for the POS tags that is solved in the third round is between ADV-AUX. This is due to shortcuts in the annotation tool ConlluEditor (Heinecke, 2019). Another confusion that is mostly solved in the third round is the confusion between AUX and VERB. For the Universal Dependency relations, the most common disagreements included amod-advmod confusions and differences in selecting the root.

4 Experiments

4.1 Data selection

First, we selected 24 treebanks of languages close to Frisian, which contained code-switching or consisted of transcribed speech. The languages included are Dutch, English, German, French, Naija, Afrikaans, Danish and Hindi-English[3]. As a baseline, 24 parsers were trained, each on a single treebank. The eight best scoring treebanks (based on LAS score) were used for further experiments.

[3]The names of all treebanks can be found in Appendix C

The eight best scoring treebanks were: Dutch Alpino (Van der Beek et al., 2002), Dutch LassySmall (Van Noord et al., 2013), German GSD, German PUD, English GUM (Zeldes, 2017), English EWT(Silveira et al., 2014), English ParTUT (Sanguinetti and Bosco, 2015) and the Tweebank by Liu et al. (2018). We chose to use these eight because we observed a drop in performance beyond the lowest scoring treebank in this selection.

4.2 Latent Dirichlet Allocation

For the data selection, we use Latent Dirichlet Allocation (LDA) with character 1-5 grams and word 1-2 grams as features. We choose LDA, because it is unsupervised, efficient and returns the probability of instances belonging to each clusters. Traditionally LDA is commonly used for topic classification, but when given data from multiple languages, we hypothesize that it will cluster based on language similarity instead. In LDA, one has to define the number of classes; we started with eight topics (because we used eight treebanks) and multiplied the number by two for the successive runs (8, 16, 32, 64 and 128).

4.3 Experimental setup

We use the full training data from all eight treebanks. For the treebanks without train, we use the test data, as we do not perform any experiments on the source data. For the LDA target data, we sampled sentences from the train split of the FAME! (Yilmaz et al., 2016) corpus. Note that we did not use the samples that are in our annotated data set. After the clustering, we select similar sentences based on the euclidean distance to the mean of the Frisian input. We ran experiments with 8, 16, 32, 64 and 128 LDA components. From the results we selected 1000, 2000 and 4000 sentences for training to see if the number of sentences in training was also influential. We did a total of 75 runs (8, 16, 32, 64, 128 components with each 1000, 2000 and 4000 sentences, 5 seeds). Training was done using a deep biaffine parser as implemented by MaChAmp 0.2 (van der Goot et al., 2020) with default parameters and mBERT embeddings (Devlin et al., 2019). Five random seeds were used for training.

5 Results

Overall, our best model consisted of 128 components and used 2000 sentences. Table 2 shows

Components	8	16	32	64	128
POS	**81.2**	80.4	81.0	79.4	79.4
UAS	72.7	71.4	70.8	72.6	**73.8**
LAS	55.2	55.1	54.8	55.5	**57.1**

Table 2: POS, UAS and LAS scores on dev data for 2000 sentences, mean over 5 random seeds. Highest scores are marked in bold.

Sentences	1000	2000	4000
POS	78.5	79.4	**79.8**
UAS	71.5	**73.8**	73.3
LAS	54.6	**57.1**	56.0

Table 3: POS, UAS and LAS scores on dev data for 128 components, mean over 5 random seeds. Highest scores are marked in bold.

the effect of changing the number of components when using 2000 sentences for training. While 128 components is the best for LAS and UAS, 8 components gave the best result for POS. When using the best performing number of components (128) and varying the amount of training data (Table 3), we can also see that the best model only needs 2000 sentences while using more sentences seemed to improve only the POS score.

Table 4 shows the results of our best model (128 components, 2000 sentences) compared to the best single treebank parser (NL_ALPINO) and training on the eight treebanks simultaneously. The scores for test are for LAS and UAS slightly lower than in the development phase. Surprisingly the POS scores are a bit higher. Our model outperforms the baselines on the test scores for LAS and UAS (but not for POS). We tested significance with random Bootstrapping as done by Udapi (Popel et al., 2017) compared to both baselines. Unfortunately, none of the results have proven to be significant at an alpha of 0.05.

	NL_ALPINO		Eight		Best model	
	Dev	Test	Dev	Test	Dev	Test
POS	79.9	81.1	80.3	80.3	79.4	80.2
UAS	72.5	69.7	70.9	69.2	73.8	70.2
LAS	55.3	54.7	54.3	53.2	57.1	55.6

Table 4: POS, UAS and LAS scores baselines versus best model (128 components/2000 sentences). Dev over five random seeds, test over the best random seed of dev.

NL_ALPINO	1514	NL_LASSYSMALL	447
DE_GSD	14	EN_EWT	14
EN_GUM	5	EN_TWEEBANK	4
EN_PUD	2		

Table 5: Sources of training data instances.

NL_ALPINO		Best Model	
INTJ-ADV	45	INTJ-ADV	48
ADV-ADJ	20	INTJ-PRON	20
DET-ADP	19	ADV-ADJ	17
AUX-VERB	14	DET-ADP	16
PRON-ADV	12	AUX-VERB	14

Table 6: Top five confusions on POS. Actual-predicted, number of confusions.

A closer look at the data selection of our model (Table 5) shows that the training set consists of mainly Dutch data. Only few sentences are selected that are not in the Dutch treebanks. This comes as no surprise, as we have seen that in the total corpus 26.1% of the words are Dutch, and the Frisian language is related to Dutch. This also agrees with the fact that the Dutch treebanks perform best in single treebank training.

6 Error Analysis

We perform an error analysis of our best model and the baseline (NL_ALPINO) on the development data. Table 6 shows the top five confusions on POS tags. The baseline is often unable to correctly predict interjections and our model does not seem to solve this confusion. Some of the difficulties that we have come across during annotation also arise here (e.g. ADV-ADJ and AUX-VERB).

The confusions on dependency labels are similar for both models (Table 7). Our model is slightly better on discourse-parataxis, but other than that it shows no big improvements. This is not surprising as our data consists mainly out of Alpino sentences.

NL_ALPINO		Best Model	
discourse-parataxis	39	discourse-parataxis	31
cc-mark	20	cc-mark	20
det-case	16	discourse-advmod	16
discourse-advmod	13	det-case	13
root-parataxis	12	advmod-amod	10

Table 7: Top five confusions on dependency labels. Actual-predicted, number of confusions.

The most occurring confusion (discourse-parataxis) was also a cause of disagreement in the annotation process.

7 What did not work?

In an attempt to obtain better results we have tried three different approaches to improve our best model. Muller et al. (2020) have shown that transliteration to a script of a related high source language on which the language model is trained leads to better results. Even though Frisian is not in a different script as the training data, it does contain a high amount of diacritics, which results in both many unseen wordpieces during testing, as well as differences in tokenization[4]. We attempt to overcome this mismatch by removing the diacritics from the characters in our Frisian data. In our development set, which consists of 150 utterances, there are 44 utterances with at least one diacritic and there are a total of 53 tokens with diacritics.

The second approach tries to make our training data more similar to our Frisian spoken data. A similar approach is taken by Blodgett et al. (2018), they create synthetic data following Internet-specific conventions and syntactic features of African-American English. This synthetic data proved to be helpful for performance.Vania et al. (2019) also try similar methods of data augmentation and found that when no source treebank is available, data augmentation can be very helpful. In our case, the utterances are not always "full sentences". An example from our development set is *"dêr kinnen we in hele hoop oer sizze mar"* ("we can say a lot about that but"). Normally the sentence would continue after "mar" (but) and "mar" would connect to this next part, but in this case the utterance stops at this point. We chose to connect this "mar" with an orphan relation to the root. These kind of "non-standard" constructions occur relatively often in our target data compared to the non-spoken treebanks in our training data. We tried to make our training data more similar by cropping sentences and adding an orphan relation. We did this for approximately the same percentage of utterances that have this construction in our development data (approximately 9 %).

As a final experiment we replaced mBERT with XLM-R. The results of all three experiments can

[4]We saw empirically that the mBERT tokenizer was splitting words containing diacritics more, presumably because diacritics were underrepresented during training of the tokenizer.

	Diacritics	Orphans	XLM-R	Best
POS	78.2	78.5	81.2	79.4
UAS	72.7	74.4	73.6	73.8
LAS	55.8	56.5	57.0	57.1

Table 8: POS, UAS and LAS scores for the additional experiments on dev set (128 components, 2000 sentences).

be found in Table 8. As can be seen, our diacritics and orphan experiments do not increase our scores. Only the UAS increases slightly when cropping some sentences, but unfortunately the LAS drops in both cases. The results with XLM-R are highly similar to the mBERT scores. Only the POS scores increase slightly but the difference in scores for UAS and LAS is very small.

8 Conclusion

In this paper we explored parsing and annotating the low-resource language Frisian and we have shown that selecting more similar training data (by using LDA) can lead to improvements in scores. These improvements were not significantly better compared to our baselines, but it did show that selecting fewer instances can outperform single treebank training. Besides slightly higher scores, using fewer instances sped up the training process. Additional experiments of removing diacritics and adjusting the training data to our development set did not show improvements. Future research can focus on improving the data selection method (using a different selection approach will probably result in different outcomes), weighing the importance of the selected instances and combining data selection with orthogonal approaches.

References

James Barry, Joachim Wagner, and Jennifer Foster. 2019. Cross-lingual parsing with polyglot training and multi-treebank learning: A Faroese case study. In *Proceedings of the 2nd Workshop on Deep Learning Approaches for Low-Resource NLP (DeepLo 2019)*, pages 163–174, Hong Kong, China. Association for Computational Linguistics.

Leonoor Van der Beek, Gosse Bouma, Rob Malouf, and Gertjan Van Noord. 2002. The Alpino dependency treebank. In *Computational linguistics in the netherlands 2001*, pages 8–22. Brill Rodopi.

Su Lin Blodgett, Johnny Wei, and Brendan O'Connor. 2018. Twitter universal dependency parsing for african-american and mainstream american english. In *Proceedings of the 56th Annual Meeting of the Association for Computational Linguistics (Volume 1: Long Papers)*, pages 1415–1425.

Anouck Braggaar and Rob van der Goot. 2021. Creating a universal dependencies treebank of spoken frisian-dutch code-switched data.

Özlem Çetinoğlu and Çağrı Çöltekin. 2019. Challenges of annotating a code-switching treebank. In *Proceedings of the 18th International Workshop on Treebanks and Linguistic Theories (TLT, SyntaxFest 2019)*, pages 82–90, Paris, France. Association for Computational Linguistics.

Sam Davidson, Dian Yu, and Zhou Yu. 2019. Dependency parsing for spoken dialog systems. In *Proceedings of the 2019 Conference on Empirical Methods in Natural Language Processing and the 9th International Joint Conference on Natural Language Processing (EMNLP-IJCNLP)*, pages 1513–1519, Hong Kong, China. Association for Computational Linguistics.

Jacob Devlin, Ming-Wei Chang, Kenton Lee, and Kristina Toutanova. 2019. BERT: Pre-training of deep bidirectional transformers for language understanding. In *Proceedings of the 2019 Conference of the North American Chapter of the Association for Computational Linguistics: Human Language Technologies, Volume 1 (Long and Short Papers)*, pages 4171–4186, Minneapolis, Minnesota. Association for Computational Linguistics.

Kaja Dobrovoljc and Matej Martinc. 2018. Er ... well, it matters, right? on the role of data representations in spoken language dependency parsing. In *Proceedings of the Second Workshop on Universal Dependencies (UDW 2018)*, pages 37–46, Brussels, Belgium. Association for Computational Linguistics.

Rob van der Goot, Ahmet Üstün, Alan Ramponi, and Barbara Plank. 2020. Massive choice, ample tasks (machamp):a toolkit for multi-task learning in nlp.

Johannes Heinecke. 2019. ConlluEditor: a fully graphical editor for Universal dependencies treebank files. In *Universal Dependencies Workshop 2019*, Paris.

Robert Litschko, Ivan Vulić, Željko Agić, and Goran Glavaš. 2020. Towards instance-level parser selection for cross-lingual transfer of dependency parsers. In *Proceedings of the 28th International Conference on Computational Linguistics*, pages 3886–3898, Barcelona, Spain (Online). International Committee on Computational Linguistics.

Yijia Liu, Yi Zhu, Wanxiang Che, Bing Qin, Nathan Schneider, and Noah A. Smith. 2018. Parsing tweets into Universal Dependencies. In *Proceedings of the 2018 Conference of the North American Chapter of the Association for Computational Linguistics: Human Language Technologies, Volume 1 (Long Papers)*, pages 965–975, New Orleans, Louisiana. Association for Computational Linguistics.

Ailsa Meechan-Maddon and Joakim Nivre. 2019. How to parse low-resource languages: Cross-lingual parsing, target language annotation, or both? In *Proceedings of the Fifth International Conference on Dependency Linguistics (Depling, SyntaxFest 2019)*, pages 112–120.

Khalil Mrini, Franck Dernoncourt, Quan Hung Tran, Trung Bui, Walter Chang, and Ndapa Nakashole. 2020. Rethinking self-attention: Towards interpretability in neural parsing. In *Findings of the Association for Computational Linguistics: EMNLP 2020*, pages 731–742, Online. Association for Computational Linguistics.

Benjamin Muller, Antonis Anastasopoulos, Benoît Sagot, and Djamé Seddah. 2020. When being unseen from mbert is just the beginning: Handling new languages with multilingual language models. *arXiv preprint arXiv:2010.12858*.

Niko Partanen, Rogier Blokland, KyungTae Lim, Thierry Poibeau, and Michael Rießler. 2018. The first Komi-Zyrian Universal Dependencies treebanks. In *Proceedings of the Second Workshop on Universal Dependencies (UDW 2018)*, pages 126–132, Brussels, Belgium. Association for Computational Linguistics.

Barbara Plank and Gertjan Van Noord. 2011. Effective measures of domain similarity for parsing. In *Proceedings of the 49th Annual Meeting of the Association for Computational Linguistics: Human Language Technologies*, pages 1566–1576.

Martin Popel, Zdeněk Žabokrtský, and Martin Vojtek. 2017. Udapi: Universal API for Universal Dependencies. In *Proceedings of the NoDaLiDa 2017 Workshop on Universal Dependencies (UDW 2017)*, pages 96–101, Gothenburg, Sweden. Association for Computational Linguistics.

Manuela Sanguinetti and Cristina Bosco. 2015. Parttut: The turin university parallel treebank. In *Harmonization and development of resources and tools for italian natural language processing within the parli project*, pages 51–69. Springer.

Djamé Seddah, Farah Essaidi, Amal Fethi, Matthieu Futeral, Benjamin Muller, Pedro Javier Ortiz Suárez, Benoît Sagot, and Abhishek Srivastava. 2020. Building a user-generated content North-African Arabizi treebank: Tackling hell. In *Proceedings of the 58th Annual Meeting of the Association for Computational Linguistics*, pages 1139–1150, Online. Association for Computational Linguistics.

Natalia Silveira, Timothy Dozat, Marie-Catherine de Marneffe, Samuel Bowman, Miriam Connor, John Bauer, and Christopher D. Manning. 2014. A gold standard dependency corpus for English. In *Proceedings of the Ninth International Conference on Language Resources and Evaluation (LREC-2014)*.

Gertjan Van Noord, Gosse Bouma, Frank Van Eynde, Daniel De Kok, Jelmer Van der Linde, Ineke Schuurman, Erik Tjong Kim Sang, and Vincent Vandeghinste. 2013. Large scale syntactic annotation of written Dutch: Lassy. In *Essential speech and language technology for Dutch*, pages 147–164. Springer, Berlin, Heidelberg.

Clara Vania, Yova Kementchedjhieva, Anders Søgaard, and Adam Lopez. 2019. A systematic comparison of methods for low-resource dependency parsing on genuinely low-resource languages. In *Proceedings of the 2019 Conference on Empirical Methods in Natural Language Processing and the 9th International Joint Conference on Natural Language Processing (EMNLP-IJCNLP)*, pages 1105–1116.

Emre Yilmaz, Maaike Andringa, Sigrid Kingma, Jelske Dijkstra, Frits van der Kuip, Hans Van de Velde, Frederik Kampstra, Jouke Algra, Henk van den Heuvel, and David van Leeuwen. 2016. A longitudinal bilingual Frisian-Dutch radio broadcast database designed for code-switching research. In *Proceedings of the Tenth International Conference on Language Resources and Evaluation (LREC'16)*, pages 4666–4669, Portorož, Slovenia. European Language Resources Association (ELRA).

Amir Zeldes. 2017. The GUM corpus: Creating multilayer resources in the classroom. *Language Resources and Evaluation*, 51(3):581–612.

Daniel Zeman, Jan Hajič, Martin Popel, Martin Potthast, Milan Straka, Filip Ginter, Joakim Nivre, and Slav Petrov. 2018. CoNLL 2018 shared task: Multilingual parsing from raw text to Universal Dependencies. In *Proceedings of the CoNLL 2018 Shared Task: Multilingual Parsing from Raw Text to Universal Dependencies*, pages 1–21, Brussels, Belgium. Association for Computational Linguistics.

Daniel Zeman, Joakim Nivre, Mitchell Abrams, Elia Ackermann, Noëmi Aepli, Hamid Aghaei, Željko Agić, Amir Ahmadi, Lars Ahrenberg, Chika Kennedy Ajede, Gabrielė Aleksandravičiūtė, Ika Alfina, Lene Antonsen, Katya Aplonova, Angelina Aquino, Carolina Aragon, Maria Jesus Aranzabe, Hórunn Arnardóttir, Gashaw Arutie, Jessica Naraiswari Arwidarasti, Masayuki Asahara, Luma Ateyah, Furkan Atmaca, Mohammed Attia, Aitziber Atutxa, Liesbeth Augustinus, Elena Badmaeva, Keerthana Balasubramani, Miguel Ballesteros, Esha Banerjee, Sebastian Bank, Verginica Barbu Mititelu, Victoria Basmov, Colin Batchelor, John Bauer, Seyyit Talha Bedir, Kepa Bengoetxea, Gözde Berk, Yevgeni Berzak, Irshad Ahmad Bhat, Riyaz Ahmad Bhat, Erica Biagetti, Eckhard Bick, Agnė Bielinskienė, Kristín Bjarnadóttir, Rogier Blokland, Victoria Bobicev, Loïc Boizou, Emanuel Borges Völker, Carl Börstell, Cristina Bosco, Gosse Bouma, Sam Bowman, Adriane Boyd, Kristina Brokaitė, Aljoscha Burchardt, Marie Candito, Bernard Caron, Gauthier Caron, Tatiana Cavalcanti, Gülşen Cebiroğlu Eryiğit, Flavio Massimiliano Cecchini, Giuseppe G. A. Celano, Slavomír

Čéplö, Savas Cetin, Özlem Çetinoğlu, Fabricio Chalub, Ethan Chi, Yongseok Cho, Jinho Choi, Jayeol Chun, Alessandra T. Cignarella, Silvie Cinková, Aurélie Collomb, Çağrı Çöltekin, Miriam Connor, Marine Courtin, Elizabeth Davidson, Marie-Catherine de Marneffe, Valeria de Paiva, Mehmet Oguz Derin, Elvis de Souza, Arantza Diaz de Ilarraza, Carly Dickerson, Arawinda Dinakaramani, Bamba Dione, Peter Dirix, Kaja Dobrovoljc, Timothy Dozat, Kira Droganova, Puneet Dwivedi, Hanne Eckhoff, Marhaba Eli, Ali Elkahky, Binyam Ephrem, Olga Erina, Tomaž Erjavec, Aline Etienne, Wograine Evelyn, Sidney Facundes, Richárd Farkas, Marília Fernanda, Hector Fernandez Alcalde, Jennifer Foster, Cláudia Freitas, Kazunori Fujita, Katarína Gajdošová, Daniel Galbraith, Marcos Garcia, Moa Gärdenfors, Sebastian Garza, Fabrício Ferraz Gerardi, Kim Gerdes, Filip Ginter, Iakes Goenaga, Koldo Gojenola, Memduh Gökırmak, Yoav Goldberg, Xavier Gómez Guinovart, Berta González Saavedra, Bernadeta Griciūtė, Matias Grioni, Loïc Grobol, Normunds Grūzītis, Bruno Guillaume, Céline Guillot-Barbance, Tunga Güngör, Nizar Habash, Hinrik Hafsteinsson, Jan Hajič, Jan Hajič jr., Mika Hämäläinen, Linh Hà Mỹ, Na-Rae Han, Muhammad Yudistira Hanifmuti, Sam Hardwick, Kim Harris, Dag Haug, Johannes Heinecke, Oliver Hellwig, Felix Hennig, Barbora Hladká, Jaroslava Hlaváčová, Florinel Hociung, Petter Hohle, Eva Huber, Jena Hwang, Takumi Ikeda, Anton Karl Ingason, Radu Ion, Elena Irimia, Ọlájídé Ishola, Tomáš Jelínek, Anders Johannsen, Hildur Jónsdóttir, Fredrik Jørgensen, Markus Juutinen, Sarveswaran K, Hüner Kaşıkara, Andre Kaasen, Nadezhda Kabaeva, Sylvain Kahane, Hiroshi Kanayama, Jenna Kanerva, Boris Katz, Tolga Kayadelen, Jessica Kenney, Václava Kettnerová, Jesse Kirchner, Elena Klementieva, Arne Köhn, Abdullatif Köksal, Kamil Kopacewicz, Timo Korkiakangas, Natalia Kotsyba, Jolanta Kovalevskaitė, Simon Krek, Parameswari Krishnamurthy, Sookyoung Kwak, Veronika Laippala, Lucia Lam, Lorenzo Lambertino, Tatiana Lando, Septina Dian Larasati, Alexei Lavrentiev, John Lee, Phuong Lê H`ông, Alessandro Lenci, Saran Lertpradit, Herman Leung, Maria Levina, Cheuk Ying Li, Josie Li, Keying Li, Yuan Li, KyungTae Lim, Krister Lindén, Nikola Ljubešić, Olga Loginova, Andry Luthfi, Mikko Luukko, Olga Lyashevskaya, Teresa Lynn, Vivien Macketanz, Aibek Makazhanov, Michael Mandl, Christopher Manning, Ruli Manurung, Cătălina Mărănduc, David Mareček, Katrin Marheinecke, Héctor Martínez Alonso, André Martins, Jan Mašek, Hiroshi Matsuda, Yuji Matsumoto, Ryan McDonald, Sarah McGuinness, Gustavo Mendonça, Niko Miekka, Karina Mischenkova, Margarita Misirpashayeva, Anna Missilä, Cătălin Mititelu, Maria Mitrofan, Yusuke Miyao, AmirHossein Mojiri Foroushani, Amirsaeid Moloodi, Simonetta Montemagni, Amir More, Laura Moreno Romero, Keiko Sophie Mori, Shinsuke Mori, Tomohiko Morioka, Shigeki Moro, Bjartur Mortensen, Bohdan Moskalevskyi, Kadri Muischnek, Robert Munro, Yugo Murawaki, Kaili Müürisep, Pinkey Nainwani, Mariam Nakhlé, Juan Ignacio Navarro Horñiacek, Anna Nedoluzhko, Gunta Nešpore-Bērzkalne, Luong Nguy˜ên Thị, Huy`ên Nguy˜ên Thị Minh, Yoshihiro Nikaido, Vitaly Nikolaev, Rattima Nitisaroj, Alireza Nourian, Hanna Nurmi, Stina Ojala, Atul Kr. Ojha, Adédayọ Olúòkun, Mai Omura, Emeka Onwuegbuzia, Petya Osenova, Robert Östling, Lilja Øvrelid, Şaziye Betül Özateş, Arzucan Özgür, Balkız Öztürk Başaran, Niko Partanen, Elena Pascual, Marco Passarotti, Agnieszka Patejuk, Guilherme Paulino-Passos, Angelika Peljak-Łapińska, Siyao Peng, Cenel-Augusto Perez, Natalia Perkova, Guy Perrier, Slav Petrov, Daria Petrova, Jason Phelan, Jussi Piitulainen, Tommi A Pirinen, Emily Pitler, Barbara Plank, Thierry Poibeau, Larisa Ponomareva, Martin Popel, Lauma Pretkalniņa, Sophie Prévost, Prokopis Prokopidis, Adam Przepiórkowski, Tiina Puolakainen, Sampo Pyysalo, Peng Qi, Andriela Rääbis, Alexandre Rademaker, Taraka Rama, Loganathan Ramasamy, Carlos Ramisch, Fam Rashel, Mohammad Sadegh Rasooli, Vinit Ravishankar, Livy Real, Petru Rebeja, Siva Reddy, Georg Rehm, Ivan Riabov, Michael Rießler, Erika Rimkutė, Larissa Rinaldi, Laura Rituma, Luisa Rocha, Eiríkur Rögnvaldsson, Mykhailo Romanenko, Rudolf Rosa, Valentin Roșca, Davide Rovati, Olga Rudina, Jack Rueter, Kristján Rúnarsson, Shoval Sadde, Pegah Safari, Benoît Sagot, Aleksi Sahala, Shadi Saleh, Alessio Salomoni, Tanja Samardžić, Stephanie Samson, Manuela Sanguinetti, Dage Särg, Baiba Saulīte, Yanin Sawanakunanon, Kevin Scannell, Salvatore Scarlata, Nathan Schneider, Sebastian Schuster, Djamé Seddah, Wolfgang Seeker, Mojgan Seraji, Mo Shen, Atsuko Shimada, Hiroyuki Shirasu, Muh Shohibussirri, Dmitry Sichinava, Einar Freyr Sigurosson, Aline Silveira, Natalia Silveira, Maria Simi, Radu Simionescu, Katalin Simkó, Mária Šimková, Kiril Simov, Maria Skachedubova, Aaron Smith, Isabela Soares-Bastos, Carolyn Spadine, Steinhór Steingrímsson, Antonio Stella, Milan Straka, Emmett Strickland, Jana Strnadová, Alane Suhr, Yogi Lesmana Sulestio, Umut Sulubacak, Shingo Suzuki, Zsolt Szántó, Dima Taji, Yuta Takahashi, Fabio Tamburini, Mary Ann C. Tan, Takaaki Tanaka, Samson Tella, Isabelle Tellier, Guillaume Thomas, Liisi Torga, Marsida Toska, Trond Trosterud, Anna Trukhina, Reut Tsarfaty, Utku Türk, Francis Tyers, Sumire Uematsu, Roman Untilov, Zdeňka Urešová, Larraitz Uria, Hans Uszkoreit, Andrius Utka, Sowmya Vajjala, Daniel van Niekerk, Gertjan van Noord, Viktor Varga, Eric Villemonte de la Clergerie, Veronika Vincze, Aya Wakasa, Joel C. Wallenberg, Lars Wallin, Abigail Walsh, Jing Xian Wang, Jonathan North Washington, Maximilan Wendt, Paul Widmer, Seyi Williams, Mats Wirén, Christian Wittern, Tsegay Woldemariam, Tak-sum Wong, Alina Wróblewska, Mary Yako, Kayo Yamashita, Naoki Yamazaki, Chunxiao Yan, Koichi Yasuoka, Marat M. Yavrumyan, Zhuoran Yu, Zdeněk Žabokrtský, Shorouq Zahra, Amir Zeldes, Hanzhi Zhu, and Anna Zhuravleva. 2020. Universal dependencies 2.7. LINDAT/CLARIAH-CZ digital library at the Institute of Formal and Applied Linguistics (ÚFAL), Faculty of Mathematics and Physics, Charles University.

A Distribution languages over POS tags

	Frisian	Dutch	Other
ADV	365	89	0
PRON	388	53	1
NUM	58	2	0
NOUN	314	158	11
ADP	396	44	1
DET	337	21	0
VERB	343	50	6
CCONJ	152	7	0
INTJ	181	8	0
ADJ	158	54	3
PROPN	158	133	14
AUX	158	4	1
SCONJ	59	2	0

Table 9: Number of tokens for the combination language and POS tag.

B Annotation guidelines

We tried to follow the universal dependency guidelines as much as possible. In cases we could not follow them precisely we discussed and made our own guidelines:

- To determine if something is an ADJ or ADV we use a dictionary. If the word is not in the dictionary we use the frequencies of the Alpino treebank. For the decision between advmod and amod, we used amod only for nominals.
- If "toen/want/tot/dan" are at the beginning of utterances we tag them as mark and not as conj. "en" is cconj or cc.
- Orphan always attaches to the root. Orphan is used in cases where utterances seem to have a "non-standard" ending. Normally the word would be attached to the right part of the utterance but this part is missing. Both Figures 2 and 3 show utterances with orphans.

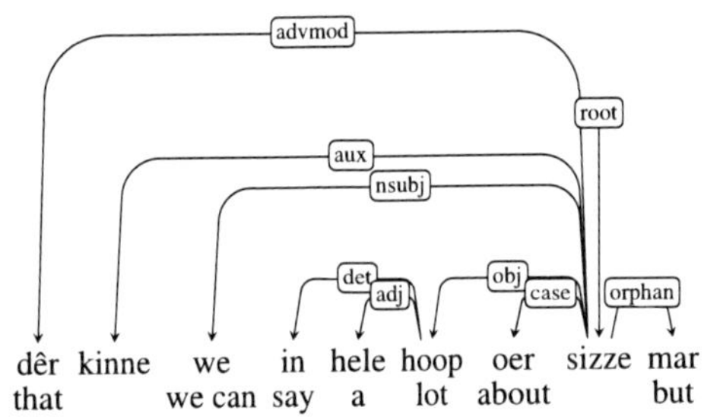

Figure 2: Utterance with orphan relation.

- Discourse is always attached to the highest node without any projectivity. Figure 3 shows an utterance with a discourse relation.

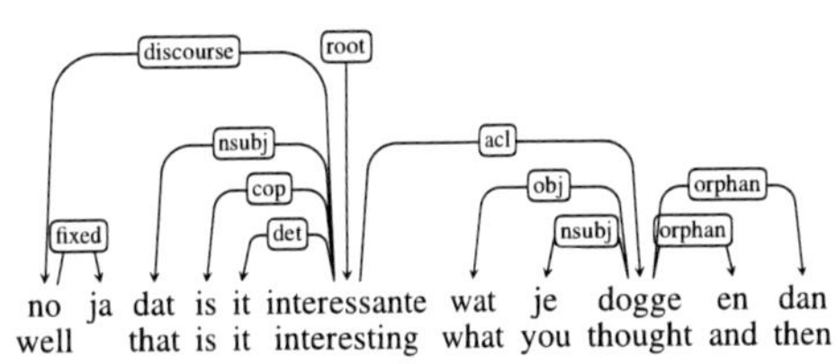

Figure 3: Utterance showing both orphan and discourse relations.

C List of treebanks

1. Treebanks in UD 2.7:
    - English ESL
    - Hindi English HIENCS
    - English GUM Reddit
    - English EWT
    - English GUM
    - English LinES
    - English ParTUT
    - English Pronouns
    - English PUD
    - French FQB
    - French ParTUT
    - French PUD
    - French Sequoia
    - French Spoken
    - German GSD
    - German LIT
    - German PUD
    - Dutch LassySmall
    - Dutch Alpino
    - Danish DDT
    - Naija NSC
    - Afrikaans AfriBooms
2. Treebanks not in UD:
    - ConvBank (English)
    - Tweebank (English)

D Standard deviations development data

Components	8	16	32	64	128
POS	**81.2**	80.4	81.0	79.4	79.4
	0.41	0.65	0.28	0.60	0.46
UAS	72.7	71.4	70.8	72.6	**73.8**
	0.96	1.0	1.16	0.95	0.49
LAS	55.2	55.1	54.8	55.5	**57.1**
	0.47	0.89	0.76	0.85	0.42

Table 10: POS, UAS and LAS scores (mean over 5 random seeds) and standard deviations on dev data for 2000 sentences. Highest scores are marked in bold.

Sentences	1000	2000	4000
POS	78.5	79.4	**79.8**
	0.26	0.46	0.87
UAS	71.5	**73.8**	73.3
	0.55	0.49	0.96
LAS	54.6	**57.1**	56.0
	1.12	0.42	0.92

Table 11: POS, UAS and LAS scores (mean over 5 random seeds) and standard deviation on dev data for 128 components. Highest scores are marked in bold.

Genres, Parsers, and BERT: The Interaction Between Parsers and BERT Models in Cross-Genre Constituency Parsing in English and Swedish

Daniel Dakota
Uppsala University
Department of Linguistics
ddakota@lingfil.uu.se

Abstract

Genre and domain are often used interchangeably, but are two different properties of a text. Successful parser adaptation requires both cross-domain and cross-genre sensitivity (Rehbein and Bildhauer, 2017). While the impact domain differences have on parser performance degradation is more easily measurable in respect to lexical differences, impact of genre differences can be more nuanced. With the predominance of pre-trained language models (LMs; e.g. BERT (Devlin et al., 2019)), there are now additional complexities in developing cross-genre sensitive models due to the infusion of linguistic characteristics derived from, usually, a third genre. We perform a systematic set of experiments using two neural constituency parsers to examine how different parsers behave in combination with different BERT models with varying source and target genres in English and Swedish. We find that there is extensive difficulty in predicting the best source due to the complex interactions between genres, parsers, and LMs. Additionally, the influence of the data used to derive the underlying BERT model heavily influences how best to create more robust and effective cross-genre parsing models.

1 Introduction

The performance degradation of models trained on one data set when used on another has been well established (Gildea, 2001; Petrov and Klein, 2007). However, how we define the source of the problem (e.g. *out-of-domain differences*) is problematic. Within domain adaption, even the term *domain* is incredibly loosely defined (Ramponi and Plank, 2020). This has allowed conflating several different properties of texts, as such properties can be difficult to distinguish given some of their inherent overlap. Relevant for this work is how we define the distinction between *genre* and *domain*.

We use Falkenjack et al. (2016) as a template and define *genre* dealing with more *abstract* and *linguistic characteristics* used within a text (Biber and Conrad, 2009). *Domain*, however, is more about the topics and content words used. Much parsing work has actively focused on handling domain differences, such as reducing lexical gap issues between target and source domains (e.g. Candito et al. (2011)), while explicit handling of genre differences is not as heavily researched, nor as well understood.

While much parsing literature uses the terms interchangeably (Rehbein and Bildhauer, 2017), they are not, however, identical concepts. By doing so we are are not effectively identifying which *out-of-domain* differences should be contributed more to out of *genre* or *domain* difference. For example, Wikipedia articles are written in a style following more of an encyclopedia. Pages on medicine and languages may contain very different vocabularies, but the linguistic characteristics are most likely similar given the encyclopedic style of writing. However, responses in a forum on medical advice may share a large amount of vocabulary overlap with Wikipedia medical pages, but would share considerably less linguistic structure given the dialogue nature of a forum (e.g. more interrogative sentences).

A treebank (in our case constituency treebanks) often contains many noticeable domains, but it is harder to gauge how many distinct genres are present. Sometimes they are explicitly marked in the annotation (Candito and Seddah, 2012; Telljohann et al., 2015), while others explicitly separate out the different genres out (McDonald et al., 2011; Adesam et al., 2015). Yet a treebank is often times a concatenation of various texts that may ultimately represent slightly different linguistic characteristics (even if annotated strictly on newspaper).

Domain differences often result in a high lexi-

Proceedings of the Second Workshop on Domain Adaptation for NLP, pages 59–71
April 20, 2021.

cal divergence. The best performing chart-based grammar-based constituency parsers were predominantly unelexicalized (Petrov and Klein, 2007), which helped reduce issues with lexical differences. However, current state-of-the-art neural span-based chart-based parsers have substantially changed this paradigm. With the use of lexical embeddings, there is now a great deal of lexicalization within the modeling architecture to an extent that was not seen before, with some state-of-the-art parsers not utilizing POS tags (Zhang et al., 2020). The use of characters and subtoken information has been shown to be beneficial in reducing lexical sparsity issues (Vania et al., 2018), which ultimately reduces domain difference disparities. However, what impact this degree of lexical contextualization has on cross-genre parsing remains unclear.

Additionally, the use of language models (LMs), such as BERT (Devlin et al., 2019), to derive contextualized embeddings presents yet another variable in selecting the best source. Given that LMs are derived on large, unannotated texts, they implicitly capture various linguistic properties of the these texts (Tenney et al., 2019a) which they they infuse into the parser via contextualized embeddings. How embeddings derived from, often, a single genre behave as a bridge between two, often, other genres presents an interesting issue.

We are interested in examining the following in cross-genre experiments:

1. What preferences do different parsing architectures exhibit?
2. What interactions do different BERT models demonstrate?
3. What behaviors are exhibited across languages?

2 Related Work

Most parsing work[1] in parser adaptation has been more explicitly focused on issues of domain differences. Early techniques focused on selecting optimal source data to boost a target set (Plank and van Noord, 2011; McDonald et al., 2011) or parameter and model optimization to handle both general and domain specific features (Daumé III, 2007; Kim et al., 2016). Both delexicalized (Rosa and Žabokrtský, 2015) and lexicalized (Falenska and Çetinoğlu, 2017) similarity metrics have shown the ability to select optimal source data.

More recent work has been focused on creating domain specific embeddings. The use of domain embeddings in Chinese dependency parsing by Li et al. (2019) built on the previous research by Stymne et al. (2018). Both showed domain and treebank specific embeddings respectively yielded better performance over direct treebank concatenation, as this allows for the capturing of domain specific and general features. Results were further improved upon with adversarial methods and BERT fine-tuning by Li et al. (2020).

Joshi et al. (2018) found that contextualized embeddings have substantially reduced the difficulty in handling lexical gap issues between domains when the target and source are syntactically similar, but then employ additional strategies to handle more syntactically dissimilar ones. Additional work by Fried et al. (2019) showed that while pretrained LMs improved parser performance over several English domains, the improvements for out-of-domain results were not relatively larger. As Rehbein and Bildhauer (2017) note, parser adaptation requires both genre and domain adaption, but that content features, such as topics, do not generalize well for genre modeling, suggesting different techniques are needed for cross-genre modeling.

While the incorporation of pre-trained LMs has become standard in many NLP tasks, understanding how different models interact with different tasks is still an area of active research. Work by Martin et al. (2020) on French shows that a smaller French specific LM model derived from more diversified source data can compete with models substantially larger across a variety of downstream NLP tasks. Specifically, tasks which showed more divergence from Wikipedia benefited the most from a mixed genre LM. The importance of source diversification is also seen in LMs for Finnish (Virtanen et al., 2019) and Chinese (Cui et al., 2020), each of which contain more text sources than simply Wikipedia. The impact of source diversification can also be seen in domain specific LMs, such as FinBERT (Liu et al., 2020), which was derived from several types of financial sources, as different financial texts are radically different stylistically.

One additional benefit by explicitly looking at specific genres is it can help further our understanding of linguistic properties of different texts, forcing us to re-evaluate earlier annotation schemes

[1] In the related work section we use the terms used in the original papers and not our definitions.

predominantly designed for an original treebank genre (Rúnarsson and Sigursson, 2020).

3 Methodology

We perform a systematic set of experiments for English and Swedish, using different neural constituency parsing architectures in combination with various BERT models to examine how this impacts cross-genre parsing. English is widely used in cross-domain and cross-genre research. Swedish, however, is not as thoroughly examined, yet possess multiple genre treebanks as well as BERT models, making it suitable for our research interests.

3.1 Parsers

We use two different neural span-based chart-based parsers, the Berkeley Neural Parser (Kitaev et al., 2019) and the SuPar Neural CRF Parser (Zhang et al., 2020).

Berkeley Neural Parser uses a self-encoder and can incorporate BERT models to generate word representations. It uses the last layer embedding of the last subtoken to represent the word.[2] It decouples predicting the optimal representation of a span (i.e. input sequence) from predicting the optimal label, requiring only that the resultant output form a valid tree. This not only removes the underlying grammars found in traditional PCFG parsers, but also direct correlations between a constituent and a label (Fried et al., 2019). A CKY (Kasami, 1965; Younger, 1967; Cocke and Schwartz, 1970) style inference algorithm is used at test time. Additionally, the parser allows the option of using POS tag prediction to be used as an auxiliary loss task (we use BNP and BNPno to represent with and without the POS loss respectively in our experiments).

SuPar Neural CRF Parser (SuPar) is a two-stage parser, that, similarly to the Berkeley parser, produces a constituent and then a label. It uses a Scalar mix (Peters et al., 2018; Tenney et al., 2019a,b) of the last four layers for each subtoken of a word. Additionally, it uses a BiLSTM encoder to compute context aware representations by employing two different MLP layers indicating both left and right word boundaries. Each candidate is scored over the two representations using a biaffine operation (Dozat and Manning, 2017), while the CKY algorithm is used when parsing to obtain the best tree.

3.2 Treebanks

We choose to experiment on two languages that contain treebanks representative of different genres, the English Webocorpus Treebank (Petrov and McDonlad, 2012) and the Koala Eukalyptus Corpus (Adesam et al., 2015).

English Webcorpus Treebank (EWT) was introduced in the 2012 shared task on Web Parsing and consists of five subareas: Yahoo answers, emails, Newsgroup texts, product reviews, and Weblog entries. The treebank follows an English Penn Treebank (Marcus et al., 1993) style annotation scheme with some additional POS tags to account for specific annotation needs, resulting in 50 POS tags and 28 phrase heads. We removed unary nodes, traces, and function labels during preprocessing.

Swedish Eukalyptus Treebank (SET) consists of: blog entries from the SIC corpus (Östling, 2013), parts of Swedish Europarl (Koehn, 2005), chapters from books, public information gathered from government and health information sites, and Wikipedia articles, and contains only 13 POS tags and 10 phrases heads. The treebank's annotation scheme is derived from the TiGer Treebank of German (Brants et al., 2004). Notably this includes discontinuous constituents, resulting in the need to uncross the branches of the extracted treebank. We follow the procedure used for TiGer, namely the transformation process proposed by Boyd (2007) using *treetools*,[3] and additionally remove all function labels.

Data Splits The EWT is traditionally used as dev and test sets for examining the out-of-domain adaptability of models developed on the English PTB (Petrov and McDonlad, 2012), and we are not aware of any standard splits for the EWT nor of standard splits for the SET. For this reason we chose to split each genre within the treebanks into approximately sequential 80/10/10 splits, with selected treebank statistics presented in Table 1. For cross-genre experiments, EWT and SET subgenres are concatenated respectively.

3.3 BERT Embeddings

We use four different embeddings in our experiments: both bert-base-multilingual-cased and

[2]The authors note they found no difference between using the last and first subtoken.

[3]`https://github.com/wmaier/treetools`

Treebank	Genre	Train Sent.	Tok	Tok. Typ.	Tok. Rat.	POS Trigram Rat.	Dev Sent.
EWT	Answers	2790	42428	6344	.1495	.1367	349
	Enail	3919	45488	7056	.1551	.1103	490
	Newsgroup	1909	33764	6769	.2005	.1498	238
	Reviews	3049	44414	6362	.1432	.1156	381
	Weblog	1623	35864	6420	.1790	.1414	203
SET	Blog	1050	15050	3659	.2431	.0713	100
	Europarl	640	14580	3074	.2108	.0565	79
	Public	900	16540	4540	.2745	.0589	89
	Novels	950	16188	4114	.2552	.0594	120
	Wiki	900	16031	4788	.2937	.0364	100

Table 1: Treebank statistics for EWT and SET genres with number of train sentences along with total tokens, token type ratios, and unique POS trigram ratios for training sets, as well as number of dev sentences

Treebank		Answers	Email	Newsgroup	Reviews	Weblog	Answers	Email	Newsgroup	Reviews	Weblog
EWT	Answers	0	.2679	.2622	**.2063**	.3180	0	.3900	.3539	**.2987**	.4416
	Email	.3689	0	**.3099**	.4755	.4721	.4820	0	**.4044**	.6236	.6194
	Newsgroup	.4157	.3845	0	.4881	**.2539**	.4038	.4215	0	.4851	**.3213**
	Reviews	**.2279**	.3870	.3613	0	.4082	**.2978**	.4926	.4390	0	.5465
	Weblog	.4125	.4523	**.1945**	.4738	0	.4860	.5767	**.3201**	.5475	0
		Blog	Europarl	Public	Novels	Wiki	Blog	Europarl	Public	Novels	Wiki
SET	Blog	0	.4108	.5060	**.2374**	.4633	0	.4942	.4942	**.4034**	.5134
	Europarl	.4660	0	**.2074**	.2165	.2526	.5109	0	**.3983**	.4965	.5572
	Public	.4816	.2443	0	.2665	**.1494**	.4413	**.3930**	0	.4217	.3983
	Novels	**.1991**	.2388	.2705	0	.2596	**.3783**	.5003	.4469	0	.4342
	Wiki	.4197	.3382	**.1622**	.2720	0	.4257	.5004	**.4179**	.4637	0

Table 2: KL Divergence for POS trigrams (left) and BERTbc and kbBERT Subtokens (right)

bert-base-cased (Devlin et al., 2019), bert-large-swedish-uncased,[4] and bert-base-swedish-cased (Malmsten et al., 2020).[5] All of these have an unknown number of domains present within each model.

bert-base-multilingual-cased (mBERT) was trained on 104 languages of Wikipedia with oversampling of low resource languages and under sampling of high resource languages.

bert-base-cased (BERTbc) was trained on a mixture of English Wikipedia (2,500M words) and BookCorpus (800M words; Zhu et al., 2015) with the BookCorpus containing sixteen identified book genres.[6]

bert-large-swedish-uncase (swBERT) was trained on Swedish Wikipedia (300M words).

bert-base-swedish-cased (kbBERT) was trained using newspapers (2,977 M words), government publications (117M words), legally available e-deposits (62M words),[7] internet forums (31M words), and Swedish Wikipedia (29M words).

4 Delexicalized and Subtoken Divergence

As noted in section 2, delexicalized comparisons of treebanks have been used to identify treebank similarity for source selection. An established delexicalized method is KL divergence (Kullback and Leibler, 1951) of POS trigrams (Rosa and Žabokrtský, 2015). In Table 2 we present results for KL divergence for POS trigrams with the closest similar genre in bold.[8]

Given that BERT works on a subtoken level, we additionally present the KL divergence for BERT subword tokens between genres. Each genre was tokenized using the specified BERT tokeinzer and counts were collected on subtokens. Identifying BERT subword tokens similarities provides insights into (sub)lexical level similarity, as well as how delexicalized and subword pattern with each other.[9]

The row (y-axis) is the target genre, and the columns (x-axis) are the source (e.g. in Table 2 .4660 is Europarl target Blog source).[10] We see

[4]https://github.com/af-ai-center/SweBERT

[5]https://github.com/Kungbib/swedish-bert-models

[6]We do not consider this to mean there are 16 distinct genres as we define the term, rather to note the more diversified domains, though author style would naturally influence any learned representations.

[7]Including governmental releases, books, and magazines.

[8]We follow Rosa and Žabokrtský (2015) and default the target genre to 1 in KL calculations.

[9]We note however that the two parsers do not necessarily use all the subtokens when generating embeddings.

[10]All future heat maps and tables have the same set-up.

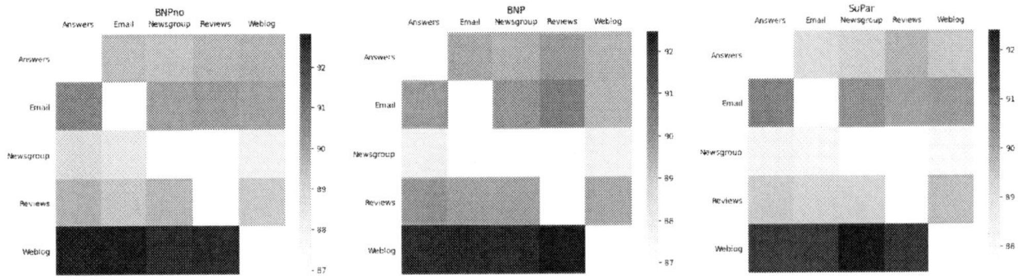

Figure 1: Heat maps for EWT with mBERT on Dev Set

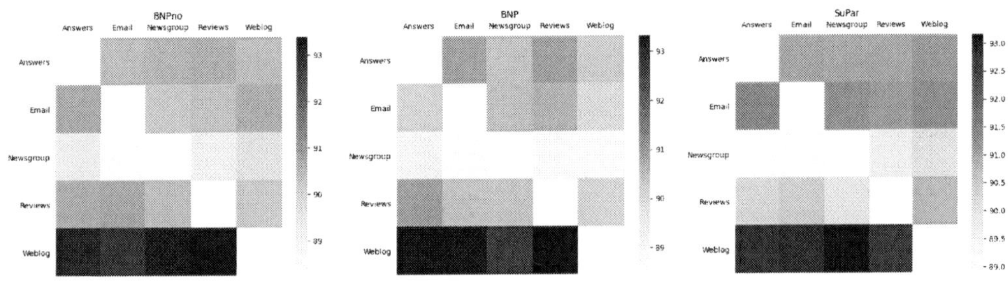

Figure 2: Heat maps for EWT with BERTbc on Dev Set

that the patterns are rather similar, with simply the degree of divergence being larger between POS trigrams and sublexical tokens. The lone exception is that on the POS level, Wiki is a better source for Public while on the subtoken level, Europarl is. We can also see that a high subword dissimilarity does not necessarily predict a proportionally high POS dissimilarity.

5 Results

5.1 EWT mBERT

Fig. 1 shows heat maps representing transfer F-scores on the dev sets for different target and source genres. Note that the diagonals are NA values, not the minimum per axis given that the diagonal represents when the target and source are the same genre. We also present a setting All[11] in which all the genres are combined in the train and indicate the absolute F-score increase over the baseline, as well as Gap which indicates the absolute increase the All setting shows compared to the best source experiment.

We see that EWT using mBert does not correlate well with the KL divergences in Table 2. There is seemingly a preference for either Answers or Reviews as the best source genre across experiments. Furthermore, no single parsing architecture can claim to be superior, as the best individual settings are quite varied across the parsers. The All setting results in the best over all performance, a trend that will continue through all results, but this is unsurprising given it has more training data across all cross-genre experiments. The individual Gap improvements show a large range of improvements, but also a lack of noted consistency about how much improvement the All setting has over the best source for each genre.

[11]Tables containing full results are found in Appendix A.

5.2 EWT BERTbc

We see noticeable improvements for all experiments when using an English specific BERT model (see Fig. 2), which is expected. However, improvements for individual settings vary greatly. In some cases, the improvements are greater than 2% absolute, while in others they are as small as .05%.

We also see a more noticeable trend to SuPar performing slightly better than BNP and BNPno in many experiments overall, particularly in the All setting, and shows consistent higher Gap increases. However, we see continued individual architectural strengths and consistency, such as that BNPno still shows strength on parsing Weblog, similar to that in Fig. 1, and BNP actually shows identical best source genres as those for mBERT.

We do, however, see more variation in source preferences for the other two architectures. For

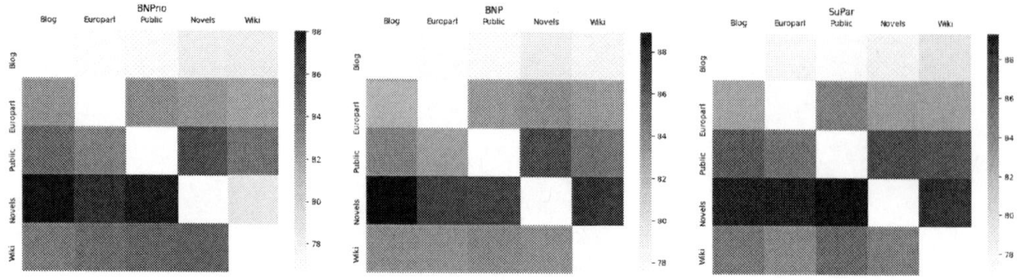

Figure 3: Heat maps for SET with mBERT on Dev Set

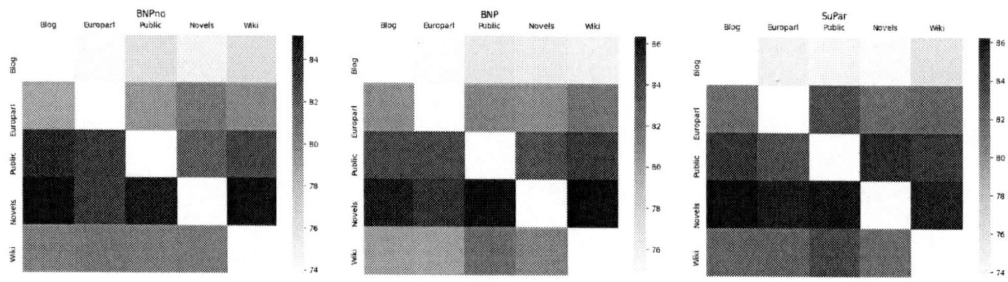

Figure 4: Heat maps for SET with swBERT on Dev Set

BNPno, Answers is no longer dominant and instead we see a great deal of variation, while for SuPar, we see a shift towards Weblog. This is particularly interesting given that Weblog is often the most dissimilar source in regards to KL.

Another interesting observation is that for both BNPno and BNP, Reviews is clearly not benefiting in the All setting as the other genres are. In fact, for BNP, we see it is is actually worse than the best source experiment.

5.3 SET mBERT

In Fig. 3 we see results using multilingual BERT on Swedish.[12] An initial observation is that SuPar performs, overall, better than both BNPno and BNP, particularly in the All setting, though there may be individual settings in which a Berkeley parser setup performs better.

In terms of individual source experiments, we see a great deal of variation intra and inter parser. While Novels is the best source for Public across three experimental setings, for all other genres, at least one of the best sources is different for that specific genre across the parsers.

For BNPno we see that Wiki is the best source for Blog, even though it is furthest in subtoken similarity, and the second furthest in POS similarity. Yet when using Wiki as a source, BNPno outperforms its BNP counterpart in every single experiment, often substantially, except in the All setting.

Europarl is seemingly a case where POS and subtoken divergences align with parser architectures in regards to lexicalization. For the BNP, Novels is preferred, which is just behind Public in POS divergence but substantially behind in subtoken divergence. However, both BNPno and SuPar prefer Public, which is by far the closest at the subtoken level, and actually perform relatively poorly using the other genres as sources.

5.4 SET swBERT

Generally, we see a decrease in performance for swBERT (Fig. 4) compared to mBERT. However, the drop is perhaps not as significant in many cases as expected, especially given the size difference of the LMs. Also remembering that swBERT is uncased, and many cased models work better, we are unsure how much this contributes to performance degradation. However, there are still several settings in which swBERT out performs mBERT. BNP also shows more volatility compared to BNPno, but we still see the trend that in the All setting, it still performs better. One interesting observation is the lack of variation in the results in the BNPno experiments using any different source for Wiki data.

[12] Tables containing full results are found in Appendix B.

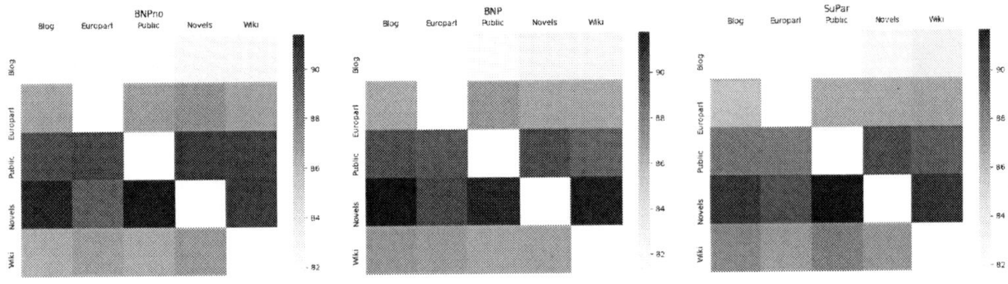

Figure 5: Heat maps for SET with kbBERT on Dev Set

Additionally, in three experiments Wiki is the best source for BNP, yet none of these sources were the best using mBERT. However, these three experiments substantially out perform their BNPno counterparts. The behavior of Blog is not intuitive, as it actually now benefits the most from one of the least similar sources in Public.

SuPar stays relatively consistent, with the only change that the best source for Novels switched from Public to Blog. However, this is actually a change to the most similar source genre, something that mBERT dispreferred.

5.5 SET kbBERT

All results for kbBERT (Fig. 5) are substantially better than both mBERT and swBERT. SuPar again shows less volatility, with Public returning as the best source for Novels, and now Wiki being the best source of Europarl.

Wiki is the best source for Blog, but we must note that for both BNPno and BNP, it is barely better than Novels, while for SuPar it is substantially better. For BNPno, we see the best performing sources are slightly different than with mBERT as now Euorparl prefers Novels and Novels prefers Public instead of Blog. For BNP, Wiki benefits the most from Blog, even though it is the most dissimilar in regards to POS divergence. Another important observation however, is that the slight performance advantage SuPar had using mBERT and swBERT over the Berkeley parsers has been somewhat reduced, and in many settings a Berkeley parser out performs SuPar again.

6 Discussion

The different parsing architectures interact differently with the underlying latent properties of the embeddings in their parsing decisions. SuPar, however, does seem to show the most consistent stable performance across all experiments, and in a majority of cases, is the best performing model.

Whether POS information is needed in neural constituency parsing is seemingly a complicated picture in terms of performance, though it has been shown to benefit certain neural dependency parsing architectures (Zhou et al., 2020). However, we can see the impact the inclusion of the POS loss has in terms of parser source preferences, as seldom were the behaviors of BNPno and BNP similar. This is to be expected, as the source of the underlying LM may have implicitly different POS distributions than either the target or source genre, and a POS loss is most likely sensitive to these differences.

BNP showed much more stable source preferences across genres and experiments, indicating how the POS task is seemingly is able to mitigate, to some degree, the influence of the LM, though whether this is positive or negative is unclear. This may indicate that embeddings derived from more mono-genre texts interact in a more consistent way when using POS information, stablizing source preferences. This is seen in both English and Swedish experiments to a degree. However, once the LM has more genre representations, this stabilizing factor no longer holds as the inherent POS distributions are most likely far more varied, as seen with kbBERT.

We can also see how other architectural choices besides the inclusion of POS information are important, as otherwise we would expect BNPno and SuPar to behave similarly, which they do not. A clear distinction is how the two parsers incorporate BERT embeddings. The choice of Scalar mixing (Liu et al., 2020; de Vries et al., 2020), embedding averages (He and Choi, 2020), and different subtoken selection (Hettiarachchi and Ranasinghe, 2020) have all shown to impact performance on NLP tasks. Another factor may be the additional word boundaries MLP layers created in SuPar's architecture, providing more context for an individual parsing decision, making it more robust to slight variations in syntactic distributions.

The influence of the LM's genre is perhaps most seen in the Swedish Wikipedia genre experiments with swBERT and BNP seen in Fig. 4. All the sources produce in similar results when Wikipedia is the target. It may simply be that when the target genre is too similar to the genre of the LM, the impact of similar sizes of different source genres is minimized, as there now exist too much latent and explicit Wikipedia data. However, in the All setting, we see a substantial increase where now there is not only more data, but more diversity to counterbalance the Wikipedia derived LM. Additionally we see that Wikipedia is the preferred source for all genres outside of Blog for BNP, and results are substantially better than their BNPno counterparts. However, this does not hold across parsers, given that SuPar shows completely different behaviors for swBERT than the Berkeley experiments. This further emphasizes the difficulty of transferring knowledge of one parser's source preference behaviors to another.

For both languages there can be substantial deviation of the best performing source genre from the closest source genre on both a delexicalized and subtoken level. Overall gains specific sources show for an individual target source can also be incredibly inconsistent across experiments. Why this is, is further complicated by the source genres interaction with the LM. An English only BERT model yielded some improvements while a Swedish only model showed varying results depending upon the LM. This can be due to several factors. The most obvious one is due to the size of the LM, as swBERT is substantially smaller, yet it still yields results close to the much larger mBERT for Swedish. However, kbBERT is approximately the same size as BERTbc, and produces much larger absolute gains than BERTbc did for English, providing counter evidence that size is not the only factor. The difficulty in identifying the reasons is due to many interacting aspects such as higher baselines for English, treebank sizes, and annotation scheme complexity. However, kbBERT was derived from a far more diverse set of genres, many of which overlap with the SET, compared to BERTbc, which was derived from mostly two distinct genres, neither of which overlap with the EWT substantially.

Importantly, we also see the impact a LM model has on closing performance gaps between parsing architectures, as kbBERT results for the Berkeley parsers are overall more on par with SuPar. This demonstrates how interactions between three distinct genres makes optimal source selection far more difficult when using LMs and different parsers than established delexicalized approaches.

7 Conclusion

We have performed a set of detailed experiments that explored the interaction between genres, parsers, and BERT models. We have shown that the LM plays the pivotal role in successful genre-sensitive parsing within our chosen parsing architectures. In addition, we have also shown that different architectures often behave dissimilarly, making determining best sources for a specific target reliant on better understanding the underlying architectures, and not transferring direct behavior of one parser to another.

Treebanks are rather static, particularly constituency treebanks. While we have often seen incremental performance gains with every new parser, how successful we are at cross-genre parsing will, for the time being, be more related to our exploitation of various other sources and methods. LMs, for example, can be trained on vast amounts of unannotated data, allowing for the the LM to become far more sensitive to genre differences than any small treebank, especially as we have control over the creation of an LM, and less so than with a treebank.

Perhaps the most practical way to currently create genre-sensitive parsing models is to better mix distinct genres within the data used to derive the LM. The LM itself does not even have to be overtly large, rather even small mixtures of other genres and domains provides noticeable benefits (Martin et al., 2020). Future research will look to create multilingual cross-genre models that work across treebanks and genres.

Acknowledgements

The author would like to thank Yvonne Adesam and Gerlof Bouma for providing the SET, Sandra Kübler and members of the Uppsala NLP Parsing Group: Joakim Nivre, Sara Stymne, and Artur Kulmizev for their feedback, and the anonymous reviewers for their comments. The author is supported by the Swedish strategic research programme eSSENCE.

References

Yvonne Adesam, Gerlof Bouma, and Richard Johansson. 2015. Defining the eukalyptus forest – the koala treebank of Swedish. In *Proceedings of the 20th Nordic Conference of Computational Linguistics (NODALIDA 2015)*, pages 1–9, Vilnius, Lithuania. Linköping University Electronic Press, Sweden.

Douglas Biber and Susan Conrad. 2009. *Register, Genre, and Style*. Cambridge Textbooks in Linguistics. Cambridge University Press.

Adriane Boyd. 2007. Discontinuity Revisited: An Improved Conversion to Context-free Representations. In *Proceedings of the Linguistic Annotation Workshop*, LAW '07, pages 41–44, Prague, Czech Republic.

Sabine Brants, Stefanie Dipper, Peter Eisenberg, Silvia Hansen, Esther König, Wolfgang Lezius, Christian Rohrer, George Smith, and Hans. Uszkoreit. 2004. TIGER: Linguistic Interpretation of a German Corpus. *Journal of Language and Computation*, 2004 (2):597–620.

Marie Candito, Enrique Henestroza Anguiano, and Djamé Seddah. 2011. A word clustering approach to domain adaptation: Effective parsing of biomedical texts. In *Proceedings of the 12th International Conference on Parsing Technologies*, pages 37–42, Dublin, Ireland.

Marie Candito and Djamé Seddah. 2012. Le corpus sequoia : annotation syntaxique et exploitation pour l'adaptation d'analyseur par pont lexical. In *Proceedings of the Joint Conference JEP-TALN-RECITAL 2012*, pages 321–334, Grenoble, France.

John Cocke and Jacob Schwartz. 1970. Programming Languages and Their Compilers. Technical report, Courant Institute of Mathematical Sciences, New York.

Yiming Cui, Wanxiang Che, Ting Liu, Bing Qin, Shijin Wang, and Guoping Hu. 2020. Revisiting pretrained models for Chinese natural language processing. In *Findings of the Association for Computational Linguistics: EMNLP 2020*, pages 657–668, Online. Association for Computational Linguistics.

Hal Daumé III. 2007. Frustratingly easy domain adaptation. In *Proceedings of the 45th Annual Meeting of the Association of Computational Linguistics*, pages 256–263, Prague, Czech Republic.

Jacob Devlin, Ming-Wei Chang, Kenton Lee, and Kristina Toutanova. 2019. BERT: Pre-training of deep bidirectional transformers for language understanding. In *Proceedings of the 2019 Conference of the North American Chapter of the Association for Computational Linguistics: Human Language Technologies*, pages 4171–4186, Minneapolis, Minnesota.

Timothy Dozat and Christopher Manning. 2017. Deep biaffine attention for neural dependency parsing. In *5h International Conference on Learning Representations (ICLR 2017)*, Toulon, France. Conference Track Proceedings.

Agnieszka Falenska and Özlem Çetinoğlu. 2017. Lexicalized vs. delexicalized parsing in low-resource scenarios. In *Proceedings of the 15th International Conference on Parsing Technologies*, pages 18–24, Pisa, Italy.

Johan Falkenjack, Marina Santini, and Arne Jönsson. 2016. An exploratory study on genre classification using readability features. In *Proceedings of the The Sixth Swedish Language Technology Conference (SLTC 2016)*, Umeå, Sweden.

Daniell Fried, Nikita Kitaev, and Dan Klein. 2019. Cross-domain generalization of neural constituency parsers. In *Proceedings of the 57th Annual Meeting of the Association for Computational Linguistics*, pages 323–330, Florence, Italy.

Daniel Gildea. 2001. Corpus Variation and Parser Performance. In *Proceedings of the 2001 Conference on Empirical Methods in Natural Language Processing (EMNLP)*, pages 167–202, Pittsburgh, PA.

Han He and Jinho D. Choi. 2020. Establishing strong baselines for the new decade: Sequence tagging, syntactic and semantic parsing with bert.

Hansi Hettiarachchi and Tharindu Ranasinghe. 2020. BRUMS at SemEval-2020 task 3: Contextualised embeddings for predicting the (graded) effect of context in word similarity. In *Proceedings of the Fourteenth Workshop on Semantic Evaluation*, pages 142–149, Barcelona (online). International Committee for Computational Linguistics.

Vidur Joshi, Matthew Peters, and Mark Hopkins. 2018. Extending a parser to distant domains using a few dozen partially annotated examples. In *Proceedings of the 56th Annual Meeting of the Association for Computational Linguistics (Volume 1: Long Papers)*, pages 1190–1199, Melbourne, Australia.

Tadao Kasami. 1965. An Efficient Recognition and Syntax-Analysis Algorithm for Context-Free Languages. Technical report, AFCRL-65-75, Air Force Cambridge Research Laboratory.

Young-Bum Kim, Karl Stratos, and Ruhi Sarikaya. 2016. Frustratingly easy neural domain adaptation. In *Proceedings of COLING 2016, the 26th International Conference on Computational Linguistics: Technical Papers*, pages 387–396, Osaka, Japan.

Nikita Kitaev, Steven Cao, and Dan Klein. 2019. Multilingual constituency parsing with self-attention and pre-training. In *Proceedings of the 57th Annual Meeting of the Association for Computational Linguistics*, pages 3499–3505, Florence, Italy.

Philipp Koehn. 2005. Europarl: A parallel corpus for statistical machine translation. In *Machine Translation Summit*, pages 79–86, Phuket, Thailand.

Solomon Kullback and Richard Leibler. 1951. On information and sufficiency. pages 79–85.

Ying Li, Zhenghua Li, and Min Zhang. 2020. Semi-supervised domain adaptation for dependency parsing via improved contextualized word representations. In *Proceedings of the 28th International Conference on Computational Linguistics*, pages 3806–3817, Barcelona, Spain (Online).

Zhenghua Li, Xue Peng, Min Zhang, Rui Wang, and Luo Si. 2019. Semi-supervised domain adaptation for dependency parsing. In *Proceedings of the 57th Annual Meeting of the Association for Computational Linguistics*, pages 2386–2395, Florence, Italy.

Zhuang Liu, Degen Huang, Kaiyu Huang, Zhuang Li, and Jun Zhao. 2020. Finbert: A pre-trained financial language representation model for financial text mining. In *Proceedings of the Twenty-Ninth International Joint Conference on Artificial Intelligence, IJCAI-20*, pages 4513–4519. International Joint Conferences on Artificial Intelligence Organization. Special Track on AI in FinTech.

Martin Malmsten, Love Börjeson, and Chris Haffenden. 2020. Playing with words at the national library of sweden – making a swedish bert.

Mitchell P. Marcus, Mary Ann Marcinkiewicz, and Beatrice Santorini. 1993. Building a Large Annotated Corpus of English: The Penn Treebank. *Computational Linguistics*, 19(2):313–330. Penn Treebank.

Louis Martin, Benjamin Muller, Pedro Javier Ortiz Suárez, Yoann Dupont, Laurent Romary, Éric de la Clergerie, Djamé Seddah, and Benoît Sagot. 2020. CamemBERT: a tasty French language model. In *Proceedings of the 58th Annual Meeting of the Association for Computational Linguistics*, pages 7203–7219, Online. Association for Computational Linguistics.

Ryan McDonald, Slav Petrov, and Keith Hall. 2011. Multi-source transfer of delexicalized dependency parsers. In *Proceedings of the 2011 Conference on Empirical Methods in Natural Language Processing*, pages 62–72, Edinburgh, Scotland, UK.

Robert Östling. 2013. Stagger: an open-source part of speech tagger for Swedish. *Northern European Journal of Language Technology*, 3:1–18.

Matthew Peters, Mark Neumann, Mohit Iyyer, Matt Gardner, Christopher Clark, Kenton Lee, and Luke Zettlemoyer. 2018. Deep contextualized word representations. In *Proceedings of the 2018 Conference of the North American Chapter of the Association for Computational Linguistics: Human Language Technologies*, pages 2227–2237, New Orleans, Louisiana. Association for Computational Linguistics.

Slav Petrov and Dan Klein. 2007. Improved Inference for Unlexicalized Parsing. In *Proceedings of Human Language Technologies 2007: The Conference of the North American Chapter of the Association for Computational Linguistics*, pages 404–411, Rochester, NY.

Slav Petrov and Ryan McDonlad. 2012. Overview of the 2012 shared task on Parsing the Web. In *Notes of the First Workshop on Syntactic Analysis of Non-Canonical Language (SANCL)*, Sapporo, Japan.

Barbara Plank and Gertjan van Noord. 2011. Effective measures of domain similarity for parsing. In *Proceedings of the 49th Annual Meeting of the Association for Computational Linguistics: Human Language Technologies*, pages 1566–1576, Portland, Oregon, USA.

Alan Ramponi and Barbara Plank. 2020. Neural unsupervised domain adaptation in NLP—A survey. In *Proceedings of the 28th International Conference on Computational Linguistics*, pages 6838–6855, Barcelona, Spain (Online).

Ines Rehbein and Felix Bildhauer. 2017. Data point selection for genre-aware parsing. In *Proceedings of the 16th International Workshop on Treebanks and Linguistic Theories*, pages 95–105, Prague, Czech Republic.

Rudolf Rosa and Zdeněk Žabokrtský. 2015. KLcpos3 - a language similarity measure for delexicalized parser transfer. In *Proceedings of the 53rd Annual Meeting of the Association for Computational Linguistics and the 7th International Joint Conference on Natural Language Processing*, pages 243–249, Beijing, China.

Kristján Rúnarsson and Einar Freyr Sigursson. 2020. Parsing Icelandic alingi transcripts: Parliamentary speeches as a genre. In *Proceedings of the Second ParlaCLARIN Workshop*, pages 44–50, Marseille, France. European Language Resources Association.

Sara Stymne, Miryam de Lhoneux, Aaron Smith, and Joakim Nivre. 2018. Parser training with heterogeneous treebanks. In *Proceedings of the 56th Annual Meeting of the Association for Computational Linguistics (Volume 2: Short Papers)*, pages 619–625, Melbourne, Australia.

Heike Telljohann, Erhard Hinrichs, Sandra Kübler, Heike Zinsmeister, and Kathrin Beck. 2015. Stylebook for the Tübingen Treebank of Written German (TüBa-D/Z). Seminar für Sprachwissenschaft, Universität Tübingen, Germany.

Ian Tenney, Dipanjan Das, and Ellie Pavlick. 2019a. BERT rediscovers the classical NLP pipeline. In *Proceedings of the 57th Annual Meeting of the Association for Computational Linguistics*, pages 4593–4601, Florence, Italy. Association for Computational Linguistics.

Ian Tenney, Patrick Xia, Berlin Chen, Alex Wang, Adam Poliak, Thomas R. McCoy, Najoung Kim, Benjamin Van Durme, Samuel R. Bowman, Dipanjan Das, and Ellie Pavlick. 2019b. What do you learn from context? probing for sentence structure in contextualized word representations.

Clara Vania, Andreas Grivas, and Adam Lopez. 2018. What do character-level models learn about morphology? the case of dependency parsing. In *Proceedings of the 2018 Conference on Empirical Methods in Natural Language Processing*, pages 2573–2583, Brussels, Belgium.

Antti Virtanen, Jenna Kanerva, Rami Ilo, Jouni Luoma, Juhani Luotolahti, Tapio Salakoski, Filip Ginter, and Sampo Pyysalo. 2019. Multilingual is not enough: BERT for Finnish.

Wietse de Vries, Andreas van Cranenburgh, and Malvina Nissim. 2020. What's so special about BERT's layers? a closer look at the NLP pipeline in monolingual and multilingual models. In *Findings of the Association for Computational Linguistics: EMNLP 2020*, pages 4339–4350, Online. Association for Computational Linguistics.

Daniel Younger. 1967. Recognition and parsing of context-free languages in n^3. *Information and Control*, 10(2):189–208.

Yu Zhang, Houquan Zhou, and Zhenghua Li. 2020. Fast and accurate neural crf constituency parsing. In *Proceedings of the Twenty-Ninth International Joint Conference on Artificial Intelligence, IJCAI-20*, pages 4046–4053.

Houquan Zhou, Yu Zhang, Zhenghua Li, and Min Zhang. 2020. Is pos tagging necessary or even helpful for neural dependency parsing? In *Natural Language Processing and Chinese Computing*, pages 179–191, Cham. Springer International Publishing.

Yukun Zhu, Ryan Kiros, Rich Zemel, Ruslan Salakhutdinov, Raquel Urtasun, Antonio Torralba, and Sanja Fidler. 2015. Aligning books and movies: Towards story-like visual explanations by watching movies and reading books. In *The IEEE International Conference on Computer Vision (ICCV)*, pages 19–27.

A Full English Results for Parsers and BERT Models

Parser		Baseline	Answers	Email	Newsgroup	Reviews	Weblog	All	Gap
BNPno	Answers	88.72	NA	89.51	89.38	89.57	**89.67**	90.66 (+1.94)	+.99
	Email	89.29	**90.62**	NA	89.92	90.03	89.93	91.16 (+1.87)	+.54
	Newsgroup	87.61	**88.67**	88.34	NA	86.90	87.82	89.05 (+1.44)	+.38
	Reviews	88.68	**89.52**	89.22	89.46	NA	89.15	90.52 (+1.84)	+1.00
	Weblog	91.13	92.75	**92.83**	92.55	92.61	NA	93.75 (+2.62)	+.92
BNP	Answers	89.01	NA	89.63	89.43	**89.81**	89.37	90.66 (+1.65)	+.85
	Email	89.03	89.86	NA	89.94	**90.44**	89.35	91.21 (+2.18)	+.77
	Newsgroup	86.50	**87.46**	86.75	NA	86.75	87.54	88.20 (+1.70)	+.74
	Reviews	88.94	**89.84**	89.65	89.62	NA	89.60	90.20 (+1.26)	+.36
	Weblog	90.66	92.22	92.18	92.16	**92.47**	NA	93.53 (+2.87)	+1.06
SuPar	Answers	88.10	NA	89.16	89.23	**89.69**	89.44	90.54 (+2.44)	+.85
	Email	89.06	**90.62**	NA	90.27	89.98	90.09	91.34 (+2.28)	+.72
	Newsgroup	86.68	**88.13**	88.00	NA	87.47	87.78	89.42 (+2.74)	+1.29
	Reviews	88.06	89.35	89.19	89.08	NA	**89.57**	90.39 (+2.33)	+.82
	Weblog	90.58	91.95	91.94	**92.41**	92.05	NA	93.56 (+2.98)	+1.15

Table 3: Full EWT Results with mBERT on Dev Set

Parser		Baseline	Answers	Email	Newsgroup	Reviews	Weblog	All	Gap
BNPno	Answers	89.68	NA	90.45	90.51	**90.58**	90.41	91.48 (+1.80)	+.90
	Email	88.75	**90.67**	NA	90.13	90.31	90.56	91.35 (+2.60)	+.68
	Newsgroup	87.96	89.07	88.25	NA	88.95	**89.51**	90.29 (+2.33)	+.78
	Reviews	89.70	90.53	**90.65**	90.34	NA	90.06	90.76 (+1.06)	+.11
	Weblog	91.48	93.14	92.87	93.28	**93.39**	NA	95.01 (+3.53)	+1.62
BNP	Answers	89.60	NA	90.87	90.45	**90.93**	90.29	91.63 (+2.03)	+.70
	Email	89.28	90.10	NA	90.41	**90.58**	89.93	91.58 (+2.30)	+1.00
	Newsgroup	87.74	**89.01**	88.47	NA	88.69	88.73	89.85 (+2.11)	+.84
	Reviews	89.88	**90.83**	90.27	90.25	NA	90.02	90.69 (+.81)	-.14
	Weblog	91.28	93.23	93.17	92.69	**93.32**	NA	94.29 (+3.01)	+.97
SuPar	Answers	89.95	NA	90.98	90.90	90.93	**91.10**	92.19 (+2.24)	+1.09
	Email	90.14	**91.38**	NA	91.20	91.06	91.23	92.51 (+2.37)	+1.13
	Newsgroup	88.57	88.90	88.97	NA	89.55	**89.89**	90.91 (+2.34)	+1.02
	Reviews	89.28	90.17	90.39	89.76	NA	**90.69**	91.73 (+2.45)	+1.04
	Weblog	91.82	92.79	92.87	**93.17**	92.67	NA	94.31 (+2.49)	+1.14

Table 4: Full EWT Results with BERTbc on Dev Set

B Full Swedish Results for Parsers and BERT Models

Parser		Baseline	Blog	Europarl	Public	Novels	Wiki	All	Gap
BNPno	Blog	75.99	NA	76.65	77.09	78.01	**78.14**	79.22 (+3.23)	+1.08
	Europarl	80.91	82.60	NA	**82.97**	82.44	81.98	83.97 (+3.06)	+1.00
	Public	83.11	84.55	83.33	NA	**85.81**	84.34	85.34 (+2.23)	-.47
	Novels	85.14	**88.04**	87.03	87.67	NA	87.33	89.75 (+4.61)	+1.71
	Wiki	82.10	83.75	84.35	84.74	**84.89**	NA	84.68 (+2.58)	-.21
BNP	Blog	75.87	NA	77.45	77.86	**78.80**	78.18	79.57 (+3.70)	+.77
	Europarl	80.71	82.22	NA	83.20	**83.55**	83.06	84.41 (+3.70)	+.86
	Public	83.25	83.99	82.94	NA	**86.51**	84.77	86.72 (+3.47)	+.21
	Novels	84.94	**88.91**	86.99	86.81	NA	87.38	89.59 (+4.65)	+.68
	Wiki	81.84	83.56	83.42	**83.88**	83.56	NA	85.03 (+3.19)	+1.15
SuPar	Blog	74.40	NA	77.55	76.90	77.77	**79.18**	80.13 (+5.73)	+.95
	Europarl	82.52	82.60	NA	**84.36**	83.03	82.81	85.01 (+2.49)	+.65
	Public	84.95	85.98	85.06	NA	**86.88**	86.43	87.99 (+3.04)	+1.11
	Novels	86.54	88.58	88.67	**89.30**	NA	88.12	90.80 (+4.51)	+1.50
	Wiki	83.13	84.61	83.72	**85.57**	84.48	NA	86.12 (+2.99)	+.55

Table 5: Full SET Results with mBERT on Dev Set

Parser		Baseline	Blog	Europarl	Public	Novels	Wiki	All	Gap
BNPno	Blog	71.81	NA	73.82	75.93	74.62	**76.07**	77.87 (+6.06)	+1.80
	Europarl	78.21	78.73	NA	79.43	**80.78**	79.89	82.12 (+3.91)	+1.34
	Public	83.60	**84.16**	83.53	NA	81.99	83.09	86.30 (+2.70)	+2.14
	Novels	81.71	**85.13**	83.34	84.80	NA	85.08	87.86 (+6.15)	+2.73
	Wiki	78.52	80.32	**80.47**	80.40	80.46	NA	82.97 (+4.45)	+2.50
BNP	Blog	72.37	NA	74.69	**76.55**	76.19	75.79	79.12 (+6.75)	+3.46
	Europarl	78.56	80.70	NA	80.97	80.66	**81.85**	83.01 (+4.45)	+1.22
	Public	82.66	83.75	83.90	NA	83.34	**84.51**	86.98 (+4.32)	+2.47
	Novels	82.70	85.69	84.96	86.14	NA	**86.33**	88.44 (+5.74)	+2.11
	Wiki	78.45	80.04	79.92	**82.13**	81.26	NA	83.13 (+4.68)	+1.00
SuPar	Blog	73.11	NA	74.85	74.41	73.72	**75.86**	80.21 (+7.10)	+4.35
	Europarl	80.86	81.89	NA	**83.35**	81.95	82.20	84.32 (+3.46)	+.97
	Public	83.30	84.54	83.22	NA	**85.06**	84.41	86.50 (+3.20)	+1.44
	Novels	83.82	**86.22**	85.57	85.97	NA	85.50	89.04 (+5.22)	+2.82
	Wiki	80.31	82.18	82.18	**83.48**	81.77	NA	85.21 (+4.90)	+1.73

Table 6: Full SET Results with swBERT on Dev Set

Parser		Baseline	Blog	Europarl	Public	Novels	Wiki	All	Gap
BNPno	Blog	79.37	NA	81.67	81.70	82.63	**82.68**	84.25 (+4.88)	+1.57
	Europarl	84.38	86.60	NA	86.82	**87.34**	86.63	86.96 (+2.58)	+.14
	Public	89.03	89.66	89.85	NA	**90.47**	90.26	90.93 (+1.90)	+.46
	Novels	87.29	91.00	89.03	**91.39**	NA	90.53	92.74 (+5.45)	+1.35
	Wiki	84.21	86.23	86.66	86.41	**87.05**	NA	87.77 (+3.56)	+.72
BNP	Blog	78.63	NA	81.18	81.74	82.44	**82.48**	83.95 (+5.32)	+1.47
	Europarl	84.63	86.33	NA	**87.00**	86.42	86.36	87.75 (+3.12)	+.75
	Public	88.90	89.77	89.50	NA	**89.86**	89.00	91.35 (+2,45)	+1.49
	Novels	88.38	**91.78**	89.88	91.26	NA	91.39	92.41 (+4.03)	+.63
	Wiki	85.47	**86.94**	86.61	86.43	86.50	NA	87.61 (+2.14)	+.67
SuPar	Blog	79.36	NA	81.79	81.76	82.64	**83.28**	84.45 (+5.09)	+1.17
	Europarl	84.92	85.90	NA	86.54	86.54	**86.74**	88.18 (+3.26)	+1.44
	Public	87.53	88.46	88.34	NA	**90.00**	89.32	90.74 (+3.21)	+.74
	Novels	88.64	90.65	89.65	**91.67**	NA	90.93	93.04 (+4.40)	+1.37
	Wiki	85.96	87.70	86.88	**87.93**	87.37	NA	89.26 (+3.30)	+1.33

Table 7: Full SET Results with kbBERT on Dev Set

Cross-Lingual Transfer with MAML on Trees

Jezabel R. Garcia, Federica Freddi, Feng-Ting Liao, Jamie McGowan, Tim Nieradzik, Da-shan Shiu, Ye Tian, Alberto Bernacchia*

*MediaTek Research, Cambourne Business Park, Cambridge CB23 6DW, United Kingdom

Abstract

In meta-learning, the knowledge learned from previous tasks is transferred to new ones, but this transfer only works if tasks are related. Sharing information between unrelated tasks might hurt performance, and it is unclear how to transfer knowledge across tasks that have a hierarchical structure. Our research extends a meta-learning model, MAML, by exploiting hierarchical task relationships. Our algorithm, TreeMAML, adapts the model to each task with a few gradient steps, but the adaptation follows the hierarchical tree structure: in each step, gradients are pooled across tasks clusters and subsequent steps follow down the tree. We also implement a clustering algorithm that generates the tasks tree without previous knowledge of the task structure, allowing us to make use of implicit relationships between the tasks.

We show that TreeMAML successfully trains natural language processing models for cross-lingual Natural Language Inference by taking advantage of the language phylogenetic tree.

This result is useful, since most languages in the world are under-resourced and the improvement on cross-lingual transfer allows the internationalization of NLP models.

1 Introduction

Deep learning models require a large amount of data in order to perform well when trained from scratch. When data is scarce for a given task, we can *transfer* the knowledge gained in a source task to quickly learn a target task, if the two tasks are related. *Multi-task learning* studies how to learn multiple tasks simultaneously with a single model, by taking advantage of task relationships (Ruder, 2017; Zhang and Yang, 2018). However, in Multi-task learning models, a set of tasks is fixed in advance and they do not generalize to new tasks. Instead, *Meta-learning* is inspired by the human ability to learn how to quickly learn new tasks by using the knowledge of previously learned ones.

Meta-learning has been widely used in multiple domains, especially in recent years since the advent of Deep Learning (Hospedales et al., 2020). A successful model for meta-learning, MAML (Finn et al., 2017), does not diversify task relationships according to their similarity and it is unclear how to modify it for that purpose. Furthermore, there is still a lack of methods for sharing information across tasks that have a hierarchical structure, and the goal of our work is to fill this gap.

The use of MAML-like algorithms in NLP has just recently been proved successful for Natural Language Inference (NLI) and Question Answering (QA) (Nooralahzadeh et al., 2020). These results represent a practical meta-learning solution to the fundamental problem of applying NLP models to under-resourced languages where data annotation is scarce. This work, combined with the fact that languages can be organized hierarchically using their phylogenetic tree (Dunn et al., 2011), motivated us to develop a hierarchical meta-learning algorithm, that we call TreeMAML.

In this work, we make the following contributions:

- We propose a novel modification of MAML to account for a hierarchy of tasks. The algorithm uses the tree structure of data during adaptation, by pooling gradients across tasks at each adaptation step and subsequent steps follow down the tree (see Figure 1a).
- We modify the hierarchical clustering from Menon et al. (2019) to allow asymmetric tree structure. We apply this clustering algorithm to learn dynamic trees that exploit the similarity between tasks.
- We apply TreeMAML to few-shot NLI, using

Proceedings of the Second Workshop on Domain Adaptation for NLP, pages 72–79
April 20, 2021.

the XNLI dataset (Conneau et al., 2018), obtaining accuracies higher than previous state-of-the-art.

2 Related work

The problem of quantifying and exploiting task relationships has a long history in Multi-task learning and is usually approached by parameter sharing, see Ruder (2017); Zhang and Yang (2018) for reviews. However, Multi-task Learning is fundamentally different from Meta-learning as it does not consider the problem of generalizing to new tasks (Hospedales et al., 2020). Recent work includes Zamir et al. (2018), who studies a large number of computer vision tasks and quantifies the transfer between all pairs of tasks. Achille et al. (2019) proposes a novel measure of task representation by assigning an importance score to each model parameter in each task. The score is based on each task's loss function gradients with respect to each model parameter. This work suggests that gradients can be used as a measure of task similarity and we use this insight in our proposed algorithm.

In Meta-learning, a few papers have been recently published on learning and using task relationships. The work of Yao et al. (2019) applies hierarchical clustering to task representations learned by an autoencoder and uses those clusters to adapt the parameters to each task. The model of Liu et al. (2019) maps the classes of each task into the edges of a graph, it meta-learns relationships between classes and how to allocate new classes by using a graph neural network with attention. However, these algorithms are not model-agnostic; they have a fixed backbone and loss function and are thus difficult to apply to new problems. Instead, we design our algorithm as a straightforward generalization of Model-agnostic meta-learning (MAML, Finn et al. (2017)) and it can be applied to any loss function and backbone.

A couple of studies looked into modifying MAML to account for task similarities. The work of Jerfel et al. (2019) finds a different initial condition for each cluster of tasks and applies the algorithm to the problem of continual learning. The work of Katoch et al. (2020) defines parameter updates for a task by aggregating gradients from other tasks according to their similarity. However, in contrast with our algorithm, both of these models are not hierarchical, tasks are clustered on one level only and cannot be represented by a tree structure.

Recently, MAML has been applied to cross-lingual meta-learning (Gu et al., 2018; Dou et al., 2019). In particular, the implementation by Nooralahzadeh et al. (2020), called XMAML, obtained good results on NLI and QA tasks. As in the previously mentioned computer vision studies, some of these NLP algorithms looked into the relationships among languages to select the support languages used in their meta-learning algorithm, but they do not use the hierarchical structure of the languages.

3 The meta-learning problem

We follow the notation of Hospedales et al. (2020). We assume the existence of a distribution over tasks $\mathcal{T}$ and, for each task, a distribution over data points $\mathcal{D}$ and a loss function $\mathcal{L}$. The loss function of the meta-learning problem, $\mathcal{L}^{meta}$, is defined as an average across both distributions of tasks and data points:

$$\mathcal{L}^{meta}(\boldsymbol{\omega}) = \mathop{\mathbb{E}}_{\mathcal{T}} \mathop{\mathbb{E}}_{\mathcal{D}|\mathcal{T}} \mathcal{L}_{\mathcal{T}}\left(\boldsymbol{\theta}_{\mathcal{T}}(\boldsymbol{\omega}); \mathcal{D}\right) \tag{1}$$

The goal of meta-learning is to minimize the loss function with respect to a vector of meta-parameters $\boldsymbol{\omega}$. The vector of parameters $\boldsymbol{\theta}$ is task-specific and depends on the meta-parameters $\boldsymbol{\omega}$. Different meta-learning algorithms correspond to a different choice of $\boldsymbol{\theta}_{\mathcal{T}}(\boldsymbol{\omega})$. We describe below the choice of MAML that will also be followed by TreeMAML.

During meta-training, the loss is evaluated on a sample of m tasks and n_v validation data points for each task.

$$\mathcal{L}^{meta}(\boldsymbol{\omega}) = \frac{1}{mn_v} \sum_{i=1}^{m} \sum_{j=1}^{n_v} \mathcal{L}_{\mathcal{T}_i}\left(\boldsymbol{\theta}_{\mathcal{T}_i}(\boldsymbol{\omega}); \mathcal{D}_{ij}\right) \tag{2}$$

For each task i, the parameters $\boldsymbol{\theta}_{\mathcal{T}_i}$ are learned by a set of n_t training data points, distinct from the validation data. During meta-testing, a new (target) task is given and the parameters $\boldsymbol{\theta}$ are learned by a set of n_r target data points. In this work, we also use a batch of training data points to adapt $\boldsymbol{\theta}$ at test time. No training data is used to compute the model's final performance, which is computed on separate test data of the target task.

3.1 TreeMAML

MAML aims at finding the optimal initial condition ω from which a suitable parameter set can be found, separately for each task, after K gradient steps (Finn et al., 2017). For task i, we define the single gradient step with learning rate α as

$$U_i(\boldsymbol{\omega}) = \boldsymbol{\omega} - \frac{\alpha}{n_t}\sum_{j=1}^{n_t} \nabla\mathcal{L}(\boldsymbol{\omega}; \mathcal{D}_{ij}) \quad (3)$$

Then, MAML with K gradient steps corresponds to K iterations of this step.

$$\boldsymbol{\theta}_{\mathcal{T}_i}(\boldsymbol{\omega}) = U_i(U_i(...U_i(\boldsymbol{\omega}))) \qquad (K \text{ times}) \quad (4)$$

This update is usually referred to as *inner loop* and is performed separately for each task, while optimization of the loss 2 is referred to as *outer loop*.

We propose to modify MAML in order to account for a hierarchical structure of tasks. The idea is illustrated in Figure 1.

At each gradient step k, we assume that tasks are aggregated into C_k clusters and the parameters for each task are updated according to the average gradient across tasks within the corresponding cluster (in Fig.1b, we use $K = 3$ steps and $C_1 = 2$, $C_2 = 4$, $C_3 = 8$). We denote by $\mathcal{T}_c$ the set of tasks in cluster c. Then, the gradient update for the parameters of each task belonging to cluster c is equal to

$$U_c(\boldsymbol{\omega}) = \boldsymbol{\omega} - \frac{\alpha}{n_t\,|\mathcal{T}_c|}\sum_{i\in\mathcal{T}_c}\sum_{j=1}^{n_t} \nabla\mathcal{L}(\boldsymbol{\omega}; \mathcal{D}_j^{(i)}) \quad (5)$$

Furthermore, we denote by c_i^k the cluster to which task i belongs at step k. Then, TreeMAML with k gradient steps corresponds to K iterations of this step.

$$\boldsymbol{\theta}_{\mathcal{T}_i}(\boldsymbol{\omega}) = U_{c_i^K}(U_{c_i^{K-1}}(...U_{c_i^1}(\boldsymbol{\omega}))) \quad (6)$$

The intuition is the following: if each task has scarce data, gradient updates for single tasks are noisy and adding up gradients across similar tasks increases the signal. Note that we recover MAML if C_k is equal to the total number of tasks m at all steps. On the other hand, if $C_k = 1$, then the inner loop would take a step with a gradient averaged across all tasks.

Because at one specific step the weight updates are equal for all tasks within a cluster, it is possible to define the steps of the inner loop update per cluster c instead of per task $\boldsymbol{\theta}_{\mathcal{T}_i}$. Given a cluster c and its parent cluster p_c in the tree, the update at step k is given by

$$\boldsymbol{\theta}_{c,k} = \boldsymbol{\theta}_{p_c,k-1} - \frac{\alpha}{n_t\,|\mathcal{T}_c|}\sum_{i\in\mathcal{T}_c}\sum_{j=1}^{n_t} \nabla\mathcal{L}(\boldsymbol{\theta}_{p_c,k-1}; \mathcal{D}_{ij}) \quad (7)$$

where $\boldsymbol{\theta}_k^c$ is the parameter value for cluster c at step k. In terms of the notation used in expression 6, we have the equivalence $\boldsymbol{\theta}_{\mathcal{T}_i}(\boldsymbol{\omega}) = \boldsymbol{\theta}_{c_i,K}$, which depends on the initial condition $\boldsymbol{\omega}$. The full procedure is described in Algorithm 1

We consider two versions of the algorithm, depending on how we obtain the tree structure similar to Srivastava and Salakhutdinov (2013):

- **Fixed TreeMAML**. The tree is fixed by the knowledge of the tree structure of tasks when this structure is available. In that case, the values of C_k are determined by such tree.
- **Learned TreeMAML**. The tree is unknown *a priori* and is learned using a hierarchical clustering algorithm. In that case, the values of C_k are determined at each step by the clustering algorithm.

In the latter case, we cluster tasks based on the gradients of each task loss, consistent with recent work Achille et al. (2019). After each step k at cluster c_i, the clustering algorithm takes as input the gradient vectors of the children tasks i

$$\mathbf{g}_{ik} = \frac{1}{n_t}\sum_{j=1}^{n_t} \nabla\mathcal{L}(\boldsymbol{\theta}_{c_i,k}; \mathcal{D}_{ij}) \quad (8)$$

and these gradients are further allocated into clusters according to their similarity. The clustering algorithm is described in subsection 3.2.

Similar to MAML, adaptation to a new task is performed by computing $\boldsymbol{\theta}^{(i)}(\boldsymbol{\omega})$ on a batch of data of the target task. In order to exploit task relationships, we first reconstruct the tree structure by using a batch of training data and then we introduce the new task.

3.2 Clustering Algorithm

We employ a hierarchical clustering algorithm to cluster the gradients of our model parameters in the learned TreeMAML case. We specifically opt for an online clustering algorithm to maximise computational efficiency at test time and scalability. When a new task is evaluated, we reuse the tree structure generated for a training batch and add the

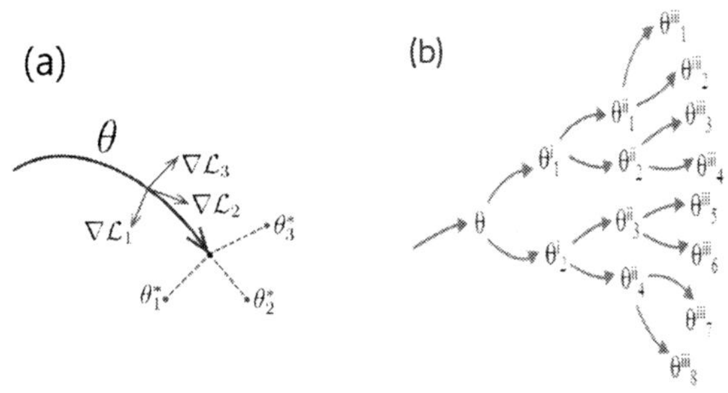

Figure 1: Illustration of the MAML(a) and TreeMAML(b) algorithms. Both algorithms are designed to quickly adapt to new tasks with a small number of training samples. MAML achieves this by introducing a gradient step in the direction of the single task. TreeMAML follows a similar approach, but it exploits the relationship between tasks by introducing the hierarchical aggregation of the gradients.

Algorithm 1 TreeMAML

Require: distribution over tasks $p(\tau)$; distribution over data for each task $p(\mathcal{D}|\tau)$;
Require: number of inner steps K; number of training tasks m; learning rates α, β;
Require: number of clusters C_k for each step k; loss function $\mathcal{L}_\tau(\boldsymbol{\omega}, \mathcal{D})$ for each task

randomly initialize $\boldsymbol{\omega}$
while not done **do**
  sample batch of $i = 1 : m$ tasks $\{\tau_i\} \sim p(\tau)$
  for all tasks $i = 1 : m$ initialize a single cluster $c_i = 1$
  initialize $\boldsymbol{\theta}_{1,0} = \boldsymbol{\omega}$
  for steps $k = 1 : K$ **do**
    for tasks $i = 1 : m$ **do**
      sample batch of $j = 1 : n_v$ data points $\{\mathcal{D}_{ij}\} \sim p(\mathcal{D}|\tau_i)$
      evaluate gradient $\mathbf{g}_{ik} = \frac{1}{n_t} \sum_{j=1}^{n_t} \nabla \mathcal{L}_{\tau_i}(\boldsymbol{\theta}_{c_i,k-1}; \mathcal{D}_{ij})$
    end for
    regroup tasks into C_k clusters $\mathcal{T}_c = \{i : c_i = c\}$
    according to similarity of $\{\mathbf{g}_{ik}\}$ and parent clusters $\{p_c\}$
    update $\theta_{c,k} = \theta_{p_c,k-1} - \frac{\alpha}{|\mathcal{T}_c|} \sum_{i \in \mathcal{T}_c} \mathbf{g}_{ik}$ for all clusters $c = 1 : C_k$
  end for
  update $\boldsymbol{\omega} \leftarrow \boldsymbol{\omega} - \beta \frac{1}{m n_v} \sum_{i=1}^{m} \sum_{j=1}^{n_v} \nabla_{\boldsymbol{\omega}} \mathcal{L}_{\tau_i}(\boldsymbol{\theta}_{c_i,K}(\boldsymbol{\omega}); \mathcal{D}_{ij})$
end while

new task. This process saves us from computing a new task hierarchy from scratch for every new task. Moreover, with offline hierarchical clustering, all the data needs to be available to the clustering algorithm simultaneously, which becomes a problem when dealing with larger batch sizes. Therefore online clustering favours scalability.

We follow the online top-down (OTD) approach set out by Menon et al. (2019) and adapt this to approximate non-binary tree structures. Our clustering algorithm is shown in Algorithm 2. Specifically, we introduce two modifications to the original OTD algorithm:

- *Maximum Tree Depth Parameter D*: This is equivalent to the number of inner steps to take in the TreeMAML since the tree is a representation of the inner loop where each layer in the tree represents a single inner step.
- *Non-binary Tree Approximation*: We introduce a hyperparameter ξ which represents how far the similarity of a new task needs to be to the average cluster similarity in order to be considered a child of that same cluster. This is not an absolute value of distance, but it is a multiplicative factor of the standard deviation of the intracluster similarities. Introducing this factor allows clusters at any level to have more than two children.

Algorithm 2 Online top down (OTD) - Non-binary

Require: origin cluster node C with a given set of children $A = \{x_1, x_2, ..x_N\}$
Require: new task x; maximum depth allowed D; similarity metric, $\omega()$
Require: standard deviation multiplicative hyper-parameter ξ;
  if $|A| = 0$ **then**
    new task becomes a new child $A = \{x\}$
  else if $|A| = 1$ **then**
    add new task to set of children $A \leftarrow A \cup \{x\}$
  else if $\omega(A \cup \{x\}) > \omega(A)$ **then**
    identify most similar child $x_* = \arg\min_{x_i}(\omega(\{x_i, x\}))$
    if reached maximum depth $C_{\text{depth}} + 1 = D$ **then**
      add new task to set of children $A \leftarrow A \cup \{x\}$
    else
      recursively perform OTD to create new node $C' = \text{OTD}(x_*, x)$
      add new node to set of children $A \leftarrow (A \setminus \{x_*\}) \cup C'$
    end if
  else if $\omega(A \cup \{x\}) < \omega(A) - \xi\sigma_T$ **then**
    current node and new task become children to new cluster $A \leftarrow \{C, x\}$
  else
    add new task to set of children $A \leftarrow A \cup \{x\}$
  end if

4 Cross-Lingual NLI

Languages can be embraced in a forest of phylogenetic trees (Dunn et al., 2011), for example, the Indo-European and Asian trees (Figure 2). TreeMAML exploits this hierarchical structure to generalize the performance of models across languages, including under-resourced languages, useing all the available languages in the tree.

We adapt a high-resource language model, Multi-BERT (Devlin et al., 2018), to a NLI task. In particular, we consider the problem of Few-Shot NLI using the XNLI data set (Conneau et al., 2018).

This dataset consists of a crowd-sourced collection of 5,000 test and 2,500 dev sentence-label pairs from the MultiNLI corpus. They are annotated with textual entailment and translated into 15 languages: English (en), French (fr), Spanish (es), German (de), Greek(el), Bulgarian (bg), Russian (ru), Turkish, Arabic, Vietnamese (vi), Thai (th), Chinese (zh), Hindi (hi), Swahili and Urdu (ur). Twelve of these languages are part of the same phylogenetic tree, and we focus our study on those languages (see Figure 2). We separately set as target language each language of the tree and we used the eleven remaining languages as auxiliary languages for meta-training.

Each sentence has also an associated topic, or genre, among a collection of 10 possible genres (Face-To-Face, Telephone, Government, 9/11, Letters, Oxford University Press (OUP), Slate, Verbatim, and Government, Fiction). We define each combination of a language and a genre as a task, and we consider the problem of few-shot meta-learning using three shots for each task during meta-training. We add the new target task to the original distribution of tasks, we apply the TreeMAML algorithm and evaluate the model on the target language test set.

We use the TreeMAML algorithm to fine-tune the top layer of Multi-BERT (layer 12), with four inner steps. We compare our results with MAML, using the same number of inner steps, with the baseline Multi-BERT, and with XMAML Nooralahzadeh et al. (2020). An important difference of our approach is that, while XMAML uses only two auxiliary languages to fine tune Multi-BERT to a target language, we use all other languages as auxiliary languages.

4.1 Fixed TreeMAML

In the case of fixed TreeMAML, we use the phylogenetic tree in Figure 2. Fine-tuning of Multi-BERT for the target language benefits not only from proximal (auxiliary) languages, but also from all other languages in the tree that share roots with the target language. For example, if the target language is German, the fine-tuning in fixed TreeMAML would use for the first step of the gradient update all the remaining languages. In the second step, the auxiliary languages would be all the training languages of the Indo-European branch. The third and last steps uses only English.

The accuracy of TreeMAML is consistently higher than the one of the Baseline or MAML and an average of $\sim 3\%$ better than the one achieved by XMAML, see Table 1.

Note that we used a relatively simple version of the phylogenetic tree. A more detailed version could be used for testing under-resourced languages, or to emphasize the dependencies inside

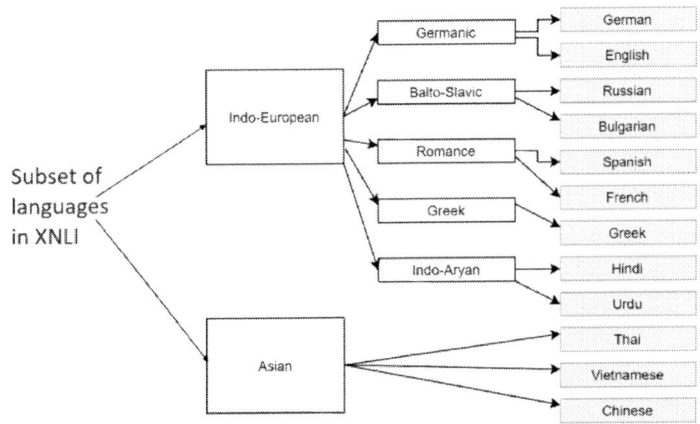

Figure 2: Simplified version of the phylogenetic language tree. The tree include 12 of the 15 languages of XNLI data set and have depth three (Three levels of hierarchy)

the tree. For example, a Bavarian testing data set would fall inside the German branch, or we could add depth to the tree by adding Germanic sub-branches, such as high-german, anglo-frisian and low-franconian.

4.2 Learned TreeMAML

While fixed TreeMAML uses previous knowledge to construct the tree, learned TreeMAML allows learning the relation between languages and genres, potentially reflecting a priory unknown relationships in the XNLI corpus, but also potentially fitting some noise. Note that learned TreeMAML has one additional parameter, the maximum tree depth, as explained in 3.2.

The relationships between languages and genres is learned at each step of gradient descent, for each batch of data. Therefore, the tree for one batch can be different from the tree for the next batch. This difference is due to the fact that the clustering algorithm only cares about the similarity of the gradients, and this similarity does not need to be always the same between two languages. It may depend on the particular words used in the sentences, or in the tasks genres. For example, for a particular batch, some sentences from the same genre in English and French could have closer gradients than other sentences in Germanic languages with a different genre.

The clustering process happens at both training and testing time, which means that learned TreeMAML may improve the accuracy by improving the training, but also by producing the best hierarchy for the target task at testing time. This may be particularly useful for under-resourced languages where non-obvious dependencies between the task in the target languages and the tasks in other languages can be exploited to improve the test accuracy.

As shown in Table 1, fixed/learned TreeMAML outperforms other methods in almost all languages. These results show that using the languages hierarchical structure helps achieving better cross-lingual transfer and higher accuracy in the XNLI task.

In the case of Greek (el), TreeMAML outperforms XMAML, but the baseline Multi-BERT obtains a slightly higher accuracy. This result could be due to the simplified structure of the tree that we use, which does not adequately reflect the actual distance in between languages from the Indo-European family. Besides Greek, Thai (th) is the only language for which TreeMAML does not get higher accuracy. This is mainly due to oversimplified tree used. We used a generic "Asian" language tree, but Chinese, Vietnamese and Thai belong to three separate language families.

Learned TreeMAML performs very similar to fixed TreeMAML in most experiments, achieving higher values for some of the languages. We believe that the difference depends on how well our clustering algorithm performs in each case. For some languages, learned TreeMAML is just learning the same tree structure that we use in fixed TreeMAML, and both algorithms produce almost

	en	fr	es	de	el	bg	ru	vi	th	zh	hi	ur	avg
two languages (Nooralahzadeh et al., 2020)													
Multi-BERT (Baseline)	81.94	75.39	75.79	73.25	69.54	71.60	70.84	73.23	61.18	73.93	64.37	63.71	71.23
XMAML	82.71	75.97	76.51	74.07	70.66	72.77	72.12	73.87	**62.5**	74.85	65.75	64.59	72.20
all languages (ours)													
Multi-BERT (Baseline)	83.56	76.22	76.89	73.11	**72.89**	72.89	71.33	74.67	57.56	74.89	63.11	63.33	71.70
MAML	83.11	78.22	77.11	73.56	69.33	71.78	71.33	74.22	57.33	75.11	63.33	63.78	71.52
Fixed TreeMAML	**84.67**	**79.78**	78.22	76.89	72.00	**74.22**	73.33	74.44	59.56	**79.11**	**66.00**	**66.89**	**73.76**
Learned TreeMAML	84.22	77.33	**79.78**	**78.00**	71.56	73.78	**74.00**	**74.89**	59.78	76.44	65.11	65.56	73.37

Table 1: The top part of the table shows the results of training with two auxiliary languages (Nooralahzadeh et al., 2020). The lower part of the table shows the performance when using all languages (except the target) as auxiliary languages. The difference in the amount of data used for training may account for a part of the difference in performance between XMAML and TreeMAML, and may also explain why our Baseline outperforms XMAML for some languages. The results are reported for each of our experiment by averaging the performance over three different runs. The standard deviation is for all our experiments below 1%.

the same results. In other cases, the clustering algorithm assigns tasks to the wrong branch, making learned TreeMAML perform worse. For some other languages, learned TreeMAML performs better, possibly because it finds other useful relationships, for example tasks belonging to the same genre in different languages.

5 Discussion and Conclusion

This paper presents a method to exploit the data hierarchy in the meta-learning framework, TreeMAML. This algorithm can use a priory knowledge of the data set (fixed TreeMAML), or learn the hierarchical structure using our modification of the OTD clustering algorithm (learned TreeMAML).

Since languages follow a hierarchical phylogenetic tree, we hypothesized that we could use TreeMAML to meta-train models for cross-lingual understanding. We applied TreeMAML to the cross-lingual XNLI problem and show an improvement in accuracy $\sim 3\%$ with respect to the state of the art obtained by XMAML (Nooralahzadeh et al., 2020) (Table 1). The improvement with respect to XMAML suggests that using all available languages results in increased performance. Furthermore, the improvement with respect to MAML suggests that using the tree structure of those languages also improves performance.

How much each auxiliary language contributes to the target language's performance may depend on its relative position in the language tree. These results are especially encouraging for meta-training of cross-lingual understanding tasks for under-resourced languages. Future work may include an improved algorithm that takes into account not only the position of a language in the tree, but also the distances between languages in a branch by, for example, introducing weighted averaging of the gradients.

In our NLI experiments, learned TreeMAML is in most cases as good or even better than fixed TreeMAML. One possible explanation is that clustering learns the tree for each batch of data at each gradient step, which allows it to pick up NLI-relevant similarities that are not described by a phylogenetic tree, as the genre of the task in the XNLI data set, structural similarities and lexical similarity, which can be the result of language contact, as for example lexical borrowings. This may help with cross-lingual understanding tasks for uncommon languages for which the exact position in the tree may be unclear or not enough data may be available.

As discussed in section 4.2, the lack of improvement in accuracy in the Greek language and the low performance in Thai can be rooted in the experimental design's naive assumptions about: which languages to include in the experiment, and the correctness of the language tree. The results in which TreeMAMl performs worse than the other algorithms speak in favour of the robustness of this algorithm to properly learn cross-lingual relationships and exploit them to perform natural language understanding tasks. Therefore, the use of learned TreeMAML could help with the internationalization of the NLP models.

References

Alessandro Achille, Michael Lam, Rahul Tewari, Avinash Ravichandran, Subhransu Maji, Charless Fowlkes, Stefano Soatto, and Pietro Perona. 2019. Task2Vec: Task Embedding for Meta-Learning. *arXiv:1902.03545*. ArXiv: 1902.03545.

Alexis Conneau, Guillaume Lample, Ruty Rinott, Adina Williams, Samuel R. Bowman, Holger Schwenk, and Veselin Stoyanov. 2018. XNLI: Evaluating Cross-lingual Sentence Representations. *arXiv:1809.05053*.

Jacob Devlin, Ming-Wei Chang, Kenton Lee, and Kristina Toutanova. 2018. BERT: Pre-training of Deep Bidirectional Transformers for Language Understanding. *arXiv:1810.04805*.

Zi-Yi Dou, Keyi Yu, and Antonios Anastasopoulos. 2019. Investigating Meta-Learning Algorithms for Low-Resource Natural Language Understanding Tasks. *arXiv:1908.10423*.

Michael Dunn, Simon J. Greenhill, Stephen C. Levinson, and Russell D. Gray. 2011. Evolved structure of language shows lineage-specific trends in word-order universals. *Nature*, 473(7345):79–82.

Chelsea Finn, Pieter Abbeel, and Sergey Levine. 2017. Model-Agnostic Meta-Learning for Fast Adaptation of Deep Networks. *arXiv:1703.03400*. ArXiv: 1703.03400.

Jiatao Gu, Yong Wang, Yun Chen, Kyunghyun Cho, and Victor O. K. Li. 2018. Meta-Learning for Low-Resource Neural Machine Translation. *arXiv:1808.08437*.

Timothy Hospedales, Antreas Antoniou, Paul Micaelli, and Amos Storkey. 2020. Meta-Learning in Neural Networks: A Survey. *arXiv:2004.05439*. ArXiv: 2004.05439.

Ghassen Jerfel, Thomas L Griffiths, Erin Grant, and Katherine Heller. 2019. Reconciling meta-learning and continual learning with online mixtures of tasks. *NIPS*, page 12.

Sameeksha Katoch, Kowshik Thopalli, Jayaraman J. Thiagarajan, Pavan Turaga, and Andreas Spanias. 2020. Invenio: Discovering Hidden Relationships Between Tasks/Domains Using Structured Meta Learning. *arXiv:1911.10600*. ArXiv: 1911.10600.

Yanbin Liu, Juho Lee, Minseop Park, Saehoon Kim, Eunho Yang, Sung Ju Hwang, and Yi Yang. 2019. Learning to Propagate Labels: Transductive Propagation Network for Few-shot Learning. *arXiv:1805.10002*. ArXiv: 1805.10002.

Aditya Krishna Menon, Anand Rajagopalan, Baris Sumengen, Gui Citovsky, Qin Cao, and Sanjiv Kumar. 2019. Online Hierarchical Clustering Approximations. *arXiv:1909.09667*. ArXiv: 1909.09667.

Farhad Nooralahzadeh, Giannis Bekoulis, Johannes Bjerva, and Isabelle Augenstein. 2020. Zero-Shot Cross-Lingual Transfer with Meta Learning. *arXiv:2003.02739*. ArXiv: 2003.02739.

Sebastian Ruder. 2017. An Overview of Multi-Task Learning in Deep Neural Networks. *arXiv:1706.05098*. ArXiv: 1706.05098.

Nitish Srivastava and Russ R Salakhutdinov. 2013. Discriminative Transfer Learning with Tree-based Priors. In C. J. C. Burges, L. Bottou, M. Welling, Z. Ghahramani, and K. Q. Weinberger, editors, *Advances in Neural Information Processing Systems 26*, pages 2094–2102. Curran Associates, Inc.

Huaxiu Yao, Ying Wei, Junzhou Huang, and Zhenhui Li. 2019. Hierarchically Structured Meta-learning. *arXiv:1905.05301*. ArXiv: 1905.05301.

Amir Zamir, Alexander Sax, William Shen, Leonidas Guibas, Jitendra Malik, and Silvio Savarese. 2018. Taskonomy: Disentangling Task Transfer Learning. *arXiv:1804.08328*. ArXiv: 1804.08328.

Yu Zhang and Qiang Yang. 2018. A Survey on Multi-Task Learning. *arXiv:1707.08114*. ArXiv: 1707.08114.

Addressing Zero-Resource Domains Using Document-Level Context in Neural Machine Translation

Dario Stojanovski and **Alexander Fraser**
Center for Information and Language Processing
LMU Munich, Germany
{stojanovski,fraser}@cis.lmu.de

Abstract

Achieving satisfying performance in machine translation on domains for which there is no training data is challenging. Traditional supervised domain adaptation is not suitable for addressing such zero-resource domains because it relies on in-domain parallel data. We show that when in-domain parallel data is not available, access to document-level context enables better capturing of domain generalities compared to only having access to a single sentence. Having access to more information provides a more reliable domain estimation. We present two document-level Transformer models which are capable of using large context sizes and we compare these models against strong Transformer baselines. We obtain improvements for the two zero-resource domains we study. We additionally provide an analysis where we vary the amount of context and look at the case where in-domain data is available.

1 Introduction

Training robust neural machine translation models for a wide variety of domains is an active field of work. NMT requires large bilingual resources which are not available for many domains and languages. When there is no data available for a given domain, e.g., in the case of web-based MT tools, this is a significant challenge. Despite the fact that these tools are usually trained on large scale datasets, they are often used to translate documents from a domain which was not seen during training. We call this scenario zero-resource domain adaptation and present an approach using document-level context to address it.

When an NMT model receives a test sentence from a zero-resource domain, it can be matched to similar domains in the training data. This is to some extent done implicitly by standard NMT. Alternatively, this matching can be facilitated by a domain adaptation technique such as using special domain tokens and features (Kobus et al., 2017; Tars and Fishel, 2018). However, it is not always easy to determine the domain of a sentence without larger context. Access to document-level context makes it more probable that domain signals can be observed, i.e., words representative of a domain are more likely to be encountered. We hypothesize that this facilitates better matching of unseen domains to domains seen during training and provide experimental evidence supporting this hypothesis.

Recent work has shown that contextual information improves MT (Miculicich et al., 2018; Voita et al., 2019b; Maruf et al., 2019), often by improving anaphoric pronoun translation quality, which can be addressed well with limited context. However, in order to address discourse phenomena such as coherence and cohesion, access to larger context is preferable. Voita et al. (2019b,a) were the first to show large improvements on lexical cohesion in a controlled setting using challenge sets. However, previous work did not make clear whether previous models can help with disambiguation of polysemous words where the sense is domain-dependent.

In this work, we study the usefulness of document-level context for zero-resource domain adaptation (which we think has not been studied in this way before). We propose two novel Transformer models which can efficiently handle large context and test their ability to model multiple domains at once. We show that document-level models trained on multi-domain datasets provide improvements on zero-resource domains. We evaluate on English→German translation using TED and PatTR (patent descriptions) as zero-resource domains. In addition to measuring translation quality, we conduct a manual evaluation targeted at word disambiguation. We also present additional experiments on classical domain adaptation where access to in-domain TED and PatTR data is allowed.

Proceedings of the Second Workshop on Domain Adaptation for NLP, pages 80–93
April 20, 2021.

Our first proposed model, which we call the domain embedding model (DomEmb) applies average or max pooling over all context embeddings and adds this representation to each source token-level embedding in the Transformer. The second model is conceptually similar to previous work on context-aware NMT (Voita et al., 2018; Stojanovski and Fraser, 2018; Miculicich et al., 2018; Zhang et al., 2018) and introduces additional multi-head attention components in the encoder and decoder in order to handle the context. However, in order to facilitate larger context sizes, it creates a compressed context representation by applying average or max pooling with a fixed window and stride size. We compare our proposed models against previous context-aware NMT architectures and techniques for handling multi-domain setups, and show they improve upon strong baselines. The proposed models encode context in a coarse-grained way. They only have a limited ability to model discourse phenomena such as coreference resolution, so the gains we see in a multi-domain setup show that they encode domain information. Evaluating on multiple and zero-resource domains allows us to show that context can be used to capture domain information.

The contributions of our work can be summarized as follows: we (i) propose two NMT models which are able to handle large context sizes, (ii) show that document-level context in a multi-domain experimental setup is beneficial for handling zero-resource domains, (iii) show the effect of different context sizes and (iv) study traditional domain adaptation with access to in-domain data.

2 Related Work

Domain adaptation Several previous works address the problem that standard NMT may fail to adequately model all domains in a multi-domain setup even when all of the domains are known in advance. Kobus et al. (2017) introduce using domain tags for this problem, a similar method to the domain embedding model in our paper. These domain tags are mapped to corresponding embeddings and are either inserted at the beginning of the sentence or concatenated to the token-level embeddings. The domain embeddings are reserved for specific domains and are fixed for all sentences in a given domain. The number of distinct domain embeddings is limited to the number of known domains. Tars and Fishel (2018) define a similar approach which uses oracle domain tags and tags obtained using supervised methods and unsupervised clustering. However, clustering limits how many domains can be taken into consideration. Furthermore, this approach assumes that sufficient domain information can be obtained from a single sentence alone. Document-level classifiers (Xu et al., 2007) address this problem, but they are not jointly trained with the MT model. Further work in multi-domain MT is Foster and Kuhn (2007) who propose mixture models to dynamically adapt to the target domain, Foster et al. (2010) who build on this work and include instance weighting, Zeng et al. (2018) where domain-specific and domain-shared annotations from adversarial domain classifiers are used and Britz et al. (2017) where a discriminator is used to backpropagate domain signals.

Continued training is an established technique for domain adaptation if access to in-domain resources is possible. The method entails initially training on out-of-domain data, and then continuing training on in-domain data (Luong and Manning, 2015). Chen et al. (2017) and Zhang and Xiong (2018) improve upon this paradigm by integrating a domain classifier or a domain similarity metric into NMT and modifying the training cost based on weights indicating in-domain or out-of-domain data. Sajjad et al. (2017) and Farajian et al. (2017) use continued training in a multi-domain setup and propose various ways of fine-tuning to in-domain data. Standard continued training (Luong and Manning, 2015) leads to catastrophic forgetting, evident by the degrading performance on the out-of-domain dataset. Freitag and Al-Onaizan (2016) address this issue by ensembling the original and the fine-tuned model. We show that our model obtains significant improvements compared to a baseline with the ensembling paradigm. In contrast to these previous works, we do not know the domains during training. Our proposed approaches model the domain implicitly by looking at document-level context. Moreover, we evaluate performance on domains not seen during training.

Naradowsky et al. (2020) adapt to unseen domains using bandit learning techniques. The method relies on explicit user feedback which is not always easily available. Bapna and Firat (2019) propose a retrieval-based method that, at inference time, adapts to domains not seen during training. However, they assume access to in-domain parallel data at inference time, and they retrieve parallel phrases from this in-domain data. In our

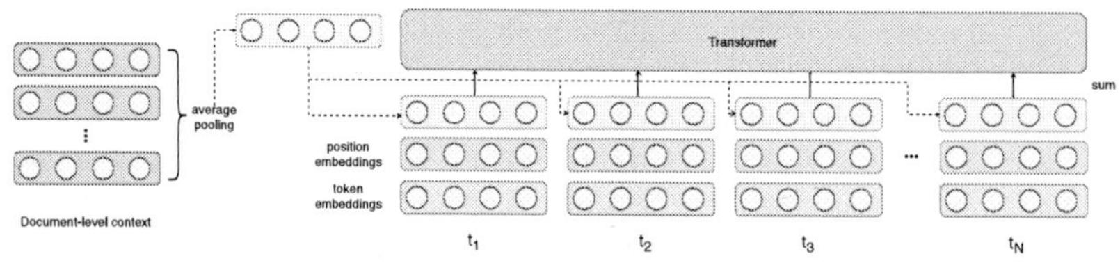

Figure 1: Domain embedding Transformer.

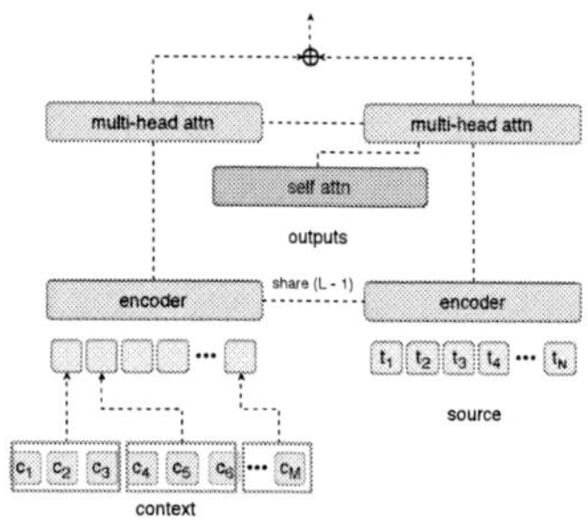

Figure 2: Context-aware Transformer with pooling.

zero-resource experiments, we have no access to in-domain parallel data.

Context-aware NMT A separate field of inquiry is context-aware NMT which proposes integrating cross-sentence context (Tiedemann and Scherrer, 2017; Bawden et al., 2018; Voita et al., 2018; Zhang et al., 2018; Stojanovski and Fraser, 2018; Miculicich et al., 2018; Tu et al., 2018; Maruf and Haffari, 2018; Voita et al., 2019b; Maruf et al., 2019; Yang et al., 2019; Voita et al., 2019a; Tan et al., 2019). These works show that context helps with discourse phenomena such as anaphoric pronouns, deixis and lexical cohesion. Kim et al. (2019) show that using context can improve topic-aware lexical choice, but in a single-domain setup.

Previous work on context-aware NMT has mostly worked with limited context. Miculicich et al. (2018) address the problem by reusing previously computed encoder representations, but report no BLEU improvements by using context larger than 3 sentences. Zhang et al. (2018) find 2 sentences of context to work the best. Maruf and Haffari (2018) use a fixed pretrained RNN encoder for context sentences and only train the document-level RNN. Junczys-Dowmunt (2019) concatenates sentences into very large inputs and outputs as in Tiedemann and Scherrer (2017). Maruf et al. (2019) propose a scalable context-aware model by using sparsemax which can ignore certain words and hierarchical attention which first computes sentence-level attention scores and subsequently word-level scores. However, for domain adaptation, the full encoder representation is too granular and not the most efficient way to obtain domain signals, for which we present evidence in our experiments. Stojanovski and Fraser (2019a); Macé and Servan (2019) propose a similar approach to our domain embedding model, but they do not investigate it from a domain adaptation perspective.

To our knowledge, our work is the first at the intersection of domain adaptation and context-aware NMT and shows that document-level context can be used to address zero-resource domains.

3 Model

The models we propose in this work are extensions of the Transformer (Vaswani et al., 2017). The first approach introduces separate domain embeddings applied to each token-level embedding. The second is conceptually based on previous context-aware models (Voita et al., 2018; Stojanovski and Fraser, 2018; Miculicich et al., 2018; Zhang et al., 2018). Both models are capable of handling document-level context. We modify the training data so that all sentences have access to the previous sentences within the corresponding source document. Access to the document-level context is available at test time as well. Sentences are separated with a special <SEP> token from the next sentence. We train and evaluate our models with a 10 sentence context.

3.1 Domain Embedding Transformer

The first model is shown in Figure 1. It is inspired by Kobus et al. (2017) which concatenates a special domain tag to each token-level embedding. Kobus et al. (2017) assume access to oracle domain tags during training. However, at inference, perfect domain knowledge is not possible. Consequently, the domain has to be predicted in advance which creates a mismatch between training and inference. An additional problem is inaccurately predicted domain tags at test time. We modify this approach by replacing the predefined special domain tag with one inferred from the document context. A disadvantage of this approach as opposed to Kobus et al. (2017) is that there is no clear domain indicator. However, the model is trained jointly with the component inferring the domain which increases the capacity of the model to match a sentence from an unseen domain to a domain seen during training.

The main challenge is producing the domain embedding from the context. We use maximum (DomEmb(max)) or average pooling (DomEmb(avg)) over all token-level context embeddings, both resulting in a single embedding representation. We do not apply self-attention over the context in this model. The intuition is that the embeddings will contain domain information in certain regions of the representation and that this can be extracted by max or average pooling. More domain-specific words will presumably increase the related domain signal. In contrast to a sentence-level model, large context can help to more robustly estimate the domain. Based on preliminary experimental results, we add a feed-forward neural network after the pooled embedding representation in DomEmb(avg), but not in DomEmb(max). We represent each token as a sum of positional, token-level embeddings and the inferred domain embedding. As the model only averages embeddings, the computational overhead is small. A computational efficiency analysis is provided in the appendix.

3.2 Context-Aware Transformer with Pooling

The second approach (CtxPool) is similar to previous work on context-aware NMT (e.g., (Stojanovski and Fraser, 2018; Zhang et al., 2018)). The model is outlined in Figure 2. It first creates a compact representation of the context by applying max or average pooling over the context with certain window and stride sizes. The intuition is similar to DomEmb, but pooling over a window provides a more granular representation. We use the concatenation of all context sentences (separated by <SEP>) as input to CtxPool.

The output of applying max or average pooling over time is used as a context representation which is input to a Transformer encoder. We share the first $L-1$ encoder layers between the main sentence and the context. L is the number of encoder layers. In the decoder, we add an additional multi-head attention (MHA) over the context. This attention is conditioned on the MHA representation from the main sentence encoder. Subsequently, these two representations are merged using a gated sum. The gate controls information flow from the context.

In contrast to DomEmb, CtxPool can be used to handle other discourse phenomena such as anaphora resolution. In this work, we use a window size of 10, suitable for domain adaptation. For anaphora, summarizing ten neighboring words makes it difficult to extract antecedent relationships. Careful tuning of these parameters in future work may allow modeling both local and global context.

4 Experiments

4.1 Experimental Setup

We train En→De models on Europarl, NewsCommentary, OpenSubtitles, Rapid and Ubuntu. TED and PatTR are considered to be zero-resource domains for which we have no parallel data. In additional experiments, we also consider classical domain adaptation where we do use TED and PatTR parallel data in a continued training setup. The models are implemented in Sockeye (Hieber et al., 2017). The code and the datasets are publicly available.[1] The preprocessing details and model hyperparameters are provided in the appendix.

4.2 Datasets

The datasets for some domains are very large. For example, OpenSubtitles contains 22M sentences and PatTR 12M. Due to limited computational resources, we randomly sample documents from these domains, ending up with approximately 10% of the initial dataset size. We keep the original size for the remaining datasets. Dataset sizes for all domains are presented in Table 1. The development and test sets are also randomly sampled from the original datasets. We sample entire documents rather than specific sentences. For TED we use tst2012 as dev and tst2013 as test set. The TED and PatTR dev sets are only used in the fine-tuning experiments where we assume access to in-domain data and are not used in any other experiment.

Europarl, NewsCommentary, OpenSubtitles, Rapid and TED are provided with document boundaries. Ubuntu lacks a clear discourse structure and PatTR is sentence-aligned, but provides document IDs. Previous work has shown that context-aware NMT performance is not significantly degraded

[1] https://www.cis.uni-muenchen.de/~dario/projects/zero_domain

domain	train	dev	test
Europarl	1.8M	3.2K	3.0K
NewsCommentary	0.3M	1.5K	1.5K
OpenSubtitles	2.2M	2.7K	3.3K
Rapid	1.5M	2.5K	2.5K
Ubuntu	11K	1.1K	0.6K
TED	0.2M	1.7K	1.0K
PatTR	1.2M	2.0K	2.2K

Table 1: Domain datasets sizes in sentences.

from lack of document boundaries (Müller et al., 2018; Stojanovski and Fraser, 2019b) or random context (Voita et al., 2018). To a large extent, both issues can be ignored, given the nature of our models. DomEmb is oblivious to the sentence order. CtxPool preserves some notion of sequentiality, but it should also be robust to these issues. Furthermore, we focus on obtaining domain signals. Even in an extreme case where the context comes from a different document (but from the same domain) we hypothesize similar performance. We later conduct an ablation study into whether arbitrary context from the same domain has a negative effect on performance. The results partially support our hypothesis by either matching or exceeding sentence-level performance, but also show that the correct context is important to obtain the best results.

4.3 Baselines

We compare our proposed methods against a sentence-level baseline (SentBase) and the domain tag (TagBase) approach (Kobus et al., 2017). We train TagBase with oracle domain tags, while at test time, we use tags obtained from a document-level domain classifier. All sentences within a document are marked with the same predicted domain tag. The domain classifier is a two-layer feed-forward network and the documents are represented as a bag-of-words. The classifier obtains an accuracy of 98.6%. By design, documents from TED and PatTR were marked with tags from the remaining domains. Additionally, we compare with a context-aware model (CtxBase) which is similar to CtxPool, but we feed the full context to the context Transformer encoder, without applying max or average pooling beforehand. This model has token-level granular access to the context. We also train a concatenation model (ConcBase) (Tiedemann and Scherrer, 2017) using source-side context.

5 Results

5.1 Zero-Resource Domain Adaptation

In zero-resource domain adaptation experiments, we do not use any data from TED or PatTR, neither as training nor development data. The models are trained on our multi-domain dataset consisting of five domains. The results are shown in Table 2. We compute statistical significance with paired bootstrap resampling (Koehn, 2004).

SentBase achieves 16.7 and 32.9 BLEU on PatTR and TED respectively. The domains seen during training are more similar to TED in comparison to PatTR which is the reason for the large BLEU score differences. Our proposed models improve on PatTR by up to 0.4 BLEU and on TED by up to 1.0 BLEU. Improvements vary, but all models increase the BLEU score. The TagBase model does not improve significantly over SentBase.

	PatTR	TED
SentBase	16.7	32.9
TagBase	16.8	33.0
DomEmb(max)	**17.1**†	**33.9**†
DomEmb(avg)	**17.1**†	33.8†
CtxPool(max)	16.9	33.6‡
CtxPool(avg)	**17.1**†	**33.9**†

Table 2: Results on zero-resource domain adaptation for PatTR and TED. Best results in bold. †- statistical significance with $p < 0.01$, ‡- $p < 0.05$.

Our document-level models are robust across the two domains. These results confirm our assumption that access to document-level context provides for a domain signal. These models are oblivious to the actual characteristics of the domain since it was not seen in training, but presumably, they managed to match the zero-resource domain to a similar one. We assume that the reason for the larger improvements on TED in comparison to PatTR is that TED is a more similar domain to the domains seen in training. As a result, matching TED to seen domains was easier for all models. Table 2 shows that our proposed models improve on PatTR and TED and provides evidence that document-level context is useful for addressing zero-resource domains.

5.2 Evaluating Domains Seen During Training

We assume that the improvements on zero-resource domains are because of document-level models having an increased capability to model domain.

domain	SentBase	TagBase	DomEmb(max)	DomEmb(avg)	CtxPool(max)	CtxPool(avg)
Europarl	31.3	31.4	32.3†	**32.5**†	32.4†	32.3†
NewsComm	32.8	32.6	32.7	33.0	**33.1**‡	32.8
OpenSub	26.6	27.1‡	27.0‡	**27.5**†	27.3†	27.4†
Rapid	40.7	40.9	41.1‡	41.5†	41.4†	**41.6**†
Ubuntu	31.5	**34.6**†	32.8‡	31.9	31.6	32.1
Average	30.4	30.9	**31.0**	**31.0**	30.9	**31.0**
Joint	29.1	29.2	29.5†	**29.8**†	29.7†	**29.8**†

Table 3: Results on the multi-domain dataset. Joint and average scores including PatTR and TED. Statistical significance computed for all scores except for Average. †- $p < 0.01$, ‡- $p < 0.05$.

As a result, we also evaluate on the other domains which were seen during training. We show average BLEU and the BLEU score on the concatenation of all test sets. This is a useful way to evaluate in a multi-domain setting because it is less sensitive to larger improvements on a smaller test set.

Table 3 shows the results. We first compare the baseline against DomEmb(avg). The smallest improvement is on NewsCommentary, only 0.2 BLEU. Improvements vary between 0.8 and 1.2 BLEU on Europarl, OpenSubtitles and Rapid. On Ubuntu, this model improves only by 0.4 BLEU. Joint and average BLEU improve by 0.7 and 0.6, respectively. Replacing average pooling with maximum pooling leads to slightly worse results on all domains except Ubuntu, but still improves upon the baseline. Our assumption is that averaging handles situations when there is a mix of domain signals because it can emphasize the more frequent domain signals. Max pooling is not able to differentiate between less and more frequent domain signals.

CtxPool(avg) and DomEmb(avg) perform similarly and have the same average and joint BLEU scores. Max pooling is slightly worse as shown by the performance of CtxPool(max). TagBase is not very effective in our experiments, improving slightly on some domains and only performing well on Ubuntu. We show that document-level context is useful for modeling multiple known domains at the same time. In the appendix we show translation examples from SentBase and DomEmb(avg).

5.3 Context Length

We also investigate the effect of context size on DomEmb(avg). Previous work on context-aware NMT (Zhang et al., 2018; Miculicich et al., 2018) typically showed that large context fails to provide for consistent gains. But this applies to more granular models which resemble the context-aware baseline CtxBase. In contrast, we observe that larger context does provide for improvements. We assume that for DomEmb, access to more context improves the likelihood of encountering domain-specific tokens.

domain	ctx=1	ctx=5	ctx=10
Europarl	31.5	32.0†‡	**32.5**†♣
NewsComm	32.7	32.9	**33.0**
OpenSub	26.8	27.2*‡	**27.5**†✧
Rapid	41.1‡	**41.5***‡	**41.5***
Ubuntu	32.5	**32.9***‡	31.9
PatTR	17.0‡	**17.2**‡	17.1
TED	33.5**	33.7‡	**33.8**
Average	30.7	**31.1**	31.0
Joint	29.3‡	29.7†‡	**29.8**†♣

Table 4: Results using the DomEmb(avg) model with different context sizes. Context size in number of previous sentences. ‡- $p < 0.01$, ** - $p < 0.05$, compared to SentBase. †- $p < 0.01$, * - $p < 0.05$, compared to *ctx=1*. ♣ - $p < 0.01$, ✧ - $p < 0.05$, compared to *ctx=5*.

We compare different context sizes and show the results in Table 4. A context size of 1 (*ctx=1*) obtains the lowest scores on all domains. Using *ctx=5* is comparable or slightly worse than *ctx=10*. Both *ctx=1* and *ctx=5* get higher scores on Ubuntu and obtain significant improvements over SentBase on the full test set. Significance indicators for *ctx=10* compared with respect to SentBase were already presented in Table 3. Due to resource limitations, we do not conduct a similar study for CtxPool.

5.4 Comparison to Context-Aware Baselines

Previous work on context-aware NMT has shown improvements in single-domain scenarios. In our work, we put two context-aware models to the test in a multi-domain setup. All models are trained with a 5 sentence context. The results in Table 5 show that all models improve to varying degrees. They perform similarly on NewsCommentary and

OpenSubtitles. CtxBase and ConcBase obtain better results on Europarl than DomEmb(avg) and worse on Ubuntu. CtxBase is best on Rapid. Both baselines obtained better scores on TED, showing they have some capacity to transfer to unseen domains. However, both failed to improve on PatTR.

domain	CtxBase	ConcBase	DomEmb(a)
Europarl	**32.4**†	**32.4**†	32.0†
NewsCo	32.8	32.7	**32.9**
OpenSub	27.2‡	**27.4**†	27.2†
Rapid	**41.8**†	40.8	41.5†
Ubuntu	31.6	29.1	**32.9**†
PatTR	16.6	14.8	**17.2**†
TED	**34.1**†	**34.1**†	33.7†
Average	30.9	30.2	**31.1**
Joint	**29.7**†	29.5	**29.7**†

Table 5: Comparison with the context-aware baseline CtxBase and the concatenation model ConcBase. †- p < 0.01, ‡- p < 0.05 compared to SentBase.

We use 5 sentences of context for this experiment. Scaling the baseline models to large context is challenging with regards to computational efficiency and memory usage. In contrast, DomEmb scales easily to larger context. Furthermore, our analysis shows that DomEmb(avg) has the best average and joint score (CtxBase obtains the same joint score), improves on both unseen domains and consistently obtains significant improvements on all domains except NewsCommentary. As previous works show (Müller et al., 2018), these context-aware baselines improve fine-grained discourse phenomena such as anaphora resolution. We show in our manual analysis that DomEmb(avg) does not improve anaphoric pronoun translation which indicates that the improvements of our proposed model and the context-aware baselines are orthogonal.

5.5 Translation of Domain-Specific Words

We also evaluated the translation of domain-specific words. We extracted the most important words from a domain based on TF-IDF scores and selected the top 100 with the highest scores which have more than 3 characters. Next, we follow Liu et al. (2018) and compute alignments using *fastalign* (Dyer et al., 2013) based on the training set and force align the test set source sentences to the references and generated translations. We then compute the F_1 score of the translation of the domain-specific words. Results are shown in Table 6. We compare SentBase with DomEmb(avg).

	SentBase	DomEmb(avg)
Europarl	0.661	**0.667**
NewsComm	0.649	**0.650**
OpenSub	0.435	**0.453**
Rapid	0.724	**0.730**
Ubuntu	0.434	**0.439**
PatTR	0.407	**0.409**
TED	0.551	**0.565**

Table 6: F_1 score for domain-specific words.

domain	SentBase	DomEmb(a)
PatTR	34.4	34.4
	ensemble	
Europarl	29.0	**29.6**†
NewsCommentary	28.7	**28.9**
OpenSubtitles	22.8	**23.4**†
Rapid	35.1	**35.7**†
Ubuntu	33.0	**33.4**
PatTR	29.2	**29.4**
TED	29.8	**30.4**‡
Average	29.7	**30.1**
Joint	30.2	**30.6**†

Table 7: Domain adaptation results on PatTR for SentBase and DomEmb(avg). †- p < 0.01, ‡- p < 0.05.

domain	SentBase	DomEmb(a)
TED	36.1	**36.6**‡
	ensemble	
Europarl	30.4	**30.8**†
NewsCommentary	31.9	**32.2**‡
OpenSubtitles	24.6	**25.4**†
Rapid	38.8	**39.5**†
Ubuntu	**32.7**	32.4
PatTR	16.9	**17.0**‡
TED	35.4	**35.8**‡
Average	30.1	**30.4**
Joint	28.4	**28.8**†

Table 8: Domain adaptation results on TED for SentBase and DomEmb(avg). †- p < 0.01, ‡- p < 0.05.

DomEmb(avg) improved the F_1 score across all domains with the largest improvements on OpenSubtitles and TED. Our assumption is that the baseline translation of OpenSubtitles domain-specific words is more formal. A large part of the seen domains contain formal language in contrast to the

domain	Europarl	NewsComm	OpenSub	Rapid	Ubuntu	PatTR	TED	True
Europarl	**31.3**	30.1	30.6	30.3	30.7	30.7	30.7	32.5
NewsComm	30.6	**32.8**	31.9	30.1	32.3	31.5	32.1	33.0
OpenSub	22.2	23.1	**27.1**	22.0	25.4	24.4	26.7	27.5
Rapid	39.5	37.0	38.7	**41.3**	40.3	40.4	38.9	41.5
Ubuntu	29.3	29.1	29.2	29.6	**31.4**	31.1	30.1	31.9
PatTR	16.6	16.2	16.3	16.5	16.9	**17.1**	16.8	17.1
TED	30.0	33.0	33.1	28.8	33.4	31.5	**33.7**	33.8

Table 9: Results from the ablation study investigating the influence of context from a different domain. Each row shows which domain is used as the test set and each column shows from which domain the context originates.

informal subtitles. Lack of context seems to have biased SentBase to generate more formal translations. We later conduct a manual analysis on the TED test set where we confirm that word sense disambiguation is indeed improved in DomEmb(avg).

5.6 Domain Adaptation with Available In-Domain Data

We also conduct a classical domain adaptation evaluation where access to in-domain data is allowed. We either use PatTR or TED as in-domain data and evaluate with SentBase and DomEmb(avg). In both cases we consider the concatenation of the remaining domains as out-of-domain. This setup differs from zero-resource domain adaptation because we assume access to in-domain training and dev data.

First, we train the baseline and DomEmb(avg) on out-of-domain data. Since these initial models are identical to the ones in the zero-resource setup, we reuse them. We then continue training on the corresponding in-domain data. Table 7 shows the results for PatTR. Fine-tuning the baseline and DomEmb(avg) on PatTR improves BLEU by a large margin, both obtaining 34.4 BLEU. The results are unsurprising because our model is tailored to multi-domain setups and is unlikely to contribute to large improvements when fine-tuning on a single domain. Identifying the domain in such a case is trivial and using large context should not be helpful.

The strengths of our approach come to light by comparing it against SentBase in an ensembling scenario as in Freitag and Al-Onaizan (2016). We ensemble DomEmb(avg) trained on out-of-domain data with DomEmb(avg) fine-tuned on in-domain data and do the same for SentBase. The DomEmb(avg) ensemble is better than the SentBase ensemble on all domains and on joint BLEU. Similar results are obtained when fine-tuning on TED which are shown in Table 8.

5.7 Ablation

We previously hypothesized that our models will benefit from context from different documents within the same domain. We conduct an ablation study to test this assumption using DomEmb(avg) model, similar to the study in (Kobus et al., 2017), where they investigated the effect of giving the wrong domain tag to every sentence.

For DomEmb(avg), we simulate this approach by replacing the real contextual representation of each test sentence with C_d, which is context representative of domain d. We first compute $C_d^{'} = \frac{1}{N_d}\sum_{i=1}^{N_d} c_i^d$ where c_i^d is the contextual representation of a test sentence in domain d and N_d is the number of test sentences in d. c_i^d is the average of the context token-level embeddings for sentence i. Finally, $C_d = \arg\max_{c_i^d} cos(c_i^d, C_d^{'})$. This procedure is conducted for each domain d separately.

Table 9 shows the results. On OpenSubtitles, Rapid, PatTR and TED, DomEmb(avg) improves on the sentence-level baseline if presented with context from the same domain (which is usually not from the same document). On Europarl, NewsCommentary and Ubuntu, it performs similarly to the baseline. In almost all cases, providing a mismatched context degrades the performance of the original DomEmb(avg). The results show that the model is relatively robust to incorrect but closely related context which provides evidence for our hypothesis that DomEmb captures domain-relevant features. However, the correct context is important to obtain the best results across all domains. Our finding is in contrast with recent results (Li et al., 2020) where they show that multi-encoder context-aware NMT models do not encode contextual information.

5.8 Manual Analysis

We conduct a manual analysis of SentBase and DomEmb(avg) by inspecting them on the TED test set. We only consider translation differences related to word senses and ignore other types of mistakes. We find 156 cases where the two models translate a word in a different sense and at least one of them outputs the correct sense. We define 3 categories: (i) one model is correct while the other wrong; (ii) both are correct, but one is closer to the actual meaning and (iii) both are correct, but one matches the reference translation. DomEmb(avg) is better on (i) in 43 cases as opposed to the 19 cases where SentBase is better. The ratio of DomEmb(avg) being correct in contrast to SentBase is 23/12 in (ii) and 38/21 in (iii). This shows that DomEmb(avg) is better at coherence which is closely related to better domain modeling in multi-domain setups where the number of probable senses is larger than in a single domain. Furthermore, we find that DomEmb(avg) does not improve on pronoun translation. In fact, in several cases it introduced errors, thus ruling out better coreference resolution as a source of improvements.

6 Conclusion

We presented document-level context-aware NMT models and showed their effectiveness in addressing zero-resource domains. We compared against strong baselines and showed that document-level context can be leveraged to obtain domain signals. The proposed models benefit from large context and also obtain strong performance in multi-domain scenarios. Our experimental results show the proposed models obtain improvements of up to 1.0 BLEU in this difficult zero-resource domain setup. Furthermore, they show that document-level context should be further explored in future work on domain adaptation and suggest that larger context would be beneficial for other discourse phenomena such as coherence.

Acknowledgments

This work was supported by the European Research Council (ERC) under the European Union's Horizon 2020 research and innovation programme (grant agreement No. 640550) and by the German Research Foundation (DFG; grant FR 2829/4-1).

References

Ankur Bapna and Orhan Firat. 2019. Non-Parametric Adaptation for Neural Machine Translation. In *Proceedings of the 2019 Conference of the North American Chapter of the Association for Computational Linguistics: Human Language Technologies, Volume 1 (Long and Short Papers)*, pages 1921–1931, Minneapolis, Minnesota. Association for Computational Linguistics.

Rachel Bawden, Rico Sennrich, Alexandra Birch, and Barry Haddow. 2018. Evaluating Discourse Phenomena in Neural Machine Translation. In *NAACL 2018*, New Orleans, USA.

Denny Britz, Quoc Le, and Reid Pryzant. 2017. Effective Domain Mixing for Neural Machine Translation. In *Proceedings of the Second Conference on Machine Translation*, pages 118–126. Association for Computational Linguistics.

Boxing Chen, Colin Cherry, George Foster, and Samuel Larkin. 2017. Cost Weighting for Neural Machine Translation Domain Adaptation. In *Proceedings of the First Workshop on Neural Machine Translation*, pages 40–46. Association for Computational Linguistics.

Chris Dyer, Victor Chahuneau, and Noah A. Smith. 2013. A Simple, Fast, and Effective Reparameterization of IBM Model 2. In *Proceedings of the 2013 Conference of the North American Chapter of the Association for Computational Linguistics: Human Language Technologies*, pages 644–648. Association for Computational Linguistics.

M. Amin Farajian, Marco Turchi, Matteo Negri, and Marcello Federico. 2017. Multi-Domain Neural Machine Translation through Unsupervised Adaptation. In *Proceedings of the Second Conference on Machine Translation*, pages 127–137. Association for Computational Linguistics.

George Foster, Cyril Goutte, and Roland Kuhn. 2010. Discriminative instance weighting for domain adaptation in statistical machine translation. In *Proceedings of the 2010 Conference on Empirical Methods in Natural Language Processing*, pages 451–459, Cambridge, MA. Association for Computational Linguistics.

George Foster and Roland Kuhn. 2007. Mixture-model adaptation for SMT. In *Proceedings of the Second Workshop on Statistical Machine Translation*, pages 128–135, Prague, Czech Republic. Association for Computational Linguistics.

Markus Freitag and Yaser Al-Onaizan. 2016. Fast Domain Adaptation for Neural Machine Translation. *CoRR*, abs/1612.06897.

Felix Hieber, Tobias Domhan, Michael Denkowski, David Vilar, Artem Sokolov, Ann Clifton, and Matt Post. 2017. Sockeye: A Toolkit for Neural Machine Translation. *ArXiv e-prints*.

Marcin Junczys-Dowmunt. 2019. Microsoft Translator at WMT 2019: Towards Large-Scale Document-Level Neural Machine Translation. In *Proceedings of the Fourth Conference on Machine Translation*

(Volume 2: Shared Task Papers, Day 1), pages 225–233, Florence, Italy. Association for Computational Linguistics.

Yunsu Kim, Thanh Tran, and Hermann Ney. 2019. When and why is document-level context useful in neural machine translation? In *DiscoMT@EMNLP*.

Catherine Kobus, Josep Crego, and Jean Senellart. 2017. Domain Control for Neural Machine Translation. In *Proceedings of the International Conference Recent Advances in Natural Language Processing, RANLP 2017*, pages 372–378. INCOMA Ltd.

Philipp Koehn. 2004. Statistical Significance Tests for Machine Translation Evaluation. In *Proceedings of the 2004 Conference on Empirical Methods in Natural Language Processing*, pages 388–395, Barcelona, Spain. Association for Computational Linguistics.

Bei Li, Hui Liu, Ziyang Wang, Yufan Jiang, Tong Xiao, Jingbo Zhu, Tongran Liu, and Changliang Li. 2020. Does multi-encoder help? a case study on context-aware neural machine translation. In *Proceedings of the 58th Annual Meeting of the Association for Computational Linguistics*, pages 3512–3518, Online. Association for Computational Linguistics.

Pierre Lison and Jörg Tiedemann. 2016. OpenSubtitles2016: Extracting large parallel corpora from movie and TV subtitles. In *Proceedings of the Tenth International Conference on Language Resources and Evaluation (LREC'16)*, pages 923–929, Portorož, Slovenia. European Language Resources Association (ELRA).

Frederick Liu, Han Lu, and Graham Neubig. 2018. Handling Homographs in Neural Machine Translation. In *Proceedings of the 2018 Conference of the North American Chapter of the Association for Computational Linguistics: Human Language Technologies, Volume 1 (Long Papers)*, pages 1336–1345.

Minh-Thang Luong and Christopher D Manning. 2015. Stanford Neural Machine Translation Systems for Spoken Language Domains. In *Proceedings of the International Workshop on Spoken Language Translation*, pages 76–79.

Valentin Macé and Christophe Servan. 2019. Using whole document context in neural machine translation. *arXiv preprint arXiv:1910.07481*.

Sameen Maruf and Gholamreza Haffari. 2018. Document Context Neural Machine Translation with Memory Networks. In *Proceedings of the 56th Annual Meeting of the Association for Computational Linguistics (Volume 1: Long Papers)*, pages 1275–1284, Melbourne, Australia. Association for Computational Linguistics.

Sameen Maruf, André F. T. Martins, and Gholamreza Haffari. 2019. Selective Attention for Context-aware Neural Machine Translation. In *Proceedings of the 2019 Conference of the North American Chapter of the Association for Computational Linguistics: Human Language Technologies, Volume 1 (Long and Short Papers)*, pages 3092–3102, Minneapolis, Minnesota. Association for Computational Linguistics.

Lesly Miculicich, Dhananjay Ram, Nikolaos Pappas, and James Henderson. 2018. Document-Level Neural Machine Translation with Hierarchical Attention Networks. In *Proceedings of the 2018 Conference on Empirical Methods in Natural Language Processing*, pages 2947–2954. Association for Computational Linguistics.

Mathias Müller, Annette Rios, Elena Voita, and Rico Sennrich. 2018. A Large-Scale Test Set for the Evaluation of Context-Aware Pronoun Translation in Neural Machine Translation. In *Proceedings of the Third Conference on Machine Translation, Volume 1: Research Papers*, pages 61–72, Brussels, Belgium. Association for Computational Linguistics.

Jason Naradowsky, Xuan Zhang, and Kevin Duh. 2020. Machine translation system selection from bandit feedback. In *Proceedings of the 14th Conference of the Association for Machine Translation in the Americas (Volume 1: Research Track)*, pages 50–63, Virtual. Association for Machine Translation in the Americas.

Hassan Sajjad, Nadir Durrani, Fahim Dalvi, Yonatan Belinkov, and Stephan Vogel. 2017. Neural Machine Translation Training in a Multi-Domain Scenario. *CoRR*, abs/1708.08712.

Dario Stojanovski and Alexander Fraser. 2018. Coreference and Coherence in Neural Machine Translation: A Study Using Oracle Experiments. In *Proceedings of the Third Conference on Machine Translation, Volume 1: Research Papers*, pages 49–60, Brussels, Belgium. Association for Computational Linguistics.

Dario Stojanovski and Alexander Fraser. 2019a. Combining local and document-level context: The lmu munich neural machine translation system at wmt19. In *Proceedings of the Fourth Conference on Machine Translation (Volume 2: Shared Task Papers, Day 1)*, pages 400–406, Florence, Italy. Association for Computational Linguistics.

Dario Stojanovski and Alexander Fraser. 2019b. Improving Anaphora Resolution in Neural Machine Translation Using Curriculum Learning. In *Proceedings of Machine Translation Summit XVII Volume 1: Research Track*, pages 140–150, Dublin, Ireland. European Association for Machine Translation.

Xin Tan, Longyin Zhang, Deyi Xiong, and Guodong Zhou. 2019. Hierarchical Modeling of Global Context for Document-Level Neural Machine Translation. In *Proceedings of the 2019 Conference on Empirical Methods in Natural Language Processing and the 9th International Joint Conference on Natural Language Processing (EMNLP-IJCNLP)*, pages 1576–1585, Hong Kong, China. Association for Computational Linguistics.

Sander Tars and Mark Fishel. 2018. Multi-Domain Neural Machine Translation. *arXiv preprint arXiv:1805.02282*.

Jörg Tiedemann and Yves Scherrer. 2017. Neural Machine Translation with Extended Context. In *Proceedings of the Third Workshop on Discourse in Machine Translation*, pages 82–92.

Zhaopeng Tu, Yang Liu, Shuming Shi, and Tong Zhang. 2018. Learning to Remember Translation History with a Continuous Cache. *Transactions of the Association for Computational Linguistics*, 6:407–420.

Ashish Vaswani, Noam Shazeer, Niki Parmar, Jakob Uszkoreit, Llion Jones, Aidan N Gomez, Łukasz Kaiser, and Illia Polosukhin. 2017. Attention is All you Need. In *Advances in Neural Information Processing Systems*, pages 6000–6010.

Elena Voita, Rico Sennrich, and Ivan Titov. 2019a. Context-Aware Monolingual Repair for Neural Machine Translation. In *Proceedings of the 2019 Conference on Empirical Methods in Natural Language Processing and the 9th International Joint Conference on Natural Language Processing (EMNLP-IJCNLP)*, pages 876–885, Hong Kong, China. Association for Computational Linguistics.

Elena Voita, Rico Sennrich, and Ivan Titov. 2019b. When a Good Translation is Wrong in Context: Context-Aware Machine Translation Improves on Deixis, Ellipsis, and Lexical Cohesion. In *Proceedings of the 57th Annual Meeting of the Association for Computational Linguistics*, pages 1198–1212, Florence, Italy. Association for Computational Linguistics.

Elena Voita, Pavel Serdyukov, Rico Sennrich, and Ivan Titov. 2018. Context-Aware Neural Machine Translation Learns Anaphora Resolution. In *Proceedings of the 56th Annual Meeting of the Association for Computational Linguistics (Volume 1: Long Papers)*, pages 1264–1274, Melbourne, Australia.

Jia Xu, Yonggang Deng, Yuqing Gao, and Hermann Ney. 2007. Domain Dependent Statistical Machine Translation. In *MT Summit*.

Zhengxin Yang, Jinchao Zhang, Fandong Meng, Shuhao Gu, Yang Feng, and Jie Zhou. 2019. Enhancing Context Modeling with a Query-Guided Capsule Network for Document-level Translation. In *Proceedings of the 2019 Conference on Empirical Methods in Natural Language Processing and the 9th International Joint Conference on Natural Language Processing (EMNLP-IJCNLP)*, pages 1527–1537, Hong Kong, China. Association for Computational Linguistics.

Jiali Zeng, Jinsong Su, Huating Wen, Yang Liu, Jun Xie, Yongjing Yin, and Jianqiang Zhao. 2018. Multi-Domain Neural Machine Translation with Word-Level Domain Context Discrimination. In *Proceedings of the 2018 Conference on Empirical Methods in Natural Language Processing*, pages 447–457. Association for Computational Linguistics.

Jiacheng Zhang, Huanbo Luan, Maosong Sun, Feifei Zhai, Jingfang Xu, Min Zhang, and Yang Liu. 2018. Improving the Transformer Translation Model with Document-Level Context. In *Proceedings of the 2018 Conference on Empirical Methods in Natural Language Processing*, pages 533–542. Association for Computational Linguistics.

Shiqi Zhang and Deyi Xiong. 2018. Sentence Weighting for Neural Machine Translation Domain Adaptation. In *Proceedings of the 27th International Conference on Computational Linguistics*, pages 3181–3190. Association for Computational Linguistics.

A Preprocessing and Hyperparameters

We tokenize all sentences using the script from Moses[2]. We apply BPE splitting[3] with 32K merge operations. We exclude TED and PatTR when computing the BPEs. The BPEs are computed jointly on the source and target data. Samples where the source or target are larger than 100 tokens are removed. We also apply a per-sentence limit of 100 tokens on the context, meaning that models trained on 10 sentences of context have a limit of 1000 tokens. A batch size of 4096 is used for all models.

We first train a sentence-level baseline until convergence based on early-stopping. All context-aware models are initialized with the parameters from this pretrained sentence-level baseline. Parameters that are specific to the models' architectures are randomly initialized. All proposed models in this work share the source, target, output and context embeddings. The models' architecture is a 6 layer encoder/decoder Transformer with 8 attention heads. The embedding and model size is 512 and the size of the feed-forward layers is 2048. The number of parameters for all models is shown in Table 10. We use label smoothing with 0.1 and dropout in the Transformer of 0.1. Models are trained on 2 GTX 1080 Ti GPUs with 11GB RAM.

Model	parameters
SentBase	61M
CtxBase	74M
CtxPool	74M
DomEmb(avg)	63M

Table 10: Number of model parameters. TagBase, ConcBase and DomEmb(max) have the same number of parameters as SentBase.

The initial learning rate for the document-level models is 10^{-4}. For the classical domain adaptation scenario with fine-tuning, we use a learning rate of 10^{-5} in order not to deviate too much from the well-initialized out-of-domain model. We lower the learning rate by a factor of 0.7 if no improvements are observed on the validation perplexity in 8 checkpoints. A checkpoint is saved every 4000 updates. We did not do any systematic hyperparameter search.

Before inference, we average the parameters of the 8 best checkpoints based on the validation perplexity. We use a beam size of 12. BLEU scores are computed on detokenized text using *multi-bleu-detok.perl* from the Moses scripts[4]. For the evaluation of translation of domain-specific words, we used the script from (Liu et al., 2018)[5].

B Datasets

We use the document-aligned versions of Europarl, NewsCommentary and Rapid from WMT 2019[6]. We also use OpenSubtitles[7][8] (Lison and Tiedemann, 2016), Ubuntu[9], PatTR[10] and TED[11].

C Validation performance

In Table 11, Table 12 and Table 13 we present BLEU scores on the development sets for all the experiments we ran. We only show results for the sets we actually used during training and therefore ignore TED and PatTR for which we had no access to data at training time. The results for TagBase are with oracle domain tags. For the experiments with continued training on TED and PatTR, we show results only on the development sets for TED and PatTR.

D Computational Efficiency

In this section, we compare the computational efficiency of our proposed methods. We compare how many seconds on average are needed to translate a sentence from the test set. The average times are 0.2588, 0.2763 ± 0.0124, 0.3662 for SentBase, DomEmb and CtxPool, respectively. DomEmb is insignificantly slower than the sentence-level baseline, in contrast to CtxPool, which is to be expected considering the additional applying of self-attention over the compressed context. In terms of training time, SentBase converged after 90 hours of training, DomEmb(avg) after 168h and CtxPool(avg) after 116h.

[2]https://github.com/moses-smt/mosesdecoder/blob/master/scripts/tokenizer/tokenizer.perl

[3]https://github.com/rsennrich/subword-nmt

[4]https://github.com/moses-smt/mosesdecoder/blob/master/scripts/generic/multi-bleu-detok.perl

[5]https://github.com/frederick0329/Evaluate-Word-Level-Translation

[6]http://statmt.org/wmt19/translation-task.html

[7]http://opus.nlpl.eu/OpenSubtitles-v2018.php

[8]http://www.opensubtitles.org/

[9]http://opus.nlpl.eu/Ubuntu.php

[10]http://www.cl.uni-heidelberg.de/statnlpgroup/pattr/

[11]https://wit3.fbk.eu/2015-01

domain	SentBase	TagBase	DomEmb(max)	DomEmb(avg)	CtxPool(max)	CtxPool(avg)
Europarl	33.3	33.6	33.6	33.7	33.8	33.8
NewsComm	34.1	34.3	34.1	34.1	34.2	34.1
OpenSub	33.3	34.2	34.2	34.5	34.1	34.2
Rapid	39.4	39.7	39.5	39.7	39.8	39.9
Ubuntu	40.2	43.0	41.3	42.6	42.0	42.2

Table 11: BLEU scores on the development sets of the multi-domain dataset.

domain	ctx=1	ctx=5	ctx=10
Europarl	33.5	33.8	33.7
NewsComm	34.0	34.2	34.1
OpenSub	33.7	34.1	34.5
Rapid	39.7	39.8	39.7
Ubuntu	41.5	43.0	42.6
domain	**CtxBase**	**ConcBase**	**DomEmb(a)**
Europarl	34.0	34.1	33.7
NewsComm	34.0	33.9	34.1
OpenSub	33.9	34.5	34.5
Rapid	40.1	39.1	39.7
Ubuntu	42.3	42.3	42.6

Table 12: Results on the development sets using the DomEmb(avg) model with different context sizes and comparing DomEmb(avg) with *ctx=10* against CtxBase and ConcBase.

domain	SentBase	DomEmb(a)
TED	33.2	33.4
PatTR	36.4	36.3

Table 13: Domain adaptation results on PatTR and TED for SentBase and DomEmb(avg) on the development sets.

E Examples

In Table 14 we show some example translations from the sentence-level baseline and our DomEmb(avg) model. We show examples where our model corrected erroneous translations from the baseline. Some of the proper translations should be evident from the main sentence itself, but some can only be inferred from context. The first four examples are from TED and the last from PatTR.

In the first example, we can see that the sentence-level baseline translates "students" as "Studenten" (university students), but the correct translation in this case is "Schüler" (elementary or high school student). The main sentence itself is not informative enough for the sentence-level model to make this distinction. In contrast, the DomEmb model has access to more information which provides for the appropriate bias towards the correct translation.

The second sentence depicts an example where it's nearly impossible for the baseline to make a correct prediction for the translation of "ambassador" because it depends on whether the person is male (Botschafter) or female (Botschafterin). In the third example, the sentence-level model translated "model" as in "a role model" (Vorbild), but the context indicates that the speaker talks about "fashion models".

Examples 4 and 5 are relatively unintuitive because the main sentences themselves should be enough to infer the correct translation. In example 4, "reflect" refers to the physical process of reflection and should not be translated as in "to reflect on oneself" ("denken"), while in example 5, "raise" refers to the action of "lifting" or "elevating"("aufwärtsbewegt" or "hochzuziehen") some object instead of "raising" as in "raising a plant (from a seed)" ("züchten").

The last example shows that the sentence-level model translates "springs" ("Federn" which is a part of the compound word "Druckfedern" in the reference) as in "water springs" ("Quellen" which is a part of the compound word "Kompressionsquellen") while it should be translated instead as in the physical elastic device. However, in other test sentences, both SentBase and DomEmb(avg) translated "spring" as a season, even though this should be less likely in PatTR, showing that our model does not always succeed in capturing domain perfectly.

Source We all knew we were risking our lives – the teacher, the **students** and our parents. *Reference* Wir alle wussten, dass wir unser Leben riskierten: Lehrer, **Schüler** und unsere Eltern. *SentBase* Wir alle wussten, dass wir unser Leben riskieren... den Lehrer, die **Studenten** und unsere Eltern. *DomEmb(avg)* Wir wussten alle, dass wir unser Leben riskierten. Der Lehrer, die **Schüler** und unsere Eltern.
Source That's why I am a global **ambassador** for 10x10, a global campaign to educate women. *Reference* Deshalb bin ich globale **Botschafterin** für 10x10, einer weltweiten Kampagne für die Bildung von Frauen. *SentBase* Aus diesem Grund bin ich ein globaler **Botschafter** für 10x10, eine weltweite Kampagne zur Ausbildung von Frauen. *DomEmb(avg)* Deshalb bin ich eine globale **Botschafterin** für 10x10, eine weltweite Kampagne zur Ausbildung von Frauen.
Source And I am on this stage because I am a **model**. *Reference* Und ich stehe auf dieser Bühne, weil ich ein **Model** bin. *SentBase* Und ich bin auf dieser Bühne, weil ich ein **Vorbild** bin. *DomEmb(avg)* Und ich bin auf dieser Bühne, weil ich ein **Model** bin.
Source It's going to bounce, go inside the room, some of that is going to **reflect** back on the door ... *Reference* Es wird abprallen, in den Raum gehen, ein Teil davon wird wieder zurück auf die Tür **reflektiert** ... *SentBase* Es wird abprallen, ins Zimmer gehen, etwas davon wird wieder an die Tür **denken** ... *DomEmb(avg)* Es wird abprallen, ins Zimmer gehen, etwas davon wird wieder über die Tür **reflektieren** ...
Source Tie member 60 is driven to **raise** movable cone 58 ... *Reference* Mit dem Zugelement 60 wird durch den An der bewegliche Kegel 58 **aufwärtsbewegt** ... *SentBase* Tie-Mitglied 60 wird angetrieben, bewegliche Konfitüre 58 zu **züchten** ... *DomEmb(avg)* Teemitglied 60 wird angetrieben, bewegliche Kegel 58 **hochzuziehen** ...
Source It is only when a certain pressure level is reached that the pistons are pushed back against the action of the **compression springs** ... *Reference* Erst bei Erreichen eines bestimmten Druckniveaus werden die Kolben gegen die Wirkung der **Druckfedern** zurückgeschoben ... *SentBase* Erst wenn ein gewisses Druckniveau erreicht ist, werden die Pistonen gegen die Wirkung der **Kompressionsquellen** zurückgedrängt ... *DomEmb(avg)* Erst wenn ein bestimmtes Druckniveau erreicht ist, werden die Pistonen gegen die Wirkung der **Kompressionsfedern** zurückgedrängt ...

Table 14: Example translations obtained using sentence-level baseline and the DomEmb(avg) model. Relevant parts of the examples are in bold.

MultiReQA: A Cross-Domain Evaluation for Retrieval Question Answering Models

Mandy Guo[a*], **Yinfei Yang**[a*], **Daniel Cer**[a], **Qinlan Shen**[b†], **and Noah Constant**[a]

[a]Google Research
Mountain View, CA, USA

[b]Carnegie Mellon University
Pittsburgh, PA, USA

Abstract

Retrieval question answering (ReQA) is the task of retrieving a sentence-level answer to a question from an open corpus (Ahmad et al., 2019). This dataset paper presents MultiReQA, a new multi-domain ReQA evaluation suite composed of eight retrieval QA tasks drawn from publicly available QA datasets [1]. We explore systematic retrieval based evaluation and transfer learning across domains over these datasets using a number of strong baselines including two supervised neural models, based on fine-tuning BERT and USE-QA models respectively, as well as a surprisingly effective information retrieval baseline, BM25. Five of these tasks contain both training and test data, while three contain test data only. Performing cross training on the five tasks with training data shows that while a general model covering all domains is achievable, the best performance is often obtained by training exclusively on in-domain data.

1 Introduction

Retrieval-based question answering (QA) investigates the problem of finding answers to questions from an open corpus (Surdeanu et al., 2008; Yang et al., 2015; Chen et al., 2017; Lee et al., 2019; Ahmad et al., 2019; Chang et al., 2020; Ma et al., 2020). There is a growing interest in building scalable end-to-end question answering systems for large scale retrieval (Ahmad et al., 2019; Roy et al., 2020). Retrieval question answering (ReQA) (Ahmad et al., 2019), illustrated in Table 1, defines the task as *directly* retrieving an answer sentence from a corpus.[2] Motivated by real applications such as Google's Talk to Books [3], where sentence-level answers from books are retrieved to answer users' queries, ReQA is different from traditional machine reading for question answering or "reading comprehension" which aims to extract a short answer span from a given passage. Rather than just identifying answers within a short preselected passage that is provided to the model effectively by an oracle, retrieving sentence-level answers from a large pool of candidates directly addresses the real-world problem of searching for answers within a corpus. Sentences retrieved as answers in this manner can be used directly to answer questions. Alternatively, retrieved sentences, as well as possibly the passages that contains them, can be provided to a traditional Open Domain QA model (Chen et al., 2017; Karpukhin et al., 2020).

Question: In what year did Cortes send the first cochineal to Spain? **Answer in Context:** [...] It worked particularly well on silk, satin and other luxury textiles. **In 1523 Cortes sent the first shipment to Spain.** Soon cochineal began to arrive in European ports aboard convoys of Spanish galleons.

Table 1: ReQA example drawn from SQuAD. The goal is to retrieve the answer sentence (**bolded**) from an open corpus based on the meaning of the sentence and the surrounding context.

Recent research has shown promising results on developing neural models for retrieval tasks including ReQA, MS MARCO, and the retrieval part of open domain question QA (Roy et al., 2020; Karpukhin et al., 2020; Xiong et al., 2020; Luan et al., 2020). One challenge of employing neural models is that it usually requires a large amount of training data. While it is possible to get such data from a general domain, it may hard to get similar data for specialized domains, which is a common

* Corresponding authors: {xyguo, yinfeiy}@google.com
† Work done during an internship at Google Research.

[1]We released the sentence boundary annotation of MultiReQA: `https://github.com/google-research-datasets/MultiReQA`

[2]This can be contrasted to a two stage approach that first retrieves supporting text and then identifies the correct answer span (Chen et al., 2017; Lee et al., 2019)

[3]`https://books.google.com/talktobooks/`

Proceedings of the Second Workshop on Domain Adaptation for NLP, pages 94–104
April 20, 2021.

Dataset	Question	Answer
SearchQA	At age 33 in 1804, he started a new symphony, his 5th, with a Da-Da-Da-Duhg	This is the first movement of Beethoven's 5th symphony.
TriviaQA	From the Greek for color, what element, with an atomic number of 24, uses the symbol Cr?	Rubies and emeralds also owe their colors to chromium compounds.
HotpotQA	Lenny Young is a collaborator on the stop motion film released in what year?	Chicken Run is a 2000 stop-motion animated comedy film produced by the British studio Aardman Animations.
NQ	when was the last episode of vampire diaries aired	The series ran from September 10, 2009 to March 10, 2017 on The CW.
SQuAD	what decade did house music hit the mainstream in the us?	The early 1990s additionally saw the rise in mainstream US popularity for house music.
BioASQ	What chromosome is affected in Turner's syndrome?	The origin of sSMC of Turner syndrome with 45, X/46, X, + mar karyotype was almost all from sex chromosomes, and rarely from autosomes.
R.E.	Which year is Bird Girl and the Man Who Followed the Sun released?	Bird Girl and the Man Who Followed the Sun is a 1996 novel by Velma Wallis.
TextbookQA	which nervous system disease causes seizures?	Epilepsy is a disease that causes seizures.

Table 2: Example questions and answers from each dataset.

situation with examples including personal search over private repositories and search within enterprise environments (Hawking, 2004; Chirita et al., 2005). It is unknown how well a general domain model can perform on domain specific QA tasks or even the extent of transfer possible across different specialized domains.

In order to further investigate these questions within the context of the ReQA task, we propose a new common evaluation suite consisting of eight new datasets extracted from existing QA datasets. Five *in-domain* tasks include training and test data, while three *out-of-domain* tasks contain only test data. We provide cross domain baselines for neural and non-neural retrieval methods. Our baseline experiments use two competitive neural models, based on BERT (Devlin et al., 2019) and USE-QA (Yang et al., 2019), respectively, and BM25, a strong information retrieval baseline. BM25 performs surprisingly well on many retrieval question answering tasks, achieving the best performance on two of five in-domain tasks and all three out-of-domain tasks. Neural models achieve the highest performance on three of five in-domain tasks, outperforming BM25 by a wide margin on tasks with less token overlap between question and answer. Comparing general models trained on a mixture of QA training sets to specialized in-domain models trained on a single QA task reveals that models trained jointly on multiple datasets rarely outperform those trained on only in-domain data.

The main contribution of this paper is summarized as follows: 1) A new evaluation suit derived from existing QA tasks for measuring retrieval question answering performance in multiple domains; 2) Establish the strong baselines with key word based retrieval approach and neural retrieval models. 3) Exploring the domain transferability and limitation for existing retrieval models. Extensive experiments show that BM25 remains a strong baseline for all domains. While a general neural model covering all domains is achievable, the best performing neural model is often obtained by training exclusively on in-domain data.

2 Retrieval QA (ReQA)

ReQA formalizes the retrieval-based QA task as the identification of a sentence in-context that answers a provided question (Ahmad et al., 2019). Retrieval QA models are evaluated using Precision at 1 (P@1) and Mean Reciprocal Rank (MRR). The P@1 score tests whether the true answer sentence appears as the top-ranked candidate[4]. MRR, introduced for the evaluation of retrieval based QA systems (Voorhees, 2001; Radev et al., 2002), is calculated as MRR $= \frac{1}{N}\sum_{i=1}^{N}\frac{1}{rank_i}$, where N is the total number of questions, and $rank_i$ is the rank of the first correct answer for the ith question.

[4]Retrieval models are often measured by P@N (N=1,3,5,10). However, as our main concern is whether the question is correctly answered, we focus on P@1.

3 Multi-domain ReQA (MultiReQA)

The multi-domain ReQA (MultiReQA) test suite is composed of select datasets drawn from the MRQA shared task (Fisch et al., 2019a).[5] We follow the training, in-domain test, out-of-domain test splits defined in MRQA. The individual datasets are described below:

SearchQA Jeopardy question-answer pairs augmented with text snippets retrieved by Google (Dunn et al., 2017).

TriviaQA Trivia enthusiasts authored question-answer pairs. Answers are drawn from Wikipedia and Bing web search results, excluding trivia websites (Joshi et al., 2017b).

HotpotQA Wikipedia question-answer pairs. This dataset differs from the others in that the questions require reasoning over multiple supporting documents (Yang et al., 2018). The annotators generate the questions knowing the answers and the supporting contexts.

SQuAD 1.1 Wikipedia question-answer pairs (Rajpurkar et al., 2016a). Given the supporting contexts from Wikipedia, the annotators were asked to write questions such that the answers could be found in the contexts. Moreover, many of the questions are directly formed from parts of the supporting contexts.

NaturalQuestions (NQ) Questions are real queries issued by multiple users to Google search that retrieve a Wikipedia page in the top five search results. Answer text is drawn from the search results (Kwiatkowski et al., 2019). We removed the duplicate question-answer pairs in the in-domain test split, since during the original dataset construction, multiple raters were asked to select answers from the paragraphs. Unlike ReQA (Ahmad et al., 2019), we did not limit the questions and candidates to be only within the HTML paragraph block, and the candidates could contain lists and tables.

BioASQ Bio-medical question-answer pairs with answers annotated by domain experts and drawn from research articles (Tsatsaronis et al., 2015).

RelationExtraction (R.E.) Entity relation question-answer pairs, created by slot filling using the WikiReading dataset (Ahmad et al., 2019).

TextbookQA Multi-modal question-answer pairs taken from middle school science curricula (Kembhavi et al., 2017). In this paper, we only consider the text aspect of this task as defined by the original MRQA shared task.

Table 2 provides example question-answer sentence pairs. Datasets are converted from a span identification task to sentence-level retrieval. The questions from the original data are used without modification. Supporting documents are split into sentences using NLTK. [6] All resulting sentences become retrieval candidates. Answer spans identify sentences containing the correct answers. Spans covering multiple sentence are excluded.[7]

Table 3 provides statistics on the number of training set pairs and the number of questions, candidates and average answers per question in the evaluation data. Table 4 shows the average length of word tokens and degree of token overlap. SearchQA and HotpotQA have supporting documents split by [DOC]/[PAR] tags, so they have comparatively shorter context length. TriviaQA has much longer context length because all supporting documents were tokenized as one due to lack of clear division among special tags in the dataset. NaturalQuestions contain lists and tables that bring up the average answer length. SearchQA and SQuAD have high degree of question/answer overlap because the supporting documents in SearchQA are retrieved by search engine, and SQuAD questions are written with advance knowledge of the answers and supporting contexts. However, even though HotpotQA questions are also written with the knowledge of the answers and contexts, the degree of overlap is quite low likely due to the inclusion of multi-document inference.

[5] We exclude NewsQA, RACE, DROP, and DuoRC, as the majority of their questions are underspecified when taken out of their original context, making them inappropriate for a large-scale retrieval evaluations.

[6] As the datasets SearchQA, TriviaQA and HotpotQA contain special tags [DOC], [PAR], [SEP], and [TLE], we perform dataset-specific pre-processing to handle context splitting and tag removal. TriviaQA has [DOC] [TLE] [PAR] tags, but with no clear divisions to mark where the span of each kind of tags ends. We remove all the tags, and tokenize the article as if it does not have special tags. SearchQA uses [DOC] to separate the supporting snippets, [TLE] to mark the start of title, and [PAR] to mark start of the snippet content. We treat contents between two [DOC] tags as individual context. We then use NLTK to split the sentences within each context. The contents between [TLE] and [PAR] are used as a title feature. If the answer appears in the title feature, we do not add it as a positive answer. There are about 500 examples where the answer span is only in the title span, and we remove the corresponding questions. We follow the same procedure for HotpotQA, which uses [PAR] to separate supporting documents, and [SEP] to separate title and document content.

[7] This is typically due to sentence splitting errors by NLTK.

Dataset	Train	Test		
		Ques.	Cand.	Avg. ans. per ques.
SearchQA	629,160	16,476	454,836	5.47
TriviaQA	335,659	7,776	238,339	5.46
HotpotQA	104,973	5,859	52,191	1.69
SQuAD	87,133	10,485	10,642	1.09
NQ	106,521	4,131	22,118	1.06
BioASQ	-	1,503	14,158	2.85
R.E.	-	2,945	3,301	1.00
TextbookQA	-	1,497	3,701	3.31

Table 3: Statistics for each constructed dataset: # of training pairs, # of questions, # of candidates, and average # of answers per question.

Dataset	Question	Answer	Context
Average Length (Tokens)			
SearchQA	17.25	31.51	55.50
TriviaQA	15.56	33.88	747.75
HotpotQA	18.52	28.31	91.57
SQuAD	11.45	29.70	140.64
NQ	9.24	107.10	220.02
BioASQ	11.18	29.01	241.52
R.E.	9.15	27.51	29.14
TextbookQA	10.20	16.37	648.23
Question/Answer Token Overlap (%)			
SearchQA	-	37.83	55.23
TriviaQA	-	25.53	74.23
HotpotQA	-	29.08	49.16
SQuAD	-	43.03	56.36
NQ	-	23.50	36.87
BioASQ	-	23.08	53.40
R.E.	-	39.21	40.98
TextbookQA	-	25.64	82.54

Table 4: Average length (# of word tokens) and degree of question/answer token overlap of each constructed dataset.

4 Baseline Models

To establish strong baselines for the MultiReQA test suite, we use two neural models, based on BERT (Devlin et al., 2019) and USE-QA (Yang et al., 2019), respectively, as well as an well established term-based information retrieval baseline, BM25.

4.1 BERT

BERT dual encoders are used for retrieval tasks like translation retrieval (Feng et al., 2020) and QA passage retrieval (Roy et al., 2020; Karpukhin et al., 2020). We explore a BERT dual encoder as our first neural baseline, using the $\text{BERT}_{\text{BASE}}$ model,[8] due to memory constraints.[9]

Questions and answers are encoded using two separate towers with tied model weights. The question is fed into one tower and we take the embedding output of the CLS token as the question encoding. The answer text and context are concatenated as a long sequence, using segment IDs to separate them. The concatenated input is fed into the other tower. As with the question encoder, we take the CLS embedding as the answer encoding. To distinguish questions and answers, we add an additional *input type embedding* to each input token.[10] The final embeddings are l_2 normalized.

4.2 Universal Sentence Encoder QA

Following Ahmad et al. (2019), we employ the Universal Sentence Encoder QA (USE-QA) (Yang et al., 2019)[11] as another neural baseline. USE-QA is a multilingual QA retrieval model pre-trained on billions of examples from web-crawled question answering corpora.[12] USE-QA encodes the question and answer separately using a transformer (Vaswani et al., 2017) based dual encoder architecture. The question embedding is obtained by average pooling over all token positions in the final transformer block follwed by fully-connected network. Answers and their context are encoded using a transformer for the answer text and a deep averaging network (DAN) (Iyyer et al., 2015) for context. Preliminary answer vectors are computed using average pooling over positions. The answer vector is then concatenated with the DAN based context vector and fed to a fully-connected network to compute the final joint representation.

4.3 BM25

Term frequency inverse document frequency (TF-IDF) based methods remain the dominant method for document retrieval, with the "Best Matching 25" (BM25) family of ranking functions providing a well established baseline (Robertson and Zaragoza, 2009). In previous work on open domain question answering, BM25 has been used to retrieve evi-

[8]The $\text{BERT}_{\text{BASE}}$ model uses 12 transformer layers with 12 attention heads, a hidden size of 768 and a filter size of 3072. The final embedding size is 768.

[9]We use in-batch negative sampling in the dual encoder training, which requires relatively large batch size. For more details of dual encoder training with negative sampling, see Gillick et al. (2018) and Guo et al. (2018).

[10]Note that we switch the final activation layer of the BERT CLS token from *tanh* to *gelu*.

[11]https://tfhub.dev/google/universal-sentence-encoder-multilingual-qa/1

[12]USE-QA uses a 6 layer transformer with 8 attention heads, a hidden size of 512 and a filter size of 2048. The context DAN encoder uses hidden sizes [320, 320, 512, 512] with residual connections. The feed-forward networks for question and answer both use hidden sizes [320, 512], so the final dimension of the encodings is 512.

dence text, and has been shown to be a particularly strong baseline on tasks where the question is written with advance knowledge of the answer (Lee et al., 2019).

The BM25 score of document D given query Q which contains words $q_1, ..., q_n$ is given by:

$$\sum_{i=1}^{n} \text{IDF}(q_i) \cdot \frac{f(q_i, D) \cdot (k_1 + 1)}{f(q_i, D) + k_1 \cdot (1 - b + b \cdot \frac{|D|}{\text{avgdl}})} \quad (1)$$

where $f(q_i, D)$ is q_i's term frequency in the document, $|D|$ is the length of the document in words, and $avgdl$ is the average document length across all documents. Scalars k_1 and b are free parameters. We concatenate the answer sentence and context as the document when applying BM25 for answer retrieval.[13]

5 Experiments

5.1 Fine-tuning and Configurations

BM25 We use the BM25 implementation in the Gensim library (Řehůřek and Sojka, 2010) with default k_1 and b settings. Inverse document frequency is calculated for each constructed dataset independently. We deploy two different tokenization methods for BM25: NLTK (Bird et al., 2009) and a WordPiece model (wpm) (Wu et al., 2016) following the BERT implementation.[14] The NLTK tokenizer does not normalize text, while the WordPiece model does by default. Our results in Table 5 for $\text{BM25}_{\text{word}}$ use NLTK without normalization, while BM25_{wpm} uses wpm with normalization.[15]

USE-QA The USE-QA model is already pre-trained specifically for retrieval QA tasks. We first evaluate the default model without any dataset specific fine-tuning. We further fine-tune USE-QA model with a discriminative ranking objective (Yang et al., 2019) on our training sets:[16]

$$P(a \mid q) = \frac{e^{\phi(q,a)}}{\sum_{\bar{a} \in \mathcal{A}} e^{\phi(q,\bar{a})}} \quad (2)$$

Above, q is the question, a is the correct answer, $\mathcal{A}$ is all answers in the same batch, which serve as sampled negatives, and $\phi(q, a)$ is the dot product of question and answer representations. We fine-tune USE-QA models on in-domain data for 10 epochs using batch size 64, and SGD with learning rate decaying exponentially from 0.01 to 0.001.

BERT Our BERT dual encoder is fine-tuned for retrieval with the same discriminative objective used for the USE-QA models.[17] We fine-tune for 10 epochs using batch size 128 and the default AdamW optimizer with learning rate 0.0001.[18]

5.2 Results

Table 5 shows baseline model performance on the MultiReQA evaluation suite for both precision at 1 (P@1) and Mean Reciprocal Rank (MRR). The highest score for each task is bolded. For P@1, the first two rows shows the results for $\text{BM25}_{\text{word}}$ and BM25_{wpm}. Notably, BM25_{wpm} performs better on 7 of 8 tasks, indicating that a careful selection of tokenization and normalization can improve the term-based model considerably. The advantage of BM25_{wpm} is particularly noticeable on datasets where the question is constructed without seeing the answer: SearchQA, TriviaQA, NQ, BioASQ and Relation Extraction. BM25_{wpm} also achieves the highest P@1 on 2 of 5 in-domain datasets and on all out-of-domain dataests.

The remaining rows show the results of the neural models: off-the-shelf USE-QA, fine-tuned versions of USE-QA and fine-tuned BERT dual encoders. We fine-tune on each in-domain dataset separately. The off-the-self USE-QA baseline is overall not competitive with BM25_{wpm}. However, when fine-tuned on in-domain data, USE-QA outperforms BM25_{wpm} on 3 of 5 in-domain datasets. Fine-tuned BERT often performs almost as well as fine-tuned USE-QA, suggesting there is only minimal benefit to QA specific pre-training.

The best neural models outperform BM25_{wpm} on Hotpot and NQ by +11.68% and +12.68% on P@1, respectively. This aligns with the statistics from Table 3, where token overlap between question and answer/context is low for these sets. BM25_{wpm} outperforms neural models, on datasets with higher token overlap between question and answer/context (e.g., SearchQA, R.E. and SQuAD w.r.t. all neural

[13]The answer sentence is included in the context, so it appears twice in the constructed documents. This allows multiple answers that share the same context to still receive unique scores.

[14]The wpm vocab is from $\text{BERT}_{\text{BASE}}$.

[15]We also experimented on SQuAD with removing normalization from wpm, and found that wpm still outperforms NLTK.

[16]Notably, this is the same discriminative objective used for the original USE-QA model

[17]Since BERT is originally pre-trained on masked language modeling and next-sentence prediction, fine-tuning is necessary to use it to perform retrieval tasks.

[18]For both USE-QA and BERT, hyper-parameters are tuned on a validation set (10%) split out from the training data.

Metric	Models	In-domain Datasets					Out-of-domain Datasets		
		SearchQA	TriviaQA	HotpotQA	NQ	SQuAD	BioASQ	R.E.	TextbookQA
P@1	$\text{BM25}_{\text{word}}$	30.94	39.35	21.04	10.07	61.50	6.38	55.75	8.39
	BM25_{wpm}	**35.86**	**43.26**	20.37	25.32	65.32	**8.31**	**64.04**	**8.52**
	USE-QA	31.17	28.60	18.12	24.71	51.02	5.58	52.05	7.52
	$\text{USE-QA}_{\text{finetune}}$	31.45	32.58	31.71	**38.00**	**66.83**	6.41	59.87	6.62
	$\text{BERT}_{\text{finetune}}$	30.20	29.11	**32.05**	36.22	55.13	5.71	49.89	6.29
MRR	$\text{BM25}_{\text{word}}$	47.75	51.58	33.07	15.51	69.16	10.37	71.27	17.23
	BM25_{wpm}	**52.25**	**55.80**	32.99	37.1	72.96	12.86	**79.86**	16.97
	USE-QA	47.52	40.26	22.65	34.73	62.08	12.31	67.41	16.92
	$\text{USE-QA}_{\text{finetune}}$	50.70	42.39	43.77	**52.27**	**75.86**	13.39	74.89	15.49
	$\text{BERT}_{\text{finetune}}$	47.08	41.34	**46.21**	52.02	64.74	**19.21**	65.21	**20.17**

Table 5: Precision at 1(P@1)(%) and Mean Reciprocal Rank (MRR)(%) on the constructed question answer retrieval datasets. $\text{USE-QA}_{\text{finetune}}$ and $\text{BERT}_{\text{finetune}}$ are fine-tuned on each in-domain dataset individually. The performance of fine-tuned models on out-of-domain datasets are the average score across all five fine-tuned models.

Metric	Train \ Test	In-domain Datasets					Out-of-domain Datasets		
		SearchQA	TriviaQA	HotpotQA	NQ	SQuAD	BioASQ	R.E.	TextbookQA
P@1	SearchQA	31.45	35.48	16.04	24.69	46.60	6.52	60.03	6.66
	TriviaQA	28.44	32.58	14.91	22.58	38.87	4.45	60.84	4.06
	HotpotQA	30.79	32.70	**31.71**	26.45	56.17	5.65	57.21	6.52
	NQ	28.80	31.77	17.64	**38.00**	52.23	6.52	55.48	7.66
	SQuAD	31.44	35.21	20.25	28.32	**66.83**	**7.65**	**63.73**	8.32
	Joint	**32.24**	37.40	26.54	36.35	60.81	7.58	62.71	7.52
	$\text{Joint}_{\text{No TriviaQA}}$	31.92	**37.71**	29.68	36.23	64.00	6.78	61.69	**8.72**
MRR	SearchQA	50.70	47.88	25.88	36.31	57.83	13.34	75.51	15.19
	TriviaQA	44.57	42.39	23.40	32.77	47.50	9.26	75.88	10.49
	HotpotQA	47.17	44.41	**43.77**	36.99	66.25	32.15	72.54	15.08
	NQ	45.08	44.39	26.57	**52.27**	62.88	13.77	70.07	17.71
	SQuAD	48.70	48.16	30.12	38.79	**75.86**	**15.75**	**78.50**	**18.71**
	Joint	**51.04**	**50.88**	38.95	50.11	71.02	14.86	78.05	16.61
	$\text{Joint}_{\text{No TriviaQA}}$	50.80	50.77	41.62	49.93	73.71	14.69	77.04	18.64

Table 6: P@1(%) and MRR(%) of USE-QA models fine-tuned on either one or all in-domain datasets, evaluated across all datasets. **Joint**: Fine-tune on all in-domain datasets together. $\textbf{Joint}_{\textbf{No TriviaQA}}$: Same as "Joint", but removing TriviaQA from the fine-tuning data pool.

models except $\text{USE-QA}_{\text{finetune}}$) and paradoxically the particularly difficult TriviaQA task.

A very similar pattern of results is seen for MRR, with the exception that $\text{BERT}_{\text{finetune}}$ performs best on BioASQ and TextbookQA. We observe that the vocabulary of BioASQ and TextbookQA are different from the other datasets, including more specialized technical terms. Superior MRR performance could be due to better representations of novel words, computed from the composition of sub-word tokens.[19] However, it's not clear why BM25^{wpm}, also using sub-word tokenization, performs best on these datasets for P@1.

5.3 Transfer Learning across Domains

The previous section shows that the strongest baselines are the USE-QA and BERT models, fine-tuned on in-domain data, with USE-QA slightly outperforming BERT. In order to better understand generalization across QA tasks, we experiment with training and evaluating on different dataset pairings, focusing on the USE-QA model. Table 6 shows the performance of models trained on each individual dataset, as well as a model trained jointly on all available in-domain datasets.

Each column compares performance of different models on a specific test set. The best numbers for each test set are bolded. In general, models trained on an individual dataset achieve the best (or near-best) performance on their associated evaluation set. TriviaQA is an exception, performing poorly on its own evaluation data and nearly all other datasets. This suggests training on the TriviaQA sentence-level retrieval task is more difficult than other datasets. Critically, TriviaQA requires reasoning across multiple sources of evidence (Joshi et al., 2017a), with the meaning of complete sentences annotated with answer spans often not directly answering their associate questions.

[19] BM23_{wpm} benefits from subword tokens but lacks the ability to understand how adjacent sub-word tokens compose a larger meaningful unit.

Joint models use combined training sets. The model denoted as Joint trains on all the datasets. $\text{Joint}_{\text{No TriviaQA}}$ trains on all datasets except TrivialQA, motivated by the poor performance of models trained on only TriviaQA data. The model trained over all available data is competitive, but the performance on some datasets, e.g. NQ and SQuAD, is significantly lower than the individually-trained models. By removing TriviaQA, the combined model gets close to the individual model performance on NQ and SQuAD, and achieves the best P@1 performance on TriviaQA and TextbookQA.

6 Analysis

6.1 Does Context Help?

Candidate answers may be not fully interpretable when taken out of their surrounding context (Ahmad et al., 2019). In this section we investigate how model performance changes when removing context. We experiment with one BM25 model and one neural model, by picking the best performing models from previous experiments: BM25_{wpm} and $\text{USE-QA}_{\text{finetune}}$. Recall, $\text{USE-QA}_{\text{finetune}}$ models are fine-tuned on each individual dataset.

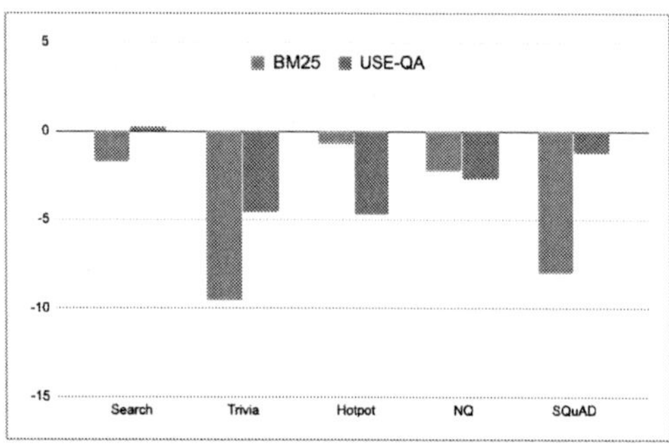

Figure 1: Performance change on P@1(%) for BM25_{wpm} and $\text{USE-QA}_{\text{finetune}}$ when candidate selection is blind to answer context.

Figure 1 illustrates the change in performance when models are restricted to evaluating candidate answers without context.[20] For the USE-QA model, the performance drop by excluding answer context is less than 5% on all datasets. The drop in BM25 performance is larger, supporting the hypothesis that BM25's token overlap heuristic is effective over large spans of text, while the neural model obtains a "deeper" semantic understanding and thus extracts more signal out of a single sentence.

[20]We report P@1 here, but observed similar trends in MRR.

6.2 Error Analysis

In this section we examine some typical failure cases of the BM25_{wpm} and $\text{USE-QA}_{\text{finetune}}$ models. As a first observation, the two models retrieve very different answers. For example, we find that on Natural Questions, the two models' top-ranked answers disagree on 64.75% questions.[21] The other datasets have similar levels of disagreement. This suggests that the models have different strengths, and that a combination of these modeling techniques could leads to a significant improvement.

Table 7 shows examples where the models retrieve different answers, and both are incorrect. In the first example, the BM25_{wpm} retrieves the correct context by matching the keyword "Salton Sea". But it fails to retrieve the correct sentence, as none of the keywords in the question appear in the target answer. On the other hand, the $\text{USE-QA}_{\text{finetune}}$ model understands the question is asking about some sort of animal living in the sea, but fails to connect to the Salton Sea specifically. Similarly, in the second example, both models retrieve sentences that match some keywords from the question. The BM25_{wpm} matches keywords "Spencer" and "Maine", but misses that the question is looking for an invention. The $\text{USE-QA}_{\text{finetune}}$ matches "Spencer", and is able to connect "invent" with "discover", but surfaces the wrong discovery. Overall, we observe term based models very often retrieve the correct context, but then fail to identify the correct sentence as the answer. Conversely, neural models seems to better understand the question, but sometimes fails to recognize important keywords.

7 Related Work

Open domain QA involves finding answers to questions within large document collections (Voorhees and Tice, 2000). The ground-truth answer for many evaluations is a span often containing a word or a short phrase (i.a., Kwiatkowski et al. (2019); Chen et al. (2017); Rajpurkar et al. (2016b)).

Karpukhin et al. (2020) and Xiong et al. (2020) explored passage level retrieval for QA. Seo et al. (2018) constructs a phrase-indexed QA challenge benchmark retrieving phrases, allowing for a direct F_1 and exact-match evaluation on SQuAD. (Seo et al., 2019) demonstrates phrase-indexed QA systems can be built using a combination of dense (neural) and sparse (term-frequency based)

[21]Note that even if the models retrieve different answers, both answers could still be correct.

Example 1 (from NQ): what kind of fish live in the salton sea

Correct Answer: [...] Due to the high salinity , very few fish species can tolerate living in the Salton Sea . *Introduced tilapia are the main fish that can tolerate the high salinity levels and pollution* . Other freshwater fish species live in the rivers and canals that feed the Salton Sea , including threadfin shad . [...]

USE-QA$_{\text{finetune}}$: [...] It may also drift in to the south - western part of the Baltic Sea (where it can not breed due to the low salinity) . *Similar jellyfish – which may be the same species – are known to inhabit seas near Australia and New Zealand* . The largest recorded specimen found washed up on the shore of Massachusetts Bay in 1870 . [...]

BM25$_{\text{wpm}}$: [...] Introduced tilapia are the main fish that can tolerate the high salinity levels and pollution . *Other freshwater fish species live in the rivers and canals that feed the Salton Sea , including threadfin shad , carp, red shiner , channel catfish , white catfish , largemouth bass , mosquitofish , sailfin molly , and the vulnerable desert pupfish* . [...]

Example 2 (from TriviaQA): What was invented in the 1940s by Percy Spencer, an American self-taught engineer from Howland, Maine, who was building magnetrons for radar sets?

Correct Answer: [...] After experimenting, he realized that microwaves would cook foods quickly - even faster than conventional ovens that cook with heat. *The Raytheon Corporation produced the first commercial microwave oven in 1954; it was called the 1161 Radarange.* It was large, expensive, and had a power of 1600 watts. [...]

USE-QA$_{\text{finetune}}$: [...] Because of his accomplishments, Spencer was awarded the Distinguished Service Medal by the U.S. Navy and has a building named after him at Raytheon. *Percy Spencer, while working for the Raytheon Company, discovered a more efficient way to manufacture magnetrons.* In 1941, magnetrons were being produced at a rate of 17 per day. [...]

BM25$_{\text{wpm}}$: [...] By the end of 1971, the price of countertop units began to decrease and their capabilities were expanded. *Spencer, born in Howland, Maine, was orphaned at a young age.* Although he never graduated from grammar school, he became Senior Vice President and a member of the Board of Directors at Raytheon, receiving 150 patents during his career [...]

Table 7: Examples where both the BM25$_{\text{wpm}}$ and USE-QA$_{\text{finetune}}$ models get wrong. *Italics* indicate the answer sentence. At most one sentence before/after the answer is shown, although the original context may be longer.

indices. Roy et al. (2020) investigates the retrieval of sentence-level answers from a language agnostic candidate pool. Chang et al. (2020) investigates the pre-training tasks for retrieving answers from a large scale candidate pool.

Surdeanu et al. (2008) provides a dataset consisting of 142,627 question-answer pairs from Yahoo! Answers "how to" questions, with the goal of retrieving the correct answer to a given question from the set of all answers. WikiQA (Yang et al., 2015) is another sentence-level answer selection dataset consisting of 3,047 questions and 29,258 candidate answers, split into train, dev, and test. These datasets, however, are either limited to a specific type of question, or limited to a small set of candidates. we propose a more comprehensive eval covering multiple domains and include tasks at a much larger scale. Additionally, folding the various MRQA in-domain and out-of-domain datasets into a single eval allows us to directly investigate cross-domain generalization.

8 Conclusion

In this paper, we convert eight existing QA tasks from the MRQA shared task (Fisch et al., 2019b) into sentence-level retrieval tasks, by treating the sentence containing the ground-truth span as the target sentence-level answer. In additional to a new evaluation suite for sentence level retrieval, we provide strong baselines using unsupervised term-based information retrieval methods (BM25), and three neural models, off-the-self USE-QA, fine-tuned USE-QA, and BERT dual encoders.

Overall, BM25's classical term-based retrieval approach is a surprisingly strong baseline, and one that could likely be improved further using additional information retrieval techniques such as normalization and synonym matching. The neural models, however, can be trained end-to-end without feature engineering, and perform particularly well on tasks with a low degree of question/answer token overlap, or in situations where context is limited. The neural model performance can also be improved through the addition of in-domain training data. However, we find that QA tasks are not all alike and having training data in the precise target domain is important.

References

Amin Ahmad, Noah Constant, Yinfei Yang, and Daniel Cer. 2019. ReQA: An evaluation for end-to-end answer retrieval models. In *Proceedings of the 2nd Workshop on Machine Reading for Question Answer-*

ing, pages 137–146, Hong Kong, China. Association for Computational Linguistics.

Steven Bird, Ewan Klein, and Edward Loper. 2009. *Natural language processing with Python: analyzing text with the natural language toolkit.* " O'Reilly Media, Inc.".

Wei-Cheng Chang, Felix X. Yu, Yin-Wen Chang, Yiming Yang, and Sanjiv Kumar. 2020. Pre-training tasks for embedding-based large-scale retrieval. In *International Conference on Learning Representations*.

Danqi Chen, Adam Fisch, Jason Weston, and Antoine Bordes. 2017. Reading Wikipedia to answer open-domain questions. In *Proceedings of the 55th Annual Meeting of the Association for Computational Linguistics (Volume 1: Long Papers)*, pages 1870–1879, Vancouver, Canada. Association for Computational Linguistics.

Paul Alexandru Chirita, Wolfgang Nejdl, Raluca Paiu, and Christian Kohlschütter. 2005. Using odp metadata to personalize search. In *Proceedings of the International ACM SIGIR Conference on Research and Development in Information Retrieval*, pages 178–185.

Jacob Devlin, Ming-Wei Chang, Kenton Lee, and Kristina Toutanova. 2019. BERT: Pre-training of deep bidirectional transformers for language understanding. In *Proceedings of the 2019 Conference of the North American Chapter of the Association for Computational Linguistics: Human Language Technologies, Volume 1 (Long and Short Papers)*, pages 4171–4186, Minneapolis, Minnesota. Association for Computational Linguistics.

Matthew Dunn, Levent Sagun, Mike Higgins, V. Ugur Güney, Volkan Cirik, and Kyunghyun Cho. 2017. Searchqa: A new q&a dataset augmented with context from a search engine. *CoRR*, abs/1704.05179.

Fangxiaoyu Feng, Yinfei Yang, Daniel Cer, Naveen Arivazhagan, and Wei Wang. 2020. Language-agnostic bert sentence embedding.

Adam Fisch, Alon Talmor, Robin Jia, Minjoon Seo, Eunsol Choi, and Danqi Chen. 2019a. MRQA 2019 shared task: Evaluating generalization in reading comprehension. In *Proceedings of the 2nd Workshop on Machine Reading for Question Answering*, pages 1–13, Hong Kong, China. Association for Computational Linguistics.

Adam Fisch, Alon Talmor, Robin Jia, Minjoon Seo, Eunsol Choi, and Danqi Chen. 2019b. MRQA 2019 shared task: Evaluating generalization in reading comprehension. In *Proceedings of 2nd Machine Reading for Reading Comprehension (MRQA) Workshop at EMNLP*.

Daniel Gillick, Alessandro Presta, and Gaurav Singh Tomar. 2018. End-to-end retrieval in continuous space. *arXiv preprint arXiv:1811.08008*.

Mandy Guo, Qinlan Shen, Yinfei Yang, Heming Ge, Daniel Cer, Gustavo Hernandez Abrego, Keith Stevens, Noah Constant, Yun-Hsuan Sung, Brian Strope, and Ray Kurzweil. 2018. Effective parallel corpus mining using bilingual sentence embeddings. In *Proceedings of the Third Conference on Machine Translation: Research Papers*, pages 165–176, Belgium, Brussels. Association for Computational Linguistics.

David Hawking. 2004. Challenges in enterprise search. In *ADC*, volume 4, pages 15–24. Citeseer.

Mohit Iyyer, Varun Manjunatha, Jordan Boyd-Graber, and Hal Daumé III. 2015. Deep unordered composition rivals syntactic methods for text classification. In *Proceedings of the 53rd Annual Meeting of the Association for Computational Linguistics and the 7th International Joint Conference on Natural Language Processing (Volume 1: Long Papers)*, pages 1681–1691, Beijing, China. Association for Computational Linguistics.

Mandar Joshi, Eunsol Choi, Daniel Weld, and Luke Zettlemoyer. 2017a. TriviaQA: A large scale distantly supervised challenge dataset for reading comprehension. In *Proceedings of the 55th Annual Meeting of the Association for Computational Linguistics (Volume 1: Long Papers)*, pages 1601–1611, Vancouver, Canada. Association for Computational Linguistics.

Mandar Joshi, Eunsol Choi, Daniel S. Weld, and Luke Zettlemoyer. 2017b. Triviaqa: A large scale distantly supervised challenge dataset for reading comprehension. In *Proceedings of the 55th Annual Meeting of the Association for Computational Linguistics*, Vancouver, Canada. Association for Computational Linguistics.

Vladimir Karpukhin, Barlas Oğuz, Sewon Min, Ledell Wu, Sergey Edunov, Danqi Chen, and Wen tau Yih. 2020. Dense passage retrieval for open-domain question answering.

Aniruddha Kembhavi, Minjoon Seo, Dustin Schwenk, Jonghyun Choi, Ali Farhadi, and Hannaneh Hajishirzi. 2017. Are you smarter than a sixth grader? textbook question answering for multimodal machine comprehension. In *The IEEE Conference on Computer Vision and Pattern Recognition (CVPR)*.

Tom Kwiatkowski, Jennimaria Palomaki, Olivia Redfield, Michael Collins, Ankur Parikh, Chris Alberti, Danielle Epstein, Illia Polosukhin, Matthew Kelcey, Jacob Devlin, Kenton Lee, Kristina N. Toutanova, Llion Jones, Ming-Wei Chang, Andrew Dai, Jakob Uszkoreit, Quoc Le, and Slav Petrov. 2019. Natural questions: a benchmark for question answering research. *Transactions of the Association of Computational Linguistics*.

Kenton Lee, Ming-Wei Chang, and Kristina Toutanova. 2019. Latent retrieval for weakly supervised open domain question answering. In *Proceedings of the*

57th Annual Meeting of the Association for Computational Linguistics, pages 6086–6096, Florence, Italy. Association for Computational Linguistics.

Yi Luan, Jacob Eisenstein, Kristina Toutanova, and Michael Collins. 2020. Sparse, dense, and attentional representations for text retrieval.

Ji Ma, Ivan Korotkov, Yinfei Yang, Keith Hall, and Ryan McDonald. 2020. Zero-shot neural retrieval via domain-targeted synthetic query generation.

Dragomir R. Radev, Hong Qi, Harris Wu, and Weiguo Fan. 2002. Evaluating web-based question answering systems. In *Proceedings of the Third International Conference on Language Resources and Evaluation (LREC'02)*, Las Palmas, Canary Islands - Spain. European Language Resources Association (ELRA).

Pranav Rajpurkar, Jian Zhang, Konstantin Lopyrev, and Percy Liang. 2016a. SQuAD: 100,000+ questions for machine comprehension of text. In *Proceedings of the 2016 Conference on Empirical Methods in Natural Language Processing*, pages 2383–2392, Austin, Texas. Association for Computational Linguistics.

Pranav Rajpurkar, Jian Zhang, Konstantin Lopyrev, and Percy Liang. 2016b. SQuAD: 100,000+ questions for machine comprehension of text. In *Proceedings of the 2016 Conference on Empirical Methods in Natural Language Processing*, pages 2383–2392, Austin, Texas. Association for Computational Linguistics.

Radim Řehůřek and Petr Sojka. 2010. Software Framework for Topic Modelling with Large Corpora. In *Proceedings of the LREC 2010 Workshop on New Challenges for NLP Frameworks*, pages 45–50, Valletta, Malta. ELRA. `http://is.muni.cz/publication/884893/en`.

Stephen Robertson and Hugo Zaragoza. 2009. The probabilistic relevance framework: Bm25 and beyond. *Found. Trends Inf. Retr.*, 3(4):333–389.

Uma Roy, Noah Constant, Rami Al-Rfou, Aditya Barua, Aaron Phillips, and Yinfei Yang. 2020. Lareqa: Language-agnostic answer retrieval from a multilingual pool. In *Conference on Empirical Methods in Natural Language Processing (EMNLP)*.

Minjoon Seo, Tom Kwiatkowski, Ankur Parikh, Ali Farhadi, and Hannaneh Hajishirzi. 2018. Phrase-indexed question answering: A new challenge for scalable document comprehension. In *Proceedings of the 2018 Conference on Empirical Methods in Natural Language Processing*, pages 559–564, Brussels, Belgium. Association for Computational Linguistics.

Minjoon Seo, Jinhyuk Lee, Tom Kwiatkowski, Ankur Parikh, Ali Farhadi, and Hannaneh Hajishirzi. 2019. Real-time open-domain question answering with dense-sparse phrase index. In *Proceedings of the 57th Annual Meeting of the Association for Computational Linguistics*, pages 4430–4441, Florence, Italy. Association for Computational Linguistics.

Mihai Surdeanu, Massimiliano Ciaramita, and Hugo Zaragoza. 2008. Learning to rank answers on large online QA collections. In *Proceedings of ACL-08: HLT*, pages 719–727, Columbus, Ohio. Association for Computational Linguistics.

George Tsatsaronis, Georgios Balikas, Prodromos Malakasiotis, Ioannis Partalas, Matthias Zschunke, Michael R. Alvers, Dirk Weissenborn, Anastasia Krithara, Sergios Petridis, Dimitris Polychronopoulos, Yannis Almirantis, John Pavlopoulos, Nicolas Baskiotis, Patrick Gallinari, Thierry Artières, Axel-Cyrille Ngonga Ngomo, Norman Heino, Éric Gaussier, Liliana Barrio-Alvers, Michael Schroeder, Ion Androutsopoulos, and Georgios Paliouras. 2015. An overview of the bioasq large-scale biomedical semantic indexing and question answering competition. In *BMC Bioinformatics*.

Ashish Vaswani, Noam Shazeer, Niki Parmar, Jakob Uszkoreit, Llion Jones, Aidan N Gomez, Ł ukasz Kaiser, and Illia Polosukhin. 2017. Attention is all you need. In I. Guyon, U. V. Luxburg, S. Bengio, H. Wallach, R. Fergus, S. Vishwanathan, and R. Garnett, editors, *Advances in Neural Information Processing Systems 30*, pages 6000–6010. Curran Associates, Inc.

Ellen M. Voorhees. 2001. The trec question answering track. *Nat. Lang. Eng.*, 7(4):361–378.

Ellen M. Voorhees and Dawn M. Tice. 2000. Building a question answering test collection. In *Proceedings of the 23rd Annual International ACM SIGIR Conference on Research and Development in Information Retrieval*, SIGIR '00, pages 200–207, New York, NY, USA. ACM.

Yonghui Wu, Mike Schuster, Zhifeng Chen, Quoc V Le, Mohammad Norouzi, Wolfgang Macherey, Maxim Krikun, Yuan Cao, Qin Gao, Klaus Macherey, et al. 2016. Google's neural machine translation system: Bridging the gap between human and machine translation. *arXiv preprint arXiv:1609.08144*.

Lee Xiong, Chenyan Xiong, Ye Li, Kwok-Fung Tang, Jialin Liu, Paul Bennett, Junaid Ahmed, and Arnold Overwijk. 2020. Approximate nearest neighbor negative contrastive learning for dense text retrieval.

Yi Yang, Wen-tau Yih, and Christopher Meek. 2015. WikiQA: A challenge dataset for open-domain question answering. In *Proceedings of the 2015 Conference on Empirical Methods in Natural Language Processing*, pages 2013–2018, Lisbon, Portugal. Association for Computational Linguistics.

Yinfei Yang, Daniel Cer, Amin Ahmad, Mandy Guo, Jax Law, Noah Constant, Gustavo Hernandez Abrego, Steve Yuan, Chris Tar, Yun-Hsuan

Sung, et al. 2019. Multilingual universal sentence encoder for semantic retrieval. *arXiv preprint arXiv:1907.04307*.

Zhilin Yang, Peng Qi, Saizheng Zhang, Yoshua Bengio, William W. Cohen, Ruslan Salakhutdinov, and Christopher D. Manning. 2018. HotpotQA: A dataset for diverse, explainable multi-hop question answering. In *Conference on Empirical Methods in Natural Language Processing (EMNLP)*.

Domain adaptation in practice: Lessons from a real-world information extraction pipeline

Timothy Miller
Computational Health Informatics Program
Boston Children's Hospital
Department of Pediatrics, Harvard Medical School
timothy.miller@childrens.harvard.edu

Egoitz Laparra and **Steven Bethard**
School of Information
University of Arizona
{laparra,bethard}
@arizona.edu

Abstract

Advances in transfer learning and domain adaptation have raised hopes that once-challenging NLP tasks are ready to be put to use for sophisticated information extraction needs. In this work, we describe an effort to do just that – combining state-of-the-art neural methods for negation detection, document time relation extraction, and aspectual link prediction, with the eventual goal of extracting drug timelines from electronic health record text. We train on the THYME colon cancer corpus and test on both the THYME brain cancer corpus and an internal corpus, and show that performance of the combined systems is unacceptable despite good performance of individual systems. Although domain adaptation shows improvements on each individual system, the model selection problem is a barrier to improving overall pipeline performance.

1 Introduction

Advances in machine learning methods and the release of annotated datasets of clinical texts (Uzuner et al., 2011; Styler IV et al., 2014) in the past decade has led to an increase of available clinical NLP systems for interesting tasks. Recent advances in pre-trained models (Devlin et al., 2019; Liu et al., 2019) have made ever more accurate clinical NLP systems possible. Unsupervised domain adaptation algorithms (e.g., Ziser and Reichart (2019)) have made it possible to reduce performance degradation when applying trained models to new domains. The great promise of these developments is that these methods can be combined into pipelines that allow for sophisticated information extraction capabilities for downstream clinical use cases. Rather than building one-off datasets for each complex downstream task that arises, standard NLP components could potentially be used as "Lego"-style building blocks that allow for flexibly approaching new tasks as they arise.

However, the existence of the building blocks alone does not solve this problem. Combining individual components into NLP pipelines can lead to cascading errors (Finkel et al., 2006). The true error rate for structured extraction tasks is potentially as high as the sum of the component tasks' errors. For example, if the goal is to extract normalized concepts with assertion status, the concept error can come from normalization error, negation detection error, uncertainty detection error, etc, and the errors may not be correlated. These problems are exacerbated in the common case where individual components are trained on data from different domains, and tested on data from yet another domain.

In this work, we quantitatively examine the issues described above in the context of extracting drug temporality signatures, with the goal of understanding drug start and stop events. We approach this task with the combination of three sub-tasks: 1) the temporal relation of these mentions to the document creation time (DocTimeRel), 2) negation status of the mention, and 3) aspectual link relations of the mention (e.g., is it being described as starting or stopping). Figure 1 shows an example sentence with a drug mention, that demonstrates how the three tasks work together to establish the status of that drug in that patient. Successfully solving this task is beneficial for understanding patient treatment course, and enabling more causal understanding in important tasks such as adverse drug event detection or relating medication courses to outcomes.

We first set state-of-the-art benchmarks for three tasks on the THYME corpus by fine-tuning large pre-trained transformer models (Devlin et al., 2019; Liu et al., 2019). We then examine how the performance of individual systems degrades when moving from the training data to our target data (a pediatric cardiology cohort), and how the overall system performs when combining multiple systems

Proceedings of the Second Workshop on Domain Adaptation for NLP, pages 105–110
April 20, 2021.

Additionally , as the patient has preserved ejection fraction , no prior history of embolic phenomena , and no significant valvular disease , it would be acceptable for him to remain off ⟨*e*⟩ ***Coumadin*** ⟨*/e*⟩ *for the interim .*

Figure 1: An example sentence with highlighted drug name *Coumadin* to be classified for all three tasks. The gold standard has this drug mention classified as *negated*, with DocTimeRel=OVERLAP, and ALINK=CONTINUES. These three facts can be used to understand that the patient is not on the drug now or going forward, and was likely not on the drug prior to the note as well.

with imperfect performance. Despite strong individual results, we find that performance suffers immensely due to both out-of-domain performance losses and the basic combinatorial math of integrating outputs from multiple systems. This is the case even though we use a metric, accuracy, that is forgiving to the worst-performing individual model.

2 Background

It is both formally and empirically understood that classifiers can suffer performance loss when the test data is drawn from a different distribution than the training data (sometimes called *domain shift*). This presents a difficult challenge in clinical NLP because data-sharing limitations make it difficult to create large and diverse training corpora. As a result, domain adaptation approaches have been applied to multiple tasks in clinical NLP (Miller et al., 2017; Liu et al., 2018; Hur et al., 2020).

Recent work in the general domain has made use of transfer learning, which can attack the problem of domain shift, but by a different mechanism than domain adaptation; by training on massive corpora, large pre-trained models both learn general features, and are able to learn from smaller new datasets without overfitting. The most prominent of these models are based on the transformer architecture (Vaswani et al., 2017).

BERT (Devlin et al., 2019) uses a transformer encoder, and has shown that pre-training with massive amounts of text on a language modeling task, then fine-tuning on a supervised task of interest, achieves large performance gains in multiple NLP tasks.[1] During fine-tuning for sentence classification tasks, a classification head with randomly initialized weights is attached to a special sentence-initial token. Fine-tuning then proceeds in a standard supervised learning paradigm, with the goal of learning the weights of the classification head, but where the weights of all of the transformer encoder layers can also be updated. We use RoBERTa-base, a 12-layer transformer encoder that provides excellent performance but manageable memory utilization for our hardware (Liu et al., 2019).

The bigger vision of our current work is extracting temporally-aware medication mentions from electronic health records data. This would enable important downstream tasks including automatically extracting drug timelines to correlate with treatments, or extracting better causal information about drugs and potential adverse events. Some other recent work has also examined this topic (Ramirez et al., 2019), but focused on a single drug class (proton pump inhibitors), was limited to the problem list section, and made the assumption that missing drug implied drug stoppage.

3 Methods

We began this work by developing several NLP components necessary to extract drug temporality signatures, including negation detection, relation to document creation time (DocTimeRel), and aspectual link extraction (ALINK), all detailed below. Detecting negation helps us avoid false positives from mentions corresponding to, for example, decisions to not use a drug. DocTimeRel helps us distinguish mentions of drugs that are current from those that predate the current time period, or are being speculated about for future use. ALINK can model drug start, stop, and continuation events, which can help to distinguish whether a missing mention in the middle of a record corresponds to a stop and restart, or an incidentally omitted mention. Figure 1 shows an example instance of a drug mention to be classified for all three tasks.

The THYME dataset (Styler IV et al., 2014), released as part of Clinical TempEval (Bethard et al., 2017), contains all three of these annotation types, on 1200 notes of patients with colon and brain cancer. We train all models on the colon cancer section (details on data are in Section 4). While our bigger

[1] The RoBERTa system that followed (Liu et al., 2019) found further gains by pre-training on even larger datasets and for more iterations.

project is specific to drug mentions, the problem is not limited to drug mentions, so we train and evaluate on all annotated events in the THYME corpus. We also assume that events are given, to allow a straightforward metric of how many events we "get right" when combining all property predictions. In the real world, events will have to be automatically detected, so our metric will be an upper bound on how often the combined models get everything correct.

Negation detection

This is the task of finding whether a given event is being negated (e.g., *statins* is negated in *not currently on statins*). We model this as a span-in-context classification – given a sentence in a document with a marked event span, classify that span as being negated or not negated. We experiment with two different machine learning models. The first is a classical feature-based support vector machine that is the default model of Apache cTAKES (Savova et al., 2010). Features include bag of words and part of speech tags in and around the event, negation cue words from lists and their relation to the event, and dependency parse features that relate negation cue words to events. Details of this system were presented by Wu et al. (2014). For comparison we train a RoBERTa-based system, where the input representation is the sentence with special tokens indicating the event to be classified. We put a binary sigmoid layer as the output, with the "[CLS]" token representation from the final layer as the classifier input, and fine-tune the entire model. Hyperparameters such as learning rate and number of training epochs are optimized on the THYME colon development set. Our implementation uses the Huggingface Transformers library (Wolf et al., 2019).

DocTimeRel

DocTimeRel classification is the task of relating an event to the document creation time. The categories are BEFORE, OVERLAP, AFTER, and BEFORE/OVERLAP. As above, we model this as a span-in-context classification, and we again compare a feature-based approach with a RoBERTa-based approach.

The feature-based approach again uses the default cTAKES SVM-based implementation (Lin et al., 2016), with features based on bags of words in and around the event, and verb tense information for verbs on either side of the event. We train a separate RoBERTa-based model with the same architecture as the negation model, with the only difference being that the output layer is a softmax over the four categories rather than a sigmoid.

Aspectual Link Extraction

Aspectual link extraction (ALINK) is the task of classifying whether an event mention is related to an aspectual temporal modifier, for example, *discontinued*. This is annotated as a relation between an event and a modifier, but we model it as an event property classification task since each event can only participate in one type of relation. The set of possible labels is INITIATES, CONTINUES, TERMINATES, and REINITIATES.

We are not aware of any existing open-source models for this task, so for our feature-based baseline we train a model with the same SVM classification approach and feature set as the DocTimeRel model in cTAKES. We did not perform extensive feature engineering for this task, so further gains in the SVM system are probably possible. For the RoBERTa-based model, we used the same architecture as both systems above, with a softmax over the 5 categories – the 4 ALINK categories above as well as NONE, indicating a drug mention does not participate in any ALINK relation. NONE is by far the most common category.

3.1 Domain Adaptation Methods

The tasks described above are trained on a single *source* dataset, and must be combined into a pipeline that will run on data from a different *target* distribution. To adapt to the target domain, we use *unsupervised* domain adaptation methods, where we have access to only unlabeled target examples.

Since large pre-trained transformer models have arrived, they have been shown to be quite robust to out-of-distribution examples (Hendrycks et al., 2020), including on clinical tasks (Lin et al., 2020), where it was shown that adding domain adaptation layers on top of BERT was no better than BERT itself for negation detection. One of the few effective methods for improving the out-of-distribution performance of pre-trained transformer models has been to continue to pre-train the language modeling objective on the target domain data, before any fine-tuning is done on the source data (Han and Eisenstein, 2019; Gururangan et al., 2020). In this work, we focus on that method, since this is currently the most promising direction for adapting large pre-trained transformers. Specifically, to use this method, we run additional masked language model training steps on the target training data from the RoBERTa-base checkpoint, before fine-tuning on the labeled colon cancer data, and then testing on target test data. We tune the learning rate for the language model pre-training on target development set data, optimizing for perplexity.

4 Evaluation

For the three tasks of interest, we evaluate in-domain (THYME colon cancer corpus), as well as one closely related out-of-domain corpus (THYME brain cancer corpus). We also use a second out-of-domain corpus, an internal data set we annotated for all three tasks (pulmonary hypertension [PH] notes). This annotation was performed by an experienced annotator who has worked on clinical annotation projects in the past.

We measure performance on negation with F1-score, on DocTimeRel with accuracy (because the classes are relatively balanced), and on ALINK extraction with the average F1 score of all categories, macro-F1 (because the high frequency NONE label makes accuracy uninformative). In addition to system-level performance, we report an evaluation of mention-level accuracy: an event is counted as correct if all three systems made the correct prediction, and we report the percentage of events that were correct. This setting estimates how usable the entire pipeline is, given different system settings.

The "Colon" columns of Table 1 show results on the THYME colon cancer data (in-domain). RoBERTa performance is stronger than the SVM on all three tasks. Negation performance is particularly strong, though we are not aware of any reported results on this dataset to compare against. DocTimeRel performance is 3 points better than the best result of Clinical TempEval 2016 (Bethard et al., 2017). ALINK scores are lower than the other tasks, though again there are no published comparisons. It is likely this is a more difficult task, in particular because the RE-INITIATES category has relatively few examples and whose low performance skews the averaging of the macro-F1.

The "Brain" and "PH" columns of Table 1 show out-of-domain performance of the same systems on the THYME brain cancer and our internal pulmonary hypertension data, respectively. On THYME brain cancer data, RoBERTa again out-performs SVM substantially on all sub-tasks, but surprisingly the SVM performs better on PH data for negation and DocTimeRel. Adapting the RoBERTa model (RoBERTa+LM) by performing additional language modeling in the target domain before fine-tuning on colon cancer data leads to gains only on DocTimeRel for the PH data and on ALINK for both corpora. However, the improvement to DocTimeRel from adapting RoBERTa still leaves it worse off than the SVM.

Mention level accuracy ("All" column) is good for the in-domain data (THYME colon cancer), but drops off substantially even for the THYME brain cancer corpus from the same institution, created with the same guidelines and using the same annotators. The mention level accuracy for our internal PH data is unusable at an accuracy of 0.506 with RoBERTa+LM. This accuracy means that roughly one of every two drug mentions will have at least one of its attributes classified incorrectly.

5 Discussion and Conclusion

The results also show that combining NLP systems for new, complex, information needs is likely to run into issues even when individual systems perform well. In particular, our experiments raise questions about real-world use of domain adaptation. If we treated THYME colon and brain sets as representative in-domain and out-of-domain datasets we would select RoBERTa or RoBERTa+LM for everything. But an oracle optimizing PH performance would tell us to use the SVM for negation and DocTimeRel and RoBERTa+LM for ALINK. One of the difficulties in even *studying* domain adaptation is model selection – if labeled target data is not available, standard practices like tuning on held out data are impossible. But the reality our results suggest is that different algorithms work well on different tasks and datasets, and selecting the best model for each task is an unsolved and under-studied problem.

One direction of research that may address these concerns is on better modeling of domains themselves. The problem has been exacerbated with the move from feature-based classifiers to pre-trained black box models, as it is now even more difficult to understand the cause of errors in new domains without interpretable features. Domain adaptation should leverage "BERTology" and interpretability research to help understand how different aspects of domains contribute to performance differences. For example, in clinical notes, variation in institutions, specialties, note types, authors, etc., all

System	Negation (F1)			DocTimeRel (Acc)			ALINK (MacroF)			All (Acc)		
	Colon	Brain	PH	Colon	Brain	PH	Colon	Brain	PH	Colon	Brain	PH
SVM	0.924	0.705	0.625	0.842	0.703	0.694	0.502	0.338	0.345	–	–	–
RoBERTa	0.950	0.833	0.583	0.874	0.757	0.542	0.684	0.633	0.674	0.860	0.732	0.454
RoBERTa+LM	–	0.831	0.582	–	0.758	0.615	–	0.660	0.694	–	0.736	0.506

Table 1: Performance on both the individual sub-tasks (Negation, DocTimeRel, and ALINK) and the complete task (All) for systems trained on the THYME colon cancer training set and tested on the in-domain THYME colon test set, the out-of-domain THYME brain test set, and the out-of-domain pulmonary hypertension (PH) test set.

probably contribute differently to domain shift, and these sources of variation should be empirically explored. Future work will explore this direction to develop unsupervised model selection algorithms that better predict target domain performance.

Acknowledgments

Research reported in this publication was supported by the National Library Of Medicine of the National Institutes of Health under Award Numbers R01LM012918 and R01LM012973. The content is solely the responsibility of the authors and does not necessarily represent the official views of the National Institutes of Health.

References

Steven Bethard, Guergana Savova, Martha Palmer, and James Pustejovsky. 2017. SemEval-2017 task 12: Clinical TempEval. In *Proceedings of the 11th International Workshop on Semantic Evaluation (SemEval-2017)*, pages 565–572, Vancouver, Canada. Association for Computational Linguistics.

Jacob Devlin, Ming-Wei Chang, Kenton Lee, and Kristina Toutanova. 2019. BERT: Pre-training of deep bidirectional transformers for language understanding. In *Proceedings of the 2019 Conference of the North American Chapter of the Association for Computational Linguistics: Human Language Technologies, Volume 1 (Long and Short Papers)*, pages 4171–4186, Minneapolis, Minnesota. Association for Computational Linguistics.

Jenny Rose Finkel, Christopher D. Manning, and Andrew Y. Ng. 2006. Solving the problem of cascading errors: Approximate Bayesian inference for linguistic annotation pipelines. In *Proceedings of the 2006 Conference on Empirical Methods in Natural Language Processing*, pages 618–626, Sydney, Australia. Association for Computational Linguistics.

Suchin Gururangan, Ana Marasović, Swabha Swayamdipta, Kyle Lo, Iz Beltagy, Doug Downey, and Noah A. Smith. 2020. Don't stop pretraining: Adapt language models to domains and tasks. In *Proceedings of the 58th Annual Meeting of the Association for Computational Linguistics*, pages 8342–8360, Online. Association for Computational Linguistics.

Xiaochuang Han and Jacob Eisenstein. 2019. Unsupervised domain adaptation of contextualized embeddings for sequence labeling. In *Proceedings of the 2019 Conference on Empirical Methods in Natural Language Processing and the 9th International Joint Conference on Natural Language Processing (EMNLP-IJCNLP)*, pages 4238–4248, Hong Kong, China. Association for Computational Linguistics.

Dan Hendrycks, Xiaoyuan Liu, Eric Wallace, Adam Dziedzic, Rishabh Krishnan, and Dawn Song. 2020. Pretrained transformers improve out-of-distribution robustness. In *Proceedings of the 58th Annual Meeting of the Association for Computational Linguistics*, pages 2744–2751, Online. Association for Computational Linguistics.

Brian Hur, Timothy Baldwin, Karin Verspoor, Laura Hardefeldt, and James Gilkerson. 2020. Domain adaptation and instance selection for disease syndrome classification over veterinary clinical notes. In *Proceedings of the 19th SIGBioMed Workshop on Biomedical Language Processing*, pages 156–166, Online. Association for Computational Linguistics.

Chen Lin, Steven Bethard, Dmitriy Dligach, Farig Sadeque, Guergana Savova, and Timothy A Miller. 2020. Does BERT need domain adaptation for clinical negation detection? *Journal of the American Medical Informatics Association*, 27(4):584–591.

Chen Lin, Dmitriy Dligach, Timothy A Miller, Steven Bethard, and Guergana K Savova. 2016. Multilayered temporal modeling for the clinical domain. *Journal of the American Medical Informatics Association*, 23(2):387–395.

Miaofeng Liu, Jialong Han, Haisong Zhang, and Yan Song. 2018. Domain adaptation for disease phrase matching with adversarial networks. In *Proceedings of the BioNLP 2018 workshop*, pages 137–141, Melbourne, Australia. Association for Computational Linguistics.

Yinhan Liu, Myle Ott, Naman Goyal, Jingfei Du, Mandar Joshi, Danqi Chen, Omer Levy, Mike Lewis, Luke Zettlemoyer, and Veselin Stoyanov. 2019.

Roberta: A robustly optimized bert pretraining approach. *arXiv preprint arXiv:1907.11692*.

Timothy Miller, Steven Bethard, Hadi Amiri, and Guergana Savova. 2017. Unsupervised domain adaptation for clinical negation detection. In *BioNLP 2017*, pages 165–170, Vancouver, Canada,. Association for Computational Linguistics.

Andrea H. Ramirez, Yaping Shi, Elliot Fielstein, Jonathan Schildcrout, Henry H. Ong, Josh C. Denny, and Josh F. Peterson. 2019. Extracting Drug Exposure Epochs and Drug Response Outcomes from Electronic Health Records. In *Proceedings of AMIA Annual Symposium (Podium Abstract)*, Washington, DC.

Guergana K Savova, James J Masanz, Philip V Ogren, Jiaping Zheng, Sunghwan Sohn, Karin C Kipper-Schuler, and Christopher G Chute. 2010. Mayo clinical Text Analysis and Knowledge Extraction System (cTAKES): architecture, component evaluation and applications. *Journal of the American Medical Informatics Association*, 17(5):507–513.

William F. Styler IV, Steven Bethard, Sean Finan, Martha Palmer, Sameer Pradhan, Piet C de Groen, Brad Erickson, Timothy Miller, Chen Lin, Guergana Savova, and James Pustejovsky. 2014. Temporal annotation in the clinical domain. *Transactions of the Association for Computational Linguistics*, 2:143–154.

Özlem Uzuner, Brett R South, Shuying Shen, and Scott L DuVall. 2011. 2010 i2b2/VA challenge on concepts, assertions, and relations in clinical text. *Journal of the American Medical Informatics Association*, 18(5):552–556.

Ashish Vaswani, Noam Shazeer, Niki Parmar, Jakob Uszkoreit, Llion Jones, Aidan N Gomez, Łukasz Kaiser, and Illia Polosukhin. 2017. Attention is all you need. In *Advances in neural information processing systems*, pages 5998–6008.

Thomas Wolf, Lysandre Debut, Victor Sanh, Julien Chaumond, Clement Delangue, Anthony Moi, Pierric Cistac, Tim Rault, R'emi Louf, Morgan Funtowicz, and Jamie Brew. 2019. Huggingface's transformers: State-of-the-art natural language processing. *ArXiv*, abs/1910.03771.

Stephen Wu, Timothy Miller, James Masanz, Matt Coarr, Scott Halgrim, David Carrell, and Cheryl Clark. 2014. Negation's not solved: generalizability versus optimizability in clinical natural language processing. *PloS one*, 9(11):e112774.

Yftah Ziser and Roi Reichart. 2019. Task refinement learning for improved accuracy and stability of unsupervised domain adaptation. In *Proceedings of the 57th Annual Meeting of the Association for Computational Linguistics*, pages 5895–5906, Florence, Italy. Association for Computational Linguistics.

BERTologiCoMix*
How does Code-Mixing interact with Multilingual BERT?

Sebastin Santy[†] **Anirudh Srinivasan**[†] **Monojit Choudhury**

Microsoft Research, India
{t-sesan, t-ansrin, monojitc}@microsoft.com

Abstract

Models such as mBERT and XLMR have shown success in solving Code-Mixed NLP tasks even though they were not exposed to such text during pretraining. Code-Mixed NLP models have relied on using synthetically generated data along with naturally occurring data to improve their performance. Finetuning[1] mBERT on such data improves it's code-mixed performance, but the benefits of using the different types of Code-Mixed data aren't clear. In this paper, we study the impact of finetuning with different types of code-mixed data and outline the changes that occur to the model during such finetuning. Our findings suggest that using naturally occurring code-mixed data brings in the best performance improvement after finetuning and that finetuning with any type of code-mixed text improves the responsivity of it's attention heads to code-mixed text inputs.

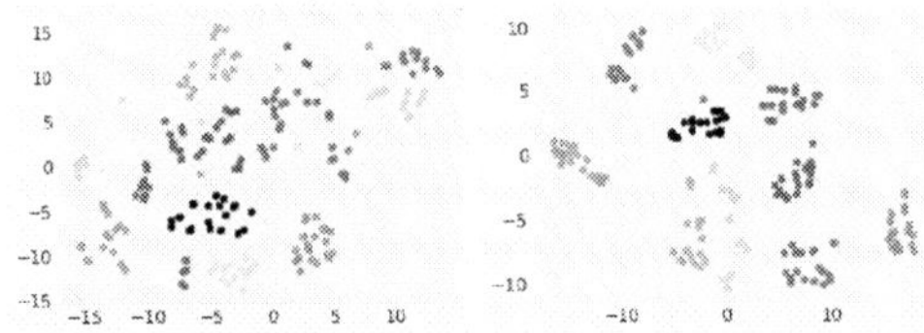

(a) Vanilla mBERT (without fine-tuning) (b) mBERT fine-tuned on En-Hi CM

Figure 1: t-SNE representations of En-Es CM sentences on the respective models. Each color represents CM sentences with the same meaning but with different amounts of mixing generated based on the g-CM method in Sec 3.1. The tight clusters in (b) shows that CM sentence representations align better in mBERT fine-tuned on any CM data regardless of the language of mixing.

1 Introduction

Massive multilingual models such as mBERT (Devlin et al., 2019) and XLMR (Conneau et al., 2020) have recently become very popular as they cover over 100 languages and are capable of zero-shot transfer of performance in downstream tasks across languages. As these models serve as good multilingual representations of sentences (Pires et al., 2019), there have been attempts at using these representations for encoding code-mixed sentences (Srinivasan, 2020; Aguilar et al., 2020; Khanuja et al., 2020). **Code-Mixing (CM)** is the mixing of words belonging two or more languages within a single sentence and is a commonly observed phenomenon in societies with multiple spoken languages. These multilingual models have shown promise for solving CM tasks having surpassed the previously achieved performances (Khanuja et al., 2020; Aguilar et al., 2020). This is an impressive feat considering that these models have never been exposed to any form of code-mixing during their pre-training stage.

Traditionally, CM has been a spoken phenomenon though it is slowly penetrating into written form of communication (Tay, 1989). However, they mostly occur in an informal setting and hence such CM data is not publicly available in large quantities. Such scarcity of data would mean that building independent CM models can be unfeasible. With the onset of pre-trained multilingual models, further training with CM data can help in adapting these models for CM processing. However, even for further training, there is a requirement for a significant amount of data albeit lesser than starting from scratch. The amount of data available even for their monolingual counterparts is very less (Joshi et al., 2020) let alone the amount of real-world CM data. This can prove to be a bottleneck. Rightly so,

* The word BERTologiCoMix is a portmanteau of BERTology and Code-Mixing, and is inspired from the title of the graphic novel: *Logicomix: An Epic Search for Truth* by Apostolos Doxiadis and Christos Papadimitriou (2009).

[†] The authors contributed equally to the work.

[1] In this paper, unless specifically stated, finetuning refers to MLM finetuning/continued pretraining and not downstream task finetuning

Proceedings of the Second Workshop on Domain Adaptation for NLP, pages 111–121
April 20, 2021.

there have been previous works exploring synthesis of CM data for the purpose of data augmentation (Bhat et al., 2016; Pratapa et al., 2018a). Synthesis of CM mostly rely on certain linguistic theories (Poplack, 2000) to construct grammatically plausible sentences. These works have shown that using the synthetic and real CM data in a curriculum setting while fine-tuning can help with achieving better performances on the downstream CM tasks. Though this is analogous to adapting models to new domains, CM differs in that the adaptation is not purely at vocabulary or style level but rather at a grammatical level. Although it is known such adaptation techniques can bring an improvement, it is not well understood how exactly fine-tuning helps in the CM domain.

Through this paper, we seek to answer these lingering questions which exist in area of CM processing. We first study the impact of finetuning multilingual models with different forms of CM data on downstream task performance. For this purpose, we rely on three forms of CM varying in their complexity of mixing, naturalness and obtainability - (i) randomly ordered code-mixing (l-CM), (ii) grammatically appropriate code-mixing (g-CM) both of which are synthetically generated and (iii) real-world code-mixing (r-CM). We perform this comparative analysis in a controlled setting where we finetune models with the same quantity of CM text belonging to different forms and then evaluate these finetuned models on 11 downstream tasks. We find that on average the r-CM performs better on all tasks, whereas the synthetic forms of CM (l-CM, g-CM) tend to diminish the performance as compared to the stock/non-finetuned models. However, these synthetic forms of data can be used in conjuction to r-CM in a curriculum setting which allows to alleviate the data scarcity issue. In order to understand the difference in the behavior of these models, we analyze their self-attention heads using a novel visualization technique and show how fine-tuning with CM causes the model to respond more effectively to CM texts. We notice that using r-CM for finetuning makes the model more robust and the representations more distributed leading to better and stable overall performances on the downstream tasks.

The rest of the paper is organized as follows. Section 2 surveys prior work done in domain adaptation of transformer-based LMs, code-mixing and interpretability and analysis techniques. Section 3 introduces the different types of code-mixing and the models that we build with them. Section 4 and 5 respectively presents the task-based and attention-head based probing experiments along with the findings. Section 6 concludes the paper by summarizing the work and laying out future directions.

2 Related Work

2.1 Domain Adaptation of BERT

Pre-trained Language Models trained on generic data such as BERT and RoBERTa are often adapted to the domain where it is required to be used. Domain adaptation benefits BERT in two ways (i) it gives exposure to text in the domain specific contexts and (ii) adds domain specific terms to the vocabulary. BERT has been adapted to several domains especially once which have its own complex jargon of communication such as the biomedical domain (Lee et al., 2020; Peng et al., 2019; Alsentzer et al., 2019), scientific texts or publications (Beltagy et al., 2019), legal domain (Chalkidis et al., 2020) and financial document processing (Yang et al., 2020b). Most of these works employ sophisticated techniques for mining large quantities of domain specific text from the internet and thus prefer to train the BERT model from scratch rather than fine-tuning the available BERT checkpoints. This is because they don't have to accommodate existing vocabulary along with the domain specific vocabulary which can lead to further fragmentation (Gu et al., 2020). While most works have looked at domain adaptation by plainly continuing the training using MLM objectives, some works have explored on different techniques to improve downstream task performance. Ma et al. (2019) uses curriculum learning and domain-discriminative data selection for domain adaptation. Adversarial techniques have been used for enforce domain-invariant learning and thus improve on generalization (Naik and Rose, 2020; Wang et al., 2019; Zhang et al., 2020). Ye et al. (2020) explores adapting BERT across languages. However, domain adaptation is not always effective and can lead to worse performances. This depends on several factors such as how different the domains are (Kashyap et al., 2020) or how much data is available (Zhang et al., 2020).

2.2 Code-Mixing

Traditionally, Code-Mixing has been used in informal contexts and can be difficult to obtain in large quantities (Rijhwani et al., 2017). This scarcity of data has been previously tackled by generation of synthetic CM data to augment the real CM data. Bhat et al. (2016); Pratapa et al. (2018a) demonstrate a technique to generate code-mixed sentences using parallel sentences and show that using these synthetic sentences can improve language model perplexity. A similar method is also proposed by Samanta et al. (2019) which uses parse trees to generate synthetic sentences. Yang et al. (2020a) generates CM sentences by using phrase tables to align and mix parts of a parallel sentence. Winata et al. (2019) proposes a technique to generate code-mixed sentences using pointer generator networks. The efficacy of synthetic CM data is evident from these works where they have been used in a curriculum setting for CM language modelling (Pratapa et al., 2018a), cross-lingual training of multilingual transformer models (Yang et al., 2020a) as well as to develop CM embeddings as a better alternative to standard cross-lingual embeddings for CM tasks (Pratapa et al., 2018b). In this work, we use grammatical theories to generate synthetic CM data from parallel sentences analogous to the aforementioned techniques.

2.3 BERT Attention based probing

Given the complex black-box nature of the BERT model, there have been a large number of works that propose experiments to probe and understand the working of different components of the BERT model. A large portion of these methods have focused on the attention mechanism of the transformer model. Clark et al. (2019); Htut et al. (2019) find that certain attention heads encode linguistic dependencies between words of the sentence. Kovaleva et al. (2019) report on the patterns in the attention heads of BERT and find that a large number of heads just attend to the `[CLS]` or `[SEP]` tokens and do not encode any relation between the words of the sentence. Michel et al. (2019); Prasanna et al. (2020) also show that many of BERT's attention heads are redundant and pruning heads does not affect downstream task performance. In this paper, we borrow ideas from these works and propose a technique for visualizing the attention heads and how their behaviour changes during finetuning.

3 Models

In this section, we describe the mBERT models, the modifications we make to them, and the types of CM data that we use for training.

3.1 Types of Code-Mixing

For the purpose of this study, we characterize CM data across two dimensions: *linguistic complexity* and *languages involved*. Here, we experiment with CM for two different language pairs: English-Spanish ($enes$) and English-Hindi ($enhi$). While Spanish has similar word order and a sizeable shared vocabulary with English, Hindi has a different word order and no shared vocabulary by virtue of using a different script. Thus, investigating through these two diverse pairs is expected to help us understand the representational variance.

The linguistic complexity of code-mixing can be categorized into the following three *types*:

Lexical Code-Mixing (l-CM): The simplest form of code-mixing is to substitute lexical units within a monolingual sentence with its counterpart from the other language. This can be achieved by using parallel sentences, and aligning the words with an aligner (Dyer et al., 2013).

Grammatical Code-Mixing (g-CM): There are grammatical constraints (Joshi, 1982; Poplack, 2000; Belazi et al., 1994) on word-order changes and lexical substitution during code-mixing that the l-CM does not take into account. Pratapa et al. (2018a) propose a technique to generate all grammatically valid CM sentences from a pair of parallel sentences. Here, we use this generated dataset as our g-CM[2].

Parse trees are generated for parallel sentences (between two languages L_1 and L_2), and common nodes between these parse trees are then replaced based on certain conditions specified by Equivalence Constraint (EC) theory (Poplack, 2000; Sankoff, 1998), thereby producing a grammatically sound code-mixing. Fine-tuning with this form of CM should ideally impart the knowledge of grammatical boundaries for CM and would let us know whether a grammatically correct CM sentence is required to improve the performance.

Real Code-Mixing (r-CM): While g-CM considers purely the syntactic structure of CM, real-world

[2]It is important to note that Pratapa et al. (2018a) uses GCM to denote "Generated CM" data, and not for "grammatical" as is used here.

	SENT		NER		POS			LID		QA	NLI
model	$enes$	$enhi$	$enes$	ehi	$enes$	$enhi$	$enhi$	$enes$	$enhi$	$enhi$	$enhi$
$m_{\langle\rangle}$	67.81$_{\pm 2.5}$	**58.42**$_{\pm 1.1}$	59.50$_{\pm 0.9}$	75.55$_{\pm 0.6}$	93.35$_{\pm 0.2}$	87.49$_{\pm 0.1}$	63.40$_{\pm 0.5}$	95.99$_{\pm 0.0}$	**95.80**$_{\pm 0.4}$	71.95$_{\pm 0.8}$	**63.25**$_{\pm 1.9}$
$m_{\langle l,\odot\rangle}$	68.07$_{\pm 1.5}$	58.08$_{\pm 0.8}$	59.39$_{\pm 1.0}$	76.53$_{\pm 1.0}$	**93.84**$_{\pm 0.1}$	88.00$_{\pm 0.2}$	**64.09**$_{\pm 0.2}$	96.09$_{\pm 0.1}$	95.32$_{\pm 0.9}$	70.53$_{\pm 3.5}$	62.94$_{\pm 2.7}$
$m_{\langle g,\odot\rangle}$	68.64$_{\pm 1.5}$	57.90$_{\pm 1.1}$	59.88$_{\pm 0.7}$	76.86$_{\pm 0.6}$	93.74$_{\pm 0.1}$	87.79$_{\pm 0.2}$	63.79$_{\pm 0.2}$	96.06$_{\pm 0.0}$	95.41$_{\pm 0.8}$	70.11$_{\pm 1.8}$	55.19$_{\pm 6.5}$
$m_{\langle r,\odot\rangle}$	**68.51**$_{\pm 0.7}$	58.25$_{\pm 0.8}$	**60.46**$_{\pm 0.6}$	**76.86**$_{\pm 0.5}$	93.68$_{\pm 0.1}$	**88.00**$_{\pm 0.0}$	63.38$_{\pm 0.0}$	**96.12**$_{\pm 0.0}$	94.60$_{\pm 0.2}$	**73.54**$_{\pm 3.9}$	60.00$_{\pm 5.7}$

Table 1: Performance of the models for different tasks along with their standard deviations. The trained model language corresponds to the language the model is tested on, and is denoted by $\odot$. r-CM trained models almost always perform better than models trained on other types of CM data.

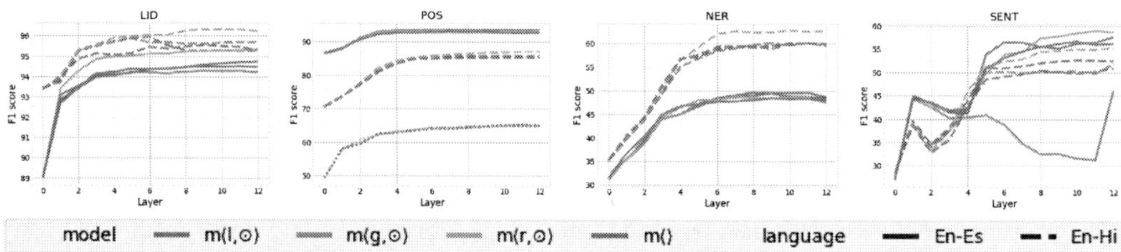

Figure 2: Layer-wise F1 scores for LID, POS, NER and SENT respectively across different layers. The dashed lines represent the $enhi$ versions and solid lines represent the $enes$ versions of different tasks.

code-mixing is influenced by many more factors such as cultural/social and/or language-specific norms which comes in the semantic and pragmatics space of language understanding. Though r-CM is a subset of g-CM, there does not exist any method which can sample realistic CM from such synthetic data, hence we rely on real-world CM datasets. Fine-tuning with this form should let the model become aware of certain nuances of real-world code-mixing which are still not completely known.

3.2 Training Procedure

There are 3 [types] $\times$ 2 [language-pairs] = 6 combinations of data which can be obtained based on the previous specifications. For l-CM and g-CM, we use the same set of parallel sentences: en-es from Rijhwani et al. (2017) and en-hi from Kunchukuttan et al. (2018). As CM is prominently used in informal contexts, it is difficult to procure textual r-CM data. We use twitter data from Rijhwani et al. (2017) for en-es; for en-hi, we use data from online forums and Twitter respectively from Chandu et al. (2018) and Patro et al. (2017). For each of the 6 combinations, we randomly sample 100,000 sentences which is then used to further train mBERT with the masked language modelling objective. We use layer-wise scaled learning rate while finetuning the models. Sun et al. (2019)

Model Notation: Let $m_{\langle\rangle}$ be the vanilla mBERT, then $m_{\langle p,q\rangle}$ are the mBERTs further trained on $\langle p, q\rangle$ data, where $p \in \{l, g, r\}$ is the complexity of mixing and $q \in \{enes, enhi\}$ is the language of mixing. For example, a model trained on English-Hindi lexical code-mixed data will be represented as $m_{\langle l,enhi\rangle}$. $\odot$ means that the model used depends on the configuration of the corresponding data. For example, $m_{\langle l,\odot\rangle}$ with $enes$ data would mean that the model used is $m_{\langle l,enes\rangle}$ while with $enhi$ data would mean that the model used is $m_{\langle l,enhi\rangle}$.

4 Task-based Probing

In this section, we describe layer-wise task-based probing of the different models.

4.1 Tasks

Recently, two benchmarks for code-mixing were released: GLUECoS (Khanuja et al., 2020) and LINCE (Aguilar et al., 2020). For this study, we probe with the following tasks from GLUECoS: Language Identification (LID), Part-of-Speech (POS) Tagging, Named Entity Recognition (NER) and Sentiment Analysis (SENT) for both $enes$ and $enhi$, and Question Answering (QA) and Natural Language Inference (NLI) for only $enhi$.

4.2 Method

We first measure the performance of these models on the aforementioned tasks. For each task, we fine-tune the models further after attaching a task specific classification layer. We report the average performances and standard deviations of each model run for 5 seeds in Table 1. [3]

In addition to getting absolute performances, we want to get an insight of how much each layer of the different models contribute to the performance of a particular task. Following Tenney et al. (2019), we measure the *solvability* of a task by finding out the *expected layer* at which the model is able to correctly solve the task. Here the mBERT weights are kept frozen and a weighted sum of representations from each layer are passed to the task specific layer. Figure 2 shows the layer-wise F1 scores for the tasks for different models and language pairs. We additionally calculate scalar mixing weights which lets us know the contribution of each layer by calculating the attention paid to each layer for the task.

4.3 Observations

From Table 1 it is clear that for almost all the tasks, $m_{\langle r,\odot\rangle}$ models perform better than the other fine-tuned models. In Particular, fine-tuning with $\boldsymbol{r}$-CM data helps with `SENT`, `NER`, `LID` *enes* as well as `QA` tasks. While for `POS`, the performance remains almost same regardless of which data the model is fine-tuned with. [4]

These differences are also reflected in the layer-wise performance of these models as shown in Figure 2. The tasks are considered solved at the knee point where the performances start plateauing. The performances of different models start at the same note, and after a certain point $m_{\langle r,\odot\rangle}$ diverges to plateau at a higher performance than others. This can be attributed to final layers adapting the most during MLM fine-tuning. (Liu et al., 2019; Kovaleva et al., 2019). `LID` gets solved around 2nd layer. $enhi$ `LID` gives a relatively high performance at the 0th layer indicating that it only needs the token+positional embeddings. This is because $enhi$ `LID` task has en and hi words in different scripts, which means it can be solved even with a simple unicode classification rule. `POS` gets solved at around 4th layer. The indifference to fine-tuning observed in case of `POS` is reflected here as well, as all the models are performing equally at all the layers for both the languages.

`NER` gets solved around the 5th layer. Here, $\boldsymbol{r}$-CM training seems to help for $enhi$, perhaps due to exposure to more world knowledge which is required for NER. `SENT` shows an interesting shift in patterns. We can see that $m_{\langle l,enes\rangle}$ solves the task at 6th layer whereas the other models solve it at around 8th layer. Thus, the general trend observed is that easier tasks like `LID`, `POS` are solved in the earlier layers and as the complexity of the tasks increase, the effective layer moves deeper - which shows a neat pattern of how BERT "re-discovers" the NLP pipeline (Tenney et al., 2019), or rather the CM pipeline in our case.

5 Structural Probing

As observed earlier, exposing mBERT to $\boldsymbol{r}$-CM help boost its overall and layer-wise performance on CM tasks. In this section, we describe three structural probing experiments, through which we will try to visualize the structural changes in the network, if any, induced by continued pre-training with CM data that are responsible for performance gains. We will first look at whether there are any changes in the behaviour of attention heads at a global level by checking the inter-head distances within a model. Further, we want to localize and identify the heads whose behaviours have changed. Finally, we take a look at how the attention heads respond to code-mixed stimulus.

5.1 Probes

The probes for conducting the experiments consist of CM and Monolingual sentences. We take a sample of 1000 sentences for each type of CM as well as monolingual sentences for each language.

Probe Notation: To denote these probes, we use $d_{\langle p,q\rangle}$ such that $p \in \{l, g, r\}$ is the complexity of mixing and $q \in \{enes, enhi, en, hi, es\}$ are the languages. For example, English-Spanish lexical CM data is represented as $d_{\langle l,enhi\rangle}$ and (real) Spanish monolingual data is represented as $d_{\langle -,es\rangle}$.

[3] As we use just 100k sentences as opposed to 3M sentences, we do not get the same performance jump reported by Khanuja et al. (2020).

[4] We also carried out training in a curriculum fashion where synthetic CM data was first introduced followed by real CM data in different ratios similar to Pratapa et al. (2018a). However, we do not include these numbers as we could not derive any meaningful insights from them. This can most probably be due to a fixed constraint of 100k sentences that we use.

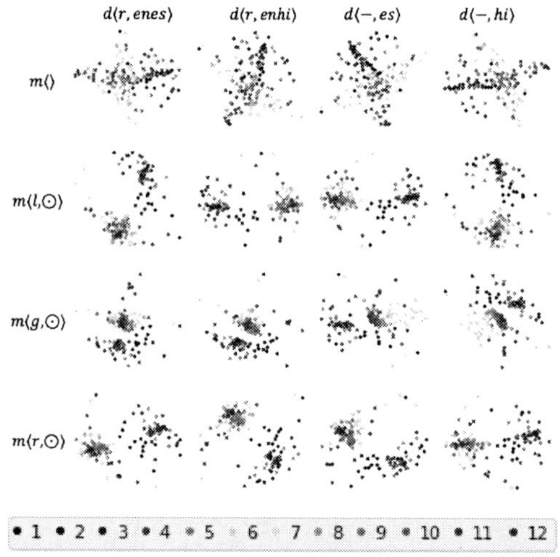

Figure 3: Intra-head distances $d(\mathbf{H}_i, \mathbf{H}_j)$ for models. The points are colored layer-wise and follows dark blue → light blue/red → dark red scheme. The rows are the models which are used and columns are the different set of probes used. ⊙ indicates that model trained in the same language (code-mixed) as probe is used.

5.2 Global Patterns of Change

Has anything changed within the models due to pre-training with CM datasets? In order to answer this question, we look at the global patterns of relative distances between the attention heads within a model.

Method: Clark et al. (2019) describes an inter-head similarity measure which allows for visualizing distances between each attention head with another within a model. The distance d between two heads $\mathbf{H}_i$ and $\mathbf{H}_j$ is calculated as,

$$d(\mathbf{H}_i, \mathbf{H}_j) = \sum_{\text{token} \in \text{ sentence}} JS(\mathbf{H}_{i(\text{token})}, \mathbf{H}_{j(\text{token})}) \tag{1}$$

where JS is the Jensen-Shannon Divergence between attention distributions. We average these distances obtained across 1000 sentences ($d_{\langle \odot, \odot \rangle}$). Further, in order to visualize these head distances, we use multidimensional scaling (Kruskal, 1964) which preserves the relative distance better than other scaling methods such as T-SNE or PCA (Van Der Maaten et al., 2009).

Observation: Figure 3 shows the two-dimensional projections of the heads labeled by the layers. There are clear differences between the patterns in $m_{\langle\rangle}$ and the other models, though the same cannot be said for the probes. $m_{\langle\rangle}$ shows a rather distributed representation of heads across layers; in particular, *g*-CM models have a tightly packed representation especially for the later layers.

5.3 Local Patterns of Change

Attention patterns of which heads have changed? We observe that there is a change in the overall internal representations based on the type of data which the models are exposed to. It would be interesting to know which specific attention heads, or layers are most affected by the exposure to CM data.

Method: In order to contrast the attention patterns of specific heads between $m_{\langle \odot, \odot \rangle}$ and the base model - $m_{\langle\rangle}$, we calculate the distance between their corresponding heads as follows:

$$\Delta_m = JS(\mathbf{H}_{i,j}^{m_{\langle \odot, \odot \rangle}}{}_{(\text{token})}, \mathbf{H}_{i,j}^{m_{\langle\rangle}}{}_{(\text{token})}) \tag{2}$$

where JS is the Jensen-Shannon Divergence, i and j are the layers and their respective heads, $m_{\langle \odot, \odot \rangle}$ is any model in the set of fine-tuned models and $m_{\langle\rangle}$ is the vanilla model. We visualize these distances in form of heatmaps (Δ_m maps). For the sake of clarity, only top 15 attention heads is plotted for each Δ_m map. The darker the head, the more the head has changed between a particular trained model and the vanilla model. Visual triangulation can let us understand if there are common heads between sets of models and probes.

Observation: Figure 4 depicts the different combinations of Δ_m maps. It can be seen how there are common heads between different configurations of trained models as well as the inference data which is used. Here, even the difference between different languages and forms of code-mixing stand out compared to the previous analysis. We also look at cross-interaction of languages: fine-tuned in one language and probed on another. Through visual examination, we highlight some of the common heads which are present among the different Δ_m plots.

5.4 Responsivity to Code-Mixing

How do attention heads respond to code-mixed probes? The common patterns in the way heads are functioning between different models and probes are easily observable from the set of Δ_m maps. These do point us to certain heads getting more activated while encoding a particular type of CM sentence. In this section, we want to understand

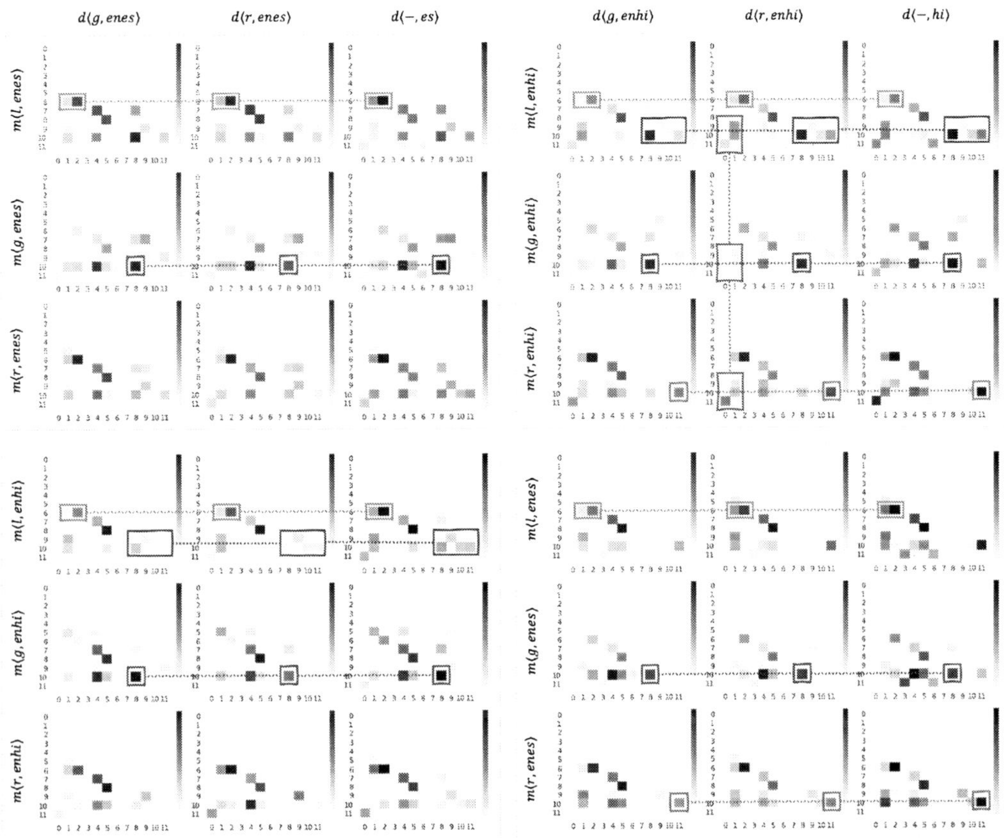

Figure 4: Δ_m maps for different configurations of trained models and probes. The first row of maps depict head interactions within same language whereas the second row of maps depict cross-language interaction i.e. trained and probed on different languages. Some of the common heads that can be observed have been marked to show the patterns which differentiate between complexity and language of models and probes.

how these heads respond to input probes. We borrow the term *responsivity*, $\mathcal{R}$, from the field of neuroscience which is used to summarize the change in the neural response per unit signal (stimulus) strength. In this context, we want to understand the change in attention head response of different models when exposed to CM data which act as the stimulus.

Method: Our aim is to understand the excitement of different heads when they see code-mixed data as a stimulus. To this end, we design a classification experiment to quantify the excitement of each head (/ neuron) while distinguishing between monolingual and CM classes. For the CM class, we randomly sample 2000 sentences from $\boldsymbol{r}$-CM in the same way as we did for probes. Similarly, for monolingual class, we sample 1000 sentences each from en and es or hi. Each probe is then passed through the different models to obtain the attentions. To summarize the net attention for each head, we average the attentions over all the tokens after removing `[CLS]` & `[SEP]` tokens present in that head. (`[CLS]` & `[SEP]`) tokens are removed as they act as a sink to non-attended tokens.

These average attention heads are then used as features (x) ($12 \times 12 = 144$ features) with the monolingual and CM classes being the predictor variable (y). To capture the relative excitement of different heads to y, we define responsivity ($\mathcal{R}$) as the gain of information of each feature (or heads) in context of the prediction variable (y). This is analogous to Information Gain used in determining feature importance. Hence, Responsivity of a head x for class y can be written as:

$$\mathcal{R}_{x,y} = H(x) - H(x|y) \tag{3}$$

where, $H(x)$ is the entropy of class distribution for x and $H(x|y)$ is the conditional entropy for x

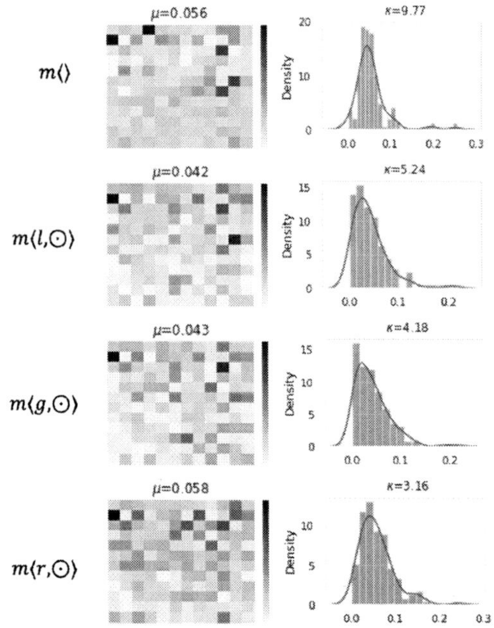

Figure 5: $\mathcal{R}$ of different models when classifying Monolingual vs. Code-mixing sentence

given y.

Observation: As shown in Figure 5, we plot the responsivity of different attention heads to CM in the form of 12×12 $\mathcal{R}$ heatmaps. We also plot the distribution of these values. We report two values, mean responsivity (μ) of a model to code-mixing and kurtosis (κ) to measure the skewness or the tailedness of the distribution compared to a normal distribution.

It can be observed from the heatmaps that there are certain common heads such as (1, 0), (2, 9) which are highly responsive to CM. As we pump in different types of CM data, we can observe that responsivity of some heads [(5, 10), (6,9)] are reducing while for other heads [(1, 7), (4, 8)] it is spiking up. A distinctive pattern that can be noticed from the heatmaps is that as CM data is fed to the models in the order of their linguistic complexity, more and more heads are responding towards the CM stimulus. Even the distribution density curve widens as confirmed by decreasing Kurtosis.

As described earlier, there is no single point in the network which responds to CM data. Previous studies (Elazar et al., 2020) involving probing of specific regions to understand their independent contributions to solving any task has been somewhat futile. It has been observed that heads collectively work towards solving tasks, and such specific regions cannot be demarcated - which means that information pertaining to task-solving is represented in a distributed fashion. In line with this, it has been shown that these models can be significantly pruned during inference with minimal drop in performance (Michel et al., 2019; Kovaleva et al., 2019). Our study confirms these observations for code-mixing as well, through a different visualization approach.

6 Conclusion & Future Work

In this work, we develop different methods of fine-tuning BERT-like models for CM processing. We then compare the downstream task performances of these models through absolute performance, their stability as well as the layer-wise *solvability* of certain tasks. To further understand the varied performances between the three types of CM, we perform structural probing. We adopted an existing approach and introduced a couple of new techniques for the visualization of the attention heads as a response to probes.

The most important finding from these probing experiments is that there are discernable changes introduced in the models due to exposure to CM data, of which a particularly interesting observation is that this exposure increases the overall *responsivity* of the attention heads to CM. As of now, these experiments are purely analytical in nature where we observed how the attention heads behave on a CM stimuli. One future direction is to expand the analysis to a wider range of domains and fine-tuning experiments to understand how generalizable are our findings of distributed information in BERT-like models. We use a fairly simple and easily replicable method for testing this through the *responsivity* metric that we propose. This method can be further improved to rigorously verify our observations.

7 Acknowledgements

We thank the anonymous reviewers for their many insightful comments and suggestions on our paper. We also thank Tanuja Ganu and Amit Deshpande for their valuable feedback on some of our experiments.

References

Gustavo Aguilar, Sudipta Kar, and Thamar Solorio. 2020. LinCE: A centralized benchmark for linguistic code-switching evaluation. In *Proceedings of the 12th Language Resources and Evaluation Conference*, pages 1803–1813, Marseille, France. European Language Resources Association.

Emily Alsentzer, John Murphy, William Boag, Wei-Hung Weng, Di Jindi, Tristan Naumann, and Matthew McDermott. 2019. Publicly available clinical BERT embeddings. In *Proceedings of the 2nd Clinical Natural Language Processing Workshop*, pages 72–78, Minneapolis, Minnesota, USA. Association for Computational Linguistics.

Hedi M Belazi, Edward J Rubin, and Almeida Jacqueline Toribio. 1994. Code switching and x-bar theory: The functional head constraint. *Linguistic inquiry*, pages 221–237.

Iz Beltagy, Kyle Lo, and Arman Cohan. 2019. SciBERT: A pretrained language model for scientific text. In *Proceedings of the 2019 Conference on Empirical Methods in Natural Language Processing and the 9th International Joint Conference on Natural Language Processing (EMNLP-IJCNLP)*, pages 3615–3620, Hong Kong, China. Association for Computational Linguistics.

Gayatri Bhat, Monojit Choudhury, and Kalika Bali. 2016. Grammatical constraints on intra-sentential code-switching: From theories to working models. *arXiv preprint arXiv:1612.04538*.

Ilias Chalkidis, Manos Fergadiotis, Prodromos Malakasiotis, Nikolaos Aletras, and Ion Androutsopoulos. 2020. LEGAL-BERT: The muppets straight out of law school. In *Findings of the Association for Computational Linguistics: EMNLP 2020*, pages 2898–2904, Online. Association for Computational Linguistics.

Khyathi Chandu, Thomas Manzini, Sumeet Singh, and Alan W. Black. 2018. Language informed modeling of code-switched text. In *Proceedings of the Third Workshop on Computational Approaches to Linguistic Code-Switching*, pages 92–97, Melbourne, Australia. Association for Computational Linguistics.

Kevin Clark, Urvashi Khandelwal, Omer Levy, and Christopher D. Manning. 2019. What does BERT look at? an analysis of BERT's attention. In *Proceedings of the 2019 ACL Workshop BlackboxNLP: Analyzing and Interpreting Neural Networks for NLP*, pages 276–286, Florence, Italy. Association for Computational Linguistics.

Alexis Conneau, Kartikay Khandelwal, Naman Goyal, Vishrav Chaudhary, Guillaume Wenzek, Francisco Guzmán, Edouard Grave, Myle Ott, Luke Zettlemoyer, and Veselin Stoyanov. 2020. Unsupervised cross-lingual representation learning at scale. In *Proceedings of the 58th Annual Meeting of the Association for Computational Linguistics*, pages 8440–8451, Online. Association for Computational Linguistics.

Jacob Devlin, Ming-Wei Chang, Kenton Lee, and Kristina Toutanova. 2019. BERT: Pre-training of deep bidirectional transformers for language understanding. In *Proceedings of the 2019 Conference of the North American Chapter of the Association for Computational Linguistics: Human Language Technologies, Volume 1 (Long and Short Papers)*, pages 4171–4186, Minneapolis, Minnesota. Association for Computational Linguistics.

Chris Dyer, Victor Chahuneau, and Noah A. Smith. 2013. A simple, fast, and effective reparameterization of IBM model 2. In *Proceedings of the 2013 Conference of the North American Chapter of the Association for Computational Linguistics: Human Language Technologies*, pages 644–648, Atlanta, Georgia. Association for Computational Linguistics.

Yanai Elazar, Shauli Ravfogel, Alon Jacovi, and Yoav Goldberg. 2020. When bert forgets how to pos: Amnesic probing of linguistic properties and mlm predictions. *arXiv preprint arXiv:2006.00995*.

Yu Gu, Robert Tinn, Hao Cheng, Michael Lucas, Naoto Usuyama, Xiaodong Liu, Tristan Naumann, Jianfeng Gao, and Hoifung Poon. 2020. Domain-specific language model pretraining for biomedical natural language processing.

Phu Mon Htut, Jason Phang, Shikha Bordia, and Samuel R. Bowman. 2019. Do attention heads in bert track syntactic dependencies?

Aravind Joshi. 1982. Processing of sentences with intra-sentential code-switching. In *Coling 1982: Proceedings of the Ninth International Conference on Computational Linguistics*.

Pratik Joshi, Sebastin Santy, Amar Budhiraja, Kalika Bali, and Monojit Choudhury. 2020. The state and fate of linguistic diversity and inclusion in the NLP world. In *Proceedings of the 58th Annual Meeting of the Association for Computational Linguistics*, pages 6282–6293, Online. Association for Computational Linguistics.

Abhinav Ramesh Kashyap, Devamanyu Hazarika, Min-Yen Kan, and Roger Zimmermann. 2020. Domain divergences: a survey and empirical analysis. *arXiv preprint arXiv:2010.12198*.

Simran Khanuja, Sandipan Dandapat, Anirudh Srinivasan, Sunayana Sitaram, and Monojit Choudhury. 2020. GLUECoS: An evaluation benchmark for code-switched NLP. In *Proceedings of the 58th Annual Meeting of the Association for Computational Linguistics*, pages 3575–3585, Online. Association for Computational Linguistics.

Olga Kovaleva, Alexey Romanov, Anna Rogers, and Anna Rumshisky. 2019. Revealing the dark secrets of BERT. In *Proceedings of the 2019 Conference on Empirical Methods in Natural Language Processing and the 9th International Joint Conference on Natural Language Processing (EMNLP-IJCNLP)*, pages 4365–4374, Hong Kong, China. Association for Computational Linguistics.

Joseph B Kruskal. 1964. Nonmetric multidimensional scaling: a numerical method. *Psychometrika*, 29(2):115–129.

Anoop Kunchukuttan, Pratik Mehta, and Pushpak Bhattacharyya. 2018. The IIT Bombay English-Hindi parallel corpus. In *Proceedings of the Eleventh International Conference on Language Resources and Evaluation (LREC 2018)*, Miyazaki, Japan. European Language Resources Association (ELRA).

Jinhyuk Lee, Wonjin Yoon, Sungdong Kim, Donghyeon Kim, Sunkyu Kim, Chan Ho So, and Jaewoo Kang. 2020. Biobert: a pre-trained biomedical language representation model for biomedical text mining. *Bioinformatics*, 36(4):1234–1240.

Nelson F. Liu, Matt Gardner, Yonatan Belinkov, Matthew E. Peters, and Noah A. Smith. 2019. Linguistic knowledge and transferability of contextual representations. In *Proceedings of the 2019 Conference of the North American Chapter of the Association for Computational Linguistics: Human Language Technologies, Volume 1 (Long and Short Papers)*, pages 1073–1094, Minneapolis, Minnesota. Association for Computational Linguistics.

Xiaofei Ma, Peng Xu, Zhiguo Wang, Ramesh Nallapati, and Bing Xiang. 2019. Domain adaptation with BERT-based domain classification and data selection. In *Proceedings of the 2nd Workshop on Deep Learning Approaches for Low-Resource NLP (DeepLo 2019)*, pages 76–83, Hong Kong, China. Association for Computational Linguistics.

Paul Michel, Omer Levy, and Graham Neubig. 2019. Are sixteen heads really better than one? In *Advances in Neural Information Processing Systems*, volume 32. Curran Associates, Inc.

Aakanksha Naik and Carolyn Rose. 2020. Towards open domain event trigger identification using adversarial domain adaptation. In *Proceedings of the 58th Annual Meeting of the Association for Computational Linguistics*, pages 7618–7624, Online. Association for Computational Linguistics.

Jasabanta Patro, Bidisha Samanta, Saurabh Singh, Abhipsa Basu, Prithwish Mukherjee, Monojit Choudhury, and Animesh Mukherjee. 2017. All that is English may be Hindi: Enhancing language identification through automatic ranking of the likeliness of word borrowing in social media. In *Proceedings of the 2017 Conference on Empirical Methods in Natural Language Processing*, pages 2264–2274, Copenhagen, Denmark. Association for Computational Linguistics.

Yifan Peng, Shankai Yan, and Zhiyong Lu. 2019. Transfer learning in biomedical natural language processing: An evaluation of BERT and ELMo on ten benchmarking datasets. In *Proceedings of the 18th BioNLP Workshop and Shared Task*, pages 58–65, Florence, Italy. Association for Computational Linguistics.

Telmo Pires, Eva Schlinger, and Dan Garrette. 2019. How multilingual is multilingual BERT? In *Proceedings of the 57th Annual Meeting of the Association for Computational Linguistics*, pages 4996–5001, Florence, Italy. Association for Computational Linguistics.

Shana Poplack. 2000. Sometimes i'll start a sentence in spanish y termino en español: Toward a typology of code-switching. *The bilingualism reader*, 18(2):221–256.

Sai Prasanna, Anna Rogers, and Anna Rumshisky. 2020. When BERT Plays the Lottery, All Tickets Are Winning. In *Proceedings of the 2020 Conference on Empirical Methods in Natural Language Processing (EMNLP)*, pages 3208–3229, Online. Association for Computational Linguistics.

Adithya Pratapa, Gayatri Bhat, Monojit Choudhury, Sunayana Sitaram, Sandipan Dandapat, and Kalika Bali. 2018a. Language modeling for code-mixing: The role of linguistic theory based synthetic data. In *Proceedings of the 56th Annual Meeting of the Association for Computational Linguistics (Volume 1: Long Papers)*, pages 1543–1553, Melbourne, Australia. Association for Computational Linguistics.

Adithya Pratapa, Monojit Choudhury, and Sunayana Sitaram. 2018b. Word embeddings for code-mixed language processing. In *Proceedings of the 2018 Conference on Empirical Methods in Natural Language Processing*, pages 3067–3072, Brussels, Belgium. Association for Computational Linguistics.

Shruti Rijhwani, Royal Sequiera, Monojit Choudhury, Kalika Bali, and Chandra Shekhar Maddila. 2017. Estimating code-switching on Twitter with a novel generalized word-level language detection technique. In *Proceedings of the 55th Annual Meeting of the Association for Computational Linguistics (Volume 1: Long Papers)*, pages 1971–1982, Vancouver, Canada. Association for Computational Linguistics.

Bidisha Samanta, Niloy Ganguly, and Soumen Chakrabarti. 2019. Improved sentiment detection via label transfer from monolingual to synthetic code-switched text. In *Proceedings of the 57th Annual Meeting of the Association for Computational Linguistics*, pages 3528–3537, Florence, Italy. Association for Computational Linguistics.

David Sankoff. 1998. The production of code-mixed discourse. In *36th Annual Meeting of the Association for Computational Linguistics and 17th International Conference on Computational Linguistics,*

Volume 1, pages 8–21, Montreal, Quebec, Canada. Association for Computational Linguistics.

Anirudh Srinivasan. 2020. MSR India at SemEval-2020 task 9: Multilingual models can do code-mixing too. In *Proceedings of the Fourteenth Workshop on Semantic Evaluation*, pages 951–956, Barcelona (online). International Committee for Computational Linguistics.

Chi Sun, Xipeng Qiu, Yige Xu, and Xuanjing Huang. 2019. How to fine-tune bert for text classification? In *China National Conference on Chinese Computational Linguistics*, pages 194–206. Springer.

Mary WJ Tay. 1989. Code switching and code mixing as a communicative strategy in multilingual discourse. *World Englishes*, 8(3):407–417.

Ian Tenney, Dipanjan Das, and Ellie Pavlick. 2019. BERT rediscovers the classical NLP pipeline. In *Proceedings of the 57th Annual Meeting of the Association for Computational Linguistics*, pages 4593–4601, Florence, Italy. Association for Computational Linguistics.

Laurens Van Der Maaten, Eric Postma, and Jaap Van den Herik. 2009. Dimensionality reduction: a comparative. *J Mach Learn Res*, 10(66-71):13.

Huazheng Wang, Zhe Gan, Xiaodong Liu, Jingjing Liu, Jianfeng Gao, and Hongning Wang. 2019. Adversarial domain adaptation for machine reading comprehension. In *Proceedings of the 2019 Conference on Empirical Methods in Natural Language Processing and the 9th International Joint Conference on Natural Language Processing (EMNLP-IJCNLP)*, pages 2510–2520, Hong Kong, China. Association for Computational Linguistics.

Genta Indra Winata, Andrea Madotto, Chien-Sheng Wu, and Pascale Fung. 2019. Code-switched language models using neural based synthetic data from parallel sentences. In *Proceedings of the 23rd Conference on Computational Natural Language Learning (CoNLL)*, pages 271–280, Hong Kong, China. Association for Computational Linguistics.

Jian Yang, Shuming Ma, Dongdong Zhang, ShuangZhi Wu, Zhoujun Li, and Ming Zhou. 2020a. Alternating language modeling for cross-lingual pre-training. *Proceedings of the AAAI Conference on Artificial Intelligence*, 34(05):9386–9393.

Yi Yang, Mark Christopher Siy UY, and Allen Huang. 2020b. Finbert: A pretrained language model for financial communications.

Hai Ye, Qingyu Tan, Ruidan He, Juntao Li, Hwee Tou Ng, and Lidong Bing. 2020. Feature adaptation of pre-trained language models across languages and domains with robust self-training. In *Proceedings of the 2020 Conference on Empirical Methods in Natural Language Processing (EMNLP)*, pages 7386–7399, Online. Association for Computational Linguistics.

Xinyu Zhang, Andrew Yates, and Jimmy Lin. 2020. A little bit is worse than none: Ranking with limited training data. In *Proceedings of SustaiNLP: Workshop on Simple and Efficient Natural Language Processing*, pages 107–112, Online. Association for Computational Linguistics.

Locality Preserving Loss: Neighbors that *Live* together, *Align* together

Ashwinkumar Ganesan, Francis Ferraro, Tim Oates
Dept. Of Computer Science & Electrical Engineering (CSEE),
University Of Maryland Baltimore County (UMBC),
MD, USA - 21250
gashwin1@umbc.edu, ferraro@umbc.edu, oates@cs.umbc.edu

Abstract

We present a **locality preserving loss** (LPL) that improves the alignment between vector space embeddings while separating uncorrelated representations. Given two pretrained embedding manifolds, LPL optimizes a model to project an embedding and maintain its local neighborhood while aligning one manifold to another. This reduces the overall size of the dataset required to align the two in tasks such as crosslingual word alignment. We show that the LPL-based alignment between input vector spaces acts as a regularizer, leading to better and consistent accuracy than the baseline, especially when the size of the training set is small. We demonstrate the effectiveness of LPL-optimized alignment on semantic text similarity (STS), natural language inference (SNLI), multi-genre language inference (MNLI) and cross-lingual word alignment (CLA) showing consistent improvements, finding up to 16% improvement over our baseline in lower resource settings.[1]

1 Introduction

Over the last few years, vector space representations of words and sentences, extracted from encoders trained on a large text corpus, are primary components to model any natural language processing (NLP) task, especially while using neural or deep learning methods. Neural NLP models can be initialized with pretrained word embeddings learned using *word2vec* (Mikolov et al., 2013) or *GloVe* (Pennington et al., 2014) and fine-tuned sentence encoders like BERT (Devlin et al., 2018) or RoBERTa (Liu et al., 2019). They show state-of-the-art performance in a number of tasks from part-of-speech tagging, named entity recognition, and machine translation to measuring textual similarity (Wang et al., 2018). BERT's success has spawned research dedicated to understanding (Rogers et al., 2020) and reducing parameters in transformer architectures (Lan et al., 2019). Despite these successes, supervised transfer learning is not a panacea. Models based on pretrained word embeddings (for bilingual induction) or BERT-based models require a large parallel corpus to train on. Can we reduce the number of training samples even further?

We approach this problem by proposing a framework that exploits the inherent relationship between word or sentence representations in their *pretrained manifolds*. These relationships help train the model with fewer samples, since each training sample represents a group of instances.

We consider three types of tasks: (1) a regression task such as semantic text similarity; (2) a classification task (e.g., natural language inference (NLI)); and (3) vector space alignment, where the purpose is to learn a mapping between two independently trained embeddings (e.g., crosslingual word alignment) Learning bilingual word embedding models alleviates low resource problems by aligning embeddings from a source language that is rich in available text to a target language with a small corpus with limited vocabulary.[2] Largely, recent work focuses on learning a linear mapping to align two embedding spaces by minimizing the mean squared error (MSE) between embeddings of words projected from the source domain and their counterparts in the target domain (Mikolov et al., 2013; Ruder et al., 2017). Minimizing MSE is useful when a large set of translated words (between source and target languages) is provided, but the mapping overfits when the parallel corpus is small or may require non-linear transformations

[1]Code Source: https://github.com/codehacken/locality-preservation

[2]*Low resource* has two interpretations i.e. one where corpus size to generate unsupervised pretrained embeddings is small and the other where the parallel corpus for alignment is minimal. We experiment with the later here.

Proceedings of the Second Workshop on Domain Adaptation for NLP, pages 122–139
April 20, 2021. ©2021 Association for Computational Linguistics

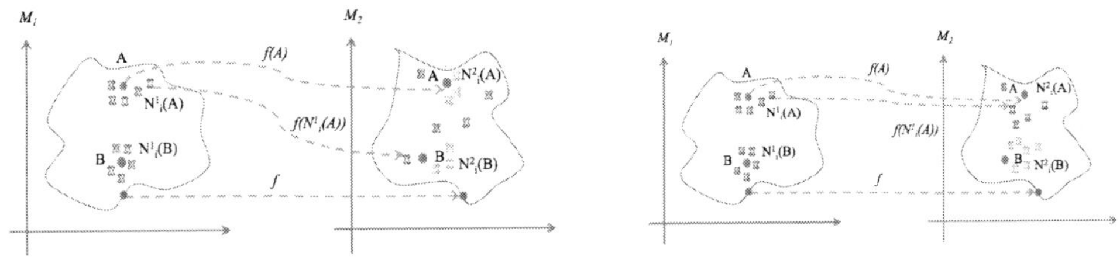

Figure 1: Quality of alignment with different types of losses. A, B are two words in two word embedding manifolds M_1 and M_2. f is the manifold alignment function while $N_i^1(A)$ and $N_i^1(B)$ are their respective neighbors in manifold M_1. $N_i^2(A)$ and $N_i^2(B)$ are their neighbors in manifold M_2. Figure (a) shows the alignment when trained with a MSE loss. The neighbors are distributed across the manifold due to overfitting. (b) shows alignment with a locality preserving loss (LPL) that reconstructs the original manifold in the target domain M_2 maintaining its local structure.

(Søgaard et al., 2018). In order to reduce overfitting and improve word alignment, we propose an auxiliary loss function called locality preserving loss (LPL) that trains the model to align two sets of word embeddings while maintaining the local neighborhood structure around words in the source domain.

With classification and regression tasks where there are two inputs (e.g., NLI and STS-B), we show how the alignment between the two input subspace acts as regularizer, improving the model's accuracy on the task with MSE alone and when MSE and LPL are combined together. LPL achieves this by augmenting existing text $\leftrightarrow$ label pairs with pseudo-pairs constructed from their neighbors.

Specifically, our main contributions are:

- We propose a loss function called **locality preserving loss (LPL)** to improve vector space alignment and show how the **alignment acts as a regularizer** while performing language inference and semantic text similarity. LPL improves correlation or accuracy of linear and non-linear mapping (deep networks) while exploiting the inherent geometries of existing pretrained embedding manifolds to optimize an alignment model (Table 1a, Figure 3).
- We show LPL is flexible and can be optimized with SGD. Hence, it can be applied to both deep neural networks and linear transformations. In contrast, previous cross-lingual word alignment models that are a linear map between source and target language, are learned using singular value decomposition.
- We show an increase in correlation on semantic text similarity (STS-B) and accuracy on SNLI in comparison with the baseline when the models are trained with small datasets. Training with LPL shows up to 16.38% (90.1% relative), on SNLI up to 8.9% (19.3% relative) improvement when trained with just 1000 samples (0.002% of the dataset). We train a crosslingual word alignment model giving up to 4.1% (13.8% relative) improvement in comparison to a MSE optimized mapping while reducing the size of the parallel corpus required to train the mapping by 40% (3K out of 5K pairs).

2 Background & Related Work

2.1 Dimensionality Reduction

Manifold learning methods represent these high dimensional datapoints in a lower dimensional space by extracting important features from the data, making it easier to cluster and search for similar data points. The methods are broadly categorized into linear, such as Principal Component Analysis (PCA), and non-linear algorithms. Nonlinear methods include multi-dimensional scaling (Cox and Cox, 2000, MDS), locally linear embedding (Roweis and Saul, 2000, LLE) and Laplacian eigenmaps (Belkin and Niyogi, 2002, LE). He and Niyogi (2004) compute the Euclidean distance between points to construct an adjacency graph and create a linear map that preserves the neighborhood structure of each point in the manifold. Another popular tool to learn manifolds is an autoencoder where a self-reconstruction loss is used to train a neural network (Rumelhart et al., 1985). Vincent et al. (2008) design an autoencoder that is robust to noise by training it with a noisy input and then reconstructing the original noise-free input.

In locally linear embedding (LLE) (Roweis and Saul, 2000), the datapoints are assumed to have a linear relation with their neighbors. To project each point, first a reconstruction loss is utilized to learn the linear relation between a point and their k neighbors. Then, the linear relation is used to learn the embeddings in the reduced dimension.[3]

Wang et al. (2014) extend autoencoders by modifying the reconstruction loss to use nearest neighbors of data points, leveraging neighborhood relationships between datapoints from non-linear dimension reduction methods like LLE and Laplacian Eigenmaps.

2.2 Manifold Alignment

Benaim and Wolf (2017) utilize a GAN to learn a unidirectional mapping. The total loss applied to train the generator is a combination of different losses, namely, an adversarial loss, a cyclic constraint (inspired by Zhu et al. (2017)), MSE and an additional distance constraint where the distance between the point and its neighbors in the source domain are maintained in the target domain. Similarly, Conneau et al. (2017) learn to translate words without any parallel data with a GAN that optimizes a cross domain similarity scale to resolve the hubness problem (Dinu et al., 2014).

These methods are the foundation to learn a mapping between two lower dimensional spaces (manifold alignment, Figure 1). Wang et al. (2011) propose a manifold alignment method that preserves the local similarity between points in the manifold being transformed and the correspondence between points that are common to both manifolds. Boucher et al. (2015) replace the manifold alignment algorithm that uses the nearest neighbor graph with a low rank alignment. Cui et al. (2014) align two manifolds without any pairwise data (unsupervised) by assuming the structure of the lower dimension manifolds are similar.

Our work is similar to Bollegala et al. (2017) where the meta-embedding (a common embedding space) for different vector representations is generated using a locally linear embedding (LLE) which preserves the locality. One drawback, though, is that LLE does not learn a singular functional mapping between the source and target vector spaces. A linear mapping between a word and its neighbor is learned for each new word. Hence, the meta-embedding must be retrained every time new words are added to the vocabulary. Nakashole (2018) propose NORMA that uses neighborhood sensitive maps where the neighbors are learned rather than extracted from the existing embedding space. Similar to NORMA, LPL uses a modified locally linear representation of each embedding but, unlike it, LPL uses actual nearest neighbors in order to learn an embedding. This is important as NNs may not be present in annotated parallel corpus. **Hence, using NNs of annotated pairs in the corpus in LPL expands the size of the training dataset.** LPL is optimized with gradient descent and can be easily added to a deep neural network (as seen in §3.5).

[3] See Appendix C for an in-depth explanation of LLE.

3 Incorporating Locality Preservation into Task-based Learning

In this section, we describe locality preserving loss, the assumption underlying the loss function and objective functions (eq. (2), eq. (3)) that are optimized. The cumulative loss function while training the model is defined in eq. (4).

3.1 Locality Preservation Criteria

The locality preserving loss (LPL, eq. (2)) is based on an important assumption about the source manifold: for a pre-defined neighborhood of k points (k is chosen manually) in the source embedding space we assume points are "close" to a given point such that it can be reconstructed using a linear map of its neighbors. This assumption is similar to that made in locally linear embedding (Roweis and Saul, 2000).

3.2 Preliminaries

As individual embeddings can represent words or sentences, we call each individual embedding a *unit*. Consider two manifolds—$M^s \in \mathbb{R}^{n\times d}$ (source domain) and $M^t \in \mathbb{R}^{m\times d}$ (target domain)—that are vector space representations of units within each domain. We do not make assumptions on the methods used to learn each manifold; they may be different. We also do not assume they share a common lexical vocabulary. For example, M^s can be created using a standard distributed representation method like word2vec (Mikolov et al., 2013) and consists of English word embeddings while M^t is created using GloVe (Pennington et al., 2014) and contains Italian embeddings. Let V^s and V^t be the respective vocabularies (collection of units) of the two manifolds. Hence $V^s = \{w_1^s \dots w_n^s\}$ and $V^t = \{w_1^t \,..\, w_m^t\}$ are sets of units in each vocabulary of size n and m. The distributed representations of the units in each manifold are $M^s = \{m_1^s \dots m_n^s\}$ and $M^t = \{m_1^t \dots m_m^t\}$.

While we do not assume that V^t and V^s must

have common items, we do assume that there is some set of unit pairs that are connected by some consistent relationship. Let $V^p = \{w_1^p \dots w_c^p\}$ be the set of the unit pairs; we consider V^p a supervised training set (though it could be weakly supervised, e.g., derived from a parallel corpus). For example, in crosslingual word alignment this consistent relationship is whether one word can be translated as another; in natural language inference, the relationship is whether one sentence entails the other (the second must logically follow from the first). We assume this common set V^p is much smaller than the individual vocabularies ($c << m$ and $c << n$). The mapping (manifold alignment) function is f.

In this paper, we experiment with three types of tasks: cross-lingual word alignment (mapping), natural language inference (classification), and semantic text similarity (regression). In cross-lingual word alignment, V^s and V^t represent the source and target vocabularies, V^p is a bilingual dictionary, and M^t and M^s are the target and source manifolds. f with θ_f parameters is a linear projection with a single weight matrix W. For NLI, V^t and V^s are target and source sentences with M^t and M^s being their manifolds. f is a 2-layer FFN.

3.3 Locality Preserving Loss (LPL)

We use a mapping function $f : M^s \to M^t$ to align manifold M^s to M^t. The exact structure of f is task-specific: for example, in our experiments f is a linear function for crosslingual word alignment and it is a 2-layer neural network (non-linear mapping) for NLI. The mapping is optimized using three loss functions: an orthogonal transform (Xing et al., 2015) $\mathcal{L}_{\text{ortho}}$ (constrain $W^{-1} = W^T$); mean squared error $\mathcal{L}_{\text{mse}}$ (eq. 1); and locality preserving loss (LPL) $\mathcal{L}_{\text{lpl}}$ (eq. 2).

The standard loss function to align two manifolds is mean squared error (MSE) (Ruder et al., 2017; Artetxe et al., 2016),

$$\mathcal{L}_{\text{mse}} = \sum_{i \in V^p} \mathcal{L}^i_{\text{mse}} = \sum_{i \in V^p} \overbrace{\left\| f(m_i^s) - m_i^t \right\|_2^2}^{\mathcal{L}^i_{\text{mse}}}, \quad (1)$$

which minimizes the distance between the unit's representation in M_t (the target manifold) and projected vector from M_s. The function $f(m_i^s)$ has learnable parameters θ_f. MSE can lead to an optimal alignment when there is a large number of units in the parallel corpus to train the mapping between the two manifolds (Ruder et al., 2017). However, when the parallel corpus V^p is small, the mapping is prone to overfitting (Glavas et al., 2019).

Locality preserving loss (LPL: eq. 2) optimizes the mapping f to project a unit together with its neighbors. For a small neighborhood of k units, the source representation of unit w_i^s is assumed to be a linear combination of its source neighbors. We represent this small neighborhood (of the source embedding m_i^s of word w_i^s) with $N_k(m_i^s)$, and we compute the local linear reconstruction using W_{ij}, a learned weight associated with each word in the neighborhood of the current word, $N_k(m_i^s)$. LPL requires that the projected source embedding $f(m_i^s)$ be a weighted average of all the projected vectors of its neighbors $f(m_j^s)$. Formally, for a particular common item i, LPL at i minimizes

$$\mathcal{L}^i_{\text{lpl}} = \left\| m_i^t - \sum_{m_j^s \in N_k(m_i^s)} W_{ij} f(m_j^s) \right\|^2 \quad (2)$$

with $\mathcal{L}_{\text{lpl}} = \sum_{m_i^s, m_i^t \in V^s} \mathcal{L}^i_{\text{lpl}}$. Intuitively, W represents the relation between a word and its neighbors in the source domain. We learn it by minimizing the LLE-inspired loss. For a common i this is

$$\mathcal{L}^i_{\text{lle}} = \left\| m_i^s - \sum_{m_j^s \in N_k(m_i^s)} W_{ij} m_j^s \right\|^2 \quad (3)$$

with $\mathcal{L}_{\text{lle}} = \sum_{m_i^s \in V^p} \mathcal{L}^i_{\text{lle}}$. The weights W are subject to the constraint $\sum W_{ij} = 1$, making the projected embeddings invariant to scaling (Roweis and Saul, 2000). We can formalize this with an objective $\mathcal{L}_{\text{ortho}} = WW^\intercal - I$. LPL reduces overfitting because the mapping function f does not simply learn the mapping between unit embeddings in the parallel corpus: it also optimizes for a projection of the unit's neighbors that are not part of the parallel corpus—effectively expanding the size of the training set by the factor k.

3.4 Model Training with LPL

The total supervised loss becomes:

$$\mathcal{L}_{\text{sup}} = \mathcal{L}_{\text{mse}}(\theta_f) + \beta * \mathcal{L}_{\text{lpl}}(\theta_f, W) + \mathcal{L}_{\text{lle}}(W) + \mathcal{L}_{\text{ortho}}(\theta_f) \quad (4)$$

We introduce a constant β to allow control over the contribution of LPL to the total loss. Although we minimize total loss (4), shown explicitly with variable dependence, the optimization can be unstable

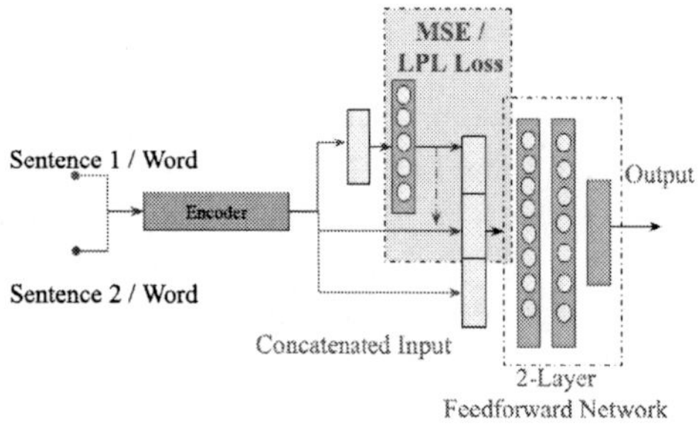

Figure 2: Use of alignment loss for the NLI and STS-B task. The pipeline consists of a 2-layer FFN used to classify sentence pairs. The output layer is of size 3 to classify the input into *entailment, contradiction* and *neutral*. It has a size of 1 to generate a continuous value between 0 and 1 for STS-B. The premise / sentence 1 and hypothesis / sentence 2 subspaces are aligned using a MSE and LPL loss that are then added as a concatenated input to train the classifier / regressor. A δ hyperparameter configured for each label provides the ability to perform *alignment* for *entailment* and *contradiction* while performing *divergence* for *neutral* input pairs.

as there are two sets of independent parameters W and θ_f representing different relationships between datapoints. To reduce the instability, we split the training into two phases. In the first phase, W is learned by minimizing $\mathcal{L}_{\text{lle}}$ alone and the weights are frozen. Then, $\mathcal{L}_{\text{mse}}$ and $\mathcal{L}_{\text{lpl}}$ are minimized while keeping W fixed.

One key difference between our work and Artetxe et al. (2016) is that they optimize the mapping function by taking the singular vector decomposition (SVD) of the squared loss while we use gradient descent to find optimal values of θ_f. As our experimental results show, while both can be empirically advantageous, our work allows LPL to be easily added as just another term in the loss function. With the exception of the alternating optimization of W, our approach does not need special optimization updates to be derived. **Euclidean distance** between embeddings is used to find NNs.

3.5 Alignment as Regularization

MSE and LPL can be used to align two vector spaces: in particular, we show that the objectives can align two subspaces in the *same* manifold. When combined with cross entropy loss in a classification task, this subspace alignment effectively acts as a regularizer. Figure 2 shows an example architecture where alignment is used as a regularizer for the NLI task. The architecture contains a two layer FFN used to perform language inference, i.e., to predict if the given sentence pairs are *entailed*, *contradictory* or *neutral*. The input to the network is a pair of sentence vectors. The initial representations are generated from any sentence/language encoder, e.g., from BERT. The source/sentence1/premise embeddings are first projected to the hypothesis space. The projected vector is then concatenated with the original pair of embeddings and given as input to the network. The alignment losses (MSE and LPL) are computed between the projected premise and original hypothesis embeddings. If the baseline network is optimized with cross entropy (CE) loss to predict label y_i, the total loss becomes:

$$\mathcal{L}_{\text{total}} = \gamma \sum_i \delta_{y_i} (\mathcal{L}^i_{\text{mse}} + \mathcal{L}^i_{\text{lpl}} + \mathcal{L}^i_{\text{lle}}(W)) + CE_{y_i} \quad (5)$$

where γ is a hyperparameter that controls the impact of the loss (learning rate). Thus, the loss (eq. (5)) is an extension of eq. (4) for a classification task but without $\mathcal{L}_{\text{ortho}}$, which is not applied as f is a 2-layer FFN (non-linear mapping) and the $WW^\intercal = I$ constraint for each layer's weights cannot be guaranteed. The alignment loss becomes a vehicle to bias the model based upon our knowledge of the task, forcing a specific behavior on the network. The behavior can be controlled with δ, which can be a positive or negative value specific to each label. A positive δ optimizes the network to align the embeddings while a negative δ is a divergence loss. In NLI we assign a constant scalar to all samples with a specific label (i.e., 100 for entailment, 1.0 for contradiction and -5.0 for neutral). The scalars were set when optimizing network hyper-parameters. As the optimizer minimizes the loss, a divergence loss tends to $-\infty$; in practice, we clip the negative loss value at -1.

4 Experiment Results & Analysis

We demonstrate the effectiveness of the locality preserving alignment on three types of tasks: semantic text similarity (regression), natural language inference (text classification) and crosslingual word alignment (mapping / regression). In order to compute local neighborhoods, as needed for, e.g., (2), we build a standard KD-Tree and find the nearest neighbors using Euclidean distance.

4.1 Semantic Text Similarity (STS)

In semantic text similarity (STS), we use the STS-B dataset (Cer et al., 2017) that is widely utilized as a part of the GLUE benchmark (Wang et al., 2018). The baseline model is the same as Siamese-BERT

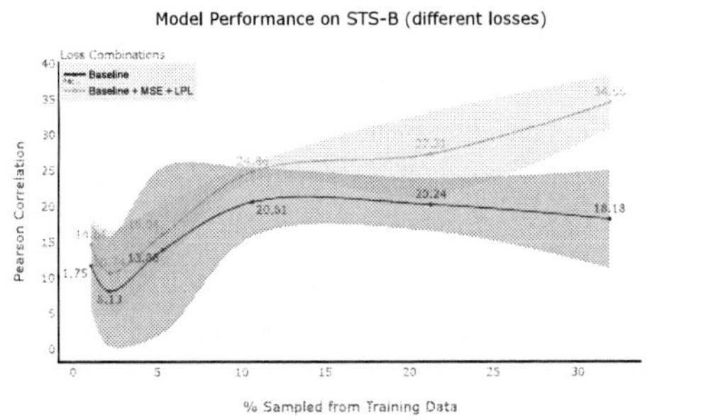

Figure 3: Pearson correlation on semantic text similarity with STS-B dataset. Locality Preserving Loss (LPL) improves sentence pair similarity in all data sizes from small (100 samples or 2% of total data) to 50% of the dataset.

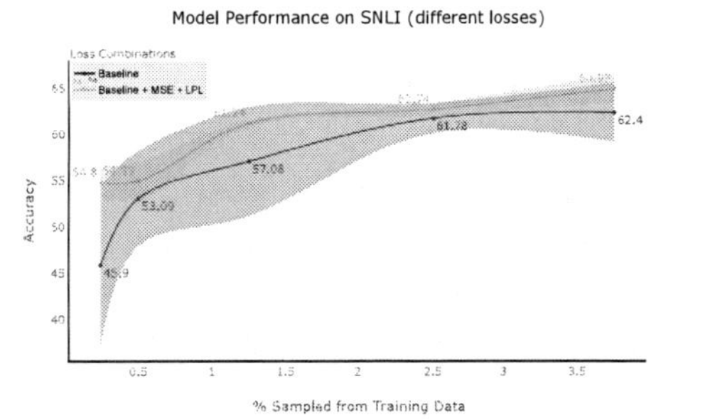

Figure 4: Accuracy of alignment regularization on SNLI. The graph shows the accuracy, averaged across 3 runs, for differing size of training samples up to 5% of the training dataset only (total: 500K).

(Reimers and Gurevych, 2019) where sentence embeddings are extracted individually using a BERT model (Devlin et al., 2018). An attached connected feedforward network (FFN) is trained to predict a sentence similarity score between 0 and 1 (optimized with squared error loss).[4]

To analyze the impact of various loss functions, the BERT model parameters are frozen so that sentence embeddings remain the same and only the parameters of the FFN are optimized. As described in §3.4, the baseline model is additionally trained with a `MSE` loss that aligns one sentence manifold to another ($m_1 \rightarrow m_2$) and the third model also trains with `LPL`. δ is set to mimic the normalized label thus generating the largest loss while aligning two sentences that are same. The contrastive loss separates the two sentence embeddings when they are dissimilar. The maximum margin is set to 0.1.

In order to study the impact on model performance when the training data is small, we limit the sampled training data size to upto 50% of the original (total dataset size is 5k).[5] Figure 3 shows the Pearson correlation between the baseline model and the same regularizer with `MSE` and `LPL` (eq. 4). As observed, the correlation of models trained with `LPL` is higher for every training dataset size. The relative increase in correlation is in the range of 10.83 to 90.1%. We note here that the correlation cannot be compared with the original BERT model as we do not fine-tune the entire network but only the FFN in order to measure the improvements with the addition of `LPL`.

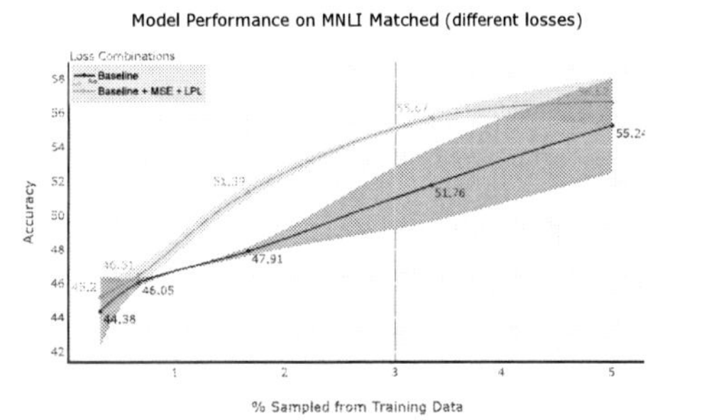

Figure 5: Accuracy of alignment regularization on MNLI dataset with a varying number of *matched* in-genre samples, up to 5% of the training dataset only (total: 300K samples).

4.2 Natural Language Inference

To test the effectiveness of alignment as a regularizer, a 2-layer FFN is used as shown in Figure 2; we measure the change in accuracy with respect to this baseline. An additional single layer network is utilized to perform the alignment with premise and hypothesis spaces. We experiment with the impact of the loss function on two datasets: the Stanford natural language inference (SNLI) (Bowman et al., 2015a) and the multigenre natural language inference dataset (MNLI) (Williams et al., 2018). SNLI consists of 500K sentence pairs while MNLI contains about 433k pairs. The MNLI dataset contains two test datasets. The *matched* dataset contains sentences that are sampled from the same genres as the training samples while *mismatched* samples test the models accuracy for out of genre text.

Figures 4, 5, and 6 show the accuracy of the models when optimized with a standard cross-entropy loss (baseline) and with `MSE` and `LPL` combined. The accuracy is measured when the size of the

[4]Appendix A.1 provides details about the dataset and FFN.

Method	Trans.	Optim.	EN-IT	EN-DE	EN-FI	EN-ES
MSE, Train T→S (Shigeto et al., 2015)	S1, S2	Linear	41.53	43.07	31.04	33.73
MSE (Artetxe et al., 2016)	S0, S2	Linear	39.27	41.87	30.62	31.40
MSE: IS (Smith et al., 2017)	S0, S2, S5	Linear	41.53	43.07	31.04	33.73
MSE: NN (Artetxe et al., 2018)	S0-S5	Linear	44.00	44.27	32.94	36.53
MSE: IS (Artetxe et al., 2018)	S0-S5	Linear	**45.27**	44.13	32.94	**36.60**
MSE	S0, S2	SGD	39.67	45.47	29.42	35.3
LPL+MSE: CSLS	S0, S2	SGD	43.33	**46.07**	**33.50**	35.13

(a) We compare our method (bottom row: LPL) on cross-lingual word alignment. In comparison to Artetxe et al. (2018), we use cross-domain similarity local scaling (CSLS) (Conneau et al., 2017) to retrieve the translated word. The *method* column lists different losses/methods used to learn the projection: *NN* is nearest neighbor search while *IS* is inverted softmax. Many mapping methods use additional transformation steps.

Trans.	Desc.	Backprop?
S0	Embedding normalization (unit / center)	Yes
S1	Whitening	No
S2	Orthogonal Mapping	Yes
S3	Re-weighting	No
S4	De-Whitening	No
S5	Dimensionality Reduction	No

(b) A map of various transformations that can be performed as described in Artetxe et al. (2018). We indicate which steps can easily be combined with backpropagation.

Table 1: The accuracy of the locality preserving method. Table 1a lists 6 high-performing supervised/semi-supervised baselines; table 1b lists the transformations used in these methods and how easily those transformations can be used with back-propagation. Notice that our method uses transformations amenable with back-propagation. In Table 1a, the first five baselines rely on algebraic updates while our method works nicely with SGD: we include the sixth row (MSE via SGD) to illustrate the comparative performance gain we obtain.

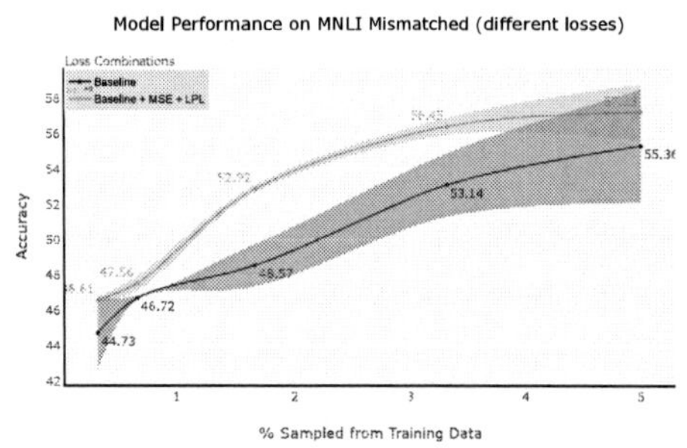

Figure 6: Accuracy of alignment regularization on MNLI dataset with a varying number of *mismatched* out-of-genre samples, up to 5% of the training dataset only (total: 300K samples).

training set is reduced.[5] The reduced datasets are created by randomly sampling the required number from the entire dataset. The graphs show that an alignment loss consistently boosts accuracy of the model with respect to the baseline. The difference in accuracy (in Figure 4) is larger initially, it reduces as the training set becomes larger. This is because we calculate the neighbors for each premise from the training dataset only rather than any external text like Wikipedia (i.e., generate embeddings for Wikipedia sentences and then use them as neighbors). As the training size increases LPL has diminishing returns, as the neighbors tend to be part of the training pairs themselves.

4.3 Crosslingual Word Alignment

The cross lingual word alignment dataset is from Dinu et al. (2014). The dataset is extracted from the Europarl corpus and consists of word pairs split into training (5k pairs) and test (1.5k pairs) respectively.[6] From the 5K word pairs available for training only 3K pairs are used to train the model with LPL and an additional 150 pairs are used as the validation set (in case of Finnish 2.5K pairs are used). This is a reduced set in comparison to the models in Table 1a that are trained with all pairs.'

Compared to previous methods that look at explicit mapping of points between the two spaces, LPL tries to maintain the relations between words and their neighbors in the source domain while projecting them into the target domain. Along with the mapping methods in Table 1a, previous methods also apply additional pre/post processing transforms on the word embeddings as documented in Artetxe et al. (2018) (described in Table 1b). Cross-domain similarity local scaling (CSLS) (Conneau et al., 2017) is used to retrieve the translated word. Table 1a shows the accuracy of our approach in comparison to other methods.

The accuracy of our proposed approach is better or comparable to previous methods that use similar numbers of transforms. It is similar to Artetxe et al. (2018) while having fewer preprocess-

[5] Model accuracy using MSE and MSE + LPL with 100% of the training data for STS-B is provided in Appendix A.1 and A.2 for SNLI / MNLI.

[6] http://opus.lingfil.uu.se/

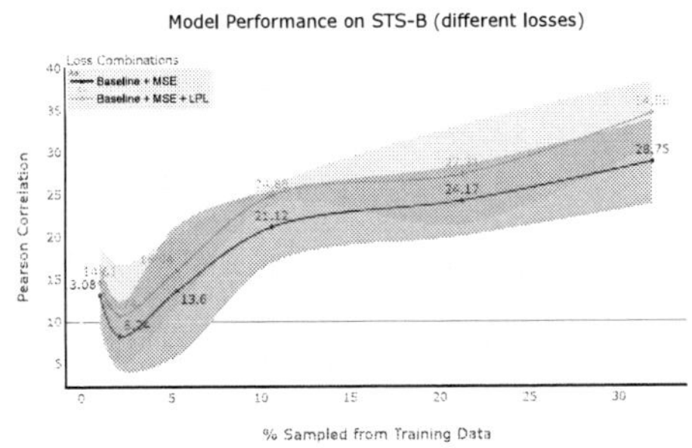

Figure 7: Pearson correlation of alignment regularization on STS-B up to 50% of the training dataset only (total: 4700 samples). The models are trained with `MSE` and `MSE + LPL`.

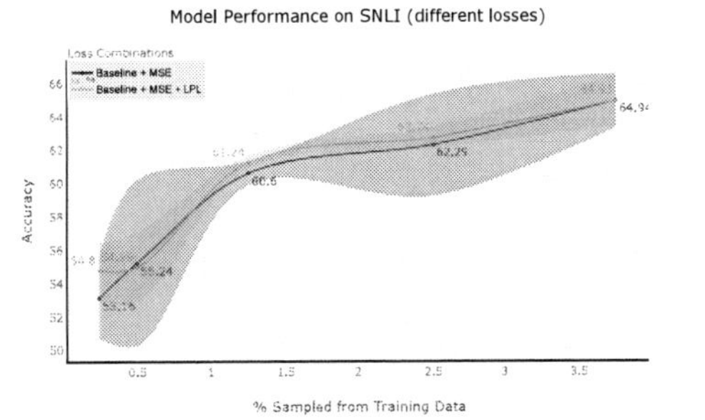

Figure 8: Accuracy of alignment regularization on SNLI up to 5% of the training dataset only. The models are trained with `MSE` and `MSE + LPL`.

ing steps. This is because we choose to optimize using gradient descent as compared to a matrix factorization approach. Thus, our implementation of Artetxe et al. (2016) (`MSE` Loss only) under performs in comparison to the original baseline while giving improvements with `LPL`. Gradient descent has been adopted in this case because the loss function can be easily adopted by any neural network architecture in the future as compared to matrix factorization methods that will force architectures to use a two-step training process.

4.4 Ablation Study

Although we introduce `LPL` in this paper, models in §4.1 and §4.2 are both trained with a combination of `MSE` and `LPL`. This raises the question: how much does `LPL` contribute to the overall performance of the model? We analyze this question by training a model separately on the STS-B dataset with `MSE` only and then comparing it with the prior model trained with the combined losses. In Figure 7, we see that the model trained with `MSE + LPL` performs better with a maximum of 20.2% relative improvement (sampled dataset size is 30%) over one trained with `MSE` alone. Additionally when the dataset size is small (less than 10% of the training data), it is observed that variation in accuracy is smaller for the model with the combined loss.

Additionally, we show the results of ablation studies on SNLI, MNLI (matched) and MNLI (mismatched). As seen in figures 8, 9, 10, `LPL`'s contribution to the model's accuracy in these tasks is lower in comparison to its contribution STS-B, but the variation in accuracy is smaller with it. Thus, we can conclude that `LPL` makes the model's performance consistent across experiments.

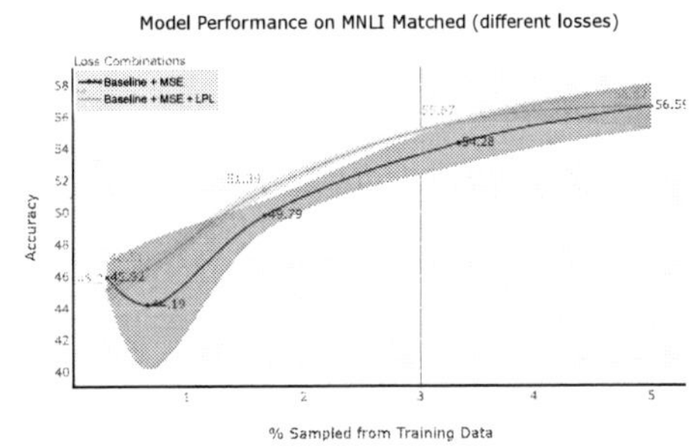

Figure 9: Accuracy of alignment regularization on STS-B up to 5% of the training dataset only. The models are trained with `MSE` and `MSE + LPL`.

4.5 Discussion

Table 2 shows the 2 nearest neighbors for a premise-hypothesis pair (P, H) taken from each classifier, i.e., baseline (B), baseline + `MSE` (BM), and baseline + `MSE + LPL` (BML) after they are trained (the dataset size is small at just 2000 samples). Since NLI is a reasoning task, the sentence pair representations ideally will cluster around a pattern that represents *Entailment* or *Contradiction* or *Neutral*. Instead what is observed is that when the samples are limited, sentence pair representations have NNs that are syntactically similar (NNs 1 and 2) for the baseline model. The predicted labels for the NN pairs are not clustered into entailment but are a combination of all 3. This problem is reduced for models trained with BM and BML (NNs 3 and 4 for BM, NNs 5 and 6 for BML). The predicted labels of the NNs are clustered into entailment only. The sentence pair representations cluster containing a single label suggest the models are better at extracting a pattern for entailment (and improving the model's ability to reason). This semantic clustering of representations can be attributed to

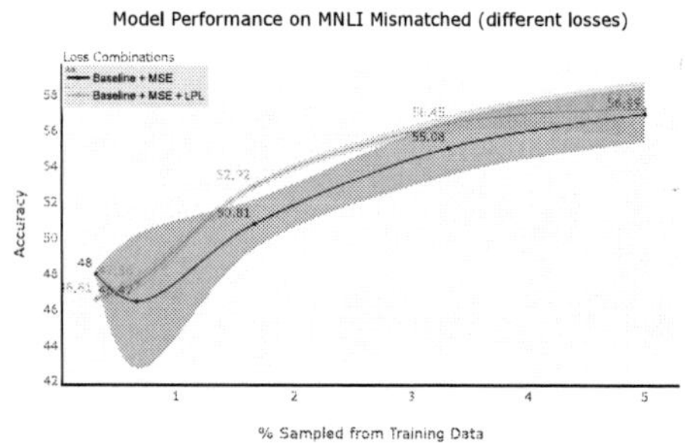

Figure 10: Accuracy of alignment regularization on STS-B up to 5% of the training dataset only. The models are trained with `MSE` and `MSE + LPL`.

Model Type	ID	Sentence
	P	Family members standing outside a home.
	H	A family is standing outside.
B	1P	People standing outside of a building.
	1H	One person is sitting inside.
	2P	Airline workers standing under a plane.
	2H	People are standing under the plane.
BM	3P	A group of four children dancing in a backyard.
	3H	A group of children are outside.
	4P	People standing outside of a building.
	4H	One person is sitting inside.
BML	5P	A family doing a picnic in the park.
	5H	A family is eating outside.
	6P	Airline workers standing under a plane.
	6H	People are standing under the plane.

Table 2: Nearest neighbors extracted from SNLI classifier for a sentence pair representation. P and H are the sample premise and hypothesis pair. The original label is *Entailment*. (nP, nH) are the nearest neighbors of this sentence pair's representation from the penultimate layer of each classifier, i.e., baseline (B), baseline + `MSE` (BM), and baseline + `MSE + LPL` (BML). 1 & 2 are nearest neighbors from the baseline, 3 & 4 are when trained with `MSE` only and 5 & 6 are when trained with `MSE` and LPL.

the initial alignment (or divergence) between the premise and hypothesis. Also, we observe that a model regularized with `MSE` and `LPL` are more likely to reach optimal parameters consistently.[7]

5 Conclusion

In this paper, we introduce a new locality preserving loss (LPL) function that learns a linear relation between the given word and its neighbors and then utilizes it to learn a mapping for the neighborhood words that are not a part of the word pairs (parallel corpus). Also, we show how the results of the method are comparable to current supervised models while requiring a reduced set of word pairs to train on. The models are trained with SGD as compared to others that learn with SVD. Additionally, the same alignment loss is applied as a regularizer in a classification task (NLI) and a regression task (STS-B) to demonstrate how it can improve the accuracy of the model over the baseline.

Broader Impact

In this section, we discuss the potential benefits and risks of using a locality preserving loss in the NLP tasks described in this paper.

Benefits of LPL. The main motivation of our work is to train models with limited data and showcase the effectiveness of locality preserving loss. When the dataset is small, models overfit the training data unable to generalize and exacerbate language biases. The main benefit of using `LPL` is that it maintains relationships between a datapoint and its neighbor in the target embedding space, restricting the model from overfitting.

Risks of Utilizing LPL. `LPL`'s ability to maintain relationships between points that are present in the source manifold after projection, can also be a risk. The weights W in equation 3 are learned by constructing a linear map between a datapoint and its neighbors using embeddings extracted from a pretrained model. Thus, any biased relationships prevalent in the pretrained model will become of a component of `LPL` and ultimately a part of the downstream fine-tuned model too. Hence it is necessary to evaluate the pretrained model thoroughly prior its use with `LPL`.

Acknowledgements

We would like to thank our anonymous reviewers from the Adapt-NLP Workshop and previous NLP conferences for their constructive reviews. We thank Prof. Konstantinos Kalpakis for his insights about manifold alignment and locality preservation methods. The hardware used in our computational studies is part of the UMBC HPCF facility and UMBC's CARTA lab. This material is also based on research that is in part supported by the Air Force Research Laboratory (AFRL), DARPA, for the KAIROS program under agreement number FA8750-19-2-1003. The U.S.Government is authorized to reproduce and distribute reprints for Governmental purposes notwithstanding any copyright notation thereon. The views and conclusions contained herein are those of the authors and should not be interpreted as necessarily representing the official policies or endorsements, either express or implied, of the Air Force Research Laboratory (AFRL), DARPA, or the U.S. Government.

[7] Check appendix section B for more details.

References

Mikel Artetxe, Gorka Labaka, and Eneko Agirre. 2016. Learning principled bilingual mappings of word embeddings while preserving monolingual invariance. In *Proceedings of the 2016 Conference on Empirical Methods in Natural Language Processing*, pages 2289–2294.

Mikel Artetxe, Gorka Labaka, and Eneko Agirre. 2018. Generalizing and improving bilingual word embedding mappings with a multi-step framework of linear transformations. In *Proceedings of the Thirty-Second AAAI Conference on Artificial Intelligence (AAAI-18)*.

Mikhail Belkin and Partha Niyogi. 2002. Laplacian eigenmaps and spectral techniques for embedding and clustering. In *Advances in neural information processing systems*, pages 585–591.

Sagie Benaim and Lior Wolf. 2017. One-sided unsupervised domain mapping. In *Advances in Neural Information Processing Systems*, pages 752–762.

Danushka Bollegala, Kohei Hayashi, and Ken-ichi Kawarabayashi. 2017. Think globally, embed locally—locally linear meta-embedding of words. *arXiv preprint arXiv:1709.06671*.

Thomas Boucher, CJ Carey, Sridhar Mahadevan, and Melinda Darby Dyar. 2015. Aligning mixed manifolds. In *AAAI*, pages 2511–2517.

Samuel R Bowman, Gabor Angeli, Christopher Potts, and Christopher D Manning. 2015a. A large annotated corpus for learning natural language inference. *arXiv preprint arXiv:1508.05326*.

Samuel R. Bowman, Gabor Angeli, Christopher Potts, and Christopher D. Manning. 2015b. A large annotated corpus for learning natural language inference. In *Proceedings of the 2015 Conference on Empirical Methods in Natural Language Processing (EMNLP)*. Association for Computational Linguistics.

Daniel Cer, Mona Diab, Eneko Agirre, Inigo Lopez-Gazpio, and Lucia Specia. 2017. Semeval-2017 task 1: Semantic textual similarity-multilingual and cross-lingual focused evaluation. *arXiv preprint arXiv:1708.00055*.

Alexis Conneau, Guillaume Lample, Marc'Aurelio Ranzato, Ludovic Denoyer, and Hervé Jégou. 2017. Word translation without parallel data. *arXiv preprint arXiv:1710.04087*.

Trevor F Cox and Michael AA Cox. 2000. *Multidimensional scaling*. CRC press.

Zhen Cui, Hong Chang, Shiguang Shan, and Xilin Chen. 2014. Generalized unsupervised manifold alignment. In *Advances in Neural Information Processing Systems*, pages 2429–2437.

Jacob Devlin, Ming-Wei Chang, Kenton Lee, and Kristina Toutanova. 2018. Bert: Pre-training of deep bidirectional transformers for language understanding. *arXiv preprint arXiv:1810.04805*.

Georgiana Dinu, Angeliki Lazaridou, and Marco Baroni. 2014. Improving zero-shot learning by mitigating the hubness problem. *arXiv preprint arXiv:1412.6568*.

Manaal Faruqui and Chris Dyer. 2014. Improving vector space word representations using multilingual correlation. In *Proceedings of the 14th Conference of the European Chapter of the Association for Computational Linguistics*, pages 462–471.

Goran Glavas, Robert Litschko, Sebastian Ruder, and Ivan Vulic. 2019. How to (properly) evaluate cross-lingual word embeddings: On strong baselines, comparative analyses, and some misconceptions. *arXiv preprint arXiv:1902.00508*.

Xiaofei He and Partha Niyogi. 2004. Locality preserving projections. In *Advances in neural information processing systems*, pages 153–160.

Zhenzhong Lan, Mingda Chen, Sebastian Goodman, Kevin Gimpel, Piyush Sharma, and Radu Soricut. 2019. Albert: A lite bert for self-supervised learning of language representations. *arXiv preprint arXiv:1909.11942*.

Yinhan Liu, Myle Ott, Naman Goyal, Jingfei Du, Mandar Joshi, Danqi Chen, Omer Levy, Mike Lewis, Luke Zettlemoyer, and Veselin Stoyanov. 2019. Roberta: A robustly optimized bert pretraining approach. *arXiv preprint arXiv:1907.11692*.

Tomas Mikolov, Ilya Sutskever, Kai Chen, Greg S Corrado, and Jeff Dean. 2013. Distributed representations of words and phrases and their compositionality. In *Advances in neural information processing systems*, pages 3111–3119.

Ndapandula Nakashole. 2018. Norma: Neighborhood sensitive maps for multilingual word embeddings. In *Proceedings of the 2018 Conference on Empirical Methods in Natural Language Processing*, pages 512–522.

Jeffrey Pennington, Richard Socher, and Christopher D. Manning. 2014. Glove: Global vectors for word representation. In *Empirical Methods in Natural Language Processing (EMNLP)*, pages 1532–1543.

Nils Reimers and Iryna Gurevych. 2019. Sentence-bert: Sentence embeddings using siamese bert-networks. *arXiv preprint arXiv:1908.10084*.

Anna Rogers, Olga Kovaleva, and Anna Rumshisky. 2020. A primer in bertology: What we know about how bert works. *arXiv preprint arXiv:2002.12327*.

Sam T Roweis and Lawrence K Saul. 2000. Nonlinear dimensionality reduction by locally linear embedding. *science*, 290(5500):2323–2326.

Sebastian Ruder, Ivan Vulic, and Anders Søgaard. 2017. A survey of cross-lingual embedding models. *CoRR, abs/1706.04902*.

Sebastian Ruder, Ivan Vulić, and Anders Søgaard. 2019. A survey of cross-lingual word embedding models. *Journal of Artificial Intelligence Research*, 65:569–631.

David E Rumelhart, Geoffrey E Hinton, and Ronald J Williams. 1985. Learning internal representations by error propagation. Technical report, DTIC Document.

Yutaro Shigeto, Ikumi Suzuki, Kazuo Hara, Masashi Shimbo, and Yuji Matsumoto. 2015. Ridge regression, hubness, and zero-shot learning. In *Joint European Conference on Machine Learning and Knowledge Discovery in Databases*, pages 135–151. Springer.

Samuel L Smith, David HP Turban, Steven Hamblin, and Nils Y Hammerla. 2017. Offline bilingual word vectors, orthogonal transformations and the inverted softmax. *arXiv preprint arXiv:1702.03859*.

Anders Søgaard, Sebastian Ruder, and Ivan Vulić. 2018. On the limitations of unsupervised bilingual dictionary induction. *arXiv preprint arXiv:1805.03620*.

Pascal Vincent, Hugo Larochelle, Yoshua Bengio, and Pierre-Antoine Manzagol. 2008. Extracting and composing robust features with denoising autoencoders. In *Proceedings of the 25th international conference on Machine learning*, pages 1096–1103. ACM.

Alex Wang, Amanpreet Singh, Julian Michael, Felix Hill, Omer Levy, and Samuel R Bowman. 2018. Glue: A multi-task benchmark and analysis platform for natural language understanding. *arXiv preprint arXiv:1804.07461*.

Chang Wang, Peter Krafft, and Sridhar Mahadevan. 2011. Manifold alignment.

Wei Wang, Yan Huang, Yizhou Wang, and Liang Wang. 2014. Generalized autoencoder: A neural network framework for dimensionality reduction. In *Proceedings of the IEEE conference on computer vision and pattern recognition workshops*, pages 490–497.

Adina Williams, Nikita Nangia, and Samuel Bowman. 2018. A broad-coverage challenge corpus for sentence understanding through inference. In *Proceedings of the 2018 Conference of the North American Chapter of the Association for Computational Linguistics: Human Language Technologies, Volume 1 (Long Papers)*, pages 1112–1122. Association for Computational Linguistics.

Adina Williams, Nikita Nangia, and Samuel R Bowman. 2017. A broad-coverage challenge corpus for sentence understanding through inference. *arXiv preprint arXiv:1704.05426*.

Chao Xing, Dong Wang, Chao Liu, and Yiye Lin. 2015. Normalized word embedding and orthogonal transform for bilingual word translation. In *Proceedings of the 2015 Conference of the North American Chapter of the Association for Computational Linguistics: Human Language Technologies*, pages 1006–1011.

Jun-Yan Zhu, Taesung Park, Phillip Isola, and Alexei A Efros. 2017. Unpaired image-to-image translation using cycle-consistent adversarial networks. In *Proceedings of the IEEE international conference on computer vision*, pages 2223–2232.

Appendix

A Experimentation Details

This section discusses in detail the various experiments conducted in this paper. For each set of experiments, we provide an overview of the dataset used, a description of the dataset (with samples), information about the training set and list of any hyper-parameters that are optimized. The computing infrastructure used is a single Tesla P100-SXM2 GPU to train a single model. The GPU consumption is driven by the base text / word encoding model. GPU usage while training the feedforward network (FFN) is limited. In practice, once the embeddings are extracted from an language encoder (like BERT), multiple FFs can be simultaneously trained on a single GPU. Additional GPUs are used to scale experiments while training models with different loss function combinations and dataset sizes.

A.1 Semantic Text Similarity (STS)

In order to understand the impact of Locality Preserving Loss (LPL) while finetuning a model to measure how similar two sentences are, we use the STS-B dataset (Cer et al., 2017) that is widely utilized as a part of the GLUE benchmark (Wang et al., 2018). STS-B consists of a total of 8628 pairs of sentences of which 5749 are for training, 1500 pairs are part of the dev set (for hyper-parameter tuning) and 1379 are test pairs. The labels are a continuous value between $0-5$ where 0 represents sentences that are not similar while 5 represents sentences are that have the same syntax and meaning. While training various models, the labels are normalized between 0 and 1. Table 3 shows a few examples of sentence pairs in the dataset.

Sentence 1	Sentence 2	Label
A plane is taking off.	An air plane is taking off.	5.0
A man is spreading shreded cheese on a pizza.	A man is spreading shredded cheese on an uncooked pizza.	3.8
Three men are playing chess.	Two men are playing chess.	2.6

Table 3: Sample sentence pairs from STS-B (Cer et al., 2017) dataset with their corresponding labels. The labels represent subjective human judgements of how similar the sentences are. It is a continuous variable.

A BERT model (Devlin et al., 2018) with an additional 2-layer feedforward network (FFN) (P_n) predicts the similarity score between sentences and is optimized with MSE (between predicted score and label). The FFN consists of 2 hidden layers, each of size 1024. The baseline model (trained only with MSE) has a concatenated input (as shown in Figure 2 - *baseline*). While using an additional alignment loss (MSE or LPL), an additional single hidden layer FFN (A_n) is attached that aligns the two sentence manifolds. The aligned projection of sentence 1 is then concatenated as input to P_n (as shown in Figure 2 - *baseline with alignment*). Although this increases the number of parameters in the P_n (by 768 x 1024) for models trained with alignment, we experimented with increasing the baseline model with the same number of hidden layer parameters and found the baseline's performance to decrease or remain constant. Hence, the size of the layers is maintained at 1024.

A.1.1 Crossvalidation

Figure 3 shows the pearson correlation between the predicted and actual similarity score. For each sample size on the X-axis, 3-fold cross validation is performed. Each time cross-validation is performed, different training pairs are randomly sampled (without replacement) from the complete dataset and the seed for initializing weights of each layer in the FFN is changed. To maintain consistency across experiments, the seed is maintained constant across trained models.

A.1.2 Hyperparameters

As described in §3.5, the hyperparameters include γ and δ. γ is a learning rate that defines how much of the alignment loss functions contribute to the overall loss. In practice, γ is set to 1.0.

Equation 5 uses LPL as a regularizer. We implement this as a contrastive divergence loss.

$$\mathcal{L}^i_{\text{mcd}} = \gamma \sum_i \max(-1.0, \delta_{y_i} * \mathcal{L}^i_{\text{mse}}) \quad (6)$$

$$\mathcal{L}^i_{\text{lcd}} = \gamma \sum_i \max(-1.0, \delta_{y_i} * \mathcal{L}^i_{\text{lpl}}) \quad (7)$$

The above equations change $\mathcal{L}_{\text{mse}}$ and $\mathcal{L}_{\text{lpp}}$ to a contrastive divergence (max margin) loss. We set the maximum margin to 0.1. The margin is manually tuned after optimizing it on validation pairs. The overall learning rate to train the model is 0.0001. The optimizer is RMSProp.

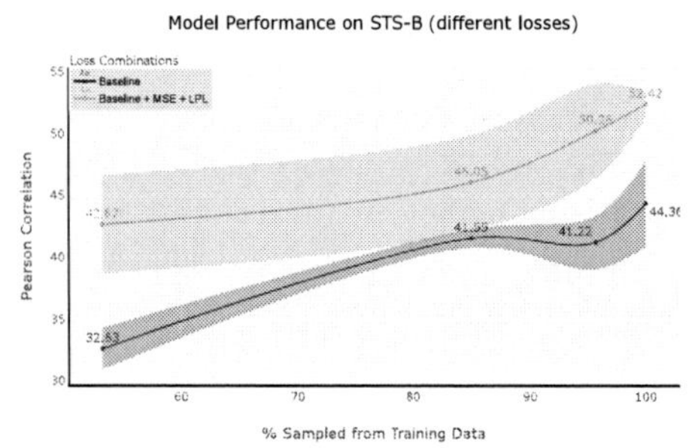

Figure 11: Pearson correlation on semantic text similarity with STS-B dataset for training sample size greater than 50% of the original dataset.

δ is the label specific hyper-parameter that defines how much loss can be contributed by a specific label. As the STS label is a continuous variable, δ is equal to the label value. This forces sentence pairs with scores that are 5.0 to have maximum loss while pairs with scores that tend towards 0 create a negative squared loss (this moves the embeddings apart) limited up-to the maximum margin.

A.1.3 Performance on Larger Dataset

In Figure 11, we see that the `LPL + MSE` loss model performs better than the baseline when dataset size is increased. The lowest bound in performance is higher than the upper bound of the baseline. `LPL`s improvement over the baseline when the entire dataset is used shows that as a whole STS-B may benefit from `LPL` irrespective of the dataset size. This is because `LPL` explicitly models a relationship between sentences present in a given sample text's neighborhood, ensuring that those relationships are maintained while computing the similarity between a given sentence pair.

A.2 Natural Language Inference (NLI)

§4.2 discusses in detail the experiments with natural language inference. Experiments are conducted on SNLI (Bowman et al., 2015b) and MNLI (Williams et al., 2017) datasets. Stanford's natural language inference dataset contains sentence pairs consisting of a premise and hypothesis. The model predicts if the hypothesis *entails* or *contradicts* the premise or if they have a neutral relationship (i.e., the two sentences are not related). The dataset contains $500K$ training pairs, $10K$ pairs in the dev set and $10K$ pairs of sentences for testing. Table 4 shows a few sentence pairs from the dataset.

MNLI (Williams et al., 2017) is an extension of the SNLI dataset where the sentences are from multiple genres such as letters promoting non-profit organizations, government reports and documents as well as fictional books. This expands the variation in language used in sentences, reducing the model's ability to memorize sentence pairs and their labels. Table 5 contains example pairs from the MNLI training data.

Premise	Hypothesis	Label
A person on a horse jumps over a broken down airplane.	A person is at a diner, ordering an omelette.	*Contradiction*
A person on a horse jumps over a broken down airplane.	A person is outdoors, on a horse.	*Entailment*
Children smiling and waving at camera	They are smiling at their parents	*Neutral*

Table 4: Samples from the SNLI (Bowman et al., 2015b) dataset. Each pair consists of two sentences and a label with one of three values *entailment, neutral, contradiction*.

Premise	Hypothesis	Label
Conceptually cream skimming has two basic dimensions - product and geography.	Product and geography are what make cream skimming work.	*Neutral*
How do you know? All this is their information again.	This information belongs to them.	*Entailment*

Table 5: Samples from the SNLI (Bowman et al., 2015b) dataset. Each pair consists of two sentences and label with one of three values *entailment, neutral, contradiction*

The model's architecture is described in Figure 2. The sentence embeddings are extracted from BERT (Devlin et al., 2018) and the NLI classification layers are trained separately. For experiments in §4.2, the trained model is a 2-layer FNN, each hidden layer with a size of 4096. The activation function is a Leaky RELU. Similar to the experiments in appendix A.1.1, we perform 3-fold crossvalidation where the training dataset is resampled and the results presented in §4.2 are an average over these 3 runs.

A.2.1 Hyperparameters

The models are trained with a learning rate of 0.0001 and the optimizer is RMSProp. In order to train the model with LPL and MSE, δ is configured. In comparison to a continuous δ variable used in the STS task, in NLI, the δ is constant for each label. For each dataset, the δ parameter is set after manual testing on the dev set. Sentence pairs that have a *neutral* label tend to be sentences

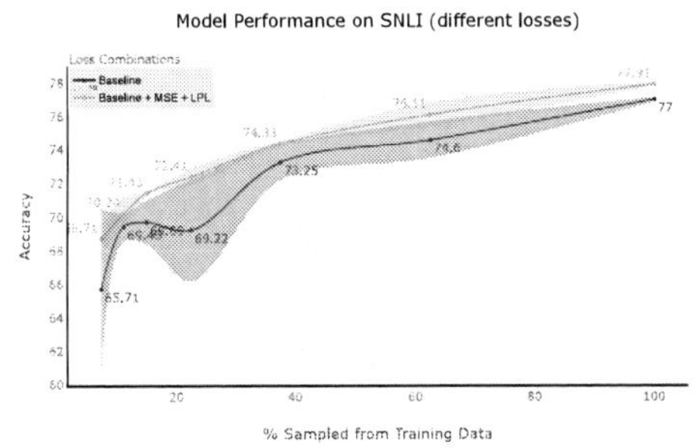

Figure 12: Accuracy of alignment regularization on SNLI. The graph shows the accuracy, averaged across 3 runs, for differing size of training samples from 5% to 100% of the training dataset only (total: 500K).

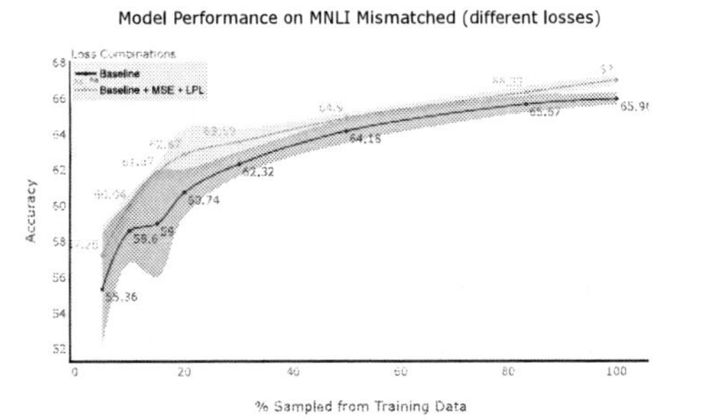

Figure 14: Accuracy of alignment regularization on MNLI dataset with a varying number of *mismatched* out-of-genre samples, from 5% to 100% of the training dataset only (total: 300K samples).

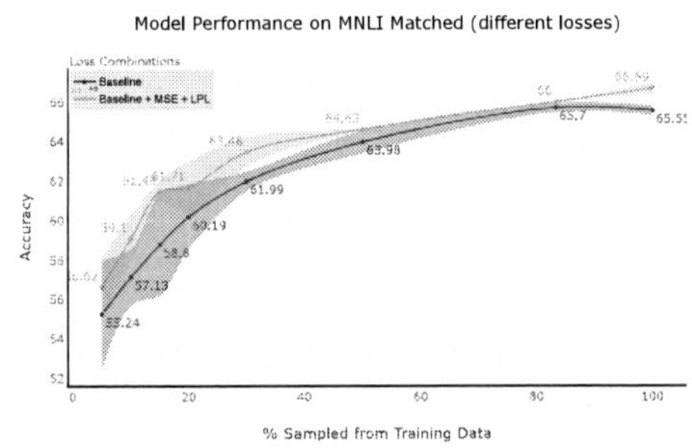

Figure 13: Accuracy of alignment regularization on MNLI dataset with a varying number of *matched* in-genre samples, from 5% to 100% of the training dataset only (total: 300K samples).

that are dissimilar. The semantic difference can be based on differing subjects, predicates or objects in the sentence, the content / topic or even genre of the sentence. Hence while training the model, these projections are **separated** with the alignment loss (and have a negative δ) rather than converged.

From our initial experiments, we found that lower δ on *entailment* and *contradiction* yielded no change in accuracy from baseline. The accuracy increases when a higher positive δ scalar multiple is attached to *entailment* & *contradiction*, and a negative scalar is multiplied to the loss generated for *neutral* label samples.

Dataset	Entailment	Neutral	Contradiction
SNLI	100.0	−5.0	0.0
MNLI	250.0	1.0	−10.0

Table 6: Samples from the SNLI (Bowman et al., 2015b) dataset. Each pair consists of two sentences and label with one of three values *entailment, neutral, contradiction*

A.2.2 Performance on Larger Dataset

Apart from better accuracy when the training dataset is small, in Figures 12,13, and 14, we observe the accuracy of models trained with the alignment loss using `MSE` alone and another in combination with `LPL` converge as the number of training samples increases. This happens because of the way k-nearest neighbor (k-NN) is computed for each embedding in the source domain. We use BERT to generate the embedding of each sentence in the SNLI and MNLI dataset. Because BERT itself is trained on millions of sentences from Wikipedia and Book Corpus, searching for k-NN embeddings for each sentence from this dataset (for each sentence in the training sample) is computationally difficult. In order to make the k-NN search tractable, neighbors are extracted from the dataset itself (500K sentences in SNLI and 300K sentences in MNLI). This impacts the overall improvement in accuracy using `LPL` as it is not a perfect reconstruction of the datapoint (using its neighbors). Initially when the dataset is small the neighbors are unique. As the dataset size increases, the unique neighbors reduce and are subsumed by the overall supervised dataset (hence `MSE` begins to perform better). The impact of `LPL` reduces as the number of unique neighbors decreases and the entire dataset is used to train the model. This is unlikely to happen when NNs from a larger unrelated text corpus reconstruct local manifolds.

A.3 Crosslingual Word Alignment

For experiments with cross lingual word alignment, we use the parallel corpus from Dinu et al. (2014). Table 7 compares our method with other methods such as Xing et al. (2015) and Faruqui and Dyer

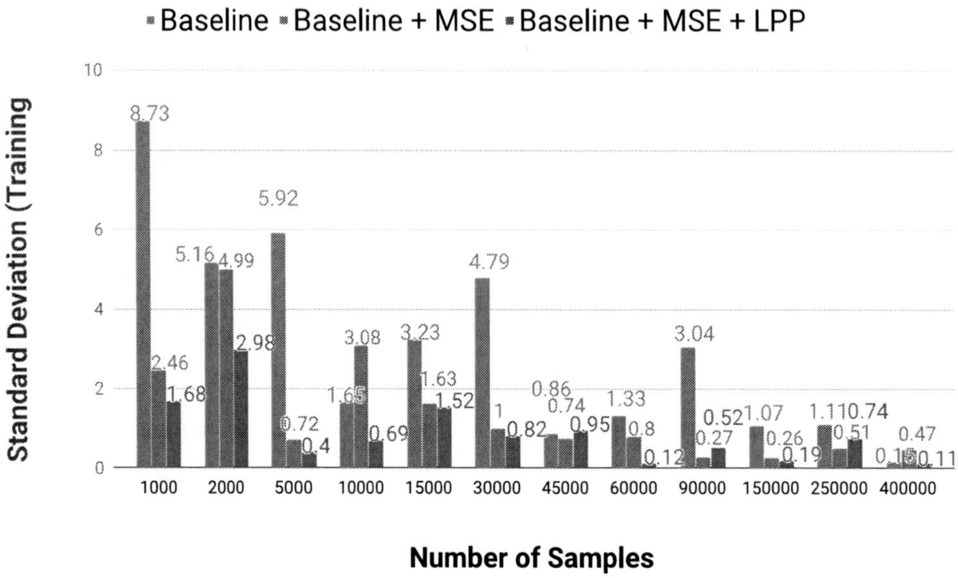

Figure 15: Standard deviation in performance. The graphs show the standard deviation in performance over 3 runs when the SNLI training dataset size varies In each case, the model trained with `LPL + MSE` + task loss has the least variation in performance, while the model trained with task loss + `MSE` or the task loss alone having a higher variance in performance.

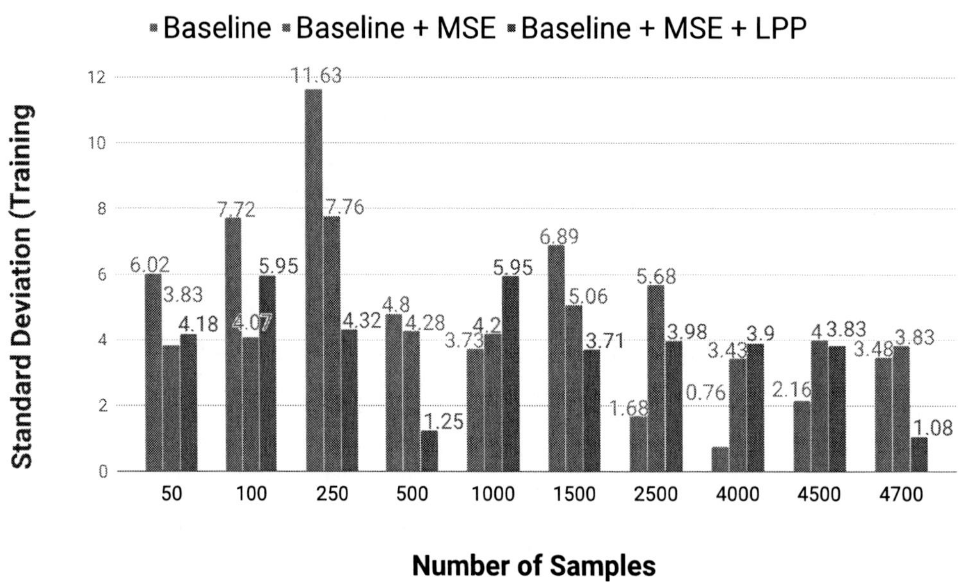

Figure 16: Standard deviation in pearson correlation. The graphs show the standard deviation in correlation over 3 runs when the STS-B training dataset size varies. In each case, the model trained with LPL + MSE + task loss has the least variation in performance, while the model trained with task loss + MSE or the task loss alone having a higher variance in performance.

(2014) and extends results in Table 1a. The dataset contains word pairs collected from the Europarl corpus. The bilingual dictionary has 5000 word pairs for training and 1500 word pairs for testing and evaluation. The language pairs in the dictionary include English $\leftrightarrow$ Italian, English $\leftrightarrow$ German, English $\leftrightarrow$ Finnish and English $\leftrightarrow$ Spanish. Figure 18 shows the pipeline to perform cross-lingual word alignment.

Method	EN - IT
Mikolov et al. (2013)	34.93
Xing et al. (2015)	36.87
Faruqui and Dyer (2014)	37.80
Artetxe et al. (2016)	39.27
Locality Preserving Loss (Our Work)	**43.33**

Table 7: Accuracy of various models predicting word translated from English to Italian.

Once the initial pretrained word vectors are selected, preprocessing can be applied. Preprocessing functions include unit normalization, whitening and z-normalization (Table 1b). Ruder et al. (2019) observe that deep neural networks are perform word alignment poorly in comparison to a linear tranformation ($Y = WX$). The linear transformation matrix W is learned by minimizing the sum of squared loss between Y and WX. Optimal parameters for W are learned by minimizing the loss with singular value decomposition (SVD) (Artetxe et al., 2016).

Locality Preserving Alignment combines preprocessing functions and training W. Also, parameters of W are learned using SGD, showcasing that LPL can be added to both linear and non-linear transformations. To find the translated word in the target embedding space, multiple inference mechanism are available such as nearest neighbor (NN), inverted softmax (Smith et al., 2017), and cross-domain similarity scaling (CSLS) (Conneau et al., 2017). We use **CSLS** to find the translated word in the target language.

In our experiments, we use original pretrained word embeddings obtained from the dataset (Dinu et al., 2014). The models are trained with a learning rate of 0.001. The β parameter is the learning rate specific to LPL (from equation 4) and is set to 0.7 and is manually tuned against the validation dataset.

Table 8 shows the neighbors for the word "windows" from the source embedding (English) and the target embedding (Italian). Compared to previous methods that look at explicit mapping of points between the two spaces, LPL tries to maintain the relations between words and their neighbors in the source domain while projecting them into the target domain.

Manifold	Nearest Neighbors of "Windows"
Source (M_1)	nt4, 95/98/nt, nt/2000, nt/2000/xp, windows98
Target (M_2)	winzozz, mac, nt, osx, msdos
Aligned ($f(M_1)$)	winzozz, nt4, ntfs, mac, 95/98/nt, nt, osx, msdos

Table 8: Neighbors of the word "windows" in source domain (English), target domain (Italian) and the combined vector space with both English & Italian vocabulary. The **Aligned** neighborhood contains a mix of the English and Italian words, not just the translation.

In this example, the word "nt/2000" is not a part of the supervised pairs available and will not have an explicit projection in the target domain to be optimized without a locality preserving loss.

B Measuring Performance Consistency

Figure 16 and 17 chart the variation in evaluated performance on each model on tasks STS-B and MNLI when the size of the training dataset varies. In each case, a model optimized with the task specific loss has higher variation in performance than models that are optimized with additional losses MSE and LPL. The variation for baseline models are higher when the size of the dataset is small. Figure 15 shows the variation in test accuracy across runs on the SNLI dataset. The variation in accuracy is highest for the baseline model when the size of the dataset is small. For example, when the baseline is trained with 1000 samples (0.002% of the dataset), the variation in accuracy is 8.73%. Similarly, when the baseline is trained with 50 samples (0.01% of the dataset) in STS-B task, the variation in accuracy is 6.02% (11.63% when sample size is 250). The variation in accuracy reduces as the sample size increases.

This occurs because when the subset of data randomly sampled, the quality of instances sampled has a large impact on the final performance of the model. Thus, measuring the consistency of the model's performance over multiple runs is a vital evaluation criteria (as much as the accuracy itself).

Hence, training the model with an alignment loss, i.e., with locality preservation ($\mathcal{L}_{mse}$ and $\mathcal{L}_{lpl}$), empirically guarantees that the model reaches near-optimal performance when the size of the supervised set is limited and that it has a narrow bound as compared to the baseline model trained without

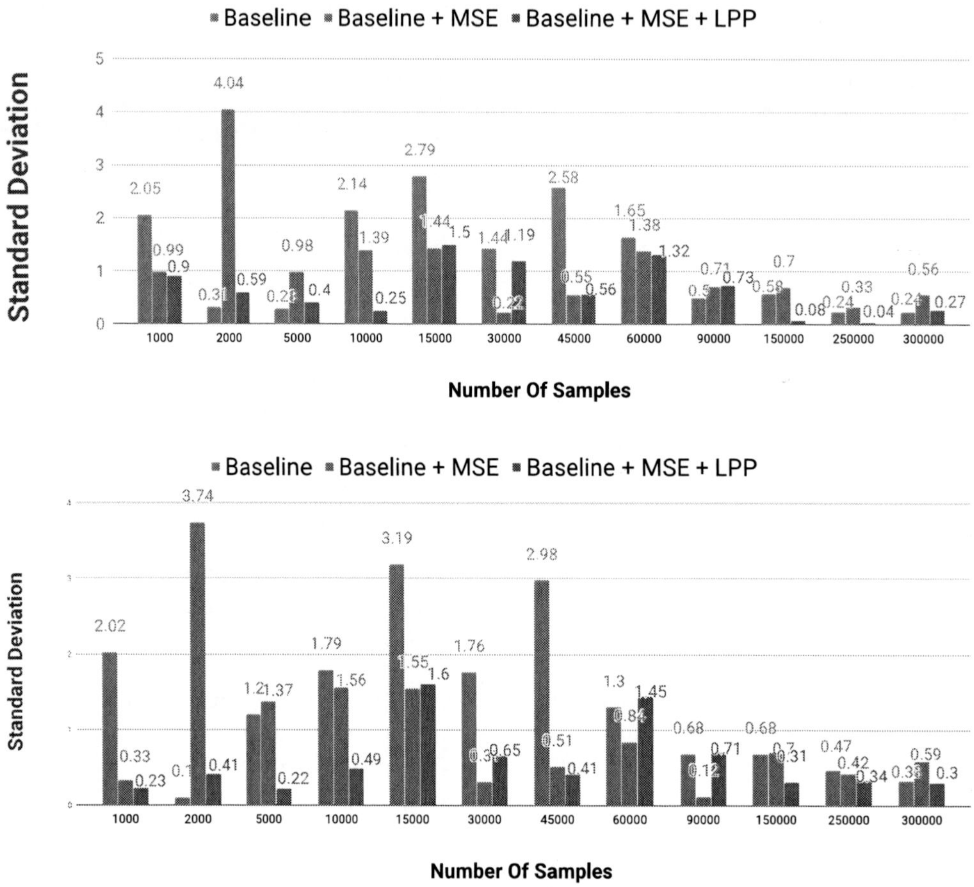

Figure 17: Standard deviation in accuracy of alignment on MNLI. The graph shows standard deviation in accuracy when size of the training sample set differs (total: 300K) for the baseline, baseline + MSE and baseline + MSE + LPL models: LPL yields more consistently optimal systems. (a) Standard deviation in accuracy when tested with in in-genre sentence pairs (matched MNLI) (b) Standard deviation in accuracy when tested with in out-of-genre sentence pairs (mismatched MNLI)

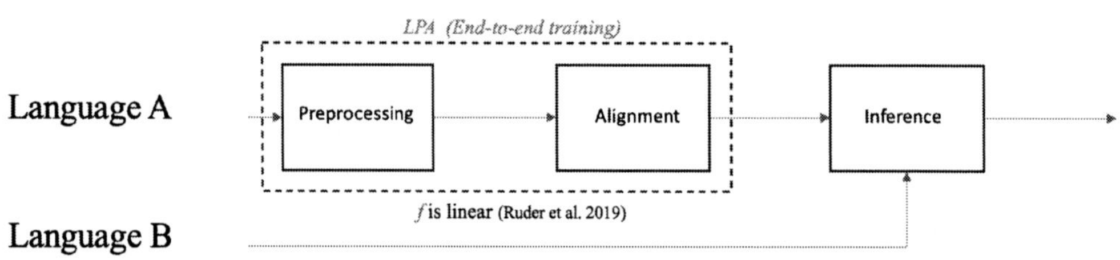

Figure 18: Crosslingual Word Alignment Pipeline (CLA). As described in Ruder et al. (2019), the CLA pipeline includes choosing an existing set of pretrained vectors that can be preprocessed. Table 1b contains a list of preprocessing functions that can be applied. Artetxe et al. (2018) evaluate each preprocessing method in detail. Alignment involves learning the transform matrix W and inference involves finding the translated word.

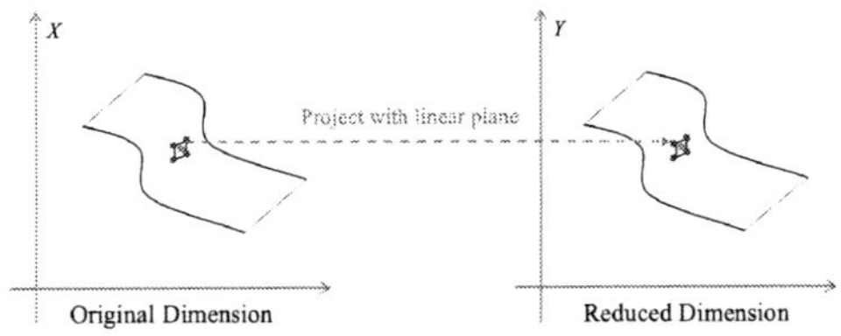

Figure 19: Locally Linear Embedding (LLE). The red point is a vector X_i that is reconstructed by a plane of its neighbors in blue. This linear plane is functionally represented by $W \in \mathbb{R}^{n \times k}$ for n points, each having k neighbors.

them. While performing these experiments, not only are the vocabularies randomly initialized, but also parameters too, making the model less dependent on how the training pairs are sampled from the dataset.

C Locally Linear Embedding

Our work is inspired from locally linear embedding (LLE) (Roweis and Saul, 2000). As discussed in §2.1, in LLE, the datapoints are assumed to have a linear relation with their neighbors (Figure 19). The reduced dimension projection of each vector is learned through a two step process: (a) Learn the linear relationship through a reconstruction loss (b) Use relation to learn low dimension representation. Assume each point in the manifold has k neighbors N_i. The reconstruction loss is:

$$\mathcal{L}_{\text{reconstruct}} = \sum_i \left\| X_i - \sum_{j \in N_i} W_{ij} X_j \right\|^2, \quad (8)$$

where X_i is the datapoint and the X_j represents each neighbor. An additional constraint is imposed on the weights ($\sum_{ij} W_{ij} = 1$) to make the transform scale invariant.

In (8) the weights W are an $N \times K$ matrix in a dataset of N points (i.e., each point has its own weights). Given a learned W from (8), we learn Y_i (a projection for X_i) by minimizing the following:

$$\sum_i \left\| Y_i - \sum_{j \in N_i} W_{ij} Y_j \right\|^2, \quad (9)$$

Y_i is typically with reduced dimensions.

On the *Hidden* Negative Transfer in Sequential Transfer Learning for Domain Adaptation from News to Tweets

Sara Meftah*, **Nasredine Semmar***, **Youssef Tamaazousti***, **Hassane Essafi***, **Fatiha Sadat**+
*CEA-List, Université Paris-Saclay, F-91120, Palaiseau, France
+UQÀM, Montréal, Canada
{firstname.lastname}@cea.fr, sadat.fatiha@uqam.ca

Abstract

Transfer Learning has been shown to be a powerful tool for Natural Language Processing (NLP) and has outperformed the standard supervised learning paradigm, as it takes benefit from the pre-learned knowledge. Nevertheless, when transfer is performed between less related domains, it brings a negative transfer, *i.e.* it hurts the transfer performance. In this research, we shed light on the *hidden* negative transfer occurring when transferring from the News domain to the Tweets domain, through quantitative and qualitative analysis. Our experiments on three NLP tasks: Part-Of-Speech tagging, Chunking and Named Entity recognition reveal interesting insights.

1 Introduction

High performing NLP neural tools often require huge volumes of annotated data to produce powerful models and prevent over-fitting. Consequently, in the case of social media content (informal texts) such as Tweets, it is difficult to achieve the performance of state-of-the-art neural models on News (formal texts).

The last few years have witnessed an escalated interest in studying Transfer Learning (TL) for neural networks to overcome the problem of the lack of annotated data. TL aims at performing a task on a target dataset using features learned from a source dataset (Pan and Yang, 2009). TL has been proven to be effective for a wide range of applications (Zamir et al., 2018; Long et al., 2015; Moon and Carbonell, 2017), especially for low-resourced domains.

However, it has been shown in many works in the literature (Rosenstein et al., 2005; Ge et al., 2014; Ruder, 2019; Gui et al., 2018a; Cao et al., 2018; Chen et al., 2019; Wang et al., 2019; O'Neill, 2019) that, when source and target domains are less related (*e.g.* languages from different families), sequential transfer learning may lead to a negative effect on the performance, instead of improving it. This phenomenon is referred to as *negative transfer*. Precisely, negative transfer is considered when transfer learning is harmful for the target task/dataset, *i.e.* the performance when using transfer learning algorithm is lower than that with a solely supervised training on in-target data (Torrey and Shavlik, 2010).

Several works (Gui et al., 2017, 2018b; Meftah et al., 2018a,b; März et al., 2019) have shown that sequential transfer learning from the News resource-rich domain to the Tweets low-resource domain enhances the performance of sequence labelling of Tweets. Hence, following the above definition of negative transfer, transfer learning from News to Tweets does not beget a negative transfer. Contrariwise, in this work, we rather consider the *hidden negative transfer*, *i.e.* the percentage of predictions which were correctly tagged by random initialisation, but using transfer learning falsified.

In this work, we take a step towards identifying and analysing the impact of transfer from News to Tweets. Precisely, we perform an empirical analysis to investigate the *hidden* negative transfer. First, we show in section.5.1 that, the final gain brought by TL can be separated into two categories: *positive transfer* and *negative transfer*. We define *positive transfer* as the percentage of tokens that were wrongly predicted by random initialisation, but the TL changed to the correct ones. In comparison, *negative transfer* represents the percentage of words which were tagged correctly by random initialisation, but using TL gives wrong predictions. Then, in section.5.2, we study the impact of pretraining state on negative and positive transfer. Finally, in section.5.3, we provide some qualitative examples of negative transfer. Our experiments on three NLP tasks (Part-Of-Speech tagging (POS), Chunking

Proceedings of the Second Workshop on Domain Adaptation for NLP, pages 140–145
April 20, 2021. ©2021 Association for Computational Linguistics

(CK) and Named Entity recognition (NER)) reveal interesting insights.

The remainder of the paper is organised as follow. We first present, briefly, the sequence tagging neural model (§2). Then, we describe the sequential transfer learning method (§3), followed by a short presentation of the involved datasets and tasks (§4.1). Then, we report the results of our analysis to highlight the hidden negative transfer occurring when transferring from News to Tweets (§5). Finally, we wrap up with a conclusion and future work (§6).

2 Sequence Tagging Neural Architecture

We perform experiments on 3 Sequence Tagging (ST) tasks: Part-Of-Speech tagging (**POS**), Chunking (**CK**) and Named Entity Recognition (**NER**). Given an input sentence of n successive tokens $S = [w_1, \ldots, w_n]$, the goal of a ST model is to predict the tag $c_i \in \mathcal{C}$ of every w_i, with $\mathcal{C}$ being the tag-set. We use a common ST neural model. It includes three main components. First, we have a WRE (Word Representation Extractor) to build, for each word w_i, a final representation $\mathbf{x}_i$ combining two hybrid representations; a word-level embedding (denoted Υ^{word}) and a character-level embedding based on a bidirectional-Long Short-Term Memory (biLSTMs) encoder (denoted Υ^{char}). Second, the $\mathbf{x}_i$ representation is fed into a Features Extractor (FE) (denoted Φ) based on a single-layer BiLSTMs network, to produce a hidden representation h_i which constitutes the input of the Classifier (denoted Ψ): a fully-connected (FC) layer used for classification. Formally, given w_i, the predictions are obtained using the following equation: w_i: $\hat{y}_i = (\Psi \circ \Phi \circ \Upsilon)(w_i)$. With Υ ensuring the concatenation of Υ^{char} and Υ^{word}.[1]

3 Transfer Learning Method

We use a simple sequential TL method to transfer knowledge from the News domain to the Tweets-domain. It consists in learning a source model on the source task with enough data from the News domain, then transferring a part of the learned parameters to initialise the target model, which is further fine-tuned on the target task with few training examples from the Tweets domain.

[1]Note that – for simplicity –, we define $\hat{y}_i$ only as a function of w_i, but in reality $\hat{y}_i$ is a function of all words in the sentence, thanks to the biLSTMs component.

Specifically, in this work we perform the TL following three simple yet effective steps: 1) The source model is learnt using a large annotated dataset from the source domain. 2) We transfer to the target model the first set of parameters (Υ and Φ) of the source model, while the second set of parameters (Ψ) of the target model is randomly initialised. Then, 3) the target model is further fine-tuned on the small target data-set.

4 Experimental Settings

4.1 Data-sets

We conduct experiments on TL from English News (source-domain) to English Tweets (target-domain) on three tasks (Datasets statistics are given in Table.1):

- **POS tagging:** we use the Wall Street Journal (**WSJ**) part of Penn-Tree-Bank (PTB) as a source-dataset. Regarding the target-datasets, we used three Tweets datasets: **TPoS** (Ritter et al., 2011), **ARK** (Owoputi et al., 2013) and **TweeBank** (Liu et al., 2018).
- **CK:** for the source dataset, we use the **CONLL2000** shared task's English data-set (Tjong Kim Sang and Buchholz, 2000). Regarding the target dataset, we use **TChunk** Tweets data-set (Ritter et al., 2011) (the same corpus as TPoS).
- **NER:** regarding the source domain, we make use of the English newswire dataset **CONLL-03** from the CONLL 2003 shared task (Tjong Kim Sang and De Meulder, 2003). target domain, we conduct our experiments on **WNUT2017** dataset (Derczynski et al., 2017).

4.2 Implementation Details

In the standard word-level embeddings, tokens are converted to lower-case while the character-level component still retains access to the capitalisation information. We set the randomly initialised character embedding dimension at 50, the dimension of hidden states of the character-level biLSTM at 100 and used 300-dimensional word-level embeddings. Word-level embeddings were pre-loaded from publicly available GloVe vectors pre-trained on 42 billions words collected through web crawling and containing 1.9M different words (Pennington et al., 2014). These embeddings are also updated during training. For the **FE** component, we

Task	Classes	Sources	Eval. Metrics	Splits (train - val - test)
POS: POS Tagging	36	WSJ	Top-1 Acc.	912,344 - 131,768 - 129,654
CK: Chunking	22	CONLL-2000	Top-1 Exact-match F1.	211,727 - n/a - 47,377
NER: Named Entity Recognition	4	CONLL-2003	Top-1 Exact-match F1.	203,621 - 51,362 - 46,435
POS: POS Tagging	17	TweeBank	Top-1 Acc.	24,753 - 11,742 - 19,112
CK: Chunking	18	TChunk	Top-1 Exact-match F1.	10,652 - 2,242 - 2,291
NER: Named Entity Recognition	6	WNUT	Top-1 Exact-match F1.	62,729 - 15,734 - 23,394

Table 1: Statistics of the datasets we used to train our models. **Top**: datasets of the source domain. **Bottom**: datasets of the target domain.

Method	POS (Accuracy %)			CK (Accuracy %)	NER (F1 %)
	TPoS	ArK	TweeBank	TChunk	WNUT
Random Initialisation	86.82	91.10	91.66	85.96	40.36
Transfer Learning	89.57	92.09	93.23	88.86	41.92

Table 2: Results on POS, CK and NER of Tweets using Transfer Learning vs Random initialisation.

use a single layer biLSTM (token-level feature extractor) and set the number of units to 200. In all of our experiments, both pretraining and fine-tuning were preformed using the same training settings, *i.e.* SGD with momentum and early stopping, and mini-batches of 16 sentences, and a fixed learning rate of 1.5×10^{-2}. Throughout this thesis, all our models are implemented with the PyTorch library (Paszke et al., 2017).

5 Analysis

First, in order to have an idea about the final impact of TL compared to randomly initialised models, we provide in Table.2 the performance of Random Initialisation and Transfer Learning. Clearly, TL enhances the performance across all data-sets and tasks. In the following sub-sections, we attempt to analyse thoroughly these results by showing that the impact of TL is two fold, *positive transfer* and *negative transfer*.

5.1 Quantifying Negative Transfer

Let us consider the gain $\mathcal{G}_i$ brought by transfer learning compared to random initialisation for the dataset i. $\mathcal{G}_i$ is defined as the difference between positive transfer $\mathcal{PT}_i$ and negative transfer $\mathcal{NT}_i$: $\mathcal{G}_i = \mathcal{PT}_i - \mathcal{NT}_i$. Where positive transfer $\mathcal{PT}_i$ represents the percentage of tokens that were wrongly predicted by random initialisation, but transfer learning changed to the correct ones. *negative transfer* $\mathcal{NT}_i$ represents the percentage of words which were tagged correctly by random initialisation, but using transfer learning gives wrong predictions.

$\mathcal{PT}_i$ and $\mathcal{NT}_i$ are defined as follows: $\mathcal{PT}_i = \frac{N_i^{corrected}}{N_i}$ and $\mathcal{NT}_i = \frac{N_i^{falsified}}{N_i}$. Where

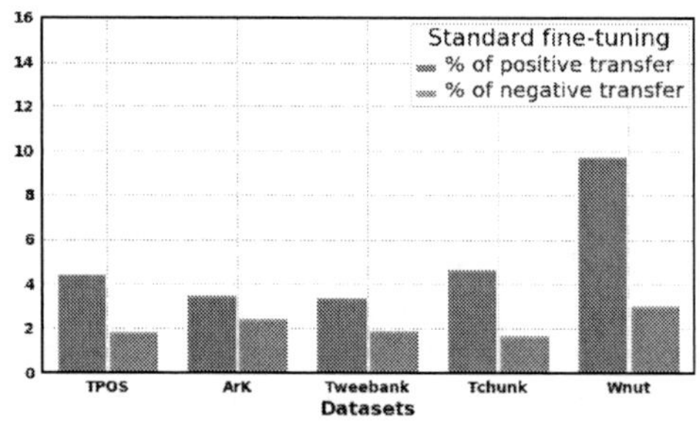

Figure 1: Impact on predictions made by TL compared to Random initialisation. Positive Transfer stands for the percentage of predictions that were wrong in the training from scratch scheme but the TL changed to the correct ones, and Negative Transfer stands for the percentage of predictions which the random model tagged correctly, but the TL falsified.

N_i the total number of tokens in the validation-set of the dataset$_i$. $N_i^{corrected}$ is the number of tokens from the validation-set of the dataset$_i$, that were wrongly tagged by the the model trained from scratch but are correctly predicted by the model using transfer learning. And $N_i^{falsified}$ is the number of tokens from the validation-set of the dataset$_i$, that were correctly tagged by the the model trained from scratch but are wrongly predicted by the model using transfer learning.

We show in Figure.1 the results on English Tweets datasets TpoS, ArK and TweeBank for POS; WNUT for NER; and Tchunk for CK. First tagged with the classic training scheme (Random) and then *using TL*. Blue bars show the percentage of *positive transfer*, and red bars give the percentage of *negative transfer*. We observe that even though TL approach is effective, since the resulting *positive transfer* is higher than *negative transfer* in all cases,

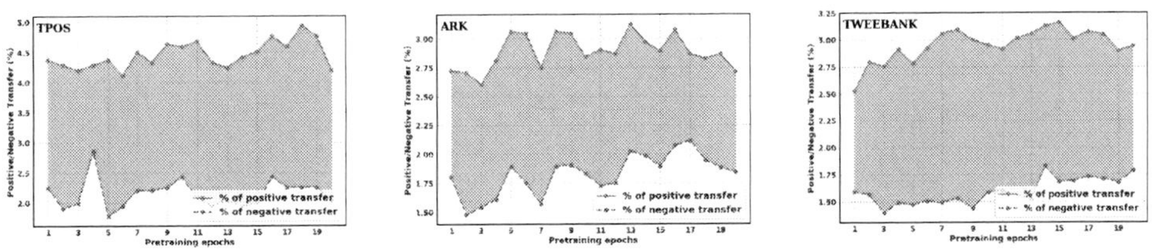

Figure 2: Positive transfer curves (blue) and negative transfer curves (red) on Tweets data-sets, according to different pretraining epochs. Transparent Gray highlights the final gain brought by TL.

this last mitigates the final gain brought by TL. For instance, on Tchunk dataset, TL corrected $\sim$4.7% of predictions but falsified $\sim$1.7%, which reduces the final gain to $\sim$3%.

5.2 The impact of pretraining state on Negative Transfer

So far in our experiments we used the pretrained parameters from the best model trained on the source dataset. In simple words, we picked the model at the epoch with the highest performance on the source validation-set. In this analysis, we study when pretrained parameters are ready to be transferred. Specifically, we pick the pretrained weights at different pretraining epochs; that we call the pretraining states. Then, we assess the performance when transferring each. In Figure.2, we plot for each target dataset, the curves of positive transfer (blue curves) and negative transfer (red curves) brought by initialisation with pretrained weights from different pretraining epochs compared to random initialisation. Clearly, both negative and positive transfer increase with pretraining epochs. More important, we can observe that for *TweeBank* and *ArK* datasets the negative transfer increases rapidly in the last pretraining epochs. However, for *TPoS* dataset, the negative transfer stays almost stable throughout pretraining epochs. This phenomenon could be explained by the fact that *TPoS* shares the same PTB tag-set as *WSJ*, whereas *TweeBank* and *ArK* use different tag-sets. Consequently, in the last states of pretraining, the pretrained parameters become well-tuned to the source dataset and specific to the source tag-set, leading to an increase of negative transfer and thus a drop in transfer performance.

5.3 Qualitative Examples of Negative Transfer:

We illustrate in Table 3[2] concrete examples of words whose predictions were falsified when using transfer learning compared to random initialisation. Among mistakes we have observed:

- **Tokens with an upper-cased first letter**: In news (formal English), only proper nouns start with an upper-case letter inside sentences. Consequently, in the transfer learning scheme, the pre-trained units fail to slough this pattern which is not always respected in social media. Hence, we found that most of the tokens with an upper-cased first letter are mistakenly predicted as proper nouns (PROPN) in POS, *e.g.* Award, Charity, Night, etc. and as entities in NER, *e.g.* Father, Hey, etc., which is consistent with the findings of Seah et al. (2012); negative transfer is mainly due to conditional distribution differences between source and target domains.

- **Contractions** are frequently used in social media to shorten a set of words. For instance, in TPoS dataset, we found that "'s" is in most cases predicted as a "possessive ending (pos)" instead of "Verb, 3rd person singular present (vbz)". Indeed, in formal English, "'s" is used in most cases to express the possessive form, *e.g.* "company's decision", but rarely in contractions that are frequently used in social media, *e.g.* "How's it going with you?". Similarly, "wont" is a frequent contraction for

[2] Classes significations: nn=N=noun=common noun / nnp=pnoun=propn=proper noun / vbz=Verb, 3rd person singular present / pos=possessive ending / prp=personal pronoun / prp$=possessive pronoun / md=modal / VBP=Verb, non-3rd person singular present / uh=!=intj=interjection / rb=R=adverb / L=nominal + verbal or verbal + nominal / E=emoticon / $=numerical / P=pre- or postposition, or subordinating conjunction / Z=proper noun + possessive ending / V=verb / adj=adjective / adp=adposition

DataSet							
TPoS	Award$^{\diamond}$	's	its*	Mum	wont*	id*	Exactly
	nn	vbz	prp	nn	MD	prp	uh
	nnp	pos	prp$	uh	VBP	nn	rb
ArK	Charity$^{\diamond}$	I'M*	2pac$^{\times}$	2$^{\times}$	Titans*	wth$^{\times}$	nvr$^{\times}$
	noun	L	pnoun	P	Z	!	R
	pnoun	E	$	$	N	P	V
TweeBank	amazin$^{\bullet}$	Night$^{\diamond}$	Angry$^{\diamond}$	stangs	#Trump	awsome$^{\bullet}$	bout$^{\bullet}$
	adj	noun	adj	propn	propn	adj	adp
	noun	propn	propn	noun	X	intj	verb
TChunk	luv$^{\times}$	**ROCKSTAR**THURSDAY		ONLY	Just$^{\diamond}$	wyd$^{\times}$	id*
	b-vp	b-np		i-np	b-advp	b-np	b-np
	i-intj	O		b-np	b-np	b-intj	i-np
Wnut	Hey$^{\diamond}$	Father$^{\diamond}$	&$^{\times}$	IMO$^{\times}$	UN	Glasgow	Supreme
	O	O	O	O	O	b-location	b-person
	b-person	b-person	i-group	b-group	b-group	b-group	b-corporation

Table 3: **Examples of falsified predictions by standard fine-tuning scheme when transferring from News-domain to Tweets-domain**. Line 1: Some words from the validation-set of each data-set. Line 2: Correct labels predicted by the classic supervised setting (Random-200). Line 3: Wrong labels predicted by TL setting. Mistake type: $\diamond$ for words with first capital letter, $\bullet$ for misspelling, $\star$ for contractions, $\times$ for abbreviations.

"will not", *e.g.* "i wont get bday money lool", predicted as "verb" instead of "modal (MD)" by transfer learning. The same for "id", which stands for "I would".

- **Abbreviations** are frequently used in social media to shorten the way a word is standardly written. We found that transfer learning scheme stumbles on abbreviations predictions, *e.g. 2pac* (Tupac), *2* (to), *ur* (your), *wth* (what the hell) and *nvr* (never) in ArK dataset; and *luv* (love) and *wyd* (what you doing?) in TChunk dataset.

- **Misspellings**: Likewise, we found that the transfer learning scheme often gives wrong predictions for misspelt words, *e.g. awsome, bout, amazin*.

6 Conclusion

Our analysis on the *hidden* negative transfer from News-domain to Tweets-domain reveals interesting insights: 1) Even if using TL improves the performance on Tweets Sequence labelling, an inherent negative transfer may minimise the final gain; and 2) the negative transfer increases with the number of pretraining epochs. This study opens a set of promising directions. We plan to 1) Extend our experiments by investigating the impact of the model's hyper-parameters (size, activation functions, learning rate, etc.). 2) Investigate the impact of the similarity between source and target datasets and source and target training datasets size on the negative transfer. 3) Tackle the negative transfer problem, by identifying automatically biased neurons in the pretrained model and proceed to a pruning of the most biased ones before fine-tuning. 4) Explore negative transfer on Transformers-based pretrained models, such as BERT, XLNet, etc.

References

Zhangjie Cao, Mingsheng Long, Jianmin Wang, and Michael I Jordan. 2018. Partial transfer learning with selective adversarial networks. In *Proceedings of the IEEE Conference on Computer Vision and Pattern Recognition*, pages 2724–2732.

Xinyang Chen, Sinan Wang, Bo Fu, Mingsheng Long, and Jianmin Wang. 2019. Catastrophic forgetting meets negative transfer: Batch spectral shrinkage for safe transfer learning. In *Advances in Neural Information Processing Systems*, pages 1908–1918.

Leon Derczynski, Eric Nichols, Marieke van Erp, and Nut Limsopatham. 2017. Results of the wnut2017 shared task on novel and emerging entity recognition. In *Proceedings of the 3rd Workshop on Noisy User-generated Text*, pages 140–147.

Liang Ge, Jing Gao, Hung Ngo, Kang Li, and Aidong Zhang. 2014. On handling negative transfer and imbalanced distributions in multiple source transfer learning. *Statistical Analysis and Data Mining: The ASA Data Science Journal*, 7(4):254–271.

Lin Gui, Ruifeng Xu, Qin Lu, Jiachen Du, and Yu Zhou. 2018a. Negative transfer detection in transductive transfer learning. *International Journal of Machine Learning and Cybernetics*, 9(2):185–197.

Tao Gui, Qi Zhang, Jingjing Gong, Minlong Peng, Di Liang, Keyu Ding, and Xuan-Jing Huang. 2018b. Transferring from formal newswire domain with hypernet for twitter pos tagging. In *Proceedings of the*

2018 Conference on Empirical Methods in Natural Language Processing, pages 2540–2549.

Tao Gui, Qi Zhang, Haoran Huang, Minlong Peng, and Xuanjing Huang. 2017. Part-of-speech tagging for twitter with adversarial neural networks. In *Proceedings of the 2017 Conference on Empirical Methods in Natural Language Processing*, pages 2411–2420.

Yijia Liu, Yi Zhu, Wanxiang Che, Bing Qin, Nathan Schneider, and Noah A Smith. 2018. Parsing tweets into universal dependencies. In *Proceedings of the 2018 Conference of the North American Chapter of the Association for Computational Linguistics: Human Language Technologies, Volume 1 (Long Papers)*, pages 965–975.

Mingsheng Long, Yue Cao, Jianmin Wang, and Michael Jordan. 2015. Learning transferable features with deep adaptation networks. In *International conference on machine learning*, pages 97–105.

Luisa März, Dietrich Trautmann, and Benjamin Roth. 2019. Domain adaptation for part-of-speech tagging of noisy user-generated text. In *Proceedings of the 2019 Conference of the North American Chapter of the Association for Computational Linguistics: Human Language Technologies, Volume 1 (Long and Short Papers)*, pages 3415–3420.

Sara Meftah, Nasredine Semmar, and Fatiha Sadat. 2018a. A neural network model for part-of-speech tagging of social media texts. In *Proceedings of the Eleventh International Conference on Language Resources and Evaluation (LREC 2018)*.

Sara Meftah, Nasredine Semmar, Fatiha Sadat, and Stephan Raaijmakers. 2018b. Using neural transfer learning for morpho-syntactic tagging of south-slavic languages tweets. In *Proceedings of the Fifth Workshop on NLP for Similar Languages, Varieties and Dialects (VarDial 2018)*, pages 235–243.

Seungwhan Moon and Jaime G Carbonell. 2017. Completely heterogeneous transfer learning with attention-what and what not to transfer. In *IJCAI*, volume 1, pages 1–2.

James O'Neill. 2019. Learning to avoid negative transfer in few shot transfer learning.

Olutobi Owoputi, Brendan O'Connor, Chris Dyer, Kevin Gimpel, Nathan Schneider, and Noah A Smith. 2013. Improved part-of-speech tagging for online conversational text with word clusters. In *Proceedings of the 2013 conference of the North American chapter of the association for computational linguistics: human language technologies*, pages 380–390.

Sinno Jialin Pan and Qiang Yang. 2009. A survey on transfer learning. *IEEE Transactions on knowledge and data engineering*, 22(10):1345–1359.

Adam Paszke, Sam Gross, Soumith Chintala, Gregory Chanan, Edward Yang, Zachary DeVito, Zeming Lin, Alban Desmaison, Luca Antiga, and Adam Lerer. 2017. Automatic differentiation in pytorch.

Jeffrey Pennington, Richard Socher, and Christopher Manning. 2014. Glove: Global vectors for word representation. In *Proceedings of the 2014 conference on empirical methods in natural language processing (EMNLP)*, pages 1532–1543.

Alan Ritter, Sam Clark, Oren Etzioni, et al. 2011. Named entity recognition in tweets: an experimental study. In *Proceedings of the conference on empirical methods in natural language processing*, pages 1524–1534. Association for Computational Linguistics.

Michael T Rosenstein, Zvika Marx, Leslie Pack Kaelbling, and Thomas G Dietterich. 2005. To transfer or not to transfer. In *In NIPS'05 Workshop, Inductive Transfer: 10 Years Later*. Citeseer.

Sebastian Ruder. 2019. *Neural Transfer Learning for Natural Language Processing*. Ph.D. thesis, NATIONAL UNIVERSITY OF IRELAND, GALWAY.

Chun-Wei Seah, Yew-Soon Ong, and Ivor W Tsang. 2012. Combating negative transfer from predictive distribution differences. *IEEE transactions on cybernetics*, 43(4):1153–1165.

Erik F Tjong Kim Sang and Sabine Buchholz. 2000. Introduction to the conll-2000 shared task: chunking. In *Proceedings of the 2nd workshop on Learning language in logic and the 4th conference on Computational natural language learning-Volume 7*, pages 127–132.

Erik F Tjong Kim Sang and Fien De Meulder. 2003. Introduction to the conll-2003 shared task: language-independent named entity recognition. In *Proceedings of the seventh conference on Natural language learning at HLT-NAACL 2003-Volume 4*, pages 142–147.

Lisa Torrey and Jude Shavlik. 2010. Transfer learning. In *Handbook of research on machine learning applications and trends: algorithms, methods, and techniques*, pages 242–264. IGI global.

Zirui Wang, Zihang Dai, Barnabás Póczos, and Jaime Carbonell. 2019. Characterizing and avoiding negative transfer. In *Proceedings of the IEEE Conference on Computer Vision and Pattern Recognition*, pages 11293–11302.

Amir R Zamir, Alexander Sax, William Shen, Leonidas J Guibas, Jitendra Malik, and Silvio Savarese. 2018. Taskonomy: Disentangling task transfer learning. In *Proceedings of the IEEE conference on computer vision and pattern recognition*, pages 3712–3722.

Trajectory-Based Meta-Learning for Out-Of-Vocabulary Word Embedding Learning

Gordon Buck
University of Cambridge
ghb28@cantab.ac.uk

Andreas Vlachos
University of Cambridge
av308@cam.ac.uk

Abstract

Word embedding learning methods require a large number of occurrences of a word to accurately learn its embedding. However, out-of-vocabulary (OOV) words which do not appear in the training corpus emerge frequently in the smaller downstream data. Recent work formulated OOV embedding learning as a few-shot regression problem and demonstrated that meta-learning can improve results obtained. However, the algorithm used, model-agnostic meta-learning (MAML) is known to be unstable and perform worse when a large number of gradient steps are used for parameter updates. In this work, we propose the use of Leap, a meta-learning algorithm which leverages the entire trajectory of the learning process instead of just the beginning and the end points, and thus ameliorates these two issues. In our experiments on a benchmark OOV embedding learning dataset and in an extrinsic evaluation, Leap performs comparably or better than MAML. We go on to examine which contexts are most beneficial to learn an OOV embedding from, and propose that the choice of contexts may matter more than the meta-learning employed.

1 Introduction

Distributional methods for learning word embeddings require a sufficient number of occurrences of a word in the training corpus to accurately learn its embedding. Even though the embeddings can be trained on raw text implying that an embedding for every word is obtained, in practice out-of-vocabulary (OOV) words do occur in the downstream applications embeddings are used, for example due to domain-specific terminology. Nevertheless, OOV words are often content words such as names which convey important information for downstream tasks; for example, drug names are key in the biomedical domain. However, the amount of downstream language data is typically much smaller than the corpus used for training word embeddings, thus methods that rely on distributional properties of words across large amounts of data perform poorly (Herbelot and Baroni, 2017).

Researchers often assign OOV words to random embeddings or to an "unknown" embedding, however these solutions fail to capture the distributional properties of words. Zero-shot approaches (Pinter et al., 2017; Kim et al., 2016; Bojanowski et al., 2017) attempt to predict the embeddings for OOV words from their characters alone. These approaches rely on inferring the meaning of a word from its subword information, such as morphemes or WordPiece tokens used in BERT (Devlin et al., 2019). While this works well for many words, it performs poorly for names and words where morphology is not informative.

Given that an OOV word occurs once, the chance of a second occurrence is much higher than the first (Church, 2000). Hence while OOV words can be rare and not seen in training, it is reasonable to expect that a limited number of occurrences will be present in the data of a downstream application. Few-shot approaches (Garneau et al., 2018; Khodak et al., 2018; Hu et al., 2019) leveraged this to predict the embeddings for OOV words from just a few contexts, often in conjunction with their morphological information. Hu et al. (2019) proposed an attention-based architecture for OOV word embedding learning as a few-shot regression problem. The model is trained to predict the embedding of a word based on a few contexts and its character sequence. Such a model is trained by simulating OOV words in the training corpus, with their target embeddings provided by learning them on the same corpus. As OOV words must have their embeddings inferred from contexts outside the training corpus, the authors show that using an adaptation of the model-agnostic meta-learning (MAML) algorithm (Finn et al., 2017) to adapt the model's

Proceedings of the Second Workshop on Domain Adaptation for NLP, pages 146–155
April 20, 2021.

parameters to the target domain improves the quality of the learned OOV word embeddings.

However, MAML is known to be unstable due to the calculation of gradients requiring backpropagation through multiple instances of the model, as the learning process must be unrolled to calculate gradients with respect to the initial parameters (Antoniou et al., 2019). In practice, the learning process is often truncated to a small number of gradient steps, but has been shown to have a short-horizon bias (Wu et al., 2018), causing it to underperform.

In this work we explore OOV word embedding learning using *Leap* (Flennerhag et al., 2019), a meta-learning framework which takes into consideration the entire learning trajectory, not only the beginning and end points. Each task is associated with a loss surface over the model's parameters on which the learning process travels, and the aim is to minimize the expected length of this process across tasks. Leap also does not require backpropagation through the learning process, allowing it to adapt over a larger number of gradient steps and thus not suffering from the short-horizon bias that MAML is prone to.

We conduct an intrinsic evaluation of MAML and Leap on the dataset of Lazaridou et al. (2017) which simulates OOV words by combining the contexts of two semantically similar words to form a 'chimera'. We find that Leap performs better than MAML at adapting model parameters to a new corpus. We also conduct an extrinsic evaluation on NER in the biomedical domain where the results are comparable to MAML, without improving in most cases on a random embedding baseline. Finally, we examine which contexts are more beneficial to learn an embedding from, and note that the contexts from which an embedding is learned matters more than the meta-learning method employed.

2 Meta-Learning

Meta-learning algorithms aim to capture knowledge across a variety of learning tasks such that fine-tuning a model on a specific task both avoids overfitting and leads to good performance. Approaches include learning a similarity function by which to cluster and classify data points (Vinyals et al., 2016; Snell et al., 2017); learning an update rule for neural network optimization (Ravi and Larochelle, 2017); and learning an initialization from which to fine-tune a model. We consider algorithms for the latter.

Formally, we consider task $\mathcal{T}$ to consist of a dataset $D_\mathcal{T}$ of labelled examples (x, y) and loss function $\mathcal{L}_\mathcal{T}(\theta) \rightarrow \mathbb{R}$ which maps a model's parameters θ to a real-valued loss. For batch gradient descent this loss is constant for a given set of parameters, however for stochastic gradient descent it depends on the sampled examples. During training, tasks $\mathcal{T} \sim p(\mathcal{T})$ are sampled from a distribution $p(\mathcal{T})$ over the tasks the model should be able to adapt to. The aim is then to train the model's parameters such that they capture features common to all tasks in $p(\mathcal{T})$, and thus are a promising initialization for any of these tasks. Below we describe the approaches taken by MAML and Leap.

2.1 MAML

During training with MAML, for each task $\mathcal{T}$ the model's parameters are updated from an initialization θ to $\theta_\mathcal{T}^K$ through K gradient steps according to $\mathcal{L}_\mathcal{T}$. The final parameters $\theta_\mathcal{T}^K$ are then used to calculate the final task losses, and the original parameters θ are updated to minimize their sum. This meta-objective is given below in equation 1, where $u_\mathcal{T}(\theta) = \theta - \alpha \nabla_\theta \mathcal{L}_\mathcal{T}(\theta)$ is a single gradient step:

$$\min_\theta \sum_{\mathcal{T} \sim p(\mathcal{T})} \mathcal{L}_\mathcal{T}(\theta_\mathcal{T}^K) = \sum_{\mathcal{T} \sim p(\mathcal{T})} \mathcal{L}_\mathcal{T}(u_\mathcal{T}^K(\theta)) \quad (1)$$

The final task losses $\mathcal{L}_\mathcal{T}(\theta_\mathcal{T}^K)$ are usually computed using examples held out from training $\theta_\mathcal{T}^K$ to simulate a testing loss. The meta-optimization is then performed by backpropagating with respect to the original parameters, θ, rather than the trained parameters $\theta_\mathcal{T}^K$. This aims to optimize θ such that a small number of gradient steps, K, on a particular task produces a low testing loss. Algorithm 1 below gives the overview of the training.

Algorithm 1: MAML

Input: $p(\mathcal{T})$: a distribution over tasks
Input: α, β: step size parameters
define $u_\mathcal{T}(\theta) = \theta - \alpha \nabla_\theta \mathcal{L}_\mathcal{T}(\theta)$;
initialize model parameters θ;
while *not done* **do**
  sample batch $\mathcal{B}$ of tasks $\mathcal{T} \sim p(\mathcal{T})$;
  forall $\mathcal{T} \in \mathcal{B}$ **do**
    $\theta_\mathcal{T}^K \leftarrow u_\mathcal{T}^K(\theta)$;
  end
  $\theta \leftarrow \theta - \beta \nabla_\theta \sum_{\mathcal{T} \in \mathcal{B}} \mathcal{L}_\mathcal{T}(\theta_\mathcal{T}^K)$;
end

Algorithm 2: Leap

Input: $p(\mathcal{T})$: a distribution over tasks
Input: α, β: step size parameters
initialize model parameters θ;
while *not done* **do**
  $\nabla \bar{F} \leftarrow 0$;
  sample batch $\mathcal{B}$ of tasks $\mathcal{T} \sim p(\mathcal{T})$;
  forall $\mathcal{T}$ **do**
    $\theta^0_{\mathcal{T}} \leftarrow \theta$;
    $\psi^0_{\mathcal{T}} \leftarrow \theta$;
    forall $i \in \{0, ..., K-1\}$ **do**
      $\theta^{i+1}_{\mathcal{T}} \leftarrow \theta^i_{\mathcal{T}} - \alpha \nabla_{\theta^i_{\mathcal{T}}} \mathcal{L}_{\mathcal{T}}(\theta^i_{\mathcal{T}})$;
      $\psi^{i+1}_{\mathcal{T}} \leftarrow \psi^i_{\mathcal{T}} - \alpha \nabla_{\psi^i_{\mathcal{T}}} \mathcal{L}_{\mathcal{T}}(\psi^i_{\mathcal{T}})$;
      $\nabla \bar{F} \leftarrow \nabla \bar{F} + \frac{(\mathcal{L}_{\mathcal{T}}(\theta^i_{\mathcal{T}}) - \mathcal{L}_{\mathcal{T}}(\psi^{i+1}_{\mathcal{T}}))\nabla_{\theta^i_{\mathcal{T}}} \mathcal{L}_{\mathcal{T}}(\theta^i_{\mathcal{T}}) + (\theta^i_{\mathcal{T}} - \psi^{i+1}_{\mathcal{T}})}{\|\bar{\gamma}^{i+1}_{\mathcal{T}} - \gamma^i_{\mathcal{T}}\|_2}$;
    end
  end
  $\theta \leftarrow \theta - \frac{\beta}{|\mathcal{B}|} \nabla \bar{F}$;
end

Computing $\nabla_\theta \sum_{\mathcal{T} \in \mathcal{B}} \mathcal{L}_{\mathcal{T}}(\theta^K_{\mathcal{T}})$ requires backpropagation through the learning process for each task $\mathcal{T} \in \mathcal{B}$. Gradients are computed by backpropagation through $K+1$ different instances of the model's parameters, which can cause both exploding and diminishing gradient problems, and becomes unstable for large K (Antoniou et al., 2019). However, truncating the learning process with a small K results in a short-horizon bias (Wu et al., 2018), where the learned parameters adapt poorly to tasks over a number of gradient steps larger than K. To extend to more steps, a first order approximation of MAML has been shown to achieve similar performance (Nichol et al., 2018; Finn et al., 2017). However, this still considers only the initial and the final parameters and loss, and for larger K the intermediate steps become more significant.

2.2 Leap

In Leap the learning process is viewed as a path along a loss surface $\mathcal{L}$, traversed by K gradient steps from initial to final parameters. The intuition behind Leap is that geometrical similarities between learning processes associated with different tasks can be exploited for transfer learning. In particular, Leap seeks to find an initialization that reduces the expected length of learning processes.

Following Flennerhag et al. (2019), we consider the learning process to be a sequence of discrete points $\{\gamma^i\}_{i=0}^K$ with $\gamma^i = (\theta^i, \mathcal{L}(\theta^i))$ corresponding to K gradient updates, and as such we consider the learning process to be the shortest path passing through these points. The length of a learning process is then approximated as the cumulative chordal distance of the path from initial parameters $\theta = \theta^0$ to final parameters θ^K.The cumulative chordal distance approximates the length of the arc passing through the points $\{\gamma^i\}_{i=0}^K$, and is key to minimizing the length of the learning process rather than simply moving the initial parameters towards the final parameters:

$$d(\theta; \mathcal{L}) = \sum_{i=0}^{K-1} \|\gamma^{i+1} - \gamma^i\|_2 \qquad (2)$$

Considering again a distribution of tasks $p(\mathcal{T})$, an initialization θ is associated with an expected learning process length $\mathbb{E}_{\mathcal{T} \sim p(\mathcal{T})}[d(\theta; \mathcal{L}_{\mathcal{T}})]$. When dealing with complex non-convex loss surfaces, minimizing only the expected learning process length makes no guarantees about the final loss $\mathcal{L}(\theta^K)$ and thus may inadvertently find final parameters θ^K with lower performance. Note that MAML takes this into account directly in its objective by optimizing for the final loss on a separate held-out set. Leap instead enforces this as part of its meta-objective by requiring that the optimized initialization θ must not converge to a higher loss than a baseline initialization $\psi = \psi^0$ for all tasks

$\mathcal{T}$. That is, $\mathcal{L}_{\mathcal{T}}(\theta^K) \le \mathcal{L}_{\mathcal{T}}(\psi^K)$ assuming convergence after K gradient steps. For this purpose, Leap defines an objective which optimizes the initialization for expected learning process length only along the task-specific learning processes originating from a baseline initialization. This ensures that the learning processes originating from the optimized initialization will have no greater final loss than their counterpart originating from the baseline initialization, given that both consist of K gradient steps. The objective is given in equation 3, where points $\{\gamma^i_{\mathcal{T}}\}^K_{i=0}$ lie along the learning process for task $\mathcal{T}$ originating from the optimized initialization θ, while points $\{\bar{\gamma}^i_{\mathcal{T}}\}^K_{i=0}$ lie along the respective learning process originating from the fixed baseline initialization ψ.

$$\begin{aligned} \bar{d}(\theta; \mathcal{L}_{\mathcal{T}}, \psi) &= \sum_{i=0}^{K-1} \|\bar{\gamma}^{i+1}_{\mathcal{T}} - \gamma^i_{\mathcal{T}}\|_2 \\ \min_{\theta} \bar{F}(\theta; \psi) &= \mathbb{E}_{\mathcal{T} \sim p(\mathcal{T})}[\bar{d}(\theta; \mathcal{L}_{\mathcal{T}}, \psi)] \end{aligned} \tag{3}$$

Gradient descent on the objective $\bar{F}$ with respect to θ pulls the parameters θ^i towards ψ^{i+1}. Parameters θ are initialized to be equal to ψ such that each gradient descent update pulls θ forward along the learning processes originating from it.

Algorithm 2 describes the training with Leap. Tasks $\mathcal{T} \sim p(\mathcal{T})$ are sampled from the distribution $p(\mathcal{T})$ and the model's parameters are updated to $\theta^K_{\mathcal{T}}$ through K gradient steps for each task $\mathcal{T}$ as in MAML (lines 1-10; the learning trajectory is expanded in lines 8, 9 and 10, as it is needed in Leap). The gradient $\nabla\bar{F}$ is incrementally computed at each point $(\theta^i_{\mathcal{T}}, \mathcal{L}_{\mathcal{T}}(\theta^i_{\mathcal{T}}))$ during the task training (line 11). $\nabla\bar{F}$ is always evaluated at $\theta = \psi$, with the update term on line 11 pulling θ^i towards $\psi^{i+1} = \theta^{i+1}$. This is performed in order to take into account each point in the learning trajectory, as opposed to the start and end points in MAML. The initialization θ is then updated according to the accumulated gradient $\nabla\bar{F}$ (line 14), and the algorithm continues with ψ set to the updated θ. This is done implicitly when θ is updated, which ensures that any future θ improves the task loss over the one already obtained, instead of just over the initial random initialization.

3 Leap for OOV Embedding Learning

In this section we describe our application of Leap to learning embeddings for OOV words. This technique is generally applicable to any word embedding regression function H_θ trainable by gradient descent, though in our experiments we use the HiCE architecture (Hu et al., 2019).

The regression function H_θ is trained to predict a word's embedding given K contexts, and possibly morphological information, with words and their contexts sampled from some large training corpus $\mathcal{D}_T$. Each word (either a training target or in a context) is represented as a pre-trained embedding in the input to H_θ. We note that H_θ can be trained only on words with sufficient occurrences in $\mathcal{D}_T$ such that their pre-trained embeddings can be accurately learned. The trained H_θ can then be used to infer the embeddings for OOV words, for which we do not have a pre-trained embedding. However, OOV words often form part of domain-specific vocabularies, the semantics of which are not captured by word embeddings trained on generic large corpora (Kameswara Sarma et al., 2018). To counteract this, we adapt the trained parameters θ_T of the word embedding regression function to the domain in which we infer the OOV embeddings.

When adapting θ_T we consider both $\mathcal{D}_T$, and the corpus on which we wish to infer OOV embeddings, $\mathcal{D}_N$. We wish to transfer the knowledge encoded in θ_T to the task of predicting OOV embeddings for words in $\mathcal{D}_N$. One approach would be to simply fine-tune θ_T on $\mathcal{D}_N$; that is, sample words and their contexts from $\mathcal{D}_N$ which have their pre-trained embeddings from $\mathcal{D}_T$ known and train H_θ as before on these words. This ignores that $\mathcal{D}_N$ is much smaller than a corpus usually used for word embedding training, and direct training on it is likely to lead to overfitting to the corpus rather than adapting to its domain, which in turn hurts the quality of inferred OOV embeddings, an instance of catastrophic forgetting (French, 1999). Instead of fine-tuning, meta-learning algorithms can be applied. Hu et al. (2019) use MAML, and we extend this work with the use of Leap.

We adapt θ_T by applying Leap across two tasks; inferring OOV words in $\mathcal{D}_T$ and $\mathcal{D}_N$. Optimizing the objective in equation 4 moves the adapted parameters θ to minimize the lengths of the two corresponding learning processes. The loss function $\mathcal{L}(\cdot|\mathcal{D})$ used throughout is the cosine distance between predicted and pre-trained embeddings.

$$\min_{\theta} \sum_{C \in \{T,N\}} \bar{d}(\theta; \mathcal{L}(\cdot|\mathcal{D}_C), \theta_T) \tag{4}$$

This pulls the model parameters θ along the learning processes for $\mathcal{D}_T$ and $\mathcal{D}_N$ originating from the pre-trained parameters θ_T. The learning process for $\mathcal{D}_T$ should already be short, as θ_T is trained to convergence on $\mathcal{D}_T$. Optimization of the pull-forward objective must naturally pull the parameters away from this point of convergence to minimize the length of the learning process for $\mathcal{D}_N$. However, as each task is weighted equally, the model parameters cannot move towards the convergence point for $\mathcal{D}_N$ if this results in a larger divergence from the convergence point for $\mathcal{D}_T$. It is thus necessary for the parameters to move into areas which encode knowledge sharing between $\mathcal{D}_T$ and $\mathcal{D}_N$. This reduces overfitting on $\mathcal{D}_N$ by ensuring θ does not move too far from the convergence point for $\mathcal{D}_T$.

While each word's embedding is inferred from only a few contexts, the total number of words available for training in $\mathcal{D}_N$ is large enough so θ can be adapted over a larger number of gradient steps. We posit that this, in conjunction with knowledge sharing that considers the entire learning trajectory rather than just the beginning and end points, results in higher quality OOV embeddings than those that can be obtained with MAML.

4 Experiments

4.1 Intrinsic Evaluation

To obtain an intrinsic evaluation of the methods proposed, we require a dataset that simulates the natural occurrences of OOV words in a real-world setting, and defines a notion for evaluating how close an embedding is to representing an OOV word's meaning. Following Hu et al. (2019), we use the 'Chimera' dataset for evaluation, a popular benchmark dataset for OOV words.

The Chimera dataset (Lazaridou et al., 2017) is constructed specifically to simulate unseen words occurring naturally in text. Each unseen word is a *chimera*, which is a novel concept created by combining two related but distinct concepts; for example a gorilla and a bear. In total there are 33 chimeras, generated by first taking a base concept, called a *pivot*, and matching this with a compatible concept by traversing a list of terms ranked by similarity to the pivot. In the case of the 'gorilla/bear' chimera, the pivot is the gorilla and the compatible term is the bear. Each chimera is then associated with passages of 2, 4 and 6 sentences, with half containing the pivot and half containing the compatible concept. The occurrences of the pivot and the compatible term are replaced with a nonce word that represents the chimera; for example 'mohalk'.

Each passage is then annotated by human subjects with similarity scores between the nonce word and six different words, called *probes*, specific to the chimera. These similarity scores are then averaged across human subjects, resulting in six scores for each passage indicating the similarity between the chimera and each probe word.

For each of the 2-shot, 4-shot and 6-shot cases the chimera's embedding is inferred given each sentence (shot) as a context and the pivot's character sequence. Following Lazaridou et al. (2017) we measure the performance of the embeddings inferred by looking at their cosine similarity to the probe embeddings and calculating the Spearman correlation to the similarity judgements by the human subjects.

Throughout all experiments HiCE is trained on WikiText-103 (Merity et al., 2017) with pre-trained embeddings provided by SkipGram (Mikolov et al., 2013) on the same corpus. Where MAML and Leap are used, word embeddings are adapted to the Chimera dataset. Both approaches were implemented using PyTorch (Paszke et al., 2017) and the code will become publicly available. To implement MAML we use `higher` (Grefenstette et al., 2020), a PyTorch library for higher order optimization such as backpropagation through gradient descent updates, as is required for MAML. This allows us to compute the second order gradients that are required for MAML, rather than using a first order approximation. The learning rates α and β for each of MAML and Leap were chosen based on each algorithm's stability during training; for MAML we used $\alpha = 5 \times 10^{-4}, \beta = 1 \times 10^{-5}$ and for Leap we used $\alpha = 5 \times 10^{-4}, \beta = 1 \times 10^{-4}$. These learning rates are in line with the publicly available code of Hu et al. (2019). The number of gradient steps used for adaptation with MAML was 4, while with Leap we increased this to 64, taking advantage of its ability to train tasks over longer horizons.[1]

Table 1 gives the average Spearman correlations for HiCE, its combination with MAML as proposed by Hu et al. (2019), and its combination with Leap as proposed in this work, for the 2-shot, 4-shot and 6-shot cases. We also include the results for related works taken from their corresponding papers. These include fasttext (Bojanowski et al., 2017); the additive method (a simple averaging of context word embeddings) (Lazaridou et al., 2017); a la

[1]The code used in our experiments is available here: `http://github.com/Gordonbuck/ml-oov-we`

	2-shot	4-shot	6-shot
fasttext	0.1775	0.1738	0.1294
additive	0.3376	0.3624	0.4080
a la carte	0.3634	0.3844	0.3941
nonce2vec	0.3320	0.3668	0.3890
HiCE	0.3611 ± 0.0054	0.3882 ± 0.0049	0.4134 ± 0.0043
+MAML	0.3574 ± 0.0058	0.3901 ± 0.0072	0.4169 ± 0.0057
+Leap	$\mathbf{0.3695 \pm 0.0022}$	$\mathbf{0.4022 \pm 0.0043}$	$\mathbf{0.4262 \pm 0.0051}$
pre-trained	0.4173	0.4367	0.4410

Table 1: Average Spearman's correlations for each k-shot case and method. Resulting of HiCE are given with 95% confidence intervals. Bold indicates the best results.

carte (a linear transformation-based modification of the averaging method) (Khodak et al., 2018); and nonce2vec (a modification of the Word2Vec algorithm for few-shot learning) (Herbelot and Baroni, 2017). We also give the scores obtained when using the pivot's pre-trained embedding as the chimera's embedding to indicate a ceiling, following Hu et al. (2019). However, we would expect the OOV embedding to differ from the pivot's pre-trained embedding, since the semantics of a chimera are a combination of the pivot and compatible concept.

HiCE+Leap achieves the best results across all k-shot settings in our experiments. The results for HiCE, HiCE+MAML and HiCE+Leap are all obtained by averaging the results over 10 different random seeds, and we give a 95% confidence interval for each. We take this approach to highlight the known instability of training MAML across random seeds (Antoniou et al., 2019), even with no hyperparameter changes. Leap consistently performs better than MAML and with a lower variance; in all cases, the average Spearman's correlation for MAML lies outside of the confidence interval range given for Leap. We also see that due to MAML's instability it can actually lower the performance of pre-trained HiCE in the 2-shot case. Outside of HiCE-based methods, a la carte performs best in the 2- and 4-shot cases, and additive performs best in the 6-shot case. These scores similarly lie outside of confidence interval ranges for HiCE+Leap, which overall performs best in each case.

Hu et al. (2019) reported 0.3781, 0.4053 and 0.4307 with HiCE+MAML in the in the 2-, 4- and 6-shot cases respectively, but did not report experiments with multiple random seeds. While were able to obtain similar results for HiCE+MAML in some of our experiments, they were outside the confidence intervals we obtained, illustrating the relative instability in training with MAML (Antoniou et al., 2019). The results of Hu et al. (2019) are also lower than the highest results we obtained with HiCE+Leap (0.3896, 0.4116 and 0.4395 for 2-, 4- and 6-shot).

4.2 Extrinsic Evaluation

To gauge the quality of the OOV embeddings for downstream tasks we evaluate their performance when applied to NER. For this purpose we use the JNLPBA 2004 Bio-Entity Recognition Task dataset (Collier and Kim, 2004). We choose this dataset as the biomedical domain differs significantly from the domain of Wikipedia that HiCE is pre-trained on, and contains many OOV technical terms. Hu et al. (2019) use this dataset also but did not provide their datasplits; thus. while we were able to confirm their results, we cannot compare against them directly.

The JNLPBA dataset is constructed from 2000 abstracts for training and 404 abstracts for testing, each extracted from a bibliographic database of biomedical information and hand annotated with 36 classes corresponding to chemical classifications. These classifications are simplified into 5 classes for the purpose of the bio-entity recognition task; *protein*, *DNA*, *RNA*, *cell-line* and *cell-type*. In total there are 18546 training and 3856 test sentences.

Following Hu et al. (2019), HiCE is trained on the WikiText-103 corpus, and we adapt word embeddings to the biomedical domain by using the JNLPBA dataset as a corpus. Contrary to the Chimera dataset, we consider contexts at the abstract level rather than only the sentence level. We train different embeddings for OOV words for each of the 2-shot, 6-shot and 10-shot cases, considering only those OOV words with 2, 6 or 10 occurrences or more respectively. In total we infer embeddings

	2-shot	6-shot	10-shot
random	**0.7226**	0.7206	0.7209
HiCE	0.7116	0.7213	0.7232
+MAML	0.7135	0.7232	0.7269
+Leap	0.7141	**0.7256**	**0.7282** †

Table 2: Micro-averaged F1 score for each of the 2-shot, 6-shot and 10-shot settings. Bold indicates the best results and (†) indicates the result is better than random embeddings at a 0.05 significance level.

for 4643 OOV distinct words (types) in the 2-shot case, 1310 in the 6-shot case and 702 in the 10-shot case.[2] The contexts used to infer the embedding of a word are chosen at random from the contexts that word appears. The inferred embeddings, alongside the embeddings for in-vocabulary words, are used as input to train the LSTM-CRF architecture of Lample et al. (2016).

For each of the k-shot cases a separate test set is created by subsampling, such that the respective test set contains only those sentences with an OOV word whose embeddings has been inferred. This ensures that the test sets focus on the quality of the inferred OOV embeddings. For the 2-shot case there are 2876 test sentences; 2451 for 6-shot; and 2134 for 10-shot. The results for each k-shot setting are given in Table 2, reported in micro-averaged F1 score. The results obtained using random OOV embeddings as input are given as a baseline.

Results are marginally improved with any of the proposed methods for the 6-shot and 10-shot cases, with HiCE+Leap producing the best results. We perform a paired t-test on each pair of results within a k-shot case. However, we do not find the differences between methods to be significant, with only HiCE+Leap in the 10-shot case performing significantly better than random embeddings, at a 0.05 significance level.

We find that performance increases across all methods as we use more contexts. However, for the 2-shot case we find that results are lower than if random embeddings are used. With fewer contexts the quality of the learned OOV embeddings is naturally lower, and inaccuracies in the embeddings add noise which hurts the performance of the downstream NER tagger. This highlights the need for a sufficient number of occurrences to effectively learn word embeddings, even with models specifically designed to handle the lack of data, and that using inaccurate embeddings can lower the performance of the entire downstream system. Our findings corroborate contemporary research which suggests that random embeddings can perform comparably to pre-trained and contextual embeddings on benchmark tasks (Arora et al., 2020).

[2]Hu et al. (2019) do not distinguish between different number of shots/contexts per word in their results.

4.3 Informative Contexts

Apart from comparing different meta-learning approaches for word embedding learning, we seek to find which contexts are invariably most informative to a word's meaning. For this purpose, we return to the Chimera dataset. Considering the 2-shot case, we rank passages by the performance of the chimera embeddings inferred from them. That is, we infer the chimera embeddings, obtain the cosine similarities against the probe embeddings, and calculate the Spearman correlation against the human scores. We then calculate the pairwise Spearman correlation between these rankings across random seeds and methods experimented with in this paper, i.e. HiCE, HiCE with MAML, and HiCE with Leap. The average Spearman correlation is 0.89 ± 0.0047 for a 95% confidence interval, indicating that the rankings of passages are largely similar across methods. Thus we conclude that the contexts which each method finds most useful to infer a chimera's meaning are largely invariable.

Ordering passages by their cumulative rank across methods, we observe that passages which consistently perform poorly are composed of sentences with more ambiguity and fewer content words. The top section in table 3 gives the lowest and highest performing passages as examples. The lowest performing passage contains little in the way of content words indicating the meaning of the chimera 'refrigerator/closet' besides the presence of 'freezers', and the second sentence is highly ambiguous. Naturally, human annotators would also struggle to pinpoint the semantic meaning of this chimera based on the two sentences given. In contrast the highest performing passage very clearly relates to organic produce and cooking, providing far more hints as to the semantic meaning of the chimera 'broccoli/spinach'.

We also look at which passages perform best for a given chimera. The bottom section in table 3 gives the lowest and highest performing passages for the 'drum/tuba' chimera. We observe the same trend within the chimera, with the lowest

chimera	probes	shot 1	shot 2	score
refrigerator / closet	cupboard, basement, mixer, dishwasher, ladle, boat	23144 security materials that may adversely affect hpc components shall not be stored in the ___ or freezers	if there is any difference from the first there are fewer of those ___	-0.68
broccoli / spinach	celery, radish, grape, salamander, budgie, pot	all manner of produce fill the fields including exotic vegetables like pumpkins spring onions ___ and asparagus	discard any bruised or yellow leaves and soak remaining leaves in a basin of cold water with ___	0.98
drum / tuba	bagpipe, harmonica, whistle, shotgun, bear, bouquet	i could nt yet hear the ___ that told you where to go on any particular day	is probably at mirage poker room income from week he borrowed was swimming ___	-0.63
drum / tuba	bagpipe, harmonica, whistle, shotgun, bear, bouquet	is there a better way to start a record or a song than with a thumpin ___ intro	they add considerably to the tone of the ___ however when used on their low notes	0.91

Table 3: Each section gives a higher and lower performing 2-shot passage with its average Spearman correlation across all methods and random seeds. The nonce word is replaced by '___'.

performing passage consisting of more ambiguous sentences, while the highest performing passage contains many content words which hint at the semantics of the chimera, such as 'song'. These two passages differ greatly in their performance, with the lowest passage averaging a Spearman correlation of -0.63 while the highest passage achieves an average of 0.91. However, if we look across methods the difference in performance for each of these passages is no higher than 0.2. This suggests that one of the most important factors to inferring an OOV word's embedding is the choice of contexts, perhaps more so than the meta-learning employed. To quantify this further, we calculate the Spearman correlation between the proportion of content words in a passage and its score, which we find to be 0.12 ± 0.0083 for a 95% confidence interval. We do this by using a standard part-of-speech tagger (Honnibal and Montani, 2017) on each passage; taking all nouns, adjectives, verbs and adverbs to be content words. While the correlation is weak, it is significant at a 95% confidence interval and further suggests that context informativeness is a suitable future area of work.

5 Conclusion

We investigated the use of meta-learning for few-shot learning of OOV word embeddings. We built on the work of Hu et al. (2019), formulating OOV word embedding learning as a few-shot regression problem and training their proposed architecture HiCE to predict OOV embeddings given K contexts and morphological features. We proposed the use of Leap as a meta-learning algorithm to adapt HiCE to a new semantic domain and compared it to the popular MAML as used by Hu et al. (2019). Experiments on a benchmark dataset show that Leap is more stable and achieves comparably higher performance than MAML in the context of OOV embedding learning. Further experimentation shows that there is little variation in which contexts perform well across both random seeds and meta-learning approaches, and a qualitative analysis indicates that performance is lower on ambiguous sentences with fewer content words. Our findings suggest a future avenue of work which focuses on the selection of contexts from which to learn an OOV embedding, such as prioritising contexts based on a notion of informativeness.

References

Antreas Antoniou, Harrison Edwards, and Amos Storkey. 2019. How to train your MAML. In *International Conference on Learning Representations*.

Simran Arora, Avner May, Jian Zhang, and Christopher

Ré. 2020. Contextual embeddings: When are they worth it? In *Proceedings of the 58th Annual Meeting of the Association for Computational Linguistics*, pages 2650–2663, Online. Association for Computational Linguistics.

Piotr Bojanowski, Edouard Grave, Armand Joulin, and Tomas Mikolov. 2017. Enriching word vectors with subword information. *Transactions of the Association for Computational Linguistics*, 5:135–146.

Kenneth W. Church. 2000. Empirical estimates of adaptation: The chance of two noriegas is closer to p/2 than p2. In *COLING 2000 Volume 1: The 18th International Conference on Computational Linguistics*.

Nigel Collier and Jin-Dong Kim. 2004. Introduction to the bio-entity recognition task at JNLPBA. In *Proceedings of the International Joint Workshop on Natural Language Processing in Biomedicine and its Applications (NLPBA/BioNLP)*, pages 73–78, Geneva, Switzerland. COLING.

Jacob Devlin, Ming-Wei Chang, Kenton Lee, and Kristina Toutanova. 2019. BERT: Pre-training of deep bidirectional transformers for language understanding. In *Proceedings of the 2019 Conference of the North American Chapter of the Association for Computational Linguistics: Human Language Technologies, Volume 1 (Long and Short Papers)*, pages 4171–4186, Minneapolis, Minnesota. Association for Computational Linguistics.

Chelsea Finn, Pieter Abbeel, and Sergey Levine. 2017. Model-agnostic meta-learning for fast adaptation of deep networks. In *Proceedings of the 34th International Conference on Machine Learning - Volume 70*, ICML'17, page 1126–1135. JMLR.org.

Sebastian Flennerhag, Pablo Garcia Moreno, Neil Lawrence, and Andreas Damianou. 2019. Transferring knowledge across learning processes. In *International Conference on Learning Representations*.

Robert M. French. 1999. Catastrophic forgetting in connectionist networks. *Trends in Cognitive Sciences*, 3(4):128 – 135.

Nicolas Garneau, Jean-Samuel Leboeuf, and Luc Lamontagne. 2018. Predicting and interpreting embeddings for out of vocabulary words in downstream tasks. In *Proceedings of the 2018 EMNLP Workshop BlackboxNLP: Analyzing and Interpreting Neural Networks for NLP*, pages 331–333, Brussels, Belgium. Association for Computational Linguistics.

Edward Grefenstette, Brandon Amos, Denis Yarats, Phu Mon Htut, Artem Molchanov, Franziska Meier, Douwe Kiela, Kyunghyun Cho, and Soumith Chintala. 2020. Generalized inner loop meta-learning. In *International Conference on Learning Representations*.

Aurélie Herbelot and Marco Baroni. 2017. High-risk learning: acquiring new word vectors from tiny data. In *Proceedings of the 2017 Conference on Empirical Methods in Natural Language Processing*, pages 304–309, Copenhagen, Denmark. Association for Computational Linguistics.

Matthew Honnibal and Ines Montani. 2017. spaCy 2: Natural language understanding with Bloom embeddings, convolutional neural networks and incremental parsing.

Ziniu Hu, Ting Chen, Kai-Wei Chang, and Yizhou Sun. 2019. Few-shot representation learning for out-of-vocabulary words. In *Proceedings of the 57th Annual Meeting of the Association for Computational Linguistics*, pages 4102–4112, Florence, Italy. Association for Computational Linguistics.

Prathusha Kameswara Sarma, Yingyu Liang, and Bill Sethares. 2018. Domain adapted word embeddings for improved sentiment classification. In *Proceedings of the Workshop on Deep Learning Approaches for Low-Resource NLP*, pages 51–59, Melbourne. Association for Computational Linguistics.

Mikhail Khodak, Nikunj Saunshi, Yingyu Liang, Tengyu Ma, Brandon Stewart, and Sanjeev Arora. 2018. A la carte embedding: Cheap but effective induction of semantic feature vectors. In *Proceedings of the 56th Annual Meeting of the Association for Computational Linguistics (Volume 1: Long Papers)*, pages 12–22, Melbourne, Australia. Association for Computational Linguistics.

Yoon Kim, Yacine Jernite, David Sontag, and Alexander M. Rush. 2016. Character-aware neural language models. In *Proceedings of the Thirtieth AAAI Conference on Artificial Intelligence*, AAAI'16, page 2741–2749. AAAI Press.

Guillaume Lample, Miguel Ballesteros, Sandeep Subramanian, Kazuya Kawakami, and Chris Dyer. 2016. Neural architectures for named entity recognition. In *Proceedings of the 2016 Conference of the North American Chapter of the Association for Computational Linguistics: Human Language Technologies*, pages 260–270, San Diego, California. Association for Computational Linguistics.

Angeliki Lazaridou, Marco Marelli, and Marco Baroni. 2017. Multimodal word meaning induction from minimal exposure to natural text. *Cognitive Science*, 41 Suppl 4.

Stephen Merity, Caiming Xiong, James Bradbury, and Richard Socher. 2017. Pointer sentinel mixture models. In *5th International Conference on Learning Representations, ICLR 2017, Toulon, France, April 24-26, 2017, Conference Track Proceedings*. OpenReview.net.

Tomas Mikolov, Ilya Sutskever, Kai Chen, Greg Corrado, and Jeffrey Dean. 2013. Distributed representations of words and phrases and their compositionality. In *Proceedings of the 26th International Conference on Neural Information Processing Systems*

- *Volume 2*, NIPS'13, page 3111–3119, Red Hook, NY, USA. Curran Associates Inc.

Alex Nichol, Joshua Achiam, and John Schulman. 2018. On first-order meta-learning algorithms.

Adam Paszke, Sam Gross, Soumith Chintala, Gregory Chanan, Edward Yang, Zachary DeVito, Zeming Lin, Alban Desmaison, Luca Antiga, and Adam Lerer. 2017. Automatic differentiation in pytorch.

Yuval Pinter, Robert Guthrie, and Jacob Eisenstein. 2017. Mimicking word embeddings using subword RNNs. In *Proceedings of the 2017 Conference on Empirical Methods in Natural Language Processing*, pages 102–112, Copenhagen, Denmark. Association for Computational Linguistics.

Sachin Ravi and Hugo Larochelle. 2017. Optimization as a model for few-shot learning. In *5th International Conference on Learning Representations, ICLR 2017, Toulon, France, April 24-26, 2017, Conference Track Proceedings*. OpenReview.net.

Jake Snell, Kevin Swersky, and Richard Zemel. 2017. Prototypical networks for few-shot learning. In I. Guyon, U. V. Luxburg, S. Bengio, H. Wallach, R. Fergus, S. Vishwanathan, and R. Garnett, editors, *Advances in Neural Information Processing Systems 30*, pages 4077–4087. Curran Associates, Inc.

Oriol Vinyals, Charles Blundell, Timothy Lillicrap, koray kavukcuoglu, and Daan Wierstra. 2016. Matching networks for one shot learning. In D. D. Lee, M. Sugiyama, U. V. Luxburg, I. Guyon, and R. Garnett, editors, *Advances in Neural Information Processing Systems 29*, pages 3630–3638. Curran Associates, Inc.

Yuhuai Wu, Mengye Ren, Renjie Liao, and Roger B. Grosse. 2018. Understanding short-horizon bias in stochastic meta-optimization. In *6th International Conference on Learning Representations, ICLR 2018, Vancouver, BC, Canada, April 30 - May 3, 2018, Conference Track Proceedings*. OpenReview.net.

Dependency Parsing Evaluation for Low-resource Spontaneous Speech

Zoey Liu
Department of Computer Science
Boston College
ying.liu.5@bc.edu

Emily Prud'hommeaux
Department of Computer Science
Boston College
prudhome@bc.edu

Abstract

How well can a state-of-the-art parsing system, developed for the written domain, perform when applied to spontaneous speech data involving different interlocutors? This study addresses this question in a low-resource setting using child-parent conversations from the CHILDES databse. Specifically, we focus on dependency parsing evaluation for utterances of one specific child (18 - 27 months) and her parents. We first present a semi-automatic adaption of the dependency annotation scheme in CHILDES to that of the Universal Dependencies project, an annotation style that is more commonly applied in dependency parsing. Our evaluation demonstrates that an *out-of-domain* biaffine parser trained only on written texts performs well with parent speech. There is, however, much room for improvement on child utterances, particularly at 18 and 21 months, due to cases of omission and repetition that are prevalent in child speech. By contrast, parsers trained or fine-tuned with *in-domain* spoken data on a much smaller scale can achieve comparable results for parent speech and improve the weak parsing performance for child speech at these earlier ages.

1 Introduction

While the task of dependency parsing has been studied extensively, in both monolingual (Eisner, 1996; Sun et al., 2019) and crosslinguistic contexts (McDonald et al., 2013; Agić et al., 2016), much of the effort thus far has been devoted to parsing data from the written domain. By contrast, dependency parsing of spontaneous speech in general has received little attention, despite the notable and sometimes quantifiable differences of syntactic variations between written and spoken registers (Biber, 1991; O'Donnell, 1974).

One obstacle to the development of dependency parsing for speech is that, in comparison to the written domain, which offers numerous corpora with gold-standard (morpho)syntactic annotations in a large variety of languages (Zeman et al., 2020), data sets annotated with comparable levels of structural details in the spoken genre are relatively rare, regardless of the particular annotation frameworks adopted. One of the most widely used and largest spoken corpora is the Switchboard corpus (Godfrey et al., 1992), which provides constituency structures for around one million tokens from transcriptions of conversational speech in English.

Other available spoken corpora are of much smaller scale. For instance, Dobrovoljc and Nivre (2016) developed a dependency treebank for spoken Slovenian also using transcripts of spontaneous speech, which contains 29,488 tokens in total. Spence et al. (2018) built a dependency treebank for Hupa, an indigenous language residing in Northern California; the treebank used mainly transcriptions of story telling from the only master speaker of the Hupa language and contained around 6,561 mannualy annotated tokens. A few treebanks in the Universal Dependencies project v2.7 (Zeman et al., 2020) (hereafter UD) include transcriptions of spoken data, but most such data is mixed in with written texts and the register is not specified for individual sentences.

The limited availability of spoken corpora leaves open the questions of how well the current state-of-the-art dependency parser, developed mainly for written texts, performs on low-resource naturalistic speech and to what extent the performance of the parser differs depending on the specific role of the speaker. It is possible that recent advances in the parsing of written texts (Kondratyuk and Straka, 2019; Bouma et al., 2020; Qi et al., 2020) will extend to speech and that errors will be restricted to cases that are unique in the spoken genre, such as omissions of frequent or short words (Ferreira and Anes, 1994).

Proceedings of the Second Workshop on Domain Adaptation for NLP, pages 156–165
April 20, 2021.

Alternatively, it is also reasonable to speculate that such parsers would not align well with speech given that they are being applied to a domain that is different from their original training data. Nevertheless, the potential differences between the dependency structure of an utterance assigned by a parser and one assigned manually might not necessarily indicate that there are *errors* but rather that there is more than one way of interpreting the utterance when the discourse context is not considered. Understanding whether and where parsers for written texts fall short in low-resource spontaneous speech has the potential to contribute to developing parsing systems for the spoken domain, as well as expanding the availability of spoken data.

This study makes a step towards the aforementioned directions. In order to investigate the parsing performance for spoken data in a low-resource setting (Vania et al., 2019; Agić et al., 2016) , especially spontaneous speech that involves different interlocutors, we focus on child-parent conversational interactions as our targeted evaluation data. Specifically, the evaluation sets contain utterance samples of one child, "Eve", and her parents from the Brown Corpus (Brown, 1973) in the CHILDES database (MacWhinney, 2000).

The remainder of the paper is structured as follows: we review related work in section 2; section 3 points out some general issues with parsing speech; section 4 describes our procedures of adapting the current dependency annotation scheme in CHILDES to that of UD; section 5 presents our experiments[1]; and we conclude with section 6.

2 Related Work

Although most work in the dependency parsing and annotation literature has examined the written domain, there have been a number of notable exceptions. Looking at the domain of human-computer interactions, Adams (2017) adapted the UD annotation scheme to a data set of 882 sentences that are mostly transcripts generated from automatic speech recognition systems. Their work showed that a parser ensemble approach (two parsers in this case) yielded the best results. Davidson et al. (2019) also investigated dependency parsing with transcripts from dialogue systems; using a data set of 1,500 sentences annotated with UD labels, they found that the best parsing accuracy was achieved when an out-of-domain parser was fine-tuned with more in-domain data.

Other work such as Kong et al. (2014) and Liu et al. (2018) has focused on dependency parsing of tweets, which can be considered a domain that lies between the spoken genre and other written contexts. The data set from Liu et al. (2018) contains a total of 3,550 tweets, four times the number used in Kong et al. (2014). Their annotation standards followed the UD style while allowing multiple roots in tweets that have more than one sentences indicated mainly by punctuation. They reported that an ensemble approach with 20 different parsers was the most effective.

3 Issues with Speech Orthography

One major challenge with parsing speech lies in finding a standard way of transcribing and formatting spoken language. In particular, syntactic parses should be developed for what the speakers have actually said, without further added facilitation during the transcription process. This general issue has not been addressed consistently, at least in the current format of CHILDES. As a demonstration, consider the following annotated examples (adapted from their initial forms in CHILDES).

(1) *that green bean white* **.**

(2) *you* ***v*** *more cookies*

(3) *well* ***(tagmarker)*** *we already did that*

Cases such as (1) contain punctuation, yet punctuation is not explicitly articulated during spontaneous speech. With transcriptions like (2), in this particular instance *v* represents an omitted verb (e.g. *want*). In example (3), a tagmarker was added in order to (mostly) indicate that the first token of the sentence is a discourse marker or communicator. All of these added items were annotated with syntactic dependencies in CHILDES.

The problems with including punctuation and tagmarkers for syntactic analyses could potentially be relaxed to some extent via automatically removing the added items from the dependency parse following certain heuristics. For example, a rule of thumb could be to change all tokens before the tagmarker to be a dependent of the root of the utterance, with the dependency relation *discourse*, then discard the tagmarker itself. However, this would not entirely alleviate the problem, since the

[1]Our annotations, code and full results for parser comparisons are in quarantine at `https://github.com/zoeyliu18/Parsing_Speech`.

parser sometimes assign dependents to punctuation or tagmarker. In our manual check of about 250 utterances of the English data from CHILDES that were not labeled as gold-standard (see section 5), this was indeed the case. While in some sentences the root can be assigned as the head of the dependents of the punctuation or tagmarker assigned by an automatic parser, in other cases, the correct syntactic heads are not easily identifiable without actually looking at the utterance.

Utterances with omitted words are even more challenging than those with punctuation or tagmarkers. Ideally, to syntactically analyze spoken data, the focus should be on the actual utterances rather than what the annotators *think* the utterance should be, especially since the inclusion of additional words in transcribed speech assumes that there were words that were omitted to begin with. This is not to deny that all manual annotations are subjective in some respects, and a less arguable dependency parse could be assigned to an utterance with potential word omissions when the preceding or following contexts are taken into account. For instance [2], in example (4) *celery* is treated as a nominal modifier of *piece*; and since the token *of*, which did not occur in the child utterance, has no further dependents, it could then be removed from the parse without causing any ambiguous issues.

(4) *Child: piece celery*

Parent: piece of celery

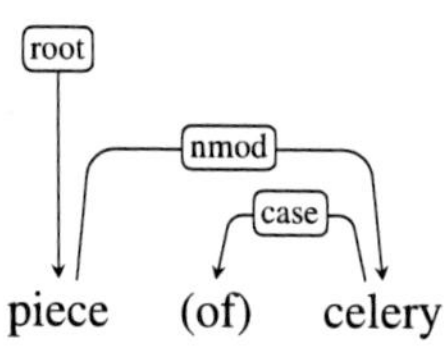

Nevertheless, that is not always the case. Consider (5), where the utterance could be interpreted in at least in three different ways , each with a different syntactic parse.

(5) *Child: man no spoon*

Parent: what

First, *man* could be the subject of the sentence an omitted verb: *man has no spoon.*

[2] All dependency graphs in this paper were annotated according to the UD annotation style.

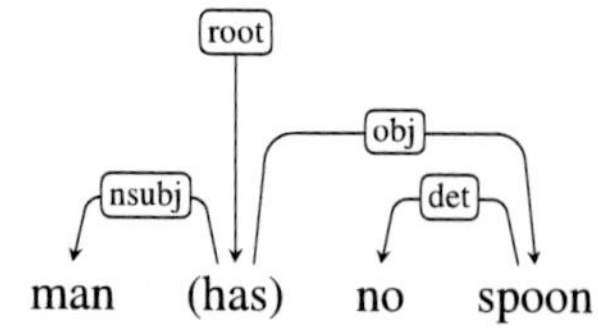

Secondly, instead of a verb, if there were indeed an omitted word, it could also be a preposition: *man with no spoon.*

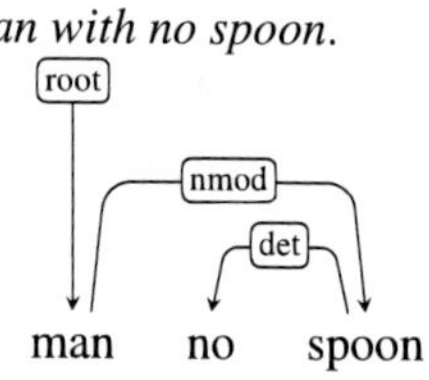

Thirdly, *man* could be a discourse marker and the sentence would have a reading of *man (!) no spoon.*

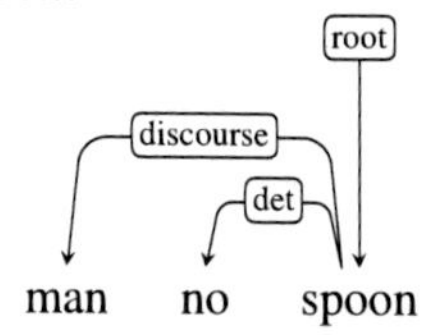

To address these issues in a consistent way, in the parsing evaluation experiments here, we did not include any punctuation, tagmarkers, or omitted words in the utterances.

4 Annotation Adaptation to UD

The dependency annotations in CHILDES, which now have 37 different dependency relations, were initially developed by Sagae et al. (2004) (see also Sagae et al. (2005)). The annotation scheme was then slightly modified by Sagae et al. (2007), with adjustments to cases such as locative phrases and verb particles. Given that most of the available dependency parsers for written texts in English abide by the style of UD (Zeman et al., 2020), we first adapted the CHILDES dependency relations so that they would be comparable to those in UD.

4.1 Direct (one-to-one) conversion

Comparing the two parsing schemes, we found that there are several dependency relations that can be converted from CHILDES to UD straightforwardly, such as subjects and objects (Table 1). Other dependencies can be changed directly with the help of part-of-speech (POS) or lexical information. For instance, in the phrase *my stool*, *my* is annotated as the determiner (DET) in CHILDES and its POS is pronoun; for cases like this, the original DET relation was changed to the possessive nominal modifier *nmod:poss* based on UD. As another example, the dependency relation LINK is used for any relativizer, complementizer, or subordinate conjunction; for such cases, the dependency can be changed to *mark* given the UD annotations if the lexical word is *if*, *because*, *so*, etc.

CHILDES	UD
SUBJ	nsubj
OBJ	obj
OBJ2	iobj
CSUBJ	csubj
APP	appos
VOC	vocative
INF	mark
DATE	nummod
ENUM (enumeration)	conj

Table 1: Examples of dependency relations in English that can be converted directly from CHILDES to UD.

4.2 Collapsing dependency relations

Additionally, we also collapsed dependency relations in CHILDES that have very similar syntactic functions, the differences of which can be easily identified automatically if needed. For instance, BEG, COM and END all describe communicators (and sometimes vocatives). The major difference between them is only their relative position in the sentence, with BEG describing sentence-initial communicators, COM sentence-medial, and END sentence-final. Therefore we combined them all to the *discourse* relation in UD. On the other hand, CHILDES has two different relations for the root of the sentence, ROOT and INCROOT, with the former applied to utterances that are considered full sentences (e.g. *I wanna go*) while the latter specifically used for cases without a verbal or copula root (e.g. *not on the couch*). When adapting to UD we annotated both with the *root* relation.

4.3 Function head vs. content head

While the aforementioned conversions are comparatively trivial, other automatic conversions require more heuristic steps. The main reason is that the annotation style of UD favors content head over function head for better crosslinguistic applicability, while this was not always the case with CHILDES. In particular, the English annotations in CHILDES choose function word as the syntactic head in structures that involve copula verb, prepositional phrase (PP), conjunction with coordinators, and negation.

Copula The treatment of copula structures in CHILDES is consistent across the utterances, where the copula verb is the root of the sentence. By contrast, UD has different annotations for the copula structures depending on whether the utterance is a statement (Figure 1), question (Figure 2), and whether there is an expletive in the sentence (Figure 3). For all utterances with a copula root from CHILDES, we determined whether they were questions/interrogatives or had expletives based on the lexical word of the annotated subjects, and the rest were treated as statements. With statements and questions in particular, the predicate of the copula verb was instead the new root of the sentence; any initial dependents of the copula that are not the subject or the predicate in the CHILDES annotations were converted to be dependents of the new root in the UD annotations.

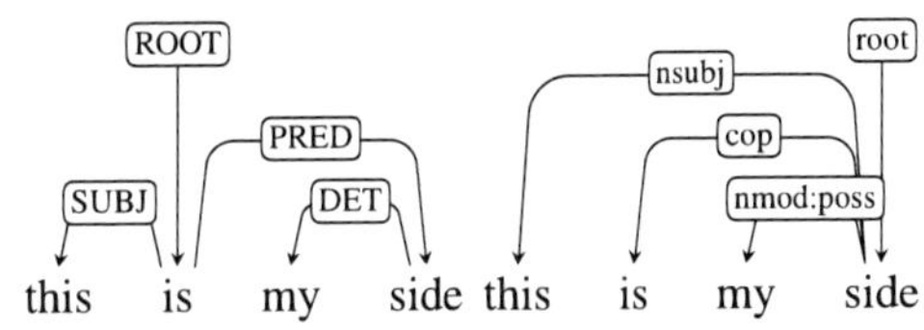

(a) CHILDES (b) UD

Figure 1: Annotations of copula structures in statements.

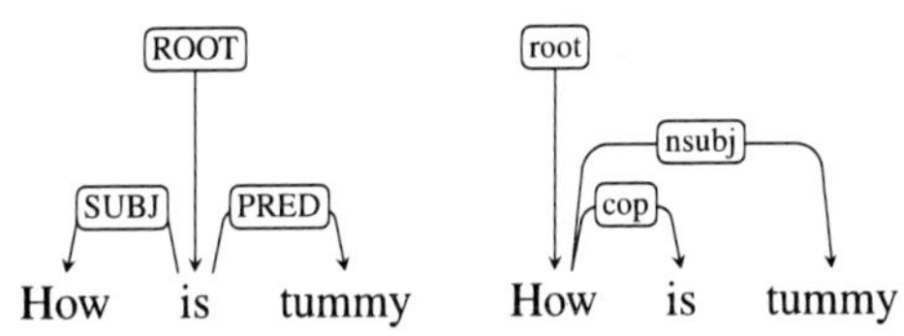

(a) CHILDES (b) UD

Figure 2: Annotations of copula structures in questions.

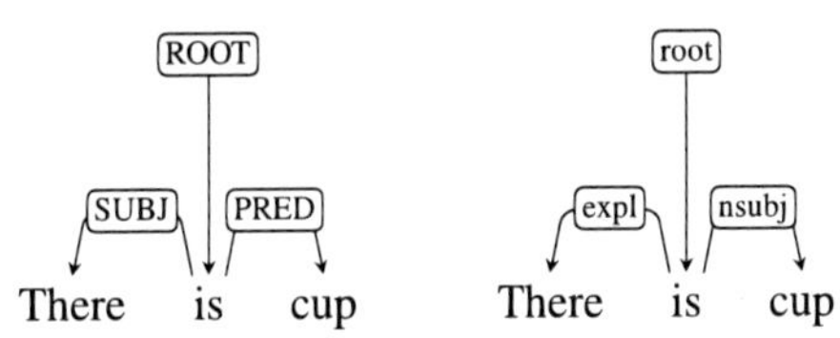

(a) CHILDES (b) UD

Figure 3: Annotations of copula structures in expletives.

Prepositional phrase In CHILDES, a PP has the preposition as its syntactic head, while UD chooses the lexical head as the head of the phrase in order for the annotations to be more comparable for languages with different case marking systems.

In our conversion, the initial prepositional object (POBJ) was the new head of the phrase and the preposition was treated as the *case* dependent (Figure 4). Any other initial dependents of the preposition were changed to be dependents of the lexical head in UD.

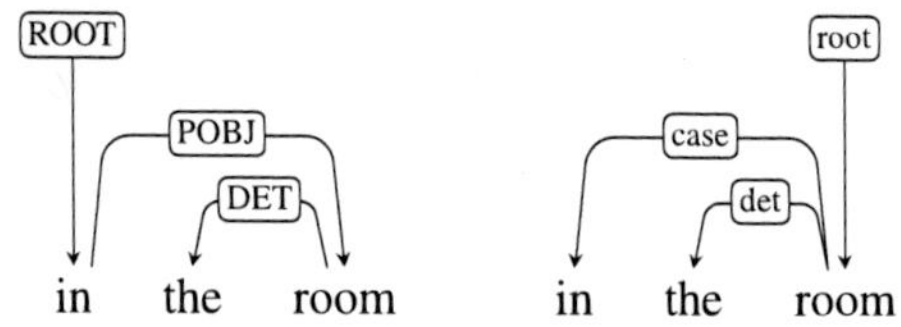

(a) CHILDES (b) UD

Figure 4: Annotations of prepositional phrases.

Conjunction The major difference in annotations of conjunctions with coordinators between CHILDES and UD, as illustrated in Figure 5, is that in CHILDES, for a series of coordinated items, the items other than the first one are dependents of their respective preceding coordinator, whereas they are all dependents of the first coordinated word in UD and also heads of their coordinators. This is distinct from structures with conjunctions that do not have coordinators (Figure 6), which have the same dependency parse in CHILDES and UD, except for the dependency relation (enumeration in CHILDES and conjunction in UD).

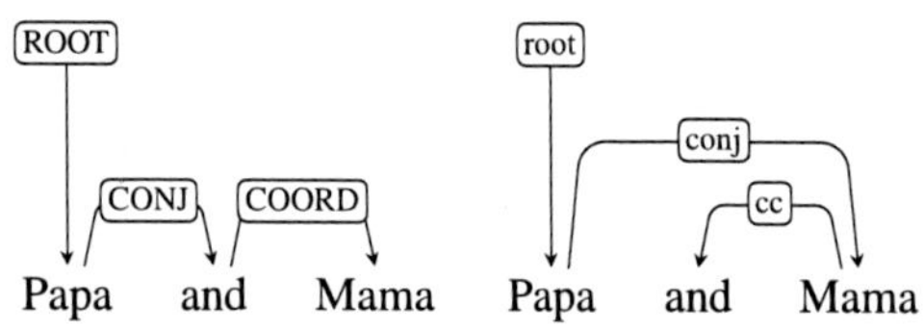

(a) CHILDES (b) UD

Figure 5: Annotations of conjunctions with coordinators.

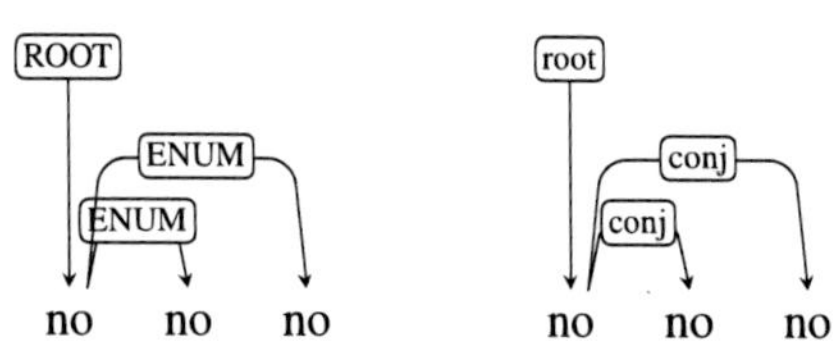

(a) CHILDES (b) UD

Figure 6: Annotations of conjunctions without coordinators.

Negation In utterances with auxiliary or copula verbs modified by negation markers such as *not* or *n't*, the negation markers are annotated as the dependents of the auxiliary/copula in CHILDES. When converting to UD, if the auxiliary/copula is not the root of the sentence, we changed the dependencies of the negation markers so they have the same syntactic heads as the auxiliary/copula.

4.4 Manual inspections

We reviewed all of the utterances thoroughly after automatic conversion. This was performed by an author of this paper, who has had extensive training in dependency linguistics. We tried to be as faithful as possible to the initial gold-standard annotations in the data and their interpretations accordingly.

Our inspections mainly concern syntactic dependencies that were not converted completely. These largely fall in three aspects. The first is temporal modifiers, which are treated as adverbial modifiers (JCT) in CHILDES. We changed them to either *obl:tmod* or *nmod:tmod* depending on whether they were modifying a verbal or nominal head. The second is clausal modifiers, which could be relative clauses or complements in CHILDES. We changed these to either *acl:relcl* or *ccomp* when converting to UD.

The third involves clausal conjunct (CJCT). These include coordinated clauses within one utterance (e.g. *I hear and watch Sarah*) that may or may not have the coordinators, or cases that seem less like one utterance but rather "side-by-side" sentences (e.g. *I say see Mommy*). The former was adapted to UD with *conj*; while for the latter we resorted to the *parataxis* relation (Figure 7). To be consistent with the UD style, we annotated the head of the first sentence to be the root of the whole utterance, and the heads of other sentences in parallel are dependents of the root.

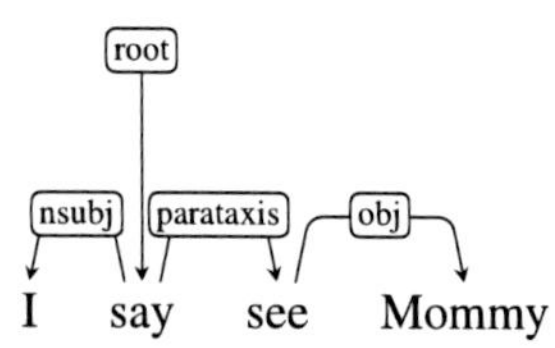

Figure 7: Annotations of clausal conjunctions.

In addition, we also carefully examined new dependencies that were added due to our modified tokenization scheme. We modified the initial tokenization of possessives (e.g. *Mommy's*), combined adverbs (e.g. *as_well*) and combined conjunctives (e.g. *in_case_that*). These are all treated as one token in CHILDES, and in the UD annotations we split them into individual tokens based on the apostrophe or the underscore. While these tokenizations were first carried out during the automatic process, we checked to ensure that their dependency relations aligned with those in UD and that we were not including cases such as rhymes or onomatopoeia, which share similar tokenization standards with combined adverbs or conjunctives.

5 Experiments

5.1 Data

	18 mos	21 mos	24 mos	27 mos
Eve				
utterances	426	341	280	235
tokens	1,023	1,018	1,025	1,041
MLU	2.40	2.99	3.66	4.43
Parent				
utterances	203	210	190	180
tokens	1,034	1,039	1,041	1,046
MLU	5.09	4.95	5.48	5.8

Table 2: Descriptive statistics of the number of utterances, words and mean utterance length (MLU) for child and parent speech, at the corresponding age of the child in months (mos).

While the available corpora of English from CHILDES contain syntactic dependency parses, most of these annotations were derived automatically from the MEGRASP developed by Sagae et al. (2010), In the English sections, the Eve Corpus from the Brown Corpus (Brown, 1973) provides gold-standard manual annotations (Sagae et al., 2007) for its first fifteen transcripts out of the twenty files in total. Given the age range of the child Eve (18-27 months), we took around 1,000 tokens from child and parent utterances respectively, at the different ages of the child (Table 2) among the twenty files. Each utterance contained at least two tokens in order to not inflate the results of parsing and evaluations. We then converted the dependency annotations of these utterances to UD-style based on the procedures described in section 4.

5.2 Out-of-domain training

To evaluate parsing systems that were mainly developed for written corpora in English, we used Stanza (Qi et al., 2020), an open-source natural language processing toolkit that was developed with the multilingual corpora from UD. Using the default parameter setting for English in Stanza as well as Glove embeddings (Pennington et al., 2014), we first trained a POS tagger and a biaffine parser (Dozat et al., 2017; Qi et al., 2018) with the predefined train-development-test sets from the UD English Web Treebank (UD-EWT). The UD-EWT tagger and parser were then applied to our evaluation sets of child and parent speech.

Unlabeled attachment score (UAS) and labeled attachment score (LAS) were taken as indexes of parsing performance (Kübler et al., 2009). Since the utterances in each of our evaluation sets came from the same speaker, and overall our data was taken from one child and her parents, this indicates that the utterances under examinations were not exactly independent from one another. Due to this reason as well as the small size of our evaluation data, we used bootstrapping (Berg-Kirkpatrick et al., 2012; Dror et al., 2018; Efron and Tibshirani, 1994) for significance testing. Given an evaluation set with a total of N utterances which have been automatically parsed, we randomly selected N sentences from the set with replacement, then calculated the UAS and LAS of the sample. This process was repeated for 10,000 iterations, which yielded an empirical distribution of the LAS and UAS values respectively. We then computed the mean and the 95% confidence intervals of these empirical distributions.

Parsing	
UAS	89.33 (88.60, 90.03)
LAS	86.30 (85.52, 87.07)

Table 3: Parsing accuracy for UD-EWT test set evaluated with the UD-EWT parser. UAS refers to unlabeled attachment score, while LAS refers to labeled attachment score. Significance testing was performed with bootstrapping.

5.3 Discrepancy analysis

As certain utterances can have multiple interpretations according to whether contexts are taken into account (see section 3), especially cases in child speech, and since our UD dependency annotations rely heavily on the existing dependency relations from CHILDES, we are hesitant to label automatic parses that are different from the annotations in our UD conversions as errors. Instead we examined the parse results as a way to see what discrepancies there were between our annotations and the parser that is targeted towards written data.

Data	Parser	18 mos	21 mos	24 mos	27 mos
Parent	*UD-EWT*				
	UAS	**95.95**	**92.18**	92.51	91.30
	LAS	**91.10**	**88.72**	**88.36**	**87.09**
Child	*UD-EWT*				
	UAS	84.86	74.24	89.94	86.26
	LAS	68.13	59.36	80.58	79.89
	UD-EWT fine-tuned with parent speech				
	UAS	82.40	74.47	92.97	89.53
	LAS	72.12	66.14	**87.19**	83.85
	UD-EWT fine-tuned with child speech				
	UAS	88.59	**82.77**†	90.15	83.09
	LAS	**77.15**	**73.38**	83.31	75.59
	Parent speech				
	UAS	78.23	74.45	92.9	89.54
	LAS	66.01	66.13	**87.24**	83.88
	Parent speech fine-tuned with child speech				
	UAS	91.02	79.53	90.64	88.29
	LAS	**81.05**	**71.68**	83.52	80.12

Table 4: Parser accuracy for (1) parent speech with the UD-EWT parser; (2) child speech with the UD-EWT parser; and (3) child speech with various parser training configurations. At each of the four ages, the scores for (1) and (3) were compared with (2). Boldface indicates a significant difference, derived by comparing their respective 95% confidence intervals after bootstrapping.

5.3.1 Parent speech

As presented in Table 4, by contrast, the UD-EWT parser appears to perform relatively well when applied to parent speech. The results are comparable to those when evaluating the parser on just the test set of UD-EWT and mostly better than those when the same parser was evaluated with child speech; these patterns seem to be more or less consistent across the different ages of the child. This pattern is possibly due to the following factors: (1) parent utterances are on average longer than those produced by the child yet still generally shorter than written texts; (2) parent speech is less likely to have omitted words and repetitions, which helps the parser to analyze the syntactic structures of the utterances more deterministically.

Manual inspection across the evaluation sets reveals three major discrepancies between the automatic parses of parent speech and our annotations. First, in CHILDES, for noun phrases where the first noun serves more or less as a modifier of the second noun, during our UD conversion, the first noun was annotated as a nominal modifier (*nmod*) of the second noun, such as the word *grape* in the phrase *grape juice*. The automatic parser, however, consistently treated the first noun as a *compound* dependent of the second. This accounts for around 9.68% of all parsing discrepancies in parent speech.

Secondly, prepositions that lack their own lexical object and co-occur with verbs are labeled in CHILDES as either adverbial modifiers or verb particles. If the meaning of the preposition is essential in deriving the compositional meaning of the verb and the preposition (e.g *look it up*), then it is treated as a particle; otherwise the preposition is considered an adverbial modifier of the verb (e.g. *tear if off*). The latter in our UD annotations was directly converted to *advmod*. On the other hand, the parser treated the prepositions in cases like this almost entirely as particles with the *compound:prt* dependency. This accounts for about 9.89% of all parsing differences in parent speech.

The discrepancies described above are not particularly crucial, since the parser annotated related cases in a consistent fashion, which could be adapted easily if necessary. Additionally, there is not always a clear criterion determining whether two nouns should be considered as a compound or whether a preposition should be a particle of a verb. In comparison, the last main difference between the automatic parse and our annotations, which accounts for around 14.41% of all discrepancies in parent speech, is related to correctly labeling words that are vocatives or discourse markers of the utterance. Such instances are less straightforward to resolve. For instance, the utterance *who are you calling Eve* is directed to the child. Thus the word *Eve* should be treated as a vocative of the root of the sentence, *calling*; yet the parser instead labeled Eve as a direct object of calling.

5.3.2 Child speech

Looking at child speech, the three main parsing discrepancies found in parent utterances are also observed (*nmod / compound*: 10.08%; *advmod / compound:prt*: 4.60%; *discourse* and *vocative*: 10.26%). That said, a large number (around 10.08%) of differences between the automatic parses of child speech and our annotations result from utterances lacking a clear syntactic structure, which potentially leads the utterance to having more than one interpretation, especially when context is disregarded. These utterances are mostly telegraphic speech consisting of two tokens.

For example, the utterance *Eve writing* could mean the writing belongs to Eve, or Eve is doing the action of writing. Based on initial annotations from CHILDES as well as the surrounding context of this sentence, *Eve* was converted to be the subject of *writing* in our annotations. Yet the parser annotated it as the *compound* or sometimes an adjective modifier (*amod*) of *writing*. This type of utterances is more common when the child is at the age of 18 or 21 months at least in our evaluation data, which drives the parsing differences for child speech at the different ages in Table 4.

Another reason why the parser does not seem to align well with our dependency annotations when the child is 18 months and especially 21 months old is due to repetition or conjunction without coordinators in speech. For example, the utterances *writing a b c* was annotated with a dependency structure as Figure 8. Nevertheless, the automatic parser's treatment of cases as such was more random; it would either label *a* as a determiner of *b*, a compound or a nominal modifier of *c*.

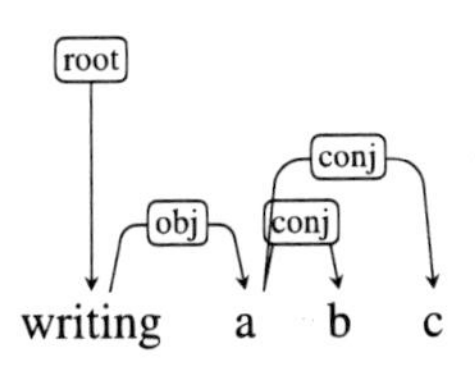

Figure 8: Annotations of *writing a b c*

5.4 In-domain training

To investigate whether the parsing performance for child speech could be improved with help from domain-specific spoken data, we experimented with four different training settings without changing our annotation decisions analyzed above.

The first and second approaches applied fine-tuning to the UD-EWT parser initially trained on just written texts with either parent or child speech. When fine-tuning with parent speech, we concatenated all parent utterances in our evaluation data. When fine-tuning with child speech, we concatenated all child utterances except for those to be evaluated (e.g. fine-tuning with data from the ages of 21, 24 and 27 months when evaluating child speech at the age of 18 months). The third approach trained an biaffine parser with the same parameter settings as those for the UD-EWT parser, except with all utterances of the parent speech in our evaluation sets. The last approach fine-tuned the parser trained with just parent speech with additional data from child speech; the fine-tuning was done in the same way as described in the second approach.

The training data of the UD-EWT parser is about 48 times larger than that of all parent utterances; yet based on results from Table 4, the parser trained with just parent speech performs on par with the UD-EWT parser. The overall best parsing performance was achieved when the parsers were fine-tuned with child speech. This is the most obvious with child speech at 18 or 21 months; whereas in cases with already decent parsing results such as child speech at 27 months, there does not appear to be a significant gain with fine-tuning.

6 Conclusion

In our low-resource evaluation settings, we found that an out-of-domain parser trained only with written texts performed well with parent speech, but not necessarily so with child speech. On the other hand, similar or better performance was achieved when the parser was fine-tuned with a very limited amount of in-domain data.

Given the relatively small size of our evaluation data and the narrow age range of the child, it is certain that there are other common phenomenon unique to child-speech that have not been covered, such as disfluency. For future work, we would like to conduct a more thorough and larger-scale parsing evaluation with speech across wider age ranges of different children. In addition, we plan to extend our study with further experimentation of different domain adaptation methods to other spoken domains such as medical conversations as well as languages. Besides English, CHILDES also provides dependency annotations in child-parent interactions in other languages, such as Spanish (Sagae et al., 2010), Japanese (Miyata et al., 2013), Dutch (Odijk et al., 2018) and Hebrew (Gretz et al., 2015). Since annotation standards in in these corpora largely abide by those of English (Sagae et al., 2007), our semi-automatic UD conversion scheme described here could be applied to these languages, along with modifications of language-specific morphosyntactic structures.

References

Allison Adams. 2017. Dependency parsing and dialogue systems: an investigation of dependency parsing for commercial application.

Željko Agić, Anders Johannsen, Barbara Plank, Héctor Martínez Alonso, Natalie Schluter, and Anders Søgaard. 2016. Multilingual projection for parsing truly low-resource languages. *Transactions of the Association for Computational Linguistics*, 4:301–312.

Taylor Berg-Kirkpatrick, David Burkett, and Dan Klein. 2012. An empirical investigation of statistical significance in NLP. In *Proceedings of the 2012 Joint Conference on Empirical Methods in Natural Language Processing and Computational Natural Language Learning*, pages 995–1005, Jeju Island, Korea. Association for Computational Linguistics.

Douglas Biber. 1991. *Variation across speech and writing*. Cambridge University Press.

Gosse Bouma, Yuji Matsumoto, Stephan Oepen, Kenji Sagae, Djamé Seddah, Weiwei Sun, Anders Søgaard, Reut Tsarfaty, and Dan Zeman, editors. 2020. *Proceedings of the 16th International Conference on Parsing Technologies and the IWPT 2020 Shared Task on Parsing into Enhanced Universal Dependencies*. Association for Computational Linguistics, Online.

Roger Brown. 1973. *A first language: The early stages*. Harvard University Press.

Sam Davidson, Dian Yu, and Zhou Yu. 2019. Dependency parsing for spoken dialog systems. In *Proceedings of the 2019 Conference on Empirical Methods in Natural Language Processing and the 9th International Joint Conference on Natural Language Processing (EMNLP-IJCNLP)*, pages 1513–1519, Hong Kong, China. Association for Computational Linguistics.

Kaja Dobrovoljc and Joakim Nivre. 2016. The Universal Dependencies treebank of spoken Slovenian. In *Proceedings of the Tenth International Conference on Language Resources and Evaluation (LREC'16)*, pages 1566–1573, Portorož, Slovenia. European Language Resources Association (ELRA).

Timothy Dozat, Peng Qi, and Christopher D. Manning. 2017. Stanford's graph-based neural dependency parser at the CoNLL 2017 shared task. In *Proceedings of the CoNLL 2017 Shared Task: Multilingual Parsing from Raw Text to Universal Dependencies*, pages 20–30, Vancouver, Canada. Association for Computational Linguistics.

Rotem Dror, Gili Baumer, Segev Shlomov, and Roi Reichart. 2018. The hitchhiker's guide to testing statistical significance in natural language processing. In *Proceedings of the 56th Annual Meeting of the Association for Computational Linguistics (Volume 1: Long Papers)*, pages 1383–1392, Melbourne, Australia. Association for Computational Linguistics.

Bradley Efron and Robert J Tibshirani. 1994. *An introduction to the bootstrap*. CRC press.

Jason M. Eisner. 1996. Three new probabilistic models for dependency parsing: An exploration. In *COLING 1996 Volume 1: The 16th International Conference on Computational Linguistics*.

Fernanda Ferreira and Michael Anes. 1994. Why study spoken language? In Morton Ann Gernsbacher, editor, *Handbook of psycholinguistics*, page 33–56. Academic Press.

John J Godfrey, Edward C Holliman, and Jane McDaniel. 1992. Switchboard: Telephone speech corpus for research and development. In *Acoustics, Speech, and Signal Processing, IEEE International Conference on*, volume 1, pages 517–520. IEEE Computer Society.

Shai Gretz, Alon Itai, Brian MacWhinney, Bracha Nir, and Shuly Wintner. 2015. Parsing hebrew childes transcripts. *Language Resources and Evaluation*, 49(1):107–145.

Dan Kondratyuk and Milan Straka. 2019. 75 languages, 1 model: Parsing Universal Dependencies universally. In *Proceedings of the 2019 Conference on Empirical Methods in Natural Language Processing and the 9th International Joint Conference on Natural Language Processing (EMNLP-IJCNLP)*, pages 2779–2795, Hong Kong, China. Association for Computational Linguistics.

Lingpeng Kong, Nathan Schneider, Swabha Swayamdipta, Archna Bhatia, Chris Dyer, and Noah A. Smith. 2014. A dependency parser for tweets. In *Proceedings of the 2014 Conference on Empirical Methods in Natural Language Processing (EMNLP)*, pages 1001–1012, Doha, Qatar. Association for Computational Linguistics.

Sandra Kübler, Ryan McDonald, and Joakim Nivre. 2009. Dependency parsing. *Synthesis lectures on human language technologies*, 1(1):1–127.

Yijia Liu, Yi Zhu, Wanxiang Che, Bing Qin, Nathan Schneider, and Noah A. Smith. 2018. Parsing tweets into Universal Dependencies. In *Proceedings of the 2018 Conference of the North American Chapter of the Association for Computational Linguistics: Human Language Technologies, Volume 1 (Long Papers)*, pages 965–975, New Orleans, Louisiana. Association for Computational Linguistics.

Brian MacWhinney. 2000. *The CHILDES Project: Tools for analyzing talk. transcription format and programs*, volume 1. Psychology Press.

Ryan McDonald, Joakim Nivre, Yvonne Quirmbach-Brundage, Yoav Goldberg, Dipanjan Das, Kuzman Ganchev, Keith Hall, Slav Petrov, Hao Zhang, Oscar Täckström, Claudia Bedini, Núria Bertomeu Castelló, and Jungmee Lee. 2013. Universal Dependency annotation for multilingual parsing. In *Proceedings of the 51st Annual Meeting of the Association for Computational Linguistics (Volume 2: Short Papers)*, pages 92–97, Sofia, Bulgaria. Association for Computational Linguistics.

Susanne Miyata, Kenji Sagae, and Brian MacWhinney. 2013. The syntax parser grasp for childes (in japanese). *Journal of Health and Medical Science*, (3):45–62.

Jan Odijk, Alexis Dimitriadis, Martijn Van der Klis, Marjo Van Koppen, Meie Otten, and Remco van der Veen. 2018. The anncor childes treebank. In *Proceedings of the Eleventh International Conference on Language Resources and Evaluation (LREC 2018), Miyazaki, Japan*, pages 2275–2283. European Language Resources Association (ELRA).

Roy C O'Donnell. 1974. Syntactic differences between speech and writing. *American Speech*, 49(1/2):102–110.

Jeffrey Pennington, Richard Socher, and Christopher Manning. 2014. GloVe: Global vectors for word representation. In *Proceedings of the 2014 Conference on Empirical Methods in Natural Language Processing (EMNLP)*, pages 1532–1543, Doha, Qatar. Association for Computational Linguistics.

Peng Qi, Timothy Dozat, Yuhao Zhang, and Christopher D. Manning. 2018. Universal Dependency parsing from scratch. In *Proceedings of the CoNLL 2018 Shared Task: Multilingual Parsing from Raw Text to Universal Dependencies*, pages 160–170, Brussels, Belgium. Association for Computational Linguistics.

Peng Qi, Yuhao Zhang, Yuhui Zhang, Jason Bolton, and Christopher D. Manning. 2020. Stanza: A python natural language processing toolkit for many human languages. In *Proceedings of the 58th Annual Meeting of the Association for Computational Linguistics: System Demonstrations*, pages 101–108, Online. Association for Computational Linguistics.

Kenji Sagae, Eric Davis, Alon Lavie, Brian MacWhinney, and Shuly Wintner. 2007. High-accuracy annotation and parsing of CHILDES transcripts. In *Proceedings of the Workshop on Cognitive Aspects of Computational Language Acquisition*, pages 25–32, Prague, Czech Republic. Association for Computational Linguistics.

Kenji Sagae, Eric Davis, Alon Lavie, Brian MacWhinney, and Shuly Wintner. 2010. Morphosyntactic annotation of childes transcripts. *Journal of child language*, 37(3):705–729.

Kenji Sagae, Alon Lavie, and Brian MacWhinney. 2005. Automatic measurement of syntactic development in child language. In *Proceedings of the 43rd Annual Meeting of the Association for Computational Linguistics (ACL'05)*, pages 197–204, Ann Arbor, Michigan. Association for Computational Linguistics.

Kenji Sagae, Brian MacWhinney, and Alon Lavie. 2004. Adding syntactic annotations to transcripts of parent-child dialogs. In *Proceedings of the Fourth International Conference on Language Resources and Evaluation (LREC'04)*, Lisbon, Portugal. European Language Resources Association (ELRA).

Justin Spence, Zoey Liu, Palakurthy Kayla, and Lee-Wynant Tyler. 2018. Syntactic annotation of a hupa text corpus. In *Working Papers in Athabaskan Languages: Alaska Native Language Center Working Papers*, pages 37–53. Fairbanks, AK: ANLC Publications.

Weiwei Sun, Yufei Chen, Xiaojun Wan, and Meichun Liu. 2019. Parsing Chinese sentences with grammatical relations. *Computational Linguistics*, 45(1):95–136.

Clara Vania, Yova Kementchedjhieva, Anders Søgaard, and Adam Lopez. 2019. A systematic comparison of methods for low-resource dependency parsing on genuinely low-resource languages. In *Proceedings of the 2019 Conference on Empirical Methods in Natural Language Processing and the 9th International Joint Conference on Natural Language Processing (EMNLP-IJCNLP)*, pages 1105–1116, Hong Kong, China. Association for Computational Linguistics.

Daniel Zeman, Joakim Nivre, Mitchell Abrams, Elia Ackermann, et al. 2020. Universal dependencies 2.7. LINDAT/CLARIAH-CZ digital library at the Institute of Formal and Applied Linguistics (ÚFAL), Faculty of Mathematics and Physics, Charles University.

An Empirical Study of Compound PCFGs

Yanpeng Zhao[ε]
[ε]ILCC, University of Edinburgh
yanp.zhao@ed.ac.uk

Ivan Titov[εæ]
[æ]ILLC, University of Amsterdam
ititov@inf.ed.ac.uk

Abstract

Compound probabilistic context-free grammars (C-PCFGs) have recently established a new state of the art for phrase-structure grammar induction. However, due to the high time-complexity of chart-based representation and inference, it is difficult to investigate them comprehensively. In this work, we rely on a fast implementation of C-PCFGs to conduct evaluation complementary to that of Kim et al. (2019). We highlight three key findings: (1) C-PCFGs are data-efficient, (2) C-PCFGs make the best use of global sentence-level information in preterminal rule probabilities, and (3) the best configurations of C-PCFGs on English do not always generalize to morphology-rich languages.

1 Introduction

Probabilistic context-free grammars (PCFGs) have been used for unsupervised constituency grammar learning since decades ago (Lari and Young, 1990), while learning PCFGs with the Expectation Maximization algorithm (Dempster et al., 1977) has been difficult as being involving non-convex optimization. Recently, Kim et al. (2019) propose compound PCFGs, an over-parameterized neural model that extends corpus-level PCFGs by defining a mixture of PCFGs per sentence. C-PCFGs have achieved the state-of-the-art performance on English and Chinese treebanks. They are also shown to be effective in a visually-grounded learning setting (Zhao and Titov, 2020). However, because of the high time-complexity of chart-based representation and inference, it is hard to inspect C-PCFGs comprehensively.

In this work, we rely on a fast implementation[1] of C-PCFGs to conduct a set of experiments complementary to those of Kim et al. (2019). Our first experiment concerns data efficiency and length generalization of C-PCFGs. We empirically find that though trained only on short sentences, e.g., shorter than 30 tokens, C-PCFGs can generalize to longer sentences while maintaining high performance (54.8% F1) at test time. We further investigate which factors contribute to the good performance of C-PCFGs. Since a major difference between C-PCFGs and vanilla PCFGs is that C-PCFGs define sentence-dependent rule probabilities by using global sentence-level information, we ablate C-PCFGs by removing it from start, preterminal, and nonterminal rules,[2] individually. Our experimental results show that sentence-level information is most effective for preterminal rules. Despite the impressive performance of C-PCFGs on English, it is still unclear whether they can generalize to other languages. We thus conduct multilingual evaluation of C-PCFGs on the SPMRL dataset (Seddah et al., 2014). The experimental results suggest that the best configurations of C-PCFGs on English do not necessarily generalize to morphology-rich languages.

2 Compound PCFGs

Compound PCFGs provide a novel parameterization of PCFGs. Unlike PCFGs, which assign each grammar rule r a non-negative *scalar* π_r such that $\sum_{r:A\to\gamma} \pi_r = 1$ for each given left-hand-side symbol A, C-PCFGs relax the strong context-free assumption of PCFGs by assuming that rule probabilities follow a compound distribution:

$$\pi_r = g_r(\mathbf{z};\theta), \quad \mathbf{z} \sim p(\mathbf{z})\,,$$

[1]https://github.com/zhaoyanpeng/cpcfg.

[2]Start rules generate a nonterminal symbol from the start symbol S (e.g., $S \to A$), preterminal rules generate a word from a nonterminal symbol (e.g., $A \to w$), and nonterminal rules are binary rules of the form $A \to BC$, which involve only nonterminal symbols.

Proceedings of the Second Workshop on Domain Adaptation for NLP, pages 166–171
April 20, 2021. ©2021 Association for Computational Linguistics

where $p(\mathbf{z})$ is a prior distribution and allows for capturing interdependencies between the rules; $g_r(\mathbf{z};\theta)$ takes a latent $\mathbf{z}$ as input and incorporates the interdependencies into rule probabilities. Typically, $g_r(\mathbf{z};\theta)$ is parameterized by flexible neural networks and is amenable to gradient-based optimization techniques (we refer interested readers to Kim et al. (2019) for the detailed parameterization).

Learning C-PCFGs is formalized as maximizing the log likelihood of each observed sentence $\boldsymbol{w} = w_1 w_2 \dots w_n$:

$$\log p_\theta(\boldsymbol{w}) = \log \int_{\mathbf{z}} \sum_{t \in \mathcal{T}_\mathcal{G}(\boldsymbol{w})} p_\theta(t|\mathbf{z}) p(\mathbf{z})\, d\mathbf{z}\,,$$

where $\mathcal{T}_\mathcal{G}(\boldsymbol{w})$ consists of all parses of a sentence $\boldsymbol{w}$ under a PCFG $\mathcal{G}$. As standard in learning latent variable models, C-PCFGs resort to variational inference for tractable learning and instead maximize the evidence lower bound (ELBO):

$$\log p_\theta(\boldsymbol{w}) \geq \text{ELBO}(\boldsymbol{w};\phi,\theta) = \\ \mathbb{E}_{q_\phi(\mathbf{z}|\boldsymbol{w})}[\log p_\theta(\boldsymbol{w}|\mathbf{z})] - \text{KL}[q_\phi(\mathbf{z}|\boldsymbol{w})||p(\mathbf{z})]\,,$$

where the first term computes the expected log likelihood under a variational posterior $q_\phi(\mathbf{z}|\boldsymbol{w})$; the KL term can be estimated analytically when $p(\mathbf{z})$ and $q_\phi(\mathbf{z}|\boldsymbol{w})$ are normally distributed. $q_\phi(\mathbf{z}|\boldsymbol{w})$ is parameterized by a neural network and defines a distribution over the latent $\mathbf{z}$.

C-PCFGs satisfy the context-free assumption conditioned on $\mathbf{z}$ and thus admit tractable inference for each given $\mathbf{z}$. Inference with C-PCFGs seeks the most probable parse t^* of $\boldsymbol{w}$:

$$t^* = \operatorname{argmax} \int_{\mathbf{z}} p_\theta(t|\mathbf{w},\mathbf{z}) p_\theta(\mathbf{z}|\boldsymbol{w})\, d\mathbf{z}\,.$$

Though given $\mathbf{z}$, the maximum a posterior (MAP) inference over $p_\theta(t|\mathbf{w},\mathbf{z})$ can be exactly solved by using the CYK algorithm, the integral over $\mathbf{z}$ renders inference intractable. The MAP inference is instead approximated by:

$$t^* \approx \operatorname{argmax} \int_{\mathbf{z}} p_\theta(t|\mathbf{w},\mathbf{z}) \delta(\mathbf{z} - \boldsymbol{\mu}_\phi(\boldsymbol{w}))\, d\mathbf{z}\,,$$

where $\delta(\cdot)$ is the Dirac delta function and $\boldsymbol{\mu}_\phi(\boldsymbol{w})$ is the mean vector of the variational posterior.

Similarly to C-PCFGs, neural PCFGs (N-PCFGs) also use neural networks to parameterize PCFGs, but their parameterization does not rely on the sentence-dependent $\mathbf{z}$. In the following discussion, we will refer to $\mathbf{z}$ as 'sentence embedding'.

3 Experimental setup

Datasets: We investigate the parsing performance of C-PCFGs across ten languages. Specifically, we conduct experiments on the Wall Street Journal (WSJ) corpus of the Penn Treebank (Marcus et al., 1994) for English, the Penn Chinese Treebank 5.1 (CTB) (Xue et al., 2005) for Chinese, and eight additional treebanks from the SPMRL 2014 shared task (Seddah et al., 2014) for the other eight languages (Basque, German, French, Hebrew, Hungarian, Korean, Polish, Swedish). We use the standard data splits for each treebank. Following Kim et al. (2019), punctuation is removed from all data; the top 10000 frequent tokens in the training data of each treebank are kept as the vocabulary.[3] Unless otherwise specified, we train C-PCFGs on sentences no longer than 40 tokens.

Model hyperparameters and evaluation: We re-implement C-PCFGs relying on Torch-Struct (Rush, 2020) and adopt the same hyperparameter settings as in Kim et al. (2019). We train C-PCFGs for each language separately. On each treebank we run C-PCFGs four times with different random seeds and for 30 epochs. The best model in each run is selected according to the perplexity on the validation data. At test time, trivial spans, such as single-word and sentence-level spans, are ignored. We report average corpus- and sentence-level F1 numbers as well as the unbiased standard deviations.

4 Results and discussion

4.1 Main results

We compare C-PCFGs against three trivial baselines (left- / right-branching model and random trees) and a neural PCFG model. In short, C-PCFGs beats all baselines in terms of corpus- and sentence-level F1 (see the second row of Table 1). Our re-implementation of C-PCFGs reaches the highest sentence-level F1, slightly outperforming the model of Kim et al. (2019) by 0.5% F1. To give an in-depth analysis of the model gains, we present recall numbers on six most frequent constituent labels in the test data (NP, VP, PP, SBAR, ADJP, ADVP). Unsurprisingly, C-PCFGs achieve the best recall for most labels (4 out of 6 constituent labels). However, on verb phrases (VPs) they fall far behind the right-branching baseline (-30.8%

[3]A unified data preprocessing pipeline is available at https://github.com/zhaoyanpeng/xcfg.

Model	NP	VP	PP	SBAR	ADJP	ADVP	C-F1	S-F1
Left Branching	10.4	0.5	5.0	5.3	2.5	8.0	6.0	8.7
Right Branching	24.1	**71.5**	42.4	**68.7**	27.7	38.1	36.1	39.5
Random Trees	$22.5_{\pm0.3}$	$12.3_{\pm0.3}$	$19.0_{\pm0.5}$	$9.3_{\pm0.6}$	$24.3_{\pm1.7}$	$26.9_{\pm1.3}$	$15.3_{\pm0.1}$	$18.1_{\pm0.1}$
†N-PCFG	71.2	33.8	58.8	52.5	32.5	45.5		50.8
N-PCFG	$72.2_{\pm4.8}$	$31.4_{\pm9.7}$	$66.8_{\pm4.7}$	$50.2_{\pm9.1}$	$46.3_{\pm5.7}$	$55.2_{\pm5.0}$	$49.0_{\pm3.5}$	$50.8_{\pm3.8}$
†C-PCFG	74.7	41.7	68.8	56.1	40.4	52.5		55.2
C-PCFG	$76.7_{\pm2.0}$	$40.7_{\pm5.5}$	$71.3_{\pm2.1}$	$53.8_{\pm3.1}$	$45.9_{\pm2.8}$	$64.2_{\pm2.8}$	$53.5_{\pm1.4}$	$55.7_{\pm1.3}$
L50C-PCFG	$\mathbf{76.9}_{\pm3.6}$	$40.7_{\pm3.7}$	$\mathbf{72.3}_{\pm0.6}$	$60.1_{\pm5.5}$	$\mathbf{46.9}_{\pm5.8}$	$63.2_{\pm5.0}$	$\mathbf{53.8}_{\pm2.1}$	$\mathbf{55.9}_{\pm1.9}$
L40C-PCFG	$76.7_{\pm2.0}$	$40.7_{\pm5.5}$	$71.3_{\pm2.1}$	$53.8_{\pm3.1}$	$45.9_{\pm2.8}$	$64.2_{\pm2.8}$	$53.5_{\pm1.4}$	$55.7_{\pm1.3}$
L30C-PCFG	$74.5_{\pm2.8}$	$38.4_{\pm1.7}$	$71.1_{\pm1.2}$	$59.7_{\pm4.8}$	$44.2_{\pm4.1}$	$\mathbf{64.3}_{\pm3.1}$	$52.5_{\pm1.5}$	$54.8_{\pm1.4}$
L20C-PCFG	$72.4_{\pm2.3}$	$36.5_{\pm1.1}$	$69.2_{\pm1.7}$	$54.1_{\pm3.2}$	$41.9_{\pm2.3}$	$58.1_{\pm7.1}$	$50.6_{\pm0.9}$	$52.8_{\pm0.7}$
L10C-PCFG	$67.1_{\pm3.8}$	$31.0_{\pm9.8}$	$61.3_{\pm2.2}$	$45.9_{\pm8.2}$	$36.7_{\pm2.3}$	$41.3_{\pm6.0}$	$45.5_{\pm2.4}$	$48.2_{\pm2.3}$

Table 1: Recall on six frequent constituent labels (NP, VP, PP, SBAR, ADJP, ADVP) in the WSJ test data, corpus-level F1 (C-F1), and sentence-level F1 (S-F1) results. The best mean number in each column is in bold. † denotes results reported by Kim et al. (2019). L# indicates that the models are trained on sentences no longer than # tokens.

recall), presumably because VPs are longer and involve more complex linguistic structures. We further plot distributions of the six labels across constituent lengths (see Figure 1). We can see that VPs are nearly uniformly distributed over different constituent lengths. In contrast, noun phrases (NPs) account for 61% of short constituents that have less than 6 tokens and cover 51% of total constituents. It suggests that C-PCFGs can recognize local and short constituents with a high accuracy but struggles with long constituents; there is clearly a room for improvement on VPs.

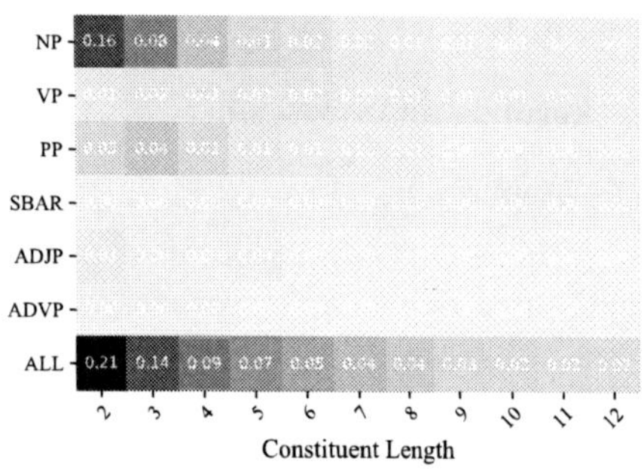

Figure 1: Label distribution over constituent lengths on the WSJ test data. *All* denotes frequencies of constituent lengths. Zero frequencies are due to the limited numerical precision.

4.2 Data efficiency and length generalization

A crucial aspect of human languages is their compositionality. Humans can derive grammar rules from a few sentences and combine the rules to generate new sentences compositionally. As C-PCFGs are backed by context-free grammar, we hypothesize that C-PCFGs are data-efficient and have a good generalizability to unseen sentences and constituents.

We design a length-generalization test to verify our hypothesis. Specifically, we train C-PCFGs using training sentences of length equal to or below a chosen sentence length. We choose five sentence lengths, 10, 20, 30, 40 and 50, indicated by L10, L20, L30, L40 and L50, respectively (see the third row of Table 1)). Figure 3 illustrates sentence-level F1 numbers on the test data of WSJ. Overall, training C-PCFGs on more / longer sentences results in higher F1 numbers. But using training sentences longer than 40 tokens only trivially improves the performance (+0.2% F1). Given that 97% test sentences are shorter than 40 tokens, we conjecture that training sentences shorter than 40 tokens can adequately cover lexical / structural characteristics in the test data. On the other hand, longer sentences have a larger tree space and probably make it harder for the model to learn. Notably, discarding training sentences longer than 30 tokens only decreases the model performance by 1.2% F1, suggesting that C-PCFGs are data-efficient.

We also conduct a constituent-length generalization test to study the generalizability of C-PCFGs on unseen long constituents. Since the test data of WSJ is too small to provide reliable statistics across constituent lengths, we test C-PCFGs on training sentences and report F1 numbers across *constituent lengths* (see Figure 2). In general, F1 numbers become lower as constituent length increases. This is reasonable because large constituents merge from

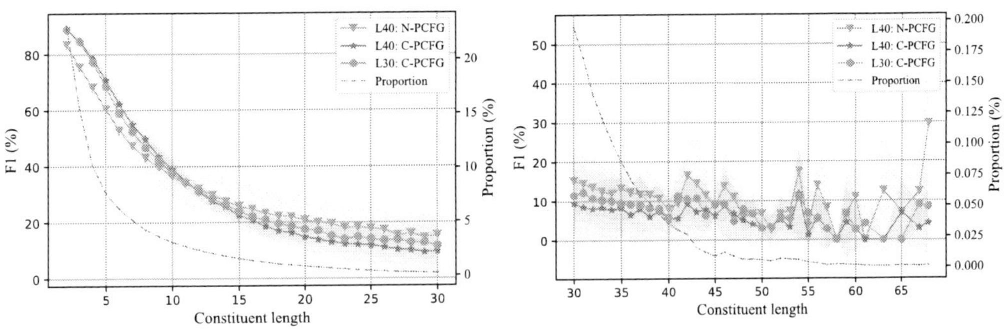

(a) F1 w.r.t. constituent length **below** 30

(b) F1 w.r.t. constituent length **above** 30

Figure 2: F1 numbers broken down by constituent lengths on the WSJ training data. During training, constituents (sentences) longer than 30 tokens (L30) are unseen to L30C-PCFG and are unseen to L40C-PCFG and L40N-PCFG when longer than 40 tokens (L40).

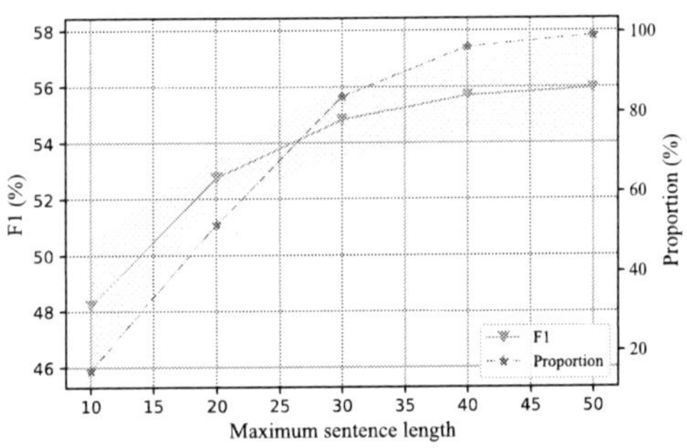

Figure 3: F1 numbers on the WSJ test data with varying maximum lengths of training sentences.

small constituents; errors in small constituents accumulate when composing larger constituents.

We further investigate the influence of training data on length generalization. We use sentence lengths 30 and 40 as an illustration. Compare with L40C-PCFG, when tested on constituents longer than 40 tokens, L30C-PCFG shows a slightly better generalizability (see Figure 2b). It consistently outperforms L40C-PCFG on sentences of length ranging from 30 to 40, though L40C-PCFG can access all sentences shorter than 40 tokens during training. This implies that C-PCFGs generalize well from short sentences; using additional long training sentences may hurt the generalizability. We also plots the proportions of constituent lengths. For example, there are about 6400 constituents of length from 30 to 40, which account for about 1.1% of total constituents, suggesting that the conclusion about the better generalizability of L30C-PCFGs is reliable.

Figure 2b visualizes the performance of an L40N-PCFG. Surprisingly, L40N-PCFG shows the best generalizability on long constituents. *Where does the F1 improvement of* C-PCFGs *over* N-PCFGs *come from?* Look at the F1 numbers on shorter constituents in Figure 2a, clearly C-PCFGs are better on constituents that are shorter than 11 tokens, while L40N-PCFGs consistently outperform C-PCFGs on constituents of length above 11. L30C-PCFGs fall in between L40C-PCFGs and L40N-PCFGs, once again showing that restricting training to short sentences can endow C-PCFGs good parsing performance as well as lead to improved generalization.

4.3 Model ablation

C-PCFGs demonstrate a significant improvement over N-PCFGs. Compare with N-PCFGs, C-PCFGs use an additional sentence embedding (i.e., the latent variable **z**, see Section 2) to parameterize sentence-specific PCFGs. Concretely, the sentence embedding is used to parameterize three types of rules: preterminal rules (P), nonterminal rules (N), and start rules (R). We would like to know *which type of rules makes the best use of the sentence embedding?* To this end, we let a C-PCFG use corpus-level parameters for each of the three types of rules, individually, i.e., parameters for a rule type are shared among sentences. Interestingly, C-PCFGs degenerate into N-PCFGs when using corpus-level parameters for preterminal rules (see Figure 4). It implies that the sentence embedding is most crucial for the parameterization of preterminal rules, presumably because the sentence embedding helps preterminal rules derive the knowledge of

Model	Chinese	Basque	German	French	Hebrew	Hungarian	Korean	Polish	Swedish	Mean
Left Branching	7.2	17.9	10.0	5.7	8.5	13.3	18.5	10.9	8.4	11.2
Right Branching	25.5	15.4	14.7	26.4	30.0	12.7	19.2	**34.2**	**30.4**	23.2
Random Trees	15.2	19.5	13.9	16.2	19.7	14.1	22.2	21.4	16.4	17.6
N-PCFG	30.1$_{\pm 4.6}$	**30.2**$_{\pm 0.9}$	**37.8**$_{\pm 1.7}$	**42.2**$_{\pm 1.4}$	**41.0**$_{\pm 0.6}$	37.9$_{\pm 0.8}$	25.7$_{\pm 2.8}$	31.7$_{\pm 1.8}$	14.5$_{\pm 12.7}$	32.3
C-PCFG	**35.1**$_{\pm 6.1}$	27.9$_{\pm 2.0}$	37.3$_{\pm 1.8}$	40.5$_{\pm 0.8}$	39.2$_{\pm 1.2}$	**38.3**$_{\pm 0.7}$	**27.7**$_{\pm 2.8}$	32.4$_{\pm 1.1}$	23.7$_{\pm 14.3}$	**33.6**

Table 2: Sentence-level F1 numbers on multilingual treebanks. Similarly to Kim et al. (2019), we observe that C-PCFGs suffer a huge variance, e.g., on the Chinese and Swedish treebanks.

part-of-speech tags, which is beneficial for parsing.

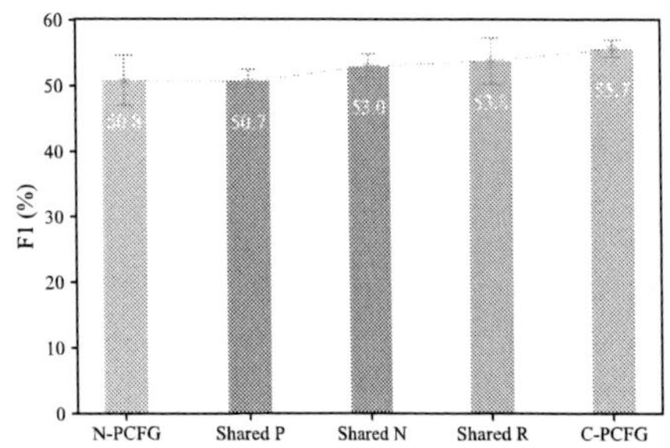

Figure 4: F1 numbers on the WSJ test data. Shared P / N / R indicates C-PCFGs that use corpus-level parameters for preterminal / nonterminal / start rules (see Section 4.3).

4.4 Multilingual evaluation

Despite the surprisingly good performance on English, it is still unclear whether C-PCFGs can generalize to languages beyond English. We thus conduct multilingual evaluation of C-PCFGs on nine additional languages (see Tablel 2). When training C-PCFGs on the nine languages, we use the hyperparameters of the best-performing C-PCFG on English, i.e., we tune C-PCFGs only on WSJ and use the best configurations on the other treebanks. We can see that C-PCFGs achieve the highest overall mean F1 (average F1 number over all treebanks), though they have two fewer winning treebanks than N-PCFGs. Notably, both C-PCFGs and N-PCFGs outperform the trivial baselines by a large margin, suggesting their nice generalizability on languages beyond English. However, they are worse than the right-branching baseline on the Polish and Swedish treebanks. As these languages have rich morphologies, we anticipate an improvement from encoding the knowledge of morphologies into the sentence embedding.

5 Conclusion

We have presented an in-depth analysis of C-PCFGs from a quantitative perspective. The analysis concerns three aspects of C-PCFGs: data efficiency and length generalization, the role of the latent sentence embedding, and multilingual performance. Our experimental results show that C-PCFGs can learn well only from short sentences and maintain good performance at test time. The latent sentence embedding is crucial for the good performance of C-PCFGs. Among the three rule types, preterminal rules make the most of it. However, the configurations of the best-performing C-PCFGs on English do not always generalize to morphology-rich languages.

Acknowledgments

We would like to thank anonymous reviewers for their suggestions and comments. The project was supported by the European Research Council (ERC Starting Grant BroadSem 678254) and the Dutch National Science Foundation (NWO VIDI 639.022.518).

References

A. P. Dempster, N. M. Laird, and D. B. Rubin. 1977. Maximum likelihood from incomplete data via the em algorithm. *Journal of the Royal Statistical Society: Series B (Methodological)*, 39(1):1–22.

Yoon Kim, Chris Dyer, and Alexander Rush. 2019. Compound probabilistic context-free grammars for grammar induction. In *Proceedings of the 57th Annual Meeting of the Association for Computational Linguistics*, pages 2369–2385, Florence, Italy. Association for Computational Linguistics.

K. Lari and S.J. Young. 1990. The estimation of stochastic context-free grammars using the inside-outside algorithm. *Computer Speech and Language*, 4(1):35 – 56.

Mitchell Marcus, Grace Kim, Mary Ann Marcinkiewicz, Robert MacIntyre, Ann Bies, Mark Ferguson, Karen Katz, and Britta Schasberger.

1994. The Penn Treebank: Annotating predicate argument structure. In *Human Language Technology: Proceedings of a Workshop held at Plainsboro, New Jersey, March 8-11, 1994*.

Alexander Rush. 2020. Torch-struct: Deep structured prediction library. In *Proceedings of the 58th Annual Meeting of the Association for Computational Linguistics: System Demonstrations*, pages 335–342, Online. Association for Computational Linguistics.

Djamé Seddah, Sandra Kübler, and Reut Tsarfaty. 2014. Introducing the SPMRL 2014 shared task on parsing morphologically-rich languages. In *Proceedings of the First Joint Workshop on Statistical Parsing of Morphologically Rich Languages and Syntactic Analysis of Non-Canonical Languages*, pages 103–109, Dublin, Ireland. Dublin City University.

Naiwen Xue, Fei Xia, Fu-dong Chiou, and Marta Palmer. 2005. The penn chinese treebank: Phrase structure annotation of a large corpus. *Natural Language Engineering*, 11(2):207–238.

Yanpeng Zhao and Ivan Titov. 2020. Visually grounded compound PCFGs. In *Proceedings of the 2020 Conference on Empirical Methods in Natural Language Processing (EMNLP)*, pages 4369–4379, Online. Association for Computational Linguistics.

User Factor Adaptation for User Embedding via Multitask Learning

Xiaolei Huang
Computer Science
University of Memphis
xiaolei.huang@memphis.edu

Michael J. Paul, Robin Burke
Information Science
University of Colorado Boulder
mpaul,robin.burke@colorado.edu

Franck Dernoncourt
Adobe Research
dernonco@adobe.com

Mark Dredze
Computer Science
Johns Hopkins University
mdredze@cs.jhu.edu

Abstract

Language varies across users and their interested fields in social media data: words authored by a user across his/her interests may have different meanings (e.g., cool) or sentiments (e.g., fast). However, most of the existing methods to train user embeddings ignore the variations across user interests, such as product and movie categories (e.g., drama vs. action). In this study, we treat the user interest as domains and empirically examine how the user language can vary across the user factor in three English social media datasets. We then propose a user embedding model to account for the language variability of user interests via a multitask learning framework. The model learns user language and its variations without human supervision. While existing work mainly evaluated the user embedding by extrinsic tasks, we propose an intrinsic evaluation via clustering and evaluate user embeddings by an extrinsic task, text classification. The experiments on the three English-language social media datasets show that our proposed approach can generally outperform baselines via adapting the user factor.

1 Introduction

Language varies across user factors including user interests, demographic attributes, personalities, and latent factors from user history. Research shows that language usage diversifies according to online user groups (Volkova et al., 2013), which women were more likely to use the word *weakness* in a positive way while men were the opposite. In social media, the user interests can include topics of user reviews (e.g., home vs. health services in Yelp) and categories of reviewed items (electronic vs kitchen products in Amazon). The ways that users express themselves depend on current contexts of user interests (Oba et al., 2019) that users may use the same words for opposite meanings and different words for the same meaning. For example, online users can use the word "fast" to criticize battery quality of the electronic domain or praise medicine effectiveness of the medical products; users can also use the words "cool" to describe a property of AC products or express sentiments.

User embedding, which is to learn a fixed-length representation based on multiple user reviews of each user, can infer the user latent information into a unified vector space (Benton, 2018; Pan and Ding, 2019). The inferred latent representations from online content can predict user profile (Volkova et al., 2015; Wang et al., 2018; Farnadi et al., 2018; Lynn et al., 2020) and behaviors (Zhang et al., 2015; Amir et al., 2017; Benton et al., 2017; Ding et al., 2017). User embeddings can personalize classification models, and further improve model performance (Tang et al., 2015; Chen et al., 2016a; Yang and Eisenstein, 2017; Wu et al., 2018; Zeng et al., 2019; Huang et al., 2019). The representations of user language can help models better understand documents as global contexts.

However, existing user embedding methods (Amir et al., 2016; Benton et al., 2016; Xing and Paul, 2017; Pan and Ding, 2019) mainly focus on extracting features from language itself while ignoring user interests. Recent research has demonstrated that adapting the user factors can further improve user geolocation prediction (Miura et al., 2017), demographic attribute prediction (Farnadi et al., 2018), and sentiment analysis (Yang and Eisenstein, 2017). Lynn et al. (2017); Huang and Paul (2019) treated the language variations as a domain adaptation problem and referred to this idea as *user factor adaptation*.

In this study, we treat the user interest as *domains* (e.g., restaurants vs. home services domains) and propose a multitask framework to model language variations and incorporate the user factor into user embeddings. We focus on three online

Proceedings of the Second Workshop on Domain Adaptation for NLP, pages 172–182
April 20, 2021.

review datasets from Amazon, IMDb, and Yelp containing diverse behaviors conditioned on user interests, which refer to genres of reviewed items. For example, if any Yelp users have reviews on items of the home services, then their user interests will include the home services.

We start with exploring how the user factor, user interest, can cause language and classification variations in Section 3. We then propose our user embedding model that adapts the user interests using a multitask learning framework in Section 4. Research (Pan and Ding, 2019) generally evaluates the user embedding via downstream tasks, but user annotations sometimes are hard to obtain and those evaluations are extrinsic instead of intrinsic tasks. For example, the MyPersonality (Kosinski et al., 2015) that was used in previous work (Ding et al., 2017; Farnadi et al., 2018; Pan and Ding, 2019) is no longer available, and an extrinsic task is to evaluate if user embeddings can help text classifiers. Research (Schnabel et al., 2015) suggests that the intrinsic evaluation including clustering is better than the extrinsic evaluation for controlling less hyperparameters. We propose an intrinsic evaluation for user embedding, which can provide a new perspective for testing future experiments. We show that our user-factor-adapted user embedding can generally outperform the existing methods on both intrinsic and extrinsic tasks.

2 Data

We collected English reviews of Amazon (health product), IMDb and Yelp from the publicly available sources (He and McAuley, 2016; Yelp, 2018; IMDb, 2020). For the IMDb dataset, we included English movies produced in the US from 1960 to 2019. Each review associates with its author and the *rated item*, which refers to a movie in the IMDb data, a business unit in the Yelp data and a product in the Amazon data. To keep consistency in each dataset, we retain top 4 frequent genres of rated items and the review documents with no less than 10 tokens.[1] We dropped non-English review documents by the language detector (Lui and Baldwin, 2012), lowercased all tokens and tokenized the corpora using NLTK (Bird and Loper, 2004). The review datasets have different score scales. We normalize the scales and encode each review score into three discrete categories: positive (> 3 for the Yelp and Amazon, > 6 for the IMDb), negative (< 3 for the Yelp and Amazon, < 5 for the IMDb) and neutral. Table 1 shows a summary of the datasets.

2.1 Privacy Considerations

To protect user privacy, we anonymize all user-related information via hashing, and our experiments only use publicly available datasets for research demonstration. Any URLs, hashtags and capitalized English names were removed. Due to the potential sensitivity of user reviews, we only use information necessary for this study. We do not use any user profile in our experiments, except, our evaluations use anonymized author ID of each review entry for training user embeddings. We will not release any private user reviews associated with user identities. Instead, we will open source our source code and provide instructions of how to access the public datasets in enough detail so that our proposed method can be replicated.

3 Exploratory Analysis of User Variations

Language varies across user factors such as user interests (Oba et al., 2019), demographic attributes (Huang and Paul, 2019), social relations (Yang and Eisenstein, 2017; Gong et al., 2020). In this section, our goal is to quantitatively analyze whether the user interests cause user language variations, which can reduce effectiveness and robustness of user embeddings. We approach this by two analysis tasks, first by measuring word feature similarity based on user interests, and second by examining how classifier performance depends on the grouped user interests in which the model is trained and applied.

3.1 Word Usage Variations

Existing methods mainly infer user embeddings from features of text contents (Pan and Ding, 2019). Therefore, word usage variations across user interests will change word distributions and further impact the stability of user embeddings. We aim to test whether there are language variations across the user interests in our datasets and how strong they are.

We consider the word usage as it relates to user embeddings by estimating the overlap of top word

[1]The top 4 rated categories of Amazon-Health, IMDb and Yelp are [sports nutrition, sexual wellness, shaving & hair removal, vitamins & dietary supplements], [comedy, thriller, drama, action] and [restaurants, health & medical, home services, beauty & spas] respectively.

Data	Users	Docs	Rated Items	Tokens	Train	Dev	Test
Amazon-Health	11,438	80,592	3,822	127	64,474	8,060	8,061
IMDb	6,089	123,184	642	187	98,548	12,319	12,320
Yelp	76,323	551,695	9,327	152	441,357	55,170	55,171

Table 1: Statistical summary of the Amazon, Yelp and IMDb review datasets. Amazon-Health refers to health-related reviews. Tokens mean the number of average tokens per document. We present the data split for the evaluation task of text classification on the right side.

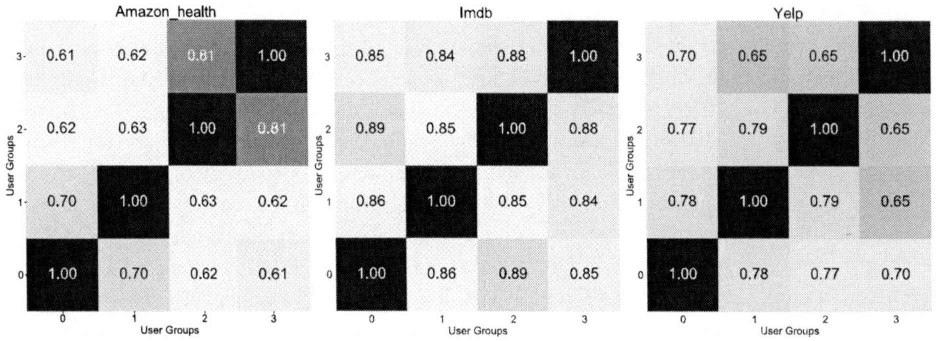

Figure 1: Word feature overlaps between every two user groups. A value of 1 means no variations of top features between two user groups, while values less than 1 indicate more feature variations.

features across the genres of rated items, the categories of reviewed products in Amazon, business units in Yelp and movies in IMDb. To solve data sparsity caused by single user preference, we grouped users and therefore their generated documents according to genres of user reviewed items. We refer to this as genre domains. We build a unified feature vectorizer (Pedregosa et al., 2011) with TF-IDF weighted n-gram features ($n \in \{1, 2, 3\}$), removing features that appeared in less than 2 documents. We rank and select the top 1000 word features for each genre domain by mutual information. We then compute the intersection percentage between every two genre domains: let F_0 is the set of top features for one genre domain and F_1 is the set of top features for the other domain, then the overlap is $|F_0 \cap F_1|/1000$.

We show the results in Figure 1. The overlap varies significantly across genre domains. This indicates that the word usage and its contexts of users change across user interests and preferences. Since the training of user embeddings relies heavily on the language features of users, this suggests that it is important to consider the language variations in user interests for the user embeddings.

3.2 Classification Performance Variations

User embeddings are effective to understand user behaviors in the classification setting (Amir et al., 2016; Ding et al., 2018). Research has found that combining user and document representations can benefit classification performance (Chen et al., 2016b; Li et al., 2018; Yuan et al., 2019). We explore how the language variations in user interests can affect classification models.

We conduct an analysis by training and testing classifiers that group users by the categories of reviewed items. We first group items and users according to item genres, which can be treated as different domains of user interests. For each domain, we downsampled documents, users and items within each group to match their numbers in the smallest group, so that classification performance differences are not due to data sizes of document, user and item. For each grouped documents, we shuffle and split the data into training (80%) and test (20%) sets. We train logistic regression classifiers with default hyperparameters from scikit-learn (Pedregosa et al., 2011) using TF-IDF weighted uni-, bi- and tri-gram features. We report weighted F1 scores across grouped users and show the results in Figure 2.

We can observe that classification performance varies across the grouped users. Higher performance variations between in- and out- user groups suggest higher user variations and vice versa. If no variations of user language exist, the performance

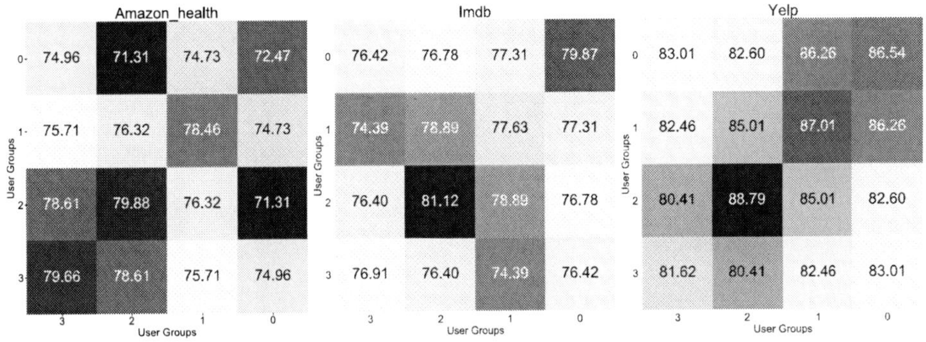

Figure 2: Document classification performance when training and testing on different groups of users. The datasets come from Amazon health, IMDb and Yelp reviews. Darker red indicates better classification performance, while darker blue means worse performance.

of classifiers should be similar across the domains. The performance variations suggest that user behaviors vary across the categories of user interests. We can also observe that classification models generally perform better when tests within the same user groups while worse in the other user groups. This suggests a variability connection between the user interests and language usage, which derives user embeddings.

4 Multitask User Embedding

We present the architecture of our proposed model in Figure 3 on the left. Methods (Pan and Ding, 2019) to train text-based user embedding mainly focus on the user-generated documents while ignoring user factors, the user interests. A close work to ours only trained user embeddings by predicting if users co-occurred with sampled words (Amir et al., 2017). We extend this line of work by adapting user interests into modeling steps. The proposed unsupervised model trains four joint tasks based on the Skip-Gram (Mikolov et al., 2013): word and word, user and word, item and word, and user and item. Note that we do not use the categories of rated items and user interests in our training steps. Then we can optimize the model by minimizing the following loss function:

$\mathcal{L} = \mathcal{L}(w, w) + \mathcal{L}(u, w) + \mathcal{L}(p, w) + \mathcal{L}(p, u)$ where w, u, p are the notations of words, users and rated items respectively. Considering the large size of the vocabulary, users and rated items, we approximate our optimization objectives by the negative sampling. Then we can treat each task as a classification problem and calculate loss values by the binary cross-entropy. We present the details of each optimization task as following:

Word and word is a standard way to train Word2vec (Mikolov et al., 2013) models. The prediction task is to predict if the sampled words have co-occurred within the window context. The training process uses the negative sampling to approximate objective function. We choose 5 as the number of negative samples. We keep the top 20,000 frequent words and finally replace the rest with a special token, $< unk >$.

User and word predicts if a user authored the sampled words by the contexts of user posts. The goal is to learn patterns of user language usage from user historical posts. Given a document i, its author u_i and the user's vocabulary $V_{u_i} = \{w_{1,i}, ..., w_{j,i}, ..., w_{n,i}\}$, where n is the number of frequent words authored by the user. Our objective is to minimize the following function:

$\mathcal{L}(u, w) = -\sum_{w_j \in V_{u_i} w_k \in V w_k \notin V_{u_i}} [log(\theta(e(u_i) \cdot e(w_j))) + log(\theta(e(u_i) \cdot e(w_k)))]$ where w_j is a negative sample from the whole vocabulary V, $e(u)$ and $e(w)$ are fixed-length user and word vectors respectively, and θ is a sigmoid function to normalize values of dot production. We extend the previous work (Amir et al., 2017) to integrate both local and global user language usage by sampling w_j from a combined token list of both the input document and the user's vocabulary. This can help the model learn contextual information of each user.

Item and word follows the prediction task of user and word to classify if sampled words describe the selected item. This task is to use review documents to train representations of rated items. Then we can have

$\mathcal{L}(p, w) = -\sum_{w_j \in V_{p_i}, w_k \in V, w_k \notin V_{p_i}} log(1 -$

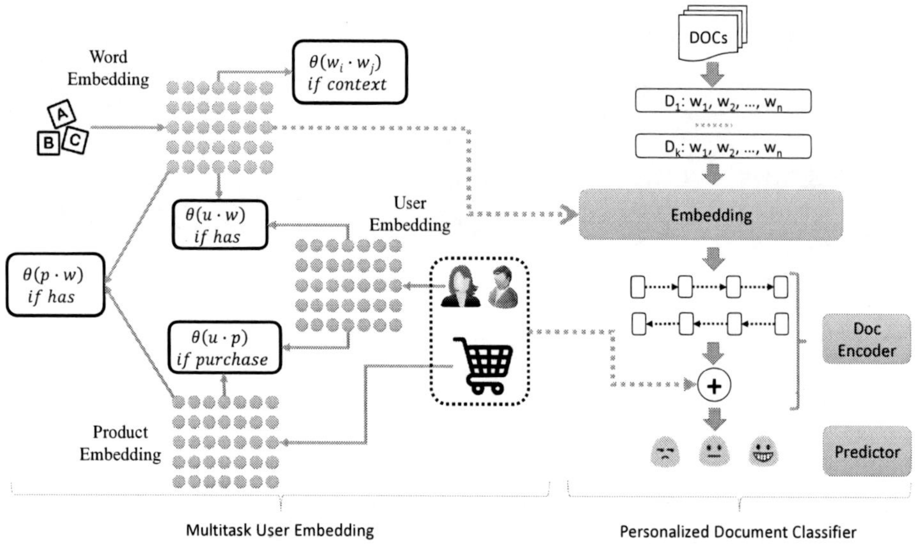

Figure 3: Illustrations of User Embedding via multitask learning framework on the left and personalized document classifiers using trained embedding models on the right. The arrows and their colors refer to the input directions and input sources respectively. We use the logos of people, shopping cart and ABC to represent users, reviewed items and word inputs. The $\bigoplus$ is the concatenation operation.

$\theta(e(p_i) \cdot e(w_j))) + log(\theta(e(p_i) \cdot e(w_k)))$ where V_{p_i} is the vocabulary of the rated item p_i and w_k is a negative sample of words. The language can be viewed as a bridge between an interactive relation of user and item, which predicts language usage for both rated items and users.

User and item learns if a user commented on the sampled items. The prediction task aims to adapt latent user factors into the user embeddings. Given a document i, its author u_i and the reviewed item p_i, we can optimize the task by minimizing $\mathcal{L}(u,p) = -\sum_{p_k \in P, p_k \notin P_{u_i}} log(\theta(e(p_i) \cdot e(u_i))) + log(\theta(e(p_k) \cdot e(u_i)))$ where the P is a collection of all items, the P_{u_i} is a reviewed item and the p_k is a negative sample that the user does not review. The constraints between reviewed items and users can help user embeddings identify language variations across domains of item genres. And in turn, the relation of user and item can help infer item vectors.

For model settings, we used Adam (Kingma and Ba, 2014) for the model optimization with a learning rate of 1e-5. We set the training epochs as 5. The model initializes embedding vectors randomly and learns 300-dimension representations for words, users and reviewed items. We empirically use 5 as the number of negative samples. For the other parameters, we keep the same as the defaults in the Keras (Chollet and Others, 2015).

5 Experiments

We evaluate the effectiveness of the user factor adapted embedding model by an intrinsic evaluation, user clustering task and an extrinsic evaluation, personalized classification task. The first task aims to measure the purity of clusters with respect to categories of user interests, and the second task uses the document classification as a proxy of qualifying quality of user embeddings. We conduct a qualitative analysis of the user embeddings comparing with our close work (Amir et al., 2017).

5.1 User Clustering Evaluation

The unsupervised evaluation of embedding models focuses on four main categories: relatedness, analogy, categorization and selectional preference (Schnabel et al., 2015). We approach the user embedding evaluation by categorizing users into different clusters. User communities or groups gather users by their interests and behaviors, such as engaging in the same filed of topics (Benton et al., 2016; Yang and Eisenstein, 2017). In our datasets, the user-purchased Amazon products, the user-visited Yelp business units and the user-watched IMDb movies have their item categories. The categories can imply user preferences and interests, and therefore can help evaluate user clusters. In this study, our proposed multitask model learns interactive relations across language, user and item instead of using the item categories. We compare our proposed model with other 5 baseline models:

word2user represents users by aggregating word representations (Benton et al., 2016). We compute a user representation by averaging embeddings of all tokens that were authored by the user. To obtain the word embeddings, for each dataset, we trained a word2vec model for 5 epochs using Gensim (Rehurek and Sojka, 2010) with 300-dimensional vectors.

lda2user generates user representations by applying Latent Dirichlet Allocation (LDA) (Blei et al., 2003) on user documents (Pennacchiotti and Popescu, 2011). We set the number of topics as 300 and leave the rest of the parameters as their defaults in Gensim (Rehurek and Sojka, 2010). We apply the LDA model on each user document to obtain a document vector, and then get a user vector by averaging the vectors of all the user's documents.

doc2user applies paragraph2vec (Le and Mikolov, 2014) to obtain user vectors. We implemented the User-D-DBOW model which achieved the best performance in the previous work (Ding et al., 2017). The implementation keeps parameters with default values in the Gensim (Rehurek and Sojka, 2010). We aggregate each user's documents as a single document. Then the User-D-DBOW model can derive a single user vector from the aggregated document.

bert2user follows a similar process of the lda2user. We use the "bert-base-uncased" pre-trained BERT model for English from the transformers toolkit (Wolf et al., 2019) with default parameter and model settings. After inserting "[CLS]" and "[SEP]" to the beginning and end of each document, the BERT model encodes a document into a fixed-length (768) document vector. We can then generate user embeddings by averaging each user's all document vectors.

user2vec trains user embeddings by predicting word usage by users. We follow the existing work (Amir et al., 2017) but set the user vector dimension as 300.

We use the `SpectralClustering` algorithm from scikit-learn (Pedregosa et al., 2011) toolkit to cluster users into three clustering sizes, 4, 8 and 12. We set the affinity as cosine and leave other parameters as their defaults. To measure cluster quality, we select every two users from the clusters without repetition. We count the user pair as a correct option if two users have overlaps within the same item genre and from the same cluster or if the user pair does not overlap and is from the different clusters. Otherwise, we will count the selection as the wrong option. Therefore, we can have a list of predicted labels and ground truths by using the item genres as a proxy. Finally, we measure the clustering purity by the F1 score.

We present results at Table 2. The results show that our multitask user embedding model outperforms the other baselines by a large portion on the IMDb and Yelp datasets. The improvements suggest the user factor adapted model can understand semantic variations in diverse user interests. The performance of our model and user2vec has similar scores on the Amazon-Health dataset. Comparing to the other two datasets, the Amazon-Health data has more similar topics of review items.

5.2 Personalized Classifier Evaluation

We train three classifiers to evaluate user embeddings on the document classification task. We split each dataset into training (80%), development (10%) and test (10%) sets, as shown in Table 1. The models oversample the minority during the training process. We test the classifiers when they achieve the best performance on the development set. Finally, we report precision, recall and F1 scores using the `classification_report` from scikit-learn (Pedregosa et al., 2011). Figure 3 illustrates personalizing classifiers by concatenating document representations with user embeddings. We compare our proposed model with classifiers using existing user2vec (Amir et al., 2017) and non-personalized classifiers. To ensure a fair comparison, classifiers use the same settings for models with and without user embeddings.

LR. We build a logistic regression classifier using `LogisticRegression` from scikit-learn (Pedregosa et al., 2011). The classifier extracts uni-, bi- and tri-gram features on the corpora with the most frequent 15K features with default parameters.

GRU. We build a bi-directional Gated Recurrent Unit (GRU) (Cho et al., 2014) classifier. We padded documents to the average document length of each corpus. We set the output dimension of GRU as 200

		Amazon-Health			IMDb			Yelp		
		F1@4	F1@8	F1@12	F1@4	F1@8	F1@12	F1@4	F1@8	F1@12
Baselines	word2user	**.929**	.909	.905	.653	.725	.762	.859	.810	.797
	lda2user	.920	**.914**	.900	.696	.726	.761	.849	.839	.832
	doc2user	.873	.891	.901	.660	.725	.748	.836	.828	.826
	bert2user	.871	.896	**.906**	.660	.714	.734	.838	.828	.830
	user2vec	.868	.891	.901	.601	.600	.593	.841	.829	.832
Ours	MTL	.870	.890	.900	**.801**	**.879**	**.884**	**.879**	**.843**	**.838**

Table 2: Performance summary of different user embedding models. We report F1 scores at multiple numbers of clusters. The bold fonts indicate the best performance in each evaluation task.

and apply a dense layer on the output. The dense layer uses ReLU (Hahnloser et al., 2000) as the activation function, applies a dropout (Srivastava et al., 2014) rate of 0.2 and outputs 200 dimensions for final document class prediction. We train the classifier for 20 epochs.

BERT. We implement a BERT-based classifier by HuggingFace's transformers toolkit (Wolf et al., 2019). The classifier loads the "bert-base-uncased" pre-trained BERT model for English, encodes each document into a fixed-length (768) vector and feeds to a linear prediction layer for prediction. We conduct fine-tuning steps for 10 epochs with a batch size of 32 and optimize the model by `AdamW` with a learning rate of $9e^{-5}$.

We show the performance results in Table 3. Comparing to the baselines, the classifiers personalized by our proposed model generally achieve the best performance across the three datasets. This highlights adapting user factors can help embedding models learn user variations and benefit the classification performance. We can also observe that the personalized classifiers generally outperform the non-personalized classifiers. This indicates personalizing the classifiers with user history boosts classification performance in our study.

5.3 Visualization Analysis

To further evaluate the effectiveness of user embedding models, we map users into a 2-D space using user embeddings and plot them in Figure 4. We group users according to user interests using the domain categories of rated items. To map the 300-d user embeddings, we use the `TSNE` algorithm from scikit-learn (Pedregosa et al., 2011) to compress the dimension into 2-d vectors. We set the n_component as 2 and leave the other parameters as their defaults in the TSNE. We can observe that the MTL user embedding model shows more clustering patterns with regard to user interests (categories of reviewed items). This indicates that the unsupervised multitask learning framework can adapt the latent user factors into the user embedding. Users may have multiple interests. In the right plot, we can also find that there is a cluster that mixes with multiple colors on the right bottom.

6 Related Work

User Profiling is a common task in natural language processing. Online generated user texts show demographic variations in the linguistic styles, and the linguistic style variability could be used for predicting user's personality and demographic attributes (Rosenthal and McKeown, 2011; Zhang et al., 2016; Hovy and Fornaciari, 2018; Wood-Doughty et al., 2020; Gjurković et al., 2020; Lynn et al., 2020). The demographic user factors influence how online users express their opinions (Volkova et al., 2013; Hovy, 2015; Wood-Doughty et al., 2017) and show promising improvements in the text classification task (Lynn et al., 2017; Huang and Paul, 2019; Lynn et al., 2019). However, in this work, the goal of modeling user factor is to train robust user embeddings via domain adaptation, rather than the end goal being demographic factor prediction and document classification itself.

Personalized classification generally improves the performance of document classifiers (Flek, 2020). The multitask learning framework has been applied for personalizing document classifiers by optimizing the classifiers on multiple document levels (Benton et al., 2017) or general and individual levels (Wu and Huang, 2016). The social relation can bridge connections between users and generalize classification models across users (Wu and Huang, 2016; Yang and Eisenstein, 2017). For example, (Wu and Huang, 2016) optimizes document

Methods	Amazon-Health			IMDb			Yelp		
	Precision	Recall	F1	Precision	Recall	F1	Precision	Recall	F1
LR	.834	.768	.793	.818	.779	.794	.856	.820	.833
LR-u	.841	.777	**.801**	.834	.791	**.807**	.860	.821	.835
LR-up	.838	.771	.796	.833	.791	**.807**	.863	.825	**.838**
GRU	.813	.844	.812	.824	.837	.823	.851	.865	.852
GRU-u	.836	.811	.821	.832	.819	.825	.868	.846	.858
GRU-up	.821	.832	**.825**	.846	.824	**.836**	.876	.864	**.867**
BERT	.866	.822	.840	.852	.809	.826	.866	.825	.840
BERT-u	.863	.812	.831	.858	.818	.833	.872	.843	**.854**
BERT-up	.873	.838	**.851**	.864	.831	**.844**	.880	.839	**.854**

Table 3: Performance scores of document classifiers on the review datasets. '-u' means personalized classifiers using user2vec (Amir et al., 2017) and '-up' indicates personalizing classifiers via our proposed method. We use the bold fonts to highlight the best performance of each classifier on separate datasets.

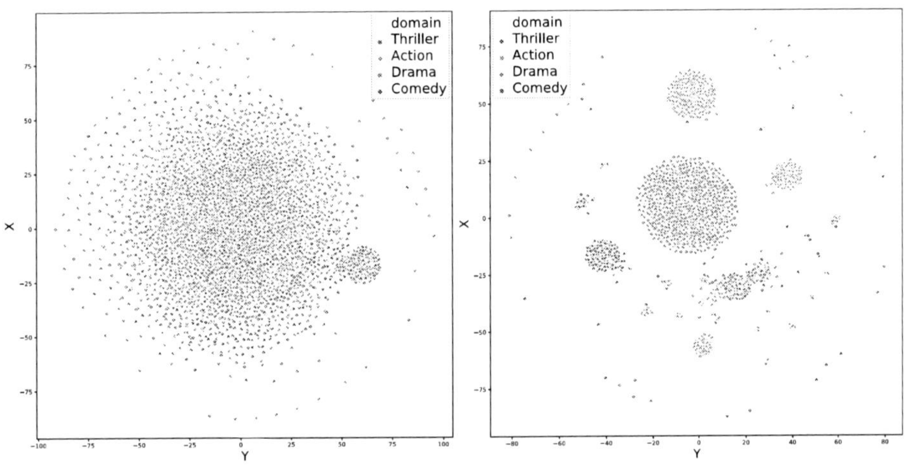

Figure 4: Visualizations of IMDb users colored concerning their interests in 4 movie genres. We plot users using the embeddings from our proposed method (right) and user2vec (Amir et al., 2017) (left). The visualizations of Yelp and Amazon are omitted for reasons of space.

classifiers by two optimization tasks, sentiment classification and user social relation minimization, which allows classifiers to minimize the impacts of user community variations. This work personalizes classifiers in a different way, where we train user embedding models under a multitask learning framework and use the personalized classifiers to evaluate user embedding models.

7 Conclusion

In this study, we have proposed user factor adaptation for building user embedding under a multitask framework. Our analyses show how the user factor causes semantic variations in relation to word usage and document classification, showing that the user factor is rooted in language. We have evaluated the proposed user embedding models in both intrinsic and extrinsic tasks. The user factor adapted model has shown its robustness to language variations in both instrinsic and extrinsic evaluations, learning user representations and personalizing classifiers. We release our source code and instructions of data access at `https://github.com/xiaoleihuang/UserEmbedding`.

Our work in user factor adaptation highlights several future directions to explore. First, our method models latent user factors inferred from user posts. A combination of user embedding and explicit attributes (e.g., demographic factors) may improve model personalization. Second, user behaviors shift over time. A time-adapted user embedding can jointly model temporality and user attributes in online social media and can be extended to other fields, such as public health.

8 Acknowledgement

The authors thank the anonymous reviews. This work was supported in part by the National Science Foundation under award number IIS-1657338. This work was also supported in part by a research gift from Adobe Research. The first author would thank the computational support from the JHU CLSP cluster.

References

Silvio Amir, Glen Coppersmith, Paula Carvalho, Mario J. Silva, and Bryon C. Wallace. 2017. Quantifying mental health from social media with neural user embeddings. In *Proceedings of the 2nd Machine Learning for Healthcare Conference*, volume 68 of *Proceedings of Machine Learning Research*, pages 306–321, Boston, Massachusetts. PMLR.

Silvio Amir, Byron C. Wallace, Hao Lyu, Paula Carvalho, and Mário J. Silva. 2016. Modelling context with user embeddings for sarcasm detection in social media. In *Proceedings of The 20th SIGNLL Conference on Computational Natural Language Learning*, pages 167–177, Berlin, Germany. Association for Computational Linguistics.

Adrian Benton. 2018. Learning representations of social media users. *arXiv preprint arXiv:1812.00436*.

Adrian Benton, Raman Arora, and Mark Dredze. 2016. Learning multiview embeddings of twitter users. In *Proceedings of the 54th Annual Meeting of the Association for Computational Linguistics (Volume 2: Short Papers)*, pages 14–19, Berlin, Germany. Association for Computational Linguistics.

Adrian Benton, Margaret Mitchell, and Dirk Hovy. 2017. Multitask learning for mental health conditions with limited social media data. In *Proceedings of the 15th Conference of the European Chapter of the Association for Computational Linguistics: Volume 1, Long Papers*, pages 152–162, Valencia, Spain. Association for Computational Linguistics.

Steven Bird and Edward Loper. 2004. NLTK: The natural language toolkit. In *Proceedings of the ACL Interactive Poster and Demonstration Sessions*, pages 214–217, Barcelona, Spain. Association for Computational Linguistics.

David M Blei, Andrew Y Ng, and Michael I Jordan. 2003. Latent {D}irichlet {A}llocation. *Journal of Machine Learning Research*, 3:993–1022.

Huimin Chen, Maosong Sun, Cunchao Tu, Yankai Lin, and Zhiyuan Liu. 2016a. Neural sentiment classification with user and product attention. In *Proceedings of the 2016 Conference on Empirical Methods in Natural Language Processing*, pages 1650–1659.

Tao Chen, Ruifeng Xu, Yulan He, Yunqing Xia, and Xuan Wang. 2016b. Learning user and product distributed representations using a sequence model for sentiment analysis. *IEEE Computational Intelligence Magazine*, 11(3):34–44.

Kyunghyun Cho, Bart van Merriënboer, Dzmitry Bahdanau, and Yoshua Bengio. 2014. On the properties of neural machine translation: Encoder–decoder approaches. In *Proceedings of SSST-8, Eighth Workshop on Syntax, Semantics and Structure in Statistical Translation*, pages 103–111, Doha, Qatar. Association for Computational Linguistics.

François Chollet and Others. 2015. Keras.

T. Ding, W. K. Bickel, and S. Pan. 2018. Predicting delay discounting from social media likes with unsupervised feature learning. In *2018 IEEE/ACM International Conference on Advances in Social Networks Analysis and Mining (ASONAM)*, pages 254–257.

Tao Ding, Warren K. Bickel, and Shimei Pan. 2017. Multi-view unsupervised user feature embedding for social media-based substance use prediction. In *Proceedings of the 2017 Conference on Empirical Methods in Natural Language Processing*, pages 2275–2284, Copenhagen, Denmark. Association for Computational Linguistics.

Golnoosh Farnadi, Jie Tang, Martine De Cock, and Marie-Francine Moens. 2018. User profiling through deep multimodal fusion. In *Proceedings of the Eleventh ACM International Conference on Web Search and Data Mining*, WSDM '18, page 171–179, New York, NY, USA. Association for Computing Machinery.

Lucie Flek. 2020. Returning the N to NLP: Towards contextually personalized classification models. In *Proceedings of the ACL*, pages 7828–7838.

Matej Gjurković, Mladen Karan, Iva Vukojević, Mihaela Bošnjak, and Jan Šnajder. 2020. Pandora talks: Personality and demographics on reddit. *arXiv preprint arXiv:2004.04460*.

Lin Gong, Lu Lin, Weihao Song, and Hongning Wang. 2020. Jnet: Learning user representations via joint network embedding and topic embedding. In *Proceedings of the 13th International Conference on Web Search and Data Mining*, WSDM '20, page 205–213, New York, NY, USA. Association for Computing Machinery.

Richard H R Hahnloser, Rahul Sarpeshkar, Misha A Mahowald, Rodney J Douglas, and H Sebastian Seung. 2000. Digital selection and analogue amplification coexist in a cortex-inspired silicon circuit. *Nature*, 405(6789):947.

Ruining He and Julian McAuley. 2016. Ups and downs: Modeling the visual evolution of fashion trends with one-class collaborative filtering. In *Proceedings of the 25th International Conference on World Wide Web (WWW)*, volume 3, pages 507–517. International World Wide Web Conferences Steering Committee.

Dirk Hovy. 2015. Demographic factors improve classification performance. In *Proceedings of the 53rd Annual Meeting of the Association for Computational Linguistics and the 7th International Joint Conference on Natural Language Processing (Volume 1: Long Papers)*, pages 752–762, Beijing, China. Association for Computational Linguistics.

Dirk Hovy and Tommaso Fornaciari. 2018. Increasing in-class similarity by retrofitting embeddings with demographic information. In *Proceedings of the 2018 Conference on Empirical Methods in Natural Language Processing*, pages 671–677, Brussels, Belgium. Association for Computational Linguistics.

Qi Huang, Chuan Zhou, Jia Wu, Mingwen Wang, and Bin Wang. 2019. Deep structure learning for rumor detection on twitter. In *2019 International Joint Conference on Neural Networks (IJCNN)*, pages 1–8. IEEE.

Xiaolei Huang and Michael J. Paul. 2019. Neural User Factor Adaptation for Text Classification: Learning to Generalize Across Author Demographics. In *Proceedings of the Eighth Joint Conference on Lexical and Computational Semantics (*{SEM} 2019)*, volume 4, pages 136–146, Minneapolis, Minnesota. Association for Computational Linguistics, Association for Computational Linguistics.

IMDb. 2020. http://www.imdb.com/interfaces/.

Diederik P. Kingma and Jimmy Ba. 2014. Adam: A Method for Stochastic Optimization. In *Proceedings of the 3rd International Conference on Learning Representations (ICLR)*.

Michal Kosinski, Sandra C Matz, Samuel D Gosling, Vesselin Popov, and David Stillwell. 2015. Facebook as a research tool for the social sciences: Opportunities, challenges, ethical considerations, and practical guidelines. *American Psychologist*, 70(6):543.

Quoc Le and Tomas Mikolov. 2014. Distributed representations of sentences and documents. In *Proceedings of Machine Learning Research*, volume 32, pages 1188–1196, Bejing, China. PMLR.

Junjie Li, Haitong Yang, and Chengqing Zong. 2018. Document-level multi-aspect sentiment classification by jointly modeling users, aspects, and overall ratings. In *Proceedings of the 27th International Conference on Computational Linguistics*, pages 925–936, Santa Fe, New Mexico, USA. Association for Computational Linguistics.

Marco Lui and Timothy Baldwin. 2012. langid.py: An off-the-shelf language identification tool. In *Proceedings of the ACL 2012 System Demonstrations*, pages 25–30, Jeju Island, Korea. Association for Computational Linguistics.

Veronica Lynn, Niranjan Balasubramanian, and H. Andrew Schwartz. 2020. Hierarchical modeling for user personality prediction: The role of message-level attention. In *Proceedings of the 58th Annual Meeting of the Association for Computational Linguistics*, pages 5306–5316, Online. Association for Computational Linguistics.

Veronica Lynn, Salvatore Giorgi, Niranjan Balasubramanian, and H. Andrew Schwartz. 2019. Tweet classification without the tweet: An empirical examination of user versus document attributes. In *Proceedings of the Third Workshop on Natural Language Processing and Computational Social Science*, pages 18–28, Minneapolis, Minnesota. Association for Computational Linguistics.

Veronica Lynn, Youngseo Son, Vivek Kulkarni, Niranjan Balasubramanian, and H. Andrew Schwartz. 2017. Human centered NLP with user-factor adaptation. In *Proceedings of the 2017 Conference on Empirical Methods in Natural Language Processing*, pages 1146–1155.

Tomas Mikolov, Ilya Sutskever, Kai Chen, Greg Corrado, and Jeffrey Dean. 2013. Distributed representations of words and phrases and their compositionality. In *Proceedings of the 26th International Conference on Neural Information Processing Systems - Volume 2*, NIPS'13, pages 3111–3119, USA. Curran Associates Inc.

Yasuhide Miura, Motoki Taniguchi, Tomoki Taniguchi, and Tomoko Ohkuma. 2017. Unifying text, metadata, and user network representations with a neural network for geolocation prediction. In *Proceedings of the 55th Annual Meeting of the Association for Computational Linguistics (Volume 1: Long Papers)*, pages 1260–1272, Vancouver, Canada.

Daisuke Oba, Naoki Yoshinaga, Shoetsu Sato, Satoshi Akasaki, and Masashi Toyoda. 2019. Modeling personal biases in language use by inducing personalized word embeddings. In *Proceedings of the 2019 Conference of the North American Chapter of the Association for Computational Linguistics: Human Language Technologies, Volume 1 (Long and Short Papers)*, pages 2102–2108, Minneapolis, Minnesota. Association for Computational Linguistics.

Shimei Pan and Tao Ding. 2019. Social media-based user embedding: A literature review. In *Proceedings of the Twenty-Eighth International Joint Conference on Artificial Intelligence, IJCAI-19*, pages 6318–6324. International Joint Conferences on Artificial Intelligence Organization.

Fabian Pedregosa, Gael Varoquaux, Alexandre Gramfort, Vincent Michel, Bertrand Thirion, Olivier Grisel, Mathieu Blondel, Peter Prettenhofer, Ron Weiss, Vincent Dubourg, Jake Vanderplas, Alexandre Passos, David Cournapeau, Matthieu Brucher, Matthieu Perrot, and Édouard Duchesnay. 2011. Scikit-learn: Machine learning in Python. *Journal of Machine Learning Research*, 12(Oct):2825–2830.

Marco Pennacchiotti and Ana-Maria Popescu. 2011. A machine learning approach to twitter user classification. In *International AAAI Conference on Web and Social Media.*

Radim Rehurek and Petr Sojka. 2010. Software Framework for Topic Modelling with Large Corpora. In *Proceedings of the LREC 2010 Workshop on New Challenges for NLP Frameworks*, pages 45–50. ELRA.

Sara Rosenthal and Kathleen McKeown. 2011. Age prediction in blogs: A study of style, content, and online behavior in pre- and post-social media generations. In *Proceedings of the 49th Annual Meeting of the Association for Computational Linguistics: Human Language Technologies*, volume 1, pages 763–772.

Tobias Schnabel, Igor Labutov, David Mimno, and Thorsten Joachims. 2015. Evaluation methods for unsupervised word embeddings. In *Proceedings of the 2015 Conference on Empirical Methods in Natural Language Processing*, pages 298–307, Lisbon, Portugal. Association for Computational Linguistics.

Nitish Srivastava, Geoffrey Hinton, Alex Krizhevsky, Ilya Sutskever, and Ruslan Salakhutdinov. 2014. Dropout: a simple way to prevent neural networks from overfitting. *The Journal of Machine Learning Research*, 15(1):1929–1958.

Duyu Tang, Bing Qin, and Ting Liu. 2015. Learning semantic representations of users and products for document level sentiment classification. In *Proceedings of the 53rd Annual Meeting of the Association for Computational Linguistics and the 7th International Joint Conference on Natural Language Processing (Volume 1: Long Papers)*, pages 1014–1023.

Svitlana Volkova, Yoram Bachrach, Michael Armstrong, and Vijay Sharma. 2015. Inferring Latent User Properties from Texts Published in Social Media. In *AAAI Conference on Artificial Intelligence (AAAI)*, Austin, TX.

Svitlana Volkova, Theresa Wilson, and David Yarowsky. 2013. Exploring demographic language variations to improve multilingual sentiment analysis in social media. In *EMNLP 2013 - 2013 Conference on Empirical Methods in Natural Language Processing, Proceedings of the Conference*, pages 1815–1827, Seattle, Washington, USA. Association for Computational Linguistics.

Jingjing Wang, Shoushan Li, Mingqi Jiang, Hanqian Wu, and Guodong Zhou. 2018. Cross-media user profiling with joint textual and social user embedding. In *Proceedings of the 27th International Conference on Computational Linguistics*, pages 1410–1420, Santa Fe, New Mexico, USA. Association for Computational Linguistics.

Thomas Wolf, Lysandre Debut, Victor Sanh, Julien Chaumond, Clement Delangue, Anthony Moi, Pierric Cistac, Tim Rault, R'emi Louf, Morgan Funtowicz, and Jamie Brew. 2019. Huggingface's transformers: State-of-the-art natural language processing. *ArXiv*, abs/1910.03771.

Zach Wood-Doughty, Michael Smith, David Broniatowski, and Mark Dredze. 2017. How does Twitter user behavior vary across demographic groups? In *Proceedings of the Second Workshop on NLP and Computational Social Science*, pages 83–89.

Zach Wood-Doughty, Paiheng Xu, Xiao Liu, and Mark Dredze. 2020. Using noisy self-reports to predict twitter user demographics. *arXiv preprint arXiv:2005.00635*.

Fangzhao Wu and Yongfeng Huang. 2016. Personalized microblog sentiment classification via multitask learning. In *Proceedings of the Thirtieth AAAI Conference on Artificial Intelligence*, AAAI'16, page 3059–3065. AAAI Press.

Zhen Wu, Xin-Yu Dai, Cunyan Yin, Shujian Huang, and Jiajun Chen. 2018. Improving review representations with user attention and product attention for sentiment classification. *arXiv preprint arXiv:1801.07861*.

Linzi Xing and Michael J. Paul. 2017. Incorporating metadata into content-based user embeddings. In *Proceedings of the 3rd Workshop on Noisy User-generated Text*, pages 45–49.

Yi Yang and Jacob Eisenstein. 2017. Overcoming language variation in sentiment analysis with social attention. *Transactions of the Association for Computational Linguistics*, 5:295–307.

Yelp. 2018. Yelp Dataset Challenge.

Zhigang Yuan, Fangzhao Wu, Junxin Liu, Chuhan Wu, Yongfeng Huang, and Xing Xie. 2019. Neural review rating prediction with user and product memory. In *Proceedings of the 28th ACM International Conference on Information and Knowledge Management*, CIKM '19, page 2341–2344, New York, NY, USA.

Xingshan Zeng, Jing Li, Lu Wang, and Kam-Fai Wong. 2019. Joint effects of context and user history for predicting online conversation re-entries. In *Proceedings of the ACL*, pages 2809–2818.

Lei Zhang, Xiaolei Huang, Tianli Liu, Ang Li, Zhenxiang Chen, and Tingshao Zhu. 2015. Using linguistic features to estimate suicide probability of chinese microblog users. In *Human Centered Computing*, pages 549–559, Cham. Springer International Publishing.

Wanru Zhang, Andrew Caines, Dimitrios Alikaniotis, and Paula Buttery. 2016. Predicting author age from Weibo microblog posts. In *Proceedings of the 10th International Conference on Language Resources and Evaluation, LREC 2016*, pages 2990–2997.

On the Effectiveness of Dataset Embeddings in Mono-lingual, Multi-lingual and Zero-shot Conditions

Rob van der Goot*
IT University of Copenhagen
robv@itu.dk

Ahmet Üstün*
University of Groningen
a.ustun@rug.nl

Barbara Plank
IT University of Copenhagen
bapl@itu.dk

Abstract

Recent complementary strands of research have shown that leveraging information on the data source through encoding their properties into embeddings can lead to performance increase when training a single model on heterogeneous data sources. However, it remains unclear in which situations these *dataset embeddings* are most effective, because they are used in a large variety of settings, languages and tasks. Furthermore, it is usually assumed that gold information on the data source is available, and that the test data is from a distribution seen during training. In this work, we compare the effect of dataset embeddings in mono-lingual settings, multi-lingual settings, and with predicted data source label in a zero-shot setting. We evaluate on three morphosyntactic tasks: morphological tagging, lemmatization, and dependency parsing, and use 104 datasets, 66 languages, and two different dataset grouping strategies. Performance increases are highest when the datasets are of the same language, and we know from which distribution the test-instance is drawn. In contrast, for setups where the data is from an unseen distribution, performance increase vanishes.[1]

1 Introduction

The performance of natural language processing systems is dependent on the amount of training data, which is often scarce. To complement existing training data, supplementary data sources can be used. Especially data annotated for the same task from other sources can be beneficial to exploit. However, because of heterogeneity in language or domain this might lead to sub-optimal performance. In early work on combining training sources, data was selected at training time (Plank and van Noord, 2011; Khan et al., 2013) for a given test set. A more nuanced way to exploit heterogeneous data is to encode properties of the language as features (Naseem et al., 2012).

Recently, Ammar et al. (2016) showed that encoding the language of an instance as an embedding in a neural model is beneficial for multi-lingual learning.[2] Follow-up work found that multiple datasets within the same language can also be combined by encoding their origin (Stymne et al., 2018; Üstün et al., 2019), thereby implicitly learning useful commonalities, while still encoding dataset-specific knowledge. These *dataset embeddings* are employed in groups of datasets which usually range in size from 2 to 10 datasets. However, it remains unclear in which situations these dataset embeddings thrive best.

Furthermore, two often overseen issues with dataset embeddings are that they are commonly learned from the *gold* data-source labels attached to each training and test instance and it is assumed that the test data is from a distribution which is seen during training. In many real world situations these assumptions are clearly violated. A common strategy when the test data is drawn from a different distribution as the training datasets (zero-shot), is to use a manually assigned proxy treebank (Smith et al., 2018; Barry et al., 2019; Meechan-Maddon and Nivre, 2019). Recent work showed that for unseen datasets in mono-lingual setups (Wagner et al., 2020), interpolated dataset embeddings can be used to improve performance for zero-shot settings. We use automatically predicted proxy data sources instead, and focus on mono-linugal as well as cross-lingual setups.

In this paper, we provide an extensive evaluation of the usefulness of dataset embeddings in existing

* Equal contributions

[1]source code is available at: https://bitbucket.org/robvanderg/dataembs/src

[2]More recently, (Conneau and Lample, 2019) showed that embedding the language can also be beneficial for training contextualized embeddings with masked language modeling.

Proceedings of the Second Workshop on Domain Adaptation for NLP, pages 183–194
April 20, 2021.

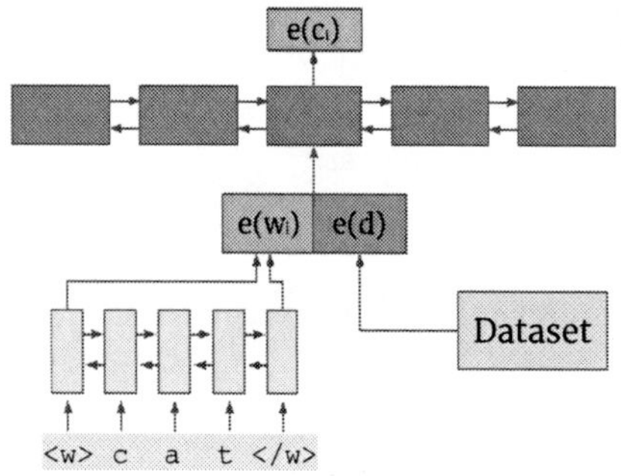

Figure 1: Overview of the model where a BiLSTM encodes the word "cat" in a sentence. Dataset embeddings (blue) are concatenated with the character-based word representation (green) which feeds into the contextual encoder (red).

setups and beyond. More concretely, we ask: 1) What are good indicators to predict the usefulness of dataset embeddings? 2) Can we effectively use dataset embeddings in the absence of gold data-source information?

2 Dataset Embeddings

Dataset embeddings enable conditioning of inputs on some property of the data when training on multiple sources. They are vector representations learned during model training, with the aim to capture distinctive properties of the sources into a continuous vector, without losing their heterogeneous characteristics. Given D data sources, technically, we learn a vector representation $e(d)$ for each data source $d \in D$ while training a single model from a group of sources. Every input instance marked with its dataset source d. For each word w_i with $i = 0, ..., n$, the word embedding $e(w_i)$ is concatenated with the dataset embedding $e(d)$, and both are updated during training. Figure 1 shows the overall architecture of the model which employs a contextual encoder that uses the resulting embedding as input and outputs $e(c_i)$ to be used for prediction.

2.1 Experimental Setup

In this work, we copy the exact setups from the UUParser 2.3 (Smith et al., 2018) and the Multi-Team tagger (Üstün et al., 2019) because they were high ranking systems in two recent shared tasks (Zeman et al., 2018; McCarthy et al., 2019) and they both showed large gains by using dataset embeddings. The UUParser is an Arc-Hybrid (Kuhlmann et al., 2011) BiLSTM (Graves and Schmidhuber, 2005) dependency parser, which exploits a dynamic oracle (Goldberg and Nivre, 2013) and supports non-projective parsing through the use of a swap action (de Lhoneux et al., 2017). The Multi-Team tagger performs morphological tagging (Kirov et al., 2018) and lemmatization jointly; to this end, they use a shared BiLSTM encoder and feed the output of the tagging as input for the lemmatization, which is predicted as a sequence of characters. For efficiency reasons and simplicity, we disabled the use of external embeddings[3] as well as POS embeddings for the UUParser.

It should be noted that besides the differences in the models and tasks, the setups also differ among several aspects; the version of UD data (2.3, 2.2) (Nivre et al., 2020), type of dataset splitting used (Multi-Team always has train-dev-test), and most interestingly, the dataset grouping strategies. Smith et al. (2018) manually designed dataset groups based on typological information, language-relatedness and empirical evidence; Üstün et al. (2019) instead propose pairs: every dataset is matched with one other dataset based on word overlap. For both of the models, we copy the exact language grouping as in the original papers[4]. For comparison of different grouping strategies, we refer to Lin et al. (2019).

2.2 Data Source Prediction

In this work, we predict data source on the sentence level, because it matches the language switches at test-time and it improves the accuracy of the classification.[5] We use a linear support vector classifier based on word and character n-grams (without tokenization). We use this approach here because of simplicity, efficiency and they have shown to reach competitive performance for text classification tasks (Zampieri et al., 2017; Medvedeva et al., 2017; Çöltekin and Rama, 2018; Basile et al., 2018). We performed a grid search with $n \in [1-7]$ and all sequential combinations (1-2, 1-3, etc.) for n-grams. For this hyper-parameter tuning, we used the eight datasets from Üstün et al. (2019), and found the most robust parameters to be 1-2 for words and 1-5 for characters. The obtained macro

[3] Üstün et al. (2019) showed that performance gains from external embeddings are highly complementary to performance gains from dataset embeddings.

[4] The full groups can be seen in Appendix C and D.

[5] However, Bhat et al. (2017) and Ravishankar (2018) have shown the usefulness of word-level language labels for processing code-switched data.

Filtering	#src	Morphological Tagging (F1) base	concat	gold	pred	Lemmatization (Accuracy) base	concat	gold	pred	#src	Dependency Parsing (LAS) base	concat	gold	pred
All	104	92.04	91.43	92.75	91.85	91.10	91.02	92.55	91.41	58	72.92	74.07	75.53	74.52
Single-lang	59	94.14	93.94	95.84	94.13	93.66	93.83	95.73	93.84	10	80.48	79.84	82.74	80.29
Multi-lang	45	89.30	88.14	88.69	88.88	87.75	87.33	88.38	88.22	48	71.35	72.87	74.03	73.32

Table 1: Results per task: overall average, and monolingual vs cross-lingual aggregates. #SRC: number of datasets sources; BASE: single dataset baseline, CONCAT: concatenation of datasets in group, GOLD: gold dataset ids, PRED: predicted dataset ids. The intensity of colors indicate the difference to the baseline performance.

average F1 on all data pairs from Üstün et al. (2019) is 95.42, and on all data groups from Smith et al. (2018) is 91.76. The performance difference can be explained by the number of datasets per group, which in the former setup is always two. To match the setup during testing, we obtain predicted dataset identifiers for the training data with 5-fold jack-knifing, and use these during training.

3 Results

We report results for all tasks in two main settings: *in-dataset*, for setups where we assume that input data is from a distribution present during training (3.1); and *zero-shot*, (3.2), a setup where this is not the case. For all reported experiments, we use Labeled Attachment Score (LAS) for parsing (Zeman et al., 2018), F1 score for morphological tagging, and accuracy for lemmatization. We do not perform any tuning, and thus only report results on development data (if no dev-split is available we use test). As a control, we compare dataset embeddings to a simple CONCAT, training on concatenation of all the data sources from a dataset group without dataset embeddings. Reported results are average over 3 runs for the UUparser, for the Multi-Team tagger we did only a single run because of the computational costs (see Appendix for more details).

3.1 In-dataset Evaluation

The average results over all datasets are shown in Table 1, as well as the results for mono-lingual and multi-lingual dataset groups (the full results can be found in the appendix). These are the takeaways:

Gold Overall, gold dataset embeddings provide substantial gains (Table 1: all). They outperform both BASE and CONCAT on all 3 tasks, which confirms previous findings (Smith et al., 2018; Üstün et al., 2019). Gains are largest for dependency parsing, followed by lemmatization and finally morphological tagging, where the increase is only 0.71.

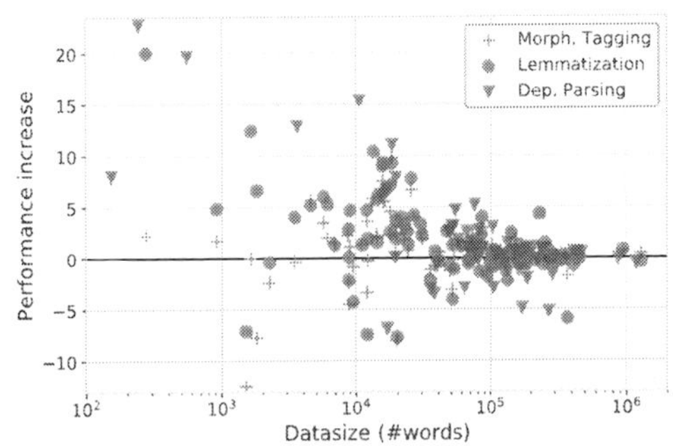

Figure 2: Absolute improvement in performance between BASE and GOLD in relation to data size (in number of words in the BASE training data) in log scale. Performance difference is absolute, and measured in the default metric for each task.

Dataset group composition Comparing the mono-lingual dataset groups with the multi-lingual groups, we can see that gold dataset embeddings improve results in both settings for 2/3 tasks. The only setup where gold dataset embeddings are not beneficial is for morphological tagging in multi-lingual groups, where the gains for lemmatization are also only marginal (+0.63 abs. compared to base). This may be attributed to the nature of the tasks, morphological tagging and lemmatization are more language-specific, making it difficult to transfer relevant information from another language. In Figure 2, we plot the performance increase from BASE to using gold dataset ID's in relation to its dataset size. Unsurprisingly, the largest gains are obtained in smaller datasets (<50,000 words) for all tasks. However, especially for the morphological tasks, the largest drops are also observed in this range, and mainly happen for low-resource languages which are paired with a distant language (e.g. Akkadian (akk_pisandub) and Irish (ga_idt)).

Gold vs Predicted The PRED columns in Table 1 shows that dataset embeddings are only beneficial

	#src	concat	pred
All	53	53.80	**53.87**
∃ same-lang	35	66.35	**66.62**
∄ same-lang	18	**29.39**	29.06

Table 2: LAS scores for zero-shot experiments.

			In-dataset training				zero-shot	
dataset	size	svm	base	concat	gold	pred	concat	pred
nl_alp	186k	0.96	84.10	84.41	**84.97**	84.74	72.03	**73.69**
af_afri	34k	1.00	79.57	78.95	79.98	**80.44**	**35.86**	34.84
nl_lassy	75k	0.88	76.76	81.59	**81.89**	81.52	74.70	**75.48**
de_gsd	268k	1.00	**79.76**	78.96	79.39	79.35	14.30	**15.09**
en_pud	0	0.00	-	-	-	-	**81.90**	81.89
en_ewt	205k	0.91	82.43	82.60	**83.42**	82.82	71.11	**71.23**
en_lines	50k	0.77	76.15	75.06	**79.20**	77.14	**74.71**	74.68
en_gum	54k	0.71	78.18	80.32	**82.77**	80.58	**80.12**	79.98

Table 3: Full results for the AF-DE-NL and EN dataset group (LAS). SIZE refers to training size in number of words. SVM accuracy of SVM language predictions.

(i.e. outperforming BASE) for lemmatization and dependency parsing when we do not have access to the gold dataset ids but use predicted ids instead. For lemmatization, the average increase compared to BASE is only 0.31 Acc., whereas for dependency parsing, it is +1.60 LAS. PRED is mostly beneficial in multi-lingual dataset groups, which is probably because the performance of the dataset classifier (Section 2.2) is higher in these cases.

3.2 Zero-shot evaluation

In many real-world situations, the basic assumption that data instances originate from the training data distribution is violated, and it becomes essential to find a good way of using data from other sources, like finding the best proxy source. To test whether dataset embeddings are still useful in a zero-shot setup, we perform experiments where we hold out the target dataset during training and then classify all development sentences into the other sets. We run this experiment only for dataset groups containing more than 2 datasets (11 groups and 53 datasets, for dependency parsing). As baseline we compare to a model trained on the concatenation of all other datasets from the group. This zero-shot setup is challenging. Results are expected to be overall lower.

Detailed results are reported in Appendix C–Table 2 summarizes the main results.[6] We aggregate over datasets for which another in-language dataset is available within its dataset group ("∃ same-lang"), and those where this is not the case. Overall, the performance increase has almost vanished, having only an 0.07 absolute increase in LAS ('all'). This increase is void in cases no in-language data exists in the group. Only for datasets for which a same language dataset exists (∃ same-lang, that is, a treebank exists for the language but it comes from another distribution/domain), slight improvements are obtained. We conclude that dataset embeddings are not useful in setups when the test instances are from another distribution.

For demonstration purposes, we highlight the full results of two dataset groups in Table 3. The first (multi-lingual) group shows that dataset-embeddings are mainly beneficial for languages with multiple datasets, both in the in-domain and zero-shot setting. In this particular dataset group, prediction of the embeddings performs on-par with the gold labels, probably because of the high performance of the classifier. In contrast, in the second (mono-lingual) group, the classifier scores lower, and PRED prediction performances are lower compared to GOLD. For this group, predicted dataset embeddings are outperformed by a simple dataset concatenation.

4 Conclusion

We provide an extensive evaluation of dataset embeddings in two large-scale settings where they were used successfully (Smith et al., 2018; Üstün et al., 2019). In setups where in-distribution training data is available, we found dataset embeddings more useful in monolingual dataset groups, compared to cross-lingual ones. In general, performance gains were the largest for 1) datasets for which another same-language datasets was available during training 2) small datasets 3) datasets which were part of a large dataset group. However, with predicted id's, their benefit is limited, contrary to gold information. When moving to zero-shot setups, the performance increases become negligible (except for some particular datasets). In particular, without in-source training data, dataset embeddings work in some cases when another treebank for the language exists; but this gain is not consistent and often small. Overall, we find dataset embeddings fail to be a viable adaptation method when no in-source data is available. Hence, in many realistic out-of-distribution setups, their benefit vanishes.

[6] Note that BASE and GOLD are not reported here, because no data from the target dataset is included in this experiments.

Acknowledgements

We would like to thank Gertjan van Noord for feedback on an earlier version of this paper. We thank NVIDIA, the HPC cluster at the ITU and the University of Groningen for computing resources. This research was supported by an Amazon Research Award, an STSM in the Multi3Generation COST action (CA18231), and grant 9063-00077B (Danmarks Frie Forskningsfond).

References

Waleed Ammar, George Mulcaire, Miguel Ballesteros, Chris Dyer, and Noah A. Smith. 2016. Many languages, one parser. *Transactions of the Association for Computational Linguistics*, 4:431–444.

James Barry, Joachim Wagner, and Jennifer Foster. 2019. Cross-lingual parsing with polyglot training and multi-treebank learning: A Faroese case study. In *Proceedings of the 2nd Workshop on Deep Learning Approaches for Low-Resource NLP (DeepLo 2019)*, pages 163–174, Hong Kong, China. Association for Computational Linguistics.

Angelo Basile, Gareth Dwyer, Maria Medvedeva, Josine Rawee, Hessel Haagsma, and Malvina Nissim. 2018. Simply the best: Minimalist system trumps complex models in author profiling. In *Experimental IR Meets Multilinguality, Multimodality, and Interaction*, pages 143–156, Cham. Springer International Publishing.

Irshad Bhat, Riyaz A. Bhat, Manish Shrivastava, and Dipti Sharma. 2017. Joining hands: Exploiting monolingual treebanks for parsing of code-mixing data. In *Proceedings of the 15th Conference of the European Chapter of the Association for Computational Linguistics: Volume 2, Short Papers*, pages 324–330, Valencia, Spain. Association for Computational Linguistics.

Çağrı Çöltekin and Taraka Rama. 2018. Tübingen-Oslo at SemEval-2018 task 2: SVMs perform better than RNNs in emoji prediction. In *Proceedings of The 12th International Workshop on Semantic Evaluation*, pages 34–38, New Orleans, Louisiana. Association for Computational Linguistics.

Alexis Conneau and Guillaume Lample. 2019. Cross-lingual language model pretraining. In *Advances in Neural Information Processing Systems*, pages 7059–7069.

Yoav Goldberg and Joakim Nivre. 2013. Training deterministic parsers with non-deterministic oracles. *Transactions of the Association for Computational Linguistics*, 1:403–414.

Alex Graves and Jürgen Schmidhuber. 2005. Framewise phoneme classification with bidirectional lstm and other neural network architectures. *Neural networks*, 18(5-6):602–610.

Mohammad Khan, Markus Dickinson, and Sandra Kübler. 2013. Towards domain adaptation for parsing web data. In *Proceedings of the International Conference Recent Advances in Natural Language Processing RANLP 2013*, pages 357–364, Hissar, Bulgaria. INCOMA Ltd. Shoumen, BULGARIA.

Christo Kirov, Ryan Cotterell, John Sylak-Glassman, Géraldine Walther, Ekaterina Vylomova, Patrick Xia, Manaal Faruqui, Sabrina J. Mielke, Arya McCarthy, Sandra Kübler, David Yarowsky, Jason Eisner, and Mans Hulden. 2018. UniMorph 2.0: Universal Morphology. In *Proceedings of the Eleventh International Conference on Language Resources and Evaluation (LREC 2018)*, Miyazaki, Japan. European Language Resources Association (ELRA).

Marco Kuhlmann, Carlos Gómez-Rodríguez, and Giorgio Satta. 2011. Dynamic programming algorithms for transition-based dependency parsers. In *Proceedings of the 49th Annual Meeting of the Association for Computational Linguistics: Human Language Technologies*, pages 673–682, Portland, Oregon, USA. Association for Computational Linguistics.

Miryam de Lhoneux, Sara Stymne, and Joakim Nivre. 2017. Arc-hybrid non-projective dependency parsing with a static-dynamic oracle. In *Proceedings of the 15th International Conference on Parsing Technologies*, pages 99–104, Pisa, Italy. Association for Computational Linguistics.

Yu-Hsiang Lin, Chian-Yu Chen, Jean Lee, Zirui Li, Yuyan Zhang, Mengzhou Xia, Shruti Rijhwani, Junxian He, Zhisong Zhang, Xuezhe Ma, Antonios Anastasopoulos, Patrick Littell, and Graham Neubig. 2019. Choosing transfer languages for cross-lingual learning. In *Proceedings of the 57th Annual Meeting of the Association for Computational Linguistics*, pages 3125–3135, Florence, Italy. Association for Computational Linguistics.

Arya D. McCarthy, Ekaterina Vylomova, Shijie Wu, Chaitanya Malaviya, Lawrence Wolf-Sonkin, Garrett Nicolai, Christo Kirov, Miikka Silfverberg, Sebastian J. Mielke, Jeffrey Heinz, Ryan Cotterell, and Mans Hulden. 2019. The SIGMORPHON 2019 shared task: Morphological analysis in context and cross-lingual transfer for inflection. In *Proceedings of the 16th Workshop on Computational Research in Phonetics, Phonology, and Morphology*, pages 229–244, Florence, Italy. Association for Computational Linguistics.

Maria Medvedeva, Martin Kroon, and Barbara Plank. 2017. When sparse traditional models outperform dense neural networks: the curious case of discriminating between similar languages. In *Proceedings of the Fourth Workshop on NLP for Similar Languages, Varieties and Dialects (VarDial)*, pages 156–163, Valencia, Spain. Association for Computational Linguistics.

Ailsa Meechan-Maddon and Joakim Nivre. 2019. How to parse low-resource languages: Cross-lingual parsing, target language annotation, or both? In *Proceedings of the Fifth International Conference on Dependency Linguistics (Depling, SyntaxFest 2019)*, pages 112–120, Paris, France. Association for Computational Linguistics.

Tahira Naseem, Regina Barzilay, and Amir Globerson. 2012. Selective sharing for multilingual dependency parsing. In *Proceedings of the 50th Annual Meeting of the Association for Computational Linguistics (Volume 1: Long Papers)*, pages 629–637, Jeju Island, Korea. Association for Computational Linguistics.

Joakim Nivre, Marie-Catherine de Marneffe, Filip Ginter, Jan Hajic, Christopher D. Manning, Sampo Pyysalo, Sebastian Schuster, Francis Tyers, and Daniel Zeman. 2020. Universal dependencies v2: An evergrowing multilingual treebank collection. In *Proceedings of The 12th Language Resources and Evaluation Conference*, pages 4034–4043, Marseille, France. European Language Resources Association.

Karl Pearson. 1901. LIII. on lines and planes of closest fit to systems of points in space. *The London, Edinburgh, and Dublin Philosophical Magazine and Journal of Science*, 2(11):559–572.

F. Pedregosa, G. Varoquaux, A. Gramfort, V. Michel, B. Thirion, O. Grisel, M. Blondel, P. Prettenhofer, R. Weiss, V. Dubourg, J. Vanderplas, A. Passos, D. Cournapeau, M. Brucher, M. Perrot, and E. Duchesnay. 2011. Scikit-learn: Machine learning in Python. *Journal of Machine Learning Research*, 12:2825–2830.

Barbara Plank and Gertjan van Noord. 2011. Effective measures of domain similarity for parsing. In *Proceedings of the 49th Annual Meeting of the Association for Computational Linguistics: Human Language Technologies*, pages 1566–1576, Portland, Oregon, USA. Association for Computational Linguistics.

Vinit Ravishankar. 2018. Parsing of texts with codeswitching. Master's thesis, Institute of Formal and Applied Linguisti, Prague.

Aaron Smith, Bernd Bohnet, Miryam de Lhoneux, Joakim Nivre, Yan Shao, and Sara Stymne. 2018. 82 treebanks, 34 models: Universal dependency parsing with multi-treebank models. In *Proceedings of the CoNLL 2018 Shared Task: Multilingual Parsing from Raw Text to Universal Dependencies*, pages 113–123, Brussels, Belgium. Association for Computational Linguistics.

Sara Stymne, Miryam de Lhoneux, Aaron Smith, and Joakim Nivre. 2018. Parser training with heterogeneous treebanks. In *Proceedings of the 56th Annual Meeting of the Association for Computational Linguistics (Volume 2: Short Papers)*, pages 619–625, Melbourne, Australia. Association for Computational Linguistics.

Ahmet Üstün, Rob van der Goot, Gosse Bouma, and Gertjan van Noord. 2019. Multi-team: A multi-attention, multi-decoder approach to morphological analysis. In *Proceedings of the 16th Workshop on Computational Research in Phonetics, Phonology, and Morphology*, pages 35–49, Florence, Italy. Association for Computational Linguistics.

Joachim Wagner, James Barry, and Jennifer Foster. 2020. Treebank embedding vectors for out-of-domain dependency parsing. In *Proceedings of the 58th Annual Meeting of the Association for Computational Linguistics*, pages 8812–8818, Online. Association for Computational Linguistics.

Marcos Zampieri, Shervin Malmasi, Nikola Ljubešić, Preslav Nakov, Ahmed Ali, Jörg Tiedemann, Yves Scherrer, and Noëmi Aepli. 2017. Findings of the VarDial evaluation campaign 2017. In *Proceedings of the Fourth Workshop on NLP for Similar Languages, Varieties and Dialects (VarDial)*, pages 1–15, Valencia, Spain. Association for Computational Linguistics.

Daniel Zeman, Jan Hajič, Martin Popel, Martin Potthast, Milan Straka, Filip Ginter, Joakim Nivre, and Slav Petrov. 2018. CoNLL 2018 shared task: Multilingual parsing from raw text to universal dependencies. In *Proceedings of the CoNLL 2018 Shared Task: Multilingual Parsing from Raw Text to Universal Dependencies*, pages 1–21, Brussels, Belgium. Association for Computational Linguistics.

A Reproducability report

The UUParser was run on two E5-2660 v3's (40 threads total, we used only 30), and took on average approximately 20 hours on a single thread per model. For three random seeds, 16 dataset groups, and approximately 5 settings (4 from Section 3.1 +1 from Section 3.2 were we only used half of the groups in two settings), the total number of models is 240. So the total computation walltime was 160 hours (approximately a week).

The Multi-Team tagger was run on two Tesla V100's (one model per V100, so two models were trained in parallel). On average this took approximately 3 hours. For this setup we had 104 dataset pairs, of which 82 were unique (if the pairs consist of the same two languages, we only trained one model). For the Multi-Team tagger, we ran four setups (Section 3.1), totaling to 328 models. The total computation time was 984 hours, which divided by 2 gpus resulted in a walltime of 492 hours (approximately three weeks).

Regarding the differences in the settings (BASE, CONCAT, GOLD and PRED), there were no clear trends in differences in run-time, even the BASE settings (where multiple models where trained for 1 dataset group) was equal in runtime compared to the other settings where one large model was trained.

It should be noted that the UUParser uses a maximum of 15,000 sentences per epoch, and the Multi-Team tagger 500,000 words (default settings), which makes training times substantially shorter (especially for the UUParser), and reduced the memory usage. Excluding external embeddings helped us reduce the running time and memory usage even further. For the UUParser, a maximum of 8GB ram is enough for training a single model (4GB on average), and the Multi-Team tagger requires a minimum of 8GB of GPU RAM.

For all the other settings and hyperparameters, we exactly replicated the original code from the Smith et al. (2018) and Üstün et al. (2019), and thus refer to their papers for experimental details. The only adaptation we made to the systems is that for the UUParser we added support for supplying the dataset information in the connlu misc-column (the adapted version is available in our repo).

B Aggregates over all results

For easier analysis, we provide average scores over aggregates of datasets. To this end, we propose to use data-filters, and report average scores over specific subsets of the data. The results are shown in Table 4. The filters show aggregates over a) whether the training portion of the dataset is small ($<$ 30,000 words) or large b) whether the dataset group to which this dataset belongs is mono-lingual or multi-lingual c) whether another dataset with the same language is available in the dataset group d) whether the svm classifier predicts the datasource id's with an accuracy of $>$95% accuracy e) whether the word overlap is larger then 10%.

C Full results for dependency parsing

Table 5 shows the results of the UUParser (Smith et al., 2018) for each dataset, grouped by dataset groups. All results are the average over three runs. We do not report scores for datasets without in-source training data in the 'parser setting' columns (which corresponds to Section 3.1 of the paper), as training data is necessary for those settings.

For the 'without train' columns (corresponding to Section 3.2 of the paper), we do not include results for dataset groups of size two; this is because we leave one training set out, and try to predict for the corresponding development set in which set it belongs. For groups of size two, this classification is trivial and non-informative, as there is only one dataset left. The left-out datasets are not taken into account for the averages. The reported results are on development splits, except for datasets which did not have a development split available, there we used test (indicated with * in the table) as we do not perform any tuning.

D Full results for morphological tagging and lemmatization

Table 6 shows the results of the Multi-Team tagger (Üstün et al., 2019) on the development data for each dataset. Because of the computational costs, results are over a single run. The second column shows the 'help-dataset' that each dataset is paired with, based on word overlap.

Note that data sizes are different compared to Table 5 due to a re-split of the data by (McCarthy et al., 2019), and different UD versions (Üstün et al. (2019) used 2.3 whereas Smith et al. (2018) used 2.2). Another effect of this re-split is that for all datasets, a train, development and test split is available. Also note that dataset prediction (SVM) scores reported are on the train data; so if the score is 1.00, PRED and GOLD can still have different scores be-

	Language Pairs				Morphological Tagging (F1)				Lemmatization (Accuracy)				Language Clusters			Dependency Parsing (LAS)			
Filtering	#sets	size	WO	svm	base	concat	gold	pred	base	concat	gold	pred	#sets	size	svm	base	concat	gold	pred
All	104	121	0.31	0.95	92.04	91.43	92.75	91.85	91.10	91.02	92.55	91.41	58	161	0.91	72.92	74.07	75.53	74.52
Large	65	186	0.28	0.94	95.40	94.78	95.72	94.98	95.92	95.08	96.00	95.19	46	200	0.92	80.80	79.62	80.98	80.06
Small	39	13	0.35	0.98	86.46	85.85	87.78	86.65	83.07	84.24	86.79	85.11	12	10	0.88	42.75	52.79	54.65	53.30
Multi-lang	45	77	0.13	0.99	89.30	88.14	88.69	88.88	87.75	87.33	88.38	88.22	48	163	0.92	71.35	72.87	74.03	73.32
Single-lang	59	154	0.44	0.92	94.14	93.94	95.84	94.13	93.66	93.83	95.73	93.84	10	149	0.86	80.48	79.84	82.74	80.29
∃ same-lang	59	154	0.44	0.92	94.14	93.94	95.84	94.13	93.66	93.83	95.73	93.84	35	187	0.86	77.32	77.33	79.29	77.76
∄ same-lang	45	77	0.13	0.99	89.30	88.14	88.69	88.88	87.75	87.33	88.38	88.22	23	121	0.98	66.23	69.11	69.80	69.60
pred<95%	33	177	0.41	0.87	95.15	94.05	96.45	94.24	94.57	94.12	95.77	94.24	24	134	0.79	73.60	75.43	78.23	76.00
pred>95%	71	95	0.26	0.99	90.60	90.21	91.02	90.75	89.49	89.57	91.05	90.10	34	179	0.99	72.45	73.11	73.62	73.48
highWO	78	139	0.39	0.94	93.22	92.98	94.69	93.36	92.82	93.11	94.94	93.38	58	161	0.91	72.92	74.07	75.53	74.52
lowWO	26	67	0.05	1.00	88.51	86.79	86.91	87.34	85.94	84.72	85.38	85.49							

Table 4: Results per tasks, with averages over different dataset filters. #SETS: number of datasets, SIZE: training data size of dataset (in 1,000 words), SVM: F1 score of dataset classifier, BASE: single dataset baseline, CONCAT: concatenation of datasets in cluster, GOLD: gold dataset ids, PRED: predicted dataset ids.

cause the dataset prediction was not equally accurate on the development data.

E PCA-analysis of gold versus predicted treebank embeddings

To gain deeper insights in what is represented in treebank embeddings, we plotted the eight largest dataset groups of the UUParser setup into a PCA space (Pearson, 1901). This is done with the default sklearn settings (Pedregosa et al., 2011). Results of the gold spaces are shown in Figure 3 and the predicted spaces are plotted in Figure 4. For some groups, there are some clear differences, however for others the plots are highly similar. There seems to be no clear trend in the amount of differences and the performance shifts in Table 5.

				In-dataset training				Zero-shot	
cluster	dataset	size	svm	base	concat	gold	pred	concat	pred
af-de-nl	nl_alpino	186,046	0.96	84.10	84.41	**84.97**	84.74	72.03	**73.69**
	af_afribooms	33,894	1.00	79.57	78.95	79.98	**80.44**	**35.86**	34.84
	nl_lassysmall	75,134	0.88	76.76	81.59	**81.89**	81.52	74.70	**75.48**
	de_gsd	268,414	1.00	**79.76**	78.96	79.39	79.35	14.30	**15.09**
e-sla	uk_iu	75,098	0.99	79.86	79.49	**80.63**	80.53	35.69	**35.99**
	ru_taiga	10,479	0.35	56.47	69.32	**71.73**	69.30	**68.81**	**68.81**
	ru_syntagrus	871,521	0.99	**87.26**	87.07	87.13	87.24	**59.52**	59.34
en	en_pud	0	0.00	-	-	-	-	**81.90**	81.89
	en_ewt	204,607	0.91	82.43	82.60	**83.42**	82.82	71.11	**71.23**
	en_lines	50,096	0.77	76.15	75.06	**79.20**	77.14	**74.71**	74.68
	en_gum	53,686	0.71	78.18	80.32	**82.77**	80.58	**80.12**	79.98
es-ca	ca_ancora	418,494	1.00	87.97	88.41	**88.55**	88.51	-	-
	es_ancora	446,145	1.00	87.44	87.74	87.97	**88.07**	-	-
finno	et_edt	287,859	1.00	**79.48**	77.47	77.79	77.66	**14.38**	14.32
	fi_tdt	162,827	0.77	**79.48**	71.43	78.27	70.45	47.21	**47.44**
	fi_ftb	127,845	0.69	**79.58**	70.48	79.05	70.88	51.46	**52.16**
	sme_giella	16,835	1.00	**63.17**	53.08	56.23	55.32	**6.58**	6.45
	fi_pud	0	0.00	-	-	-	-	74.58	**74.94**
fr	fr_spoken	14,952	0.93	71.39	76.15	**77.48**	76.72	**53.50**	53.35
	fr_gsd	366,372	0.96	88.23	88.09	**88.43**	88.30	75.65	**76.36**
	fr_sequoia	51,906	0.69	85.72	85.35	**88.75**	87.13	80.62	**80.78**
indic	ur_udtb	108,690	1.00	78.15	78.43	**78.58**	**78.58**	-	-
	hi_hdtb	281,057	1.00	89.20	89.27	**89.38**	**89.38**	-	-
iranian	fa_seraji	122,180	1.00	82.45	82.26	82.41	**82.48**	-	-
	kmr_mg	242	0.99	12.24	34.76	34.96	**35.38**	-	-
it	it_isdt	294,397	0.99	87.71	87.58	87.78	**87.89**	-	-
	it_postwita	103,553	0.98	75.17	77.72	**78.15**	77.83	-	-
ko	ko_gsd	56,687	0.68	76.70	65.62	**78.42**	63.56	-	-
	ko_kaist	296,446	0.95	**83.08**	79.90	83.03	80.93	-	-
n-ger	no_nynorsklia	3,583	0.90	50.05	62.27	62.87	**62.91**	52.89	**53.27**
	fo_oft	0	0.00	-	-	-	-	39.57	**40.87**
	sv_talbanken	66,673	0.94	77.37	76.35	**78.37**	77.57	70.49	**71.97**
	no_bokmaal	243,887	0.97	87.21	87.67	**87.97**	87.76	**76.79**	76.12
	sv_pud	0	0.00	-	-	-	-	**77.89**	77.65
	sv_lines	48,325	0.91	76.48	77.71	**78.95**	78.37	71.66	**72.18**
	no_nynorsk	245,330	0.98	85.67	85.49	**86.27**	85.93	73.50	**74.36**
	da_ddt	80,378	0.97	**76.97**	73.79	76.84	76.06	52.04	**52.27**
old	cu_proiel	37,432	1.00	**76.62**	73.91	73.12	74.22	**5.36**	4.95
	got_proiel	35,024	1.00	**71.46**	69.02	68.29	69.06	**8.53**	8.25
	grc_proiel	187,049	1.00	**76.09**	74.32	74.03	74.35	**53.90**	53.51
	la_perseus	18,184	0.88	42.55	50.45	**53.51**	52.61	**42.61**	41.12
	la_proiel	171,928	0.99	**71.18**	67.03	66.22	66.94	42.68	**43.68**
	grc_perseus	159,895	1.00	**61.78**	61.46	61.46	61.36	46.42	**47.87**
	la_ittb	270,403	1.00	**79.40**	74.29	74.14	74.69	**41.66**	40.61
pt-gl	gl_ctg	86,676	0.95	80.21	79.85	**81.11**	80.56	63.78	**64.19**
	pt_bosque	222,069	1.00	**87.68**	87.11	87.54	87.59	49.85	**50.26**
	gl_treegal	16,707	0.62	69.15	67.24	**75.76**	69.03	61.62	**61.71**
sw-sla	sl_sst	19,473	0.96	58.65	65.65	**66.42**	66.31	**52.06**	51.81
	sr_set	65,764	0.86	83.91	84.07	**86.42**	85.91	75.63	**75.66**
	hr_set	154,055	0.94	80.66	80.22	**81.23**	81.07	65.74	**66.08**
	sl_ssj	112,530	0.99	85.27	84.89	**85.46**	85.23	65.28	**65.83**
turkic	ug_udt	19,262	1.00	61.43	60.86	**61.45**	60.88	1.88	**2.80**
	bxr_bdt	153	0.98	9.95	**17.99**	17.92	17.04	4.85	**5.37**
	tr_imst	39,169	1.00	**57.01**	55.51	56.29	56.63	**9.51**	9.38
	kk_ktb	547	1.00	11.54	30.52	**31.16**	29.14	**7.03**	6.19
w-sla	sk_snk	80,575	0.98	80.39	82.49	**83.07**	82.51	**59.77**	59.57
	cs_pud	0	0.00	-	-	-	-	**83.79**	83.77
	cs_pdt	1,175,374	0.92	**87.92**	87.41	87.40	87.39	79.07	**79.33**
	pl_sz	63,070	0.46	**85.31**	80.88	82.31	81.49	67.40	**67.88**
	hsb_ufal	460	0.90	6.40	45.24	**46.30**	44.99	**39.10**	38.55
	pl_lfg	104,750	0.71	**90.98**	86.51	87.96	87.53	**70.76**	70.49
	cs_fictree	134,059	0.78	85.77	86.92	**87.14**	87.08	**83.75**	82.91
	cs_cac	473,622	0.83	86.86	**87.40**	87.32	**87.40**	**83.73**	83.57

Table 5: LAS scores on all development splits of the dependency parser. *: datasets for which no development data was available, we report results on test data instead. The 'in-dataset setting' results corresponds to Section 3, and 'zero-shot' to Section 3.2, where we assume no in-source training data. SIZE: size of training data in words. SVM: F1 score of svm classifier on dataset prediction. BASE: single dataset baseline. CONCAT: concatenation of datasets. GOLD: gold dataset embeddings. PRED: predicted dataset embeddings.

dataset	additional	size	wo	svm	Morphological Tagging (F1)				Lemmatization (Accuracy)			
					base	concat	gold	pred	base	concat	gold	pred
af_afribooms	nl_alpino	40,390	0.20	99.85	96.50	96.42	**96.96**	96.87	95.25	94.97	96.01	**96.93**
akk_pisandub	cs_pdt	1,505	0.02	100.00	**81.96**	67.99	69.49	71.96	**41.33**	34.67	34.22	35.11
ar_padt	ar_pud	231,625	0.18	96.64	95.29	95.46	**96.17**	95.44	90.79	91.52	**95.08**	91.80
ar_pud	ar_padt	17,645	0.56	96.64	89.97	87.49	**92.24**	87.20	77.36	62.83	**84.39**	57.39
be_hse	ru_syntagrus	6,855	0.08	99.98	80.51	80.61	82.01	**83.49**	78.48	75.67	79.75	**81.58**
bg_btb	ru_syntagrus	133,659	0.12	99.60	**97.85**	96.67	96.89	96.97	**96.95**	94.54	94.70	94.95
bm_crb	cs_pdt	12,025	0.09	99.98	**94.03**	89.49	90.64	89.92	**87.86**	78.40	80.40	80.09
br_keb	no_bokmaal	8,772	0.07	99.87	**90.89**	90.53	88.45	89.67	88.75	**89.77**	88.86	88.35
bxr_bdt	ru_syntagrus	8,770	0.04	99.94	**83.46**	80.65	78.94	79.96	**82.71**	80.65	80.56	81.63
ca_ancora	es_ancora	441,014	0.18	99.71	**98.61**	98.48	98.57	98.56	98.35	98.42	98.56	**98.69**
cs_cac	cs_pdt	414,810	0.57	90.62	**97.19**	96.71	96.98	96.72	**98.03**	97.05	97.27	97.24
cs_cltt	cs_pdt	29,549	0.81	99.87	94.62	96.65	**97.16**	96.62	94.02	**97.56**	97.35	**97.56**
cs_fictree	cs_pdt	143,508	0.58	95.01	95.89	94.89	**96.54**	95.36	95.21	97.07	**97.65**	97.15
cs_pdt	cs_cac	1,278,252	0.27	90.62	96.65	96.78	**97.05**	96.76	**97.50**	97.10	97.12	97.19
cs_pud	cs_pdt	15,614	0.79	98.98	87.38	96.26	94.88	**96.38**	87.03	96.84	96.03	**97.00**
cu_proiel	ru_syntagrus	50,963	0.04	99.98	**94.71**	92.94	91.62	92.12	**95.17**	92.66	91.09	91.28
da_ddt	no_bokmaal	85,373	0.25	97.38	92.58	95.21	**95.52**	95.26	92.27	95.60	**96.25**	95.30
de_gsd	fr_gsd	246,633	0.06	99.94	**93.48**	92.18	93.16	93.05	**96.55**	94.95	95.94	95.60
el_gdt	grc_proiel	52,583	0.04	99.96	**96.51**	96.25	96.36	96.45	95.00	94.52	93.93	**95.15**
en_ewt	en_gum	218,154	0.30	89.27	95.73	**95.75**	95.49	95.32	**97.02**	96.79	96.81	96.46
en_gum	en_ewt	67,381	0.57	89.27	94.45	94.39	**95.11**	94.29	**96.94**	93.94	96.37	94.63
en_lines	en_ewt	70,079	0.56	91.20	95.14	93.33	**95.88**	94.71	**97.39**	94.98	97.34	96.59
en_partut	en_ewt	40,974	0.63	95.66	93.45	90.75	**94.03**	91.83	**97.58**	96.53	97.27	95.83
en_pud	en_ewt	17,727	0.68	95.14	90.87	95.08	**95.40**	94.91	93.55	95.62	**96.17**	94.68
es_ancora	es_gsd	454,069	0.47	87.10	98.34	97.46	**98.48**	97.97	**98.60**	97.15	98.59	97.80
es_gsd	es_ancora	358,355	0.42	87.10	97.35	96.15	**97.55**	96.97	**98.59**	95.81	98.43	97.65
et_edt	cs_pdt	371,564	0.02	99.75	**96.60**	94.65	94.86	94.68	**94.73**	89.62	88.80	89.09
eu_bdt	es_ancora	104,530	0.05	99.96	**95.10**	93.62	94.41	94.38	**96.32**	95.35	95.47	95.52
fa_seraji	ur_udtb	127,371	0.12	100.00	97.15	97.24	97.26	**97.31**	95.00	94.24	**95.29**	94.97
fi_ftb	fi_tdt	142,514	0.37	71.46	95.25	94.94	**96.18**	94.94	92.15	90.99	**92.75**	90.85
fi_pud	fi_tdt	13,356	0.49	94.58	91.56	96.97	**97.41**	96.81	78.62	86.06	**88.98**	86.78
fi_tdt	fi_ftb	173,899	0.30	71.46	96.54	95.32	**97.07**	95.18	**92.42**	90.27	92.22	90.03
fo_oft	no_nynorsk	8,960	0.12	99.83	90.36	86.49	**91.46**	90.38	83.87	81.59	**88.52**	86.66
fr_gsd	fr_sequoia	333,477	0.15	93.23	97.71	97.65	**98.07**	97.40	**97.74**	96.52	97.50	96.14
fr_partut	fr_gsd	23,443	0.82	97.28	94.72	96.33	**97.51**	96.13	94.20	95.13	**96.78**	95.10
fr_sequoia	fr_gsd	58,963	0.66	93.23	96.74	96.79	**98.07**	96.21	96.99	96.90	**98.17**	95.81
fr_spoken	fr_gsd	30,410	0.77	99.33	95.81	97.10	**97.64**	97.44	96.77	98.79	98.98	**99.07**
ga_idt	cs_pdt	19,812	0.04	99.95	**83.38**	76.03	75.27	77.94	**84.63**	76.48	76.91	79.01
gl_ctg	es_ancora	114,228	0.40	99.88	97.33	97.22	**97.38**	97.36	98.12	98.14	98.16	**98.37**
gl_treegal	gl_ctg	21,366	0.53	92.26	91.56	82.76	**94.64**	84.77	92.69	94.69	**96.66**	95.57
got_proiel	no_nynorsk	48,980	0.01	99.91	**95.20**	94.61	93.97	93.94	**95.35**	94.60	94.58	94.23
grc_perseus	grc_proiel	173,299	0.25	99.95	94.86	94.74	**95.05**	**95.05**	**93.24**	92.67	93.15	93.19
grc_proiel	grc_perseus	185,142	0.31	99.95	96.92	96.98	97.08	**97.11**	95.85	95.90	**96.46**	96.30
he_htb	ru_gsd	134,397	0.00	100.00	**96.26**	96.17	96.07	96.23	96.62	96.52	96.44	**96.71**
hi_hdtb	mr_ufal	295,265	0.01	100.00	96.70	96.87	96.77	**96.89**	**98.57**	98.34	98.52	98.40
hr_set	sr_set	164,557	0.28	88.98	95.14	94.85	**95.50**	94.59	**95.81**	94.53	95.25	94.52
hsb_ufal	cs_pdt	9,475	0.08	99.95	**79.92**	77.49	79.09	76.84	**82.68**	74.70	78.39	76.76
hu_szeged	et_edt	34,903	0.03	99.95	**92.27**	91.05	91.15	89.75	**90.09**	88.37	87.94	84.66
hy_armtdp	ru_pud	19,419	0.00	100.00	90.34	**91.31**	90.81	91.13	90.00	**92.15**	91.87	92.01
id_gsd	es_gsd	101,687	0.11	99.92	92.72	92.87	93.30	**93.39**	98.77	98.87	**98.97**	98.81
it_isdt	it_partut	250,714	0.28	79.42	98.07	97.91	**98.26**	97.77	97.52	96.70	**97.87**	96.85
it_partut	it_isdt	46,228	0.94	79.42	96.11	98.47	**98.73**	98.30	96.07	97.78	**98.68**	97.21
it_postwita	it_isdt	104,437	0.46	98.49	95.76	96.13	96.15	**96.53**	94.15	**96.14**	94.89	95.20
it_pud	it_isdt	19,634	0.69	94.02	94.30	85.62	**96.69**	84.00	93.32	96.64	**97.00**	95.22

ja_gsd	ja_pud	154,453	0.14	92.59	94.59	96.10	**96.31**	95.96	98.06	**98.81**	98.77	98.77
ja_modern	ja_gsd	12,213	0.29	99.78	**95.93**	95.69	95.65	95.86	93.67	95.96	95.55	**96.59**
ja_pud	ja_gsd	22,450	0.64	92.59	95.85	**97.91**	97.66	97.29	96.08	99.30	**99.34**	99.01
kmr_mg	es_gsd	8,680	0.03	100.00	86.43	86.93	**88.64**	87.61	88.38	90.72	**91.19**	90.44
ko_gsd	ko_kaist	69,382	0.33	92.29	93.53	86.94	**94.97**	87.35	89.88	89.30	**91.47**	85.59
ko_kaist	ko_gsd	302,384	0.12	92.29	95.86	95.48	**95.97**	95.39	**94.30**	94.20	93.88	92.37
ko_pud	ko_kaist	14,106	0.55	97.97	93.41	82.62	**95.62**	83.29	92.36	75.41	**98.08**	75.41
kpv_ikdp	ru_syntagrus	916	0.26	99.95	61.38	48.34	**63.10**	55.79	56.63	55.42	**61.45**	**61.45**
kpv_lattice	ru_syntagrus	1,805	0.09	99.96	**75.26**	66.32	67.50	67.36	57.69	58.24	**64.29**	61.54
la_ittb	la_proiel	298,460	0.37	99.98	97.08	97.23	97.03	**97.36**	98.54	97.98	**98.65**	98.54
la_perseus	la_proiel	25,157	0.49	99.89	82.04	87.64	**88.67**	87.95	80.99	87.44	**88.76**	87.37
la_proiel	la_ittb	174,977	0.20	99.98	**95.30**	95.15	94.83	95.10	**96.65**	94.54	96.03	95.47
lt_hse	lv_lvtb	4,511	0.05	99.83	72.44	77.53	**78.12**	77.94	72.96	77.25	**78.11**	77.68
lv_lvtb	hr_set	129,982	0.02	99.81	**95.13**	94.58	94.34	94.54	93.78	93.41	92.60	**93.85**
mr_ufal	hi_hdtb	3,427	0.16	100.00	76.63	77.98	76.28	**78.61**	70.12	72.47	**74.12**	72.00
nl_alpino	nl_lassysmall	178,169	0.23	93.27	95.88	95.49	**96.18**	95.98	95.60	94.57	**95.61**	95.43
nl_lassysmall	nl_alpino	84,612	0.41	93.27	93.67	95.15	**96.04**	95.60	93.34	94.24	**95.61**	94.99
no_bokmaal	no_nynorsk	264,958	0.24	96.34	97.24	97.41	97.25	**97.65**	98.23	97.86	**98.31**	98.01
no_nynorsk	no_bokmaal	255,088	0.25	96.34	96.68	97.10	97.03	**97.31**	96.59	97.50	**98.02**	97.66
no_nynorsklia	no_nynorsk	11,959	0.65	99.18	92.16	95.44	**95.77**	95.11	92.93	**98.09**	97.64	97.72
pcm_nsc	en_ewt	11,038	0.74	99.99	92.95	93.28	**94.26**	94.15	98.55	**99.92**	99.84	99.76
pl_lfg	pl_sz	118,526	0.41	60.73	95.71	94.43	**96.43**	93.91	**95.93**	94.67	95.49	94.96
pl_sz	pl_lfg	73,011	0.53	60.73	92.68	88.62	**94.82**	89.33	95.78	93.96	**95.79**	94.81
pt_bosque	pt_gsd	188,265	0.48	87.08	96.38	88.48	**96.84**	92.15	97.43	86.31	**97.84**	90.18
pt_gsd	pt_bosque	265,352	0.41	87.08	97.63	94.92	**98.03**	93.49	97.53	94.37	**98.36**	94.38
ro_nonstandard	ro_rrt	164,375	0.24	97.63	95.19	95.83	95.55	**96.14**	94.49	**96.06**	95.71	96.02
ro_rrt	ro_nonstandard	182,366	0.11	97.63	97.25	97.16	97.19	**97.30**	97.09	97.11	96.47	**97.36**
ru_gsd	ru_syntagrus	84,013	0.55	96.08	93.72	91.02	**94.67**	91.26	95.69	91.96	**96.90**	92.36
ru_pud	ru_syntagrus	16,233	0.74	98.69	88.38	87.34	**93.93**	87.87	86.92	**94.09**	93.46	93.51
ru_syntagrus	ru_gsd	937,395	0.13	96.08	96.69	96.84	**97.36**	96.40	96.73	96.42	**97.50**	95.68
ru_taiga	ru_syntagrus	18,173	0.66	98.05	82.67	**92.42**	92.38	92.23	83.24	92.07	92.47	**92.98**
sa_ufal	hi_hdtb	1,634	0.10	99.98	69.59	68.81	69.60	**70.68**	52.58	62.89	64.95	**66.49**
sk_snk	cs_pdt	93,740	0.22	99.22	**94.69**	92.39	93.30	93.51	**95.13**	91.31	93.31	92.61
sl_ssj	hr_set	118,536	0.12	99.33	95.38	94.98	95.09	**95.65**	96.13	95.58	95.97	**96.32**
sl_sst	sl_ssj	26,309	0.55	99.20	89.49	92.91	93.47	**93.75**	91.76	95.64	95.93	**96.38**
sme_giella	no_nynorsk	23,877	0.02	99.89	91.20	90.44	**91.94**	91.85	87.31	86.19	**88.69**	**88.69**
sr_set	hr_set	72,045	0.62	88.98	95.52	95.24	**97.47**	96.09	95.77	95.96	**97.02**	95.96
sv_lines	sv_talbanken	67,016	0.31	90.90	94.33	94.98	**95.30**	95.14	**95.29**	94.73	95.12	94.57
sv_pud	sv_talbanken	15,758	0.39	93.08	89.65	93.78	**95.12**	94.20	83.86	88.30	**93.11**	90.35
sv_talbanken	sv_lines	82,088	0.25	90.90	96.28	96.62	**96.97**	96.81	**96.67**	95.93	95.34	95.41
tl_trg	es_gsd	274	0.13	99.98	74.73	82.22	76.92	**83.15**	60.00	72.00	**80.00**	76.00
tr_imst	tr_pud	50,925	0.13	93.10	92.59	90.83	**93.79**	90.79	92.94	92.57	**94.22**	92.20
tr_pud	tr_imst	14,180	0.33	93.10	91.82	86.88	**93.83**	87.66	84.80	84.92	**86.32**	84.34
uk_iu	ru_syntagrus	98,865	0.10	99.55	**92.69**	91.14	92.41	92.13	**93.67**	91.59	93.07	92.86
ur_udtb	fa_seraji	114,786	0.16	100.00	**91.69**	91.30	91.64	91.40	**96.20**	95.51	95.68	95.93
vi_vtb	en_ewt	37,637	0.02	99.87	**89.82**	88.84	89.02	89.39	99.18	99.83	99.83	**99.90**
yo_ytb	es_gsd	2,238	0.06	99.99	87.46	89.49	85.04	**91.00**	94.00	95.20	93.60	**96.00**
yue_hk	zh_gsd	5,641	0.42	99.93	86.32	87.42	**89.77**	88.27	92.97	**98.97**	**98.97**	**98.97**
zh_cfl	zh_gsd	6,048	0.34	99.93	86.15	88.92	88.13	**89.72**	91.00	95.57	**96.26**	95.98
zh_gsd	ja_gsd	102,731	0.15	99.99	89.62	**91.40**	90.87	91.24	98.46	99.05	98.97	**99.09**
Average		121,049	0.31	95.42	92.04	91.43	**92.75**	91.85	91.10	91.02	**92.55**	91.41

Table 6: Joint morphological tagging and lemmatization results for all datasets. First column is the dataset for which the results are reported, the second column is the 'helper' dataset. SIZE: size of training data for the target dataset in words. WO: % word overlap with 'helper' dataset. SVM: F1 score of svm classifier on dataset prediction. BASE: single dataset baseline. CONCAT: simple concatenation of datasets. GOLD: using gold dataset embeddings. PRED: predicted dataset embeddings.

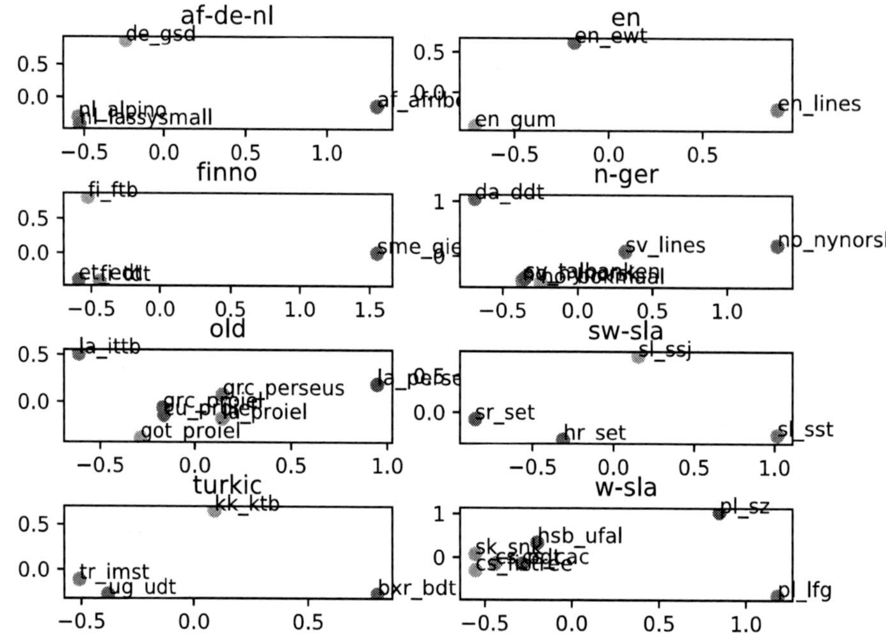

Figure 3: PCA-projection of the gold dataset embeddings of the dataset groups.

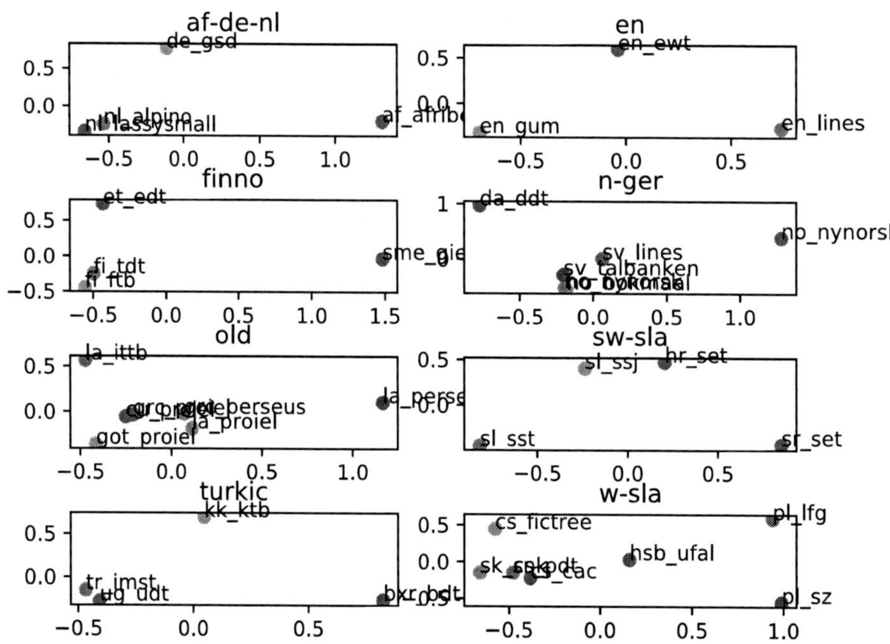

Figure 4: PCA-projection of the predicted dataset embeddings of the dataset groups.

Effective Distant Supervision for Temporal Relation Extraction

Xinyu Zhao **Shih-ting Lin** **Greg Durrett**
Department of Computer Science
The University of Texas at Austin
{xinyuzhao, j0717lin}@utexas.edu gdurrett@cs.utexas.edu

Abstract

A principal barrier to training temporal relation extraction models in new domains is the lack of varied, high quality examples and the challenge of collecting more. We present a method of automatically collecting distantly-supervised examples of temporal relations. We scrape and automatically label event pairs where the temporal relations are made explicit in text, then mask out those explicit cues, forcing a model trained on this data to learn other signals. We demonstrate that a pre-trained Transformer model is able to transfer from the automatically labeled examples to human-annotated benchmarks in both zero-shot and few-shot settings, and that the masking scheme is important in improving generalization.[1]

1 Introduction

Temporal relation extraction has largely focused on identifying pairwise relationships between events in text. Past work on annotating temporal relations has struggled to devise annotations schemes which are both comprehensive and easy to judge (Pustejovsky et al., 2003; Cassidy et al., 2014). However, even simplified annotation schemes designed for crowdsourcing (Ning et al., 2018b; Vashishtha et al., 2019) can struggle to acquire high-accuracy judgments about nebulous phenomena, leading to a scarcity of high-quality labeled data. Compared to tasks like syntactic parsing (Bies et al., 2012) or natural language inference (Williams et al., 2018), there are thus fewer resources for temporal relation extraction in other domains.

In this work, we present a method of automatically gathering distantly-labeled temporal relation examples. Unlike traditional distant supervision methods (Mintz et al., 2009), we do not rely on a knowledge base, but instead on heuristic cues that we will then mask out, forcing the model to make inferences from the remaining context. We explore two types of cues, but focus primarily on events that are anchored to orderable timexes (Goyal and Durrett, 2019). These examples can be collected and labeled using an automatic system (Chambers et al., 2014). By then masking the explicit temporal indicators, a model trained on these examples can no longer learn trivial timex-based rules, but must instead attend to more general temporal context cues. We show that a pre-trained model fine-tuned on this data learns general, implicit cues that transfer more broadly to human-annotated benchmarks. This observation follows a trend of recent work showing pre-trained models' ability to generalize from synthetic data to natural data (Xu et al., 2020; Marzoev et al., 2020).

We implement our approach with pre-trained Transformer models (Devlin et al., 2019; Liu et al., 2019; Clark et al., 2020) similar to a state-of-the-art temporal relation extraction model from the literature (Han et al., 2019). Our model is able to effectively transfer from a distantly-labeled dataset to the MATRES benchmark (Ning et al., 2018b) when used to supplement a small number of in-domain or out-of-domain samples.

2 Classification Model

Our base classification model consists of a pre-trained Transformer (Vaswani et al., 2017) model with an appended linear classification layer, represented in Figure 1. For the majority of our experiments, we use RoBERTa (Liu et al., 2019), which we found to work better than BERT (Devlin et al., 2019) and ELECTRA (Clark et al., 2020) for domain transfer. We chose a single set of hyper-parameters by tuning to match the performance of Han et al. (2019); for details see Appendix A.

A single example consists of an event pair

[1]Code and datasets available at: https://github.com/xyz-zy/distant-temprel

Proceedings of the Second Workshop on Domain Adaptation for NLP, pages 195–203
April 20, 2021. ©2021 Association for Computational Linguistics

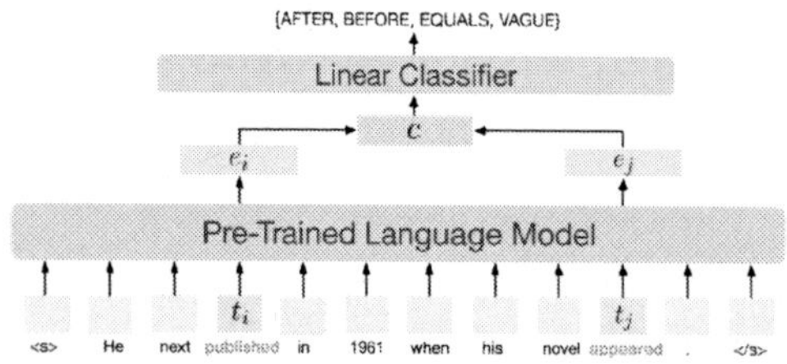

Figure 1: Classification model consisting of a pre-trained transformer model and a linear layer. Event tokens are represented by t_i, t_j and correspond to output embeddings e_i, e_j, which are used by the linear classifier to produce a distribution over labels.

in context, which may be a single sentence or two sentences, and a label from {AFTER, BEFORE, EQUALS, VAGUE}, following the annotation scheme in MATRES. Each example is tokenized to yield input tokens $T = [t_1, t_2, ..., t_n]$, with event tokens $t_i, t_j \in T$. For events consisting of multiple sub-word tokens, we track only the first token position. We use the convention of passing events in text order, where $1 \leq i < j \leq n$.

The language model then produces output embeddings $[e_1, e_2, ..., e_n]$. For classification, we select the embeddings e_i, e_j corresponding to the event token positions, and combine them into a classification vector, $c = [e_i; e_j; e_i \odot e_j; e_i - e_j]$ where $\odot$ represents elementwise multiplication. Finally, a linear classification layer produces a distribution over the four relation labels. Training is done by maximizing likelihood of labeled samples. We implement this model using PyTorch (Paszke et al., 2019) and pre-trained models from HuggingFace's Transformers library (Wolf et al., 2019).

We benchmark our classification model by training and evaluating on MATRES. We achieve an F1 of 79.8 with RoBERTa (Liu et al., 2019) and an F1 of 80.3 with ELECTRA (Clark et al., 2020), demonstrating that our model replicates state-of-the-art performance achieved by local models (only considering arcs in isolation), currently 80.3 F1 (Han et al., 2019).

3 Learning from Distant Data

We aim to create a method of automatically gathering high-quality data that can be applied to unlabeled text. To this end, we focus on two techniques identifying explicit temporal indicators. First, we identify single-sentence examples where event pairs are automatically labeled via explicit discourse connectives. Second, we scrape occurrences of event pairs that are anchorable to timexes which determine their relation. We will see that this second technique is substantially better, and analyze some factors contributing to the performance delta. Although neither technique captures the gamut of phenomena found in human-labeled data, pre-trained models' generalization capabilities and a masking technique tailored for this setting are two tools that enable effective transfer.

For both techniques, we scrape distant examples from English Gigaword Fifth Edition (Parker et al., 2011). We extract samples from a balance of the different news sources present in the dataset. In both cases, we use the Stanford CoreNLP lexicalized parser (Manning et al., 2014) to generate parse trees for the source text, which can be time-consuming at scale. However, we can pre-filter sentences based on the presence of timexes or target discourse connectives, and so in practice we only rarely need to invoke the parser. Table 9 in the Appendix shows collected data samples, and we describe these two collection methods in more detail below.

3.1 Temporal Connectives

Words like *before*, *after*, *during*, *until*, *prior to*, and others can indicate the temporal status of events in text explicitly. Past work has shown that complex relations can be learned from discourse connectives in non-temporal settings (Nie et al., 2019), so such connectives can be powerful indicators. We focus on *before* and *after* in this work, as these are the most common and straightforward to map to a temporal relation.

To identify connected event pairs, we use the Stanford CoreNLP lexicalized parser (Manning et al., 2014) to produce parse trees. We then search for a related event pair by 1) identifying the connective, 2) finding the closest parent verb phrase, and 3) finding the closest child verb phrase. These become the events for the example. When this identifies modals or auxiliaries, we take the corresponding main verb. The label for the example is simply determined by the *before* or *after* connective. Examples are listed in Appendix E; on inspection, we found this method to be reliable.

3.2 Events Anchored to Time Expressions

Beyond connectives, another cue is the explicit presence of timexes. An example is shown in Figure 2: the years *1951* and *1961* determine the order-

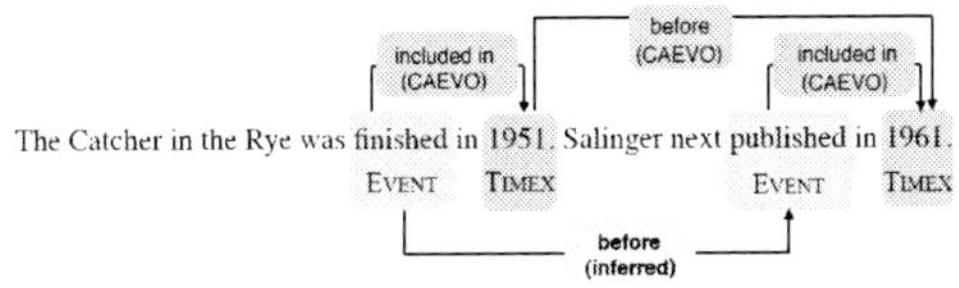

Figure 2: Process of identifying distantly labeled event-event relations using CAEVO. First, events and timexes are identified and two of CAEVO's sieves are applied. Then, using transitivity, event-event relation is inferred from associated timexes.

ing of their associated events, assuming each event can be appropriately linked to the timex.

We use CAEVO (Chambers et al., 2014) to detect event pairs and link events to timexes, which include explicit datetimes (*January, 1961*), relative times (*tomorrow*) and other natural language indicators (*now, until recently*). This approach, which yields both single- and cross-sentence examples, was explored by Goyal and Durrett (2019), who noisily labeled data to evaluate their timex embedding model.

First, the input document is annotated by CAEVO with events and timexes using its parse trees. Two of its sieves are then applied: the ADJACENTVERBTIMEX sieve identifies events that are anchored to time expressions via a direct path in the syntactic parse tree, then the TIMETIMESIEVE uses a small set of deterministic rules to label relations between timexes. These two sieves have high precisions, of 0.74 and 0.90, respectively (Chambers et al., 2014). Figure 2 shows the result of applying both sieves. Finally, the system is able to infer the relations between events that are anchored to comparable timexes (i.e *finished* before *published*), giving us event pairs usable for training.

The resulting datasets are reasonably balanced between BEFORE and AFTER, with sparse EQUAL examples and *no* VAGUE examples. A more detailed label breakdown is included in Appendix B.

3.3 Example Masking

These distant examples are gleaned from "trivial" indicators in the text, which a model like BERT (Devlin et al., 2019) will overfit to. We observe that our RoBERTa classifier yields 99.8% accuracy on a held out BeforeAfter dataset, and evaluating with the same DistantTimex train/test split of Goyal and Durrett (2019) results in 96.6% test accuracy.

In order to combat this, we *mask* the explicit temporal cues identified by our weak labeling process. Our goal is to induce the model to learn the label from the remaining tokens, including the event instances themselves and the broader context. Masking is performed *prior to* subword tokenization, so each word or timex gets one mask token per word. For our BeforeAfter examples, we simply mask the temporal connective. For our DistantTimex examples, we use the timex tags generated by CAEVO to mask all identified timexes present in the context. This results in masking of not only explicit timexes (e.g. dates, times), but also of natural language timexes (e.g. *previously, recently*). This may occasionally result in "sparse" training examples that have a high proportion of mask tokens. Refer to Tables 7-8 in Appendix E for concrete examples.

In spite of this masking, our model is able to classify distantly-labeled timex examples with 85% accuracy when evaluating on a held-out set, well above a majority baseline. This indicates that there are other temporal cues that the model can use to determine the temporal relation.

4 Results

We evaluate our distant dataset on several axes. (1) In zero-shot, few-shot, or transfer settings, to what extent can this help existing models? (2) How important is each facet of our distant extraction setup? (3) What can we say about the distribution of our data from these techniques? We focus our evaluation on the English MATRES dataset (Ning et al., 2018b), a four-class temporal relation dataset of chiefly newswire data drawn from a number of different sources.[2]

We found significant variance in model performance in our transfer for small data settings, so most results use average best performance or majority-vote ensembled performance of three randomly seeded models trained in the same setting.

Comparison of Distant Datasets To get the clearest picture of the differences in our distant setups, we first evaluate in a setting of zero-shot adaptation to MATRES. We train on different distantly labeled dataset sizes in order to establish a

[2]We choose **not** to evaluate on the UDS-T dataset (Vashishtha et al., 2019), treating it solely as a training source. In our experiments, converting from real-valued time span annotations into categorical event-pair labels required dealing with significant disagreement among annotators. Despite trying several resolution strategies, none of our *in-domain* fine-tuned Transformer models performed much better than a majority baseline, indicating high noise or an extremely challenging setting.

Training Data		Split	MATRES P	R	F1
Majority Label		Dev	52.6	60.2	56.1
		Test	50.7	58.6	54.3
MATRES		Dev	77.1	85.5	81.1
		Test	75.1	84.8	79.6
DistantTimex	1k	Dev	54.1	61.9	57.7
	1k	Test	50.8	58.7	54.5
	5k	Dev	60.4	69.1	64.5
	5k	Test	61.9	71.5	66.4
	10k	Dev	64.0	73.2	68.3
	10k	Test	61.5	71.1	66.0
BeforeAfter	10k	Dev	53.4	61.1	57.0
	10k	Test	51.6	59.7	55.3

Table 1: Results on MATRES after training on distant data, with explicit temporal cues masked. Results are esembled from three models trained in the same setting.

Labeled Set	Eval	DistantTimex Examples None	1k	5k	10k
MATRES 1k	Avg. Dev F1	64.2	67.4	75.2	75.6
	Avg. Test F1	60.9	66.1	73.6	73.7
	Ens. Dev F1	70.2	74.5	76.7	76.6
	Ens. Test F1	66.5	72.0	75.0	75.5
UDS-T 5k	Avg. Dev F1	68.7	62.8	72.0	70.8
	Avg. Test F1	66.2	60.9	69.5	69.8
	Ens. Dev F1	70.1	64.6	73.2	72.1
	Ens. Test F1	68.2	62.3	70.7	71.8

Table 2: Evaluation results on MATRES when adding automatically collected examples to small amounts of human-annotated training data. Using more DistantTimex data is able to improve performance substantially over not using any (**None**).

relationship between example quantity and generalization performance. Our results presented in Table 1 show that the DistantTimex data works substantially better than BeforeAfter: with the DistantTimex data, there is a correlation between adding more distantly-labeled examples and increased performance. While both of these rules target particular narrow slices of data, the set with explicit timexes appears to be broader than that with before/after connectives, and hence BERT can learn to generalize better.[3]

Using Fewer Labeled Examples In a more realistic setting, we assume access to small amounts of pre-existing labeled data, using roughly 10% of existing datasets. Table 2 shows results from evaluating on MATRES using small amounts of either MATRES or UDS-T data in conjunction with our distant data; three models are randomly initialized and trained for each setting. In both settings, adding distant data improves substantially over just using the in-domain MATRES data, and the best model performance is only around 4 F_1 worse than the in-domain MATRES results using the entire train set. We also show that this data can stack with data from UDS-T (Vashishtha et al., 2019) and improve transfer over raw UDS-T. This is in spite of very different event distributions between UDST and MATRES and a complete lack of examples of VAGUE relations during training.

[3]One possible reason is that explicit indicators like *before* and *after* may be used explicitly to communicate temporal information where it cannot be otherwise inferred, but timexes are often used to communicate more specific details about events where the relation may already be clear.

Training Data		MATRES Test P	R	F1
Distant Timex No Mask	5k	57.9	67.0	62.1
Distant Timex Masked	5k	61.9	71.5	66.4
BeforeAfter No Mask	5k	51.5	59.5	55.2
BeforeAfter Masked	5k	51.6	59.7	55.3

Table 3: Transfer comparison for data with and without masking. Results are ensembled from three models trained in the same setting.

MATRES		DistantTimex		BeforeAfter		UDST 5k	
said	16.0%	won	2.02%	was	2.60%	is	5.8%
killed	1.2%	died	1.69%	said	2.08%	was	3.3%
found	1.0%	said	1.67%	came	1.70%	have	2.9%
says	0.9%	began	1.41%	is	1.06%	are	2.5%
told	0.8%	joined	1.10%	began	0.99%	be	2.2%
called	0.8%	took	1.10%	made	0.85%	get	1.5%
reported	0.7%	set	1.04%	have	0.78%	had	1.4%
saying	0.7%	killed	1.04%	left	0.77%	know	1.4%
say	0.7%	born	0.96%	had	0.77%	do	1.1%
was	0.6%	held	0.93%	be	0.73%	go	1.9%

Table 4: Top 10 events for each dataset as a percentage of total event mentions.

Effect of Masking In Table 3, we test the effect of masking on model generalization. We train our model on the collected distant examples with and without masking, and report ensembled evaluation results on the MATRES test set. Our comparison shows that masking causes an increase in generalization for DistantTimex examples, but little change in BeforeAfter transfer, which still performs similar to the majority baseline.

Understanding the data distribution We report the most frequent events from each dataset in Table 4. MATRES is highly focused on reporting verbs, but the distant data has a much flatter distribution. BeforeAfter features more light verbs whereas DistantTimex features events with more complex semantics; possibly the model can learn more regular and meaningful patterns from such data, or relevant cues from a more similar event distribution (than found in BeforeAfter). We present event-label tuples in Appendix D.

5 Related Work

There is little direct prior work on using this kind of distant supervision for temporal relation extraction. Past work has studied automatic extraction of typical inter-event orderings (Chklovski and Pantel, 2004; Ning et al., 2018a; Yao and Huang, 2018) to aid downstream temporal tasks, but these approaches represent events as single words (predicates) taken out of context, so the knowledge they can capture is limited. The commonsense acquisition method of Zhou et al. (2020) learns more sophisticated information, but more about unary properties of events (typical time, duration) rather than relational knowledge. Lin et al. (2020) achieve a somewhat similar goal, but make a strong assumption about narrative-structured corpora and do not evaluate on in-context temporal relation extraction.

Our technique does not use a knowledge base like classic distant supervision methods (Mintz et al., 2009). However, because we eventually mask out the explicit temporal indicators, we are still using temporal information "external" to the final example to derive the label, hence why we invoke this term. A related concept is the idea of labeling functions (Ratner et al., 2016; Hancock et al., 2018), which are used to automatically construct training data for new domains. However, to our knowledge, these techniques have not been applied to temporal relation extraction, nor used in conjunction with masking as we do.

6 Discussion

We use explicit temporal cues to automatically identify examples of temporal relations between events in text. By masking these trivial features, a pre-trained Transformer model can learn from the remaining context and generalize to human-annotated benchmarks. Comparing performance for two distant labeling methods–using discourse connectives and linking events to time expressions–indicates that richer temporal cues exist in the second case. The scope of identified time expressions encompasses both explicit datetimes and natural language indicators ("now", "recently", etc.).

While datetimes may be more common in news and historical articles, relative time expressions are present in diverse domains such as literature and colloquial texts. Where such indicators exist, our approach may be used to automatically collect distantly labeled temporal relations. More broadly, we believe that this label-and-mask paradigm could be used to collect targeted training data for a variety of NLP tasks.

Acknowledgments

Thanks to the anonymous reviewers for their helpful comments. This material is also based on research that is in part supported by the Air Force Research Laboratory (AFRL), DARPA, for the KAIROS program under agreement number FA8750-19-2-1003. The U.S. Government is authorized to reproduce and distribute reprints for Governmental purposes notwithstanding any copyright notation thereon. The views and conclusions contained herein are those of the authors and should not be interpreted as necessarily representing the official policies or endorsements, either expressed or implied, of the Air Force Research Laboratory (AFRL), DARPA, or the U.S. Government.

References

Ann Bies, Justin Mott, Colin Warner, and Seth Kulick. 2012. *English Web Treebank*. LDC2012T13. Linguistic Data Consortium, Philadelphia, PA.

Taylor Cassidy, Bill McDowell, Nathanael Chambers, and Steven Bethard. 2014. An Annotation Framework for Dense Event Ordering. In *Proceedings of the 52nd Annual Meeting of the Association for Computational Linguistics (Volume 2: Short Papers)*, pages 501–506, Baltimore, Maryland. Association for Computational Linguistics.

Nathanael Chambers, Taylor Cassidy, Bill McDowell, and Steven Bethard. 2014. Dense Event Ordering with a Multi-Pass Architecture. *Transactions of the Association for Computational Linguistics*, 2:273–284.

Timothy Chklovski and Patrick Pantel. 2004. VerbOcean: Mining the web for fine-grained semantic verb relations. In *Proceedings of the 2004 Conference on Empirical Methods in Natural Language Processing*, pages 33–40, Barcelona, Spain. Association for Computational Linguistics.

Kevin Clark, Minh-Thang Luong, Quoc V. Le, and Christopher D. Manning. 2020. Electra: Pre-training text encoders as discriminators rather than generators. In *International Conference on Learning Representations*.

Jacob Devlin, Ming-Wei Chang, Kenton Lee, and Kristina Toutanova. 2019. BERT: Pre-training of Deep Bidirectional Transformers for Language Understanding. In *Proceedings of the 2019 Conference of the North American Chapter of the Association for Computational Linguistics: Human Language Technologies, Volume 1 (Long and Short Papers)*, pages 4171–4186, Minneapolis, Minnesota. Association for Computational Linguistics.

Tanya Goyal and Greg Durrett. 2019. Embedding Time Expressions for Deep Temporal Ordering Models. In *Proceedings of the 57th Annual Meeting of the Association for Computational Linguistics*, pages 4400–4406, Florence, Italy. Association for Computational Linguistics.

Rujun Han, Qiang Ning, and Nanyun Peng. 2019. Joint Event and Temporal Relation Extraction with Shared Representations and Structured Prediction. In *Proceedings of the 2019 Conference on Empirical Methods in Natural Language Processing and the 9th International Joint Conference on Natural Language Processing*, pages 434–444.

Braden Hancock, Paroma Varma, Stephanie Wang, Martin Bringmann, Percy Liang, and Christopher Ré. 2018. Training classifiers with natural language explanations. In *Proceedings of the 56th Annual Meeting of the Association for Computational Linguistics (Volume 1: Long Papers)*, pages 1884–1895, Melbourne, Australia. Association for Computational Linguistics.

Shih-Ting Lin, Nathanael Chambers, and Greg Durrett. 2020. Conditional Generation of Temporally-ordered Event Sequences. *arXiv cs.CL 2012.15786*.

Yinhan Liu, Myle Ott, Naman Goyal, Jingfei Du, Mandar Joshi, Danqi Chen, Omer Levy, Mike Lewis, Luke Zettlemoyer, and Veselin Stoyanov. 2019. RoBERTa: A Robustly Optimized BERT Pretraining Approach. *CoRR*, abs/1907.11692.

Christopher D. Manning, Mihai Surdeanu, John Bauer, Jenny Finkel, Steven J. Bethard, and David McClosky. 2014. The Stanford CoreNLP Natural Language Processing Toolkit. In *Association for Computational Linguistics (ACL) System Demonstrations*, pages 55–60.

Alana Marzoev, Samuel Madden, M. Frans Kaashoek, Michael Cafarella, and Jacob Andreas. 2020. Unnatural language processing: Bridging the gap between synthetic and natural language data.

Mike Mintz, Steven Bills, Rion Snow, and Daniel Jurafsky. 2009. Distant supervision for relation extraction without labeled data. In *Proceedings of the Joint Conference of the 47th Annual Meeting of the ACL and the 4th International Joint Conference on Natural Language Processing of the AFNLP*, pages 1003–1011, Suntec, Singapore. Association for Computational Linguistics.

Allen Nie, Erin Bennett, and Noah Goodman. 2019. DisSent: Learning Sentence Representations from Explicit Discourse Relations. In *Proceedings of the 57th Annual Meeting of the Association for Computational Linguistics*, pages 4497–4510, Florence, Italy. Association for Computational Linguistics.

Qiang Ning, Hao Wu, Haoruo Peng, and Dan Roth. 2018a. Improving Temporal Relation Extraction with a Globally Acquired Statistical Resource. In *Proceedings of the 2018 Conference of the North American Chapter of the Association for Computational Linguistics: Human Language Technologies, Volume 1 (Long Papers)*, pages 841–851, New Orleans, Louisiana. Association for Computational Linguistics.

Qiang Ning, Hao Wu, and Dan Roth. 2018b. A Multi-Axis Annotation Scheme for Event Temporal Relations. In *Proceedings of the 56th Annual Meeting of the Association for Computational Linguistics (Volume 1: Long Papers)*, pages 1318–1328, Melbourne, Australia. Association for Computational Linguistics.

Robert Parker, David Graff, Junbo Kong, Ke Chen, and Kazuaki Maeda. 2011. *English Gigaword Fifth Edition*. LDC2011T07. Linguistic Data Consortium, Philadelphia, PA.

Adam Paszke, Sam Gross, Francisco Massa, Adam Lerer, James Bradbury, Gregory Chanan, Trevor Killeen, Zeming Lin, Natalia Gimelshein, Luca Antiga, Alban Desmaison, Andreas Kopf, Edward Yang, Zachary DeVito, Martin Raison, Alykhan Tejani, Sasank Chilamkurthy, Benoit Steiner, Lu Fang, Junjie Bai, and Soumith Chintala. 2019. PyTorch: An Imperative Style, High-Performance Deep Learning Library. In H. Wallach, H. Larochelle, A. Beygelzimer, F. d'Alché Buc, E. Fox, and R. Garnett, editors, *Advances in Neural Information Processing Systems 32*, pages 8024–8035. Curran Associates, Inc.

James Pustejovsky, Patrick Hanks, Roser Saurí, Andrew See, Rob Gaizauskas, Andrea Setzer, Dragomir Radev, Beth Sundheim, David Day, Lisa Ferro, and Marcia Lazo. 2003. The TimeBank corpus. *Proceedings of Corpus Linguistics*.

Alexander Ratner, Christopher De Sa, Sen Wu, Daniel Selsam, and Christopher Ré. 2016. Data programming: Creating large training sets, quickly. NIPS'16, page 3574–3582, Red Hook, NY, USA. Curran Associates Inc.

Siddharth Vashishtha, Benjamin Van Durme, and Aaron Steven White. 2019. Fine-Grained Temporal Relation Extraction. In *Proceedings of the 57th Annual Meeting of the Association for Computational Linguistics*, pages 2906–2919, Florence, Italy. Association for Computational Linguistics.

Ashish Vaswani, Noam Shazeer, Niki Parmar, Jakob Uszkoreit, Llion Jones, Aidan N. Gomez, undefinedukasz Kaiser, and Illia Polosukhin. 2017. Attention is All You Need. In *Proceedings of the 31st International Conference on Neural Information Processing Systems (NeurIPS)*,.

Adina Williams, Nikita Nangia, and Samuel Bowman. 2018. A broad-coverage challenge corpus for sentence understanding through inference. In *Proceedings of the 2018 Conference of the North American Chapter of the Association for Computational Linguistics: Human Language Technologies, Volume 1 (Long Papers)*, pages 1112–1122, New Orleans, Louisiana. Association for Computational Linguistics.

Thomas Wolf, Lysandre Debut, Victor Sanh, Julien Chaumond, Clement Delangue, Anthony Moi, Pierric Cistac, Tim Rault, Rémi Louf, Morgan Funtowicz, and Jamie Brew. 2019. HuggingFace's Transformers: State-of-the-art Natural Language Processing. *ArXiv*, abs/1910.03771.

Silei Xu, Sina Semnani, Giovanni Campagna, and Monica Lam. 2020. AutoQA: From databases to QA semantic parsers with only synthetic training data. In *Proceedings of the 2020 Conference on Empirical Methods in Natural Language Processing (EMNLP)*, pages 422–434, Online. Association for Computational Linguistics.

Wenlin Yao and Ruihong Huang. 2018. Temporal Event Knowledge Acquisition via Identifying Narratives. In *Proceedings of the 56th Annual Meeting of the Association for Computational Linguistics (Volume 1: Long Papers)*, pages 537–547, Melbourne, Australia. Association for Computational Linguistics.

Ben Zhou, Qiang Ning, Daniel Khashabi, and Dan Roth. 2020. Temporal common sense acquisition with minimal supervision. In *Proceedings of the 58th Annual Meeting of the Association for Computational Linguistics*, pages 7579–7589, Online. Association for Computational Linguistics.

A Model Implementation

As mentioned previously, we selected a set of hyperparameters by fine-tuning to approximate the performance of recent state of the art on MATRES, achieving an F1 of 79.8 with RoBERTa (base) and 80.3 with ELECTRA. Specifically, we arrived at a learning rate of 2e-5 with a warmup proportion of 0.1. Our batch size varied from 16-25 based on hardware.

Full implementation can be found at `https://github.com/xyz-zy/distant-temprel`

B Label Composition Across Datasets

Table 5 compares the label distribution of our distant data against the human-annotated MATRES dataset. In comparison, our datasets are lacking in VAGUE relations (which have the lowest IAA in MATRES, and are particularly difficult to resolve) but emphasize the two most prominent classes. In few-shot settings, our model sees and trains on VAGUE relations from MATRES.

	BEFORE	AFTER	EQUAL	VAGUE
MATRES	34.5%	50.2%	3.5%	11.8%
DistantTimex	67.4%	31.4%	1.3%	–
BeforeAfter	50.7%	49.3%	–	–

Table 5: Training data label distribution. Both of our distant datasets contain 10k examples; the MATRES training set contains 9.7k examples.

Training Data		Split	MATRES P	R	F1	–Vague Acc.
Majority Label		Dev	52.6	60.2	56.1	–
		Test	50.7	58.6	54.3	–
MATRES		Dev	77.1	85.5	81.1	85.5
		Test	75.1	84.8	79.6	84.8
DistantTimex	1k	Dev	54.1	61.9	57.7	61.9
	1k	Test	50.8	58.7	54.5	58.7
	5k	Dev	60.4	69.1	64.5	69.1
	5k	Test	61.9	71.5	66.4	69.2
	10k	Dev	64.0	73.2	68.3	73.2
	10k	Test	61.5	71.1	66.0	71.1
BeforeAfter	10k	Dev	53.4	61.1	57.0	61.1
	10k	Test	51.6	59.7	55.3	59.7

Table 6: Expanded view of results on MATRES, comparing performance on only on {BEFORE, AFTER, EQUALS} examples ("– Vague") versus the entire eval set. Presented results are majority-vote ensembled from three models trained in the same setting.

C Performance without VAGUE Examples

The VAGUE label is defined to express indeterminacy and also has the lowest inter-annotator agreement in the MATRES dataset. These examples are also relatively more difficult for models to learn. Tables 6 and 7 present an expanded view of our results, adding the evaluation accuracy on only {BEFORE, AFTER, EQUALS} examples. As expected, we observe that model performance increases across the board under this evaluation.

D Most Common Event-Label Tuples

Table 8 presents a comparison of the most common (event1, event2, label) tuples across datasets. In MATRES, the most common tuples are largely (event, "said", BEFORE) events. The DistantTimex data features many examples of same-verb pairs

Labeled Set	+Distant	Full Test Set Acc.	F1	−Vague Acc.
MATRES 1k	1k	67.0	72.0	77.5
	5k	69.2	75.0	79.1
	10k	70.1	75.5	80.8
UDS-T 5k	1k	58.1	62.3	67.1
	5k	65.9	70.7	76.2
	10k	67.9	71.8	78.5

Table 7: Comparison of majority-vote ensembled performance on {BEFORE, AFTER, EQUALS} examples ("−Vague") versus performance on the entire test set. Performance is higher without vague examples, and increases with the number of DistantTimex examples added.

MATRES	
('said', 'said', BEFORE)	1.69%
('said', 'said', VAGUE)	0.67%
('said', 'said', AFTER)	0.25%
('said', 'told', BEFORE)	0.21%
('called', 'said', BEFORE)	0.21%
('killed', 'said', BEFORE)	0.16%
('found', 'said', BEFORE)	0.15%
('added', 'said', BEFORE)	0.15%
('found', 'said', AFTER)	0.14%
('declined', 'said', BEFORE)	0.14%
DistantTimex	
('won', 'won', BEFORE)	0.44%
('died', 'died', BEFORE)	0.26%
('annexed', 'seized', BEFORE)	0.26%
('born', 'graduated', BEFORE)	0.25%
('crashes', 'killed', AFTER)	0.20%
('killed', 'torched', AFTER)	0.19%
('crashed', 'crashed', AFTER)	0.17%
('died', 'married', BEFORE)	0.16%
('end', 'remove', BEFORE)	0.14%
('died', 'killed', BEFORE)	0.14%

Table 8: Top 10 event-event-relation tuples per dataset as a percentage of total event mentions.

(*won-won*, *died-died*). These examples frequently come from sentences or sentence pairs discussing related events of the same type, using dates to contrast them.

E Distant Examples

Table 9 presents a sample of our distantly labeled data. Examples (a-b) show that our BeforeAfter parsing scheme can correctly identify linked events across sentence spans. Examples (c-d) display a variety in parsed syntactic structures that link events to timexes.

Distant Example Masking Tables 10 and 11 present examples of our masking scheme on BeforeAfter and DistantTimex examples respectively.

Notably in Table 11, multi-word timexes result in one mask token per word. All identified timexes in the examples are masked, even if they are not directly linked to the events in consideration.

	Example Text	Heuristic	Label
(a)	A child prodigy, he **studied** music at the Julliard School of Music before **turning** to art.	BeforeAfter	BEFORE
(b)	Hill's support **came** only a few days after former Prime Minister Paul Keating **made** a speech at the University of New South Wales in which he revived his campaign for a republic.	BeforeAfter	AFTER
(c)	1903: General Electric **introduces** the first light set for the public sale for $12, then the average weekly wage of a typical American worker. 1962: General Electric **designs** the National Christmas Tree for the first time.	DistantTimex	BEFORE
(d)	Batista's EBX, the holding company for his five Rio-based companies, **increased** its workforce fivefold since 2006 to 2,000 employees. State-run oil producer Petroleo Brasilero... plans to **add** 6,000 more by 2013.	DistantTimex	BEFORE
(e)	It **took** until recently, the official **said**, for everyone to realize "it didn't work."	DistantTimex	BEFORE

Table 9: Weakly labeled data examples, with the identifying heuristics underlined. Examples (a-b) show different instances of labeling based on "before/after" mentions. Examples (c-e) show instances of labeling event pairs based on anchoring time expressions, which range from datetimes to natural language indicators (e.g. "recently"). While other timexes are identified in the examples shown, only the anchoring expressions for the induced labels are indicated.

	Example Text	Masked	Label
(a)	A child prodigy, he **studied** music at the Julliard School of Music before **turning** to art.	A child prodigy, he **studied** music at the Julliard School of Music [mask] **turning** to art.	BEFORE
(b)	Hill's support **came** only a few days after former Prime Minister Paul Keating **made** a speech at the University of New South Wales in which he revived his campaign for a republic.	Hill's support **came** only a few days [mask] former Prime Minister Paul Keating **made** a speech at the University of New South Wales in which he revived his campaign for a republic.	AFTER

Table 10: Masking of of weakly labeled data examples identified by before/after mentions.

	Example Text	Masked	Label
(a)	Batista's EBX, the holding company for his five Rio-based companies, **increased** its workforce fivefold since 2006 to 2,000 employees. State-run oil producer Petroleo Brasilero has hired 22,000 employees in the past six years, ... and plans to **add** 6,000 more by 2013.	Batista's EBX, the holding company for his five Rio-based companies, **increased** its workforce fivefold since [mask] to 2,000 employees. State-run oil producer Petroleo Brasilero has hired 22,000 employees in [mask] [mask] [mask] [mask], ... and plans to **add** 6,000 more by [mask].	BEFORE
(b)	It **took** until recently, the official **said**, for everyone to realize "it didn't work."	It **took** until [mask], the official **said**, for everyone to realize "it didn't work."	BEFORE

Table 11: Masking of of weakly labeled data examples identified by anchoring timexes.

Zero-Shot Cross-Lingual Dependency Parsing through Contextual Embedding Transformation

Haoran Xu and **Philipp Koehn**
Johns Hopkins University
hxu64@jhu.edu, phi@jhu.edu

Abstract

Linear embedding transformation has been shown to be effective for zero-shot cross-lingual transfer tasks and achieve surprisingly promising results. However, cross-lingual embedding space mapping is usually studied in static *word-level* embeddings, where a space transformation is derived by aligning representations of translation pairs that are referred from dictionaries. We move further from this line and investigate a contextual embedding alignment approach which is *sense-level* and dictionary-free. To enhance the quality of the mapping, we also provide a deep view of properties of contextual embeddings, i.e., the anisotropy problem and its solution. Experiments on zero-shot dependency parsing through the concept-shared space built by our embedding transformation substantially outperform state-of-the-art methods using multilingual embeddings.

1 Introduction

Cross-lingual embedding space alignment (Mikolov et al., 2013b; Artetxe et al., 2016; Xing et al., 2015; Conneau et al., 2018) recently has been attracted a lot of attention because cross-lingual model transfer is effectively facilitated by shared semantic spaces in NLP tasks, e.g., named entity recognition (Xie et al., 2018), part-of-speech tagging (Hsu et al., 2019), and dependency parsing (Schuster et al., 2019), where dependency paring is scoped out in this paper. Compared with the delexicalized parsers (McDonald et al., 2011), multilingual word embeddings have been demonstrated to significantly improve the performance of zero-shot dependency parsing by bridging the lexical feature gap (Guo et al., 2015).

With the remarkable development of monolingual contextual pre-trained models (Peters et al., 2018; Devlin et al., 2019; Radford et al., 2019), which dramatically outperform static word embeddings (Mikolov et al., 2013a; Pennington et al., 2014; Bojanowski et al., 2017) in broad NLP applications, increasing number of researchers have started focusing on contextual representation alignment for cross-lingual dependency parsing (Schuster et al., 2019; Wang et al., 2019). Moreover, with the appearance of multilingual pre-trained models, such as Multilingual BERT (mBERT) (Devlin et al., 2019), zero-shot dependency parsing becomes easier by utilizing the large vocabulary of the multilingual models (Kondratyuk and Straka, 2019).

Our approach is most similar to Schuster et al. (2019), which maps a target language space into a source language space through a linear transformation to realize zero-shot transfer in dependency parsing. Typically, a transformation is usually derived by word-level embedding alignment, while we explore a sense-level embedding alignment method to map bilingual spaces more precisely, where sense-level representations are split from multi-sense word-level embeddings. Furthermore, our mapping approach is dictionary-free which utilizes the silver token pairs from parallel corpora and eliminates the necessity of gold dictionaries. The experimental results of zero-shot dependency parsing demonstrate that two parser evaluation scores (UAS and LAS) of sense-level mapping are always better than of word-level one. Moreover, we also notice the anisotropy problem (Ethayarajh, 2019) (defined in Section 3.2) in contextual embeddings, which potentially deteriorate the performance of the zero-shot transfer task. We significantly mitigate this drawback by leveraging a prepossessing step, **i**terative **n**ormalization (IN) (Zhang et al., 2019), which is originally used for improving the performance of static embedding mapping on the bilingual dictionary induction task.

Zero-shot dependency parsing experiments are conducted on *Universal Dependencies treebank*

Proceedings of the Second Workshop on Domain Adaptation for NLP, pages 204–213
April 20, 2021. ©2021 Association for Computational Linguistics

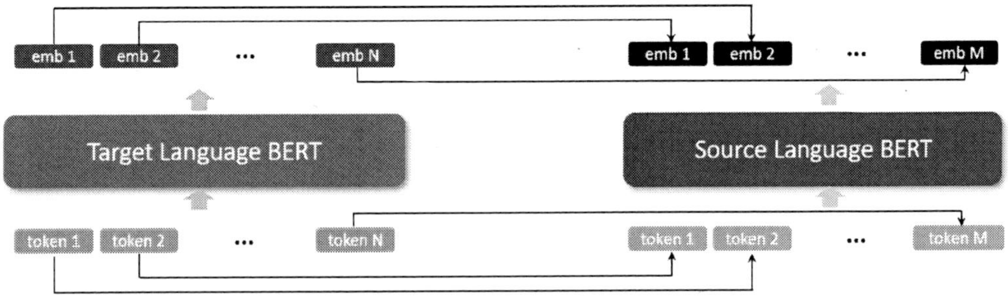

Figure 1: The target tokens (left, blue) and the source tokens (right, black) are aligned by *Fast Align*, so their contextual embeddings can be aligned as well.

v2.6 (Zeman et al., 2020), which shows that our results obtain a substantial gain compared with state-of-the-art methods using multilingual fastText and mBERT [1].

2 Linear Cross-lingual Space Alignment

Let denote $X \in \mathbb{R}^{d \times N}$ as the word embedding matrix for a target language [2], and Y as the word embedding matrix for a source language. For each column of the target embedding matrix $x_i \in \mathbb{R}^d$, it has one source embedding vector $y_i \in \mathbb{R}^d$ corresponding to a source word translated from the target word i. We aim to derive a linear transformation matrix $\hat{W}$ used for mapping from the target language space to the source language space. This can be learned by minimizing the Frobenius norm:

$$\hat{W} = \underset{W \in \mathbb{R}^{d \times d}}{\arg\min} \|WX - Y\|_F \quad (1)$$

Furthermore, Xing et al. (2015) show that the quality of space alignment is successfully improved with the orthogonal restriction, i.e, $W^T W = I$. Thus, the problem can be solved by Procrustes approach (Schönemann, 1966):

$$\begin{aligned} \hat{W} &= \underset{W \in \mathbb{O}^{d \times d}}{\arg\min} \|WX - Y\|_F = UV^T \\ &\text{s.t. } U\Sigma V^T = \text{svd}(YX^T) \end{aligned} \quad (2)$$

where $\mathbb{O}^{d \times d}$ is the set of orthogonal matrices.

3 Method

3.1 Contextual Embedding Transformation

An unsupervised bidirectional word alignment algorithm based on *IBM Model 2* (Brown et al., 1993), *Fast Align* (Dyer et al., 2013), is first applied to a parallel corpus to derive silver aligned token pairs. We then respectively feed the parallel corpus to the BERTs of the target and the source languages and extract the outputs as contextual embeddings. As shown in Figure 1, *Fast Align* bridges "links" between silver token pairs, and between the embeddings of the token pairs as well. Thus, for each target type, a collection of its contextual embeddings can be obtained, as well as a collection of contextual embeddings of its aligned source tokens. Vectors are normalized to satisfy the orthogonal condition.

Motivated by the assumption that multiple senses of a type can construct multiple distinct clusters in its collection (Schuster et al., 2019), we derive several sense-level (cluster-level) embeddings for a type by averaging vectors in each cluster. This splits the representations of multi-sense words and helps the anchor-driven space mapping in a finer resolution. To find clusters, we utilize k-means to cluster contextual embeddings in the vector collection of each type, and adaptively find the optimal k by an elbow-based method Satopaa et al. (2011). Contextual vectors are only clustered in the target side to obtain sense-level embeddings, while the aligned sense-level embeddings in the source side can also be simultaneously derived because embeddings have been already "linked" by *Fast Align*. We next build a sense embedding matrix X_s for the target language by putting the sense-level embeddings in each column, and meanwhile construct a column-wise aligned sense embedding matrix Y_s in the source side. Finally, we obtain the optimal linear mapping $\hat{W}$ from X_s to Y_s by Equation 2. Pseudo code of transformation method is in Appendix A.

[1]Code is available at: `https://github.com/felixxu/ZeroShot-CrossLing-Parsing`.

[2]Different from usual settings, we use x-related symbols for target data and y-related ones for source data.

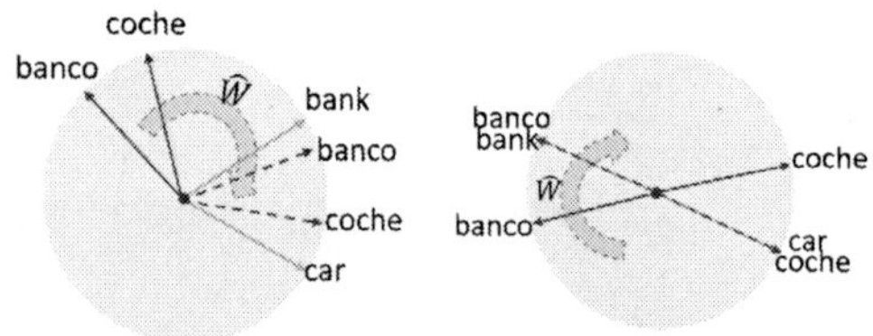

(a) (b)

Figure 2: (a) Spanish vectors (purple arrows) cannot well fit to English vectors (pink arrows) by a linear transformation because they gather in different degrees of cones (different angles between vectors), where dash lines are mapped vectors. (b) After iterative normalization, Spanish and English vectors are uniformly distributed (same angles between vectors). They can be perfectly fit after mapping now.

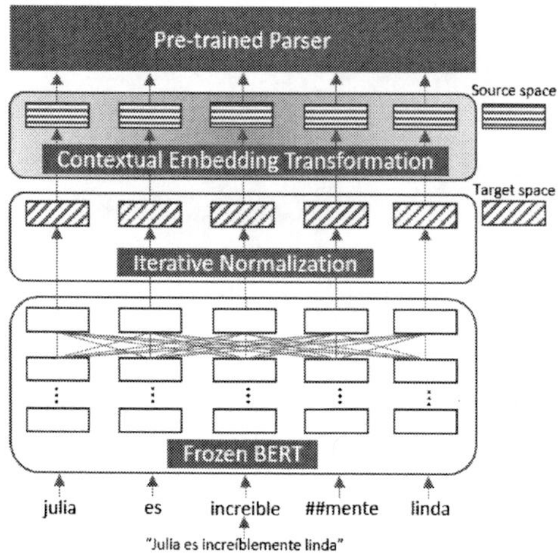

Figure 3: The workflow of how zero-shot transfer processes in our model architecture.

3.2 Anisotropy in Embedding Spaces

Our findings show that contextual embeddings always hold anisotropic property, i.e., they are not uniformly distributed in the space and gather toward a narrow range of orientations. Importantly, degrees of anisotropy across languages are various, which undermines the quality of cross-lingual mappings. A toy example of how the anisotropy affect mappings is illustrated in Figure 2a. One metric for anisotropy is to calculate the average cosine similarity distance of randomly selected vectors. The higher the distance is, the narrower directions vectors point to. Note that the distance for an isotropic space is 0. To mitigate this problem, we introduce iterative normalization. For each token i, the embedding vector x_i is forced to be zero-mean firstly in each iteration:

$$x_i = x_i - \frac{1}{N}\sum_{i=1}^{N} x_i \tag{3}$$

and then normalize it to a fixed length:

$$x_i = \frac{x_i}{\|x_i\|_2} \tag{4}$$

The two steps are repeated until convergence. N is the total number of embeddings. The iterative preprocessing enforces the space to be uniformally distributed, and relative angles between vectors across languages to be more similar (Figure 2b).

3.3 Zero-shot Transfer

A parser is first trained on a source language treebank, where outputs of a frozen BERT are used as embeddings. To apply the pre-trained parser to the target languages, we first replace the source BERT with the target BERT. Then, iterative normalization is operated to enforce contextual embeddings in a near-isotropic space. At last, we map the embeddings to the source language space. Specifically, for each target token i, its contextual representation x_i is mapped by $\hat{W}x_i$. The processing of zero-shot dependency parsing is visualized in Figure 3. Note that the space of pre-trained model has already fit to be near-isotropic by utilizing iterative normalization during training.

4 Experiment

Our parser is the deep biaffine model from Dozat and Manning (2016) where hyperparameters are almost unchanged. The settings of all hyperparameters are listed in Appendix B. English is set as the source language and other languages are targets. In our experiments, we select 6 target languages from 4 language families for which we have off-the-shelf monolingual pre-trained BERT models (base-size). We train the parsing model only in the English treebank, and directly evaluate zero-shot transfer performance on the target languages.

4.1 Baseline

Aligned fastText: Our first baseline is multilingual fastText aligned by the RCSLS method (Joulin et al., 2018; Bojanowski et al., 2017) which is straightforwardly employed to the embedding layer for the corresponding language.

lang (*treebank*)	**en** (*ewt*)		**es** (*gsd*)		**pt** (*gsd*)		**ro** (*rrt*)		**pl** (*lfg*)		**fi** (*tdt*)		**el** (*gdt*)	
	UAS	LAS	UAS	LAS	UAS	LAS	UAS	LAS	UAS	LAS	UAS	LAS	UAS	LAS
aligned fastText	88.55	86.36	73.57	65.13	72.41	60.69	60.27	46.79	75.88	59.48	62.32	40.78	71.51	61.46
mBERT uncased	93.45	91.52	82.11	72.51	80.89	68.90	72.08	56.91	**85.27**	69.76	72.76	49.64	81.72	68.35
mBERT cased	93.32	91.34	82.83	74.08	80.80	68.68	70.76	56.04	83.77	68.01	71.82	48.84	78.24	65.92
word-level	93.70	91.78	82.43	73.86	79.77	67.35	71.13	57.28	84.58	69.53	74.65	51.06	82.29	69.88
sense-level			82.55	73.92	80.34	67.80	71.46	57.57	84.71	69.56	74.81	51.14	82.33	70.10
word-level + IN	**94.21**	**92.01**	83.70	75.14	81.48	69.04	74.65	59.68	84.32	70.45	75.07	51.75	83.76	71.11
sense-level + IN			**83.91**	**75.39**	**81.99**	**69.49**	**74.78**	**59.83**	84.57	**70.52**	**75.31**	**51.99**	**84.05**	**71.26**

Table 1: UAS and LAS of zero-shot evaluation for various languages on test files. The highest scores are bolded and the second highest scores are underlined. Language families are split by dash lines. lang = language, en = English, es = Spanish, pt = Portuguese, ro = Romanian, pl = Polish, fi = Finnish, el = Greek.

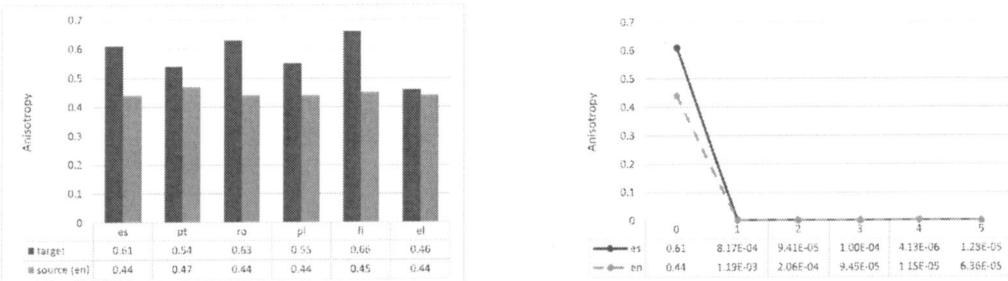

(a) (b)

Figure 4: (a) Discrepancy of anisotropic degrees for all tested language pairs, where scores of anisotropic degree are calculated by the mean cosine similarity between 1000 randomly selected vectors in their language spaces. (b) The isotropic degrees basically decrease to 0 at the first iteration and converge afterwards.

mBERT: We compare our approach with both uncased and cased version of mBERT. Outputs of mBERT are directly used for the embedding layer.

4.2 Settings

Following the analysis that top layers of BERT contain more semantic information (Jawahar et al., 2019), our contextual representation are normalized mean vector of the last 4 layers of BERT. The parallel corpora used to extract contextual embeddings are obtained from *ParaCrawl v6.0* [3]. For each language pairs, we select 1M parallel sentences whose length is shorter than 150. Since some noisy alignments are produced during *Fast Align*, we only take one-to-one token alignment into consideration. The dataset used for cross-lingual dependency parsing is the *Universal Dependencies treebank v2.6* [4] (Zeman et al., 2020).

We store up to 10K contextual vectors extracted from BERT for non-OOV tokens [5]. Vectors in the collection of a target type are clustered to derive sense-level embeddings only if the token occurs more than 100 times. Otherwise, the representation for the token is the basic word-level embedding, i.e., the mean vector of its vector collection. Experiments of word-level embedding alignment are also conducted to compare with sense-level results.

4.3 Iterative Normalization Preprocessing

Forcing contextual embedding vectors in X_s and Y_s to be zero-mean is straightforward. Nevertheless, it is difficult to look for the universal mean vector of contextual embeddings when we train the English parser, because we do not have such an exact mean vector for all possible contextual embeddings. Thus, to successfully implement IN for pre-training the parser, we calculate the approximate universal mean vector by averaging all contextual vectors of every occurrence of tokens from the given training dataset in each iteration. IN runs for 5 iterations, which is sufficient for convergence.

5 Discussion

5.1 Why Contextual Embedding Mapping?

Compare with Previous Methods: Overall results are shown in Table 1. In the first place, our contextual-aware embedding mapping (row 4 - 7)

[3] `www.paracrawl.eu`

[4] `https://lindat.mff.cuni.cz/repository/xmlui/handle/11234/1-3226`

[5] We do not use the composition of subword vectors to approximately represent OOV tokens, because our preliminary results show this hurts the mapping.

exceeds the aligned fastText (row 1) by a large margin. Moreover, our sense-level mapping without IN preprocessing outperforms uncased and cased mBERT by 0.67% and 1.42% on LAS on average, and mapping with preprocessing further outperforms them by 2.07% and 2.82% on average.

Dictionary-free Mapping: Typically, aligned embeddings take a static dictionary as reference but high-quality manual dictionaries are still rare (Ruder et al., 2019). Our mapping skips the word-level alignment in dictionaries, and directly aligns the embeddings from parallel corpora which offers a large scope of token alignments.

Sense-level Mapping: Different from static embeddings whose words only have one unique representation, our contextual embeddings also take advantage of multiple representations for multi-sense words to improve the quality of anchor-driven mapping. In Table 1, the performance of sense-level mapping always surpasses word-level mapping.

5.2 Effect of Iterative Normalization

Figure 4a illustrates the various degrees of anisotropy among different language pairs. As we expect, the anisotropic degree for English (pink, right) is basically constant, but there is large discrepancy between other target languages (blue, left). After IN preprocessing, all language spaces are approximately isotropic, where their scores of anisotropy dramatically reduce near to zero. One example of how the anisotropic degree drops down in each iteration of IN for the Spanish-English pair is illustrated in Figure 4b. IN assists the aligned embeddings in building more similar relative angles across embeddings in different language spaces. As shown in Table 1, this preprocessing improves an absolute gain of 1.37% for word-level mapping and 1.40% for sense-level mapping on average.

6 Conclusion

We proposed a linear, dictionary-free and sense-level contextual mapping approach by exploiting parallel corpus which has shown promising results and substantial improvement compared with multilingual fastText and mBERT in the zero-shot dependency parsing task. We also revealed that various degrees of anisotropy hurts the performance of mapping, and introduced iterative normalization to alleviate it by enforcing contextual embeddings to be uniformly distributed, which also has indicated the benefits of isotropy.

Acknowledgments

We thank the anonymous reviewers for their valuable comments.

References

Mikel Artetxe, Gorka Labaka, and Eneko Agirre. 2016. Learning principled bilingual mappings of word embeddings while preserving monolingual invariance. In Proceedings of the 2016 Conference on Empirical Methods in Natural Language Processing, pages 2289–2294, Austin, Texas. Association for Computational Linguistics.

Piotr Bojanowski, Edouard Grave, Armand Joulin, and Tomas Mikolov. 2017. Enriching word vectors with subword information. Transactions of the Association for Computational Linguistics, 5:135–146.

Peter F. Brown, Stephen A. Della Pietra, Vincent J. Della Pietra, and Robert L. Mercer. 1993. The mathematics of statistical machine translation: Parameter estimation. Computational Linguistics, 19(2):263–311.

Alexis Conneau, Guillaume Lample, Marc'Aurelio Ranzato, Ludovic Denoyer, and Hervé Jégou. 2018. Word translation without parallel data. In International Conference on Learning Representations.

Jacob Devlin, Ming-Wei Chang, Kenton Lee, and Kristina Toutanova. 2019. BERT: Pre-training of deep bidirectional transformers for language understanding. In Proceedings of the 2019 Conference of the North American Chapter of the Association for Computational Linguistics: Human Language Technologies, Volume 1 (Long and Short Papers), pages 4171–4186, Minneapolis, Minnesota. Association for Computational Linguistics.

Timothy Dozat and Christopher D Manning. 2016. Deep biaffine attention for neural dependency parsing. arXiv preprint arXiv:1611.01734.

Chris Dyer, Victor Chahuneau, and Noah A. Smith. 2013. A simple, fast, and effective reparameterization of IBM model 2. In Proceedings of the 2013 Conference of the North American Chapter of the Association for Computational Linguistics: Human Language Technologies, pages 644–648, Atlanta, Georgia. Association for Computational Linguistics.

Kawin Ethayarajh. 2019. How contextual are contextualized word representations? comparing the geometry of BERT, ELMo, and GPT-2 embeddings. In Proceedings of the 2019 Conference on Empirical Methods in Natural Language Processing and the 9th International Joint Conference on

Natural Language Processing (EMNLP-IJCNLP), pages 55–65, Hong Kong, China. Association for Computational Linguistics.

Jiang Guo, Wanxiang Che, David Yarowsky, Haifeng Wang, and Ting Liu. 2015. Cross-lingual dependency parsing based on distributed representations. In Proceedings of the 53rd Annual Meeting of the Association for Computational Linguistics and the 7th International Joint Conference on Natural Language Processing (Volume 1: Long Papers), pages 1234–1244, Beijing, China. Association for Computational Linguistics.

Tsung-Yuan Hsu, Chi-Liang Liu, and Hung-yi Lee. 2019. Zero-shot reading comprehension by cross-lingual transfer learning with multi-lingual language representation model. In Proceedings of the 2019 Conference on Empirical Methods in Natural Language Processing and the 9th International Joint Conference on Natural Language Processing (EMNLP-IJCNLP), pages 5933–5940, Hong Kong, China. Association for Computational Linguistics.

Ganesh Jawahar, Benoît Sagot, and Djamé Seddah. 2019. What does BERT learn about the structure of language? In Proceedings of the 57th Annual Meeting of the Association for Computational Linguistics, pages 3651–3657, Florence, Italy. Association for Computational Linguistics.

Armand Joulin, Piotr Bojanowski, Tomas Mikolov, Hervé Jégou, and Edouard Grave. 2018. Loss in translation: Learning bilingual word mapping with a retrieval criterion. In Proceedings of the 2018 Conference on Empirical Methods in Natural Language Processing.

Dan Kondratyuk and Milan Straka. 2019. 75 languages, 1 model: Parsing universal dependencies universally. In Proceedings of the 2019 Conference on Empirical Methods in Natural Language Processing and the 9th International Joint Conference on Natural Language Processing (EMNLP-IJCNLP), pages 2779–2795.

Ryan McDonald, Slav Petrov, and Keith Hall. 2011. Multi-source transfer of delexicalized dependency parsers. In Proceedings of the 2011 Conference on Empirical Methods in Natural Language Processing, pages 62–72, Edinburgh, Scotland, UK. Association for Computational Linguistics.

Tomas Mikolov, Kai Chen, Greg Corrado, and Jeffrey Dean. 2013a. Efficient estimation of word representations in vector space. arXiv preprint arXiv:1301.3781.

Tomas Mikolov, Quoc V Le, and Ilya Sutskever. 2013b. Exploiting similarities among languages for machine translation. arXiv preprint arXiv:1309.4168.

Jeffrey Pennington, Richard Socher, and Christopher D Manning. 2014. Glove: Global vectors for word representation. In Proceedings of the 2014 conference on empirical methods in natural language processing (EMNLP), pages 1532–1543.

Matthew Peters, Mark Neumann, Mohit Iyyer, Matt Gardner, Christopher Clark, Kenton Lee, and Luke Zettlemoyer. 2018. Deep contextualized word representations. In Proceedings of the 2018 Conference of the North American Chapter of the Association for Computational Linguistics: Human Language Technologies, Volume 1 (Long Papers), pages 2227–2237, New Orleans, Louisiana. Association for Computational Linguistics.

Alec Radford, Jeffrey Wu, Rewon Child, David Luan, Dario Amodei, and Ilya Sutskever. 2019. Language models are unsupervised multitask learners. OpenAI Blog, 1(8):9.

Sebastian Ruder, Ivan Vulić, and Anders Søgaard. 2019. A survey of cross-lingual word embedding models. Journal of Artificial Intelligence Research, 65:569–631.

Ville Satopaa, Jeannie Albrecht, David Irwin, and Barath Raghavan. 2011. Finding a" kneedle" in a haystack: Detecting knee points in system behavior. In 2011 31st international conference on distributed computing systems workshops, pages 166–171. IEEE.

Peter H Schönemann. 1966. A generalized solution of the orthogonal procrustes problem. Psychometrika, 31(1):1–10.

Tal Schuster, Ori Ram, Regina Barzilay, and Amir Globerson. 2019. Cross-lingual alignment of contextual word embeddings, with applications to zero-shot dependency parsing. In Proceedings of the 2019 Conference of the North American Chapter of the Association for Computational Linguistics: Human Language Technologies, Volume 1 (Long and Short Papers), pages 1599–1613, Minneapolis, Minnesota. Association for Computational Linguistics.

Yuxuan Wang, Wanxiang Che, Jiang Guo, Yijia Liu, and Ting Liu. 2019. Cross-lingual bert transformation for zero-shot dependency parsing. In Proceedings of the 2019 Conference on Empirical Methods in Natural Language Processing and the 9th International Joint Conference on Natural Language Processing (EMNLP-IJCNLP), pages 5725–5731.

Jiateng Xie, Zhilin Yang, Graham Neubig, Noah A. Smith, and Jaime Carbonell. 2018. Neural cross-lingual named entity recognition with minimal resources. In Proceedings of the 2018 Conference on Empirical Methods in Natural Language Processing, pages 369–379, Brussels, Belgium. Association for Computational Linguistics.

Chao Xing, Dong Wang, Chao Liu, and Yiye Lin. 2015. Normalized word embedding and orthogonal transform for bilingual word translation. In Proceedings of the 2015 Conference of the North American Chapter of the Association for Computational Linguistics: Human Language Technologies, pages 1006–1011, Denver, Colorado. Association for Computational Linguistics.

Daniel Zeman, Joakim Nivre, Mitchell Abrams, Elia Ackermann, Noëmi Aepli, Željko Agić, Lars Ahrenberg, Chika Kennedy Ajede, Gabrielė Aleksandravičiūtė, Lene Antonsen, Katya Aplonova, Angelina Aquino, Maria Jesus Aranzabe, Gashaw Arutie, Masayuki Asahara, Luma Ateyah, Furkan Atmaca, Mohammed Attia, Aitziber Atutxa, Liesbeth Augustinus, Elena Badmaeva, Miguel Ballesteros, Esha Banerjee, Sebastian Bank, Verginica Barbu Mititelu, Victoria Basmov, Colin Batchelor, John Bauer, Kepa Bengoetxea, Yevgeni Berzak, Irshad Ahmad Bhat, Riyaz Ahmad Bhat, Erica Biagetti, Eckhard Bick, Agnė Bielinskienė, Rogier Blokland, Victoria Bobicev, Loïc Boizou, Emanuel Borges Völker, Carl Börstell, Cristina Bosco, Gosse Bouma, Sam Bowman, Adriane Boyd, Kristina Brokaitė, Aljoscha Burchardt, Marie Candito, Bernard Caron, Gauthier Caron, Tatiana Cavalcanti, Gülşen Cebiroğlu Eryiğit, Flavio Massimiliano Cecchini, Giuseppe G. A. Celano, Slavomír Čéplö, Savas Cetin, Fabricio Chalub, Ethan Chi, Jinho Choi, Yongseok Cho, Jayeol Chun, Alessandra T. Cignarella, Silvie Cinková, Aurélie Collomb, Çağrı Çöltekin, Miriam Connor, Marine Courtin, Elizabeth Davidson, Marie-Catherine de Marneffe, Valeria de Paiva, Elvis de Souza, Arantza Diaz de Ilarraza, Carly Dickerson, Bamba Dione, Peter Dirix, Kaja Dobrovoljc, Timothy Dozat, Kira Droganova, Puneet Dwivedi, Hanne Eckhoff, Marhaba Eli, Ali Elkahky, Binyam Ephrem, Olga Erina, Tomaž Erjavec, Aline Etienne, Wograine Evelyn, Richárd Farkas, Hector Fernandez Alcalde, Jennifer Foster, Cláudia Freitas, Kazunori Fujita, Katarína Gajdošová, Daniel Galbraith, Marcos Garcia, Moa Gärdenfors, Sebastian Garza, Kim Gerdes, Filip Ginter, Iakes Goenaga, Koldo Gojenola, Memduh Gökırmak, Yoav Goldberg, Xavier Gómez Guinovart, Berta González Saavedra, Bernadeta Griciūtė, Matias Grioni, Loïc Grobol, Normunds Grūzītis, Bruno Guillaume, Céline Guillot-Barbance, Tunga Güngör, Nizar Habash, Jan Hajič, Jan Hajič jr., Mika Hämäläinen, Linh Hà Mỹ, Na-Rae Han, Kim Harris, Dag Haug, Johannes Heinecke, Oliver Hellwig, Felix Hennig, Barbora Hladká, Jaroslava Hlaváčová, Florinel Hociung, Petter Hohle, Jena Hwang, Takumi Ikeda, Radu Ion, Elena Irimia, Ọlájídé Ishola, Tomáš Jelínek, Anders Johannsen, Hildur Jónsdóttir, Fredrik Jørgensen, Markus Juutinen, Hüner Kaşıkara, Andre Kaasen, Nadezhda Kabaeva, Sylvain Kahane, Hiroshi Kanayama, Jenna Kanerva, Boris Katz, Tolga Kayadelen, Jessica Kenney, Václava Kettnerová, Jesse Kirchner, Elena Klementieva, Arne Köhn, Abdullatif Köksal, Kamil Kopacewicz, Timo Korkiakangas, Natalia Kotsyba, Jolanta Kovalevskaitė, Simon Krek, Sookyoung Kwak, Veronika Laippala, Lorenzo Lambertino, Lucia Lam, Tatiana Lando, Septina Dian Larasati, Alexei Lavrentiev, John Lee, Phng Lê H`ông, Alessandro Lenci, Saran Lertpradit, Herman Leung, Maria Levina, Cheuk Ying Li, Josie Li, Keying Li, KyungTae Lim, Yuan Li, Nikola Ljubešić, Olga Loginova, Olga Lyashevskaya, Teresa Lynn, Vivien Macketanz, Aibek Makazhanov, Michael Mandl, Christopher Manning, Ruli Manurung, Cătălina Mărănduc, David Mareček, Katrin Marheinecke, Héctor Martínez Alonso, André Martins, Jan Mašek, Hiroshi Matsuda, Yuji Matsumoto, Ryan McDonald, Sarah McGuinness, Gustavo Mendonça, Niko Miekka, Margarita Misirpashayeva, Anna Missilä, Cătălin Mititelu, Maria Mitrofan, Yusuke Miyao, Simonetta Montemagni, Amir More, Laura Moreno Romero, Keiko Sophie Mori, Tomohiko Morioka, Shinsuke Mori, Shigeki Moro, Bjartur Mortensen, Bohdan Moskalevskyi, Kadri Muischnek, Robert Munro, Yugo Murawaki, Kaili Müürisep, Pinkey Nainwani, Juan Ignacio Navarro Horñiacek, Anna Nedoluzhko, Gunta Nešpore-Bērzkalne, Lng Nguy˜ên Thị, Huy`ên Nguy˜ên Thị Minh, Yoshihiro Nikaido, Vitaly Nikolaev, Rattima Nitisaroj, Hanna Nurmi, Stina Ojala, Atul Kr. Ojha, Adédayọ Olúòkun, Mai Omura, Emeka Onwuegbuzia, Petya Osenova, Robert Östling, Lilja Øvrelid, Şaziye Betül Özateş, Arzucan Özgür, Balkız Öztürk Başaran, Niko Partanen, Elena Pascual, Marco Passarotti, Agnieszka Patejuk, Guilherme Paulino-Passos, Angelika Peljak-Łapińska, Siyao Peng, Cenel-Augusto Perez, Guy Perrier, Daria Petrova, Slav Petrov, Jason Phelan, Jussi Piitulainen, Tommi A Pirinen, Emily Pitler, Barbara Plank, Thierry Poibeau, Larisa Ponomareva, Martin Popel, Lauma Pretkalniņa, Sophie Prévost, Prokopis Prokopidis, Adam Przepiórkowski, Tiina Puolakainen, Sampo Pyysalo, Peng Qi, Andriela Rääbis, Alexandre Rademaker, Loganathan Ramasamy, Taraka Rama, Carlos Ramisch, Vinit Ravishankar, Livy Real, Petru Rebeja, Siva Reddy, Georg Rehm, Ivan Riabov, Michael Rießler, Erika Rimkutė, Larissa Rinaldi, Laura Rituma, Luisa Rocha, Mykhailo Romanenko, Rudolf Rosa, Valentin Roșca, Davide Rovati, Olga Rudina, Jack Rueter, Shoval Sadde, Benoît Sagot, Shadi Saleh, Alessio Salomoni, Tanja Samardžić, Stephanie Samson, Manuela Sanguinetti, Dage Särg, Baiba Saulīte, Yanin Sawanakunanon, Salvatore Scarlata, Nathan Schneider, Sebastian Schuster, Djamé Seddah, Wolfgang Seeker, Mojgan Seraji, Mo Shen, Atsuko Shimada, Hiroyuki Shirasu, Muh Shohibussirri, Dmitry Sichinava, Aline Silveira, Natalia Silveira, Maria Simi, Radu Simionescu, Katalin Simkó, Mária Šimková, Kiril Simov, Maria Skachedubova, Aaron Smith, Isabela Soares-Bastos, Carolyn Spadine, Antonio Stella, Milan Straka, Jana Strnadová, Alane Suhr, Umut Sulubacak, Shingo Suzuki, Zsolt Szántó, Dima Taji, Yuta Takahashi, Fabio Tamburini, Takaaki Tanaka, Samson Tella, Isabelle Tellier, Guillaume Thomas, Liisi Torga, Marsida Toska, Trond Trosterud, Anna Trukhina, Reut Tsarfaty, Utku Türk, Francis Tyers, Sumire Uematsu, Roman Untilov, Zdeňka Urešová, Larraitz Uria, Hans Uszkoreit, Andrius Utka, Sowmya Vajjala, Daniel van Niekerk, Gertjan van Noord, Viktor

Varga, Eric Villemonte de la Clergerie, Veronika Vincze, Aya Wakasa, Lars Wallin, Abigail Walsh, Jing Xian Wang, Jonathan North Washington, Maximilan Wendt, Paul Widmer, Seyi Williams, Mats Wirén, Christian Wittern, Tsegay Woldemariam, Tak-sum Wong, Alina Wróblewska, Mary Yako, Kayo Yamashita, Naoki Yamazaki, Chunxiao Yan, Koichi Yasuoka, Marat M. Yavrumyan, Zhuoran Yu, Zdeněk Žabokrtský, Amir Zeldes, Hanzhi Zhu, and Anna Zhuravleva. 2020. Universal dependencies 2.6. LINDAT/CLARIAH-CZ digital library at the Institute of Formal and Applied Linguistics (ÚFAL), Faculty of Mathematics and Physics, Charles University.

Mozhi Zhang, Keyulu Xu, Ken-ichi Kawarabayashi, Stefanie Jegelka, and Jordan Boyd-Graber. 2019. Are girls neko or shōjo? cross-lingual alignment of non-isomorphic embeddings with iterative normalization. In Proceedings of the 57th Annual Meeting of the Association for Computational Linguistics, pages 3180–3189, Florence, Italy. Association for Computational Linguistics.

A Pseudo Code of Contextual Embedding Transformation

Pseudo Code is shown in Alogirthm 1.

B Hyperparamters

Here we list all hyperparamters for our pre-trained parser in Table 2.

Hyperparameters	Value
Batch size	128
Arc representation dim	500
Tag representation dim	100
Dropout	0.3
LSTM hidden size	500
LSTM # layers	3
Pos tag embedding dim	100
Grad norm	5
# epochs	200
Patience	25
Optimizer	Dense Sparse ADAM
Learning rate	0.0008
Encoding Layer	Bi-LSTM

Table 2: Hyperparameters for deep biaffine dependency parser training.

C pre-trained Monolingual BERTs

In Table 3, we list the names of pre-trained monolingual BERTs from huggingface [6] that we used in our experiments.

Language	Model name
mbert uncased	bert-base-multilingual-uncased
mbert cased	bert-base-multilingual-cased
en	bert-base-uncased
es	dccuchile/bert-base-spanish-wwm-uncased
pt	neuralmind/bert-base-portuguese-cased
ro	dumitrescustefan/bert-base-romanian-uncased-v1
pl	dkleczek/bert-base-polish-uncased-v1
fi	bert-base-finnish-uncased-v1
el	nlpaueb/bert-base-greek-uncased-v1

Table 3: Names of Pre-trained BERT models.

[6] https://huggingface.co/models

Algorithm 1 Contextual Embedding Transformation

Require: Target Corpus $\mathcal{X}$, source Corpus $\mathcal{Y}$, target pre-trained BERT $\mathcal{B}_x$, source pre-trained BERT $\mathcal{B}_y$, where $\mathcal{X}$ is the translation corpus of $\mathcal{Y}$

function CONTEXTUAL-TRANSFORMATION($\mathcal{X}, \mathcal{Y}, \mathcal{B}_x, \mathcal{B}_y$)
    # Part 1: Collect embeddings
    $\mathcal{I} \leftarrow$ FAST-ALIGN($\mathcal{X}, \mathcal{Y}$) ▷ $\mathcal{I}$ is an index-aligned corpus, where each line is composed of index pairs of aligned tokens for each parallel sentence.
    Initialize $\mathcal{C} \leftarrow$ Empty Hash Map
    for index i in LENGTH($\mathcal{X}$) **do** ▷ number of sentences in the corpus
        $X \leftarrow \mathcal{X}[i], Y \leftarrow \mathcal{Y}[i], I \leftarrow \mathcal{I}[i]$
        $E_X \leftarrow \mathcal{B}_x(X)$ ▷ Contextual embeddings of tokens:
        $E_Y \leftarrow \mathcal{B}_y(Y)$
        for index j in LENGTH(X) **do** ▷ number of tokens in the sentence
            $x \leftarrow X[j], e_x \leftarrow E_X[j]$
            $e_y \leftarrow E_Y[I(j)]$ ▷ Find the aligned embedding by looking at I, where $I(j)$ is the index of aligned source token.
            $\mathcal{C}[x]$.append((e_x, e_y))
        end for
    end for

    # Part 2: Obtain aligned sense-level embeddings
    Initialize Empty matrix X_s, Y_s
    for target type x in $\mathcal{C}$.keys() **do**
        $c_x \leftarrow$ all target embeddings e_x in $\mathcal{C}[x]$
        $c_y \leftarrow$ all target embeddings e_y in $\mathcal{C}[x]$
        $k \leftarrow$ ELBOW-BASED(c_x) ▷ Find optimal number of clusters
        for Subcluster c_{x_i} in K-MEANS(k, c_x) **do**
            Get subcluster c_{y_i} due to aligned pair $((e_x, e_y))$ in $\mathcal{C}[x]$
            $mean_x \leftarrow$ mean vector of c_{x_i}
            $mean_y \leftarrow$ mean vector of c_{y_i}
            Put $mean_x$ in X_s as a column
            Put $mean_y$ in Y_s as a column
        end for
    end for

    # Part 3: Derive embedding transformation
    $U\Sigma V^T = \text{svd}(YX^T)$
    $\hat{W} = UV^T$
    return $\hat{W}$
end function

Gradual Fine-Tuning for Low-Resource Domain Adaptation

Haoran Xu[1], Seth Ebner[1], Mahsa Yarmohammadi[1], Aaron Steven White[2], Benjamin Van Durme[1], Kenton Murray[1]

[1]Johns Hopkins University, [2]University of Rochester

{hxu64,seth,mahsa,vandurme,kenton}@jhu.edu,
aaron.white@rochester.edu

Abstract

Fine-tuning is known to improve NLP models by adapting an initial model trained on more plentiful but less domain-salient examples to data in a target domain. Such domain adaptation is typically done using one stage of fine-tuning. We demonstrate that gradually fine-tuning in a multi-stage process can yield substantial further gains and can be applied without modifying the model or learning objective.

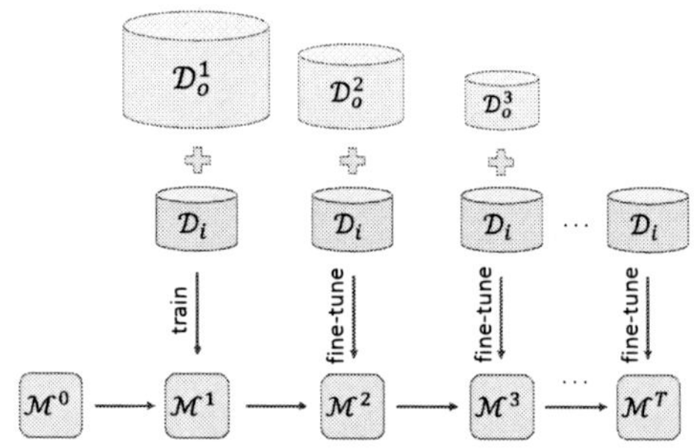

Figure 1: Stages of gradual fine-tuning: 1) Train the model, $\mathcal{M}$, on a mixture of in-domain data, $\mathcal{D}_i$, and out-of-domain data, $\mathcal{D}_o$; 2) iteratively fine-tune on mixed domain data with decreasing amounts of out-of-domain data; 3) fine-tune on only in-domain data.

1 Introduction

Domain adaptation is a technique for practical applications in which one wants to learn a model for a task in a particular domain with too few instances of in-domain data to directly learn a model. Common approaches for domain adaptation make use of fine-tuning (Dabre et al., 2019; Li and Specia, 2019; Imankulova et al., 2019), in which a model is pretrained on a large amount of out-of-domain but task-relevant data and then refined toward the target domain by subsequently training on in-domain data. This fine-tuning procedure is often performed in one stage: the pretrained model is trained on the in-domain data until convergence (Chu et al., 2017; Min et al., 2017a). We propose a *gradual* fine-tuning approach, in which a model is iteratively trained to convergence on data whose distribution progressively approaches that of the in-domain data. Intuitively, the model is eased toward the target domain rather than abruptly shifting to it.

Inspired by the general approach of curriculum learning of training a model on a trajectory from easier instances to more difficult instances (Bengio et al., 2009), we train a model on a sequence of datasets, each of which would be increasingly difficult to learn on its own due to its size. Each dataset in the sequence interpolates between the data in the previous iteration and the target domain data. We hypothesize that just as in curriculum learning where first learning from easier instances helps models subsequently learn from more difficult instances, the interpolation process yields datasets with distributions that are increasingly useful for helping models learn during subsequent stages of the gradual fine-tuning procedure. We begin by training the model on data that contains a mix of out-of-domain and in-domain instances, then increase the concentration of in-domain data in each fine-tuning stage. In this way, at each stage of fine-tuning we increase the similarity between the current domain and the target domain, which enables the model to potentially better fit the distribution of the target domain. The approach is illustrated in Figure 1.

We conduct experiments on two NLP tasks to demonstrate the effectiveness of gradual fine-tuning. We first look at (1) dialogue state tracking with the MultiWOZ v2.0 dataset (Budzianowski et al., 2018), which is a collection of human-to-human conversation transcriptions in multiple domains. We focus on single dialogue domains and utilize out-of-domain data to improve accuracy of

Proceedings of the Second Workshop on Domain Adaptation for NLP, pages 214–221
April 20, 2021.

slot classification in the target domain. We then consider (2) an event extraction task from the ACE 2005 dataset (LDC2006T06) for which we augment the Arabic target domain data with English data.

Gradual fine-tuning is also simple to implement. If fine-tuning is already supported by the code, then only new configuration files need to be created to specify the (amount of) data used at each iteration.[1] No adjustments to model or training code are needed. Just by modifying the training approach, one can obtain substantial improvements.[2]

2 Related Work

Howard and Ruder (2018) propose an effective inductive transfer learning method for language model fine-tuning and demonstrate improvements on text classification tasks. Gururangan et al. (2020) also show improvements on target task performance by fine-tuning pretrained language models on in-domain data and on the target task's training data. In this work, we focus on adapting the entire model, not just the underlying language model encoder. Our approach is a form of transductive transfer (Pan and Yang, 2009), in which the pretraining and fine-tuning tasks are the same. In the transductive transfer setting, we hope to learn task-specific information by training on a large (potentially out-of-domain) dataset, and then subsequently adjust model parameters based on domain-specific information learned from in-domain data.

Transductive transfer has been effective for tasks such as question answering (Min et al., 2017b), machine translation (Sennrich et al., 2015), and open information extraction (Sarhan and Spruit, 2020). Wu et al. (2019) fine-tune toward a target domain for dialogue state tracking using Gradient Episodic Memory (Lopez-Paz and Ranzato, 2017) to avoid catastrophic forgetting (McCloskey and Cohen, 1989). Ahn et al. (2019) introduce an uncertainty-based regularization method to overcome catastrophic forgetting in the continual learning setting. There have also been successful approaches for cross-lingual information extraction and semantic role labeling using no target language data (Subburathinam et al., 2019), mixed source and translated target language data (Fei et al., 2020), and language-independent model transfer (Daza and Frank, 2019; Fei et al., 2020).

Jiang and Zhai (2007) propose a method for upweighting the importance of target domain instances relative to source domain instances to improve domain adaptation. The iterative increase in concentration of target domain data in the mixed domain data used in gradual fine-tuning can be seen as analogous to giving target domain instances more weight. In contrast to all the aforementioned approaches, gradual fine-tuning requires no modification to existing models or learning objectives, so it can be applied to any system.

Domain adaptation can also be achieved using curriculum learning. Zhang et al. (2019) use a curriculum learning approach to adapt a general-domain machine translation model to a target domain while also using data whose domain is unknown. Inspired by curriculum learning (Bengio et al., 2009), which highlights the importance of the order of training instances, we propose a multi-stage fine-tuning strategy for domain adaptation. In this work, we order a sequence of fine-tuning datasets from least similar to the target domain to most similar.

3 Method

Domain adaptation via fine-tuning aims to improve performance on a target domain by using information learned from general domain data when training on data in the target domain. In other words, it is expected that training on general domain data would provide better initialization for subsequently training on target domain data than random initialization would provide (Erhan et al., 2010).

3.1 Mixed Domain Training

Given training data for the target domain, $\mathcal{D}_i$, we augment it with out-of-domain data $\mathcal{D}_o$ mapped to the target task schema.[3] The in-domain and out-of-domain data are concatenated to form a mixed domain training set. A mixed domain model is obtained by training on the mixed dataset.

3.2 One-Stage Fine-tuning

The distribution of the mixed domain data is different from that of the target domain data. However, regardless of how diverse the mixed domain training data is, subsequently fine-tuning the model on

[1] One may also need to implement data subsampling.

[2] Supporting code: `https://github.com/felixxu/Gradual-Finetune`.

[3] Portions of the target task schema corresponding to fields not available in the out-of-domain data could be masked in the mapped data.

the target in-domain data is a direct way to encourage the model to converge to the distribution of the target domain. The model is expected to use task knowledge learned from the mixed domain data to yield improved performance over a model trained only on data from the target domain. Because the model is fine-tuned to convergence on the target domain data once, we refer to this procedure as one-stage fine-tuning.

Algorithm 1 Gradual Fine-Tuning

Require: in-domain data $\mathcal{D}_i$, out-of-domain data $\mathcal{D}_o^0$, initial model $\mathcal{M}^0$, out-of-domain data schedule $\mathcal{S}$

function GRADUAL-FT($\mathcal{D}_i$, $\mathcal{D}_o^0$, $\mathcal{M}^0$, $\mathcal{S}$)
  $t \leftarrow 0$
  for $amount$ in $\mathcal{S}$ **do**
    $t \leftarrow t + 1$
    $\mathcal{D}_o^t \leftarrow$ SAMPLE($\mathcal{D}_o^{t-1}$, $amount$)
    $\mathcal{D}_{train}^t \leftarrow \mathcal{D}_i \cup \mathcal{D}_o^t$
    $\mathcal{M}^t \leftarrow$ TRAIN($\mathcal{M}^{t-1}$, $\mathcal{D}_{train}^t$)
  end for
  return $\mathcal{M}^t$
end function

3.3 Gradual Fine-tuning

Instead of adapting the model to the target domain by one-stage fine-tuning, we propose an iterative multi-stage approach that transitions from the initial mixed domain to the target domain. Each iteration incorporates less out-of-domain data than the preceding iteration as specified by a data schedule $\mathcal{S}$, bringing the data distribution closer to that of the target domain every training cycle. At each iteration, the model is trained to convergence. The number of iterations and the out-of-domain data schedule $\mathcal{S}$ are hyperparameters that can be tuned for a particular task. Pseudocode for gradual fine-tuning is presented in Algorithm 1. In our implementation, the out-of-domain data is uniformly randomly sampled from the out-of-domain data used in the previous iteration.

4 Experiments

4.1 Dialogue State Tracking

Dialogue state tracking (DST) involves estimating at each dialogue turn the probability distribution over slot-values enumerated in an ontology. For example, we may be interested in the distribution over cuisines given the dialogue history and an utterance indicating the *restaurant* domain and food slot. We show that gradual fine-tuning can substantially improve slot accuracy—the accuracy of predicting each slot separately—and joint accuracy—the percentage of turns in which all slots are predicted correctly—in a given dialogue domain.

	Rest.	Hotel	Attract.	Taxi	Train
# Slots	7	10	3	4	6
# Turns	3011	3472	577	1667	1771
# Dialogues					
Train	523	513	127	326	282
Dev	50	56	11	57	30
Test	61	65	12	52	33

Table 1: Data statistics for five domains from MultiWOZ v2.0.

Dataset We run experiments on the MultiWOZ v2.0 dataset (Budzianowski et al., 2018), which is a multi-domain conversational corpus with seven domains and 35 slots. Following Wu et al. (2019), we focus on five domains: *restaurant*, *hotel*, *attraction*, *taxi*, and *train*, which amounts to 2198 single-domain dialogues and 5459 multi-domain dialogues from the original dataset across all data splits. Statistics for single-domain dialogues of the five domains are presented in Table 1. Among the five domains, *restaurant* and *hotel* are adopted as the target domains for our experiments. We consider single-domain dialogues in the target domain as in-domain data and the rest of the (single-domain or multi-domain) dialogues excluding the target domain as out-of-domain data.

Settings The gradual fine-tuning data schedule of out-of-domain dialogues is $\mathcal{S}$ = 4K $\rightarrow$ 2K $\rightarrow$ 0.5K $\rightarrow$ 0 (K=thousand), where the in-domain data is mixed with the out-of-domain data at each stage.[4] We use the Slot-Utterance Matching Belief Tracker (SUMBT) model by Lee et al. (2019), as well as their hyperparameters. The SUMBT model is composed of four parts: BERT encoders for encoding slots, values, and utterances, a slot-utterance matching network, a belief tracker, and a nonparametric discriminator. SUMBT achieves state-of-the-art performance on the MultiWOZ v2.0 dataset. More training details can be found in Appendix A.

Baselines Three baselines are considered in this experiment. The first one is a model trained only on in-domain data (no data augmentation). The second is a model trained with the one-stage fine-

[4] Experiments starting with 2K (2K $\rightarrow$ 0.5K $\rightarrow$ 0) augmented data examples were also conducted to further explore the effect of data size (Appendix B).

tuning strategy ($\mathcal{S} = 4\text{K} \rightarrow 0$). The last baseline is a model trained with the same settings as Lee et al. (2019), which has seen the full training set.[5]

Result and Analysis The main results are shown in Table 2. Compared with the model trained without data augmentation, gradual fine-tuning yields an absolute gain of 3.6% for slot accuracy and 15.11% for joint accuracy in the *restaurant* domain and 1.7% slot accuracy and 5.82% joint accuracy in the *hotel* domain. Moreover, gradual fine-tuning also considerably outperforms both the one-stage strategy as well as the mixed data training.

Figure 2 shows increasing slot accuracy at each stage of (gradual) fine-tuning, which supports our hypothesis that gradually fine-tuning the model consistently improves performance as the data distribution approaches that of the target domain.

	Restaurant Slot/Joint	Hotel Slot/Joint
No FT (single domain)	90.70/52.16	90.79/46.30
No FT* (all domains)	92.19/58.63	91.48/50.26
One-stage FT	93.47/61.15	91.43/46.30
Gradual FT	**94.30/67.27**	**92.49/52.12**

Table 2: Slot and joint accuracy in the restaurant and hotel domains under various training methods. * indicates that the model uses the full training set. *No FT (single domain)* is the model trained only on in-domain data and *No FT (all domains)* is the training regime from Lee et al. (2019). FT=fine-tuning.

4.2 Event Extraction

We also employ gradual fine-tuning on an event extraction task to show the general applicability of the approach. Event extraction involves predicting event triggers, event arguments, and argument roles. We perform event extraction on the ACE 2005 corpus by considering Arabic as the target domain and English as the auxiliary domain.

Settings For data processing, model building, and performance evaluation, we use the DYGIE++ framework,[6] which achieved state-of-the-art results on ACE 2005 event extraction (Wadden et al., 2019). We replace the BERT encoder (Devlin et al., 2019) with XLM-R (Conneau et al., 2020) to train models on monolingual and mixed bilingual datasets. Because no standard splits were found for the Arabic portion of the ACE 2005 dataset, the train/dev/test splits for Arabic are randomly selected. Table 3 shows statistics of the ACE 2005 events dataset for our experiments. The gradual fine-tuning data schedule of preprocessed English documents, $\mathcal{S}$, is $1\text{K} \rightarrow 0.5\text{K} \rightarrow 0.2\text{K} \rightarrow 0$.[7] We report four metrics for the evaluation: a trigger is correctly identified if its offsets find a match in the ground truth (TrigID), and it is correctly classified if their event types match (TrigC). An argument is correctly identified if its offsets and event type find a match in the ground truth (ArgID), and it is correctly classified if their event roles match (ArgC).

	English	Arabic
# Event types	33	30
# Role types	22	21
# Events/Arguments		
Train	4202/4859	1743/2506
Dev	450/605	117/174
Test	403/576	198/287

Table 3: Statistics for English and Arabic ACE 2005.

Baselines The first baseline in Table 4 is the model from Wadden et al. (2019) (with an XLM-R encoder) trained only on Arabic data, the second baseline is trained on mixed data (Arabic + 1K English data) without any fine-tuning, and the third baseline uses the one-stage fine-tuning strategy.

Results The results are given in Table 4. Mixed data training and one-stage fine-tuning achieve slight improvements over no data augmentation and even hurt performance on the TrigID and ArgID metrics. Gradual fine-tuning outperforms all baselines by a substantial margin on all four metrics, especially TrigC, which achieves an absolute gain of 5.84% compared to the state-of-the-art model trained only on the Arabic dataset.

	TrigID	TrigC	ArgID	ArgC
No FT (Ar)	64.77	57.03	47.76	42.83
No FT (mixed)	64.12	59.48	46.57	43.21
One-stage FT	63.61	59.88	46.79	43.44
Gradual FT	**66.29**	**62.87**	**48.11**	**44.21**

Table 4: Identification and classification F1 scores for triggers and arguments on Arabic ACE 2005. FT=fine-tuning, Ar=Arabic, mixed=Arabic + 1K English.

[5]Note that use of the full training set means the model sees multi-domain dialogues which may include the target domain. The full training set contains approximately 4K more dialogues than what we use for gradual fine-tuning.

[6]https://github.com/dwadden/dygiepp

[7]1K, 0.5K, and 0.2K preprocessed documents correspond to 85%, 35%, and 5% of total events/arguments in the English training set.

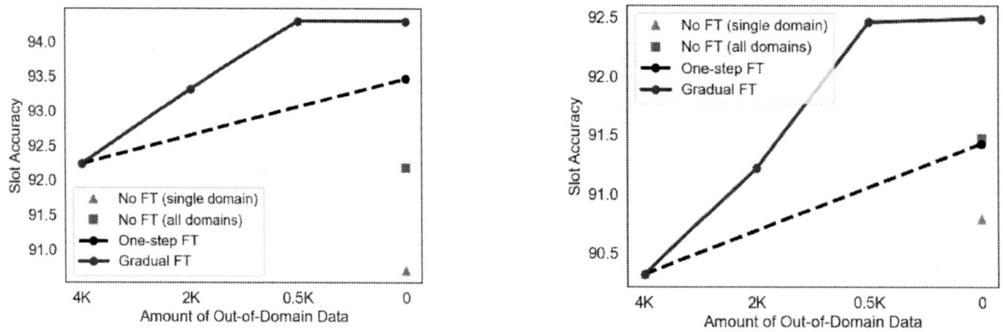

(a) Restaurant

(b) Hotel

Figure 2: Slot accuracy for the *restaurant* and *hotel* domains in MultiWOZ v2.0. Gradual fine-tuning yields higher performance than fine-tuning in a one-stage process. Both fine-tuning approaches perform better than not doing any fine-tuning. Results at the end of training are the rightmost points (Table 2).

5 Conclusion

We have proposed a gradual fine-tuning technique that iteratively steers the distribution of augmented training data toward that of a target domain. Gradual fine-tuning can be straightforwardly applied to an existing codebase without changing the model architecture or learning objective. Through experiments on dialogue state tracking and event extraction tasks, we have demonstrated that gradual fine-tuning outperforms standard one-stage fine-tuning for domain adaptation.

Acknowledgments

We thank the anonymous reviewers for their valuable comments. This work was supported in part by IARPA BETTER (#2019-19051600005) and DARPA KAIROS (FA8750-19-2-0034). The views and conclusions contained in this work are those of the authors and should not be interpreted as necessarily representing the official policies, either expressed or implied, or endorsements of DARPA, ODNI, IARPA, or the U.S. Government. The U.S. Government is authorized to reproduce and distribute reprints for governmental purposes notwithstanding any copyright annotation therein.

References

Hongjoon Ahn, Sungmin Cha, Donggyu Lee, and Taesup Moon. 2019. Uncertainty-based continual learning with adaptive regularization. In *Advances in Neural Information Processing Systems*, volume 32. Curran Associates, Inc.

Yoshua Bengio, Jérôme Louradour, Ronan Collobert, and Jason Weston. 2009. Curriculum learning. In *Proceedings of the 26th Annual International Conference on Machine Learning*, ICML '09, page 41–48, New York, NY, USA. Association for Computing Machinery.

Paweł Budzianowski, Tsung-Hsien Wen, Bo-Hsiang Tseng, Iñigo Casanueva, Ultes Stefan, Ramadan Osman, and Milica Gašić. 2018. MultiWOZ - A Large-Scale Multi-Domain Wizard-of-Oz Dataset for Task-Oriented Dialogue Modelling. In *Proceedings of the 2018 Conference on Empirical Methods in Natural Language Processing (EMNLP)*.

Chenhui Chu, Raj Dabre, and Sadao Kurohashi. 2017. An empirical comparison of domain adaptation methods for neural machine translation. In *Proceedings of the 55th Annual Meeting of the Association for Computational Linguistics (Volume 2: Short Papers)*, pages 385–391, Vancouver, Canada. Association for Computational Linguistics.

Alexis Conneau, Kartikay Khandelwal, Naman Goyal, Vishrav Chaudhary, Guillaume Wenzek, Francisco Guzmán, Edouard Grave, Myle Ott, Luke Zettlemoyer, and Veselin Stoyanov. 2020. Unsupervised cross-lingual representation learning at scale. In *Proceedings of the 58th Annual Meeting of the Association for Computational Linguistics*, pages 8440–8451, Online. Association for Computational Linguistics.

Raj Dabre, Atsushi Fujita, and Chenhui Chu. 2019. Exploiting multilingualism through multistage fine-tuning for low-resource neural machine translation. In *Proceedings of the 2019 Conference on Empirical Methods in Natural Language Processing and the 9th International Joint Conference on Natural Language Processing (EMNLP-IJCNLP)*, pages 1410–1416.

Angel Daza and Anette Frank. 2019. Translate and label! an encoder-decoder approach for cross-lingual semantic role labeling. In *Proceedings of the*

2019 Conference on Empirical Methods in Natural Language Processing and the 9th International Joint Conference on Natural Language Processing (EMNLP-IJCNLP), pages 603–615, Hong Kong, China. Association for Computational Linguistics.

Jacob Devlin, Ming-Wei Chang, Kenton Lee, and Kristina Toutanova. 2019. BERT: Pre-training of deep bidirectional transformers for language understanding. In *Proceedings of the 2019 Conference of the North American Chapter of the Association for Computational Linguistics: Human Language Technologies*, pages 4171–4186, Minneapolis, Minnesota. Association for Computational Linguistics.

Dumitru Erhan, Aaron Courville, Yoshua Bengio, and Pascal Vincent. 2010. Why does unsupervised pre-training help deep learning? In *Proceedings of the Thirteenth International Conference on Artificial Intelligence and Statistics*, pages 201–208.

H. Fei, M. Zhang, F. Li, and D. Ji. 2020. Cross-lingual semantic role labeling with model transfer. *IEEE/ACM Transactions on Audio, Speech, and Language Processing*, 28:2427–2437.

Hao Fei, Meishan Zhang, and Donghong Ji. 2020. Cross-lingual semantic role labeling with high-quality translated training corpus. *arXiv preprint arXiv:2004.06295*.

Suchin Gururangan, Ana Marasović, Swabha Swayamdipta, Kyle Lo, Iz Beltagy, Doug Downey, and Noah A. Smith. 2020. Don't stop pretraining: Adapt language models to domains and tasks. In *Proceedings of the 58th Annual Meeting of the Association for Computational Linguistics*, pages 8342–8360, Online. Association for Computational Linguistics.

Jeremy Howard and Sebastian Ruder. 2018. Universal language model fine-tuning for text classification. In *Proceedings of the 56th Annual Meeting of the Association for Computational Linguistics*, pages 328–339, Melbourne, Australia. Association for Computational Linguistics.

Aizhan Imankulova, Raj Dabre, Atsushi Fujita, and Kenji Imamura. 2019. Exploiting out-of-domain parallel data through multilingual transfer learning for low-resource neural machine translation. In *Proceedings of Machine Translation Summit XVII Volume 1: Research Track*, pages 128–139, Dublin, Ireland. European Association for Machine Translation.

Jing Jiang and ChengXiang Zhai. 2007. Instance weighting for domain adaptation in NLP. In *Proceedings of the 45th Annual Meeting of the Association of Computational Linguistics*, pages 264–271, Prague, Czech Republic. Association for Computational Linguistics.

Hwaran Lee, Jinsik Lee, and Tae-Yoon Kim. 2019. SUMBT: Slot-utterance matching for universal and scalable belief tracking. In *Proceedings of the 57th Annual Meeting of the Association for Computational Linguistics*, pages 5478–5483, Florence, Italy. Association for Computational Linguistics.

Zhenhao Li and Lucia Specia. 2019. Improving neural machine translation robustness via data augmentation: Beyond back-translation. In *Proceedings of the 5th Workshop on Noisy User-generated Text (W-NUT 2019)*, pages 328–336, Hong Kong, China. Association for Computational Linguistics.

David Lopez-Paz and Marc'Aurelio Ranzato. 2017. Gradient episodic memory for continual learning. In *Advances in neural information processing systems*, pages 6467–6476.

Michael McCloskey and Neal J Cohen. 1989. Catastrophic interference in connectionist networks: The sequential learning problem. In *Psychology of learning and motivation*, volume 24, pages 109–165. Elsevier.

Sewon Min, Minjoon Seo, and Hannaneh Hajishirzi. 2017a. Question answering through transfer learning from large fine-grained supervision data. In *Proceedings of the 55th Annual Meeting of the Association for Computational Linguistics (Volume 2: Short Papers)*, pages 510–517, Vancouver, Canada. Association for Computational Linguistics.

Sewon Min, Minjoon Seo, and Hannaneh Hajishirzi. 2017b. Question answering through transfer learning from large fine-grained supervision data. *arXiv preprint arXiv:1702.02171*.

Sinno Jialin Pan and Qiang Yang. 2009. A survey on transfer learning. *IEEE Transactions on knowledge and data engineering*, 22(10):1345–1359.

Injy Sarhan and Marco Spruit. 2020. Can we survive without labelled data in nlp? transfer learning for open information extraction. *Applied Sciences*, 10(17):5758.

Rico Sennrich, Barry Haddow, and Alexandra Birch. 2015. Improving neural machine translation models with monolingual data. *arXiv preprint arXiv:1511.06709*.

Ananya Subburathinam, Di Lu, Heng Ji, Jonathan May, Shih-Fu Chang, Avirup Sil, and Clare Voss. 2019. Cross-lingual structure transfer for relation and event extraction. In *Proceedings of the 2019 Conference on Empirical Methods in Natural Language Processing and the 9th International Joint Conference on Natural Language Processing (EMNLP-IJCNLP)*, pages 313–325, Hong Kong, China. Association for Computational Linguistics.

David Wadden, Ulme Wennberg, Yi Luan, and Hannaneh Hajishirzi. 2019. Entity, relation, and event extraction with contextualized span representations. In *Proceedings of the 2019 Conference on Empirical Methods in Natural Language Processing and the*

9th International Joint Conference on Natural Language Processing (EMNLP-IJCNLP), pages 5784–5789, Hong Kong, China. Association for Computational Linguistics.

Chien-Sheng Wu, Andrea Madotto, Ehsan Hosseini-Asl, Caiming Xiong, Richard Socher, and Pascale Fung. 2019. Transferable multi-domain state generator for task-oriented dialogue systems. In *Proceedings of the 57th Annual Meeting of the Association for Computational Linguistics*, pages 808–819, Florence, Italy. Association for Computational Linguistics.

Xuan Zhang, Pamela Shapiro, Gaurav Kumar, Paul McNamee, Marine Carpuat, and Kevin Duh. 2019. Curriculum learning for domain adaptation in neural machine translation. In *Proceedings of the 2019 Conference of the North American Chapter of the Association for Computational Linguistics: Human Language Technologies, Volume 1 (Long and Short Papers)*, pages 1903–1915, Minneapolis, Minnesota. Association for Computational Linguistics.

A Learning Rate Schedule

A.1 Potential Model Collapse

If we use the same constant learning rate for each fine-tuning stage, the model may collapse. Accuracy on the train and dev sets may drop to 0 or near-zero at the beginning of a stage of gradual fine-tuning. This phenomenon is often caused by using an overly large learning rate. This suggests that one must carefully schedule the learning rates for each stage of gradual fine-tuning.

A.2 Learning Rates for MultiWOZ v2.0

In the MultiWOZ v2.0 experiments, we use 4e-5 for the learning rate in the last stage of fine-tuning and 1e-4 (default settings from Lee et al. (2019)) for the other stages.

A.3 Learning Rates for ACE 2005

The network is split into 2 parameter groups: the parameters of the XLM-R encoder and all other parameters. We set the base learning rate of XLM-R to 5e-5 and to 1e-3 for the other parameters (default settings from Wadden et al. (2019)). We do not change the base learning rate for the first two stages of fine-tuning. At the third stage, we reduce the learning rate of XLM-R to 1e-5 and of other parameters to 4e-4. We further reduce the learning rate of XLM-R to 8e-6 and the all other learning rates to 2e-4 for the final stage of gradual fine-tuning.

B Additional MultiWOZ v2.0 Results

Here we present additional results of gradual fine-tuning on MultiWOZ v2.0 to augment Table 2. Table 5 shows the results of one-stage fine-tuning and gradual fine-tuning using the data schedule $S = 4\text{K} \rightarrow 2\text{K} \rightarrow 0.5\text{K} \rightarrow 0$ as well as suffixes of S. Figure 3 shows the trend of slot accuracy for all training strategies at each stage of fine-tuning.

	Restaurant Slot/Joint	Hotel Slot/Joint
No FT (single domain)	90.70/52.16	90.79/46.30
No FT* (all domains)	92.19/58.63	91.48/50.26
One-stage 0.5k FT	93.11/64.75	91.61/46.30
One-stage 2k FT	94.04/62.23	91.24/47.35
One-stage 4k FT	93.47/61.15	91.43/46.30
Gradual 2k FT	94.30/66.91	91.35/46.30
Gradual 4k FT	**94.30/67.27**	**92.49/52.12**

Table 5: Slot and joint accuracy in the *restaurant* and *hotel* domains under various training methods. * indicates that the model uses the full training set. *FT*=fine-tuning.

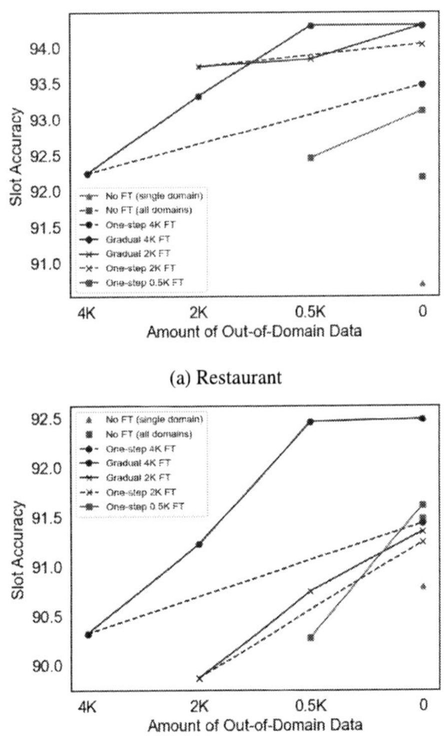

(a) Restaurant

(b) Hotel

Figure 3: Slot accuracy for the *restaurant* and *hotel* domains in MultiWOZ v2.0.

Analyzing the Domain Robustness of Pretrained Language Models, Layer by Layer

Abhinav Ramesh Kashyap[α], **Laiba Mehnaz**[β], **Bhavitvya Malik**[γ], **Abdul Waheed** [δ], **Devamanyu Hazarika**[α], **Min-Yen Kan**[α], **Rajiv Ratn Shah**[β]
[α] National University of Singapore, Singapore
[β] MIDAS Lab, IIIT-Delhi
[γ] Independent Researcher
[δ] Maharaja Agrasen Institute of Technology, New Delhi, India.
{abhinav, hazarika, kanmy}@comp.nus.edu.sg
{laibamehnaz, bhavitvya.malik, abdulwaheed1513}@gmail.com
{rajivratn}@iiitd.ac.in

Abstract

The robustness of pretrained language models (PLMs) is generally measured using performance drops on two or more domains. However, we do not yet understand the inherent robustness achieved by contributions from different layers of a PLM. We systematically analyze the robustness of these representations layer by layer from two perspectives. First, we measure the robustness of representations by using domain divergence between two domains. We find that *i)* Domain variance increases from the lower to the upper layers for vanilla PLMs; *ii)* Models continuously pretrained on domain-specific data (DAPT) (Gururangan et al., 2020) exhibit more variance than their pretrained PLM counterparts; and that *iii)* Distilled models (e.g.,DistilBERT) also show greater domain variance. Second, we investigate the robustness of representations by analyzing the encoded syntactic and semantic information using diagnostic probes. We find that similar layers have similar amounts of linguistic information for data from an unseen domain.

1 Introduction

Pretrained Language Models (PLMs) have improved the downstream performance of many natural language understanding tasks on *standard* data (Devlin et al., 2019).[1] Recent works attest to the surprising out-of-the-box robustness of PLMs on out-of-distribution tasks (Hendrycks et al., 2020; Brown et al., 2020; Miller et al., 2020). These works measure robustness in terms of the performance invariance of PLMs on end tasks like Natural Language Inference (Bowman et al., 2015; Williams et al., 2018), Sentiment Analysis (Maas et al., 2011), Question Answering (Zhang et al., 2018), among others. However, they do not investigate the domain invariance of PLM representations from different layers when presented with data from distinct domains. Studying the invariance of PLM representations has been useful in advancing methods for unsupervised domain adaptation. For example, in building domain adaptation models that explicitly reduce the divergence between layers of a neural network (Long et al., 2015; Shen et al., 2018a), for data selection (Aharoni and Goldberg, 2020; Ma et al., 2019) *et cetera.*

Given the importance of PLMs, a glass-box study of the internal robustness of PLM representations is overdue. We thus study these representations, dissecting them layer by layer, to uncover their internal contributions in domain adaptation. Firstly, we use the tools of domain divergence and domain invariance, without subscribing to the performance of a model on any end task. The theory of domain adaptation (Ben-David et al., 2010), shows that reducing $\mathcal{H}$-divergence between two domains results in higher performance in the target domain. Many works have since adopted this concept for domain adaptation in NLP (Ganin et al., 2016; Bousmalis et al., 2016). The aim is to learn representations that are invariant to the domain, while also being discriminative of a particular task. Other divergence measures such as Maximum Mean Discrepancy (MMD) (Gretton et al., 2012a), Correlational Alignment (CORAL), Central Moment Discrepancy (CMD) (Zellinger et al., 2017), have been subsequently defined and used (Ramponi and Plank, 2020; Kashyap et al., 2020). However, our community does not yet understand the inherent domain-invariance of PLM representations, particularly across different layers.

We ask key questions concerning domain invariance of PLM representations and find surpris-

[1]We borrow the term *standard data* from (Plank, 2016) to refer to news and web-like text and *non-standard data* to refer to other text like biomedical and Twitter.

Proceedings of the Second Workshop on Domain Adaptation for NLP, pages 222–244
April 20, 2021.

ing results. First, we consider vanilla PLM representations (e.g., BERT) which are trained on standard data like Wikipedia and Books (Plank, 2016). We ask: *do they exhibit domain invariance when presented with non-standard data like Twitter and biomedical text?* (§3), and *are lower layers of PLMs general and invariant compared to higher layers?* To answer these, we measure the domain divergence of PLM representations considering standard and non-standard data. We find that the lower layers of PLMs are more domain invariant compared to the upper layers (§3.2). We find that it is similar in spirit to computer vision models where lower layers of the neural network learn Gabor filters and extract edges irrespective of the image and are more transferable across tasks compared to the upper layers (Yosinski et al., 2014).

While PLMs improve the performance of tasks on standard data, Gururangan et al. (2020) improve on domain-specific tasks by continuing to pretrain RoBERTa on domain-specific data (DAPT). We thus also ask: *what happens to the domain invariance of DAPT models?* We find that compared to pretrained RoBERTa, the divergence of DAPT at a given layer either remains the same or increases, providing evidence of their specialization to a domain (§3.3). Lastly, given that standard PLMs have high training cost, we also consider the distilled model DistilBERT (Sanh et al., 2019). *What happens to the domain invariance in distilled model representations?* We find that such representations produce more domain-specific representations across layers (§3.4).

We further analyze the robustness of representations from the perspective of the encoded syntactic and semantic information across domains (§4). *Do contextualized word-level representations encode similar syntactic and semantic information even for unseen domains?* We experiment with zero-shot probes where the probes are trained on standard data only. We consider syntactic tasks like POS and NER and a semantic task – coreference resolution and find that the probes indicate similar layers encode similar amount of information, even on non-standard data.

In summary, our contributions are as follows:

- We investigate the domain invariance of PLMs layer by layer and find that lower layers are more domain invariant than upper layers, which is useful for transfer learning and domain adaptation.
- Further, we analyze the robustness in terms of the syntactic and semantic information encoded in the representations across unseen domains and find that similar layers have similar amounts of linguistic information, which is a preliminary exposition of their overall performance robustness.

2 Experimental Setup

The majority of current PLMs like BERT (Devlin et al., 2019) are transformer (Vaswani et al., 2017) based models. As such we focus on the representations from different transformers. They are unsupervisedly pretrained using masked language-modeling and next sentence prediction objectives, over large amounts of English standard data such as the Books corpus (Zhu et al., 2015) and Wikipedia articles. We consider varitaion in size: two differently sized versions of the BERT model, `bert_base_uncased` — a 12 layer model and `bert_large_uncased` — a 24 layer model, both trained on lower-cased text, for comparing matters of size in representations. Next, to analyze whether training with larger data scale aids in robustness, we consider RoBERTa (Liu et al., 2019b), which is similar to BERT, but trained on a magnitude larger standard data. Further, we check the effect of distillation on domain-invariance and hence, consider DistilBERT (Sanh et al., 2019). Finally, training of models on domain-specific data is known to increase their performance on domain-specific tasks. To analyze the effect of continued fine-tuning on invariance, we consider RoBERTa pretrained on non-standard Biomedical (Gururangan et al., 2020), and Twitter (Barbieri et al., 2020) domain data. We refer to this as **DAPT-biomed** and **DAPT-tweet**, respectively. For our experiments, we use the models hosted on the `huggingface-transformer` library (Wolf et al., 2020).

Divergence Measures. We consider three different divergence measures that are widely used in the unsupervised domain adaptation literature. Correlation Alignment (CORAL) measures the difference between covariance of features – a second-order moment. Sun and Saenko (2016) reduce the distributional distance between features for unsupervised domain adaptation (UDA) in computer vision models. In contrast to CORAL, Central moment Discrepancy (CMD) considers higher-order moments of random variables to

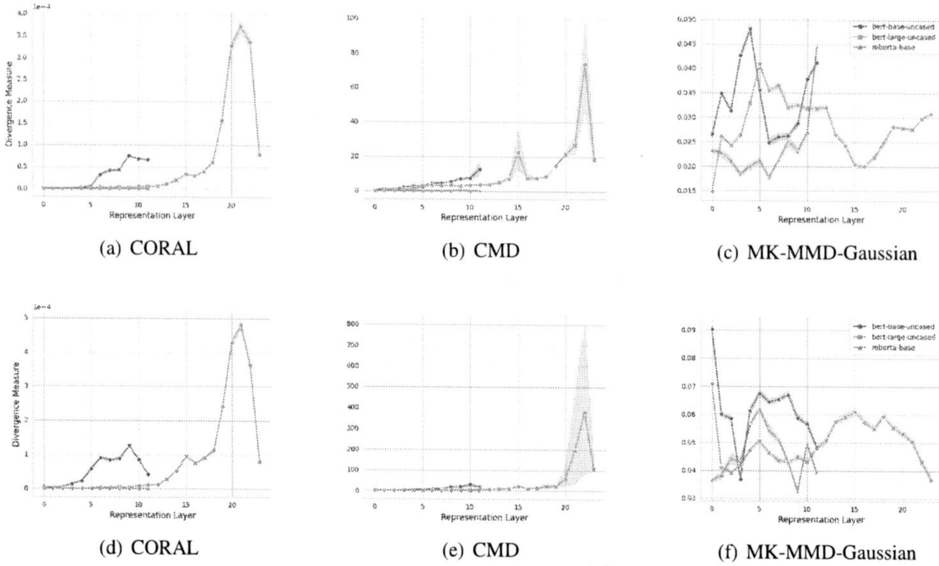

(a) CORAL (b) CMD (c) MK-MMD-Gaussian

(d) CORAL (e) CMD (f) MK-MMD-Gaussian

Figure 1: **Top**: Comparing divergence for the standard vs. biomedical samples **Bottom**: Comparing divergence for the standard vs. twitter samples. The plots consider three divergence measures: CORAL, CMD, and MK-MMD Gaussian, for three encoders `bert-base-uncased`, `bert-large-uncased` and `roberta-base`. The values are the mean and standard deviation of divergence measures calculated over 5 splits of 1000 samples.

measure the distributional difference between features, and has been used in both NLP (Peng et al., 2018) and multimodal UDA (Hazarika et al., 2020). Finally we consider another popular measure of measuring divergence — Maximum Mean Discrepancy (Gretton et al., 2012a). Specifically, we consider the Multi-Kernel Gaussian variate (MK-MMD-Gaussian), which ensures that the statistical two sample test for the difference in distributions have high power and low test error (Gretton et al., 2012b; Long et al., 2015). We chose these measures because of their popularity, relevance and inexpensive calculations, and provide their technical details in Appendix A.

3 How Domain-Invariant are PLM Representations?

Most of the current techniques in unsupervised domain adaptation explicitly reduce the divergence between different layer representations during training (Yu et al., 2020). A common post-hoc analysis from such works shows the reduction of domain invariance at different layers. However, they do not pay much heed to the domain-invariance of representations that already exist in such models prior to domain-adapted training. Thus, we use domain divergence measures to investigate whether domain-invariance is an inherent property of pretrained transformer models, by the virtue of large-scale self-supervised learning.

3.1 Datasets and Method

We randomly sample 5000 standard data sentences from the Toronto Books corpus (Zhu et al., 2015), which is similar to the data used to train pretrained language models. We further split them into five groups of 1000 sentences for calculating our divergence measures and report the mean and variance of our results. We consider two non-standard domains. The biomedical domain similarly consists of 5000 sentences from publicly available PubMed abstracts[2] and for the Twitter domain, we sample 5000 tweets from the year 2011 made available by the archive team.[3] We follow the same procedure as Nguyen et al. (2020) to preprocess tweets: we use fastText (Joulin et al., 2017) to consider only English tweets and use the `emoji` package [4] to translate emojis into text strings, normalize all the user mentions to `@USER` and URLs to `HTTPURL`.

[2]https://www.nlm.nih.gov/databases/download/pubmed_medline.html
[3]https://archive.org/details/twitterstream
[4]https://pypi.org/project/emoji

Layer	1	2	3	4	5	6	7	8	9	10	11	12
NMI (standard-biomed)	0.004	0.365	0.046	0.63	0.722	0.596	0.245	0.092	0.164	0.312	0.63	0.588
NMI (standard-twitter)	0.256	0.252	0.215	0.233	0.698	0.699	0.727	0.695	0.753	0.772	0.762	0.68

Table 1: NMI values measuring the clustering performance at different layers of `bert-base-uncased`.

We make forward passes of 1000 samples from one pair of domains (standard–biomedical / standard–twitter) separately through the transformers, obtaining two sets of representations. We then use these to calculate divergence measures. We consider the representations of `[CLS]` token as the representation of a sentence, as done in other works. Note that we do not fine-tune any of our models on the non-standard data.

3.2 Results

Across Layers: Overall, the divergence measures increase from the lower layers to the upper layers (Figure 1). CORAL and CMD for `bert-base-uncased` and `bert-large-uncased` indicate that the divergence strictly increases. Surprisingly, the models trained on standard data extract invariant representations at the lower layers, becoming more domain-specific at the upper layers, irrespective of the domain. Both CORAL and CMD indicate a sharp decrease in divergence for the last layer for all the models. Since they are language models trained to predict the next word, they might encode representations related to the pretraining objective itself (Liu et al., 2019a). Compared to BERT-base, the divergence measures of BERT-large, at layers where they can be compared, is lower (c.f. Fig. 1 and Fig. 5 in Appendix B). Even though both the models are trained on a similar amount of data and similar training procedures, it is surprising that BERT-base has lower divergence than BERT-large.

But, MK-MMD-Gaussian does not indicate a clear increase in divergence. We attribute this to the divergence measure, since MK-MMD-Gaussian is sensitive to the kernel and choosing an optimal value for its parameters is non-trivial (Gretton et al., 2012b). We confirm this by plotting the PCA representations of these data points (Figs. 8 to 13 in Appendix E.), which show that the representations from the two domains are interspersed in the lower layers and separated in the upper layers, as done in many previous works (Ganin et al., 2016; Long et al., 2015). We further quantify this by performing k-means clustering where $k = 2$ (the number of domains). We evaluate the clusters using Normalized Mutual Information (c.f. Table 1). Clustering quality is higher for upper layers compared to lower layers where representations are interspersed.

The increasing divergence across layers has plausible implications in making decisions in many scenarios. For example, in deciding the number of layers in the gradual unfreezing of layers in transfer learning (Howard and Ruder, 2018), in unsupervised domain adaptation where divergence between representations from different layers are reduced (Long et al., 2015). Recently, Aharoni and Goldberg (2020) show the final transformer layer representations cluster while Ma et al. (2019) consider penultimate layer representations. The high domain divergence of the upper layers is a plausible explanation for the clustering (Figs. 8 to 13 in Appendix E.). Clustering of representations plays a key role in downstream applications, such as data selection for machine translation and curriculum learning, data points in the source domain closest to the target domain are chosen (Axelrod et al., 2011; Moore and Lewis, 2010).

BERT vs. RoBERTa: Compared to BERT, RoBERTa has uniform divergence across layers (c.f. Fig. 1). RoBERTa is similar to BERT, but a major difference is the amount of pre-training data used (one magnitude; 160GB vs. 16GB). We speculate that the domain-invariance is because the pretraining data is an unintended mixture of different domains. Recent works have shown the impact of training models with large and diverse datasets on the robustness of image classification models (Taori et al., 2020) and text classification models (Tu et al., 2020) with similar trends observed where RoBERTa is more robust.

3.3 What happens to the domain-invariance of DAPT models?

To create domain-specific PLM, the simplest methods train models from scratch on domain-specific data like scientific publications (Beltagy et al., 2019), BioBERT (Lee et al., 2019), ClinicalBERT (Alsentzer et al., 2019) among others. In

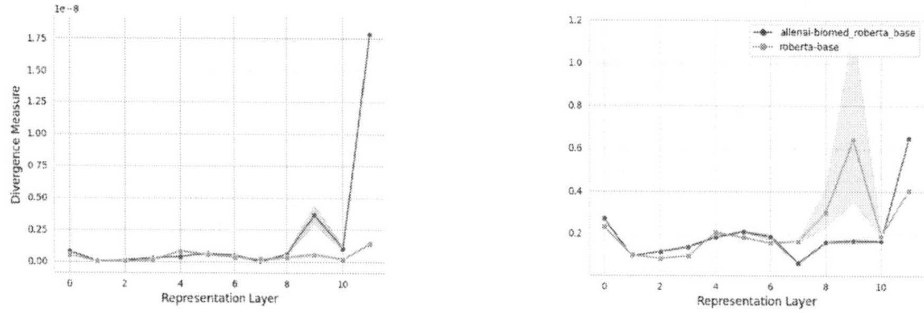

(a) CORAL (b) CMD

Figure 2: Comparing CORAL and CMD divergences for `roberta-base` and DAPT-biomed (Gururangan et al., 2020). Considers standard and biomedical samples.

contrast, instead of pretraining from scratch, recent work shows impressive benefits of continuing to pretrain on domain-specific data — termed domain adaptive pretraining (DAPT) (Gururangan et al., 2020). Although there are improvements on domain-specific end tasks, the domain-invariance of these representations is not analyzed. We consider only the CORAL and CMD divergence measures from now, due to our observations from the previous section.

Figure 2 shows that the divergence across the layers for **DAPT-biomed** is the same as RoBERTa or is higher (c.f. Fig. 6 in Appendix C for **DAPT-twitter**). The main aim of continuing to pretrain is to make the models more domain-specific. We expect the representations to diverge from the standard representations after model training. DAPT representations possibly serve as good initial representations for fine-tuning on domain-specific end tasks like natural language inference, text classification *et cetera* (Hao et al., 2019). Teasing out the benefits of domain-specific pretraining from the task-specific fine-tuning is still unclear and warrants careful attention.

3.4 What happens to the domain-invariance after distillation?

Knowledge Distillation (Hinton et al., 2015) has been successfully used to reduce the size and inference time of PLMs. Here, a smaller student network mimics the output of a larger teacher network. We consider the DistilBERTmodel. Fig. 3 shows the comparison of divergence measures between DistilBERT with BERT for the standard and the biomedical domain pair (c.f. Fig. 7 in Appendix D for comparison with Twitter domain). DistilBERT contains half the number of layers compared to BERT. At a comparable layers, DistilBERT always has higher divergence values for both CMD and CORAL. Sanh et al. (2019) show that distillation loss that mimics the teacher's output and cosine embedding loss which aligns the student and teacher hidden states vectors, are the major contributors to the student's performance. Yet, we find that DistilBERT still has greater variance which may affect downstream tasks like text classification. Although a few models (Jiao et al., 2020; Sanh et al., 2019) reduce some notion of geometric distance between the intermediate representations of the student and the teacher, it does not guarantee that the entire linguistic knowledge and the domain-invariance of the teacher are transferred to the student model. Recent work in NLP have tried to incorporate rich information from teacher networks using contrastive learning (Tian et al., 2020; Sun et al., 2020) and by reducing the Earth Mover's distance between the hidden representations in the transformer architecture (Li et al., 2020). Related computer vision work also to impart adversarial robustness, even in the student network (Goldblum et al., 2020). The benefits of such enhanced distillation techniques on the robustness of the model is an under-explored area.

4 Robustness of Linguistic Information

How much linguistic information do representations from pretrained language models still encode for data from a different domain? Here, we evaluate the robustness of representations in `bert-base-uncased`. Do word-level repre-

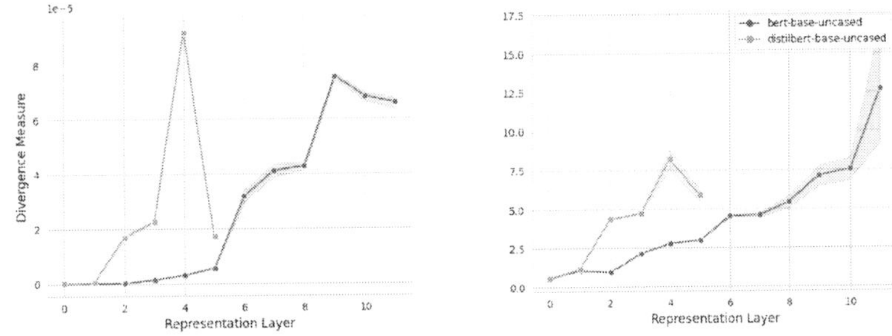

(a) CORAL

(b) CMD

Figure 3: CORAL and CMD divergence measures for standard vs biomedical samples. Two encoders are considered here: `bert-base-uncased` and `distilbert-base`.

sentations from PLMs encode similar levels of linguistic knowledge irrespective of the domain?

4.1 Datasets and Method

Edge Probes: Edge probes (Tenney et al., 2019b) measure the magnitude of linguistic information present in contextualized word representations. Representations of spans from a specific layer are passed through a shallow, multi-layer perceptron which predict their linguistic label. The performance of the probes indicates the magnitude of linguistic information.

To evaluate the linguistic information in BERT representations regardless of the domain, we train probes on source domain data and test on a held-out test dataset from the target domain. Since the *non-standard* data is *unseen* during training, this is a form of *zero-shot probing*, as also experimented in (Ravichander et al., 2020b). Training separate probes on every domain would yield inaccurate information about the linguistic information in the representations. The probes themselves may learn the linguistic task and overfit on the target domain data which can serve as a confounding factor.

A performance drop in probing performance between domains should not be interpreted as an absence of linguistic information. Other confounding factors like distribution difference (Recht et al., 2019; Miller et al., 2020) may be responsible. We are interested in the underlying pattern, and one has to exercise caution in interpreting the absolute performance numbers.

We chose three tasks from the suite of tasks defined by (Tenney et al., 2019b), where POS tagging (part-of-speech tagging), and NER (Named entity recognition) are considered syntactic, and where Coreference resolution (Coref) is considered a semantic task. We chose these tasks guided by the availability of similar datasets in both domains. For all our experiments involving probing, we use the `jiant` framework (Wang et al., 2019)
.

Data: Following (Tenney et al., 2019b) we use the OntoNotes 5.0 corpus (Weischedel, Ralph et al., 2013) for probing. Since they are from newswire and web text, which is similar to the pretraining corpus of BERT (Devlin et al., 2019), we consider this dataset as *standard* data (source domain). We choose Twitter to represent *non-standard* data (target domain) for the probing task since our previous experiments showed a greater divergence, and thus are significantly different from the pretraining corpus used in BERT.

For POS tagging, we use the dataset described by (Derczynski et al., 2013). We remove the following POS tags from the dataset: USR, URL, HT, RT, "(", and ")", to normalize the labels across the domains. For NER, we use the dataset released for the shared task of the Workshop on Noisy User-generated Text (W-NUT) (Baldwin et al., 2015). For coreference resolution, we use the dataset presented in (Aktaş et al., 2018), whose annotations were later modified by (Aktaş et al., 2020) so that they were conceptually parallel to OntoNotes 5.0 corpus (Weischedel, Ralph et al., 2013). The size of the datasets across train, development and test splits were kept similar for both the domains (c.f. Appendix F).

4.2 Results

Even though the probes had not seen examples from the target domain, we observe from Fig. 4

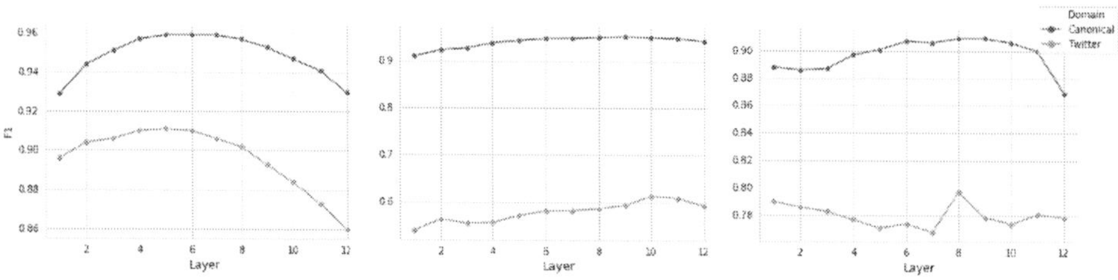

(a) POS (b) NER (c) Coref

Figure 4: Micro F1 scores for probing POS, NER, and Coref information from `bert-base-uncased` for the standard and the non-standard Twitter domain.

that the best performing layer is the same across domains for each task. The F1 scores peak at the same layers for both the domains, across all tasks. In both domains, the F1 for the task of POS tagging peaks at layer 5; for NER and Coref, at layer 10 and 8, respectively. Considering the knowledge discovered by the probes, it can be seen that similar layers are the most important for syntactic and semantic tasks across domains.

Concerning which part of the model encodes syntactic information required for POS and NER, we observe that the middle layers perform the best for both tasks, invariant of domain. This result is consistent with the results reported for non-domain adaptation work (Liu et al., 2019a; Jawahar et al., 2019). For Coref, the upper layers perform better on the task for the source domain. This indicates that the models store the information required for Coref (Liu et al., 2019a), but that the lower layers perform better when it comes to the target domain. We speculate that this is due to the nature of Twitter-coref dataset (target domain). For tasks like coreference resolution, there is a need for the presence of semantic information to identify the co-referring entities. But as tweets are naturally shorter, they contain co-referring entities that are close to each other, and do not require long-range information. This might make it easier for BERT models to use syntactic information from the lower layers to perform well on the target domain dataset.

We note that Merchant et al. (2020) show PLM representations do not experience catastrophic forgetting when fine-tuned on different end tasks such as MNLI, SQuAD and dependency parsing. With the limited capabilities that probes have, the results of this work show that similar information is being encoded for a task in similar layers without fine-tuning on any domain-specific data. This indicates that PLM representations might encode similar linguistic information across domains to begin with, potentially aiding performance on domain-specific end tasks.

5 Limitations

Our analysis using probes for different domains is intended to be an initial exploration of this topic. We inherit all the limitations of the probing classifiers highlighted by recent works (Tenney et al., 2019a; Voita and Titov, 2020; Pimentel et al., 2020). Since probing trains shallow models, there exists a possibility that the performance confounds with the models learning the task rather than being diagnostic about the linguistic power of representations. It also does not indicate that the model uses this information effectively (Hewitt and Manning, 2019) which requires further analysis. We also consider only one target domain — Twitter — and analyze `bert-base-uncased` for our probes. The availability and varying characteristics of the dataset across domains dictates our choice. For example, compared to standard coreference, biomedical text exhibits co-referring terms across sentences in long documents.

6 Related Work

6.1 NLP Robustness

Pretrained language models (PLMs) perform well on a wide range of NLP tasks, but they do not generalize well when the test distribution is different. A robust model must adapt to the shift in distributions (Quionero-Candela et al., 2009) and generalize to out-of-distribution (OOD) examples. (Hendrycks et al., 2020) study the OOD robustness of PLMs, finding that the performance drop is substantially smaller than their shallow LSTM and CNN counterparts. Much of the literature on PLM robustness use the notion of performance drop in a new target domain (Hendrycks et al., 2020; Tu et al., 2020; Miller et al., 2020). However, analyzing the robustness and invariance of the representations under data from different domains or adversarial examples (Zhu et al., 2020) has not received much attention thus far in domain adaptation.

Concerning the robustness of linguistic information stored in representations, Merchant et al. (2020) analyze the syntactic and semantic information preserved by PLMs, both before and after fine-tuning the models on task-specific data. Similarly, Tamkin et al. (2020) analyze the role of different layers in transfer learning on end tasks. Different from their study, we are interested in the intrinsic invariance of the PLM representations under data from different domains.

6.2 Unsupervised Domain Adaptation

For unsupervised domain adaptation, a popular method is use the adversarial training between a domain and a task classifier (DANN) (Ganin et al., 2016). Compared to DANN, where domain-specific peculiarities are lost, (Bousmalis et al., 2016) introduce domain-specific networks, which where domain-specific and domain-invariant representations are formed in a shared-private network. Another method to obtain invariant representations is to explicitly reduce the domain divergence between different layers of a neural network (Miller et al., 2020; Sun and Saenko, 2016; Shen et al., 2018b,a). For a complete treatment on UDA refer to (Ramponi and Plank, 2020) and for a review on divergence measure refer to (Kashyap et al., 2020). Considering the inherent domain-invariance of representations is thus important for UDA models.

6.3 Probing

As pretrained transformer models provide improvements on end tasks, understanding their internals and knowledge they encode has become increasingly important. For a review on efforts to understand pretrained transformers, see Rogers et al. (2021). Probing is a popular method to understand the linguistic information stored in continuous representations (Conneau et al., 2018). Tenney et al. (2019a,b) use probes to understand the linguistic information that the representations capture.

Recent work has questioned the premise of using a probe. Hewitt and Liang (2019) propose control tasks to ensure that the performance of probe is diagnostic about the linguistic information and is not because of learning the task. (Pimentel et al., 2020) utilize information theory to show that contextual representations contain similar amounts of information as lexical tokens. They suggest that better performing probes are increasingly accurate of detecting linguistic information regardless of their complexity and propose *ease of probing* as an alternative solution. This is similar to minimum description length suggested by Voita and Titov (2020). Contrary to previous works Ravichander et al. (2020a); Elazar et al. (2020) argue that presence of linguistic information does not guarantee its utility for end tasks. In contrast to these works that consider only a single domain, we provide experiments to diagnose cross domain linguistic information using probes.

7 Conclusion

We consider domain robustness from the perspective of domain-invariance of pretrained language model (PLM) representations. We observe that the lower layers of PLMs are generally domain-invariant. We also find that domain variance increases on continuously pretrained (DAPT) models and distilled models (DistilBERT). We have seen that RoBERTa is robust, possibly by virtue of training with more data. Domain adaptation methods using it should be careful in assessing the empirical benefits of their methods. As distillation becomes a mainstay method in NLP for retaining accuracy and saving training and inference costs on large models, considering distillation techniques to retain domain invariance and broadly applicable linguistic properties is of interest to the community.

Considering the inherent domain-invariance of PLM representations at various layers is possibly useful in understanding their performance on out of domain distribution data(Hendrycks et al., 2020) and for domain adaptation in general. For example, since we understand that the lower layers of BERT are domain-invariant compared to higher layers, we can freeze them during domain adaptation (Peters et al., 2019; Shen et al., 2018a) or drop them to make the models smaller and more efficient (Sajjad et al., 2020). In the future, we will incorporate this information for domain adaptation of models.

We used edge probes (Tenney et al., 2019b) to identify the linguistic information in representations of data from different domains. One has to note that edge probes consider span representations for probing and not the representations of the entire sentence. To answer *Is there any correlation between domain-invariance of a sentence and the amount of linguistic information contained in them*?, we should consider sentence-level probes, similar to (Conneau et al., 2018; Jawahar et al., 2019) But, we are restricted by the lack of sentence-level probing data for different domains. We believe that this is a ripe area for future work.

Acknowledgements

The authors would like to thank Yisong Miao for reading a draft of this paper and providing insightful comments. We would also like to acknowledge the support of the NExT research grant funds, supported by the National Research Foundation, Prime Ministers Office, Singapore under its IRC @ SG Funding Initiative, and to gratefully acknowledge the support of NVIDIA Corporation with the donation of the GeForce GTX Titan X GPU used in this research.

References

Roee Aharoni and Yoav Goldberg. 2020. Unsupervised domain clusters in pretrained language models. In Proceedings of the 58th Annual Meeting of the Association for Computational Linguistics, pages 7747–7763, Online. Association for Computational Linguistics.

Berfin Aktaş, Tatjana Scheffler, and Manfred Stede. 2018. Anaphora resolution for Twitter conversations: An exploratory study. In Proceedings of the First Workshop on Computational Models of Reference, Anaphora and Coreference, pages 1–10, New Orleans, Louisiana. Association for Computational Linguistics.

Berfin Aktaş, Veronika Solopova, Annalena Kohnert, and Manfred Stede. 2020. Adapting coreference resolution to Twitter conversations. In Findings of the Association for Computational Linguistics: EMNLP 2020, pages 2454–2460, Online. Association for Computational Linguistics.

Emily Alsentzer, John Murphy, William Boag, Wei-Hung Weng, Di Jindi, Tristan Naumann, and Matthew McDermott. 2019. Publicly available clinical BERT embeddings. In Proceedings of the 2nd Clinical Natural Language Processing Workshop, pages 72–78, Minneapolis, Minnesota, USA. Association for Computational Linguistics.

Amittai Axelrod, Xiaodong He, and Jianfeng Gao. 2011. Domain adaptation via pseudo in-domain data selection. In Proceedings of the 2011 Conference on Empirical Methods in Natural Language Processing, pages 355–362, Edinburgh, Scotland, UK. Association for Computational Linguistics.

Timothy Baldwin, Marie Catherine de Marneffe, Bo Han, Young-Bum Kim, Alan Ritter, and Wei Xu. 2015. Shared tasks of the 2015 workshop on noisy user-generated text: Twitter lexical normalization and named entity recognition. In Proceedings of the Workshop on Noisy User-generated Text, pages 126–135, Beijing, China. Association for Computational Linguistics.

Francesco Barbieri, Jose Camacho-Collados, Luis Espinosa Anke, and Leonardo Neves. 2020. TweetEval: Unified benchmark and comparative evaluation for tweet classification. In Findings of the Association for Computational Linguistics: EMNLP 2020, pages 1644–1650, Online. Association for Computational Linguistics.

Iz Beltagy, Kyle Lo, and Arman Cohan. 2019. SciBERT: A pretrained language model for scientific text. In Proceedings of the 2019 Conference on Empirical Methods in Natural Language Processing and the 9th International Joint Conference on Natural Language Processing (EMNLP-IJCNLP), pages 3615–3620, Hong Kong, China. Association for Computational Linguistics.

Shai Ben-David, John Blitzer, Koby Crammer, Alex Kulesza, Fernando Pereira, and Jennifer Wortman Vaughan. 2010. A theory of learning from different domains. Mach. Learn., 79(1-2):151–175.

Konstantinos Bousmalis, George Trigeorgis, Nathan Silberman, Dilip Krishnan, and Dumitru Erhan. 2016. Domain separation networks. In Advances in Neural Information Processing Systems 29: Annual Conference on Neural Information Processing Systems 2016, December 5-10, 2016, Barcelona, Spain, pages 343–351.

Samuel R. Bowman, Gabor Angeli, Christopher Potts, and Christopher D. Manning. 2015. A large annotated corpus for learning natural language inference. In Proceedings of the 2015 Conference on Empirical Methods in Natural Language Processing, pages 632–642, Lisbon, Portugal. Association for Computational Linguistics.

Tom B Brown, Benjamin Mann, Nick Ryder, Melanie Subbiah, Jared Kaplan, Prafulla Dhariwal, Arvind Neelakantan, Pranav Shyam, Girish Sastry, Amanda Askell, et al. 2020. Language models are few-shot learners. arXiv preprint arXiv:2005.14165.

Alexis Conneau, German Kruszewski, Guillaume Lample, Loïc Barrault, and Marco Baroni. 2018. What you can cram into a single $&!#* vector: Probing sentence embeddings for linguistic properties. In Proceedings of the 56th Annual Meeting of the Association for Computational Linguistics (Volume 1: Long Papers), pages 2126–2136, Melbourne, Australia. Association for Computational Linguistics.

Leon Derczynski, Alan Ritter, S. Clark, and Kalina Bontcheva. 2013. Twitter part-of-speech tagging for all: Overcoming sparse and noisy data. In RANLP.

Jacob Devlin, Ming-Wei Chang, Kenton Lee, and Kristina Toutanova. 2019. BERT: Pre-training of deep bidirectional transformers for language understanding. In Proceedings of the 2019 Conference of the North American Chapter of the Association for Computational Linguistics: Human Language Technologies, Volume 1 (Long and Short Papers), pages 4171–4186, Minneapolis, Minnesota. Association for Computational Linguistics.

Yanai Elazar, Shauli Ravfogel, Alon Jacovi, and Yoav Goldberg. 2020. Amnesic probing: Behavioral explanation with amnesic counterfactuals.

Yaroslav Ganin, Evgeniya Ustinova, Hana Ajakan, Pascal Germain, Hugo Larochelle, François Laviolette, Mario Marchand, and Victor Lempitsky. 2016. Domain-adversarial training of neural networks. J. Mach. Learn. Res., 17(1):2096–2030.

Micah Goldblum, Liam Fowl, Soheil Feizi, and Tom Goldstein. 2020. Adversarially robust distillation. In The Thirty-Fourth AAAI Conference on Artificial Intelligence, AAAI 2020, The

Thirty-Second Innovative Applications of Artificial Intelligence Conference, IAAI 2020, The Tenth AAAI Symposium on Educational Advances in Artificial Intelligence, EAAI 2020, New York, NY, USA, February 7-12, 2020, pages 3996–4003. AAAI Press.

Arthur Gretton, Karsten M. Borgwardt, Malte J. Rasch, Bernhard Schölkopf, and Alexander J. Smola. 2012a. A kernel two-sample test. J. Mach. Learn. Res., 13:723–773.

Arthur Gretton, Bharath K. Sriperumbudur, Dino Sejdinovic, Heiko Strathmann, Sivaraman Balakrishnan, Massimiliano Pontil, and Kenji Fukumizu. 2012b. Optimal kernel choice for large-scale two-sample tests. In Advances in Neural Information Processing Systems 25: 26th Annual Conference on Neural Information Processing Systems 2012. Proceedings of a meeting held December 3-6, 2012, Lake Tahoe, Nevada, United States, pages 1214–1222.

Suchin Gururangan, Ana Marasović, Swabha Swayamdipta, Kyle Lo, Iz Beltagy, Doug Downey, and Noah A. Smith. 2020. Don't stop pretraining: Adapt language models to domains and tasks. In Proceedings of the 58th Annual Meeting of the Association for Computational Linguistics, pages 8342–8360, Online. Association for Computational Linguistics.

Yaru Hao, Li Dong, Furu Wei, and Ke Xu. 2019. Visualizing and understanding the effectiveness of BERT. In Proceedings of the 2019 Conference on Empirical Methods in Natural Language Processing and the 9th International Joint Conference on Natural Language Processing (EMNLP-IJCNLP), pages 4143–4152, Hong Kong, China. Association for Computational Linguistics.

Devamanyu Hazarika, Roger Zimmermann, and Soujanya Poria. 2020. Misa: Modality-invariant and -specific representations for multimodal sentiment analysis. In Proceedings of the 28th ACM International Conference on Multimedia, MM '20, page 1122–1131, New York, NY, USA. Association for Computing Machinery.

Dan Hendrycks, Xiaoyuan Liu, Eric Wallace, Adam Dziedzic, Rishabh Krishnan, and Dawn Song. 2020. Pretrained transformers improve out-of-distribution robustness. In Proceedings of the 58th Annual Meeting of the Association for Computational Linguistics, pages 2744–2751, Online. Association for Computational Linguistics.

John Hewitt and Percy Liang. 2019. Designing and interpreting probes with control tasks. In Proceedings of the 2019 Conference on Empirical Methods in Natural Language Processing and the 9th International Joint Conference on Natural Language Processing (EMNLP-IJCNLP), pages 2733–2743, Hong Kong, China. Association for Computational Linguistics.

John Hewitt and Christopher D. Manning. 2019. A structural probe for finding syntax in word representations. In Proceedings of the 2019 Conference of the North American Chapter of the Association for Computational Linguistics: Human Language Technologies, Volume 1 (Long and Short Papers), pages 4129–4138, Minneapolis, Minnesota. Association for Computational Linguistics.

Geoffrey E. Hinton, Oriol Vinyals, and Jeffrey Dean. 2015. Distilling the knowledge in a neural network. CoRR, abs/1503.02531.

Jeremy Howard and Sebastian Ruder. 2018. Universal language model fine-tuning for text classification. In Proceedings of the 56th Annual Meeting of the Association for Computational Linguistics, ACL 2018, Melbourne, Australia, July 15-20, 2018, Volume 1: Long Papers, pages 328–339. Association for Computational Linguistics.

Ganesh Jawahar, Benoît Sagot, and Djamé Seddah. 2019. What does BERT learn about the structure of language? In Proceedings of the 57th Annual Meeting of the Association for Computational Linguistics, pages 3651–3657, Florence, Italy. Association for Computational Linguistics.

Xiaoqi Jiao, Yichun Yin, Lifeng Shang, Xin Jiang, Xiao Chen, Linlin Li, Fang Wang, and Qun Liu. 2020. TinyBERT: Distilling BERT for natural language understanding. In Findings of the Association for Computational Linguistics: EMNLP 2020, pages 4163–4174, Online. Association for Computational Linguistics.

Armand Joulin, Edouard Grave, Piotr Bojanowski, and Tomas Mikolov. 2017. Bag of tricks for efficient text classification. In Proceedings of the 15th Conference of the European Chapter of the Association for Computational Linguistics: Volume 2, Short Papers, pages 427–431, Valencia, Spain. Association for Computational Linguistics.

Abhinav Ramesh Kashyap, Devamanyu Hazarika, Min-Yen Kan, and Roger Zimmermann. 2020. Domain divergences: a survey and empirical analysis.

Jinhyuk Lee, Wonjin Yoon, Sungdong Kim, Donghyeon Kim, Sunkyu Kim, Chan Ho So, and Jaewoo Kang. 2019. BioBERT: a pre-trained biomedical language representation model for biomedical text mining. Bioinformatics, 36(4):1234–1240.

Jianquan Li, Xiaokang Liu, Honghong Zhao, Ruifeng Xu, Min Yang, and Yaohong Jin. 2020. BERT-EMD: Many-to-many layer mapping for BERT compression with earth mover's distance. In Proceedings of the 2020 Conference on Empirical Methods in Natural Language Processing (EMNLP), pages 3009–3018, Online. Association for Computational Linguistics.

Nelson F. Liu, Matt Gardner, Yonatan Belinkov, Matthew E. Peters, and Noah A. Smith. 2019a. Linguistic knowledge and transferability of contextual representations. In Proceedings of the 2019 Conference of the North American Chapter of the Association for Computational Linguistics: Human Language Technologies, Volume 1 (Long and Short Papers), pages 1073–1094, Minneapolis, Minnesota. Association for Computational Linguistics.

Yinhan Liu, Myle Ott, Naman Goyal, Jingfei Du, Mandar Joshi, Danqi Chen, Omer Levy, Mike Lewis, Luke Zettlemoyer, and Veselin Stoyanov. 2019b. Roberta: A robustly optimized BERT pretraining approach. CoRR, abs/1907.11692.

Mingsheng Long, Yue Cao, Jianmin Wang, and Michael I. Jordan. 2015. Learning transferable features with deep adaptation networks. In Proceedings of the 32nd International Conference on Machine Learning, ICML 2015, Lille, France, 6-11 July 2015, volume 37 of JMLR Workshop and Conference Proceedings, pages 97–105. JMLR.org.

Xiaofei Ma, Peng Xu, Zhiguo Wang, Ramesh Nallapati, and Bing Xiang. 2019. Domain adaptation with BERT-based domain classification and data selection. In Proceedings of the 2nd Workshop on Deep Learning Approaches for Low-Resource NLP (DeepLo 2019), pages 76–83, Hong Kong, China. Association for Computational Linguistics.

Andrew L. Maas, Raymond E. Daly, Peter T. Pham, Dan Huang, Andrew Y. Ng, and Christopher Potts. 2011. Learning word vectors for sentiment analysis. In Proceedings of the 49th Annual Meeting of the Association for Computational Linguistics: Human Language Technologies, pages 142–150, Portland, Oregon, USA. Association for Computational Linguistics.

Amil Merchant, Elahe Rahimtoroghi, Ellie Pavlick, and Ian Tenney. 2020. What happens to BERT embeddings during fine-tuning? In Proceedings of the Third BlackboxNLP Workshop on Analyzing and Interpreting Neural Networks for NLP, pages 33–44, Online. Association for Computational Linguistics.

John Miller, Karl Krauth, Benjamin Recht, and Ludwig Schmidt. 2020. The effect of natural distribution shift on question answering models. In Proceedings of the 37th International Conference on Machine Learning, volume 119 of Proceedings of Machine Learning Research, pages 6905–6916. PMLR.

Robert C. Moore and William Lewis. 2010. Intelligent selection of language model training data. In Proceedings of the ACL 2010 Conference Short Papers, pages 220–224, Uppsala, Sweden. Association for Computational Linguistics.

Dat Quoc Nguyen, Thanh Vu, and Anh Tuan Nguyen. 2020. BERTweet: A pre-trained language model for English Tweets. In Proceedings of the 2020 Conference on Empirical Methods in Natural Language Processing: System Demonstrations, pages 9–14.

Minlong Peng, Qi Zhang, Yu-gang Jiang, and Xuanjing Huang. 2018. Cross-domain sentiment classification with target domain specific information. In Proceedings of the 56th Annual Meeting of the Association for Computational Linguistics (Volume 1: Long Papers), pages 2505–2513, Melbourne, Australia. Association for Computational Linguistics.

Matthew E. Peters, Sebastian Ruder, and Noah A. Smith. 2019. To tune or not to tune? adapting pretrained representations to diverse tasks. In Proceedings of the 4th Workshop on Representation Learning for NLP (RepL4NLP-2019), pages 7–14, Florence, Italy. Association for Computational Linguistics.

Tiago Pimentel, Josef Valvoda, Rowan Hall Maudslay, Ran Zmigrod, Adina Williams, and Ryan Cotterell. 2020. Information-theoretic probing for linguistic structure. In Proceedings of the 58th Annual Meeting of the Association for Computational Linguistics, pages 4609–4622, Online. Association for Computational Linguistics.

Barbara Plank. 2016. What to do about non-standard (or non-canonical) language in NLP. In Proceedings of the 13th Conference on Natural Language Processing, KONVENS 2016, Bochum, Germany, September 19-21, 2016, volume 16 of Bochumer Linguistische Arbeitsberichte.

Joaquin Quionero-Candela, Masashi Sugiyama, Anton Schwaighofer, and Neil D. Lawrence. 2009. Dataset Shift in Machine Learning. The MIT Press.

Alan Ramponi and Barbara Plank. 2020. Neural unsupervised domain adaptation in NLP—A survey. In Proceedings of the 28th International Conference on Computational Linguistics, pages 6838–6855, Barcelona, Spain (Online). International Committee on Computational Linguistics.

Abhilasha Ravichander, Yonatan Belinkov, and Eduard Hovy. 2020a. Probing the probing paradigm: Does probing accuracy entail task relevance?

Abhilasha Ravichander, Eduard Hovy, Kaheer Suleman, Adam Trischler, and Jackie Chi Kit Cheung. 2020b. On the systematicity of probing contextualized word representations: The case of hypernymy in BERT. In Proceedings of the Ninth Joint Conference on Lexical and Computational Semantics, pages 88–102, Barcelona, Spain (Online). Association for Computational Linguistics.

Benjamin Recht, Rebecca Roelofs, Ludwig Schmidt, and Vaishaal Shankar. 2019. Do ImageNet classifiers generalize to ImageNet? In Proceedings of the 36th International Conference on Machine Learning, volume 97 of Proceedings of Machine Learning Research, pages 5389–5400. PMLR.

Anna Rogers, Olga Kovaleva, and Anna Rumshisky. 2021. A primer in bertology: What we know about how bert works. Transactions of the Association for Computational Linguistics, 8(0):842–866.

Hassan Sajjad, Fahim Dalvi, Nadir Durrani, and Preslav Nakov. 2020. Poor man's bert: Smaller and faster transformer models.

Victor Sanh, Lysandre Debut, Julien Chaumond, and Thomas Wolf. 2019. Distilbert, a distilled version of BERT: smaller, faster, cheaper and lighter. CoRR, abs/1910.01108.

Jian Shen, Yanru Qu, Weinan Zhang, and Yong Yu. 2018a. Wasserstein distance guided representation learning for domain adaptation. In Proceedings of the Thirty-Second AAAI Conference on Artificial Intelligence, (AAAI-18), the 30th innovative Applications of Artificial Intelligence (IAAI-18), and the 8th AAAI Symposium on Educational Advances in Artificial Intelligence (EAAI-18), New Orleans, Louisiana, USA, February 2-7, 2018, pages 4058–4065. AAAI Press.

Jian Shen, Yanru Qu, Weinan Zhang, and Yong Yu. 2018b. Wasserstein distance guided representation learning for domain adaptation. In Proceedings of the Thirty-Second AAAI Conference on Artificial Intelligence, (AAAI-18), the 30th innovative Applications of Artificial Intelligence (IAAI-18), and the 8th AAAI Symposium on Educational Advances in Artificial Intelligence (EAAI-18), New Orleans, Louisiana, USA, February 2-7, 2018, pages 4058–4065. AAAI Press.

Baochen Sun and Kate Saenko. 2016. Deep CORAL: correlation alignment for deep domain adaptation. CoRR, abs/1607.01719.

Siqi Sun, Zhe Gan, Yuwei Fang, Yu Cheng, Shuohang Wang, and Jingjing Liu. 2020. Contrastive distillation on intermediate representations for language model compression. In Proceedings of the 2020 Conference on Empirical Methods in Natural Language Processing (EMNLP), pages 498–508, Online. Association for Computational Linguistics.

Alex Tamkin, Trisha Singh, Davide Giovanardi, and Noah Goodman. 2020. Investigating transferability in pretrained language models. In Findings of the Association for Computational Linguistics: EMNLP 2020, pages 1393–1401, Online. Association for Computational Linguistics.

Rohan Taori, Achal Dave, Vaishaal Shankar, Nicholas Carlini, Benjamin Recht, and Ludwig Schmidt. 2020. Measuring robustness to natural distribution shifts in image classification.

Ian Tenney, Dipanjan Das, and Ellie Pavlick. 2019a. BERT rediscovers the classical NLP pipeline. In Proceedings of the 57th Annual Meeting of the Association for Computational Linguistics, pages 4593–4601, Florence, Italy. Association for Computational Linguistics.

Ian Tenney, Patrick Xia, Berlin Chen, Alex Wang, Adam Poliak, R. Thomas McCoy, Najoung Kim, Benjamin Van Durme, Samuel R. Bowman, Dipanjan Das, and Ellie Pavlick. 2019b. What do you learn from context? probing for sentence structure in contextualized word representations. In 7th International Conference on Learning Representations, ICLR 2019, New Orleans, LA, USA, May 6-9, 2019. OpenReview.net.

Yonglong Tian, Dilip Krishnan, and Phillip Isola. 2020. Contrastive representation distillation. In 8th International Conference on Learning Representations, ICLR 2020, Addis Ababa, Ethiopia, April 26-30, 2020. OpenReview.net.

Lifu Tu, Garima Lalwani, Spandana Gella, and He He. 2020. An empirical study on robustness to spurious correlations using pre-trained language models. Transactions of the Association for Computational Linguistics, 8:621–633.

Ashish Vaswani, Noam Shazeer, Niki Parmar, Jakob Uszkoreit, Llion Jones, Aidan N. Gomez, Lukasz Kaiser, and Illia Polosukhin. 2017. Attention is all you need. In Advances in Neural Information Processing Systems 30: Annual Conference on Neural Information Processing Systems 2017, December 4-9, 2017, Long Beach, CA, USA, pages 5998–6008.

Elena Voita and Ivan Titov. 2020. Information-theoretic probing with minimum description length. In Proceedings of the 2020 Conference on Empirical Methods in Natural Language Processing (EMNLP), pages 183–196, Online. Association for Computational Linguistics.

Alex Wang, Ian F. Tenney, Yada Pruksachatkun, Phil Yeres, Jason Phang, Haokun Liu, Phu Mon Htut, , Katherin Yu, Jan Hula, Patrick Xia, Raghu Pappagari, Shuning Jin, R. Thomas McCoy, Roma Patel, Yinghui Huang, Edouard Grave, Najoung Kim, Thibault Févry, Berlin Chen, Nikita Nangia, Anhad Mohananey, Katharina Kann, Shikha Bordia, Nicolas Patry, David Benton, Ellie Pavlick, and Samuel R. Bowman. 2019. `jiant` 1.3: A software toolkit for research on general-purpose text understanding models. `http://jiant.info/`.

Weischedel, Ralph, Palmer, Martha, Marcus, Mitchell, Hovy, Eduard, Pradhan, Sameer, Ramshaw, Lance, Xue, Nianwen, Taylor, Ann, Kaufman, Jeff, Franchini, Michelle, El-Bachouti, Mohammed, Belvin, Robert, and Houston, Ann. 2013. Ontonotes release 5.0.

Adina Williams, Nikita Nangia, and Samuel Bowman. 2018. A broad-coverage challenge corpus for sentence understanding through inference. In Proceedings of the 2018 Conference of the North American Chapter of the Association for Computational Linguistics: Human Language Technologies, Volume 1 (Long Papers), pages 1112–1122, New Orleans, Louisiana. Association for Computational Linguistics.

Thomas Wolf, Lysandre Debut, Victor Sanh, Julien Chaumond, Clement Delangue, Anthony Moi, Pierric Cistac, Tim Rault, Remi Louf, Morgan Funtowicz, Joe Davison, Sam Shleifer, Patrick von Platen, Clara Ma, Yacine Jernite, Julien Plu, Canwen Xu, Teven Le Scao, Sylvain Gugger, Mariama Drame, Quentin Lhoest, and Alexander Rush. 2020. Transformers: State-of-the-art natural language processing. In Proceedings of the 2020 Conference on Empirical Methods in Natural Language Processing: System Demonstrations, pages 38–45, Online. Association for Computational Linguistics.

Jason Yosinski, Jeff Clune, Yoshua Bengio, and Hod Lipson. 2014. How transferable are features in deep neural networks? In Advances in Neural Information Processing Systems 27: Annual Conference on Neural Information Processing Systems 2014, December 8-13 2014, Montreal, Quebec, Canada, pages 3320–3328.

Weijie Yu, Chen Xu, Jun Xu, Liang Pang, Xiaopeng Gao, Xiaozhao Wang, and Ji-Rong Wen. 2020. Wasserstein distance regularized sequence representation for text matching in asymmetrical domains. In Proceedings of the 2020 Conference on Empirical Methods in Natural Language Processing (EMNLP), pages 2985–2994, Online. Association for Computational Linguistics.

Werner Zellinger, Thomas Grubinger, Edwin Lughofer, Thomas Natschläger, and Susanne Saminger-Platz. 2017. Central moment discrepancy (CMD) for domain-invariant representation learning. In 5th International Conference on Learning Representations, ICLR 2017, Toulon, France, April 24-26, 2017, Conference Track Proceedings. OpenReview.net.

Sheng Zhang, Xiaodong Liu, Jingjing Liu, Jianfeng Gao, Kevin Duh, and Benjamin Van Durme. 2018. Record: Bridging the gap between human and machine commonsense reading comprehension. CoRR, abs/1810.12885.

Sicheng Zhu, Xiao Zhang, and David Evans. 2020. Learning adversarially robust representations via worst-case mutual information maximization. In Proceedings of the 37th International Conference on Machine Learning, ICML 2020, 13-18 July 2020, Virtual Event, volume 119 of Proceedings of Machine Learning Research, pages 11609–11618. PMLR.

Yukun Zhu, Ryan Kiros, Rich Zemel, Ruslan Salakhutdinov, Raquel Urtasun, Antonio Torralba, and Sanja Fidler. 2015. Aligning books and movies: Towards story-like visual explanations by watching movies and reading books. In Proceedings of the 2015 IEEE International Conference on Computer Vision (ICCV), ICCV '15, page 19–27, USA. IEEE Computer Society.

A Divergence Measures

Maximum Mean Discrepancy (MMD): MMD is a non-parametric method to estimate the distance between distributions based on Reproducing Kernel Hilbert Spaces (RKHS). Given two random variables $X = \{x_1, x_2, ..., x_m\}$ and $Y = \{y_1, y_2, ..., y_n\}$ that are drawn from distributions P and Q, the empirical estimate of the distance between distribution P and Q is given by

$$MMD(X,Y) = \left\|\left(\frac{1}{m}\sum_{i=1}^{m}\phi(x_i) - \frac{1}{n}\sum_{i=1}^{n}\phi(y_i)\right)\right\|_{\mathcal{H}} \tag{1}$$

Here $\phi : \mathcal{X} \rightarrow \mathcal{H}$ are nonlinear mappings or of the samples to a feature representation in a RKHS, called kernels. In this work, we map the contextual word representations of the text to RKHS. Various kernels can be used for this purpose. Some of the kernels are given below.

Rational Quadratic Kernel

$$\phi(x,y) = \left(1 + \frac{1}{2\alpha}(x-y)^T\Theta^{-2}(x-y)\right)^{-\alpha}$$

Energy

$$\phi(x,y) = -\|x-y\|_2$$

Gaussian

$$\phi(x,y) = exp(-\frac{\|x-y\|_2^2}{\gamma})$$

Laplacian

$$\phi(x,y) = exp(-\frac{\|x-y\|_2}{\sigma})$$

In this work we use a mixture of Gaussian Kernels rather than a single kernel which is known to be more stable than just using a single kernel. The mixture of kernels are given by

$$\mathcal{K} = \left\{\sum_{i=1}^{m}\lambda_i k_i \mid \sum_{i=1}^{m}\lambda_i = 1\right\} \tag{2}$$

We set λ_i to be $\frac{1}{m}$. We follow (Long et al., 2015) and use the Gaussian kernel. We calculate a initial value γ_s and set it to the median pairwise distances between two samples, also known as *median heuristic*. For every kernel k_i, the value of γ is set from $2^{-8}\gamma_s$ and $2^8\gamma_s$, increasing it by a multiple of 2.

Correlation Alignment (CORAL): Correlation alignment is the distance between the second-order moment of the source and target samples. If d is the representation dimension, $\|\|_F$ represents Frobenius norm and Cov_S, Cov_T is the covariance matrix of the source and target samples, then CORAL is defined as

$$D_{CORAL} = \frac{1}{4d^2}\|Cov_S - Cov_T\|_F^2 \tag{3}$$

Central Moment Discrepancy (CMD): Central Moment Discrepancy is another metric that measures the distance between source and target distributions. It not only considers the first moment and second moment, but also other higher-order moments. While MMD operates in a projected space, CMD operates in the representation space. If P and Q are two probability distributions and $X = \{X_1, X_2, ..., X_N\}$ and $Y = \{Y_1, Y_2, ..., Y_N\}$ are random vectors that are independent and identically distributed from P and Q and every component of the vector is bounded by $[a, b]$, CMD is then defined by

$$\begin{aligned} CMD(P,Q) &= \frac{1}{|b-a|}\|E(X) - E(Y)\|_2 \\ &+ \sum_{k=2}^{\infty}\frac{1}{|b-a|^k}\|c_k(X) - c_k(Y)\|_2 \end{aligned} \tag{4}$$

where $E(X)$ is the expectation of X and c_k is the $k-th$ order central moment which is defined as

$$c_k(X) = E\left(\prod_{i=1}^{N}(X_i - E(X_i))^{r_i}\right) \tag{5}$$

and $r_1 + r_2 + r_N = k$ and $r_1....r_N \geq 0$

B Domain Divergence Plots

Fig. 5 shows the domain divergence measures for `bert-base-uncased` and `bert-large-uncased` models only for greater quality. We consider only the CORAL and CMD divergence measures. Even though both the models are trained on similar amounts of data, with similar training procedures, at comparable layers `bert-large-uncased`-models are more domain-invariant compared to `bert-base-uncased`.

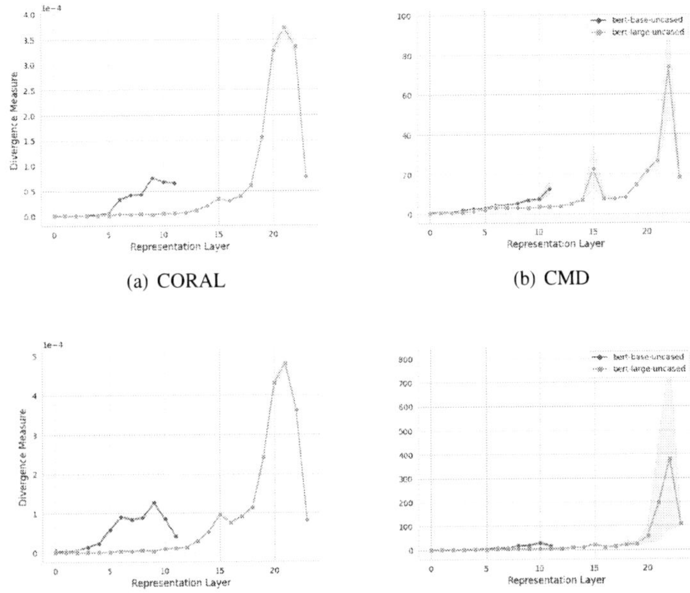

(a) CORAL (b) CMD

(c) CORAL (d) CMD

Figure 5: Comparing divergence of `bert-base-uncased` and `bert-large-uncased` models. **Top:** Divergence for standard and biomedical domain **Bottom**: Divergence for the standard and twitter domain.

C DAPT Twitter Divergence Plots

Divergence plots for DAPT-twitter compared with its `roberta-base` counterpart are shown in Fig. 6. Here we consider the CORAL and CMD divergence measures. The plots show that for DAPT-twitter the divergence measures are either the same or more than their `roberta-base` counterpart which indicates their specialization for a domain.

D DistilBERTvs BERT for twitter

Fig. 7 shows the comparison between DistilBERT – the student network and the `bert-base-uncased` which is the teacher network in knowledge distillation (Hinton et al., 2015). We consider the CORAL and CMD divergence measures. The plots show that at comparable layers DistilBERT divergence measures are strictly more than `bert-base-uncased`.

E PCA Plots for PLM Representations

Figures 8 to 15 show the 2 dimensional PCA plots for representations from different layers for all the encoders – `bert-base-uncased` , `bert-large-uncased` , `roberta-base` , `distilbert-base`. Interspersed representations in the plots indicate more domain-invariance (less domain divergence) between the representations and clearer separation indicates lesser domain divergence (more domain divergence).

F Probing classifiers' training details

Task	Train	Dev	Test
POS	110,514	15060	11,462
NER	720	150	690
Coref	2255	101	101

Table 2: Train/dev/test split used for the probing experiments in §4 for each task.

The statistics about the datasets used for training the probes are consolidated in Table 2.

For all the three tasks (POS, NER and coreference resolution) we train the probing classifiers on the source domain for 3 epochs. We use Adam as the optimizer with a learning rate of 1e-4, and a batch size of 32. We also evaluate on the validation dataset every 1000 steps, and halve the learning rate if no improvement is seen in 5 validations. The rest of the hyperparameters are the

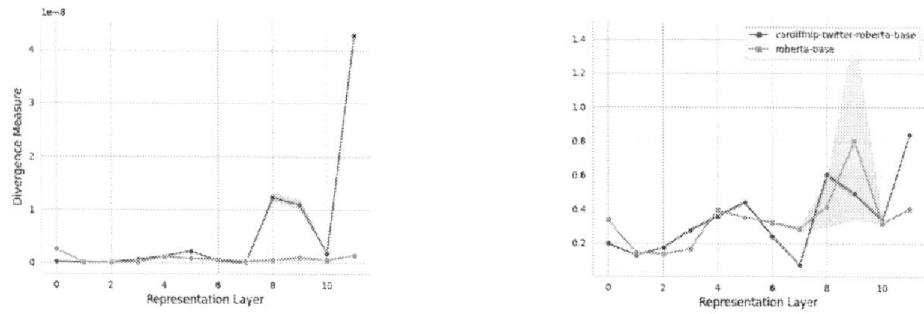

(a) CORAL (b) CMD

Figure 6: Comparing divergences for RoBERTa vs DAPT-twitter (Barbieri et al., 2020). We consider the CORAL and CMD divergence measures for standard vs twitter samples. The plots are shown for CORAL and CMD divergence measures.

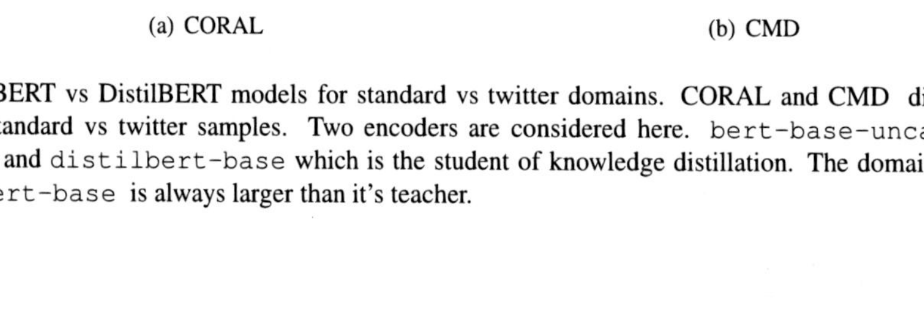

(a) CORAL (b) CMD

Figure 7: BERT vs DistilBERT models for standard vs twitter domains. CORAL and CMD divergence measures for standard vs twitter samples. Two encoders are considered here. `bert-base-uncased` which is the teacher and `distilbert-base` which is the student of knowledge distillation. The domain-invariance of `distilbert-base` is always larger than it's teacher.

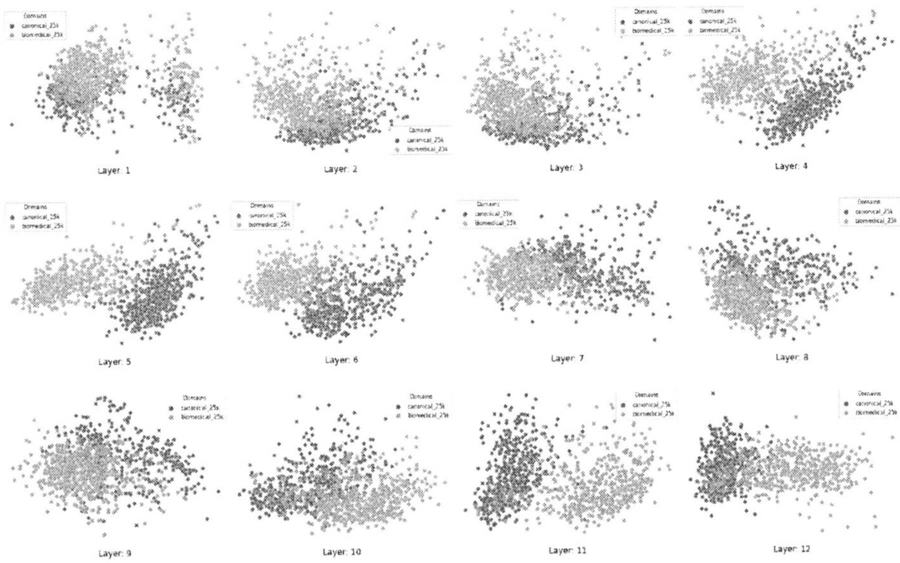

Figure 8: PCA plots for representation of `bert-base-uncased` for the pair of standard and the biomedical domain for different layers. The PCA representations show that representations are interspersed in the lower layers with a progressively clearer separation in the later layers.

same as defined by (Tenney et al., 2019a) in their edge probing experiments.

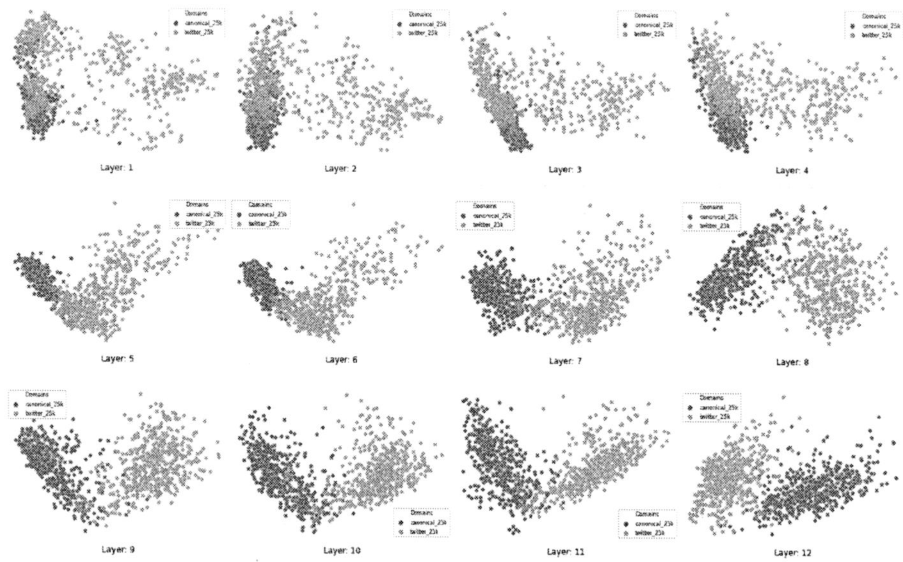

Figure 9: PCA plots for representation of `bert-base-uncased` for the pair of standard and the twitter domain for different layers. The PCA representations show that representations are interspersed in the lower layers with a progressively clearer separation in the later layers.

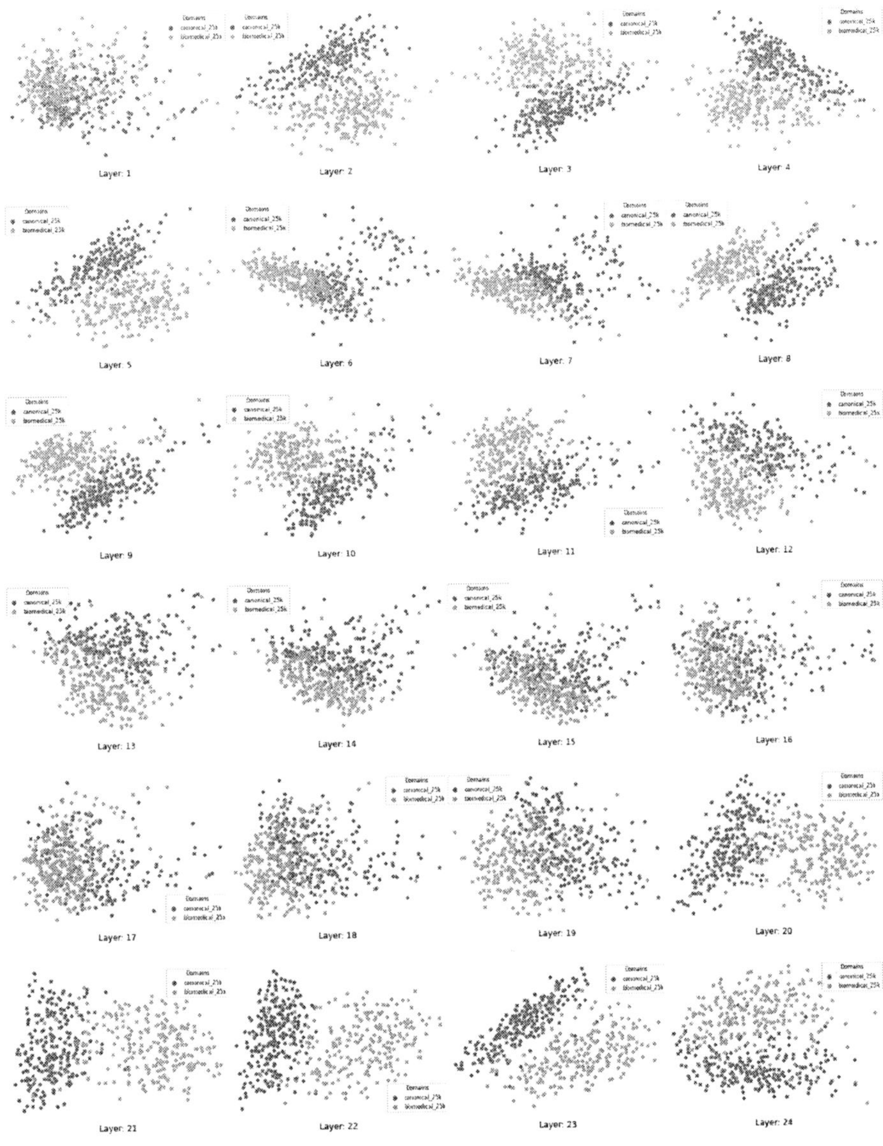

Figure 10: PCA plots for representation of `bert-large-uncased` for the pair of standard and the biomedical domain for different layers. The PCA representations show that representations are interspersed in the lower layers with a progressively clearer separation in the later layers.

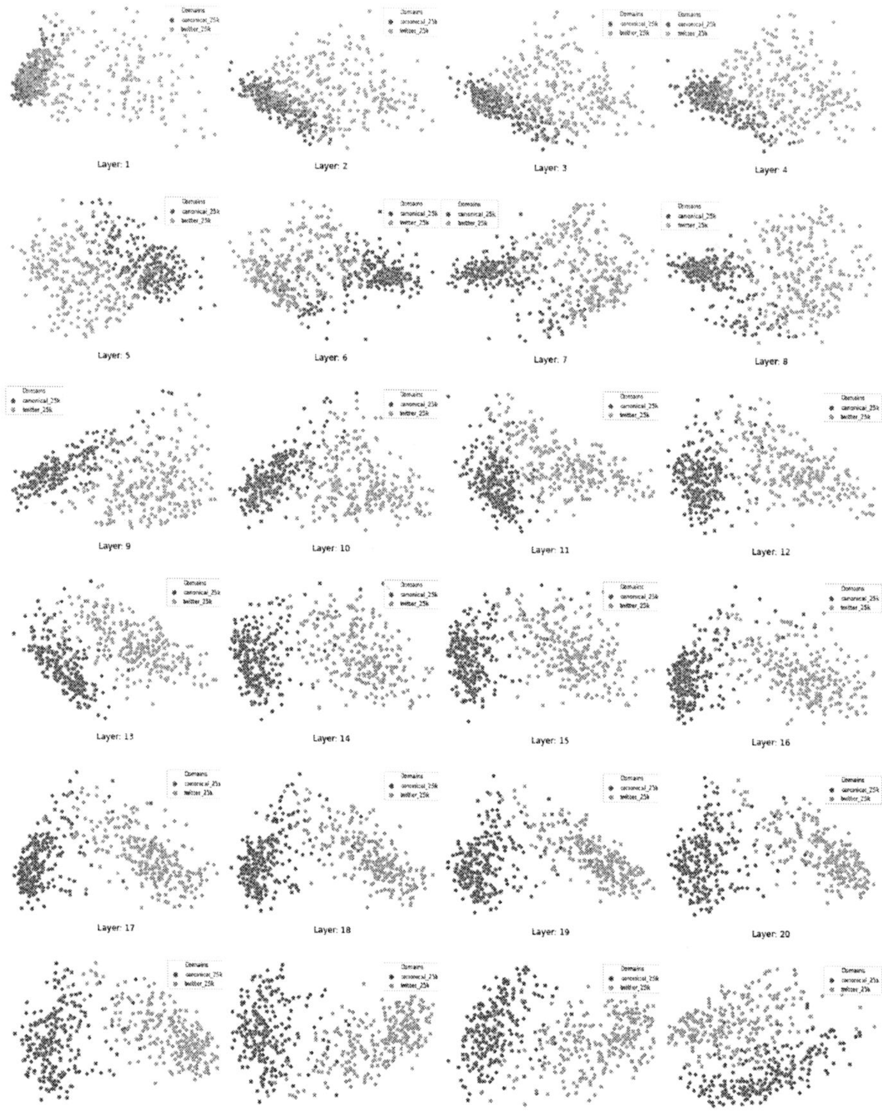

Figure 11: PCA plots for representation of `bert-large-uncased` for the pair of standard and the twitter domain for different layers. The PCA representations show that representations are interspersed in the lower layers with a progressively clearer separation in the later layers.

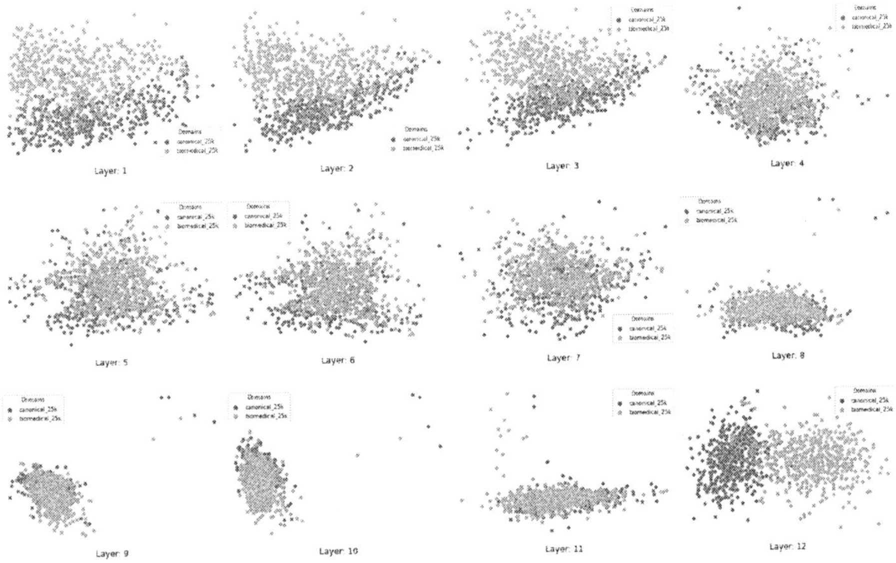

Figure 12: PCA plots for representation of `roberta-base` for the pair of standard and the biomedical domain for different layers. The PCA representations compared to the `bert-base-uncased` and `bert-large-uncased` models, the representations are interspersed across all the layers

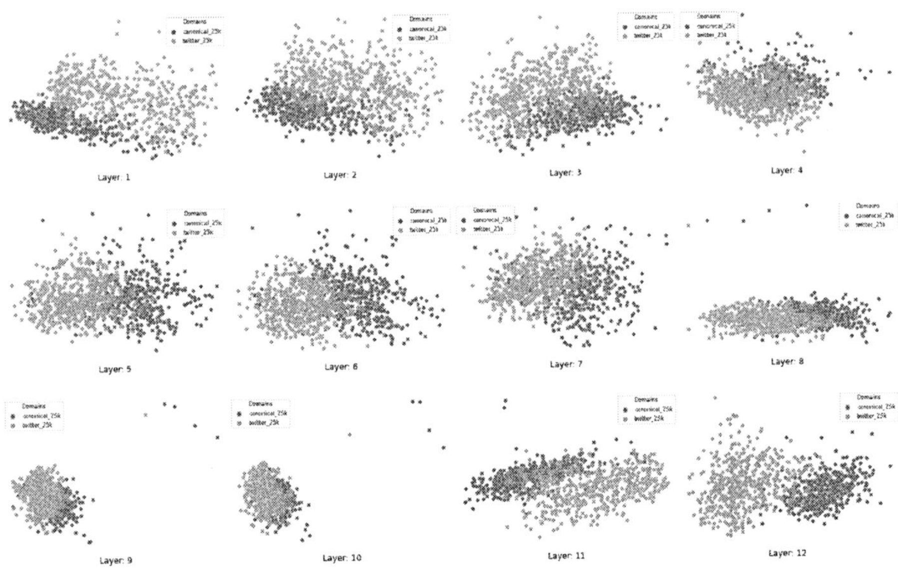

Figure 13: PCA plots for representation of `roberta-base` for the pair of standard and the twitter domain for different layers. The PCA representations compared to the `bert-base-uncased` and `bert-large-uncased` models, the representations are interspersed across all the layers

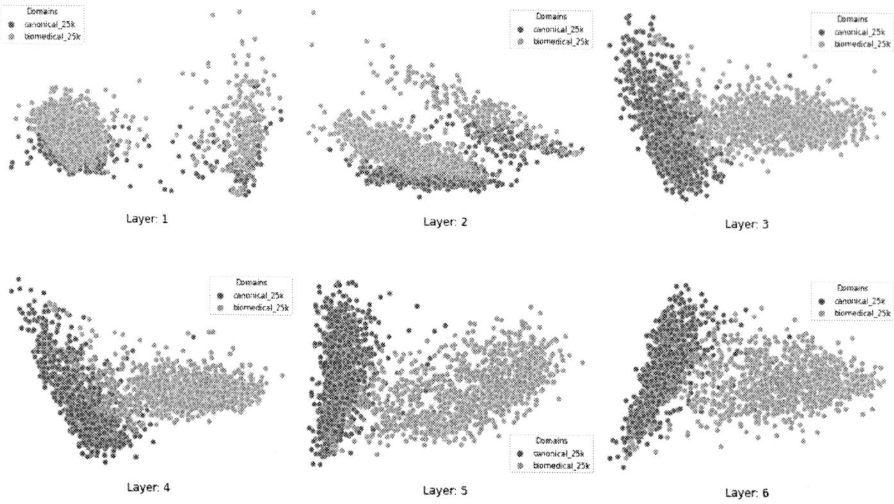

Figure 14: PCA plots for representation of `distilbert-base` for the pair of standard and the biomedical domain for different layers. The lower layers are still interspersed, with a clearer separation in the higher layers. We can see a corresponding increase in the divergence measures for these layers.

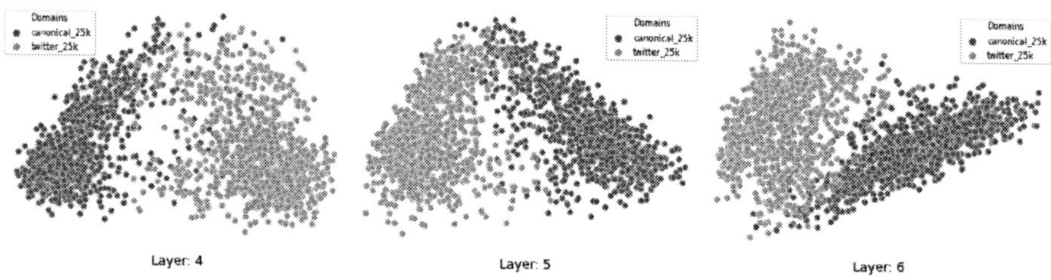

Figure 15: PCA plots for representation of `distilbert-base` for the pair of standard and the biomedical domain for different layers. The lower layers are still interspersed, with a clearer separation in the higher layers. We can see a corresponding increase in the divergence measures for these layers.

Few-Shot Learning of an Interleaved Text Summarization Model by Pretraining with Synthetic Data

Sanjeev Kumar Karn[1,2], **Francine Chen** , **Yan-Ying Chen**[3], **Ulli Waltinger**[4] **and Hinrich Schütze**[1]

[1]Center for Information and Language Processing (CIS), LMU Munich
[2]Machine Intelligence, Siemens Healthineers, Princeton
[3]Toyota Research Institute, Los Altos, California
[4]Machine Intelligence, Siemens AG, Munich

skarn@cis.lmu.de francine@acm.org yan-ying.chen@tri.global
ulli.waltinger@siemens.com inquiries@cislmu.org

Abstract

Interleaved texts, where posts belonging to different threads occur in a sequence, commonly occur in online chat posts, so that it can be time-consuming to quickly obtain an overview of the discussions. Existing systems first disentangle the posts by threads and then extract summaries from those threads. A major issue with such systems is error propagation from the disentanglement component. While end-to-end trainable summarization system could obviate explicit disentanglement, such systems require a large amount of labeled data. To address this, we propose to pretrain an end-to-end trainable hierarchical encoder-decoder system using synthetic interleaved texts. We show that by fine-tuning on a real-world meeting dataset (AMI), such a system out-performs a traditional two-step system by 22%. We also compare against transformer models and observed that pretraining with synthetic data both the encoder and decoder outperforms the BertSumExtAbs transformer model which pretrains only the encoder on a large dataset.

1 Introduction

Interleaved texts are increasingly common, occurring in social media conversations such as Slack and Stack Exchange, where posts belonging to different threads may be intermixed in the post sequence; see a meeting transcript from the AMI corpus (McCowan et al., 2005) in Table 1. Due to the mixing, getting a quick sense of the different conversational threads is often difficult.

In conversation disentanglement, interleaved posts are grouped by the thread. However, a reader still has to read all posts in each cluster of threads to get the gist. Shang et al. (2018) proposed a two-step system that takes an interleaved text as input and first disentangles the posts thread-wise by clustering, and then compresses the thread-wise posts to single-sentence summaries. However, disentanglement e.g., Wang and Oard (2009), propagates error to the downstream summarization task. An end-to-end supervised summarization system that implicitly identifies the conversations would eliminate error propagation. However, labeling of interleaved texts is a difficult and expensive task (Barker et al., 2016; Aker et al., 2016; Verberne et al., 2018).

AMI Utteracnes
. . . Who is gonna do a PowerPoint presentation ? Think we all Huh. You will . . .
. . . $^{\xi}$and uh the sender will send to the telly itself an **infra-red signal** to tell it to switch on or switch. . .
. . . $^{\zeta}$so y so it's so it's so you got so that's something we should have a look into then i when desi when designing the ergonomics of see have a look . . .
. . . $^{\psi}$,the little tiny weeny **batteries**, all like special long-lasting **batteries**. . .
. . .
Summary
1) the project manager had the team members re-introduce
. . .
2) the industrial designer discussed the interior workings of a remote and the team discussed **options for batteries** and **infra-red signals**.
5) the marketing expert prěsėnted research on consumer preferences on remotes in general and on voice recognition and the team discussed the option to have an ergonomically designed remote.
. . .

Table 1: The top section shows AMI ASR transcripts and the bottom section shows human-written summaries. ξ=150th, ζ=522th and ψ=570th utterances. a) refer to the ath sentence in a multi-sentence summary.

We propose a pretraining approach to tackle these issues. We synthesized a corpus of interleaved text-summary pairs out of a corpus of regular document-summary pairs and train an end-to-end trainable encoder-decoder system. To generate the summary the model learns to infer (disentangle) the major topics in several threads. We show

Proceedings of the Second Workshop on Domain Adaptation for NLP, pages 245–254
April 20, 2021.

on synthetic and real-world data that the encoder-decoder system not only obviates a disentanglement component but also enhances performance. Thus, the summarization task acts as an auxiliary task for the disentanglement. Additionally, we show that fine-tuning of the encoder-decode system with the learned disentanglement representations on a real-world AMI dataset achieves a substantial increment in evaluation metrics despite a small number of labels.

We also propose using a hierarchical attention in the encoder-decoder system with three levels of information from the interleaved text; posts, phrases, and words, rather than traditional two levels; post and word (Nallapati et al., 2017, 2016; Tan et al., 2017; Cheng and Lapata, 2016).

The remaining paper is structured as follows. In Section 2, we discuss related work. In Section 3, we provide a detailed description of our hierarchical seq2seq model. In Section 4, we provide a detailed description on the synthetic data creation algorithm. In Section 5, we describe and discuss the experiments. And in Section 6, we present our conclusions.

2 Related Work

Ma et al. (2012); Aker et al. (2016); Shang et al. (2018) each designed a system that summarizes posts in multi-party conversations in order to provide readers with overview on the discussed matters. They broadly follow the same two-step approach: cluster the posts and then extract a summary from each cluster.

There are two kinds of summarization: abstractive and extractive. In abstractive summarization, the model utilizes a corpus level vocabulary and generates novel sentences as the summary, while extractive models extract or rearrange the source words as the summary. Abstractive models based on neural sequence-to-sequence (seq2seq) (Rush et al., 2015) proved to generate summaries with higher ROUGE scores than the feature-based abstractive models.

Li et al. (2015) proposed an encoder-decoder (auto-encoder) model that utilizes a hierarchy of networks: word-to-word followed by sentence-to-sentence. Their model is better at capturing the underlying structure than a vanilla sequential encoder-decoder model (seq2seq). Krause et al. (2017) and Jing et al. (2018) showed multi-sentence captioning of an *image* through a hierarchical Recurrent Neural Network (RNN), topic-to-topic followed by word-to-word, is better than seq2seq. These works suggest a hierarchical decoder, thread-to-thread followed by word-to-word, may intrinsically disentangle the posts, and therefore, generate more appropriate summaries.

Integration of attention into a seq2seq model (Bahdanau et al., 2014) led to further advancement of abstractive summarization (Nallapati et al., 2016; Chopra et al., 2016). Nallapati et al. (2016) devised a hierarchical attention mechanism for a seq2seq model, where two levels of attention distributions over the source, i.e., sentence and word, are computed at every step of the word decoding. Based on the sentence attentions, the word attentions are rescaled. Our hierarchical attention is more intuitive, computes post(sentence)-level and phrase-level attentions for every new summary sentence, and is trained end-to-end.

Semi-supervised learning has recently gained popularity as it helps training parameters of large models without any training data. Researchers have pre-trained masked language models, in which only an encoder is used to reconstruct the text, e.g., BERT (Devlin et al., 2018). Liu and Lapata (2019) used BERT as seq2seq encoder and showed improved performance on several abstractive summarization tasks. Similarly, researchers have published pre-trained seq2seq models using a different semi-supervised learning technique, where a seq2seq model is learned to reconstruct the original text, e.g., BART (Lewis et al., 2019) and MASS (Song et al., 2019). In this work, we rely on transfer learning and demonstrate that by pretraining with appropriate interleaved text data, a seq2seq model readily transfers to a new domain with just a few examples.

3 Model

Our hierarchical encoder (see Figure 1 left hand section) is based on Nallapati et al. (2017), where word-to-word and post-to-post encoders are bi-directional LSTMs. The word-to-word BiLSTM encoder (E_{w2w}) runs over word embeddings of post P_i and generates a set of hidden representations, $\langle \mathbf{h}_{i,0}^{E_{w2w}}, \ldots, \mathbf{h}_{i,p}^{E_{w2w}} \rangle$, of d dimensions. The average pooled value of the word-to-word representations of post P_i ($\frac{1}{p}\sum_{j=0}^{p} \mathbf{h}_{i,j}^{E_{w2w}}$) is input to the post-to-post BiLSTM encoder (E_{t2t}), which then generates a set of representations, $\langle \mathbf{h}_{0}^{E_{p2p}}, \ldots, \mathbf{h}_{n}^{E_{p2p}} \rangle$, corresponding to the posts.

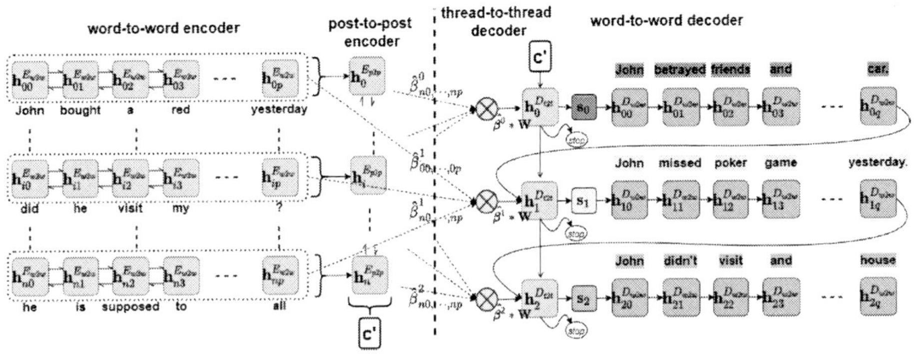

Figure 1: Hierarchical encoder-decoder architecture. On the left, interleaved posts are encoded hierarchically, i.e., word-to-word (E_{w2w}) followed by post-to-post (E_{p2p}). On the right, summaries are generated hierarchically, thread-to-thread (D_{t2t}) followed by word-to-word (D_{t2t}).

Overall, for a given channel C, output representations of word-to-word, $\mathbf{W}$, and post-to-post, $\mathbf{P}$, has $n \times p \times 2d$ and $n \times 2d$ dimensions respectively. The hierarchical decoder has two uni-directional LSTM decoders, thread-to-thread and word-to-word (see right-hand side in Figure 1).

At step k of thread decoder (D_{t2t}), we compute elements of post-level attention as $\gamma_i^k = \sigma(\text{attn}^\gamma(\mathbf{h}_{k-1}^{D_{t2t}}, \mathbf{P}_i)\ i \in \{1, \ldots, n\}$, where attn^γ aligns the current thread decoder state vector $\mathbf{h}_{k-1}^{D_{t2t}}$ to vectors of matrix $\mathbf{P}_i$. A phrase is a short sequences of words in a sentence/post. Phrases in interleaved texts are equivalent to visual patterns in images, and therefore, attending phrases are more relevant for thread recognition than attending posts. Thus, we have phrase-level attentions focusing on words in a channel and with a responsibility of disentangling threads. At step k of thread decoder, we also compute a sequence of attention weights, $\boldsymbol{\beta^k} = \langle \beta_{0,0}^k, \ldots, \beta_{n,p}^k \rangle$, corresponding to the set of encoded word representations, $\langle \mathbf{h}_{0,0}^{w2w}, \ldots, \mathbf{h}_{n,p}^{w2w} \rangle$, as $\beta_{i,j}^k = \sigma(\text{attn}^\beta(\mathbf{h}_{k-1}^{D_{t2t}}, \mathbf{a}_{i,j}))$ where $\mathbf{a}_{i,j} = add(\mathbf{W}_{i,j}, \mathbf{P}_i),\ i \in \{1, \ldots, n\},\ j \in \{1, \ldots, p\}$. add aligns a post representation to its word representations and does element-wise addition, and attn^β maps the current thread decoder state $\mathbf{h}_{k-1}^{D_{t2t}}$ and vector $\mathbf{a}_{i,j}$ to a scalar value. Then, we use the post-level attention, $\boldsymbol{\gamma}^k$, to rescale the sequence of attention weights $\boldsymbol{\beta^k}$ to obtain phrase-level attentions $\hat{\boldsymbol{\beta}}^{\boldsymbol{k}}$ as $\hat{\beta}_{i,j}^k = \beta_{i,j}^k * \gamma_i^k$.

A weighted representation of the words (crossed blue circle), $\sum_{i=1}^n \sum_{j=1}^p \hat{\beta}_{i,j}^k \mathbf{W}_{ij}$, is used as an input to compute the next state of the thread-to-thread decoder, D_{t2t}. Additionally, we also use the last hidden state $\mathbf{h}_{k-1,q}^{D_{w2w}}$ of the word-to-word decoder LSTM (D_{w2w}) of the previously generated summary sentence as the second input to D_{t2t}. The motivation is to provide information about the previous sentence.

The current state $\mathbf{h}_k^{D_{t2t}}$ is passed through a single layer feedforward network and a distribution over STOP=1 and CONTINUE=0 is computed: $p_k^{STOP} = \sigma(\text{g}\left(\mathbf{h}_k^{D_{t2t}}\right))$, where g is a feedforward network. In Figure 1, the process is depicted by a yellow circle. The thread-to-thread decoder keeps decoding until p_k^{STOP} is greater than 0.5.

Additionally, the new state $\mathbf{h}_k^{D_{t2t}}$ and inputs to D_{t2t} at that step are passed through a two-layer feedforward network, r, followed by a dropout layer to compute the thread representation $\mathbf{s}_k$. Given a thread representation $\mathbf{s}_k$, the word-to-word decoder, a unidirectional attentional LSTM (D_{w2w}), generates a summary for the thread; see the right-hand side of Figure 1. Our word-to-word decoder is based on Bahdanau et al. (2014).

At step l of word-to-word decoding of summary of thread k, we compute elements of word level attention, i.e., $\boldsymbol{\alpha}_{i,\cdot}^{k,l}$; we refer to Bahdanau et al. (2014) for further details on it. However, we use phrase-level word attentions for rescaling the word level attention as $\hat{\alpha}_{i,j}^{k,l} = norm(\hat{\beta}_{i,j}^k \times \alpha_{ij}^{k,l})$, where $norm$ (softmax) renormalizes the values. Thus, contrary to popular two-level hierarchical attention (Nallapati et al., 2016; Cheng and Lapata, 2016; Tan et al., 2017), we have three levels of hierarchical attention and each with its responsibility and is coordinated through the rescaling operation.

We train our model end-to-end to minimize the following objec-

Notations	
C	A sequence of pairs of single-thread texts and single-sentence summaries
a	A minimum number of threads
b	A maximum number of threads
m	A minimum number of posts
n	A maximum number of posts
WINDOW	returns an iterator object that traverse a given sequence elements in windowed manner
w	window size
t	step size
O	An iterator object that returns a window size sequence of pairs of single-thread texts and single-sentence summaries
E	A window size sequence of pairs of single-thread texts and single-sentence summaries
I'	A sequence of sentences
M'	A sequence of single-sentence summaries
$\mathcal{U}$	A uniform sampling function
A	A single thread text as a sequence of sentences
T	A single-sentence summary as a sequence of words
$\hat{I}$	A multi-thread interleaved text
$\hat{M}$	A multi-sentence summary of an interleaved text
$\{a_{\times b}\}$	A set in which variable a is repeated b times
S	A sequence of positive integers
REVERSE	reverses an array
POP	removes the last element from an array
P	A sentence/post as a sequence of words
$[\cdot]$	array indexing operation
$X \setminus Y$	A set of elements that belong to X but not to Y
Z	A sequence of pairs of multi-thread interleaved texts and multi-sentence summaries

Table 2: We use lowercase italics for variables, uppercase italics for sets and sequences, math symbols for mathematical operations and uppercase words for methods.

tive: $\sum_{k=1}^{m}\sum_{l=1}^{q} \log p_\theta\left(y^{k,l}|w_{k,\cdot<l}, \mathbf{W}\right) + \lambda\sum_{k=1}^{m} y_k^{STOP}\log(p_k^{STOP})$, where $\langle w^{k,0},\ldots,w^{k,q}\rangle$ and $\langle y^{k,0},\ldots,y^{k,q}\rangle$ are words in a ground-truth summary and D_{w2w} generation respectively.

4 Synthetic Dataset

Obtaining labeled training data for interleaved conversation summarization is challenging. The available ones are either extractive Verberne et al. (2018) or too small (Barker et al., 2016; Anguera et al., 2012) to train a neural model and thoroughly verify the architecture. To get around this issue, we synthesized a dataset by utilizing a corpus of conventional texts for which summaries are available. We created a corpus of interleaved texts from the abstracts and titles of articles from the PubMed corpus (Dernoncourt and Lee, 2017). We chose PubMed abstracts as it has, in contrast to other corpora such as news articles or StackOverflow posts, a single-sentence summary that can only be comprehended out of a whole abstract. Further, the number of sentences more closely resembles that of a conversationalist in a conversation.

Algorithm 1 Interleaving Algorithm

```
procedure INTERLEAVE(C, a, b, m, n)
    O, Z ← WINDOW(C, w, t), Array()
    while O ≠ ∅ do
        E, I', M', S ← O.NEXT(), Array(), Array(), {}
        r ~ U(a, b)
        for j = 1 to r do                          ▷ Selection
            A, T ← E[j]
            q ~ U(m, n)
            I'.ADD(A[1:q])
            M'.ADD(T)
            S ← S ∪ {j_×q}
        Î, M̂, l ← Array(), Array(), |S|
        for 1 to l do                              ▷ Interleaving
            k ← U(S)
            P ← REVERSE(I'[k]).POP()
            Î.ADD(P)
            T ← M'[k]
            if T ∉ M̂ then:
                M̂.ADD(T)
            S ← S \ k
        Z.ADD(Î;M̂)
    return Z
```

Random interleaving of the sentences from a small number of PubMed abstracts roughly resembles interleaved texts, and, correspondingly, interleaving of titles resembles its multi-sentence summary. We devised an algorithm for creating synthetic interleaved texts based on this idea.

Interleave Algorithm: The Interleave Algorithm generates interleaved texts, each containing randomly interleaved sentences from a small number of abstracts, where the number is a random value within a specified range. The number of sentences used per abstract is also a random value within a specified range. Abstracts to be included in an interleaved text are first selected, then the selected abstracts are interleaved, and finally the interleaved texts together with a concatenation of the titles of the selected abstracts are returned.

We first refer to Table 2 for terms and notations used in Algorithm. 1. INTERLEAVE takes a corpus of abstract-title pairs, $C = \langle A_1;T_1,A_2;T_2,\ldots,A_N;T_N\rangle$, and returns a sequence of pairs of multi-thread interleaved texts and multi-sentence summaries, Z. Each interleaved text in the generated sequence will contain a number of threads ranging between a to b, where the number is randomly selected. Each thread, in turn, will contain a number of posts or sentences ranging between m and n, where this number is also randomly selected. The WINDOW function is given C, a desired window size, w, and step size, t, and it returns an iterator object, O, of size $\frac{|N|-w}{t}+1$.

WINDOW helps to enlarge the interleaved corpus without redundancy as abstracts are randomly sampled out of an iterator element, E, and also new abstracts are always included in the next element through sliding. Similarly, sets of sentences are randomly sampled out of the selected abstracts. Thus, interleaved text-summary pairs in the corpus are different. The two parts of the INTERLEAVE algorithm, Selection and Interleaving, will be described next.

Selection: $\mathcal{U}$ in step 5 determines the number of threads, r. Then, thread candidates for an interleaved text are chosen out of an iterator element E, a window size sequence of pairs of single-thread texts and single-sentence summaries. Next, post candidates for each selected thread, A, are chosen. $\mathcal{U}$ in step 8 determines the number of posts, q. Thread indices are repeated as many times as its posts and stored in a set, S.

Interleaving: In every step in a loop of a size equivalent to the length of indices S, $\mathcal{U}$ randomly selects a thread index. REVERSE and POP in step 15 help in selecting a post, P, in the selected thread in a FIFO manner. The single-sentence summary, T, of the thread is added to the multi-sentence summary sequence, $\hat{M}$, if it didn't exist previously.

As an interleaved text-summary pair in the corpus has a thread size between a and b and post size per thread between m and n, the larger the difference between a and b and m and n in a corpus, the harder the disentangling and summarization task. So, we vary these parameters and create different synthetic corpora of varying difficulty for the experiments. Table 3 shows an example of a data instance from a Interleaved PubMed corpus compiled using a=2, b=5, m=2 and n=5.

Interleaved text
$^{\pi}$ ...conducted to evaluate the influence of excessive sweating during long-distance running on the urinary concentration of caffeine...
$^{\omega}$ ...to assess the effect of a program of supervised fitness walking and patient education on functional status...
...
$^{\pi}$ ...102 patients with a documented diagnosis of primary osteoarthritis of one or both knees participated...
$^{\phi}$ ...examined the effects of intensity of training on ratings of perceived exertion (...
...
Summary
$^{\pi}$ caffeine in sport. influence of endurance exercise on the urinary caffeine concentration.
$^{\omega}$ supervised fitness walking in patients with osteoarthritis of the knee. a randomized , controlled trial.
$^{\phi}$ the effect of training intensity on ratings of perceived exertion.

Table 3: An example of a synthetic Interleaved text and summary pair compiled using PubMed corpus and Algorithm. 1. It includes three threads (abstracts) identifiable through superscribed symbols π, ω, and ϕ.

Input Text	Model	Rouge-1	Rouge-2	Rouge-L
dis (upper bd)	hier2hier	**39.09**	**30.11**	**15.22**
(Shang et al., 2018)		29.11	15.76	10.13
ent	hier2hier	**37.11**	**27.97**	**14.26**

Table 4: Synthetic interleaved text summarization performance (Rouge Recall-Scores) comparing models when the threads are disentangled (top section, upper bound) and when the threads are entangled (bottom section, real-world) on an Interleaved PubMed Corpus. **dis** = disentangled (ground-truth) and **ent** = entangled.

5 Experiments

Parameters: For the word-to-word encoder, the steps are limited to 20, while the steps in the word-to-word decoder are limited to 15. The steps in the post-to-post encoder and thread-to-thread decoder depend on the corpus type, e.g., a Hard corpus compiled using a=2, b=5, m=2 and n=5 has 25 steps in post-to-post encoder, i.e., $b \times n$ (the maximum possible size of posts in an item in the corpus) and 5 steps in thread-to-thread decoder, i.e., b (the maximum possible threads in an item in the corpus). We initialized all weights, including word embeddings, with a random normal distribution with mean 0 and standard deviation 0.1. The embedding vectors and hidden states of the encoder and decoder in the models are set to dimension 100. Texts are lowercased. The vocabulary size is limited to 8000. We pad short sequences with a special token, $\langle PAD \rangle$. We use Adam (Kingma and Ba, 2014) with an initial learning rate of .0001 and batch size of 64 for training. The training, evaluation and test sets in a Hard Interleaved PubMed corpus (a=2, b=5, m=2 and n=5) are of sizes of 170k, 4k and 4k respectively.

We report ROUGE-1, ROUGE-2, and ROUGE-L as the quantitative evaluation of the models.

Upper-bound: In upper-bound experiments, we check the impact of disentanglement on the abstractive summarization models. In order to do this, we first evaluate the performance of a model when provided the ground-truth disentanglement (thread indices) information. We also evaluate the performance of models for either end-to-end or two-step summarization.

Ground-truth Disentangled: The ground-truth

disentanglement information is used and posts of threads are disentangled and concatenated (posts are thread-wise sequentially arranged, i.e., non-interleaved). The first row in Table 4 shows performance of the hier2hier summarization model. Clearly, the model can easily detect a thread boundary in concatenated threads and perform very well, and therefore, sets an upper bound for the task.

No disentanglement: In real-world scenarios, i.e., with no disentanglement, Shang et al. (2018)'s unsupervised two-step system first disentangles/clusters the posts thread-wise and then compresses clusters to single-sentence summaries. While hier2hier is trained end-to-end, and therefore, generates multi-sentence summaries for a given interleaved text. Table 4 shows Shang et al. (2018) performs worse than hier2hier (compare rows 2 and 3), indicating that a hier2hier model trained on a sufficiently large dataset is better at summarization than the unsupervised sentence compression method, especially in fluency as indicated by an approximately 12 point increase in Rouge-2. Additionally, the hier2hier model trained on entangled texts achieves slightly lower performance to when it is trained on disentangled texts (compare rows 1 and 3), indicating that the disentanglement component can be avoided if summaries are available. The bottom section in Table 5 show an example of the model generations (shown in color). The top indexes of the phrase-level attention ($\hat{\beta}$) is directly visualized in the table through the color coding matching the generation. This shows phrase level attention actually supports in learning to disentangle the interleaved texts.

Transfer Learning: We utilize our interleaving algorithm and PubMed data to compile an interleaved corpus with a similar thread distribution as a corpus of real meetings, the AMI meeting corpus. AMI is a very small size corpus, so we have a train, eval and test split of 112, 10 and 20 respectively. Our analysis of the AMI corpus show that 90% of meetings have ≤ 12 summary sentences while 60% of meetings have ≥ 8 summary sentences, so we used 8 and 12 as the min (a) and max (b) number of threads respectively in the algorithm and create a synthetic corpus. We pretrain the hier2hier model for several iterations on the synthetic corpus, and then transfer and fine-tune the model on the AMI corpus with all parameters fixed except for the word-to-word decoder and hierarchical attention parameters. As PubMed and AMI are from

Interleaved text
...conducted to evaluate the influence of excessive sweating during long-distance running on the urinary concentration of caffeine...
...to assess the effect of a program of supervised fitness walking and patient education on functional status...
...
...102 patients with a documented diagnosis of primary osteoarthritis of one or both knees participated...
...examined the effects of intensity of training on ratings of perceived exertion (...
...
Generation
effect of excessive [UNK] during [UNK] running on the urinary concentration of caffeine .
effect of a physical fitness walking on functional status , pain , and pain
effects of intensity of training on perceived [UNK] in [UNK] athletes .

Table 5: An example of hier2hier generated summary sentences of a three thread interleaved text. Summaries are coloured differently and colors of attended phrases (β) in the text are identical to those of the generations. The table is best viewed in color.

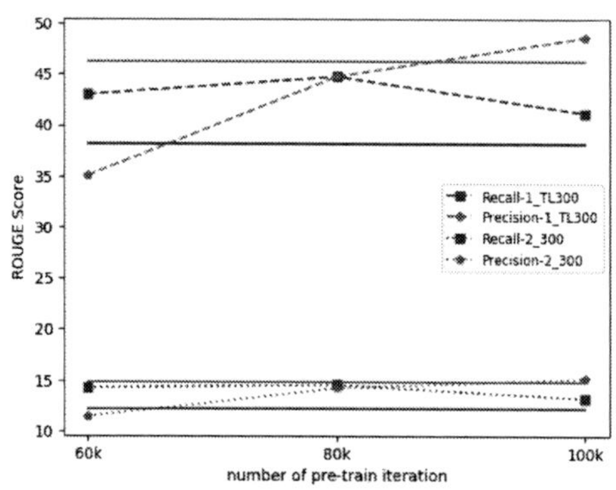

Figure 2: ROUGE uni- and bi-gram precision (green) and recall (blue) of AMI fine-tuned hier2hier models with different numbers of pretraining iterations. Maximum words in a summary is 300. As a reference, solid horizontal lines show the scores of a model trained only on AMI.

different domains, we use the byte pair encoding (BPE) (Sennrich et al., 2016) based subword dictionary. As shown in Table 6, hier2hier readily transfers its disentangling knowledge, and therefore, obtains a boost in recall while maintaining its precision. The Li et al. (2019) system has the best ROUGE-1 scores, however their model is not directly comparable as unlike Shang et al. (2018) and our text-based model, it uses audio and video in addition to text.

Additionally, we also performed transfer learning experiments with models pre-trained for a different number of iterations, and as seen in Figure 2, hier2hier readily transfers its disentangling knowledge, and therefore, obtains a boost in recall while maintaining its precision. However, longer pretraining drives the model to generate shorter summaries similar to PubMed abstracts, and thereby, results in increasing precision and decreasing recall.

We also experimented with state of the art transformer-based seq2seq models, e.g., BertSumExtAbs (Liu and Lapata, 2019) and BART (Lewis et al., 2019). BertSumExtAbs requires fine-tuning of the encoder and a de novo training of decoder while both encoder and decoder of BART are only fine-tuned. We use only AMI data for the de novo training and fine-tuning purpose, and the bottom two rows in Table 6 show the results from these models.[1] Although our hier2hier_t-learn also only requires fine-tuning of the decoder and hierarchical attention, a highly-sophisticated semi-supervised training of both the encoder and decoder of BART and larger model size (100x) yields better performance. However, for applications that have limited memory, as on some mobile devices, our model may be more desirable. Furthermore, despite a pre-trained encoder of BertSumExtAbs, a de novo training of a large size decoder with a tiny AMI data lead to over-fitting, and therefore, lower scores.

Human Evaluation: We also performed a qualitative evaluation of our system using human judgments. Following Chen and Bansal (2018), we performed a comparative evaluation, where we provided six human judges (graduate students fluent in English) with meetings ($\approx$ 6000 words) and summaries from three sources, i.e., human reference, two-step baseline and hier2hier_t-learn (here after referred to as the "our model"), and asked them to rate on a scale of 1 to 5 the two questions: 1) is the summary concise, fluent and grammatical (**fluency**) and 2) does the summary retain key information from the meeting (**relevancy**)?

We sampled six meetings (each with three summaries corresponding to three sources), duplicated them, and then randomly sampled two dissimilar meetings and assigned them to each judge to annotate. For reference, an annotation sample would be an ASR transcript and human written summaries as in Table 1 and our model and Shang et al. (2018) summaries as in Table 7. The judges were not shown the source of the summaries. The twelve ratings that we received are converted into two binary comparisons and are summarized in Table 8. Our model summaries were often judged to be better than the Shang et al. (2018) system summaries in both fluency and relevancy. Gwet's AC1 and Brennan's and Prediger's kappa inter-rater agreement statistics show strong agreement for fluency.[2] However, compared to human summaries, our model summaries were similar in terms of fluency but were lower in terms of relevancy, with inter-rater statistics indicating fair strength of agreement.

	ROUGE-1			ROUGE-2		
Model	P	R	F1	P	R	F1
two-step (Shang et al., 2018)	34.61	41.84	37.37	6.92	8.29	7.45
hier2hier	46.30	38.17	41.30	14.84	12.23	13.13
hier2hier_t-learn	**47.68**	**44.37**	**45.56**	**16.02**	**14.98**	**15.35**
(Li et al., 2019)	-	-	**53.29**	-	-	13.51
BertSumExtAbs	**55.95**	36.21	43.24	**18.35**	12.16	14.39
BART(base)	42.17	**59.19**	49.03	16.52	**23.05**	**19.15**

Table 6: Rouge Scores for summary size 300 words on the AMI Corpus. t-learn=transfer-leaning. BART(base) = BART with 6 encoder and decoder layers and 140M parameters. Li et al. uses audio+video in addition to text and the transformer models (the bottom two rows) have lots of extra data for pre-training.

h2h_t-learn summaries
1) the project manager opened the meeting and went over the minutes of the previous...
...
3) the industrial designer discussed the interior workings of a remote and the team...
...
5) the group discussed the shape of the device and decided to make the device easier...
...
two-step (Shang et al., 2018) summaries
1) marketing report uh we observed remote control users in a usability lab
...
7) majority except for the forty five to fifty five year olds for some reason didnt want a voice act speech...
...
14) headed towards like a b a big yellow and black remote as far as maybe thats our next meeting that we discuss that
...

Table 7: The top and bottom sections show our hierarchical and the Shang et al. (2018) system summaries respectively for ASR transcripts in Table 1. a) refer to the ath sentence in a multi-sentence summary.

[1]Due to the small AMI data size, batch size and initial learning rate of BERTSumExt are set to 8 and 5e-4 respectively, batch size in BERTSumExtAbs is 16 and initial learning rates of BERT and transformer decoder in BERTSumExtAbs are 0.001 and 0.01 respectively.

[2]Gwet's AC(1) and Brennan and Prediger's Kappa adjust the impact of the empirical distributions over the chance agreement, and therefore, are better suited for cases where the proportion of agreements on one class differs from that of another.

Metric	Win	Tie	Lose	gwet ac1	bp
Our Model vs. Shang et al. (2018)					
Fluency	9	2	1	0.72	0.63
Relevancy	9	1	2	-0.02	-1.3
Our Model vs. Human Reference					
Fluency	3	2	7	0.27	0.25
Relevancy	2	0	10	0.38	0.25

Table 8: Comparative ratings by human judges of summaries on fluency and relevancy metrics. gwet ac1 and bp refer to Gwet's AC(1) and Brennan-Prediger Kappa coefficients respectively.

We also compared statistics of reference summaries against Our and Shang et al. (2018) model generated summaries of maximum 300 words. We observe our model generates approximately 145 words outputs, which is close to ground-truth human written summaries of size approximately 165 words. However, the Shang et al. (2018) system generates summaries of average 290 words. Further, the median number of threads (number of summaries) of our model, human written summaries and Shang et al. (2018) are 8, 8.5, 17, respectively. This indicates our model is learning to generate human-like summaries, while Shang et al. (2018) aims to distill words up to the permissible limit, and therefore, has high recall and very low precision; see Table 6. Additionally, our model has twice the Shang et al. (2018) Rouge-2 values, which indicates high readability and was supported by human judges. Further, the difference in number of threads (summaries) between our model and reference are ≤ 3, 2, and 1 for 85%, 65%, and 40% of cases, respectively. This clearly indicates the strength of our hierarchical model in disentangling threads.

6 Conclusion

We investigated the use of an end-to-end hierarchical encoder-decoder model, hier2hier, with three levels of hierarchical attention for jointly summarizing and implicitly disentangling interleaved text. To train this model, we examined the use of pretraining using synthesized data and fine-tuning for adaptation to a new domain with limited labeled real-world data. On real-world AMI data, our fine-tuned end-to-end system outperforms a two-step system by 22% (Rouge-1). Experiments were also conducted against the transformer-based BertSumExtAbs and BART systems, which indicate that these transformer models can also summarize interleaved texts. Specifically our hier2hier model also outperformed the transformer-based BertSumExtAbs but not BART, which suggests that use of pretraining of both the decoder as well as the encoder is important, and also indicates the utility of our synthetic data.

References

Ahmet Aker, Monica Paramita, Emina Kurtic, Adam Funk, Emma Barker, Mark Hepple, and Rob Gaizauskas. 2016. Automatic label generation for news comment clusters. In *Proceedings of the 9th International Natural Language Generation Conference*, pages 61–69.

Xavier Anguera, Simon Bozonnet, Nicholas Evans, Corinne Fredouille, Gerald Friedland, and Oriol Vinyals. 2012. Speaker diarization: A review of recent research. *IEEE Transactions on Audio, Speech, and Language Processing*, 20(2):356–370.

Dzmitry Bahdanau, Kyunghyun Cho, and Yoshua Bengio. 2014. Neural machine translation by jointly learning to align and translate. *CoRR*, abs/1409.0473.

Emma Barker, Monica Lestari Paramita, Ahmet Aker, Emina Kurtic, Mark Hepple, and Robert Gaizauskas. 2016. The sensei annotated corpus: Human summaries of reader comment conversations in on-line news. In *Proceedings of the 17th annual meeting of the special interest group on discourse and dialogue*, pages 42–52.

Yen-Chun Chen and Mohit Bansal. 2018. Fast abstractive summarization with reinforce-selected sentence rewriting. In *Proceedings of the 56th Annual Meeting of the Association for Computational Linguistics (Volume 1: Long Papers)*, pages 675–686, Melbourne, Australia. Association for Computational Linguistics.

Jianpeng Cheng and Mirella Lapata. 2016. Neural summarization by extracting sentences and words. In *Proceedings of the 54th Annual Meeting of the Association for Computational Linguistics (Volume 1: Long Papers)*, pages 484–494.

Sumit Chopra, Michael Auli, and Alexander M. Rush. 2016. Abstractive sentence summarization with attentive recurrent neural networks. In *NAACL HLT 2016, The 2016 Conference of the North American Chapter of the Association for Computational Linguistics: Human Language Technologies, San Diego California, USA, June 12-17, 2016*, pages 93–98. The Association for Computational Linguistics.

Franck Dernoncourt and Ji Young Lee. 2017. Pubmed 200k rct: a dataset for sequential sentence classification in medical abstracts. In *Proceedings of the Eighth International Joint Conference on Natural Language Processing (Volume 2: Short Papers)*, pages 308–313. Asian Federation of Natural Language Processing.

Jacob Devlin, Ming-Wei Chang, Kenton Lee, and Kristina Toutanova. 2018. Bert: Pre-training of deep bidirectional transformers for language understanding. *arXiv preprint arXiv:1810.04805*.

Baoyu Jing, Pengtao Xie, and Eric Xing. 2018. On the automatic generation of medical imaging reports. In *Proceedings of the 56th Annual Meeting of the Association for Computational Linguistics (Volume 1: Long Papers)*, pages 2577–2586. Association for Computational Linguistics.

Diederik P. Kingma and Jimmy Ba. 2014. Adam: A method for stochastic optimization. *CoRR*, abs/1412.6980.

Jonathan Krause, Justin Johnson, Ranjay Krishna, and Li Fei-Fei. 2017. A hierarchical approach for generating descriptive image paragraphs. In *Computer Vision and Patterm Recognition (CVPR)*.

Mike Lewis, Yinhan Liu, Naman Goyal, Marjan Ghazvininejad, Abdelrahman Mohamed, Omer Levy, Veselin Stoyanov, and Luke Zettlemoyer. 2019. Bart: Denoising sequence-to-sequence pretraining for natural language generation, translation, and comprehension. *arXiv preprint arXiv:1910.13461*.

Jiwei Li, Thang Luong, and Dan Jurafsky. 2015. A hierarchical neural autoencoder for paragraphs and documents. In *Proceedings of the 53rd Annual Meeting of the Association for Computational Linguistics and the 7th International Joint Conference on Natural Language Processing (Volume 1: Long Papers)*, pages 1106–1115. Association for Computational Linguistics.

Manling Li, Lingyu Zhang, Heng Ji, and Richard J. Radke. 2019. Keep meeting summaries on topic: Abstractive multi-modal meeting summarization. In *Proceedings of the 57th Annual Meeting of the Association for Computational Linguistics*, pages 2190–2196, Florence, Italy. Association for Computational Linguistics.

Yang Liu and Mirella Lapata. 2019. Text summarization with pretrained encoders. In *Proceedings of the 2019 Conference on Empirical Methods in Natural Language Processing and the 9th International Joint Conference on Natural Language Processing (EMNLP-IJCNLP)*, pages 3730–3740, Hong Kong, China. Association for Computational Linguistics.

Zongyang Ma, Aixin Sun, Quan Yuan, and Gao Cong. 2012. Topic-driven reader comments summarization. In *Proceedings of the 21st ACM international conference on Information and knowledge management*, pages 265–274. ACM.

I. McCowan, J. Carletta, W. Kraaij, S. Ashby, S. Bourban, M. Flynn, M. Guillemot, T. Hain, J. Kadlec, V. Karaiskos, M. Kronenthal, G. Lathoud, M. Lincoln, A. Lisowska, W. Post, Dennis Reidsma, and P. Wellner. 2005. The ami meeting corpus. In *Proceedings of Measuring Behavior 2005, 5th International Conference on Methods and Techniques in Behavioral Research*, pages 137–140. Noldus Information Technology.

Ramesh Nallapati, Feifei Zhai, and Bowen Zhou. 2017. Summarunner: A recurrent neural network based sequence model for extractive summarization of documents. In *AAAI Conference on Artificial Intelligence*.

Ramesh Nallapati, Bowen Zhou, Cícero Nogueira dos Santos, Çaglar Gülçehre, and Bing Xiang. 2016. Abstractive text summarization using sequence-to-sequence rnns and beyond. In *Proceedings of the 20th SIGNLL Conference on Computational Natural Language Learning, CoNLL 2016, Berlin, Germany, August 11-12, 2016*, pages 280–290. ACL.

Alexander M. Rush, Sumit Chopra, and Jason Weston. 2015. A neural attention model for abstractive sentence summarization. In *Proceedings of the 2015 Conference on Empirical Methods in Natural Language Processing, EMNLP 2015, Lisbon, Portugal, September 17-21, 2015*, pages 379–389. The Association for Computational Linguistics.

Rico Sennrich, Barry Haddow, and Alexandra Birch. 2016. Neural machine translation of rare words with subword units. In *Proceedings of the 54th Annual Meeting of the Association for Computational Linguistics (Volume 1: Long Papers)*, pages 1715–1725, Berlin, Germany. Association for Computational Linguistics.

Guokan Shang, Wensi Ding, Zekun Zhang, Antoine Tixier, Polykarpos Meladianos, Michalis Vazirgiannis, and Jean-Pierre Lorré. 2018. Unsupervised abstractive meeting summarization with multi-sentence compression and budgeted submodular maximization. In *Proceedings of the 56th Annual Meeting of the Association for Computational Linguistics (Volume 1: Long Papers)*, pages 664–674. Association for Computational Linguistics.

Kaitao Song, Xu Tan, Tao Qin, Jianfeng Lu, and Tie-Yan Liu. 2019. Mass: Masked sequence to sequence pre-training for language generation. *arXiv preprint arXiv:1905.02450*.

Jiwei Tan, Xiaojun Wan, and Jianguo Xiao. 2017. From neural sentence summarization to headline generation: A coarse-to-fine approach. In *IJCAI*, pages 4109–4115.

Suzan Verberne, Emiel Krahmer, Iris Hendrickx, Sander Wubben, and Antal van Den Bosch. 2018. Creating a reference data set for the summarization of discussion forum threads. *Language Resources and Evaluation*, pages 1–23.

Lidan Wang and Douglas W Oard. 2009. Context-based message expansion for disentanglement of interleaved text conversations. In *Proceedings of human language technologies: The 2009 annual conference of the North American chapter of the association for computational linguistics*, pages 200–208. Association for Computational Linguistics.

Semantic Parsing of Brief and Multi-Intent Natural Language Utterances

Logan Lebanoff[1] **Charles Newton**[1] **Victor Hung**[1]
Beth Atkinson[2] **John Killilea**[2] **Fei Liu**[3]

[1]Soar Technology, Inc. [2]U.S. Navy [3]University of Central Florida

{logan.lebanoff, charles.newton, victor.hung}@soartech.com
{beth.atkinson, john.killilea}@navy.mil
feiliu@cs.ucf.edu

Abstract

Many military communication domains involve rapidly conveying situation awareness with few words. Converting natural language utterances to logical forms in these domains is challenging, as these utterances are brief and contain multiple intents. In this paper, we present a first effort toward building a weakly-supervised semantic parser to transform brief, multi-intent natural utterances into logical forms. Our findings suggest a new "projection and reduction" method that iteratively performs projection from natural to canonical utterances followed by reduction of natural utterances is the most effective. We conduct extensive experiments on two military and a general-domain dataset and provide a new baseline for future research toward accurate parsing of multi-intent utterances.

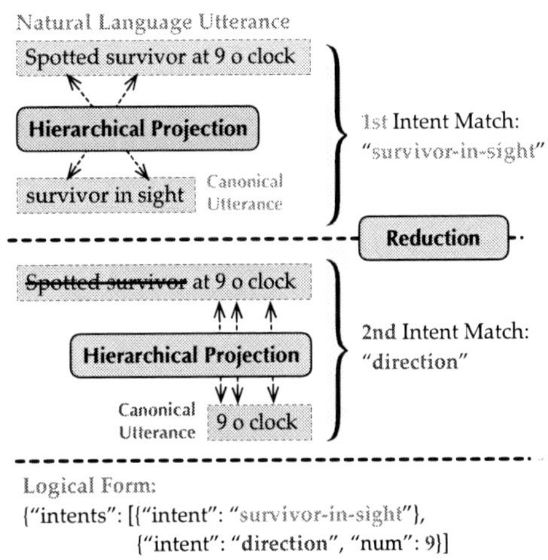

Figure 1: Example generated semantic parse. A parser must (1) understand paraphrases of canonical utterances and (2) parse multiple intents in one utterance.

1 Introduction

Semantic parsing to map a natural language utterance to its logical form is regarded as a challenging task partly due to a lack of annotated data (Berant and Liang, 2014; Yin et al., 2018; Gardner et al., 2018). A promising avenue of research is to generate a set of candidate logical forms paired with their canonical realizations in natural language. Then, the canonical utterance that best matches the input is identified by a model, and its logical form is used as output (Berant and Liang, 2014). A paraphrase/sequence-to-sequence model may additionally be used to translate a canonical utterance to a logical form (Wang et al., 2015; Herzig and Berant, 2019; Cao et al., 2020; Marzoev et al., 2020). While the results are promising, most existing works do not handle natural language utterances with multiple intents. We refer to an *intent* as a goal intended by a user's utterance. Multi-intent utterances allow people to communicate core aspects of a situation in a consistent and timely manner, as illustrated in Figure 1.

Multi-intent semantic parsing is especially suitable for military domains where emphasis is placed on communication skills, terminology, and brevity (Weinstein, 1990). While communication protocols are often published, variations are allowed given the current situation. An area of interest is Intelligence, Surveillance, and Reconnaissance (ISR) domains where contact reports (e.g., "*Arriving at home base and ready to descend*") often contain multiple intents, and a system must determine the number of intents, interpret the natural language and predict the exact logical forms for every intent, which can be highly challenging.

We investigate new methods for semantic parsing of utterances with multiple intents. Importantly, and distinguishing our work from earlier literature (Iyer et al., 2017; Zhong et al., 2017; Yu et al., 2018; Dong and Lapata, 2018; Zeng et al., 2020), our domain areas have no supervised training data, nor can pseudo-language utterances be created through crowdsourcing due to their sensi-

Proceedings of the Second Workshop on Domain Adaptation for NLP, pages 255–262
April 20, 2021.

tive nature and requirement of expert knowledge. We thus operate in a weakly-supervised setting by assuming only access to a grammar that generates canonical utterances and logical forms. Obtaining a comprehensive collection of natural utterances for military applications is difficult; it can be easier to create a grammar that generates canonical utterances for the application. In addition, there are scenarios where there is insufficient time or funding to obtain supervised data, e.g. quickly building a virtual assistant for a new mobile app. Our goal is distinct from related efforts in dialog systems (Gupta et al., 2018; Vanzo et al., 2019; Lee et al., 2019; Ham et al., 2020); the parser does not have additional context or interaction but focuses on modeling complex compositional intents. We build on methods that project natural utterances to the canonical space (Marzoev et al., 2020) and investigate novel adaptations for handling multi-intent utterances. Our contributions are as follows.

- We present a first effort at parsing brief, multi-intent utterances into logical forms; this work sheds light on parsing of airborne communications for which parallel resources are limited.
- We perform experiments on two military communications datasets and a general-domain dataset. Our findings suggest that a new approach that iteratively projects the natural language utterance to a canonical utterance, followed by a reduction step can achieve the best performance.

2 Hierarchical Projection

Let X and Y be the set of all natural language utterances and logical forms (LF), respectively. Given a natural language utterance $x \subseteq X$, we wish to produce $y \subseteq Y$. We assume only access to a grammar G that defines a set of n production rules whose union forms a canonical set of utterances Z. A grammar is assumed to be in the form $G = R_1| \ldots |R_n$, where each production rule $R_i \rightarrow (\alpha, \tau)$ is defined as rule expansion α and a tag τ. Tags define the semantic content associated with a rule, which can be used to build LFs. Figure 2 shows an example grammar. Canonical utterances found in Z do not cover the full range of variation available in natural language. A viable option, described below, is to develop a projection function π which maps X directly into Z and obtain an appropriate y through G.

We follow Marzoev et al. (2020) and use a pre-trained language model (LM) to obtain semantic

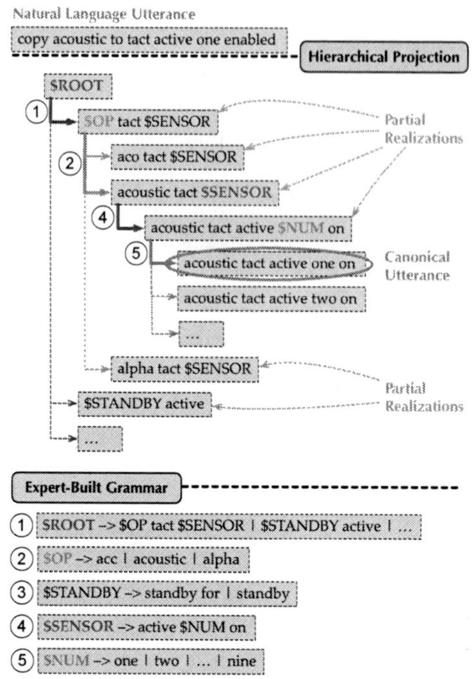

Figure 2: (Top) Method to project a natural language utterance to a canonical utterance; the logical form can then be inferred directly. (Bottom) Grammar from our ISR data.

representations of utterances in $\mathbb{R}^d$. A distance function δ is used to compute the closest canonical utterance in vector space to the natural language utterance. The projection function is defined as:

$$\pi(x) = \arg\min_{z \in Z} \delta(\text{LM}(x), \text{LM}(z)) \quad (1)$$

$\text{LM}(\cdot)$ is calculated as the average of BERT-Base (Devlin et al., 2018) representations, and δ is cosine similarity. Computing the $\arg\min$ requires $O(Z)$ operations which can be intractable for many grammars. To handle this, we use a hierarchical projection method by performing a search through the grammar (Marzoev et al., 2020). The $\$root$ is expanded by taking one step in the grammar to yield several partial instantiations z', which takes the place of z in Eq. 1. We refer to a partial instantiation z' as a canonical utterance that still contains non-terminals. The z' closest to x is chosen in the next search iteration. Non-terminals in z' are expanded until only terminals remain (Figure 2).

3 Adaptation

3.1 Non-Terminal Averaging

Vector representations of partial instantiations introduce difficulty as non-terminals are not well-

Dataset	Single-Intent Can.	NL	Multi-Intent Can.	NL	Avg Len
ISR	445	790	20,000	600	7.4
HELI	45	170	8,000	2,000	3.0
OVERNIGHT	302	2,416	20,000	2,000	10.8

Table 1: Number of canonical (*Can.*) and natural language utterances (*NL*) and average length of utterances. Each *Can.* and *NL* utterance is paired with a gold standard LF. *Can.* pairs are used for training and *NL* pairs are for evaluation. OVERNIGHT numbers are averaged over its eight subdomains.

understood by pre-trained LMs. This can be somewhat resolved by replacing non-terminals with the [MASK] token (Marzoev et al., 2020). It conveys to the LM that a word or phrase should exist at that position, but it's not clear yet what exactly belongs there, and allows the LM to form representations for the other tokens with the knowledge that something will exist there. However, partial instantiations may contain few or no terminals at all, meaning LM input will be dominated by [MASK] tokens. For example, for the given partial instantiation – *$TypeNP whose $RelNP is $EntityNP* – it is not clear what values may be used for the non-terminals, and the resulting utterance representation will not be useful.

We introduce a strategy to mitigate this issue that we call non-terminal averaging. We observe that a non-terminal is restricted to certain values defined by the grammar. We obtain a representation of the non-terminal by averaging over the representations of these possible values, which gives a much better representation than the [MASK] token. This is important when projecting over multiple intents, as discussed in the next section.

3.2 Multi-Intent Projection

We explore two methods for parsing utterances with multiple intents.

Meta-Grammar A simple method for handling multiple intents is to create a meta-grammar based on the original grammar. The $\$root$ is renamed to $\$subroot$ while keeping all other rules unchanged. A new $\$root$ is created with the rule $\$root \rightarrow \$subroot \mid \$subroot\, \$subroot \mid \ldots$ It encapsulates all combinations of multiple intents, where each combination is a concatenation of ≥ 1 intents.

Reduction Another approach is to first greedily project to the closest canonical utterance, remove all tokens in the input utterance that appear in the canonical utterance, and repeat to find another similar canonical utterance. This iterative process of projection and reduction is repeated until no tokens remain or a continuation threshold is met. Figure 1 presents an example.

To more accurately perform token removal for our *Reduction* method, we compare BERT representations of tokens rather than comparing exact string matches between tokens, similar to BERTScore (Zhang et al., 2019). If the cosine similarity scores between two tokens meet a certain similarity threshold, then those two tokens are treated as equivalent, and the token will then be removed. This technique can better handle slight variations in word choice (e.g. "survivor" and "survivors", or "spotted" and "in sight"). We used 0.5 as the similarity threshold, but the model is not very sensitive to this value.

4 Data

Most semantic parsers are given access to (natural language utterance, LF) pairs during training. Our setting, however, assumes no access to these pairs and are only given a grammar to generate canonical utterances and their LFs. We use two proprietary military communication datasets and a general-purpose dataset OVERNIGHT (see Table 1).

ISR Intelligence, surveillance, and reconnaissance (ISR) subject matter experts were consulted to develop a corpus of known utterances that an intelligence operator would say during a mission. The LFs appear in JSON format containing an intent and slots to be filled. The utterances are consolidated into a grammar with a relatively deep structure where an intent may contain slots for nested intents, making it closer to semantic parsing datasets like TOP (Gupta et al., 2018). It consists of domain-specific words and acronyms outside of ordinary vernacular, making this dataset particularly challenging. The grammar contains 37 rules, 36 non-terminals, and approximately 60 terminals.

HELI Short commands were collected from helicopter communications and consolidated into a similar grammar to ISR. The grammar has a shallow structure and does not contain many nested intents, but each utterance is short (1–5 tokens), which has its own challenges. The grammar contains 48 rules, 47 non-terminals, and approximately 60 terminals. Example in Fig. 1.

Natural language utterances in both datasets are wholly defined by its grammar. For evaluation,

		ISR	HELI
Single Intent	seq2seq (Lewis et al., 2020)	34.4	58.2
	proj (Marzoev et al., 2020)	82.5	**74.1**
	NT-Avg	**85.9**	**74.1**
Multi Intent	seq2seq (Lewis et al., 2020)	48.1	**45.5**
	NT-Avg + MetaGrammar	16.3	25.2
	NT-Avg + Reduction	**49.1**	38.8

Table 2: Logical form accuracies for internal ISR and HELI datasets

we expand to a set of paraphrased canonical utterances using an English-to-$X \rightarrow X$-to-English procedure similar to those used for augmentation in paraphrase datasets (Wieting and Gimpel, 2018; Hu et al., 2019).

OVERNIGHT (Wang et al., 2015) is a semantic parsing dataset over eight domains, including sports, restaurants, and social media. Each domain contains a grammar to generate canonical utterances and LFs, as well as natural language paraphrases. As we are interested in weakly-supervised parsing, we ignore natural language utterances in training and only use those in the test set for evaluation. The datasets we use contain grammars and natural language data for utterances with a single intent, but they lack multi-intent data. We create simulated multi-intent utterances by concatenating natural language utterances together, with target LFs as concatenations of the utterances' LFs. We enforce a limit of three intents to keep task difficulty manageable.

5 Results

We present several baselines in our experiments. We train a sequence-to-sequence (*seq2seq*) model on sequence pairs of the form (canonical utterance, LF). At evaluation, the model is given a natural language utterance associated with a canonical utterance and evaluated based on the original LF. We make use of pre-trained BART (Lewis et al., 2020) by fine-tuning on task-specific data. *Proj* is the technique of projecting a natural language utterance to a canonical utterance in the grammar, described in Section 2. *NT-Avg* is the proposed method of averaging the representations of a non-terminal's possible values. For the single-intent OVERNIGHT datasets, we display baseline results presented in Marzoev et al. (2020). Finally, we experiment with two methods on top of NT-Avg for multi-intent parsing – *Meta-Grammar* and *Reduction*.

Table 2 presents LF exact match accuracies for our internal datasets in both single-intent and multi-intent settings. We observe that projection techniques outperform seq2seq methods for single-intent, consistent with prior work (Marzoev et al., 2020). Our proposed method (NT-Avg) achieves a sizeable improvement in ISR, but equal performance on HELI. This disparity may be due to HELI's shallow grammar, demonstrating that non-terminal averaging provides gains on domains with deep, hierarchical grammars but less on simple grammars. For multi-intent, Reduction outperforms MetaGrammar by a wide margin. MetaGrammar must simultaneously predict the number, type, and location of intents. Reduction iteratively simplifies the process by searching for one intent at a time. We also observe that seq2seq achieves much stronger performance for multi-intent with similar accuracy to Reduction on ISR and achieving much higher accuracy on HELI. We believe the improvement is due to the larger amount of data available to train seq2seq models, since we can concatenate multiple single-intent canonical utterances together to form large simulated training sets.

The OVERNIGHT dataset contains a more complex grammar and longer utterances and LFs compared to our internal datasets (Table 3). NT-Avg outperforms other approaches on single-intent utterances, similar to results on ISR and HELI.

All systems evaluated on the multi-intent split of OVERNIGHT struggle to perform well. A system must be able to determine the number of intents in an utterance, interpret the natural language in each intent, and predict LFs that exactly match the LFs for every intent. Accuracies range between 0% and 2% (see supplementary). This demonstrates that it is non-trivial to transfer parsing systems from the single-intent setting to multi-intent. To tease out performance differences between systems, we instead evaluate a system prediction to be correct if *at least one* predicted LF has an exact match with any one of the gold standard LFs.

For multi-intent utterances, Reduction achieves the highest accuracies. We believe the long structure of the LFs in OVERNIGHT provide a challenge for current seq2seq models to generate accurately. Meanwhile, grammar-based approaches can easily side-step this issue by producing LFs directly from the grammar, evidenced by the higher accuracies.

An additional phenomenon appearing in all datasets is lower layers of BERT used for projection perform better than higher layers (Figure 3). How-

		Bas	Blo	Cal	Hou	Pub	Rec	Res	Soc	Avg
Single Intent	seq2seq+BERT (Marzoev et al., 2020)	**60.0**	21.0	31.0	31.0	34.0	36.0	36.0	**31.0**	35.0
	proj (Marzoev et al., 2020)	47.0	27.0	32.0	36.0	34.0	49.0	43.0	28.0	37.0
	NT-Avg	32.7	**37.0**	**42.2**	**48.6**	**51.5**	**52.3**	**56.3**	30.0	**43.8**
Multi Intent	seq2seq (Lewis et al., 2020)	18.0	16.0	11.5	7.5	23.0	21.5	27.5	7.0	16.5
	NT-Avg + MetaGrammar	18.0	11.4	22.9	16.9	21.1	40.0	23.6	22.3	22.0
	NT-Avg + Reduction	**31.7**	**24.2**	**38.8**	**36.4**	**41.5**	**57.7**	**42.0**	**23.4**	**36.9**

Table 3: Logical form accuracies against OVERNIGHT datasets. Partial accuracies are reported for multi-intent data.

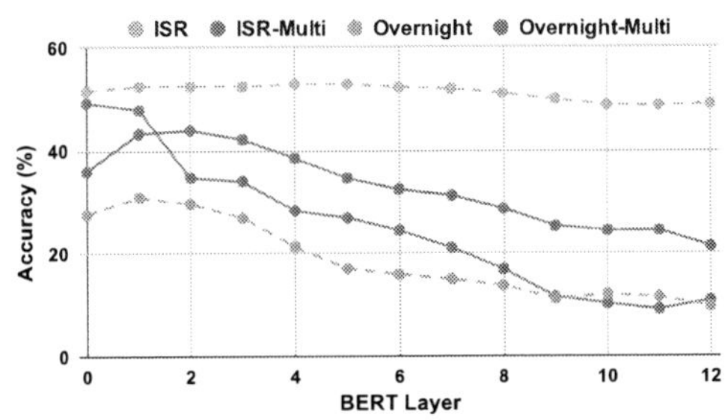

Figure 3: LF accuracies for NT-Avg system by varying BERT layer. Lower layers result in higher accuracies, especially in the multi-intent setting.

ever, we notice that layers 0-1 achieve higher accuracies in ISR and HELI, while layers 1-3 achieve higher accuracies in OVERNIGHT. We believe this is due to the role that context plays in each domain. In terse military domains, words often carry unambiguous meaning and require little context to understand. In traditional domains, context is required to interpret the meaning of a word.

6 Conclusion

We tackle multi-intent semantic parsing using weakly-supervised methods. Our results show that an iterative approach of projecting the natural utterance to a canonical utterance followed by a token reduction step achieves the best performance. Potential further improvement could be achieved by fine-tuning the BERT model on free text in the desired domain (e.g. military training materials) to create better utterance embeddings. Future research includes parsing more complex multi-intent utterances, borrowing ideas from dialogue systems and capturing dependencies between intents (Gangadharaiah and Narayanaswamy, 2019).

7 Ethics and Broader Impacts

Military Applications It is vital for military personnel to use precise language in the field to minimize confusion. This work is part of an effort to train operators of specialized military equipment to accurately communicate in search-and-rescue team and aircraft management operations. Improvement in these occupations leads to better airspace safety and rescue outcomes.

Broader Impacts This work has a larger societal impact outside of military domains. For example, natural language understanding systems in healthcare require the use of audio data or transcripts of patient interactions, and the collection of this sensitive data has major ethical considerations. Our technology is flexible enough to be used in these specialized domains without the need for training on sensitive data and thus has a positive impact in the healthcare field. Potential misuses of this technology, however, could lead to decreased privacy for individuals whose voice is recognized.

Environmental Impact As stated in the paper, our models do not require any training, which greatly reduces the number of computations and thus lessens the environmental impact of natural language technology. Instead our models are based on pre-trained language models used in an unsupervised manner, so the only computation time comes from inference and experiments.

Acknowledgments

This research is based upon work supported by the Naval Air Warfare Center Training Systems Division and the Department of the Navy's Small Business Innovation Research (SBIR) Program, contract N68335-19-C-0052. The views and conclusions contained herein are those of the authors and should not be interpreted as necessarily representing the official policies or endorsements, either expressed or implied, of the Department of the Navy or the U.S. Government. The U.S. Government is authorized to reproduce and distribute reprints for Governmental purposes notwithstanding any copyright annotation thereon.

References

Jonathan Berant and Percy Liang. 2014. Semantic parsing via paraphrasing. In *Proceedings of the 52nd Annual Meeting of the Association for Computational Linguistics (Volume 1: Long Papers)*, pages 1415–1425, Baltimore, Maryland. Association for Computational Linguistics.

Ruisheng Cao, Su Zhu, Chenyu Yang, Chen Liu, Rao Ma, Yanbin Zhao, Lu Chen, and Kai Yu. 2020. Unsupervised dual paraphrasing for two-stage semantic parsing. In *Proceedings of the 58th Annual Meeting of the Association for Computational Linguistics*, pages 6806–6817, Online. Association for Computational Linguistics.

Jacob Devlin, Ming-Wei Chang, Kenton Lee, and Kristina Toutanova. 2018. BERT: pre-training of deep bidirectional transformers for language understanding. *arXiv:1810.04805*.

Li Dong and Mirella Lapata. 2018. Coarse-to-fine decoding for neural semantic parsing. In *Proceedings of the 56th Annual Meeting of the Association for Computational Linguistics (Volume 1: Long Papers)*, pages 731–742, Melbourne, Australia. Association for Computational Linguistics.

Rashmi Gangadharaiah and Balakrishnan Narayanaswamy. 2019. Joint multiple intent detection and slot labeling for goal-oriented dialog. In *Proceedings of the 2019 Conference of the North American Chapter of the Association for Computational Linguistics: Human Language Technologies, Volume 1 (Long and Short Papers)*, pages 564–569, Minneapolis, Minnesota. Association for Computational Linguistics.

Matt Gardner, Pradeep Dasigi, Srinivasan Iyer, Alane Suhr, and Luke Zettlemoyer. 2018. Neural semantic parsing. In *Proceedings of the 56th Annual Meeting of the Association for Computational Linguistics: Tutorial Abstracts*, pages 17–18, Melbourne, Australia. Association for Computational Linguistics.

Sonal Gupta, Rushin Shah, Mrinal Mohit, Anuj Kumar, and Mike Lewis. 2018. Semantic parsing for task oriented dialog using hierarchical representations. In *Proceedings of the 2018 Conference on Empirical Methods in Natural Language Processing*, pages 2787–2792, Brussels, Belgium. Association for Computational Linguistics.

Donghoon Ham, Jeong-Gwan Lee, Youngsoo Jang, and Kee-Eung Kim. 2020. End-to-end neural pipeline for goal-oriented dialogue systems using GPT-2. In *Proceedings of the 58th Annual Meeting of the Association for Computational Linguistics*, pages 583–592, Online. Association for Computational Linguistics.

Jonathan Herzig and Jonathan Berant. 2019. Don't paraphrase, detect! rapid and effective data collection for semantic parsing. In *Proceedings of the 2019 Conference on Empirical Methods in Natural Language Processing and the 9th International Joint Conference on Natural Language Processing (EMNLP-IJCNLP)*, pages 3810–3820, Hong Kong, China. Association for Computational Linguistics.

J Edward Hu, Rachel Rudinger, Matt Post, and Benjamin Van Durme. 2019. Parabank: Monolingual bitext generation and sentential paraphrasing via lexically-constrained neural machine translation. In *Proceedings of the AAAI Conference on Artificial Intelligence*, volume 33, pages 6521–6528.

Srinivasan Iyer, Ioannis Konstas, Alvin Cheung, Jayant Krishnamurthy, and Luke Zettlemoyer. 2017. Learning a neural semantic parser from user feedback. In *Proceedings of the 55th Annual Meeting of the Association for Computational Linguistics (Volume 1: Long Papers)*, pages 963–973, Vancouver, Canada. Association for Computational Linguistics.

Sungjin Lee, Qi Zhu, Ryuichi Takanobu, Zheng Zhang, Yaoqin Zhang, Xiang Li, Jinchao Li, Baolin Peng, Xiujun Li, Minlie Huang, and Jianfeng Gao. 2019. ConvLab: Multi-domain end-to-end dialog system platform. In *Proceedings of the 57th Annual Meeting of the Association for Computational Linguistics: System Demonstrations*, pages 64–69, Florence, Italy. Association for Computational Linguistics.

Mike Lewis, Yinhan Liu, Naman Goyal, Marjan Ghazvininejad, Abdelrahman Mohamed, Omer Levy, Veselin Stoyanov, and Luke Zettlemoyer. 2020. BART: Denoising sequence-to-sequence pre-training for natural language generation, translation, and comprehension. In *Proceedings of the 58th Annual Meeting of the Association for Computational Linguistics*, pages 7871–7880, Online. Association for Computational Linguistics.

Alana Marzoev, Samuel Madden, M Frans Kaashoek, Michael Cafarella, and Jacob Andreas. 2020. Unnatural language processing: Bridging the gap between synthetic and natural language data. *arXiv preprint arXiv:2004.13645*.

Andrea Vanzo, Emanuele Bastianelli, and Oliver Lemon. 2019. Hierarchical multi-task natural language understanding for cross-domain conversational AI: HERMIT NLU. In *Proceedings of the 20th Annual SIGdial Meeting on Discourse and Dialogue*, pages 254–263, Stockholm, Sweden. Association for Computational Linguistics.

Yushi Wang, Jonathan Berant, and Percy Liang. 2015. Building a semantic parser overnight. In *Proceedings of the 53rd Annual Meeting of the Association for Computational Linguistics and the 7th International Joint Conference on Natural Language Processing (Volume 1: Long Papers)*, pages 1332–1342, Beijing, China. Association for Computational Linguistics.

Clifford J. Weinstein. 1990. Opportunities for advanced speech processing in military computer-based systems*. In *Speech and Natural Language: Proceedings of a Workshop Held at Hidden Valley, Pennsylvania, June 24-27,1990.*

John Wieting and Kevin Gimpel. 2018. ParaNMT-50M: Pushing the limits of paraphrastic sentence embeddings with millions of machine translations. In *Proceedings of the 56th Annual Meeting of the Association for Computational Linguistics (Volume 1: Long Papers)*, pages 451–462, Melbourne, Australia. Association for Computational Linguistics.

Pengcheng Yin, Chunting Zhou, Junxian He, and Graham Neubig. 2018. Structvae: Tree-structured latent variable models for semi-supervised semantic parsing. In *Proceedings of the 56th Annual Meeting of the Association for Computational Linguistics (Volume 1: Long Papers)*, pages 754–765.

Tao Yu, Rui Zhang, Kai Yang, Michihiro Yasunaga, Dongxu Wang, Zifan Li, James Ma, Irene Li, Qingning Yao, Shanelle Roman, Zilin Zhang, and Dragomir Radev. 2018. Spider: A large-scale human-labeled dataset for complex and cross-domain semantic parsing and text-to-SQL task. In *Proceedings of the 2018 Conference on Empirical Methods in Natural Language Processing*, pages 3911–3921, Brussels, Belgium. Association for Computational Linguistics.

Jichuan Zeng, Xi Victoria Lin, Caiming Xiong, Richard Socher, Michael R Lyu, Irwin King, and Steven CH Hoi. 2020. Photon: A robust cross-domain text-to-sql system. *arXiv preprint arXiv:2007.15280.*

Tianyi Zhang, Varsha Kishore, Felix Wu, Kilian Q Weinberger, and Yoav Artzi. 2019. Bertscore: Evaluating text generation with bert. In *International Conference on Learning Representations.*

Victor Zhong, Caiming Xiong, and Richard Socher. 2017. Seq2sql: Generating structured queries from natural language using reinforcement learning. *arXiv preprint arXiv:1709.00103.*

	Bas	Blo	Cal	Hou	Pub	Rec	Res	Soc	Avg
Multi-Intent									
seq2seq (Lewis et al., 2020)	0.00	0.00	0.00	0.00	0.00	0.00	0.00	0.00	0.00
NT-Avg + MetaGrammar	0.00	0.00	0.00	0.00	0.00	0.00	0.00	0.00	0.00
NT-Avg + Reduction	**0.35**	**0.35**	**0.35**	**1.30**	**1.30**	**1.95**	**1.75**	**0.30**	**0.96**

Table 4: Exact match logical form accuracies against OVERNIGHT multi-intent datasets

A Model Details

We use BART-base (Lewis et al., 2020) to closely match the number of parameters and amount of pre-training data used by BERT-base (Devlin et al., 2018), which is used for the projection approaches. BART-base uses the Transformer encoder-decoder architectures with 6 layers in the encoder and decoder, 12 attention heads in the encoder and decoder, and hidden size of 768. We train with a batch size of 4, optimized with Adam, a learning rate of 4e-5. The model converged after an average of five epochs for the OVERNIGHT single-intent datasets and one epoch for multi-intent. The model took longer to converge on the ISR and HELI datasets taking 20 epochs and 40 epochs, respectively. This is likely because of the unfamiliar military terms and terse utterances. A beam size of 10 is used for all projection techniques (including the proposed approaches).

Our results for *proj* differ from those presented in (Marzoev et al., 2020) because we use the hierarchical projection method, which forces a search through the grammar to find the closest canonical utterances. Marzoev et al. (2020) use a linear projection method, which instead compares to all canonical utterances directly, which generally performs better but is not tractable for complex grammars.

B Full Logical Form Results

All semantic parsing systems that we evaluated OVERNIGHT struggle to perform well on parsing multi-intent utterances. It can be difficult to simultaneously determine the number of intents in an utterance, interpret the natural language in each intent, and predict LFs that exactly match the LFs for every intent. Table 4 presents the exact match logical form accuracies for OVERNIGHT multi-intent.

Domain Adaptation for NMT via Filtered Iterative Back-Translation

Surabhi Kumari, Nikhil Jaiswal, Mayur Patidar, Manasi Patwardhan,
Shirish Karande, Puneet Agarwal[1], Lovekesh Vig
TCS Research, New Delhi, India
{surabhi.kumari6, nikhil.jais, patidar.mayur,
manasi.patwardhan, shirish.karande, lovekesh.vig} @tcs.com
[1]dr.puneet.a@outlook.com

Abstract

Domain-specific Neural Machine Translation (NMT) model can provide improved performance, however, it is difficult to always access a domain-specific parallel corpus. Iterative Back-Translation can be used for fine-tuning an NMT model for a domain even if only a monolingual domain corpus is available. The quality of synthetic parallel corpora in terms of closeness to in-domain sentences can play an important role in the performance of the translation model. Recent works have shown that filtering at different stages of the back translation and weighting the sentences can provide state-of-the-art performance. In comparison, in this work, we observe that a simpler filtering approach based on a domain classifier, applied only to the pseudo-training data can consistently perform better, providing performance gains of 1.40, 1.82 and 0.76 in terms of BLEU score for Medical, Law and IT in one direction, and 1.28, 1.60 and 1.60 in the other direction in low resource scenario over competitive baselines. In the high resource scenario, our approach is at par with competitive baselines.

1 Introduction

Neural Machine Translation (NMT) (Bahdanau et al., 2015; Vaswani et al., 2017) systems heavily rely on the availability of the parallel corpora to produce good quality translations (Koehn and Knowles, 2017). Even for high resource language pairs, in-domain parallel corpora are scarce. Chu and Wang (2018); Chu et al. (2018) address this challenge of domain adaptation with the objective of improving the performance of an NMT system by exploiting the in-domain monolingual corpora and out-of-domain parallel corpora for a given language pair.

In the current work, we build on top of the existing data centric approaches for domain adaptation (Chu and Wang, 2018), i.e., Back-Translation (BT) (Sennrich et al., 2016a) and Iterative Back-Translation (IBT) (Hoang et al., 2018). IBT is a variant of BT, which leverages both source and target-side monolingual corpora along with the out-of-domain parallel corpora and train $NMT_{s\rightarrow t}$ and $NMT_{t\rightarrow s}$ in alternate fashion till convergence, where $NMT_{s\rightarrow t}$ generates the synthetic parallel corpora for $NMT_{t\rightarrow s}$ and vice versa.

The performance of the NMT is influenced by the quality of synthetic parallel corpora as noted by Poncelas et al. (2018); Fadaee and Monz (2018). Hence, for the domain adaptation task, Dou et al. (2020) proposed a curriculum-based approach (*DDSWIBT*) for sentence selection from the in-domain monolingual corpora and use Junczys-Dowmunt (2018) for weight assignment to synthetic parallel corpora. In initial iterations of *IBT*, *DDSWIBT* prefer simple sentences over representative in-domain sentences, in later iterations they use more representative sentences as compared to simple sentences. Meanwhile, Imankulova et al. (2017) use an in-domain language model (*sent-LM*) and "Round-Trip BLEU" score for synthetic parallel corpora filtering.

In this paper, we propose a "classifier augmented filtered iterative back-translation" (*CFIBT*) for the domain adaptation task. We train two Convolutional Neural Network (CNN) (Kim, 2014) based binary classifiers, one in source and the other in the target language on the combination of in-domain and out-of-domain corpora. We use *IBT* for synthetic parallel corpora generation and classifier-based filtering to remove the pair of sentences where the synthetic sentence in the pair does not belong to the domain. This entire procedure is depicted in Figure 1. We do not employ sentence selection over the monolingual corpora, or a weighting mechanism for the synthetic corpora, and neither utilize any "Round-Trip" criteria for scoring the synthetic parallel corpora.

Proceedings of the Second Workshop on Domain Adaptation for NLP, pages 263–271
April 20, 2021. ©2021 Association for Computational Linguistics

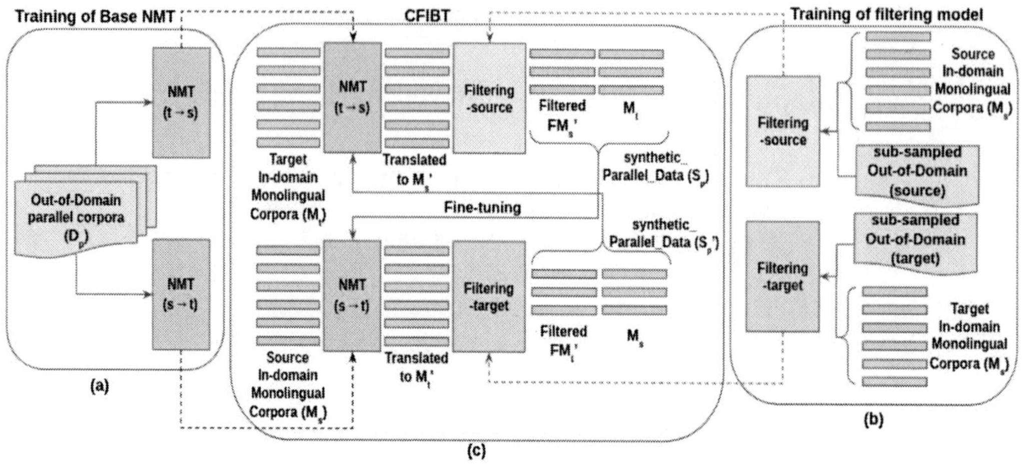

Figure 1: Overall procedure of our proposed approach. (a) We first train two Base NMT models - one in each direction on the out-of-domain parallel corpora. (b) We train two classifier-based filtering models - one for each source and target language to distinguish between in-domain and out-domain translated sentences. (c) We then use the trained NMT models to translate in-domain monolingual corpora. The translated sentences are then filtered to remove out of domain sentences. The remaining sentences along with their corresponding true source/target sentences are used to curate synthetic parallel data which is then utilized to fine-tune the NMT models and this entire cycle is iterated until convergence.

In the current work, we present our domain adaptation results for the German (de) - English (en) language pair on three different domains - Medical, Law and IT under low and high resource scenarios. In the low resource scenario, our proposed method *CFIBT* outperforms all the baselines in every domain. In the high resource settings, *CFIBT* outperforms the baselines in most of the scenarios, whereas it performs competitively with the best baseline results in the rest of the scenarios.

The rest of the paper is organized as follows: We describe related work in Section 2, our problem statement in Section 3, the proposed approach in Section 4. We present the results of the proposed and other baseline approaches in Section 5 and conclude in Section 6.

2 Related Work

In the current work, our objective is to improve the performance of the NMT model on in-domain sentences given out-of-domain parallel corpora and in-domain monolingual corpora in both source and target language, which is known as domain-adaptation for NMT (Chu and Wang, 2018; Chu et al., 2018). Approaches for domain-adaptation (Chu and Wang, 2018) are categorized into data-centric and model-centric. Data-Centric approaches for domain adaptation focuses on the use of in-domain monolingual corpora (Zhang and Zong, 2016; Cheng et al., 2016), synthetic corpora (Sennrich et al., 2016a; Hoang et al., 2018; Hu et al., 2019), or parallel corpora (Luong and Manning, 2015; Chu et al., 2017) along with the out-of-domain parallel corpora. On the other hand, model-centric approaches modify the NMT architecture to include domain information i.e. domain-tags (Britz et al., 2017), domain embedding with word embeddings (Kobus et al., 2017) and assign higher weights to in-domain sentences as compared to out-of-domain sentences (Wang et al., 2017). In our current work, we use the data-centric approach for domain adaptation to generate synthetic parallel data via Iterative Back-Translation.

Shimodaira (2000); Jiang and Zhai (2007); Foster et al. (2010); Søgaard (2011); Sgaard (2013) have proposed different instance weighting based approaches for domain adaptation in NLP, where in-domain instances are assigned more weight as compared to the out-of-domain instances. In NMT, Poncelas et al. (2018); Fadaee and Monz (2018) observe that noisy sentences in synthetic parallel corpora can affect the performance of the translation model. Round-Trip BLEU score (Papineni et al., 2002) between the authentic and synthetic versions of the same sentence is used by Imankulova et al. (2017, 2019) to filter noisy synthetic corpora. And they also use the language model trained on in-domain monolingual data to filter the noisy sentences. Similarly, Jaiswal et al. (2020) use a semantic similarity technique based on the sentence

Dataset	Train	Dev	Test
High	4.5M	3K	3K
Low	100K	3K	3K

Table 1: Out-of-domain Dataset description in high and low resource scenario, where Train, Dev and Test set consists of bilingual sentences.

Dataset	Monolingual	Dev	Test
Medical	400K	2K	2K
Law	500K	2K	2K
IT	240K	2.5K	1.8K

Table 2: In-domain Dataset description for three domains Medical, Law and IT where Monolingual refers to in-domain sentences both in source and target language. Dev and Test set consists of in-domain bilingual sentences.

embeddings of the source and synthetic corpus to filter out noisy pairs. Instead of filtering the noisy sentences from the training data, He et al. (2016); Zhang et al. (2018); Wang et al. (2019) assign the lower weight to them during model training. In Dou et al. (2020), they use a variant of Moore and Lewis (2010) for data selection from in-domain monolingual corpora and use Junczys-Dowmunt (2018) for weight assignment to synthetic corpora generated by IBT. In the current approach, we use the whole in-domain monolingual data and filter the noisy synthetic corpora with the help of a simple binary classifier which is trained on in-domain and out-of-domain corpora.

3 Problem Description

Given out-of-domain parallel corpora D_p, and in-domain monolingual corpora M_s, M_t in source and target language respectively. Our objective is to create a pair of in-domain NMT models $NMT_{s \to t}$, $NMT_{t \to s}$ which can translate in-domain sentences with high efficacy from source to target ($s \to t$) and target to source language ($t \to s$) respectively. Similar to Edunov et al. (2018), we use more D_p in high resource scenario as compared to low resource scenario and the same amount of M_s, M_t in both the scenario.

4 Proposed Approach

We describe our proposed approach "classifier augmented filtered iterative back-translation" (*CFIBT*) in Algorithm 1. We assume that we have access to out-of-domain parallel corpora and in-domain

Algorithm 1 Filtering Augmented Iterative Back-Translation for Domain Adaptation

Require: D_p ▷ Out-of-Domain parallel Corpora
Require: M_s ▷ In-Domain monolingual Corpora in source language
Require: M_t ▷ In-Domain monolingual Corpora in target language
$NMT_{s \to t} \leftarrow$ Train NMT using D_p for $s \to t$
$NMT_{t \to s} \leftarrow$ Train NMT using D_p for $t \to s$
while $NMT_{s \to t}$ and $NMT_{t \to s}$ not converged **do**
  $M'_s \leftarrow$ Translate M_t using $NMT_{t \to s}$
  $M'_t \leftarrow$ Translate M_s using $NMT_{s \to t}$
  $FM'_s \leftarrow$ Filtering(M'_s)
  $FM'_t \leftarrow$ Filtering(M'_t)
  $S_p \leftarrow$ synthetic_Parallel_Data(FM'_s, M_t)
  $S'_p \leftarrow$ synthetic_Parallel_Data(FM'_t, M_s)
  $NMT_{s \to t} \leftarrow$ Fine-tune $NMT_{s \to t}$ using S_p
  $NMT_{t \to s} \leftarrow$ Fine-tune $NMT_{t \to s}$ using S'_p
end while
return $NMT_{s \to t}$, $NMT_{t \to s}$

monolingual corpora in both source and target languages. Firstly, we train $NMT_{s \to t}$ and $NMT_{t \to s}$ using out-of-domain parallel corpora D_p. Then we use these trained $NMT_{s \to t}$, $NMT_{t \to s}$ for translating M_s to M'_t and M_t to M'_s respectively. We then apply a classifier-based filtering technique which is described below on these translated sentences. The filtered sentences FM'_s and FM'_t and their corresponding in-domain monolingual sentences M_t and M_s are used to curate synthetic parallel data. Thereafter, $NMT_{s \to t}$ and $NMT_{t \to s}$ are fine-tuned on this synthetic parallel data. This entire process repeats until convergence. We consider $NMT_{s \to t}$ and $NMT_{t \to s}$ to be converged when there is no improvement in both the models when compared to its preceding iteration model.

Filtering Model: We propose a naive "classifier-based filtering model" using a Convolutional Neural Network. The filtering model consists of a binary classifier trained to distinguish between in-domain and out-of-domain sentences. For each domain, we train two such models - one for source and other for the target language. The classifier is trained only once at the beginning, and we utilize the same classifier in each successive iterations. Given a translated sentence as input, the classifier

Source (de)	warnhinweis, dass das arzneimittel fr kinder unerreichbar und nicht sichtbar aufzubewahren ist
Target (en)	special warning that the medicinal product must be stored out of the reach and sight of children
BASE	warning that drugs for children is unvisible and not visible .
***CFIBT*$_1$**	warning that the medicinal product is being unabsorbed and has not been visible .
***CFIBT*$_2$**	warning that the medicines for children are not being able and not visible .
***CFIBT*$_3$**	warning that the medicinal product must be stored out of the reach and sight of children

Table 3: Translation of a German (de) sentence to English (en) via different *CFIBT*$_i$ models, where i represent the ith iteration of *CFIBT*.

predicts the probability of this sentence as being in-domain. All translated sentences having a probability greater than a certain threshold are considered in-domain sentences.

5 Results and Discussion

Here, we describe the datasets and the training details of our experiments. We also discuss and analyze the results and key observations.

5.1 Dataset Description

We perform our experiments on German-English (de-en) language pair. In both low and high resource scenarios, we use the same out-of-domain News dataset as used by Dou et al. (2020), which is described in Table 1.

For in-domain data, as described in Table 2, we use the same dev and test set as used by Dou et al. (2020) for Medical (EMEA), Law (Acquis) and also the same number of monolingual sentences during domain adaptation. In addition to Medical and Law, in the current work, we also report results on the IT domain and for that, we use the dataset described in Tiedemann (2012).

We tokenize the out-of-domain sentence pairs as well as in-domain sentences using moses (Koehn et al., 2007) and apply byte-pair-encoding (Sennrich et al., 2016b) with $37K$ merge operations.

5.2 Training Details

We train two types of models i.e. filtering models and NMTs.

Filtering Models: We train the filtering models in English and German languages for each domain. We use language model and classifier as filtering models for *sent-LM* and *CFIBT* respectively. For the *language model*, we use one layer LSTM (Hochreiter and Schmidhuber, 1997) having 512 embedding size and 50 sequence length using TF-LM Toolkit (Verwimp et al., 2018). The model is trained till convergence with the patience of three. We train on the tokenized monolingual in-domain dataset for each domain in English and German with vocabulary size $\approx 60K$ and $\approx 80K$ respectively. The *Classifier* architecture is inspired by Kim (2014). For training the binary classifier, we use sub-sampled out-of-domain data as one class and in-domain as another. The tokenized sentences are used with a vocabulary size of $50K$. For filtering models, we obtain the optimal values of thresholds based on the development set, where the objective is to maximize the true positives (i.e. in-domain sentences) and minimize the false positives (i.e. out-of-domain sentences) in the synthetic parallel corpus. The overall intuition is that the classifier should help to select the in-domain sentences, which could then be utilized to further train the NMT models. In *sent-LM* for all domains, we use 60 and 80 as a value of perplexity to filter-out out-of-domain sentences from synthetic sentences in English and German respectively. For *CFIBT*, we use 0.6 for Medical and 0.5 for Law and IT as a threshold over classifier probability for filtering sentences in English and German.

NMT: We use Base-Transformer (Vaswani et al., 2017) for our experiments. We use FairSeq (Ott et al., 2019) for training all the NMT models. We use out-of-domain parallel corpora to train the initial NMT model i.e. *BASE* in both low and high resource scenarios. We finetune the model obtained from *BASE* in *BT*, *IBT*, *sent-LM* and *CFIBT* with the synthetic parallel in-domain dataset, curated with respective approaches. We use the value of patience as five for all approaches.

5.3 Results and Analysis

Here, we compare and discuss the results of our proposed approach along with other baseline methods. As shown in Table 4, we compare the BLEU scores in two different scenarios,

Domain →	Medical		Law		IT	
LP →	de-en	en-de	de-en	en-de	de-en	en-de
High Resource						
BASE	33.61	24.98	33.07	23.33	21.93	16.27
BT	41.05	36.32	38.27	28.32	35.31	24.80
sent-LM	47.44	37.85	40.82	30.35	39.24	**30.11**
IBT	**47.71**	**38.01**	39.46	29.04	38.93	29.37
DDSWIBT	45.46	36.45	39.11	29.04	-	-
CFIBT	47.59	37.61	**40.99**	**30.38**	**40.06**	29.93
Low Resource						
BASE	10.05	6.53	8.52	6.84	5.05	3.70
BT	22.64	14.02	18.47	10.53	13.07	10.79
sent-LM	36.21	29.35	25.36	17.28	28.80	24.32
IBT	33.14	24.31	22.96	14.31	28.06	24.16
DDSWIBT	31.22	28.12	22.06	13.28	-	-
CFIBT	**37.61**	**30.63**	**27.18**	**18.88**	**29.56**	**25.82**

Table 4: We use the BLEU (Papineni et al., 2002) score to compare *CFIBT* with existing baselines, *BASE* (Vaswani et al., 2017), *BT* (Sennrich et al., 2016a), *sent-LM* (Imankulova et al., 2017), *IBT* (Hoang et al., 2018) and *DDSWIBT* (Dou et al., 2020). Except *DDSWIBT*, we implemented all baselines.

viz., high resource and low resource, on three different domains i.e. Medical, Law and IT in both directions for German-English (de-en) language pair on in-domain test set. With monolingual data only in both source and target language, we get performance gains of 27.56, 18.66 and 24.51 in terms of BLEU score for Medical, Law and IT in one direction (de-en), and 24.1, 12.04 and 22.12 in the other direction (en-de) in low resource scenario over the *BASE*. In the low resource scenario, *CFIBT* outperformed *sent-LM* in both directions and all the domains. *CFIBT* also outperformed *sent-LM* in high resource scenario except in one direction for the IT domain. In the low resource scenario, filtering based approaches performs better than the IBT. And *CFIBT* outperformed in all the cases. Our results show that *CFIBT* is efficient when the base model is not adequately trained. In high resource scenario results of *CFIBT* are comparable with other baselines. *CFIBT* outperformed in both directions for Law and one direction IT domain, respectively.

Why *CFIBT* works? According to Figure 2 (Appendix), IBT is trained with all synthetic bilingual sentences without filtering, which may hurt the performance of IBT in subsequent iterations because the current model is used to generate the data for the next iteration. But in *CFIBT*, as shown in Figure 3, filtering prevents training of the NMT model on out-of-domain sentence pairs which leads to a better domain model in subsequent iterations.

6 Conclusion

In the context of domain adaptation for NMT, we propose a simple and effective approach for filtering the synthetic parallel corpus, which is as good as more involved approaches for the same task. In the low resource scenario, the proposed approach outperforms all the existing baselines whereas we get similar results to baselines in the high resource scenario. As a part of future work, we would like to validate our findings on different language pairs and multiple domains and also would like to explore the combination of different filtering techniques. And instead of training different filtering models for source and target language, we would like to use a single multilingual filtering model.

Acknowledgements

We would like to thank Dr. Gautam Shroff for his valuable comments.

References

Dzmitry Bahdanau, Kyunghyun Cho, and Yoshua Bengio. 2015. Neural machine translation by jointly learning to align and translate. In *3rd International Conference on Learning Representations,*

ICLR 2015, San Diego, CA, USA, May 7-9, 2015, Conference Track Proceedings.

Denny Britz, Quoc Le, and Reid Pryzant. 2017. Effective domain mixing for neural machine translation. In *Proceedings of the Second Conference on Machine Translation*, pages 118–126, Copenhagen, Denmark. Association for Computational Linguistics.

Yong Cheng, Wei Xu, Zhongjun He, Wei He, Hua Wu, Maosong Sun, and Yang Liu. 2016. Semi-supervised learning for neural machine translation. In *Proceedings of the 54th Annual Meeting of the Association for Computational Linguistics (Volume 1: Long Papers)*, pages 1965–1974, Berlin, Germany. Association for Computational Linguistics.

Chenhui Chu, Raj Dabre, and Sadao Kurohashi. 2017. An empirical comparison of domain adaptation methods for neural machine translation. In *Proceedings of the 55th Annual Meeting of the Association for Computational Linguistics (Volume 2: Short Papers)*, pages 385–391, Vancouver, Canada. Association for Computational Linguistics.

Chenhui Chu, Raj Dabre, and Sadao Kurohashi. 2018. A comprehensive empirical comparison of domain adaptation methods for neural machine translation. *Journal of Information Processing*, 26:529–538.

Chenhui Chu and Rui Wang. 2018. A survey of domain adaptation for neural machine translation. In *Proceedings of the 27th International Conference on Computational Linguistics*, pages 1304–1319, Santa Fe, New Mexico, USA. Association for Computational Linguistics.

Zi-Yi Dou, Antonios Anastasopoulos, and Graham Neubig. 2020. Dynamic data selection and weighting for iterative back-translation. In *Proceedings of the 2020 Conference on Empirical Methods in Natural Language Processing (EMNLP)*, pages 5894–5904, Online. Association for Computational Linguistics.

Sergey Edunov, Myle Ott, Michael Auli, and David Grangier. 2018. Understanding back-translation at scale. In *Proceedings of the 2018 Conference on Empirical Methods in Natural Language Processing*, Brussels, Belgium. Association for Computational Linguistics.

Marzieh Fadaee and Christof Monz. 2018. Back-translation sampling by targeting difficult words in neural machine translation. In *Proceedings of the 2018 Conference on Empirical Methods in Natural Language Processing*, pages 436–446, Brussels, Belgium. Association for Computational Linguistics.

George Foster, Cyril Goutte, and Roland Kuhn. 2010. Discriminative instance weighting for domain adaptation in statistical machine translation. In *Proceedings of the 2010 Conference on Empirical Methods in Natural Language Processing*, pages 451–459, Cambridge, MA. Association for Computational Linguistics.

Di He, Yingce Xia, Tao Qin, Liwei Wang, Nenghai Yu, Tie-Yan Liu, and Wei-Ying Ma. 2016. Dual learning for machine translation. In D. D. Lee, M. Sugiyama, U. V. Luxburg, I. Guyon, and R. Garnett, editors, *Advances in Neural Information Processing Systems 29*, pages 820–828. Curran Associates, Inc.

Vu Cong Duy Hoang, Philipp Koehn, Gholamreza Haffari, and Trevor Cohn. 2018. Iterative back-translation for neural machine translation. In *Proceedings of the 2nd Workshop on Neural Machine Translation and Generation*, pages 18–24, Melbourne, Australia. Association for Computational Linguistics.

Sepp Hochreiter and Jrgen Schmidhuber. 1997. Long short-term memory. *Neural computation*, pages 1735–80.

Junjie Hu, Mengzhou Xia, Graham Neubig, and Jaime Carbonell. 2019. Domain adaptation of neural machine translation by lexicon induction. In *Proceedings of the 57th Annual Meeting of the Association for Computational Linguistics*, pages 2989–3001, Florence, Italy. Association for Computational Linguistics.

Aizhan Imankulova, Takayuki Sato, and Mamoru Komachi. 2017. Improving low-resource neural machine translation with filtered pseudo-parallel corpus. In *Proceedings of the 4th Workshop on Asian Translation (WAT2017)*, pages 70–78, Taipei, Taiwan. Asian Federation of Natural Language Processing.

Aizhan Imankulova, Takayuki Sato, and Mamoru Komachi. 2019. Filtered pseudo-parallel corpus improves low-resource neural machine translation. *ACM Trans. Asian Low-Resour. Lang. Inf. Process.*, 19(2).

Nikhil Jaiswal, Mayur Patidar, Surabhi Kumari, Manasi Patwardhan, Shirish Karande, Puneet Agarwal, and Lovekesh Vig. 2020. Improving NMT via filtered back translation. In *Proceedings of the 7th Workshop on Asian Translation*, pages 154–159, Suzhou, China. Association for Computational Linguistics.

Jing Jiang and ChengXiang Zhai. 2007. Instance weighting for domain adaptation in NLP. In *Proceedings of the 45th Annual Meeting of the Association of Computational Linguistics*, pages 264–271, Prague, Czech Republic. Association for Computational Linguistics.

Marcin Junczys-Dowmunt. 2018. Dual conditional cross-entropy filtering of noisy parallel corpora. In *Proceedings of the Third Conference on Machine Translation: Shared Task Papers*, pages 888–895, Belgium, Brussels. Association for Computational Linguistics.

Yoon Kim. 2014. Convolutional neural networks for sentence classification. In *Proceedings of the*

2014 Conference on Empirical Methods in Natural Language Processing (EMNLP)*, pages 1746–1751, Doha, Qatar. Association for Computational Linguistics.

Catherine Kobus, Josep Crego, and Jean Senellart. 2017. Domain control for neural machine translation. In *Proceedings of the International Conference Recent Advances in Natural Language Processing, RANLP 2017*, pages 372–378, Varna, Bulgaria. INCOMA Ltd.

Philipp Koehn, Hieu Hoang, Alexandra Birch, Chris Callison-Burch, Marcello Federico, Nicola Bertoldi, Brooke Cowan, Wade Shen, Christine Moran, Richard Zens, Chris Dyer, Ondřej Bojar, Alexandra Constantin, and Evan Herbst. 2007. Moses: Open source toolkit for statistical machine translation. In *Proceedings of the 45th Annual Meeting of the Association for Computational Linguistics Companion Volume Proceedings of the Demo and Poster Sessions*, pages 177–180, Prague, Czech Republic. Association for Computational Linguistics.

Philipp Koehn and Rebecca Knowles. 2017. Six challenges for neural machine translation. In *Proceedings of the First Workshop on Neural Machine Translation*, pages 28–39, Vancouver. Association for Computational Linguistics.

Minh-Thang Luong and Christopher D. Manning. 2015. Stanford neural machine translation systems for spoken language domain. In *International Workshop on Spoken Language Translation*.

Robert C. Moore and William Lewis. 2010. Intelligent selection of language model training data. In *Proceedings of the ACL 2010 Conference Short Papers*, pages 220–224, Uppsala, Sweden. Association for Computational Linguistics.

Myle Ott, Sergey Edunov, Alexei Baevski, Angela Fan, Sam Gross, Nathan Ng, David Grangier, and Michael Auli. 2019. fairseq: A fast, extensible toolkit for sequence modeling. In *Proceedings of NAACL-HLT 2019: Demonstrations*.

Kishore Papineni, Salim Roukos, Todd Ward, and Wei-Jing Zhu. 2002. Bleu: a method for automatic evaluation of machine translation. In *Proceedings of the 40th Annual Meeting of the Association for Computational Linguistics*, pages 311–318, Philadelphia, Pennsylvania, USA. Association for Computational Linguistics.

Alberto Poncelas, Dimitar Sht. Shterionov, Andy Way, Gideon Maillette de Buy Wenniger, and Peyman Passban. 2018. Investigating backtranslation in neural machine translation. *CoRR*, abs/1804.06189.

Rico Sennrich, Barry Haddow, and Alexandra Birch. 2016a. Improving neural machine translation models with monolingual data. In *Proceedings of the 54th Annual Meeting of the Association for Computational Linguistics (Volume 1: Long Papers)*, pages 86–96, Berlin, Germany. Association for Computational Linguistics.

Rico Sennrich, Barry Haddow, and Alexandra Birch. 2016b. Neural machine translation of rare words with subword units. In *Proceedings of the 54th Annual Meeting of the Association for Computational Linguistics (Volume 1: Long Papers)*, pages 1715–1725. Association for Computational Linguistics.

Hidetoshi Shimodaira. 2000. Improving predictive inference under covariate shift by weighting the log-likelihood function. *Journal of Statistical Planning and Inference*, 90(2):227–244.

Anders Søgaard. 2011. Data point selection for cross-language adaptation of dependency parsers. In *Proceedings of the 49th Annual Meeting of the Association for Computational Linguistics: Human Language Technologies*, pages 682–686, Portland, Oregon, USA. Association for Computational Linguistics.

Anders Sgaard. 2013. Semi-supervised learning and domain adaptation in natural language processing. *Synthesis Lectures on Human Language Technologies*, 6(2):1–103.

Jörg Tiedemann. 2012. Parallel data, tools and interfaces in OPUS. In *Proceedings of the Eighth International Conference on Language Resources and Evaluation (LREC'12)*, pages 2214–2218. European Language Resources Association (ELRA).

Ashish Vaswani, Noam Shazeer, Niki Parmar, Jakob Uszkoreit, Llion Jones, Aidan N Gomez, Ł ukasz Kaiser, and Illia Polosukhin. 2017. Attention is all you need. In I. Guyon, U. V. Luxburg, S. Bengio, H. Wallach, R. Fergus, S. Vishwanathan, and R. Garnett, editors, *Advances in Neural Information Processing Systems 30*, pages 5998–6008. Curran Associates, Inc.

Lyan Verwimp, Hugo Van hamme, and Patrick Wambacq. 2018. TF-LM: TensorFlow-based language modeling toolkit. In *Proceedings of the Eleventh International Conference on Language Resources and Evaluation (LREC 2018)*, Miyazaki, Japan. European Language Resources Association (ELRA).

Rui Wang, Masao Utiyama, Lemao Liu, Kehai Chen, and Eiichiro Sumita. 2017. Instance weighting for neural machine translation domain adaptation. In *Proceedings of the 2017 Conference on Empirical Methods in Natural Language Processing*, pages 1482–1488, Copenhagen, Denmark. Association for Computational Linguistics.

Shuo Wang, Yang Liu, Chao Wang, Huanbo Luan, and Maosong Sun. 2019. Improving back-translation with uncertainty-based confidence estimation. In *Proceedings of the 2019 Conference on Empirical Methods in Natural Language Processing and the*

9th International Joint Conference on Natural Language Processing (EMNLP-IJCNLP), pages 791–802, Hong Kong, China. Association for Computational Linguistics.

Jiajun Zhang and Chengqing Zong. 2016. Exploiting source-side monolingual data in neural machine translation. In *Proceedings of the 2016 Conference on Empirical Methods in Natural Language Processing*, pages 1535–1545, Austin, Texas. Association for Computational Linguistics.

Zhirui Zhang, S. Liu, Mu Li, M. Zhou, and E. Chen. 2018. Joint training for neural machine translation models with monolingual data. In *AAAI*.

A Appendix

A.1 Results and Analysis

Figure 2 describes the variation in the number of synthetic parallel sentence pairs as well as BLEU score on test data with the different number of iterations for the *IBT*, *sent-LM* and *CFIBT* models for low resource scenario. For *IBT*, the number of synthetic sentence pairs remains the same for all the iteration. For filtering models, the number of filtered synthetic sentences increases with every upcoming iteration. This increase in good quality synthetic pairs helps in the improvement of the translation model resulting in a better BLEU score. This process is iterated until we do not observe any improvement in the BLEU score compared to the last iteration. Since one direction translation model creates synthetic data for the other direction, we observe that if there is an improvement in the former case for a given iteration, then there is an improvement in the later model for the next iteration.

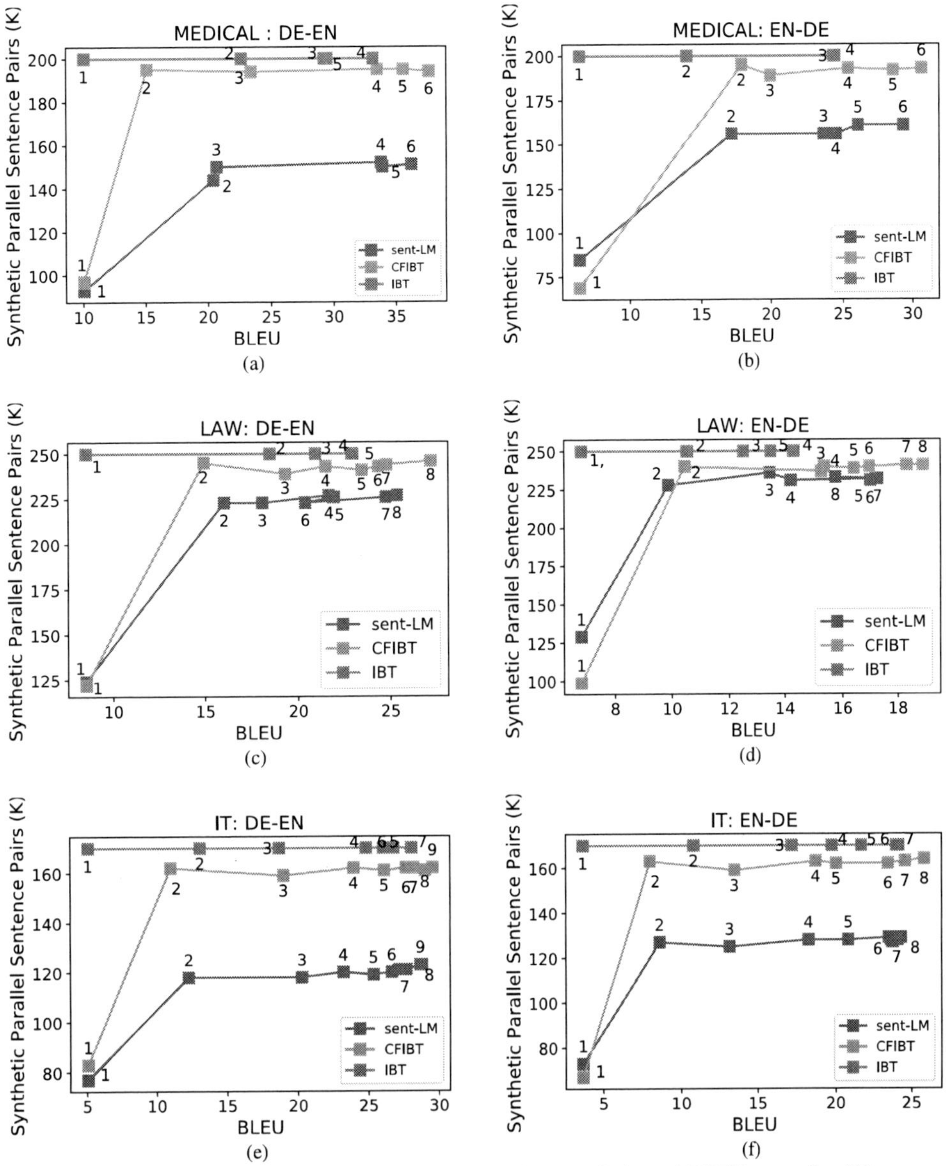

Figure 2: We represent the variation in Synthetic Parallel Sentence Pairs and BLEU scores for different number of iterations in *IBT*, *CFIBT* and *sent-LM* models for low resources. The numerical value represents the iteration number for that particular model (a) & (b) represents de-en and en-de models for Law domain, (c) & (d) represents de-en and en-de models for Medical domain, (e) & (f) represents de-en and en-de models for IT domain